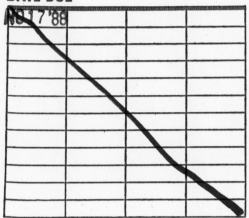

Financing the 1972 Election

Financing the 1972 Election

Herbert E. Alexander
Citizens' Research Foundation
Princeton, New Jersey

With chapters co-authored by
Eugenia Grohman, Caroline D. Jones,
and Clifford W. Brown, Jr.

Lexington Books
D.C. Heath and Company
Lexington, Massachusetts
Toronto   London

Library of Congress Cataloging in Publication Data

Alexander, Herbert E
    Financing the 1972 election.

    Includes index.
    1. Elections–United States. 2. United States. Congress–Elections–
1972. 3. Presidents–United States–Election–1972. I. Title.
JK1991.A684   329'.025'0973   75-16624
ISBN 0-669-00055-8

Published simultaneously in Canada

Printed in the United States of America

International Standard Book Number: 0-669-00055-8

Library of Congress Catalog Card Number: 75-16624

To William H. Vanderbilt who had the prescience to know many years ago that political finance was an important subject to study.

Contents

List of Figures

List of Tables

Table

Preface

This is my fourth quadrennial book on the financing of presidential election campaigns. The 1960, 1964, and 1968 studies were briefer and less comprehensive. This time, however, vast amounts of data regarding political receipts and expenditures in 1972 were available—more than in any previous presidential election in American history. New laws, voluntary disclosures, and official and media exposures, particularly about Watergate, produced a new data base. This required a reexamination of research and analytical techniques used previously, and caused us to make considerable modifications to cope with the new data. Our analyses of the data led us to some conclusions about amounts of money raised and spent that differ markedly from figures released by various government agencies and used heretofore by the media, and academic and other sources. This book also makes some interpretations of events that differ markedly from news accounts at the time, because perspectives change a year or two after the event.

So many events and facts required description independently by topic that it was difficult to organize the book efficiently. An individual item often relates to several topics; for example, "illegal corporate contributions" relates to the Nixon and other campaigns, to sources of funds, to fund-raising techniques, to the role of business in politics, to enforcement, and to the aftermath. There would have been so many footnotes cross-referencing topics that for the most part we dispensed with these, and accordingly, the reader should use both the table of contents and the index.

Each successive study is an educational experience for the author and 1972 was notable in the diversity of ways and means found to raise, handle, and spend the large amounts of money used. This study attempts to update and to keep active analyses and categories of data developed over the years by Professors James Pollock, Louise Overacker, and Alexander Heard, and by the Senate Subcommittee on Privileges and Elections (under the chairmanship of Senator Albert Gore) in 1956.

The data in this study were collected by the Citizens' Research Foundation. Special appreciation is due to many individuals for providing information in personal interviews, through correspondence, and by telephone. Many finance managers and others preferred to remain anonymous. As it would be unfair to name some and not others, I regretfully will not list the many persons in such capacities who graciously cooperated.

One innovation in this book is that three of the chapters — 4, 5, and 11 — were co-authored. The chapters speak for themselves but would not have been possible without the perseverance and skill provided by each co-author in analyzing the data and initially drafting the chapter.

Chapter 4, "Spending in the 1972 Elections," was co-authored by Caroline D. Jones. Ms. Jones has been CRF's research associate in Washington, D.C. for more than ten years, and she has always been able to make sense of the mass of figures contained in campaign filings made under federal law.

Chapter 5, "The Prenomination Campaigns," was co-authored by Eugenia Grohman. This is the second book in my series of four that Ms. Grohman helped to write and edit; her help was invaluable on the entire 1968 volume, as well as here in drafting and editing this chapter.

Chapter 11, "Sources of Funds: A Computer Analysis of Contributions by Size, Region, and Date," was co-authored by Clifford W. Brown, Jr. Dr. Brown, who is Assistant Professor of Political Science at the State University of New York in Albany, undertook the massive task of aggregating and analyzing large contributions in the April 7 to December 31, 1972 period, making possible a computer analysis revealing in its findings and pioneering in its concept. The groundwork for Chapter 11 was laid in a preliminary study conducted by Dr. Brown and the Ripon Society. It was published as an appendix to Ripon Society, *Jaws of Victory* (Boston-Toronto: Little, Brown and Company, 1973) pp. 361-77. The data analysis published in *Financing the 1972 Election* was performed at the Computer Center of the State University of New York at Albany. We wish to acknowledge the assistance of John Watson, assistant director of the computer center, Mark Aronson and Ray McQuade who served as programmers, and Mike Bibbo and Karen Pollastrino, students at SUNYA who assisted in the preparation of the data.

I am happy to give special acknowledgment to Carolyn Ford Eagle who helped write and rewrite drafts, analyzed and edited the entire book, and prepared the index. Without her command of the files and subject matter, this book would never have been completed.

Special thanks go to Linda Sheldon, who miraculously made readable copy out of more scribblings than I care to remember, and who met every deadline with a smile.

Portions of the manuscript were drafted by John M. Fenton, Richard M. Dykeman, Anthony Podesta, and Peter Slavin, and my appreciation goes to each, although none will recognize his handiwork.

Special analyses were provided by Barbara D. Paul, who along with her co-editors, Mary Jo Long and Elizabeth C. Burns, of *Political Contributors and Lenders of $10,000 or More in 1972,* a companion to this book, published by the Citizens' Research Foundation, brought order and meaning to the extensive contributor listing available for the 1972 election, and matched contributor lists against lists of officers and directors of corporations and other groups analyzed.

Theodore Jacqueney was helpful in early interviewing of campaign managers and fund raisers. Norman A. Moscowitz helped to analyze the broadcasting data and to arrange the tables.

Others who contributed importantly to the final product were Katherine C. Fisher, Jean Soete, Kaye Stegenga, Hanna Fox, Lynn Fielden-Smith, Barbara Gislason, Joseph Harkins, and James Kelley.

None of those who were so helpful is responsible for errors of omission or commission; for those, as for interpretations, the author bears sole responsibility.

I am happy to acknowledge also the encouragement and forebearance of my wife, Nancy, and the good cheers of my children, Michael, Andrew, and Kenneth.

I always appreciate the co-operation and encouragement received from officers and members of the Board of Trustees of the Citizens' Research Foundation, but the presentation is mine and does not reflect their views.

This study was made possible by grants from the Ford Foundation, the Irwin-Sweeney-Miller Foundation, and by the contributions of numerous supporters of the Citizens' Research Foundation.

Herbert E. Alexander

Financing the 1972 Election

1 Introduction

Political finance is an issue whose time finally came *Began* in 1972. It was a surprise issue, achieving higher levels of attention than ever before in American history. The means by which money was raised, handled, spent, and regulated had major impact on the politics of the presidential campaigns of 1972 and their aftermath. The issue carried strong implications for the future course of political funding—how the rules should be changed to prevent the abuses of 1972 from happening again, whether new consideration should be given to the role of government in the ways campaigns should be financed and regulated, whether more urgent consideration should be given to forms of government funding, and what implications change would have on the political system.

The series of events known as Watergate, and other disclosures such as the reasons for the Agnew resignation, have produced many issues relating to our democratic system. The problem is how to apply democratic principles to elections in an age of media politics seemingly dominated by an atmosphere of dollar politics.

The 1972 Nixon reelection campaign and some committees for Democratic candidates have provided documentation for almost every corrupt practice. Observers had known that the American system of private financing of politics had its share of secret money, unreported money, extorted money, corporate money, laundered money, foreign money, and tax-free money. But the known instances were only rarely revealed and were thought to occur mostly in campaigns at the state and local levels. In 1972 a presidential campaign conducted by an incumbent at the pinnacle of the system was found replete with abuses relating to all aspects of funding. All this has now gone on the official record in court proceedings, congressional testimony under oath, and numerous depositions. Questions have also arisen concerning certain fund-raising practices of Democratic presidential contenders—Senator Hubert H. Humphrey and Representative Wilbur Mills, among others. The facts uncovered by Special Prosecutors Archibald Cox and Leon Jaworski, the Senate Select Committee on Presidential Campaign Activities, the House Judiciary Committee in its impeachment proceedings, and the General Accounting Office, have combined to make the 1972 election one of unsurpassed disclosure and awakening. All this promises to make 1972 the end of an era probably never to be equalled in the sizes of contributions and the numbers of violations.

"Watergate" became a code word for all the excesses of political campaigning. As a case history it contains elements of both reality and drama. If

1

written as a political novel, events and developments flowing from Watergate would seem incredible, involving wiretapping, burglary, breaking and entering, perjury, bribery, forgery, obstruction of justice, conspiracy, and violations of election and campaign finance laws.

In politics, too much money can be as damaging as too little money. Nixon's reelection campaign was tainted by the politics of affluence. With a lean budget there are no excess funds for sabotage or espionage. The Republicans have generally been more efficient and effective fund raisers than the Democrats. They have had a more stable financial base, more supporters in higher income brackets who are able to give, more habitual givers, and they have been better at systematically soliciting funds from the business community. The Nixon fund-raising team, from Maurice Stans and Herbert Kalmbach down the line, was experienced from the successful 1968 effort and had the added advantages of incumbency and a divided opposition. In these circumstances, it was too easy to raise more than $60 million, twice as much as had ever been recorded on behalf of a presidential candidate.

The Democrats, suffering from a large debt from the 1968 campaign and a chronic shortage of funds, have always seemed more vulnerable to special interest demands in return for contributions. It is ironic that while the Republicans criticized the Democrats for adopting delegate quotas at their convention, the Nixon campaign target amounts were considered by some of those being solicited as corporate and industry quotas. It is also ironic that the Republicans, the traditional exponents of private financing of politics, did more through the excesses and abuses of the Nixon campaign in 1972 to create an atmosphere conducive to public financing than all the lobbies or Democrats could have achieved alone.

A few examples of misdeeds that have been uncovered and were woven into the patchquilt of politicking in the operation of the Nixon reelection campaign follow:

1. Dairy co-operatives gave a probable total of $777,000[a] and milk price supports were raised; as much as $2 million or more had been promised by these groups, although they backed down after adverse publicity of their benefactions. Democratic congressional critics were unable to exploit fully the alleged links between contributions from the dairy lobby to the administration and the price support levels; records show there were many recipients of dairy funds on both sides of the aisle.

2. International Telephone and Telegraph (I.T.T.) offered to contribute amounts ranging from $100,000 to $400,000 (depending on whether one

---

[a]This total depends on whether all or part of $95,000 given to nonpresidential Republican committees in 1971 went to Nixon's campaign, which could bring the known total dairy support from $682,500 to over $777,000.

believes the company or the Watergate Committee) to the Republican National Convention. The dropping of an antitrust investigation was thought by some to have been a consequence.

3. Funds were laundered in Mexico and were given to the Nixon campaign, later becoming a source for financing the Watergate break-in.

4. Former Attorney General John Mitchell and former Commerce Secretary Maurice Stans were indicted for their involvement in the $200,000 contribution by financier Robert Vesco, but both were acquitted; nevertheless many questions will remain unanswered as long as Vesco does not talk.

5. Requests for funds were perceived by those being asked as extortion, particularly in the cases of American Airlines and American Ship Building contributions.

These and other episodes have forced students of political finance to rethink their approach to the problems. A fine line separates contributions and bribes. Many public officials do not need to be bribed because they hold views congenial to the contributor, and that is why the giver gives anyway. Yet, recent political history shows several other examples of how certain contributions have been used illegally to influence political decisions. Bobby Baker, formerly Secretary to the Senate Majority, got a cinch amendment introduced on the Senate floor that posed a threat to the savings and loan industry, then promised to kill it in return for cash contributions.[b] Similarly, allegations were made about contributions to LBJ's President's Club in return for government contracts.[1] And it has generally been forgotten that the Justice Department prosecuted 18 corporations in 1968-71 for violating the federal prohibition of use of corporate funds, in some cases for paying public relations firms and advertising agencies for work done on behalf of candidates, following false billing.

Political finance in the United States has long been undemocratic, with undue reliance on large gifts and a strong tendency toward corruption. The system of private financing survived because for many years it managed to provide sufficient funds. It also served the purposes of certain dominant special interests. The system came increasingly under attack in the 1960s not only because of past corruptions, but also because it began to fail to provide the funds needed as campaigning became more sophisticated and more expensive. The increased incidence of deficit campaign financing during the 1960s is striking evidence of this failure.

President Kennedy helped to get a reform movement underway by establishing a bipartisan Commission on Campaign Costs, taking the first presidential

---

[b]While serving as an employee of the United States Senate, Baker received $99,000 in cash from savings and loan executives, reportedly for distribution to senators up for reelection, and kept about $80,000 for himself. See Jerry Landauer, "Trial of Bobby Baker May Illustrate Dealings of Politics and Business," *Wall Street Journal*, January 11, 1967.

initiative on this subject since Theodore Roosevelt. It took a decade between the report of that commission and the reforms of 1971-72. Toward the end of that decade, organizations such as the National Committee for an Effective Congress and Common Cause began dramatizing the issue while lobbying for change. Media focus on campaign finance served as a catalyst, and the initiatives of the 1960s became a full-fledged movement for reform in the early 1970s.

A historical review of legislation covering the twentieth century shows that reaction to criticism of the political finance system through the years invariably yielded piecemeal legislation that imposed negative controls, restricting spending even as needs and costs were rising. To prevent candidates from becoming obligated to special interests, limits were set on the amounts of contributions. Funds from suspect sources were prohibited. To dilute the "spoils system," career civil servants were protected from political demands for cash. If there was danger that partisans would dominate the airwaves, all sides were guaranteed equal opportunity for free time, although opportunities to buy time were equal only for those who could pay for it. One after another, traditional sources of political funds were cut down without provision for new sources of supply.

Until recently no major reform movement concentrated on money raised for politics. Many reforms were made around the turn of the century but the demands then for prohibition against corporate giving were peripheral to other concerns about corporate power, such as demands for antitrust legislation. The movement then for giving publicity to contributors was only part of the movement against political corruption. In shielding the civil service from politics, the central issue was patronage as it affected hiring and firing practices and the quality of government performance. In short, instead of trying to put political spending on a rational and equitable footing, Americans did almost everything to institutionalize undemocratic methods, to encourage undesirable contributors, and to protect devious customs by disguise, subterfuge, evasion, and lack of candor. The main body of campaign law has been archaic and inadequate and is only now beginning to receive the serious scrutiny it deserves.

There have been few compensatory positive features to the generally negative character of laws regarding political finance. Historically, when the assessment of government employees was prohibited, no pattern of alternative statutory provisions followed to ease fund-raising problems or to reduce political costs; the gap or income loss was filled by corporate contributions. When corporate giving was prohibited, again no statutory alternatives were enacted; the gap was filled by contributions of wealthy individuals. When the wealthy were restricted in their giving (although there were many loopholes in these restrictions), again no permissive or enabling legislation was enacted to help make available new sources of funds; the gap this time was filled by a miscellany of measures, such as fund-raising dinners and other devices currently in use. This last gap has never been adequately filled.

The impact of the new technology—television, jets, polling—was felt increasingly in politics. Costs mounted, outpacing contributions. The givers, too often large contributors and special interests, were squeezed to give more. New contributors and new sources emerged as improved solicitation and collection systems developed in computerized mail drives and through associational networks. Labor and business pioneered in forming political action committees. Other organizations, especially trade associations, then peace groups, environmentalists, and other issue-oriented groups emulated them. Millionaire candidates raised the ante for other candidates, escalating costs but also focusing attention on wealth as a factor in electoral candidacy.

So the scene was set for the implementation of major campaign reforms. In 1970 a political broadcast bill passed the Congress but was vetoed by President Nixon. The reaction to the veto led to much broader change, including the disclosure features of the Federal Election Campaign Act of 1971 (FECA),[c] which had not been in the earlier limited bill giving broadcast price breaks to candidates.

Remarkably, the FECA preceded rather than followed the scandals of Watergate, considering how many observers had said for so long that only serious scandal would bring reform. The Bobby Baker and Tom Dodd cases may be considered causal, but reform came before the greatest of all recent scandals, Watergate, because of the persistence and leadership of a few members of Congress, a few groups, and some media attention. Once legislation reached the floors of the Senate and the House, pressure for it to be recorded for reform became overriding. Before the FECA, a tradition of disclosure dated back to 1910, but inadequacies in the predecessor law, the Federal Corrupt Practices Act of 1925, and inadequacy in enforcement led to a habitual failure of many political practitioners to take certain election laws seriously. For too many years in too many jurisdictions, candidates, other participants, and constituted enforcement authorities tended to wink at certain election laws. Loose and strained legal interpretations designed to assist friends and opponents alike helped keep the rules of the game agreeable to fellow politicians.

After the FECA went into effect, several more illegal financial acts associated with Watergate were uncovered, which strengthened the case for more effective enforcement of all election laws. Most of the evidences of misconduct were violations of laws already on the books, a culmination of the traditional failure of some candidates to take certain election laws seriously, or to interpret them loosely. Some aspects of Watergate, particularly in its early stages, would not have had as much impact had the old Corrupt Practices Act been in effect and the General Accounting Office (GAO) not available to investigate events that turned out to be violations of the new law. The findings and referrals of the GAO in ferreting out violations have been widely acclaimed and considered

---

[c]For a description, see Appendix A.

fair and impartial. Watergate focused attention on the FECA and educated the public to its provisions better than any designed publicity program could have done. In turn, the FECA focused attention on the financing of Watergate, so the interaction caused publicity about both to escalate.

A companion to the FECA, the Revenue Act of 1971,[d] also became effective in 1972. The tax incentives of the Revenue Act and the improved disclosure provisions of the FECA were designed to encourage small contributions to political campaigns. Improved public reporting of contributions were aimed at putting pressure on parties and candidates to raise more money in small sums and less in large amounts. That purpose was abetted by the companion enactment of tax credits or deductions for political contributions. The theory was that the tax benefits—if accompanied by an educational campaign to acquaint the American people of their availability, and if the candidates and committees stepped up their solicitation campaigns accordingly—could bring in more small funds. Tax incentives signifying government encouragement of the act of giving are in effect a "sales tool" enabling solicitors to ask small contributors—perhaps those giving up to $25 in the past—to double the amount of their gifts since the government is now sharing the cost. In short, the combination of disclosure of large contributions and of tax incentives could, if properly exploited, serve to broaden the financial base of politics. Needless to say, this promise was not fully exploited. There was no great educational or publicity campaign to inform the people of the tax incentives in the law. Nevertheless, more than a million contributors supported the Nixon and McGovern campaigns.

The Revenue Act of 1971 also contained a provision for a tax checkoff, an opportunity for taxpayers to check off on their tax returns $1 if a single return, $2 if a joint return, with the funds to be used to subsidize presidential elections. But this was not operative during the 1972 campaigns. There was no educational campaign in 1973 to inform taxpayers of the checkoff on federal income taxes. On the contrary, the Internal Revenue Service, in a seemingly conscious effort to subvert the checkoff availability, failed to include the checkoff on the main 1040 form. In its first year of operation, only 3.1 percent of the nation's taxpayers checked off about $4 million for that purpose. Responding to congressional pressure and law suits, the IRS did a credible turnaround in the second year of the checkoff. In 1974 a five-fold increase to 15 percent of the nation's taxpayers added $17.5 million to the fund, plus $8.4 million collected retroactively from taxpayers who missed the checkoff in the first year.[2] In 1975 the response increased to about 24 percent of taxpayers and brought in $31.3 million more, to make a three-year total of $61.5 million.

Various disclosures resulting from investigations into the Watergate burglary

---

[d]For a description, see Appendix B.

of Democratic headquarters and from legal depositions and suits provided over a year of headlines. Some interesting details revealed by the disclosures were:

1. Nixon committees raised $11.4 million in the month before the new law took effect, taking in $2.3 million on April 5 and $3 million on April 6, the two days before the FECA became applicable.

2. Nixon campaigners spent almost $5 million on April 5 and 6, more than half of their total expenditures of $9.7 million for the pre-April 7 period. In those two days, large sums went to direct mail and polling firms as prepayments that it was thought would never have to be disclosed.

3. Nixon campaigners had access to a portion of $1.7 million in funds left over from the 1968 campaign (some of which had been spent in 1969-70-71 for political or "intelligence" purposes not directly related to the 1972 reelection effort) and added several million dollars more in cash contributions, providing the basis for several secret cash funds used, among other purposes, for election-related "dirty tricks."

4. Of the record $63 million fund raised by the Nixon campaign, $19.8 million, or close to one-third, was in contributions from 153 donors giving $50,000 or more. Seventy-five of the 153 donors, including one of the wealthiest Americans, J. Paul Getty, contributed $100,000 or more.

5. Illegal corporate contributions that were returned to seven corporations by the Committee to Re-Elect the President amounted to $465,000; 21 corporations either requested return or were tried and fined for contributing $960,000 illegally during the election to several recipients (almost $850,000 to Nixon).

6. Contributions from eight individuals amounting to $1,250,000 also were returned by the Nixon campaign.

7. The largest contributions to the Nixon campaign came from Wall Street, banking and finance industries, oil, gas, trucking, and drug industries, and United States ambassadors.

The matter of the pre-April 7 contributions suggests a number of characteristics of American politics circa 1972. One was the propensity of some politicians to take advantage of loopholes in the law. A second was the role of a public interest group—Common Cause—in resorting to the courts to settle political issues. Other public interest groups also have become involved. Ralph Nader's Public Citizen group sued, for example, for records on the milk industry's alleged connection with price supports.

Although the abuses of the 1972 election are many, the headlines have failed to stress the series of advances and positive steps that were made. When the emotionalism subsides and the quest to rout out the perpetrators of the misdeeds ends, perhaps the political system will recall the positive gains:

8. Various candidates, both Republican and Democratic, contesting for presidential nomination made voluntary disclosure of their contributors and lenders in the pre-April 7 period. There were gaps in the disclosures but nevertheless the effort was made.

9. The disclosures of the pre-April 7 receipts and expenditures of the Nixon reelection campaign put the Nixon campaign fully on the record, the first presidential campaign in history so fully revealed. The McGovern voluntary disclosure put that campaign mostly on the record, but was so widely decentralized with spontaneous grass-roots organizations not fully accounted for by the national campaign, that comprehensive disclosure was difficult to achieve for the pre-April 7 period. In other actions, too, Common Cause kept pressure on and helped dramatize the issue of political finance.

10. Ralph Nader's Congress Project released political studies of all members of Congress, which included information about the patterns of financing their campaigns.

11. The Democratic National Committee reduced its 1968 debt through a convention telethon, which netted $2 million in pledges from 300,000 contributors, most of them small givers, and then repeated with successful telethons in 1973, 1974, and 1975.

12. The McGovern campaign raised funds from 600,000 contributors during 1971-72 for the first truly broad-based Democratic presidential campaign. The McGovern campaign is the only Democratic presidential campaign not to leave a deficit since the days of FDR.

13. The U.S. General Accounting Office showed the way to vigorous, even-handed administration of the FECA, although the powers of enforcement continued to rest in the Department of Justice. The GAO could only refer "apparent violations" of the law to the Attorney General, but in publicizing such referrals, tried to put pressure on the Justice Department to prosecute cases. Justice moved slowly, and where convictions were achieved, as in two cases involving the Finance Committee to Re-Elect the President, no individuals were charged and only fines were levied.

The FECA and the Revenue Act of 1971 represented meaningful regulation of the financing of politics, but were only first steps, with major amendments following in 1974.[e] Nixon's 1972 victory will be recorded in history for its excesses and misjudgments, but also as an example of how political finance laws can be made effective, even against an incumbent administration, if vigorously enforced by independent investigators such as GAO and by independent agencies such as the Special Prosecutor and his staff, and if the media and the public play their essential role of vigilence.

---

[e]For a description, see Appendix C.

2

The Impact of the New Federal Election Laws: Part I

Implementing the Federal Election Campaign Act, 1971

President Richard M. Nixon signed the Federal Election Campaign Act of 1971 (FECA) on February 7, 1972. The Act became effective 60 days later, on April 7, in the midst of the 1972 presidential and congressional campaigns. The FECA began a process of improving the administration and enforcement of laws regulating political finance, particularly in making available the investigative and auditing capabilities of the U.S. General Accounting Office (GAO). The timing of the new law could not have been more appropriate, given the gross irregularities that were occurring in the Nixon reelection campaign as disclosed later by Watergate investigations; some of the practices in that campaign, of course, were designed to take place before the new law became effective.[a]

The FECA gave 14 specific statutory responsibilities to the Comptroller General (Elmer B. Staats) who heads the GAO, the Secretary of the Senate (Francis R. Valeo), and the Clerk of the House of Representatives (W. Pat Jennings).[b] Under the predecessor law, the Federal Corrupt Practices Act of 1925 (FCPA), the two supervisory officers, the Secretary and the Clerk, were limited to operating little more than passive repositories of political fund reports. The 1972 law added the GAO as the agency responsible for presidential and vice-presidential campaigns. The Comptroller General, the Clerk, and the Secretary all began preparatory work in late 1971, even before the law was fully enacted, and joint discussion among the three supervisory office staffs began in December 1971. After the bill was signed by the President on February 7, 1972, all three supervisory officers set up task forces to establish

---

[a]For earlier appraisals of the operation of the law, see Herbert E. Alexander, "Impact of New Federal Election Laws in the United States" (A paper presented at the International Political Science Association Congress, Montreal, August 1973); Alexander, "The Federal Election Campaign Act of 1972: Is It Working?", *Politeia*, vol. I, no. 4 (1972), 21; and Jeffrey M. Berry and Jerry Goldman, "Congress and Public Policy: A Study of the Federal Election Campaign Act of 1971," *Harvard Journal on Legislation*, vol. 10, no. 2 (February 1973), 331-65. For an account of the legislative history of the law, see Robert L. Peabody, Jeffrey M. Berry, William G. Frasure, and Jerry Goldman, *To Enact a Law: Congress and Campaign Financing* (New York: Praeger Publishers, Inc., 1972); and Alexander, *Money in Politics* (Washington, D.C.: Public Affairs Press, 1972).

[b]For FECA provisions, see Appendix A.

offices and procedures to carry out their duties relating to federal elections. On March 24, 1972 Comptroller General Staats established the Office of Federal Elections (OFE) within the GAO.[c] The FECA required the supervisory officers to receive, examine, audit, tabulate, publish, and preserve reports about political contributions and expenditures from the almost 5,000 committees that were to register in 1972 under the requirements of the act. Each officer had the authority to investigate complaints, conduct audits on his own initiative, and refer "apparent violations" to appropriate enforcement authorities. A full-time staff of administrators, lawyers,[d] accountants, and computer specialists assisted each supervisory officer in dealing with his responsibilities.

The GAO received most attention because of its focus on the presidential campaigns of 1972 and it led the way in the public disclosure of investigations, audits, and referrals of apparent violations to the Justice Department and by maximizing the impact of Watergate events throughout 1973 and 1974. In 1974, of course, a new round of Senate and House campaigns drew public attention to the work of the Secretary and the Clerk. The FECA served as a major factor in forwarding investigations of the Watergate break-in at critical times when the investigative momentum might otherwise have been lost. Some aspects of Watergate's early stages, when information was being developed about the $89,000 laundered in Mexico and funnelled through Watergate burglar Bernard Barker's bank account, would not have had as much impact had the old law been in effect and the OFE not available to investigate events that turned out to be violations of the new law. This is also true of the $25,000 contribution of Dwayne Andreas, similarly discovered in Barker's records.

Although the responsibilities of the GAO related specifically to presidential campaigns, its involvement in the field of political regulation had broad consequences. Its insulation from political pressures put the Comptroller General in a unique position, giving him more latitude than either the Secretary of the Senate or the Clerk of the House. The GAO had an image to preserve as the elite corps of accountants in the federal government, and the Comptroller General's vigorous public disclosure policy had implications for the other supervisory officers. On the other hand, GAO administration at times lagged behind the Secretary and the Clerk in preparing and updating on a daily basis computer indexes of filings and in other matters.

The Clerk and the Secretary were initially slow to make public disclosures of their referrals to the Justice Department, while the Comptroller General began to issue in 1972 audit reports on political committees, available for public

---

[c]For a detailed accounting of the work of the GAO Office of Federal Elections, see Larry D. McCoy, "GAO's Responsibilities in Federal Elections," *Policy Studies Journal*, II, no. 4 (Summer 1974), 242.

[d]Counsel to the Secretary of the Senate were private attorneys on contract for intermittent service.

inspection, detailing findings and conclusions, and recommending either no further action or referral (usually to the Attorney General) for apparent violation(s) of the FECA. By publicizing each case, the GAO sought to prod the Justice Department to prosecute; as noted later, the Justice Department was not easily moved to resolute action. The GAO also published in the Comptroller General's annual report such information as a summary of the audit and investigative activities of the OFE, and in appendixes such lists as the number of audit reports issued, and names of committees audited, with dates of the reports.[e] In some cases, this policy came perilously close to unwitting entanglement with politics; for example, one publicized referral of apparent violations by Senator Humphrey's campaign was announced by the GAO on the day of the California primary in which he was a candidate.

The Clerk and the Secretary made public their enforcement totals later but did not publicize each case, or name the candidate or committee, at the time of their audits or referrals.[f] The Clerk referred over 6,000 cases to Justice in 1972-73. The Secretary referred 565 cases of late and nonfilers by March 30, 1973, and published progress reports on audits and field investigations in 33 Senate elections involving 306 candidates and 1,169 committees, in March 1973 and August 1974.

Each officer established his own set of standards to determine apparent violations. While the law did not define the meaning of "report apparent violations of law," the Comptroller General evaluated cases and referred what he considered to be major rather than technical violations of any federal or state law to the Attorney General. On the other hand, the Clerk questioned whether

[e]See Comptroller General of the United States, United States General Accounting Office, *Annual Report 1973*, pp. 11-15, 179, 223-25, 273-81; see also *Report of The Office of Federal Elections of the General Accounting Office In Administering the Federal Election Campaign Act of 1971*, February 6, 1975.

[f]For detailed reports by the Secretary of the Senate, see *The Federal Election Campaign Act: Report on Audits, Field Investigations, Complaints and Referrals in Connection with Elections for the U.S. Senate in 1972*, prepared by Orlando B. Potter under the direction of Francis R. Valeo, Secretary of the Senate (Washington, D.C.: U.S. Government Printing Office, 1974); *Technical Report on the Implementation of the Act with Respect to Elections for the Senate*, prepared by Marilyn E. Courtot under the direction of Francis R. Valeo, Secretary of the Senate (Washington, D.C.: U.S. Government Printing Office, 1973); *Federal Campaign Disclosure at the State Level with Respect to Elections for the U.S. Senate in 1972*, prepared by Alicia Rae Fisher under the direction of Francis R. Valeo, Secretary of the Senate (Washington, D.C.: U.S. Government Printing Office, 1974). For information on investigations by the House of Representatives, see Campaign Expenditures Committee, *Report of the Special Committee to Investigate Campaign Expenditures*, 1972, House Report No. 93-1, 93rd Cong., 1st sess. (Washington, D.C.: U.S. Government Printing Office, January, 1973); House Report No. 93-1, part II, February 1973. (Part II is a separately bound supplement, which covers the period January 3-31, 1973.) See also Campaign Expenditures Committee, House Report No. 93-286, 93rd Cong., 1st sess. (Washington, D.C.: U.S. Government Printing Office, June 1973). See also *Supplementary Statement of W. Pat Jennings, Clerk of the House of Representatives, to the Subcommittee on Legislative Branch Appropriations of the House Committee on Appropriations on the Fiscal Year 1975 Budget Estimates for the U.S. House of Representatives and Certain "Joint Items,"* February 27, 1974.

the supervisory officers had any choice in referring all violations, major or minor, for the Attorney General to evaluate as to degree of seriousness. However, the Clerk did classify referrals, categorizing types of violations for the guidance of the Department of Justice. The Secretary felt disclosure policy should serve to protect the rights of the parties concerned in situations that ultimately could involve legal action, while at the same time seeking to insure the integrity of the enforcement process—admittedly a difficult balance to achieve. The Secretary did not start referrals until 1973. The Comptroller General chose to refer only the major cases that were serious violations and had a chance of being acted on. The Clerk's and the Secretary's rationale for not disclosing the names of candidates or committees was that the vast majority of violations were minor or inadvertent record-keeping errors, and that publicizing the referral might have needlessly embarrassed and perhaps adversely affected those cited.[g] This policy had the effect of protecting alleged noncompliers, particularly incumbents whose votes elect the Clerk and the Secretary every new Congress. Of course, the Department of Justice had discretion to sort out and surface the major cases, but it did not regularly release information either. This policy had the effect of shifting responsibility from the Clerk and the Secretary to another branch of government, and as will be seen, the Department of Justice did not have a previous record nor did it establish a new one of tough enforcement of election laws.

One problem faced in administering the FECA was that the Comptroller General, the Clerk, and the Secretary each received thousands of detailed reports. For the period covering April 7 to December 31, 1972, the GAO received approximately 83,000 pages of reports, the Clerk 117,000, and the Secretary 69,500, for a total 269,500 pages of data. Some of these figures excluded instruction pages and audit notices but others did not; all included registration forms and reports of hundreds of state and local, labor, business, professional, and miscellaneous committees, which qualified as political committees under the law.

The tri-partite arrangement of supervisory officers brought considerable overlap and duplication in filings. For example, a single committee that supported candidates for President, the Senate, and the House had to file reports containing the same information with all three officers. Of 4,744 separate

[g]For example, in the midst of the 1974 congressional debates on new campaign reform laws, more than 200 senators, challengers, and political committees were found to have violated the campaign disclosure laws already in force. As discussed in Jack Anderson's March 30, 1974 column, "Many Lawmakers Violate Law," The Center for Public Financing of Elections found the following violators of the FECA failed to file the required report by the March 10 deadline, and faced maximum penalties of a year in prison and a $1,000 fine: 34 senators, challengers, and their personal committees; and 132 special interest committees, ranging from savings and loan groups to bankers, doctors, clothing workers, firearms zealots, and realtors. These figures are unverified by the Secretary's staff.

committees registered under the FECA, more than 1,000 committees filed with two or three of the supervisory officers. The supervisory officers were required by law to make annual tabulations of campaign receipt and expenditure information, broken down by candidate and party, but the products were unnecessarily confusing and duplicative. Researchers encountered problems in distinguishing the discrete information on campaigns for President, Senate, and House from the overlapping. Each officer developed his own procedures for publishing findings: GAO devised its own computer program for annual reports, the first of which was published in August 1973. After consulting with the Clerk and the Secretary on a common format, GAO published a later, cleaner version in December 1973 as shown in Appendix D. The Clerk's report was published in April 1974, with an improved addendum published in June 1974, and the Secretary's was published in October 1974.[h] The GAO also published in October 1972 the only preelection official listing of contributors, compiled before the computer program was completed.

Each of the supervisory officers built a small staff to deal with his responsibilities under the law, and each tended to be somewhat jealous of his own prerogatives; the GAO used additional personnel from its regional offices for many audits. Although the three supervisory officers met jointly only a few times, their respective staffs met frequently, and particularly at the outset when discussions were held on administering and implementing the law. Much bargaining and negotiation occurred at these meetings. Among priority tasks were the devising of reporting forms and the drafting of regulations. The Clerk took and maintained the initiative in drafting revision upon revision of disclosure forms, in spite of GAO's accounting expertise. On the other hand, GAO's initial proposals for regulations were stronger than those of the Clerk and the Secretary, and many of these had to be revised before being accepted by the two more politically constrained officers.

A significant decision was to omit the use of social security numbers for identification purposes under the disclosure provisions of the new law. Staats had favored this, but Jennings and Valeo knew that their use would be very unpopular in Congress. The GAO won an important decision, however, in the matter of what the law meant by "filing"—merely mailing by a certain date, or

---

[h]Printouts included: *Alphabetical Listing of 1972 Presidential Campaign Receipts*, volumes I and II, Office of Federal Elections, General Accounting Office (Washington, D.C.: U.S. Government Printing Office, November 1973); *The Annual Statistical Report of Contributions and Expenditures Made During the 1972 Election Campaigns for the U.S. House of Representatives*, parts I and II, by W. Pat Jennings, as Clerk of the House of Representatives and Supervisory Officer (Washington, D.C.: U.S. Government Printing Office, April/June 1974); *The Annual Statistical Report of Receipts and Expenditures Made in Connection with Elections for the U.S. Senate in 1972*, prepared under the direction of Francis R. Valeo, Secretary of the Senate, Supervisory Officer for Senate Elections (Washington, D.C.: U.S. Government Printing Office, October 1974).

actually requiring that the report be in the hands of the appropriate office by
that date. This was particularly meaningful in the case of the last preelection
report, which the law said should be "filed" five days prior to an election. If
simply mailed, much information might not be available in time for dissemina-
tion to voters before an election. The House office wanted the more lax
definition. The GAO staff, however, was backed by the Senate staff, leading
to agreement that filing meant delivery before the declared dates or deposit as
certified airmail no later than midnight of the second day preceding the filing
(within 500 miles of Washington, airmail was not necessary, but mail still had
to be certified). This decision was finalized in mid-March when the three supervisory officers met privately for the first time.

For another example, the original GAO draft would have required that if
a committee treasurer were unable to secure the necessary identifying information about contributors giving more than $500, the money would have to be
returned to the contributor. After negotiation, the final regulations required
only that the treasurer use his best efforts to obtain the information, and keep
a record of his efforts in doing so. The GAO regulations finally issued were
longer and more explanatory than those of the Clerk and the Secretary, who
issued shorter and simpler ones that permitted more flexibility in interpretation. Notwithstanding these cooperative efforts, there was inevitable incon-
venience and duplication resulting from the tri-partite arrangement, which
emphasized the need for a single agency to monitor reports from all federal
candidates.

A Federal Election Commission to serve as a single repository for all
federal campaigns had been a part of the original Senate bill in 1971, but it
was traded out in joint conference committee. A major reason for proposing
the commission was to isolate the functions of the FECA as much as possible
from political pressures, combining the supervisory offices into one independent
agency. This was partially accomplished in the FECA Amendments of 1974.
Unlike the Comptroller General, who has no statutory role in the election field
under the 1974 law, the Secretary and the Clerk survived as ex-officio members
of the Federal Election Commission. The roles of the Clerk and the Secretary
mandated by the 1974 Amendments to serve as custodians of reports filed by
or on behalf of candidates to their respective houses, are unclear until the commission decides the meaning of the law.

GAO Reports

All the GAO reports—simple audits, nonreferrals, and referrals—were made
public and specifics were detailed. This was designed to: (1) put pressure on
the Justice Department, which had a history of nonenforcement, to prosecute
cases involving violations of election laws; and (2) show candidates and the

public that the GAO was serious about its enforcement role. Since the GAO first published its audit reports in June 1972, 420 committees were audited through December 16, 1974, as shown in Appendix E. Of these, most were undertaken in 1973 and 1974. Of the total, 49 committees had no apparent violations, 260 had technical violations that did not warrant referral, and violations of 111 committees warranted referrals to the Justice Department for further investigation or action. Forty Democratic committees were cited for minor technical violations, and 12 committees were referred to Justice; 65 Republican committees were cited, and 13 were referred. In addition, 36 McGovern committees were cited for minor technical violations, and 42 others were referred to Justice; and 45 Nixon committees were cited, and eight committees were referred. Fifteen labor committees had minor technical violations, and eight were referred; nineteen business-professional committees had minor technical violations, and four were referred; two newspapers were referred; and three individuals were referred to the Justice Department.

The GAO undertook in January 1973 a program of routine audits of the 1972 activity of all candidates and their personal committees and many nationally oriented committees. It also investigated apparent violations brought to the GAO's attention by complaints or concerned persons. Most of the reports dealt with committees supporting the two major party nominees. In addition to making a number of reports on the Finance Committee to Re-Elect the President (FCRP) and other Nixon committees, and the McGovern for President and other McGovern committees, GAO investigated a number of matters relating to the preconvention campaigns of other nominees. It issued audit reports on committees ranging from the Harris County (Texas) Republican Executive Committee to the Peabody for Vice President Committee. And it undertook systematically to audit every major party state central committee; some had filed and some had not. Among other audit purposes was the effort to determine whether those that had not filed had been involved sufficiently in federal elections to have been required to file.

The GAO developed certain guidelines to determine whether apparent violations should be referred to the Justice Department.[i] Noncooperation or serious violations, usually involving large sums of money or deliberate evasion of the law, were reasons for referring cases to Justice.

Typical of the violations that the GAO considered amendable, and on which it accepted a revised report were:

1. Failure to report organizational changes in principal officers, usually the treasurer
2. Failure of political committees to register with the GAO

---

[i]At least one of the other supervisory officers privately questioned the setting of such guidelines, claiming the law gave no such discretion to make judgments.

3. Failure to disclose or to fully disclose information about donors contributing in excess of $100, including name, address, occupation, principal place of business, and date of contribution
4. Nondisclosure of receipts and expenditures in excess of $100
5. Failure to include required notice on literature soliciting contributions
6. Failure to list all depositories
7. Inaccurate reporting of cash on hand
8. Errors in reporting expenditures and receipts
9. Incomplete or inaccurate reporting of transfers between committees
10. Failure to report contributions received the last few days before and after the election within the required 48 hours after receipt
11. Unreported or inadequately reported loans, debts, contributions of shares of stock, and in-kind contributions
12. Incorrect dates, reporting periods, and cutoff dates for reports
13. Incorrectly reporting transfers, expenditures, or receipts on wrong forms

These violations were often due to ambiguities in the new law or in the GAO regulations, or confusion about the reporting procedures. In some of its audits, GAO admitted deficiencies or ambiguities in its procedures. During the initial audits, GAO personnel refined their techniques, and everyone involved learned by doing. For example, in the GAO report of October 6, 1972, concerning the McGovern for President–D.C. Committee and other related committees, GAO admitted that its regulations were not explicit on procedures for reporting payments for advertising "made by such committee or on behalf of such committee."

As another example, in its February 13, 1973 report on the Finance Committee to Re-Elect the President (FCRP), the GAO recognized a clear need to make the law more explicit. GAO proposed an amendment to the Comptroller General's regulations, never promulgated, which expressly would have required that contributions which totalled more than $5,000 be reported under the 48-hour provision regardless of whether the contribution was to be divided among committees. GAO also contemplated applying a similar requirement to the regular reports so that any contribution aggregating more than $100 would have to be reported in total by the political committee initially receiving it, even if it was divided among committees.

Referrals to the Justice Department included some of the following violations:

1. Accepting corporate contributions and those of foreign nationals
2. Improper handling of cash contributions
3. Contributions made by one person but in the name of another
4. Failure of newspapers to obtain the required written statement from political committees and failure to receive certification from candidates for advertisements stating that the expense was within the candidate's total limit for media expenditures

5. Failure to keep detailed and exact accounting of certain contributions after April 7, 1972, the effective date of the FECA
6. Failure to keep and maintain adequate books and records on a current basis on checks and their proceeds and large balances of cash
7. Failure to keep and maintain detailed and exact accounting of currency funds and contributions that may have been received on or after April 7, 1972 and failure to disclose details of such contributions
8. Incomplete or inaccurate reporting of contributions and expenditures
9. Overreporting receipts and expenditures by large sums
10. Use of fictitious expenditure amounts to balance receipts and expenditures
11. Use of altered invoices and duplicate receipts to support expenditures
12. Officials "knowingly and willfully making false, fictitious, or fraudulent statements"
13. Unreported large cash transactions after April 7, 1972
14. Patronage contributions from state patronage employees who receive compensation "provided for or made possible in whole or part by an act of Congress"

In some of these cases, the GAO referred certain violations to other appropriate agencies in addition to the Justice Department. For example, in its July 27, 1973 review of the Indiana Republican State Central Committee, GAO investigated assessed contributions, presumably in violation of the Hatch Act, made by highway employees working under federal grant funds. Copies of the report were forwarded to the Secretary of Transportation and the chairman of the Civil Service Commission. The GAO also recommended that the matter be brought to the attention of Congress to see if legislative action was warranted. In several instances referrals were made to the Internal Revenue Service, a particular state attorney general, or the Federal Communications Commission.

GAO had a formidable task, but under the circumstances it performed generally well in covering 1972 financial activity. Philip S. Hughes, director of the Office of Federal Elections at GAO, received the Rockefeller Award for Distinguished Government Service as a result of his stewardship of OFE, although his previous government service was thought to be an important factor. Hughes' handling of the difficult administrative and enforcement problems was widely heralded.

Some of GAO's efforts, such as the state audit program, were too ambitious to suit some. In June 1974 Republican National Chairman George Bush, and Democratic National Chairman Robert Strauss, jointly approached GAO and the Justice Department after receiving complaints from some state chairmen that state party committees were "receiving unfair treatment." Bush and Strauss met with Comptroller General Staats and cited a number of apparent inequities that occurred during the course of GAO audits. The following suggestions were given to Staats:

1. That GAO make available any report of an audit of the state central com-
    mittee to the governor of the state if he is of the same party
2. That GAO more actively aid state parties in establishing separate campaign
    committees to participate in exclusively federal campaign activities. This
    would exempt the state committees from reporting under federal law their
    activities on behalf of state and local nonfederal candidates
3. That GAO develop better ways to inform party officials in the states
    regarding reporting procedures
4. That GAO agree to work with the national parties to develop realistic pro-
    posals for campaign reform legislation

The GAO agreed to reevaluate its general policies, developed as experience was
gained under the FECA. As a result of the meeting, the policy of requiring
political committees to register and report because they made travel and accom-
modation arrangements for delegates to national conventions was dropped.
Also, senior officials of GAO agreed to meet with any state representatives who
would come to Washington with questions or problems relating to the FECA.

Next, Bush and Strauss met with Attorney General William Saxbe, to discuss the problems both parties were having complying with the FECA. They
discussed the need for remedial legislation with him and were encouraged by his
"helpful attitude." Saxbe assured them that the Justice Department would conduct separate and careful studies of each report referred by one of the supervisory officers before seeking indictments. The party chairman wrote to their
state party organizations and to members of Congress to explain their represen-
tations.

While the 1974 FECA Amendments were nearing final congressional action
and it appeared that the new Federal Election Commission would be structured
so as to be dominated by Congress, the GAO decided to withdraw from active
participation in the administration of the new law, rather than accept ex officio
membership on the commission. At the same time, some members of Congress
wanted to bar the GAO from further responsibility in elections, and the final
enactment reflected that position. While the bill for the FECA Amendments
of 1974 was still in joint Senate-House conference committee, quietly GAO
began to disband the OFE—somewhat prematurely in view of the long transition
period that ensued without any effective supervision of 1972 debt repayments
or early fund-raising efforts for the 1976 presidential campaigns. The GAO
was also criticized for never auditing 1973 or 1974 political activity. Staff
members sought new jobs and the OFE prepared for the required orderly transfer of information and responsibilities to the newly created Federal Election
Commission. As of October 15, 1974, when the Amendments were signed into
law, the OFE had scheduled 565 audits of 1972 political committees. Of these,
426 were completed, 383 reports issued, leaving 43 audits completed by letter
but not published, and others stopped in process. The GAO received

surprisingly few press mentions when replaced by the FEC, but was the object of much media and editorial support for its vigorous administration of the law while it was still in effect.

Some notion of the difficulties the GAO had were illustrated when the Finance Committee to Re-Elect the President agreed a few days before the 1972 election to release the names of some of its pre-April 7 contributors in a partial settlement of a Common Cause disclosure suit. Comptroller General Elmer Staats said the next day, "We had been told orally [by FCRP] that all those records had been destroyed." After exclaiming that the current situation in campaign financing was "nothing short of a national scandal," he went on to suggest the limitations of the current mechanisms: "We do not have subpoena powers. We have to ride with whatever information we can develop through access to open records. And we cannot prosecute."[j] In spite of these shortcomings in the laws, the GAO effort was considered by some to be too enthusiastic, and so the GAO is no longer involved in the election field.

Clearinghouse

A lesser-known provision of the FECA provided for a Clearinghouse on Election Administration in the GAO. The Clearinghouse contracted for independent studies on such topics as selection and duties of boards of elections, practices in registering voters, and variations in voting and counting methods. Some studies have been published[1] and others are in process; as of January 1, 1974 14 separate contract studies were either completed or underway, at a total contract cost of just under $1 million, with administration, publication, and dissemination costs amounting to another $200,000. The Clearinghouse contracted with the Congressional Research Service of the Library of Congress to publish a monthly

---

[j]Quoted in David Nyhan, "Chief U.S. Auditor Calls Campaign Financing 'A National Scandal'," *The Boston Globe*, November 3, 1972. One unusual audit conducted by the GAO illustrates this point. In this case, there was a refusal of access to financial records. The group being audited was the Republican Victory Committee of Wilmington, Delaware. Questions arose concerning its relationship with the Legislative Dinner Committee, in particular the sale of tickets to a September 1972 fund-raising event. The event was held to raise funds in support of both federal and state candidates, and was jointly sponsored by the two committees. The Republican Victory Committee had reported under the FECA, the Legislative Dinner Committee had not. The latter committee had ticket sales of a least $9,900, requiring its reporting, and two contributions were discovered where the name of the original payee, the Victory Committee, had been crossed out and changed to the Legislative Dinner Committee. On the basis of this evidence, the GAO requested access to the latter committee's financial records, a request refused by the committee's counsel, Rodney M. Layton, on grounds of safeguarding confidentiality and alleging that the GAO did not have this legal authority. He offered access to expenditure but not contribution records, a partial access deemed not acceptable by the GAO. In October 1974 the Comptroller General referred the matter to the Justice Department for further action.

Federal-State Election Law Survey analyzing federal and state legislation and judicial decisions,[k] and also to issue a periodic survey of state election laws. The Clearinghouse has been a useful national center in the neglected field of election administration and has served as a catalyst in election law research and in the interchange of ideas. The Clearinghouse publications have been well received among federal, state, and local election officials, and among students of the electoral process. Speakers were provided at meetings of the Association of Secretaries of State and other such groups. The Clearinghouse also provided advice when sought, and consultation when needed. Although the FECA Amendments of 1974 relieved the Comptroller General of his responsibility, the clearinghouse function was maintained, vested in the Federal Election Commission.

House and Senate Procedures

Under the United States Constitution, each house of Congress is the judge of its own membership. Under the FECA, the Clerk and the Secretary were supervisory officers, and each had his own traditions to protect and pressures to meet. At first the two congressional officers were overshadowed in the media by the Comptroller General, who had comparatively massive resources available to him. The focus on the GAO and on the presidential campaigns in 1972 served to draw attention away from congressional campaigns, giving the Capitol Hill offices lower visibility and less public exposure. Of course, Common Cause monitored the congressional campaigns and filed numerous complaints on the failure of candidates and committees to comply fully. The GAO had only the 1972 election to monitor in its three years under the FECA, whereas the Clerk and the Secretary had to cope with 1972 problems while preparing for a new cycle of elections starting in 1974, when new regulations were also issued.

House

As indicated earlier, the Clerk referred approximately 6,000 cases to the Justice Department relating to 1972-73 alleged violations, some 4,900 in 1972,

---

[k]July 1, 1973 marked the first publication of the Office of Federal Elections' *Federal-State Election Law Survey*, which comprises major election legislation, both federal and state, from January 1, 1973, with analyses of relevant Supreme Court, federal, and state cases involving election matters. The *Survey* aims primarily "to furnish in the form of a brief analysis the essential provisions of state elections laws and important court decisions in the election law field," and proposed bills in the Congress.

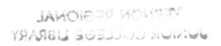

and 1,200 in 1973. Of these cases, the majority failed to file any reports, some failed to file all required reports, some failed to file duplicates with their secretaries of state, and some filed late. There was some duplication in these referrals and some classification of types of violations. During the first 16 months under FECA, it has been learned, there were what the Clerk's staff considered to be 13 major House referrals (nine candidates and ten committees) involving corporate and union contributions and loans, candidates exceeding their media expenditure limits, and other similar violations. Undoubtedly, the Clerk's task was the largest because there are so many candidates for the House—in 1972 some 1,700 candidates and 2,200 committees. He had the highest volume of paperwork, and was able to establish an operation that operated smoothly given the huge amount of work.

Every election year, the House of Representatives has established independently a Special Committee to Investigate Campaign Expenditures. The Clerk tried to get the committee abolished in 1972 (he was successful in 1974) but instead was ordered by House Resolution 819 of February 28, 1972 to assist it by reviewing jointly cases in which complaints were made. During 1972, under the chairmanship of Representative Thomas P. (Tip) O'Neill, Jr., most of the Clerk's referrals were not acted upon positively. For example, of the 21 major cases referred to the Special Committee by the Clerk, only one case was referred to the Attorney General for apparent violations of the FECA. This and one other case in which the complaint was ultimately dismissed, were investigated jointly by the Clerk's and Special Committee's staffs. But under 1973 Chairman Neal Smith, who succeeded O'Neill, the committee forwarded 11 referrals to the Attorney General out of 14 major cases referred by the Clerk for further investigation, and referred one case to the House Administration Committee for possible remedial action.[1] The Clerk was closely monitored in the administration of his duties by the House Administration Committee, and its chairman, Representative Wayne Hays, D-Ohio. Some interpreted this involvement of the committees as diluting the statutory responsibility the law gave the Clerk, although the Clerk retained and exercised ultimate judgment.

For example, the new law was not long in effect—a little over three weeks—before it was attacked. Chairman Hays announced that he would seek, through amendment, to reduce the number of reports required in election years from six to four, as well as to redefine the word "filing." Later that month, he said his committee was considering changing the disclosure requirements relating to

---

[1]The (House) Campaign Expenditures Committee *Reports of the Special Committee, op. cit.*, detail investigations of matters relating to corrupt tactics and practices in House elections including during adjournment of Congress, and report to the incoming House on vioations of United States statutes and state statutes pertaining to elections and other matters involving the election process. Each *Report* includes a summary of "Activity of the Special Committee in Conjunction with the Clerk of the House."

the occupation and principal place of business of a contributor. Hays wanted to add the qualifier "if known" to this requirement for information—obviously making it more difficult to link contributions with their private interests. At one point, Hays even suggested that the House share of the supervisory tasks be shifted from the Clerk's office to his own House Administration Committee.

Hays made his displeasure known when House Clerk Jennings went before the House Administration Committee in 1972 to ask for an annual appropriation of $399,030 for 38 additional staff to administer the law. The committee approved $156,984 for 12 new positions.[2] Hays also ordered that the price for photocopying copies of the filed reports be raised from ten cents to $1.00 per page. Common Cause, which was to make the monitoring of the new law one of its major projects, responded by suing the Clerk of the House in federal court; Hays backed down to ten cents a page before the suit was adjudicated.

If the House Administration Committee, its chairman, and the Special Committee when extant, had interfered less with the administration of the law, the Clerk would have had a freer hand to administer the law as he deemed necessary. The tensions between the Clerk and the House Administration Committee indicate the problems the Federal Election Commission could also have under the 1974 Amendments if the Congress' desirable function of oversight is overzealous; a conflict of interest arises because members of Congress are among the groups being regulated. The problems of reconciling constitutional authority of each house to judge its own members, and to establish regulatory bodies and appropriate money for them, with the need for independent judgment on elections of members, will remain difficult.

By 1973 refinement and streamlining of the Clerk's operation allowed nearly all statements and reports by the candidates and their committees to be available for public inspection within 24 hours of receipt—24 hours earlier than required by law. After receipt, each statement and report was given a desk check for completeness and correctness. This resulted in more than 3,500 notifications of omissions or errors on the statements and reports being mailed to candidates and committees in 1972, and more than 6,800 letters dunning noncompliers. In addition, several field audits, investigations, and hearings were conducted. During 1973 the Clerk referred 418 apparent violations by candidates, and 779 apparent violations by political committees, to the Attorney General. Also in 1973 one joint investigation was conducted by the Clerk and the Special Committee, resulting in a referral of the case to the Attorney General.[3] The Justice Department's response to these referrals, as to GAO's, was minimal, if not nonexistent, even though the Justice Department stated it considered about 20 percent of referrals to be substantial cases.

Senate

The Secretary of the Senate devised a systematic plan of enforcement of the

Act that encompassed major candidates in all 33 Senate races and their respective committees. It involved a detailed review of all reports filed in each case, and a rigorous schedule of field investigations in 27 states, using professional auditors detailed from the GAO at the Secretary's request. It also involved publication of a formal report, which explained these procedures in detail and summarized the results.[m]

In a letter transmitting this report to the majority and minority leaders of the Senate on August 8, 1974, the Secretary stated:

> In my judgment, the large number of referrals is by no means indicative of lack of effort on the part of candidates, committees and other participants in the electoral process, to comply with the requirements of the law. Rather, it seems to me the referrals result preponderantly from the newness of the legislation, the extreme complexity of its requirements and the stringent provisions for disclosure which it contains.

The Secretary referred a total 1,098 cases to the Justice Department relating to the 1972 elections, of which 564 referred for lateness or failure to submit reports. Of a total of 306 candidates for the Senate, and 1,169 registered political committees supporting them, 19 candidates and three political committees failed to submit reports, while 173 candidates and 369 committees failed to file reports within the prescribed time limits. Of the committees, 195 were waived from the reporting requirements.

The Secretary's compliance procedure began with preliminary desk checks of each report, registration, or other document submitted as it was received in the Senate Office of Public Records. This was a prompt examination to identify obvious omissions or errors, which could usually be corrected by amendment or additional submissions. Table 2-1 shows the results of the 1972 preliminary audits.

While the preliminary checking procedures and resulting notifications of errors and omissions prompted corrections and further disclosures, they were not used to determine apparent violations for referral to enforcement agencies in 1972. On March 30, 1973 Secretary of the Senate Valeo issued a press release announcing the completion of the first phase of enforcement activity on disclosures relating to the 1972 Senate elections. The need for a systematic review of all reports and statements to determine the degree of substantive compliance over an established period was met by a year-end desk audit. This effort identified more significant types of violations in reports submitted during

---

[m]See *Report on Audits, Field Investigations, Complaints and Referrals in connection with Elections for the U.S. Senate in 1972, op.cit.,* pp. 28-29. This volume describes the procedures and criteria used by the Secretary in auditing and referring cases to the Attorney General.

Table 2-1
Summary of 1972 Notifications of Error Sent to Major Candidates
and Supporting Committees by Secretary of the Senate

	Democrat		Republican		Independent		Total	
	Num-ber	Per-cent	Num-ber	Per-cent	Num-ber	Per-cent	Num-ber	Per-cent
Number of candidates and committees sent notifications	171	44.77	209	54.71	2	0.52	382	100
Number of notifications sent requiring response	325	46.90	363	52.38	5	0.72	693	100
Number of notifications sent not requiring response	64	52.89	57	47.11	0	0.00	121	100
Number of responses	204	50.12	202	49.63	1	0.25	407	100

Source: *The Federal Election Campaign Act: Report on Audits, Field Investigations, Complaints and Referrals in Connection with Elections for the U.S. Senate in 1972,* prepared by Orlando B. Potter under the direction of Francis R. Valeo, secretary of the Senate (Washington, D.C.: U.S. Government Printing Office, 1974), p. 14.

the 1972 reporting cycle, and covered the period April 7, 1972 through January 31, 1973. The desk audits of the Democratic Senatorial Campaign Committee, the Republican Senatorial Campaign Committee, and 475 political committees for 96 candidates in 33 states resulted in 454 referrals to the Attorney General. These referrals encompassed a total of 1,835 different technical violations, some of which may have recurred several times within various reports.

As a result of ambiguities and discrepancies noted in the desk check reports, field investigations of 78 committees supporting 59 candidates in 27 states led to referral of 59 cases to the Attorney General involving 220 apparent violations of the FECA and related statutes. One additional referral was made on the basis of a complaint. The field audits, from October 4, 1973 to July 1, 1974, in some cases supplemented the findings of the desk checks, but for the most part, the referrals were in addition to those resulting from the desk checks. The field investigations were conducted by four auditors detailed from the GAO, several of whom were veterans of prior service with the OFE.

The most frequently occurring types of apparent violations were minor ones, due to errors of omission or simple misunderstandings, such as omissions or incorrect listings of occupation, name, or address of contributors, debtors, and creditors; amount and date of contribution; purpose of expenditure; and disclosure of media expenditure on a separate form.

The Secretary's office developed a unique system for processing the reports, using computer and microfilm technology. Each report was filmed upon receipt and referenced in a computerized index, updated daily. The microfilm file constituted a retrievable public record serviced by reader-printer machines that produced paper copies on request. The Clerk's office also used a microfilm system, whereas the OFE did not, preferring a simpler photocopying system. The relative utility of these systems deserves further study by the FEC, among others.

The Secretary of the Senate, like the other supervisory officers, sent packets containing reporting forms, supporting schedules, preprinted return envelopes, and copies of the *Manual for Senate Candidates* to a large list. Between April 7 and December 31, 1972, a total of 17,500 committee registration forms, 34,000 report forms, 12,500 candidate report forms, and 6,900 manuals were distributed. The Clerk sent out a total of 2,000,000 pages of materials and forms.

Of course, spokesmen from the three supervisory offices gave speeches to groups when invited, and initiated efforts to reach candidates and political committees in order to apprise them of their responsibilities under the law. The three staffs also conferred from time to time to coordinate answers and interpretations given to inquirers about the meaning of the law.

As provided by the three supervisory officers, the annual costs of operation are shown in Table 2-2.

Table 2-2
Annual Costs of Operation of Supervisory Offices under FECA

Fiscal Year	Clerk[a]	Secretary	Comptroller General[b]
1972	$263,223	n.a.	$ 165,916
1973	375,317	$504,245	1,630,254
1974	574,064	491,873	2,642,698

[a]Calendar year costs.

[b]Includes the yearly operation of the Clearinghouse on Election Administration.

Litigation

A 1973 decision of the U.S. District Court (D.C.) declared unconstitutional certain implementation and enforcement procedures of the FECA with regard to limitations on political advertising in newspapers, magazines, and on television.[4] It was appealed to the Supreme Court, but was still pending when the 1974 Amendments rendered it moot; the case could have been pursued by the Justice Department, but was dropped.

It is instructive to recount the case and the opinion. The procedure the law

required was that before a newspaper could charge for an advertisement supporting a candidate, it had to obtain from the candidate a certification stating
that the cost of the ad would not cause him to exceed his media spending
limitation. A three-judge court declared unconstitutional the basic procedure,
saying this gave veto authority to a candidate over a citizen's ability to express
his support for the candidate through a newspaper ad, thereby constituting a
"prior restraint" on the citizen's (or a group's) right to freedom of speech as
guaranteed by the First Amendment. When the GAO was drafting regulations
for Title I of the FECA, constitutional problems regarding the communications
media limitations were kept in mind, and efforts were made to try to minimize
through regulations the sections of the law considered most vulnerable to constitutional challenge. That effort clearly was unsuccessful in this case, but
regulations cannot be written at great variance with the law, and so cannot make
unconstitutional provisions acceptable to the courts.

The first action taken under the FECA was against the National Committee
for Impeachment when it ran an advertisement in *The New York Times* calling
for President Nixon's impeachment on May 31, 1972. The ad advocated the
impeachment of the President (long before Watergate) and listed nine members
of Congress (all candidates for reelection) who were on its "honor roll" for
supporting the impeachment resolution. The GAO felt the group apparently
violated the FECA by not registering as a political committee, and not submitting records of contributions and expenditures. The committee ignored a
request by GAO to register and report, claiming it was not a political committee.
The Justice Department filed suit on August 18, charging the committee had
violated the FECA by sponsoring the ad, and an injunction was issued against
soliciting and spending funds until it submitted reports. The committee won a
stay of injunction one week later, which freed it to continue activities until a
hearing on September 21. The Justice Department announced that it would
not press charges against *The New York Times* for publishing the two page
advertisement. Then, on October 30, 1972 the United States Court of Appeals
for the Second Circuit overturned the injunction.[5] The 13-page ruling applied
a "major purpose" test, saying the advertisement itself was an insufficient
reason to classify the sponsoring organization as a political committee. To
support a candidate incidentally is not sufficient reason for a group to be
defined as a political committee.

Another challenge to the FECA came in the form of a suit from the
Socialist Workers Party (SWP), supported by the American Civil Liberties Union
(ACLU). The suit, filed in U.S. District Court in the District of Columbia on
September 10, 1974, challenged the constitutionality of disclosure of contri-
butions to political parties. The suit claimed the FECA violated the SWP's
freedom of speech and association, the rights of privacy and due process, and
the right to petition for redress of grievances. It was still pending when the
Amendments became effective. In another case at the state level, the SWP of

Minnesota won a victory for its position when it was partially exempted from its state disclosure law. In hearings before the state Campaign Ethics Commission, the Trotskyite party had charged that it was the target of police and FBI surveillance and harassment, later confirmed. In view of the refusal by FBI and U.S. Postal Service officials to testify about alleged surveillance and mail interception, the commission ruled that the SWP's 1974 Minnesota Campaign Committee could keep secret the names of individual donors or lenders, but must disclose the amounts received and expended.

Although officials of government agencies denied the SWP charges, alleged evidence of a ten-year record of harassment subsequently came to light in a civil suit brought in Federal District Court, when 3,138 pages of FBI internal documents were ordered released in March 1975.[6]

The documents evinced 31 years of FBI attention to the SWP and in the years 1961-71, a covert effort to destroy the party and frighten its 2,500 members. And at no time during these years were any charges brought against the SWP or its youth arm, the Young Socialist Alliance. The FBI had continued its investigations, claiming authority from federal statutes that years before had been declared unconstitutional. The alleged harassment efforts directed against the SWP included attempts at having party members dismissed from their jobs, at leaking unsavory items about their personal lives to the press, and encouraging police agencies to press petty prosecutions. The alleged harassments were directed both at those official party functions in the SWP as well as those claiming only membership in the party. In one covert effort, the FBI sought to have a scoutmaster in Orange, N.J. removed from his job because his wife was a party member.

A Common Cause suit, resolved through out-of-court settlement in May 1974, alleged improper enforcement of the FECA by the Secretary of the Senate and the Clerk of the House in the critical controversy over "earmarked" campaign contributions for specific candidates. A settlement was forecast on July 20, 1973, when both the Secretary and the Clerk issued revised regulations requiring full disclosure of earmarked contributions. The Comptroller General's revision followed on August 16, 1973. This practice had allowed contributors to designate a specific recipient when giving money to a party campaign committee. Then the favored candidate would receive the contribution from the committee, rather than from the actual contributor, and public records would not reveal the true source of the funds. Both Republican and Democratic party campaign committees, among others, concealed contributions earmarked for specific candidates, and the public could not distinguish earmarked funds from money given by the party committees.

Recent evidence from a well-documented case of a Democratic campaign committee being used to funnel contributions to a number of Senate candidates in 1972 revealed that the practice was widespread. Other evidence indicated, for example, that U.S. Senators Thomas J. McIntyre, D-New Hampshire;

John J. Sparkman, D-Alabama; and Walter F. Mondale, D-Minnesota, received earmarked money. Funds from the Associated Milk Producers, Inc. (AMPI) were also offered to a number of campaign committees for congressmen of both parties. But with the unfavorable publicity associated with milk contributions, some candidates publicly refused the offers; others were ignorant of the fact that their staffs had accepted the money. The Senate Watergate Committee determined that $200,000 from the milk producers was laundered through two Republican committees for Richard Nixon's presidential campaign.[7]

The settlement of the Common Cause suit resolved a two-year legal battle, with the House and Senate officers agreeing to issue and distribute better rules for full identification of original donors, and disclosure of the intended recipient at every stage of the transaction.

The laws that went into effect for the 1972 election generated considerable discussion in the Congress and among national opinion leaders. Disclosures from Watergate investigations extended those discussions and served to point up the strengths and weaknesses of the FECA. The new law served as a catalyst in opening up major aspects of the Watergate affair. The law and the scandal fed on one another, revealing many financial practices of American politics, legal, illegal, and extralegal.

It took nearly ten years of reform activity for the FECA to become reality, and it may take even longer for the various reforms to become fully effective. The FECA Amendments of 1974, signed by President Ford under pressure of the events from Watergate and earlier FECA revelations, take a further step in election regulation. But continued awareness and pressure by such organizations as Common Cause, the National Committee for an Effective Congress, and Public Citizen, and by the media is necessary if full implementation is ever to be realized. If the nation is to recover from the trauma of Watergate, even-handed administration and enforcement is needed to restore public confidence in the electoral process.

Justice Department Actions

The Justice Department has prosecuted few violators of the FECA who committed various infractions of the law in 1972. When referrals were made, the Justice Department moved very slowly. The public referrals by the GAO did not seem to prod the Justice Department, nor did the thousands of referrals by the Clerk and the Secretary find the department properly staffed to cope. Election law was never a major concern, and little was done to improve staff or competence. The Attorney General has too often been appointed as a reward for service in the most partisan of political roles, that of campaign manager. Thus was John Mitchell appointed as Attorney General by Nixon, Robert Kennedy by John Kennedy, Herbert Brownell by Eisenhower, and J. Howard McGrath by Truman. In such circumstances, almost any action toward politically sensitive prosecution could lead to political trouble. If the Attorney General prosecutes persons in his own party for election violations, he will be considered disloyal. If he prosecutes persons in the other party for such violations, he will be considered politically motivated and subject his party to retribution when the opposition obtains power.

Although the supervisory officers referred numerous possible violations of the FECA to the Justice Department, the Attorney General determined that most of the matters were not prosecutable violations. Over three years, the GAO referred more than 100 cases to the Justice Department for possible violations in 1972; so few were prosecuted that the Comptroller General was moved to urge, on April 27, 1973, in the strongest terms "that the Attorney General take the initiative with regard to . . . reported violations of the Federal Election Campaign Act. . . ."[n] Some of the referrals that the Comptroller General felt had prosecutable merit were kept under review and active investigation for many months without results being publicly announced.

Following a June 20, 1973 conviction of the FCRP that brought a $3,000 fine, Director Hughes of the OFE said he understood that the Justice Department felt these were "prosecutable offenses" against the committee but not against any individuals, but he did "not understand the legal reasoning." He stated he was "concerned" that there be effective penalties in the administration of the law, and questioned "whether $3,000 is that."[8]

As of August 19, 1974 the department had closed 38 GAO referrals without further action, 12 were pending with the Special Prosecutor, and 18 were pending with the department; the remaining GAO referrals occurred after that date.

Under the 1974 Amendments, the Federal Election Commission has been empowered to subpoena witnesses and records and to prosecute civil cases directly, based on its findings; criminal cases will continue to be referred to the Justice Department. However, the Justice Department must report back to the commission its action on each referral within 60 days, and every 30 days thereafter, until final disposition of the case.

Several of the cases prosecuted under the FECA, mostly referred to the Justice Department by the GAO, are detailed below to illustrate methods employed in circumventing the law, and in one case, unintentional violation of the FECA.

---

[n]This was when about one-fourth of the GAO's total referrals had been made. See "Report to the Comptroller General on Unreported Cash Expenditures made by the Finance Committee to Re-Elect the President," U.S. General Accounting Office, Office of Federal Elections, April 27, 1973, p. 10.

John L. Loeb

The first prosecution and conviction of a contributor under the FECA was
the case of John L. Loeb, Sr., a prominent Wall Street investment banker. Loeb,
senior partner in the brokerage firm of Loeb, Rhoades & Co., and his wife Frances,
were major contributors to both sides in the 1972 campaigns, giving $50,000 to
the Humphrey organization and, later, $62,000 to the Nixon cause. However,
$48,000 for Humphrey was given illegally in the names of eight other persons,
seven employees of Loeb's firm and Mrs. Loeb's personal secretary.[o] Each was
credited with a $6,000 donation, violating the FECA's requirement that money
be given in the name of the true donor, not in the name of another.

The GAO became suspicious when a newspaper reporter drew attention to
a report listing eight $6,000 contributions to Humphrey, all made on the same
day from New York City or vicinity, with several bearing the same address. Presumably, to avoid the federal gift tax, the donations were in the form of 14 checks
for $3,000 each, and one check for $6,000, made out to 12 committees for
Humphrey. All the donations were reported as given to one committee by the
Humphrey staff. When GAO began an inquiry, the Loebs wrote letters to the 12
committees admitting the donations should have been disclosed in their own
names. The case was referred to the Justice Department on June 5, 1972; Justice
filed the information on May 15, 1973, almost a year later, charging Loeb with
eight violations of soliciting others to make contributions for him and later
reimbursing them. No charges were brought against Mrs. Loeb.[P]

Loeb's $62,000 contribution to the Nixon campaign came after disclosure

---

[o]In the GAO *Alphabetical Listing of 1972 Presidential Campaign Receipts*, Arthur
Griffirths (*sic*), Anne E. Schmidt, Carol L. Novak, Sybil M. Senoff, Donald J. (and Mrs.)
Sheehan, Arthur W. Sebastian, Jr., Yudita J. Uselyte, and Elizabeth H. Pearson are all listed
as May 12, 1972 contributors of $6,000 each to the Committee for the Nomination of
Hubert Humphrey; Frances L. Loeb is credited with $24,000 on May 12, and John L. Loeb,
Sr. is credited with $24,000 on May 12, and $2,000 on June 5, 1972. The Senate Select
Committee on Presidential Campaign Activities, *Final Report*, No. 93-981, 93rd Cong., 2d
sess. (Washington, D.C.: U.S. Government Printing Office, June 1964), pp. 894-98, explains
that Loeb did not want to be known publicly as a wealthy donor, so he arranged to reimburse
those individuals who agreed to contribute $6,000 in their names to the Humphrey cam-
paign, and added $2,000 for a total package of $50,000. The required May 24, 1972 pre-
California primary report by the Humphrey committees to the GAO listed the $48,000 contri-
butions by check, but the $2,000 from Loeb was not reported until June 10, 1972. GAO
was later notified that the committee reports should be amended to show Mr. and Mrs. Loeb
as the true donors of the $48,000, each giving $24,000. In the Watergate testimony, Loeb's
secretary stated that Loeb gave $2,000 in cash, which conflicts with an FBI report of a
July 18, 1972 interview with Griffiths, in which he states that Loeb gave the $2,000 by check.

[P]A similar case involving contributions to Senator Henry Jackson was referred to the
Justice Department on June 13, 1972 by GAO, but the Department did not prosecute. Three
contributions of $3,000 each were made in the names of Leo Harvey of Los Angeles, his
wife, and his secretary, and an additional $1,000 contribution was made by Mr. Harvey's
bookkeeper.

of the GAO's referral of his case to the Justice Department. It was suggested by some that this contribution was given as insurance against prosecution, but the Justice Department proceeded anyway. Loeb was indicted in federal court on the eight counts, but five were dropped in plea bargaining when he agreed to plead "nolo contendere" to three. The no-contest plea had the same legal effect as a plea of guilty. Each count carried a maximum penalty of three years in prison and a $3,000 fine. Loeb was fined $3,000 on June 7, 1973, but no prison term was imposed on the 70-year-old stockbroker.

Finance Committee to Re-Elect the President

The Justice Department brought the Finance Committee to Re-Elect the President (FCRP) to federal court twice as a result of GAO investigations.[q] The Finance Committee (but none of its officers, including Hugh Sloan, Jr., who was tagged with the responsibility), was charged in a criminal information on January 26, 1973 with eight counts for failure to report certain Watergate burglary-related receipts and expenditures. FCRP lawyers pleaded "nolo contendere" to the eight violations, which were misdemeanors, and on January 26 the FCRP was fined $8,000. This use of campaign contributions to pay the fines and legal fees of the committee that collected the donations must be included in the list of unique ways the FCRP found to spend money for the 1972 election.

The FCRP was brought into court again following a GAO report of March 12, 1973, citing four violations in connection with a $200,000 cash contribution from financier Robert L. Vesco to the committee. On May 3, 1973 the Justice Department charged the FCRP on three of these counts: receipt of the $200,000 and failure to report it; failure of the committee to keep records of the amount of the contribution, the name, address, occupation, and principal place of business of the donor; and failure to report the contributor to the GAO. The FCRP was found guilty again, on June 20, 1973, and fined $3,000. This was appealed on grounds that the law was unconstitutional; the court rejected the appeal in December 1974, without ruling on the constitutionality issue, saying no facts had been shown to bear out the contention. Again, no FCRP officers were named.

These were the first times a campaign committee has been penalized since nonfiling of required reports became an offense under the FCPA of 1925. The

---

[q]The first GAO audit was initiated when Director Hughes read the August 1, 1972 Woodward-Bernstein story in the *Washington Post* revealing the existence of the $25,000 Dahlberg check, and was requested by Senators Cannon and Proxmire to investigate the FCRP. Although a report on the GAO findings was ready for release on August 22, just hours before Nixon was due to be nominated at the Republican Convention, it was not made public until four days later.

Vesco contribution was pledged before April 7, 1972, when the new law became effective, but was not delivered until April 10. The committee's lawyers claimed the contribution had been constructively made before April 7, when it was pledged, and therefore it did not need to be reported after / April 7, under their interpretation of the definitions in the law.

Agnew Night

The GAO charged the FCRP, the Salute to Ted Agnew Night Committee, its treasurer, Blagden H. Wharton, and other Agnew supporters with a variety of apparent violations. Charges centering on the committee's Salute to Ted Agnew Night dinner of May 19, 1972 were filed as a result of a GAO report released on July 5, 1973.

Shortly after the April 7 effective date of the FECA, the FCRP loaned the Agnew Committee $49,900, which the committee used to inflate the receipts of its April dinner. The Agnew Committee was given the cash by Maryland State Republican Party Chairman Alexander Lankler, who had received it from the FCRP treasurer, Hugh Sloan, Jr. The transfer was not reported at the time. Instead, officials of the Agnew Committee contacted friends to get permission to use their names as contributors on the Maryland campaign fund reports. In the Maryland report the $49,900 was falsely filed as donations from 31 persons who had not actually bought tickets, but who had given permission to use their names. The scheme boosted apparent proceeds from an actual $94,859 to a more impressive $144,759. The investigation proved that the organizers had requested and obtained $50,000 in cash from the FCRP in order to inflate the proceeds from the affair and make it appear more successful than it was. The FCRP received the returned $50,000 in late July, and reported it as a receipt in its next report, thus bringing the funds into its accounts.

The Senate Watergate hearings made public the FCRP's failure to report to the GAO the transfer of the $50,000, and further revealed that the FCRP received $150,000 from Florenz R. Ourisman, a Maryland real estate developer, on the understanding that $50,000 would be channeled back to the presidential campaign within his state. The FCRP claimed it was not required to report the transfer because the $50,000 had been committed to the Maryland committee before April 7, 1972, and under the law a commitment to make payment before April 7 was in fact equivalent to a payment. The GAO cited both the Agnew Committee and the FCRP for reported violations, holding that the actual transfer was made after April 7, and referred the case to the Justice Department. The Agnew Committee and its officials violated the law in not reporting the transfer, and in knowingly and willfully falsifying facts on the state report in which the 31 fictitious contributions were reported. Agnew denied any personal knowledge of the financial arrangements. The FCRP was not charged by the Justice Department with a violation of the law.

Public disclosure of the transfer of Nixon funds induced the Agnew Committee to admit its charade. The committee set the record straight when an amended state report was filed, deleting the 31 fictitious donors. The switch came a few days before the original transaction was revealed at the Senate Watergate Hearings by Hugh Sloan, Jr., treasurer of the FCRP.

The Agnew Committee was also charged with apparent violations for receiving and not reporting $47,600 in corporate contributions. These funds had been reported to the state but not to the GAO. Limited corporate gifts are permitted by Maryland but prohibited under federal law. The Agnew Committee kept the money in a separate account, contending it was used only to support state and local candidates and therefore did not have to be shown on federal reports. The GAO maintained that the committee had violated the federal requirement that all contributions be reported, and also noted that $4,000 of the corporate funds were spent to plan and stage the gala.[r]

The gala was followed by a party catered without charge by a Baltimore firm whose parent conglomerate was at the time under investigation by the Federal Trade Commission. The circumstances suggested the gift of food and services may have been an attempt to influence Agnew to intercede. The committee failed to report these items and the donated lighting for the gala as contributions-in-kind. The GAO requested the committee to amend its reports to include the contributions-in-kind. Meanwhile, after a long battle with the Food and Drug Administration and Justice Department lawyers in Washington, D.C., the original charges against the firm were dismissed by U.S. Attorney George Beall in Baltimore. The caterer was known to have provided food and services for Baltimore-area Republican and Democratic political affairs for years, but this was apparently the first time the firm had contributed its services.

The Agnew Committee was indicted on August 14, 1973 for violating the Maryland Fair Election Practices law. While the seven co-conspirators were not indicted as individuals, the committee was charged with failing to name contributors, keep accurate records, issue donor receipts, and file proper reports. Each count carried a maximum fine of $1,000. On November 19, 1973 the committee pleaded guilty to violating the Maryland election laws on four counts in the Anne Arundel County Circuit Court. The committee was fined $500 on each count, totalling $2,000. Blagden H. Wharton, the only committee member to be charged individually, was indicted separately and charged with signing false campaign contribution reports.

Discovery of the Watergate burglars and the ensuing revelations helped

---

[r] Agnew's Maryland campaign finance reports, subpoenaed in Baltimore on August 10, 1973, in connection with a different investigation, showed this particular case fit into the larger pattern of contributions to Agnew from persons known to be under investigation for alleged kickbacks and bribes. This led to the Grand Jury investigation of Agnew for alleged bribery, extortion, and tax fraud while he was Baltimore County executive and Governor of Maryland, and his resignation as Vice-President less than two months later. See pp. 44 and 578-81.

expose other situations, in addition to the Agnew Night dinner, that presumably violated the FECA. Publicity surrounding the Watergate scandal apparently led to the May 24, 1973 suicide of Representative William O. Mills, R-Maryland. Investigators discovered that the FCRP had made a $25,000 contribution to the Mills campaign in 1971, with Interior Secretary Rogers C.B. Morton acting as intermediary, and with approval by John Mitchell and H.R. Haldeman. The funds were transferred in cash, and were unreported by the Mills committee, in apparent violation of state and federal disclosure statutes. The inquiry was launched, but because of Mills' death, and the earlier death by automobile accident of his campaign manager, James L. Webster, doubt was cast whether the money could ever be traced.

Shirley Chisholm

The fund reports of Representative Shirley Chisholm, D-New York, who ran in 1972 as the first black woman to seek the presidency, overlooked several important requirements of the FECA provisions. In September 1973 the GAO referred four apparent violations to the Justice Department for investigation. Chisholm said at the time of the referral that the Nixon administration was out to get her, that her inexperienced, amateur staff had not known all the rules, and that she was singled out for investigation and harassment because of her independent political stance against many administration policies. The Chisholm campaign maintained that it would have taken six full-time accountants plus supervisory personnel to keep track of all the records, costing nearly one-half of the total contributions received, and making the campaign impossible. Clearly, the magnitude of the task had been misjudged. A Justice Department report of April 23, 1974 found the charges of misconduct to be unfounded, and the case was substantially closed.[9] Some observers thought the GAO courageous and the Justice Department weak on this case.

The apparent violations reported by the GAO were failure to have and name a chairman; failure to keep detailed and exact accounts of contributions and expenditures, and failure to obtain and keep receipted bills for expenditures of over $100; failure to file all required reports of receipts and expenditures; failure to make adequate disclosure; failure to obtain certification for campaign advertising; and violations in the acceptance of several contributions from corporations.[s]

---

[s]According to a GAO report of November 7, 1974, covering an audit of the Shirley Chisholm for President Committee in Los Angeles and Affiliated Organizations throughout California, the Comptroller General referred four of the affiliates to the Attorney General for refusal to register as political committees. GAO felt that the affiliated organizations exercised sufficient independence and authority to be defined, and required to register and report, as separate political committees.

Conrad Chisholm, the candidate's husband and designated financial supervisor, said that the campaign was not aware of the FECA requirements, and he admitted that the campaign's final report of a $6,000 debt was erroneous. A GAO audit reported a cash balance of $18,000 on hand at the close of the campaign, and a balance of $3,000 as of February 28, 1973.

Congressional Candidates

On January 26, 1973, U.S. District Judge George L. Hart, Jr. took action against three congressional candidates who were charged with violating the law after repeated warnings by the Clerk of the House and by the Justice Department to submit reports on campaign contributions and expenditures. The candidates and actions were:

Fritjof P. Thygeson of the Peace and Freedom Party, who was defeated in his bid to represent the 40th District of California, for whom a bench warrent was issued. The FBI was unable to locate Thygeson when the warrant was issued.

Charles W. Johnson, Democrat, of Ohio's 17th District, who lost his Democratic bid for office in a May primary, asked that his case be transferred to federal court in Ohio. His request was approved.

William C. Haden, Democrat, of Pennsylvania's 14th District, received a suspended sentence and was placed on probation for one hour after pleading guilty.

Hansen Case

The first sitting member of Congress to be charged under the FECA was Representative George V. Hansen, R-Idaho, who in February 1975 pleaded guilty in U.S. District Court in Washington to two federal campaign financing misdemeanors. The two counts involved failure to file one campaign fund report and lying on another that had been filed during his 1974 congressional campaign. The law provided maximum penalties of up to one year in jail and a $1,000 fine on each count.

The first count charged that Hansen did not file a report with the Clerk of the House on June 10, 1974, as required by law. The second charged him with filing a sworn report on July 22, in which he claimed he had received no money from June 1 through July 15, when in fact he had received $2,150 and knew it. Hansen claimed that these represented "technical violations," but Judge Hart,

before passing sentence, said that the violations appeared to be intentional.[10]
One of the original allegations had been that Hansen personally handled some
corporate contributions, but this was not a final charge. Hansen was sentenced
to serve two months in prison, but a week later the prison term was set aside and
a $2,000 fine imposed instead. George Hart, chief judge of the Federal District
Court in the District of Columbia, said at the original sentencing: "If the people
who make the laws can't obey them, who can be expected to obey them?"[11]
At the reversal, Judge Hart said, "I assumed when I sentenced him to jail he was
evil. . . . Now I am not so sure. Stupid, surely."[12]

Watergate developments brought pressure on President Nixon to appoint a
Special Watergate Prosecutor. A number of illegal corporate contributions were
investigated by the Prosecutor's office, which had offered reduced fines and
sentences for those corporations and officers who voluntarily admitted giving
illegally. Also prosecuted for election law offenses were Tim M. Babcock,
Harry Dent, Jack Gleason, Herbert Kalmbach, and Maurice H. Stans. All these
matters are discussed later in this book.

The 1974 Amendments

Unlike the FECA, which took effect on April 7, 1972, leaving a gap of
several weeks after the March 10 reporting date required by its predecessor, the
FECA Amendments of 1974 took effect simultaneous to the termination of the
FECA. The 1974 Amendments were signed into law by President Gerald Ford
on October 15, 1974, and were to go into effect on January 1, 1975. However,
delay in appointing members of the Federal Election Commission and in their
confirmation kept the commission from functioning until April 1975. The
supervisory officers under the 1971 law continued to administer Titles I and III
of that law until the transfer of authority took place. This meant, in effect, that
certain provisions of the 1974 Amendments did not go into effect on January 1,
1975, as the law specified. The limitations and prohibitions in the 1974 Amendments became effective then, but the disclosure sections were delayed until the
commission took over responsibilities of the supervisory offices.

Professionalization and Mechanization

Expertise developed in the political arena as candidates and political committees turned to lawyers, accountants, and computer specialists for advice on
how to keep books and make reports that would comply with the law. The
FECA was termed by some as the "Lawyers and Accountants Full Employment
Act," and in the process of compliance a corps of well-informed advisors and

operatives outside the government emerged. In this regard, the FECA can be compared with the Securities Exchange Act of 1934. That act required public corporations to discipline their bookkeeping, which led private lawyers and accountants to set up standards which in turn brought about a far greater degree of voluntary compliance than the agency alone would have been able to command.

The new law required substantial employment of legal services, for counseling and interpretation as well as for enforcement. A corrolary development occurred in legal scholarship and litigation. For the first time, courses on the electoral process were taught in a few law schools and an increasing number of law review articles on various aspects of the new laws appeared.[t]

In addition, tax attorneys were drawn in more and more with reference to laws and IRS regulations relating to the gift tax, appreciated property, contributions to national conventions, and advertising in convention books. Public interest lawyers began to undertake a variety of court tests on disclosure and limitation aspects and on corporate and labor activity. Also, litigation concerning the dairy cooperative contributions to the Nixon reelection campaign, civil suits arising out of Watergate, and the Mitchell-Stans case related in part to provisions of the FECA; they also provided new information about financial practices, and especially new documentation that will absorb legislators and scholars for many years. Competence grew out of experience with new laws at the state level as well. Initiative 276, a wide-ranging proposal to regulate and limit contributions and expenditures, was passed overwhelmingly in 1972 by the voters in the state of Washington, triggering an avalanche of activity in the states and leading to 37 states changing their laws in a two-year period following 1972.[13]

The newly required accuracy, accountability, and attention to detail necessitated that campaigns and committees expend a significant share of their time and resources to pursue compliance with the record-keeping and disclosure sections of the FECA. Presidential and Senate campaigns in particular turned increasingly in 1972 to certified public accounting firms and computer consultants for advice and even day-to-day bookkeeping, and at least one accounting firm issued a comprehensive manual.[14] One campaign consultant issued and sold a campaign media manual outlining all relevant laws in nonlegal language.[15]

The new responsibilities thrust upon committee treasurers by the new law

---

[t]For a paper listing cases brought early regarding the 1971 FECA, see Elizabeth Yadlosky, "Constitutional Issues Raised With Respect to the Federal Election Campaign Act of 1971, P.L. 92-225," in *Hearings* before the Subcommittee on Communications of the Committee on Commerce, U.S. Senate, 93rd Cong., 1st sess., pp. 228-52. For one of the first publications on the subject, see Albert J. Rosenthal, *Federal Regulation of Campaign Finance: Some Constitutional Questions,* Milton Katz, ed. (Princeton: Citizens' Research Foundation, 1972). Exemplary among the many relevant law review articles was the entire issue of the *Harvard Law Review* devoted to "Developments in the Law—Elections," *Harv. L. Rev.,* vol. 88 (1975).

made it essential that persons accepting such positions be prepared to undergo thorough audits and be criminally liable for financial decisions that in earlier years would have gone unreported and unpublicized. More than one 1972 treasurer vowed never again to assume that role, possibly leaving such positions more and more to paid professionals.

It is ironic that one of the impacts of legislation that, in part, was drafted to limit campaign spending was to increase costs in certain categories. But in order to meet the law, sizable campaigns spent thousands of dollars for mechanization. Even photocopying costs were high when voluminous reports had to be duplicated for filing with three supervisory officers as well as numerous secretaries of state; many national-level committees contributing to a large number of congressional candidates filed in all 50 states to be on the safe side. Indeed, while computer science assisted the new politics in registering voters, in direct mail, in telephoning lists, and in bookkeeping, the mechanization of politics is a phenomenon increasing costs for politics as well.

3 The Impact of Watergate: Part I

The 1972 campaign witnessed the breaking of the most serious political scandal in American history. Watergate began with the burglary and bugging of the Democratic National Committee (DNC), but in time an ever-widening circle of acts of political espionage and sabotage, abuse of government power, and cover-up was disclosed within the Nixon administration.[a] This chapter details the initial investigations of Watergate, and presents evidence of the secret funds maintained and the dirty tricks practiced by the Nixon reelection forces.

From Caper to Affair to Scandal to Tragedy

From one perspective, Watergate began as a case of misuse of political funds. Many of the abuses that contributed to the downfall of the highest men in government, to the President himself, might never have occurred had money been strictly controlled. The ways the President's men raised, handled, and spent campaign funds were subjected to intense scrutiny. The burglary, spying, fraud, conspiracy, and use of agents and provocateurs could not have occurred without adequate funding. Espionage was not new in American politics, but the President's entourage carried it to unprecedented lengths while resorting to sometimes absurd practices.

In the spring of 1972 campaign officials accepted a plan conceived by G. Gordon Liddy, then counsel to the Finance Committee to Re-Elect the President (FCRP). The plan called for the entry, bugging, and photographing of documents at Democratic National Committee headquarters in the Watergate office building in Washington. Secondary targets were the offices of certain Democratic presidential contenders.

Liddy had originally proposed a $1 million operation that included the temporary abduction of radical leaders who might cause trouble at the Republican National Convention, the presence of squads to "rough up" demonstrators, and the anchoring of a yacht off Miami Beach, equipped with hidden microphones, cameras, and call girls who would try to extract information

---

[a]Watergate, the name of the Washington, D.C. office-hotel-apartment-shopping complex, became widely used to describe not only the break-in at DNC headquarters, but the entire scandal involving Nixon reelection campaign politics.

from Democratic officials. When the scheme was judged unacceptable, Liddy came back with a $500,000 plan focusing on wiretapping and photography, which was also rejected as too costly. A third proposal was then discussed and a $250,000 budget authorized, with John Mitchell, Jeb Magruder, and Liddy as the main actors in the scheme.

The first successful Watergate break-in was completed in the early morning hours of May 28, 1972 after two failures, one on or about May 26, and an unsuccessful attempt to enter surreptitiously McGovern's headquarters. A team of Cuban exiles, recruited by E. Howard Hunt, plus James W. McCord, Jr., security coordinator for the Nixon Re-Election Committee, photographed documents and planted wiretaps on the phones of Lawrence O'Brien, Democratic National Chairman, and R. Spencer Oliver, executive director of the Association of State Democratic Chairmen.[b] The tap on O'Brien's phone, however, proved faulty and monitoring of Oliver's phone yielded little of value, as did the photos. When Nixon campaign officials complained, Liddy decided to invade the DNC again.

In the early morning hours of June 17, 1972 the band raided Watergate again. But this time an alert security guard, Frank Wills, became suspicious about tape on the door locks, and called the police, who caught the four Cuban-Americans and McCord inside the DNC office. Later, in the hotel rooms where the men had been staying at the Watergate, the police found address books that led first to Hunt, later to Liddy.

When the group broke into the DNC offices (they said later) they thought they were looking for evidence that Fidel Castro's government had made contributions to the Democrats. Just before they set out, they were each given money, in $100 bills, by "Eduardo" (the name by which they knew Hunt), who told them, according to Eugenio Martinez, it was to use as a bribe if they were caught.[1] (No such attempt was reported.) The money in their possession at the time, amounting to $4,200, led investigators to the Miami bank account of one of the burglars, Bernard Barker.[2] The FBI established that $89,000 in four Mexican bank drafts and a $25,000 check from Minnesota businessman Dwayne O. Andreas, given through industrialist Kenneth Dahlberg, chairman of the Minnesota FCRP, had been deposited and withdrawn in cash at one time in Barker's account. Further investigation revealed that the $114,000 in checks had come directly from the treasurer of the FCRP, who had given them to Gordon Liddy on Liddy's legal advice. This established a link between the Watergate burglars and the Nixon campaign. The White House first attempted to stall this early phase of the FBI investigation. It was the disclosure two

---

[b]Oliver's father worked for the same Washington public relations firm, Mullen and Company, that had Hunt on its payroll, and where he maintained an office at the time of the break-in. The senior Oliver, a former CIA agent, handled the interests of Howard Hughes.

years later of the conversation between Nixon and Haldeman planning that stall that proved to be the "smoking pistol" that brought on the President's resignation.

The four Mexican bank drafts and $11,000 in cash had been issued by the Banco Internacional of Mexico City to an attorney, Manuel Ogarrio. From there the trail led back to Texas and Gulf Resources & Chemical Corp. executive Robert Allen, who laundered the $100,000 before donating it to the FCRP on April 6, 1972.

A few days after the break-in, Democratic National Chairman O'Brien announced the Democrats were filing a $1 million civil lawsuit against the Committee to Re-Elect the President (CRP), the President, and the burglars. The CRP countersued, as did Maurice Stans. A welter of litigation ensued, a dozen suits were filed in all by both sides, and as of this writing, nearly three years after the initial suits, the matter is still before the courts.

The seven men implicated in the burglary—Hunt, Liddy, McCord, and the four Cuban-Americans—were indicted in the District of Columbia on September 15, 1972. Attorney General Richard G. Kleindienst praised the investigation which led to the indictments as one of the most far-reaching, intensive, objective, and thorough in years. A Justice Department spokesman further said there was no evidence to indicate others should be charged. The seven were released on bonds ranging from $10,000 to $50,000 after pleading not guilty. When John Dean brought news of the indictments to Nixon, he was congratulated for helping to hold the Watergate circle to just the seven men.

Over the summer, however, two *Washington Post* reporters, Carl Bernstein and Bob Woodward, began bringing to light new facts about the Watergate affair in a job of investigative reporting that won the Pulitzer Prize for the newspaper.[c] On August 1, 1972 the *Post* reported that the $25,000 check from Dahlberg, which had gone into Barker's bank account, had been given originally to Stans for the FCRP. The story provoked an immediate General Accounting Office (GAO) audit of the FCRP by Philip S. Hughes, director of the GAO's newly created Office of Federal Elections; it was requested by Senators Cannon and Proxmire. Hughes knew that no such transaction had been reported by the FCRP to his office, and determined he would "conduct a full audit to see what's up."[3] By August 22 Hughes was ready with a first audit report, noting the existence of a secret "security fund" maintained by the FCRP (which had at one point included the Dahlberg and the Mexican checks), and listing apparent violations of the election finance law by the FCRP. Just hours before its official release time, however, it was held up. The Republican Convention was approaching a high point with Nixon due to be nominated on the evening of August 22.

---

[c]Their story is retold in Carl Bernstein and Bob Woodward, *All the President's Men* (New York: Simon & Schuster, 1974).

Hughes had been phoned from Miami by Stans, who asked him to fly down to get some more material, which had been collected by the FCRP for the audit; Hughes (who had been the top career man at the Bureau of the Budget when Stans was its director in the Eisenhower administration) felt he had no choice but to comply and hold up release. It seemed at the time that to have done otherwise would have made Hughes appear derelict in his search for material. Hughes was criticized for not requiring Stans to come to Washington in spite of the convention, and he later admitted his embarrassment in going to Miami Beach. In any case, the news of Nixon's nomination was covered by the news media that evening and the following morning without having to compete for space with the still unpublished news that the GAO had found his campaign organization violating the federal election law. The report, finally released four days later, led ultimately to Justice Department charges against the FCRP and a fine of $8,000. No individuals were charged.

Bernstein and Woodward also reported on a secret fund, controlled by John Mitchell, which was to be used for obtaining information about Democrats; the fund fluctuated between $350,000 and $700,000, and Mitchell had been approving withdrawals from it for more than a year before taking over as Nixon campaign chairman. In late October came exposure of Donald Segretti's "dirty tricks" campaign, and also news of another cash fund, known as the Treasurer's Fund, which at one time also held as much as $350,000.

In spite of the disclosure, Nixon was elected by an overwhelming margin in November (although the turnout was the lowest in years for a presidential contest). During the last few months of the campaign, McGovern had tried to stress the corruption theme but was unsuccessful in that, too. On January 8, 1973, with Judge John J. Sirica presiding in Federal District Court of the District of Columbia, the first Watergate trial began. Just one month earlier, Hunt's wife, Dorothy, was killed in an airplane crash in Chicago, and it was disclosed that she was carrying $10,000 in $100 bills in her purse; it was later established that Mrs. Hunt had served as a courier for payments to the break-in defendants, although it was claimed and never disproved that this money was for a personal investment by the Hunts.

From the beginning, the seven defendants demanded money in exchange for their silence about who had ordered the break-in. After the CIA refused a White House request to pay the defendants from its covert funds, Herbert Kalmbach, the President's personal attorney, was asked to raise the money. Although he claimed he did not realize this was to be hush money, he collected up to $230,000 over the summer of 1972. Without disclosing the purpose, he got $75,000 from Stans, $30,000 of which had been donated by Philippine interests (the Filipino money was soon returned to the donors, however). From Frederick LaRue, an aide to John Mitchell, he got about $70,000, and another $75,000 from a campaign contribution by Thomas V. Jones, chairman of the Northrop Corporation (an illegal contribution as it happened—part of the total $150,000 illegal corporate gift by Northrop). This money was never reported under the FECA requirements because both Jones and Stans were told by Kalmbach that it was not for election purposes.

After the election, with the trial impending, the defendants' demands increased; Hunt in particular escalated his demands. Some $350,000 from a secret White House fund controlled by H.R. Haldeman apparently for polling costs was used for hush money. In all, an estimated $550,000 was paid to the defendants (including lawyers' fees) for their silence, about half of it going to Hunt, who investigators said was blackmailing the White House. He reportedly had William O. Bittman, his attorney, read a letter to CRP Attorney Kenneth Parkinson threatening "to blow the White House out of the water."[4]

The first Watergate trial ran through most of January, 1973. The prosecution contended that the CRP had given Hunt at least $235,000 for intelligence operations. Five defendants—Hunt and his group—pleaded guilty, while steadfastly denying that a wider conspiracy existed. Judge Sirica criticized the prosecution for not asking more questions about the planning and financing of the break-in. He questioned some witnesses himself and urged the prosecution to call others. The trial ended with the conviction of the other two defendants, Liddy and McCord. Sirica jailed all seven men, postponing decisions on bond pending sentences.

Congressional action then began moving apace. Congressional Democrats had sought since shortly after the break-in to launch a probe but had been effectively stymied by White House efforts and the calendar. Representative Wright Patman of Texas, through his House Banking and Currency Committee, had initiated efforts, but had been blocked. Senator Edward Kennedy also tried, but the late date in the campaign at which he began his probe all but precluded the prospect of its leading to public hearings before the election.

In February 1973, however, the Senate created a bipartisan Senate Select Committee on Presidential Campaign Activities (hereafter known as the Watergate Committee or the Ervin Committee) to investigate and hold public hearings; Senator Sam Ervin of North Carolina became chairman. His selection reflected the fact that, in contrast to Kennedy, he was considered one of the least partisan men in Congress. Kennedy turned the findings of his subcommittee's three-month inquiry over to Ervin's staff.

The White House cover-up began to come apart in late March when McCord admitted to Judge Sirica that his family feared for his life, and that higher echelon officials were involved in the break-in. Sirica read McCord's letter to the court on March 21, 1973, charging also that some of the defendants had perjured themselves, and that pressure to plead quilty had been applied. McCord's charges led to further disclosures implicating Presidential Counsel John Dean, and Magruder, and produced denials that the President was involved. McCord and the others, with the exception of Liddy, agreed to cooperate with investigators and ultimately earned reductions of their sentences of from 35 to 40 years to shorter terms.

Liddy, who refused to break his vow of silence, received a sentence of six years and eight months to 20 years, plus a $40,000 fine. Hunt received two and one-half to eight years and a $10,000 fine, McCord one to five years, Barker one and one-half to six. Sturgis, Martinez, and Gonzalez, who got one to four years, spent the minimum time in prison and were then paroled.

In May two separate lines of investigation into the Watergate affairs were initiated. The seven-member Ervin Committee began its televised hearings focusing on three subjects: (1) the Watergate break-in and conduct of the investigation by various federal agencies; (2) campaign espionage and sabotage; and (3) campaign financing. The hearings ran through November. The Senate also drafted a resolution calling for a special prosecutor to try the Watergate case. When Elliot Richardson was nominated to replace Kleindienst as Attorney General, his confirmation was held up until he agreed to appoint Harvard Law Professor Archibald Cox, a liberal Democrat, as Special Watergate Prosecutor. Given a broad mandate by Congress, Cox divided his staff into five task forces to pursue the investigation of: Watergate, political espionage, the Plumbers, campaign contributions, and I.T.T.

During the Senate Watergate hearings, the existence of tape recordings of presidential conversations in the Oval Office was disclosed by Alexander Butterfield, former Nixon aide who became head of the Federal Aviation Agency. Both the Watergate Committee and Cox asked the President for nine of the tapes, but were refused on the constitutional grounds of separation of powers and executive privilege. A historic constitutional battle ensued in which Nixon lost in the lower courts, and facing the Supreme Court test, proposed an out-of-court agreement. Cox refused the compromise and in the so-called Saturday Night Massacre of October 20, 1973, Cox was fired, Richardson resigned, and Assistant Attorney General William Ruckelshaus was fired for refusing to dismiss Cox.

Other bombshells were in the offing. A week after Cox's dismissal, the White House said two of the sought-after tapes did not exist. A few weeks later one of the tapes that did exist was found to have an 18 1/2-minute gap in it, inexplicably, the White House said. In this atmosphere, the House Judiciary Committee, on October 30, began consideration of impeachment procedures, and its chairman, Peter W. Rodino of New Jersey, was granted subpoena power. Leon Jaworski, a Houston lawyer, was appointed Special Prosecutor to succeed Cox.

Not directly related to Watergate, yet further deepening public suspicions about high-level corruption, was the resignation of Vice-President Spiro T. Agnew on October 10, 1973. Agnew was under investigation for bribery, extortion, and tax evasion in connection with real estate development in Baltimore County, both before and during his vice-presidency. Publicly Agnew fought the charges, while privately his attorneys plea-bargained with the White House and federal prosecutors to limit the charges and avoid a prison sentence. On his resignation he pleaded no contest to one count of income tax evasion, received a sentence of three years of unsupervised probation, and a $10,000 fine.

Throughout the summer and fall of 1973, at the Senate hearings and elsewhere, attention focused increasingly on the question of Nixon's involvement in the scandal. His chief accuser, John Dean, accused the President of actively conspiring in the cover-up by saying, among other things, that it would be no problem to raise a million dollars hush money for the Watergate burglars; this charge later was upheld by transcripts of the tapes. For his part, Nixon's public statements through these months took the White House ever deeper into the scandal.

The affair that a year before could be dismissed as a "third rate burglary" had by November 1973 so altered the political climate that the President of the United States felt compelled to state—before the Associated Press Managing Editors in Orlando, Florida—"I'm not a crook." Nixon's reference was to yet new hints of scandal involving his personal finances. The suspicions centered on the purchase of his vacation home at San Clemente and subsequent improvements there, improvements on his Key Biscayne home, and on his personal income taxes.

Other problems with Nixon's personal finances included valuable jewels given by foreigners to the Nixon family—but not recorded as gifts to the presidency—which belong to the government. The Nixons said they intended to give them to the government when he left office, as earlier Presidents had. It also was alleged that Nixon confidant Charles "Bebe" Rebozo had spent $50,000 including campaign funds, for Nixon's personal benefit, including platinum and diamond earrings for Mrs. Nixon's birthday gift. Further questions were raised about the source of $45,621 reported used to make improvements on the President's two Key Biscayne properties. There was also speculation that a $100,000 cash campaign contribution from multimillionaire Howard Hughes had actually been spent by Rebozo on the President, F. Donald and Edward Nixon, Rose Mary Woods, and others.

The income tax controversy concerned the backdating of the deed of Nixon's gift of his vice-presidential papers to the National Archives, and the appraisal of the value of these papers. A White House aide, Edward L. Morgan, was subsequently jailed for his action; two others, the appraiser, Ralph Newman, and Nixon's California tax lawyer, Frank DeMarco, Jr., were indicted for their part in the fraud. Morgan, who Nixon rewarded by appointment as Assistant Secretary of the Treasury, handled the White House arrangements under which Newman certified the value of a collection he had never reviewed, and DeMarco allegedly backdated the deed of gift in order for it to comply before a new law curbing deductions for such gifts took effect.

The question of the President's taxes was brought before the Congressional Joint Committee on Internal Revenue Taxation, which reported a delinquency of $476,431. Within hours, the White House announced that Nixon would pay about $465,000 in back taxes and interest, while disclaiming any responsibility for preparation of the return. The state of California also asked Nixon to pay back taxes of $5,302 for time spent at San Clemente on "working vacations" where he earned part of his salary.

The political impact of Watergate was beginning to show in dramatic fashion during late 1973 and early 1974. The Republican National Committee (RNC) set a goal in 1973 of $6.3 million in contributions, but fell drastically short of that by year's end. With projections of a $1 million deficit, the RNC made a 25 percent cut in its 135-member staff, while from Chairman George Bush on down, those remaining took ten percent salary cuts. The all but defunct Committee to Re-Elect the President still had nearly a $2.5 million surplus from 1972, but had the RNC accepted these funds it might have become liable in the law suits pending against CRP.

In early 1974 the Republicans lost three of four special elections to the House of Representatives, two in traditional GOP strongholds. In all four the Republican percentage of the vote was off sharply from previous years. Post-election studies showed that perhaps a third of the voters, in some cases, were voting Democratic as a protest against the President. The national polls showed Nixon's popularity down to 26 percent, a low level not reached by a President since Truman at the depths of public discontent with the Korean war and corruption in his White House. On March 1, 1974 seven former Nixon aides—H.R. Haldeman, John Ehrlichman, John N. Mitchell, Charles W. Colson, Robert C. Mardian, Gordon C. Strachan, and Kenneth W. Parkinson—were indicted for their roles in covering up Watergate. On March 19, 1974 an important sign of erosion in Nixon's conservative support showed in the call by New York Senator James Buckley for the President's resignation.

One of the first bright spots in months for the Republicans was the April 28, 1974 acquittal in New York City of John Mitchell and Maurice Stans of charges growing out of the campaign contribution from fugitive financier Robert L. Vesco. This removed the Vesco issue from consideration by the House Judiciary Committee and, more importantly, it seemed to cast doubt on the credibility of Nixon's chief accuser, John Dean, who testified for the prosecution.

The day following the Mitchell-Stans acquittal, in a nationally televised address, Nixon made a move which many observers felt badly backfired—he released to the public 1,200 pages of edited transcripts of taped White House conversations. The revelations in the transcripts—even as edited and bowdlerized by the White House—shocked many.

On May 9 the House Judiciary Committee began impeachment hearings, with Chairman Rodino announcing six areas of inquiry including initially the question of presidential responsibility for the Watergate break-in. The committee declined to accept Nixon's edited transcripts, and notified him that he had failed to comply with its subpoena for tapes of 42 Watergate-related conversations. The committee also said that significant discrepancies were detected between the White House-approved transcripts and some actual tapes obtained previously. On May 29 Jeb Magruder, former deputy director of the CRP, was sentenced to prison for ten months to four years for conspiracy to obstruct justice and defraud the United States.

In June legal action proceeded against several other key Watergate figures. Former White House Counsel Charles Colson pleaded guilty to a felony charge that he impeded and obstructed the trial of Pentagon Papers defendant Daniel Ellsberg, and was sentenced to one to three years and fined $5,000. Former Attorney General Kleindienst pleaded guilty to a misdemeanor charge of failing to testify accurately before a Senate hearing and received a suspended sentence of one month in jail and $100 fine. Herbert Kalmbach, the President's personal attorney and a chief fund-raiser, was sentenced to six to eighteen months and fined $10,000 for violating the federal disclosure law governing campaign funds and six months on a misdemeanor, to be served concurrently. Meanwhile, the GAO reported the federal government had spent $6.5 million to that time in legal fees and expenses related to Watergate.

Also in June the secret Grand Jury report naming Nixon as an unindicted co-conspirator with his former aides was made public. The jury reportedly had been prepared to indict Nixon, but was dissuaded when Special Prosecutor Jaworski said a president could not be indicted while still in office.

Pressure for Nixon to resign built during July as Ehrlichman, along with Liddy, Barker, and Martinez, were convicted in Los Angeles of conspiring to violate the civil rights of Dr. Lewis Fielding, Ellsberg's psychiatrist. The Judiciary Committee released evidence of White House misuse of the IRS for political gain—helping friends while attempting to hurt political enemies.

A devastating blow to Nixon came on July 24 when the Supreme Court ruled eight to none that the President must comply with the subpoena issued by the Special Prosecutor for 64 Watergate tapes. The decision defined the limits of Presidential privilege narrowly, further eroding the defense fought on a broad interpretation of such privilege.

A few days later, in televised hearings, the Judiciary Committee completed approval of three impeachment articles, charging Nixon with obstruction of justice, abuse of presidential power, and attempting to impede the impeachment process by defying the committee's subpoenas. Two other articles, one charging Nixon with usurping the powers of Congress by ordering the secret bombing of Cambodia in 1969, and the other concerning income tax fraud and unconstitutional use of government funds, were rejected by the committee.[d] Ten of the 17 Republicans had stayed with Nixon through all the charges, voting nay on each.

---

[d]As the possibility of Presidential impeachment became more likely, an increasing number of studies were published to prepare, persuade, or educate Americans about the process. A number of them were the result of efforts by pro-impeachment groups working during 1973 and 1974 for the impeachment or resignation of Nixon (see pp. 576-78). See American Civil Liberties Union, *Why President Richard Nixon Should Be Impeached* (Washington, D.C.: Public Affairs Press, n.d.); ――― , *High Crimes and Misdemeanors: What They Are, What They Aren't*, The Second Pamphlet for Committees of Correspondence on the Impeachment of Richard M. Nixon (Washington, D.C.); The Committee on Federal Legislation, *The Law of Presidential Impeachment*, The Association of the Bar of the City of New York, January 21, 1974; William A. Dobrovir, Joseph D. Gebhardt, Samuel J. Buffone, and

The final turning point came on August 5 when Nixon, under pressure from his counsel, James St. Clair, released three transcripts of his taped conversations on June 23, 1972, with Haldeman. Nixon admitted that just six days after the Watergate break-in he had originated plans to have the FBI stop its investigation, which was then on the verge of tracing the Mexican checks in Barker's Miami bank account back to the CRP. He admitted he had kept the evidence from his lawyers, his staff, and his supporters on the Judiciary Committee. Within 48 hours, all ten Republicans said they had reversed their decisions and would now vote to impeach.

On the evening of August 8—after several tense days during which delicate pressure was brought to bear on him by certain members of the White House staff and congressional leaders—[e] Nixon announced to the nation that he was resigning the presidency the next day. Shortly after noon the next day, with Nixon then airborne for San Clemente, Gerald Ford was sworn in as the first President in United States history not to have won election to that office. He himself had been nominated Vice-President by Nixon ten months earlier, following the Agnew resignation, in the first use of the Twenty-fifth Amendment.

Ford rode a crest of national relief during his first month in office, with 71 percent in the first national poll taken approving his conduct in office. Concurrently, some 56 percent of the public favored prosecution of Nixon for his admitted role in the cover-up.

Suddenly, without warning, on Sunday, September 8, Ford granted Nixon a full and unconditional pardon for all federal crimes he had committed or may have been a party to while in office. This was a reversal of his position in his first press conference as President, when he said he opposed such a pardon. In accepting the pardon, Nixon admitted making misjudgments in not acting more decisively.[f]

Andra N. Oakes, *The Offenses of Richard M. Nixon: A Guide For the People of the United States of America*, with a foreword by Raoul Berger (Washington, D.C. and New York: Published jointly by Public Issues Press, Inc. and Quadrangle/The New York Times Book Co., 1974):———, *The Offenses of Richard M. Nixon: A Lawyer's Guide For the People of the United States of America* (Washington, D.C.: November 1973; *Impeachment and The U.S. Congress* (Washington, D.C.: Congressional Quarterly, Inc., 1974); Charles Morgan, Jr., "The September 15th White House Conversation: Cause for Impeachment of Richard Nixon and An Investigation of the Department of Justice," American Civil Liberties Union, Washington, D.C. (For submission to the members of the House Committee on the Judiciary in the matter of its Impeachment Inquiry (and) for submission to the Senate Committee on the Judiciary in the matter of its investigation of the role of the Department of Justice in the investigation and prosecution of the Watergate case).

[e]See Theodore H. White, *Breach of Faith: The Fall of Richard Nixon* (New York: Atheneum/Reader's Digest Press, 1975) for an examination of Nixon's resignation and the events leading up to it. The work begins with Nixon's last days in the White House, when those closest and most devoted to him felt he had deceived them and were urging his resignation, and traces Nixon's political development.

[f]On September 24, 1974 the House Subcommittee on Criminal Justice of the Committee on the Judiciary began hearings on "bills and resolutions that seek to insure public access to information relative to Watergate and its related activities." See *Pardon of Richard M. Nixon*

Public reaction to the pardon was immediate, and sharply against Ford's decision. His high rating plummeted to 49 percent, a drop in size and speed unlike any recorded for a President in 40 years (and six chief executives) of polling history. With the nation headed into a period of economic recession, Ford had spent heavily the political capital he had as successor to Richard Nixon.

Ford's nominee as his Vice-President was Nelson A. Rockefeller, the former New York Governor, who underwent throughout the fall of 1974 the most intense scrutiny of any candidate for the office, touching on his personal wealth, his political contributions through the years, his several terms as New York Governor, and his gifts of money to friends and associates. The new Vice-President was not confirmed until December 19, 1974, the second appointed under the terms of the Twenty-fifth Amendment.

Secret Funds

The secret campaign fund is not new in American politics, nor in the Nixon experience. It was a secret fund that Richard Nixon sought to explain in his 1952 "Checkers" speech, bringing him an unusual degree of national prominence for a vice-presidential candidate.[g] But in his 1972 reelection effort, the use of undisclosed funds became something of a high political art, with the total in millions of dollars in contrast to the $18,235 fund that stirred such a storm in 1952.

At least three secret funds emerged from transcripts and testimony over Watergate—and possibly there were more. The funds overlap, go back in some cases to the 1968 campaign, and accounts of their sources and uses often conflict: they were, of course, kept secret with exactly that intent of making them difficult to trace.

One fund was Herbert Kalmbach's, the earliest to be created and the largest. A second was called the Treasurers Cash Fund. It was administered by FCRP Treasurer, Hugh Sloan, but, as with all funds at the FCRP, was ultimately the responsibility of the chairman, Maurice Stans. This fund was most directly linked to the payments to Gordon Liddy, Herbert Porter, and others, enabling illegalities tied to Watergate itself. A third, H.R. Haldeman's fund, was kept in the White House until after the election; it helped pay for John Dean's honeymoon trip and much of the cover-up "hush money." A fourth fund, held by Charles "Bebe" Rebozo, was composed of $100,000 from Howard Hughes;

---

and Related Matters: Hearings before the House Subcommittee on Criminal Justice of the Committee on the Judiciary, 93rd Cong., 2d sess., September 24, October 1 and 17, 1974, Serial No. 60 (Washington, D.C.: U.S. Government Printing Office, 1975).

[g]Rebutting a critic who claimed that Nixon's "Checkers" speech cost him the presidency in 1960, Nixon himself argued, in *Six Crises*, that "If it hadn't been for that broadcast, I would never have been around to run for the Presidency." Nixon, *Six Crises* (Garden City, N.Y.: Doubleday & Co., 1962), p. 129.

Rebozo claims the money was returned to Hughes unspent, in the face of some evidence to the contrary. The Rebozo fund, some of the investigations hinted, may have been a great deal larger, swelled by Arab or Iranian contributions; that, however, remains highly speculative with no known evidence, and at this writing no indictments have resulted.

The Kalmbach Fund

The Kalmbach money—listed officially by the FCRP as the "Herbert W. Kalmbach Trust Fund"[h]—had its origins in the 1968 campaign. Shortly after Nixon's inauguration, Kalmbach was entrusted with nearly $1.7 million left over from Nixon's 1968 prenomination campaign, which he administered under the direction of H.R. Haldeman, the White House chief of staff. Between 1969 and the end of 1971 Kalmbach collected another $300,000 in donations toward the reelection effort, bringing the fund to about $2 million. Part of the money came from the Associated Milk Producers, Inc. in a $100,000 gift in August 1969, and was kept in a safe deposit box at the Security Pacific National Bank in Newport Beach, California, where Kalmbach lived.

One of the earliest "dirty tricks" came out of the Kalmbach fund in 1970, when some $400,000 was sent to Alabama as a contribution to George Wallace's Democratic primary opponent, Albert Brewer, in his gubernatorial bid; it was an effort to thwart a Wallace third-party candidacy in 1972, which CRP strategists feared would hurt Nixon's chances. Wallace, however, defeated Brewer in a run-off primary.

During this period, Kalmbach also was instrumental in a separate fund-raising operation for the 1970 congressional campaign, which was dubbed "Operation Townhouse."[i] The money did, in fact, go toward Republican congressional and gubernatorial support.

The FCRP disclosure covered a period beginning in early 1971, and the record of expenditures from the Kalmbach fund shows a total of $549,642 spent through April 7, 1972. Kalmbach himself drew $30,437 of this for his travel and meetings expenses. Other names now familiar in the Watergate litany show up on vouchers. One of the earliest was Anthony Ulasewicz, the newly retired detective from the New York City Police Department, who was hired in May 1969 on recommendation of Jack Caulfield. (Caulfield, also a former member of the New York Police Department, was put on the White House payroll to develop an

---

[h]The filing with the Clerk of the House, made in September 1973 by the FCRP as a result of the Common Cause civil suit, was used for details throughout this section.

[i]This effort raised $3.9 million, and was so-named because it operated out of a Washington, D.C. town house.

in-house investigative capability for obtaining sensitive political information.)
Ehrlichman made the decision to hire Ulasewicz, who achieved a sort of instant
celebrity status four years later with his droll accounts of his activities to the
Ervin Committee at the televised hearings.

Ulasewicz received $51,918 from the Kalmbach fund for his investigative
services and expenses. His first major assignment, on orders from Ehrlichman,
came in July 1969, after Senator Edward Kennedy's accident at Chappaquiddick;
he spent a good portion of the summer and fall in the vicinity of Chappaquiddick
trying to dig up information that might be of value to political strategists at the
White House. Over the next three years Ulasewicz visited 23 states in various investigations, and then in 1973, as the Watergate cover-up began to unravel, he was
at the heart of the payoff of hush money.[5]

Jack Caulfield also received $30,000 from the Kalmbach fund for purposes
that have not been established. Donald Segretti, whose activities, when disclosed by *Washington Post's* Woodward and Bernstein, first added "dirty tricks"
to the Watergate lexicon, was paid $40,836 from the fund. Of that, $10,500
went for his expenses; additionally, $5,336 was listed in the FCRP filing for
"Field Operations," and $25,00 for "Field Operations Expenses."

Murray Chotiner, Nixon's long-time political strategist, was paid a total of
$32,080 from the Kalmbach fund for the operation in which he paid two people
posing as journalists to cover the Democratic campaigns. Another anti-Wallace
effort—set up in California in 1971 under the directions of Lyn Nofziger—got
$10,000.

Money from the Kalmbach fund went, in some instances, to other than the
Nixon reelection campaign. In the fall of 1971, for example, former Governor
Louis Nunn of Kentucky (brother of Lee Nunn, a FCRP fund raiser) got $100,000
apparently toward his upcoming, and subsequently unsuccessful, Senate race
against Walter "Dee" Huddleston.[j]

One of the personal tragedies of the money's use resulted apparently from a
$25,000 contribution from the Kalmbach fund to the congressional campaign of
Representative William O. Mills of Maryland. Mills had been an aide to Rogers
C.B. Morton when Morton represented the Eastern Shore Congressional District.
When Morton was named Secretary of the Interior after Walter Hickel was dis-
missed, a special election was held for his seat, and Mills was asked to step in

---

[j]With Nunn's gubernatorial term ending in 1971 and his protégé, Tom Emberton, losing
to Lt. Gov. Wendell Ford, Nunn had planned to run again for Governor in 1975. But at White
House urging, he entered the race for retiring Senator Cooper's seat 28 minutes before the
filing deadline. He won the primary easily, but lost the general election to Democrat Huddleston, receiving 48 percent of the vote to Huddleston's 51 percent. An unconfirmed news
story ("Governor Favored in Ky. Primary," *Washington Post*, April 3, 1975) suggests that
the $100,000 went to Emberton, noting Kalmbach's 1973 testimony that he delivered the
money to Kentucky in late September, 1971. The donation was never reported, in violation
of Kentucky state law, but since the statute of limitations expired there was no prosecution.

before a campaign apparatus could be fully developed. Under these circumstances, Morton intervened and received a promise of money for his former aide's campaign. The funds were transferred in cash and were unreported by the Mills committee. The publicity surrounding this gift apparently led to Mills' suicide on May 24, 1973, as investigators tracing Kalmbach's funds followed the trail of the contribution to his campaign.[k]

Not all of the uses to which the Kalmbach money was put were tainted. David Derge, a political scientist who had been overall supervisor of opinion survey work done for Nixon in the 1968 race, received just under $172,000 from this fund for work he did during Nixon's first term. His variety of public opinion surveys and analyses that were directed by the White House represented a completely legitimate type of expenditure.

The Treasurer's Fund

In early 1972, with the CRP and FCRP now becoming fully operational, the Kalmbach fund was closed out and the balance of $716,234 was deposited in FCRP bank accounts. The remaining $234,000 was transferred to the treasurer's fund, and shortly afterward became part of a $350,000 fund requested by the White House for Haldeman to use for nonelection polling. While amounts in the treasurer's fund fluctuated, a listing in the CRP's later filing cites the aggregated cash fund at $919,000. During the early months of 1972, when fund raisers were striving to meet the April 7 disclosure deadline, cash constantly flowed in and out of the treasurer's fund. The list of donors to this fund was destroyed prior to April 7, but was later reconstructed from other records. It is now known that the $200,000 cash contribution from Robert Vesco went through this fund, as did the laundered Mexican money ($89,000) from Robert Allen, and many of the contributions made illegally by corporations.

Some idea of how the cash poured into the FCRP during the final six weeks before the disclosure deadline may be gained from the following chronological but not definitive account of illegal corporate gifts, all in cash, during that period.

In late February 1972 Gulf Oil delivered $50,000 in cash (having previously

---

[k]For an examination of the implications of a totally different aspect of Nixon White House policy, regarding the FCRP funding of Democratic political campaigns, see Walter Dean Burnham, "Rejoinder to 'Comments' by Philip Converse and Jerrold Rusk, " *The American Political Science Review*, vol. LXVIII, no. 3 (September 1974), 1057. Burnham calls attention to Gordon Strachan's July 23, 1973 testimony before the Watergate Committee where "[he] claims that a policy decision was made in the White House to use funds so as to avoid serious Republican contests to two classes of legislators: Democrats who supported the president's Vietnam war position, and another group of Democrats backed by organized labor, whose support Nixon sought for himself in 1972."

given $50,000 in May 1971). On March 9 Goodyear executives turned over $20,000 in cash, and then another $20,000 five days later. In March American Airlines delivered $55,000 that it had laundered through a Lebanese agent. On March 26 a 3M executive handed Stans $30,000 in a St. Paul hotel suite. In late March or early April Braniff Airways delivered $40,000. On April 3 an Ashland Oil official gave $100,000 in cash to Stans, who said, "Thanks," dumped it in his desk, and passed it on to Sloan. Late in the evening on April 5 $700,000 arrived in cash and checks from Texas on a Pennzoil company plane.

The outgoing trail of the cash was obscured in various ways. For example, Herbert Porter, the scheduling director of CRP, had a $52,000 cash fund, which was for the purpose of making prompt payments of campaign expenses. Established before April 7, 1972, it was periodically replenished from the larger cash fund whose outflow was implemented by Hugh Sloan, under the overall direction of Magruder. G. Gordon Liddy got $31,000 from the Porter fund toward the total $235,000 he drew from secret funds. Porter also used the fund to make post-April 7 payments, unreported, to help support intelligence efforts among youth groups.[6] Some of the money that Gordon Liddy received wound up in Bernard Barker's Miami bank account, where it established a link between Watergate, the CRP, and the White House.

Other money from the fund was returned to Kalmbach in the summer of 1972, following the break-in, as he sought to raise hush money. Kalmbach got an additional $75,000 for this purpose from Thomas V. Jones, president of Northrop Corp.; in tapping his friend for a "special need," Kalmbach did not tell Jones the intended use for the funds. Jones had already pledged and paid part of an illegal $100,000 corporate contribution.

The Haldeman Fund

The secret fund controlled by H.R. Haldeman was created when $350,000 in cash from the FCRP (mostly left over from Kalmbach's 1968 fund) was turned over to the chief White House aide prior to April 7, allegedly for private political polling purposes. The White House transcripts show that Nixon himself, in talking about the $350,000 with Haldeman and Ehrlichman, thought of it as "1970 money";[7] one place where 1970 money had been raised secretly was in the "Operation Townhouse" project, directed by Kalmbach, but there is no further indication that any such 1970 money was carried over.

The Haldeman fund was untouched during the election, except for $22,000, which John Dean withdrew to pay for a pro-administration Vietnam advertisement and as a loan, he later testified, for his honeymoon. At the end of November Dean requested an immediate loan from Stans to restore the fund to its full amount; Stans advanced him $22,000 out of a November 3 contribution from

Tim Babcock, expecting to receive it back promptly. Then as pressure began to mount after the election for more hush money, Haldeman agreed to its release for this purpose. By January 1973 the entire amount had been transferred to Frederick LaRue; a total $155,000 of the money was passed on to various Watergate defendants or their lawyers in the spring of 1973. When LaRue decided to tell prosecutors that he knew of the fund's existence in April, the remaining funds were returned to the FCRP.

The Rebozo Fund

A fourth secret fund was held by Rebozo. His story is that $100,000 came to him, in two payments of $50,000 each, from representatives of the billion-aire recluse Howard Hughes. He says he did not turn the money over to the FCRP in early 1972 because at that time the Hughes hierarchy was involved in litigation (linked to the Clifford Irving hoax biography), and that the gift was subsequently returned untouched. Other accounts link the money to the pur-chase of San Clemente, to improvement at Key Biscayne, and to fear of presi-dential involvements that could provide a motivation for the Watergate break-in. But none of these accounts are known to have been true.

Further indications exist that the Rebozo fund may have been substantially larger than $100,000; transcripts held back by the White House, but which came to light in the Watergate cover-up trial, show Nixon offering Haldeman and Ehrlichman compensation for their legal fees from a fund held by Rebozo that the president described as $200,000 to $300,000. Investigators have yet to determine if Nixon's figures were correct, or where the additional money might have come from, but there have been unverified suggestions: one was a Saudi Arabian banker who had known Nixon and Rebozo for about a decade;[8] a sec-ond stemmed from reports that the Shah of Iran may have made a large contribu-tion from a Swiss bank account through a Mexico City laundering operation.[9]

Yet another Haldeman fund came to light in testimony from Ralph Nader's civil suit in connection with milk price supports. Former Haldeman assistant Lawrence M. Higby said that a fund, consisting of a two-inch stack of $20 and $100 bills, had been kept by Haldeman for the apparent purpose of covering moving expenses when White House staffers joined or left the executive offices. He said he knew of only several occasions when the fund had been used for moving costs, and that it was apparently not replenished. The fund, Higby be-lieved, had been created in 1968, but he did not know how.[10]

Dirty Tricks

The 1972 campaign was subjected to an unparalleled array of "dirty tricks," mostly well-financed CRP efforts to disrupt presidential primary campaigns of opponents, active and potential. The Nixon strategy, fueled by surplus CRP funds and lack of serious Republican opposition, was designed to cause division among Democratic presidential contenders, making it more difficult to unite behind the party's eventual nominee; weaken the perceived strong candidates, primarily Muskie, and help secure the nomination of McGovern, considered by White House strategists to be the least formidable general election opponent; and attack the Democratic front-runner at any given time. This negative strategy, as initially proposed by White House speech writer Patrick Buchanan in the spring of 1971 when polls showed Muskie running ahead of both Nixon and Wallace in popularity, was not necessarily improper. But, in the words of the Senate Watergate Committee, "[it] was ultimately converted by others into gross abuses and unethical manipulations of the electoral process by persons who had little political experience, and by persons, including some with considerable political experience, who had little respect for fair play in elections."[11]

After losing the nomination, Muskie complained he had been victimized by a "systematic campaign of sabotage," including theft of documents, middle-of-the-night phone calls to voters made by imposters claiming to be Muskie canvassers, false items in newspapers, and—the best known incident—a phony letter, publicized by New Hampshire's largest newspaper, the *Manchester Union-Leader,* less than two weeks before the New Hampshire primary, claiming that Muskie had humorously condoned an aide's use of the derogatory term "Canuck" (a description of Americans of French-Canadian descent).[1]

At the direction of Jeb Magruder, Hugh Sloan, Jr., deputy finance director of the CRP, paid $100,000 to Herbert L. Porter, the campaign scheduling director, who in turn made available about $45,000 for dirty tricks under the direction of Donald Segretti. Another portion of the Porter money, $31,000, went to G. Gordon Liddy. Segretti, a California attorney, was perhaps the best known operative in the dirty tricks field, primarily because much of his story came out first—revealed during the 1972 campaign by the *Washington Post* reporters Woodward and Bernstein. Other efforts at trickery, however, were supervised by Howard Hunt, Jeb Magruder, and the late Murray Chotiner, a long-time Nixon strategist.

Segretti had been hired by the President's appointment secretary, Dwight Chapin, an old college friend from the University of Southern California, just

---

[1]The exact origins of the letter remain unclear. White House aide Kenneth Clawson initially told one of his former colleagues on the *Washington Post*, Marilyn Bender, that he had written it, then later told her he would "deny it on a stack of Bibles . . ." if it became public (Woodward and Bernstein, *All the President's Men*, pp. 142 ff). A year later, in an August 14, 1973 interview with the Senate Watergate staff, he denied he wrote it (Senate Select Committee on Presidential Campaign Activities, *Final Report*, No. 93-981, 93rd Cong., 2d sess. (Washington, D.C.: U.S. Government Printing Office, June 1974), p. 207, (fn. 96).

after he left the army. Segretti in turn recruited other agents who received $6,000 for their work. After an effective White House cover-up of his activities during the first grand jury investigation of the Watergate break-in, Segretti pleaded guilty in October 1973 to three counts of political sabotage and conspiracy to disrupt the Florida Democratic presidential primary. A month later he received a prison sentence of six months out of a possible maximum of three years. Segretti admitted to helping distribute materials that attributed to Muskie a pro-busing policy; likening George Wallace to Hitler; and making gross accusations of sexual misconduct and drunken driving against Senators Humphrey and Jackson, typed on Muskie stationery. In fact, Segretti and his operatives had disrupted and infiltrated Democratic primary campaigns in Florida (where they were most successful), California, New York, Florida, Washington, D.C., Pennsylvania, and by direct mail efforts attributed to various Democratic candidates. The most frequent activities involved hiring phony pickets to demonstrate, to carry harassing signs (strategically located to insure press notice and photographs), and to distribute false and misleading campaign literature at Democratic rallies; placing infiltrators in campaign headquarters to gather information and mailing lists; false advertising; and disruption of candidates' schedules in a number of ways, causing embarrassment to the candidates and inconvenience to their potential supporters and to the press.

George Hearing, a local recruit of Segretti's Florida operative, Robert Benz, was indicted in May 1973, prosecuted, and convicted on one count of violating 18 U.S.C. 612, which prohibits distribution of unsigned political literature. Hearing had been directed to reproduce and mail the scurrilous "Muskie" letter by Benz, who had given him materials including authentic Muskie stationery, and a list of Jackson supporters. For this, Hearing received one year in prison. Benz was given immunity and was not prosecuted.

One of the earliest of the unethical activities was the attempt to defeat George Wallace in his 1970 gubernatorial bid—thereby seriously damaging his potential as a third party presidential candidate in 1972—by funneling Republican money into the Democratic gubernatorial primary in Alabama to support Wallace's primary opponent, incumbent Governor Albert P. Brewer. In all, some $400,000 was authorized by Haldeman for Brewer's unsuccessful campaign. Haldeman testified that he had authorized the transfer of funds from the 1968 surplus funds entrusted to Kalmbach's care.[12] The relay man for the money was Lawrence Higby, Haldeman's staff assistant at the White House.

In 1971 the sum of $10,000 was funneled into California in the hope of eliminating Wallace's American Independent Party (AIP) from the ballot. Members of Wallace's former campaign staff said that Gordon Liddy and Harry Dent, a former White House aide, made repeated attempts to block a third-party Draft-Wallace movement within the AIP even after Wallace was shot in Maryland, in May 1972.[13]

As the campaign tempo picked up in 1972, so too did the variety of dirty tricks by the CRP. The separate operations were at times examples of the right hand not knowing about the left hand. The Segretti operation, under the loose direction of Dwight Chapin, at one point began to cause reports back to the CRP, by individuals Segretti was recruiting, about some mysterious individual who seemed bent on doing the reelection effort harm. When such a complaint from a leader of the Young Republicans at Madison, Wisconsin reached Jeb Magruder, Anthony Ulasewicz was sent to Wisconsin to see who it could be. While there, he never found Segretti, but soon received a phone call from Jack Caulfield who informed him that Segretti was the person and was working for the CRP.[14]

Magruder himself was the originator of the operation known as "Ruby I," which began in August 1971, with the help of Kenneth Rietz, the head of the Nixon youth campaign. Rietz recruited John R. Buckley, former chief of the inspections division of the Office of Economic Opportunity, who said he had spied on Muskie during his lunch hours in 1971 and early 1972. Buckley hired a cab driver, Elmer Wyatt, to volunteer at Muskie's Washington campaign headquarters, where Wyatt subsequently worked as a courier performing errands and transporting documents between Muskie's Senate office and his campaign headquarters in downtown Washington. En route, he would stop at an office rented by Buckley where they were photographed. Buckley then passed the photographs to Hunt, who would forward them to the CRP. Buckley told the Senate Watergate Committee that he was given $1,000 a month to carry out his mission.[15]

One of the filmed Muskie documents was a staff memo suggesting that the Senator, chairman of the Intergovernmental Relations Subcommittee, might get good coverage if he held hearings in California at government expense. This was sent, retyped on plain bond paper, to Evans and Novak who printed it and the hearings were cancelled.[16]

The operation code named "Ruby II" was another attempt to infiltrate the Muskie camp, this one using a student named Thomas Gregory from Brigham Young University, hired by Hunt on the recommendation of the nephew of Hunt's employer at the Mullen Company.[m] At a salary of $175 a week from CRP, Gregory worked as a volunteer for the Muskie campaign; he would meet weekly with Hunt to deliver typed reports of anything he had learned at the headquarters. Then in mid-April 1972 the surveillance operation—on orders from Haldeman—was transferred from Muskie to McGovern. Gregory switched to become a McGovern volunteer where his assignment was to provide diagrams of the headquarters and other material, which could be used by Hunt, Liddy, and McCord in a break-in and bugging of McGovern's campaign offices. Shortly before the Watergate break-in on June 17, Gregory resigned, bothered by what

---

[m]President of the Mullen Company was Robert Bennett, son of the Utah Senator. The Washington PR firm was also a cover for the CIA; Hunt had an office there at the time of the Watergate break-in.

he felt were the improprieties of his assignment. He had been paid approximately $3,400 for his services.[17]

Another part of the Ruby II operation was an effort to make a donation to the New Hampshire primary campaign of Representative Pete McCloskey, a Republican congressman challenging Nixon, that would appear to have come from radical leftist groups. Such a contribution—amounting to $135 in small bills and coins—was apparently made. As part of the effort to discredit McCloskey, it was suggested at one point that a political operative make a contribution to McCloskey seemingly from the Gay Alliance. This was vetoed and the contribution came instead from the Young Socialists Alliance. After the contribution had been made, an anonymous letter was drafted and sent to the *Manchester Union-Leader* reporting this apparent McCloskey support.

Along with the two Rubys were two other operational code names—two Sedan Chairs. Sedan Chair I was conceived by Magruder as a Republican response to the sort of prankster escapades of a Dick Tuck whose humorous tricks against the Republicans in previous elections had won the Democrats favorable publicity.[n]

In an effort to get similar headlines, Magruder instructed Porter to obtain advance schedules for the leading Democratic contenders as part of a plan to carry out disruptive activities—arranging, for example, to have a crowd bearing Nixon signs greet a Muskie arrival. Several such operations were carried out but were not productive. Porter occasionally paid his operatives from CRP funds.

Porter then hired Roger Greaves, a friend of a campaign advance man, at a salary of $2,000 per month; he was given the code name "Sedan Chair" after a Marine Corps operation that Porter remembered. Before setting out for New Hampshire, however, Greaves, on instructions from Gordon Liddy, had his picture taken. Liddy explained to Porter that some of his operatives in New Hampshore might be engaging in some rough work and he did not want them to confuse Greaves by mistake and possibly injure him. By all accounts, Greaves' work in New Hampshire—as it had been on a trial basis in California—never produced much publicity of the sort Magruder had in mind originally, and he resigned from the campaign shortly thereafter.[18]

Sedan Chair II was the code name for Michael W. McMinoway who was hired to infiltrate Democratic organizations in the presidential primary states by Roger Stone of CRP. This operation allegedly was initiated at the suggestion of John Mitchell; when McMinoway had information it went back into Magruder's office and from there, through Gordon Strachan, to Haldeman.

McMinoway, from Louisville, Kentucky, worked in the campaigns of Muskie,

---

[n]One of Tuck's best known pranks had come when, during the course of Nixon's 1962 gubernatorial "whistle stop" campaign, he donned a railroadman's cap and, while the candidate was midway through his speech from the back of the train, signaled the engineer to move the train out. Nixon's surprised look as his captive audience clustered around his car began suddenly to recede in the distance had been widely quoted in the press.

McGovern, and Humphrey for the CRP, and at times provided rival Democratic camps with information he picked up. From February through July 1972 McMinoway spied successively on the Muskie campaign in Wisconsin, the Humphrey campaigns in Pennsylvania and California, and on McGovern at the Democratic National Convention (where he was a volunteer security guard of the McGovern floors). CRP paid him $1,500 a month. In addition to supplying information (including tidbits about alleged prostitutes seen in a McGovern hospitality room in Miami), he also told Watergate investigators that he had on occasion harassed the Humphrey campaign, such as by mixing up canvassers' card files to cause extra work.[19]

Another operation, initiated by Charles Colson, was the infiltration of the peace vigil being conducted outside the White House by a group of Quakers. Colson told Magruder that someone should find out what the group was doing, and Magruder turned to Ken Rietz, who had been involved in the Ruby I plan. Rietz's assistant, George Gorton, subsequently located Ted Brill, former chairman of The George Washington University's Young Republican organization, and arranged to pay him to monitor the Quaker group, particularly to determine their plans for the Republican Convention in Miami. Brill received some $675 for his reports; his job ended a few days after the Watergate break-in.[20]

A long-time political strategist for Nixon, the late Murray Chotiner, ran another operation in which he hired writers to travel with the opposition campaigns, posing as legitimate reporters, and sending back to him information that might be of interest. He first hired Seymour Freidin, former foreign editor for the *New York Herald Tribune,* who was a free-lance writer when approached by Chotiner. Freidin, who had done similar work in the 1968 campaign, was paid about $1,000 a week; he got his credentials by claiming he was writing a book about the campaign. Chotiner code named himself "Chapman," and the Freidin reports were from "Chapman's Friend."

When Freidin was offered the post of London bureau chief for Hearst newspapers, he resigned from the campaign in September, and a new "Chapman's Friend" took over, at the same rate of pay. This was Lucianne Cummings Goldberg, author of the anti-Women's Liberation work, *Purr, Baby, Purr.* Mrs. Goldberg told reporters on the McGovern press plane that she was writing columns and a book; some were mystified at her methods, which included constant use of a tape recorder and frequent phone calls (to Chotiner's secretary who relayed the contents of the call to CRP)—an unlikely pattern for someone doing that kind of writing.

Both Freidin and Goldberg were paid their weekly salaries and expenses from checks drawn on Chotiner's law office account, and were listed as "survey" expenses. The operation, which cost $32,000, came under investigation by the GAO for FCRP's use of this manner of describing campaign expenses,[21] but no charges resulted. FCRP claimed it had paid the amounts at the direction of the CRP.

Operations were also staged to make Nixon look good. The White House set up "volunteer" Vietnam veterans groups to back the President. Presidential support was also faked with regard to Nixon's decision in May 1972 to mine North Vietnamese harbors to halt the flow of war materiel from the Soviet Union. The nationwide protests, which greeted this escalation, alarmed the White House, and led to the CRP financing rallies and vigils in support of the move. When *The New York Times* ran an editorial criticizing the mining as "counter to the will and conscience of a large segment of the American people," the Nixon campaign's November Group, which handled media advertising, placed a counter ad in the *Times,* costing $4,400. Entitled "The People vs. *The New York Times*," the ad cited public endorsement of the President's step in the polls; it was signed by 14 obscure people who had been rounded up by the campaign staff.

Campaign workers also were used to manufacture a ground swell of backing of the President for the mining. Shortly after the President's announcement, the White House reported that telegrams and phone calls were running six-to-one in favor of the step. Many, if not most, of these messages resulted from private White House appeals to organizations such as the American Legion, or telegrams sent and paid for by the CRP itself (through campaign offices in several cities). The CRP sent between 2,000 and 4,000 phony ballots to a poll conducted by a Washington television station—the station's final count showed 5,157 backing the President, 1,158 against. At least $8,400 in cash funds, mostly in the seemingly ubiquitous $100 bills, were spent on the various drives to manufacture pro-mining opinion.[22]

Many of those used in the staged vigils and rallies were part of an operation by Rietz with his Young Voters for the President to counter or neutralize the Democratic youth vote. After McGovern was nominated, Ed Failor, a special assistant at CRP, was directed by Magruder to organize "McGovern-Shriver Confrontations." At times during the fall Rietz and Failor were able to report on daily orchestrated demonstrations at McGovern or Shriver campaign stops, which apparently caused McGovern to cancel some of his planned activities.[23]

The CRP also secretly financed several vote siphoning schemes designed to weaken or eliminate an opposition candidate. In an attempt to take votes away from Muskie in New Hampshire, Colson initiated a project he says was approved by both Nixon and Haldeman, in which as much as $10,000 may have been spent. Colson launched a Kennedy write-in campaign in New Hampshire by drafting a letter supporting such a campaign, then working through an intermediary, getting it signed by a Maryland Democrat, Robin Ficker, who had been running a Kennedy-for-President headquarters for some months. Ficker signed the letter because he agreed with what it said; he later learned that between 150,000 and 180,000 copies of the letter were mailed to New Hampshire Democrats. Ficker himself went to New Hampshire and campaigned for Kennedy. At the suggestion of the same "Mike Abramson" who had first called Ficker about the letter, but whom Ficker never saw, he placed an ad in the *Manchester Union-Leader,* credited it to United Democrats for Kennedy, and paid for it himself; Ficker was under the impression he was working with Kennedy aides in the write-in campaign, which in reality was a Colson creation. It was not successful; Kennedy received less than one percent of the Democratic write-in vote. The same tactic was employed in the Illinois primary with secret support from the CRP to Eugene McCarthy's campaign, purporting to be legitimate aid, with the aim of weakening Muskie.[24]

A far more complicated effort was that mentioned earlier, which aimed at denying Wallace's American Independent Party a place on the ballot in California in 1972. The effort failed, but not before it went through some of the more bizarre meanderings of the reelection campaign, including a brief fling with the American Nazi Party.

The plan was conceived in 1971 by Robert Walters, a disillusioned Wallace supporter, who had come to feel that the AIP was drawing support away from conservative candidates of the two major parties. Under California law, as of January 1 of an election year a political party must have registered voters exceeding 1/15 of one percent of the total voter registration in the state to qualify for the ballot. Walters' plan was to convince enough of the approximately 140,000 registered AIP voters to reregister in another party, thus dropping the AIP below the level needed. At the same time, he sought to disenfranchise as many AIP voters as possible under an interpretation he devised of California election law; it was his understanding that voters who had moved since the 1970 elections without notifying county authorities could be purged from voting lists. From this he reasoned he could send registered letters to AIP voters; those that went undelivered due to a change of address would provide sufficient evidence to ask election officials to purge their names.

Seeking both financial and volunteer support for his plan, Walters contacted conservative groups and the CRP in Washington. In mid-September 1971 he heard from and subsequently met with Magruder. Magruder then got approval from Mitchell to put $10,000 into the project, and through Lyn Nofziger (a Californian then at the Republican National Committee, with years of political experience), a Los Angeles businessman named Jack Lindsey was lined up to supervise the project and pay the expenses. Nofziger got the $10,000 from Hugh Sloan and sent it to Lindsey.

Walters was paid $150 a week plus expenses, but the reregistration effort never amounted to much; when it folded, Walters had received $9,000, and Lindsey donated the remaining $1,000, in his own name, to a Nixon fundraising dinner in Los Angeles. Many county officials refused to purge the AIP voters who had moved, and the personal canvass, faltering from the start, ended involving the American Nazi Party. When efforts to find either volunteer or paid canvassers failed, a Walters assistant turned to Joseph Tomassi, head of the regional Nazi party, who needed mortgage payments for party headquarters. Tomassi got $1,200 of the CRP money, but he and his associates were no more successful than any of the others involved in reregistering AIP members.[25]

As to "dirty tricks" played on the Nixon reelection effort, Watergate investigators noted a number of "improper, unethical, or illegal activities." These included some violently destructive acts against campaign headquarters: a CRP office in Phoenix, Arizona was gutted by fire set by arsonists, attempted arson was reported in New Mexico and New Hampshire, and gunshots were fired into headquarters in Massachusetts and Pennsylvania. Violent demonstrations also occurred against campaign appearances by Nixon in Tulsa, Oklahoma; Agnew in Tampa, Florida, and Chicago; and Mrs. Nixon in Boston. In New York City CRP offices were harassed by people who dumped cockroaches and threw paint on Nixon volunteers.

The Watergate investigators noted, however, that except for a few isolated instances—McGovern workers in California, for example, permitting demonstrators to use their phone banks to organize a protest against Nixon's campaign appearance in Los Angeles—they found no pattern or evidence that the anti-Nixon activities were the direct or indirect responsibility of a Democratic candidate or Democratic campaign organization.[26]

The total impact of the CRP-linked dirty tricks on the 1972 campaign will be debated for years. For all save the stop-Wallace efforts, the operations were initially launched against Muskie—Segretti, Ruby I and II, Sedan Chair I and II, Chotiner, and "Chapman's Friend," and Colson's creation of a Kennedy write-in drive in New Hampshire. Muskie was feared by the White House strategists and, for whatever combination of circumstances, Muskie was stopped—with the CRP dirty tricks undoubtedly contributing to that result. Both Muskie's and McGovern's campaign directors, moreover, later testified to the "unparalleled atmosphere of rancor and discord within the Democratic Party" at the conclusion of the presidential primary season.

This account of "dirty tricks" does not include the break-ins in Dr. Fielding's office or the DNC because both are recounted elsewhere. It aims to illustrate illegitimate if not illegal uses of campaign funds, and to describe abuses that characterize an insensitivity to the essential free and open election process fundamental to a democratic society. It also points up uses of money that can only turn off political contributors who it must be assumed do not appreciate seeing their money misused. "Dirty tricks" permeated the Nixon campaign. Permission, tacit or explicit, emanated from the White House through Haldeman and Chapin; from the CRP through Mitchell, Magruder, Porter, and Liddy; and through Kalmbach working with both the White House and the CRP. The money came from various of the secret funds, controlled by Kalmbach and Porter, and directed by Haldeman, Chapin, and Magruder.

The Patman Committee

During the fall of 1972 the House Banking and Currency Committee was partly responsible for keeping Watergate alive as a public issue. The committee staff made a preliminary investigation into certain financial transactions relating to aspects of Watergate and wrote two reports presenting alleged revelations about money handling by Nixon operatives. The first, September 12, report was covered by a memo—from committee chairman Wright Patman to All Members of the Banking and Currency Committee—which cautioned: "This document is to be regarded as confidential and for the use of the Members of this Committee only. . . ." The second, October 31, staff report was an update of the September report, requested by Patman during an open session of the committee on October 12, In addition, Patman, a Democrat, mounted an unsuccessful effort to override White House opposition and win his committee's consent to subpoena witnesses to appear at public hearings on Watergate. This struggle too gained considerable publicity.

The Banking Committee claimed jurisdiction to investigate Republican campaign funds because of the evident use of foreign banks to transfer and conceal funds in what appeared to be a criminal conspiracy. The committee's first report disclosed that $100,000 in contributions to the Nixon campaign had been routed through a Mexican bank to insure the anonymity of their Texas donors; this ruse was to become known as "the Mexican laundering operation." The report accused Maurice Stans, Nixon's finance chairman, of personally clearing the legally suspect Mexican detour. Stans denounced the report as "rubbish,"[27] and later developments failed to show Stans had any link to the laundering.

According to the report, the $100,000 was part of $700,000 that was rushed across the country in a suitcase to beat the starting date of the new federal law requiring public disclosure of campaign gifts. Of the $100,000, $89,000 had been cashed through the Miami bank account of Bernard Barker, one of five men involved in the Watergate break-in.

The initial report also noted that shortly after Minnesota soybean magnate Dwayne Andreas gave $25,000 to the Nixon cause, he and several associates were granted a federal bank charter, the Treasury Department approving their application in "unusually" short time through an unusual procedure. The $25,000 Andreas check also was cashed through Barker's bank account.

In its second report the committee pointed out that the CRP had accepted $305,000—its largest single known contribution at the time—from Walter Duncan, a Texan who at the time was being sued for $2.2 million on a land deal. He later faced foreclosure on four land holdings after defaulting on notes totalling almost $6 million. He also faced expensive lawsuits. Duncan made the $305,000 contribution in the form of an IOU, borrowing heavily from banks to do so. He claimed he had not been promised anything in return for his generosity.

Elaborating on the Mexican laundering operation, the report noted the $100,000 donation originated in the Houston bank account of Gulf Resources and Chemical Corp., and speculated that the money was either a corporate campaign gift disguised by the Mexican routing or a contribution from a foreign national. The former definitely would have been illegal; the latter, quite possibly was illegal.

The report also charged that additional gifts, perhaps as much as $750,000, had been "laundered" in foreign bank accounts; as it turned out, the allegation was approximately correct, and later discoveries showed that some contributors had laundered their gifts. It also cited at least $30,000 channelled to the Nixon campaign from a Luxembourg bank just before the April 7 reporting deadline.

After the first report appeared, Patman, a 79-year-old Texas Populist, sought authorization from his committee to conduct a full-scale investigation into Republican campaign financing before the election. This would have meant the use of subpoenas to compel high-ranking Nixon campaign officials to turn over documents and testify at televised public hearings. In the White House the prospect of such hearings in the weeks just prior to the election seemed a threat to the President's reelection.

With Democrats enjoying a 22-15 majority on the committee, Patman normally could have expected to have his way easily. However, on October 3, the committee voted 20 to 15 against the subpoena power necessary for public hearings, with six Democrats joining the Republicans to doom the inquiry. Opponents claimed the hearings would prejudice the rights of the seven men yet to stand trial for the Watergate burglary. Republicans asserted that the probe was a partisan move to smear the White House and GOP.

Patman claimed White House pressure had quashed the hearings and immediately requested that the General Accounting Office investigate Republican campaign financing. He then asked four of the president's advisers (Mitchell, MacGregor, Stans, and Dean) to testify voluntarily before the committee, but they refused. The committee staff called the refusal of witnesses to cooperate unprecedented in the committee's recent history. Patman followed up with a second attempt to win committee approval of a full probe but failed even to muster enough Democrats to get a quorum. The collapse of Patman's efforts all but assured there would be no effective congressional investigation of Watergate before the elections.

Light was shed later on the scuttling of Patman's investigation in an article[28] pointing out that the argument that public hearings might jeopardize the rights of criminal defendants had been heard—and rejected—by congressional committees many times before. But rarely had Congress yielded on this ground its right to investigate and the public's right to know. For that matter, Patman's staff had maintained his investigation would carefully avoid reflecting on the guilt or innocence of the seven Watergate defendants. According to the article, it was political pressure, not legal principles, that carried the day; heavy lobbying by House Republican leaders and the Justice Department were sufficient to keep committee Republicans in line.

Some of the steps the White House took to prevent the investigation were revealed months later by former presidential counsel John W. Dean, III, who had orchestrated the opposition to the Patman hearings. Dean told the Senate Watergate hearings that the White House opposed the Patman inquiry for two reasons: "First, the hearings would have resulted in more adverse pre-election publicity regarding Watergate, and second, they just might stumble into something that would start unraveling the coverup."[29] He testified that White House measures to block the hearings included the following: (1) a check of campaign contribution reports filed by each committee member; (2) a search for a "soft spot" in Patman's political or personal life; (3) the persuasion of the Justice Department to oppose the hearings publicly on grounds they would deprive the Watergate defendants of a fair trial and imperil a prompt and successful prosecution. The department's chief of the Criminal Division, Henry Petersen, wrote a letter to that effect on October 2 to every committee member; its statement became a focus of committee debate over whether to hold public hearings; and (4) an attempt to influence the General Accounting Office to go easy on any investigation of campaign finances for Patman.

Patman did not quit, however. In December he wrote Attorney General Richard Kleindienst, telling him that an "aggressive 'no holds barred' investigation" of Watergate by the Justice Department was long overdue.[o] Patman said the investigation should cover not only the matters noted in his committee's reports but all the issues raised by the scandal, and suggested that Kleindienst appoint an independent task force—outside the political arena—to conduct it.

Four weeks later the Justice Department replied, saying it was investigating three of the matters noted in the committee reports: (1) the Mexican laundering operation; (2) any unreported disbursements from the alleged cash fund kept in the treasurer's safe at the FCRP; and (3) allegations of fraudulent financial statements to several banks involving Walter Duncan. The department reported it was not pursuing the other matters raised by the reports either because the evidence was insufficient or it lacked jurisdiction.

Patman responded harshly, accusing the department of purposely ignoring the question of an independent, full-scale inquiry and dragging its feet on Watergate to avoid embarrassment to the administration. He also criticized the department for "dealing superficially" with the allegations in the committee

---

[o]*Remarks of the Honorable Wright Patman (D., Tex.) on the Floor of the House of Representatives, Wednesday, January 3, 1973: The Attorney General's Silence on the Watergate Burglary.* At that time Patman placed in the record copies of his two letters to the Attorney General (dated December 15 and December 30, 1972).

reports and quarrelled with it for closing the probe of the $25,000 Andreas con-
tribution and for concluding that the $114,000 deposited in Bernard Barker's
bank account was not an unreported outlay of the CRP. He suggested Kleindienst resign if he could not investigate Watergate freely because of his political
loyalty to the administration.

A week after the Patman investigation collapsed, Senator Edward Kennedy
won approval from the Senate Judiciary Subcommittee, which he headed, for a
closed-door inquiry into the Watergate scandal. Kennedy had been under some
pressure from Senator McGovern and other leading Democrats to launch an
investigation, but reportedly was reluctant because he felt such an inquiry would
be suspected as politically inspired. The end of the Patman investigation coupled
with several other developments persuaded Kennedy to act. The other influences
were delays in civil suits involving Watergate, the opening of new areas of inquiry
by the disclosure of political sabotage by Donald Segretti, and encouragement to
proceed from Senator Sam Ervin, who some were thinking might head a special
Senate inquiry himself.

Armed with subpoena power, Kennedy set the staff of his Subcommittee
on Administrative Practice and Procedure to work gathering evidence. The inquiry focused heavily on reports of political espionage and sabotage apart from
the Watergate break-in itself and on the question of adequacy of the Justice
Department, FBI, and White House investigations of Watergate matters. The
late date at which Kennedy began his probe all but precluded the prospect of it
leading to public hearings before the election.

A full-scale probe by Kennedy never materialized, for after the election the
new Senate appointed Senator Ervin to head a comprehensive Watergate investigation. Ervin's selection reflected the fact that, in contrast to Kennedy, he was
considered one of the least partisan men in Congress. Kennedy subsequently
turned the findings of his subcommittee's three-month inquiry over to Ervin's
staff.

Other Investigative Organizations

Three institutions came to play an important role in uncovering the Watergate scandals and attendant government abuses. One was a totally new creation
in American government—the Office of the Special Prosecutor. A second was a
Senate committee specifically created to look into the problem area, a device
used in the past when the concern was major. The third was a standing committee of the House of Representatives, considering for only the second time in
United States history the issue before it—the impeachment of a President.

Senate Watergate Committee

The first institution to get involved was the Senate Select Committee on Presidential Campaign Activities, created by Senate Resolution 60, which was passed by a unanimous (77-0) vote on February 7, 1973. In the fall of 1972 Senator Edward M. Kennedy, as chairman of the Senate Judiciary Committee's Subcommittee on Administrative Practice and Procedure, had conducted an investigation into Watergate, and on the basis of Kennedy's findings, a new Senate's Democratic leadership decided to establish the Select Committee, with Senator Sam J. Ervin, Jr., D-North Carolina, as its chairman.

Over the next 19 months the members of this committee, in particular its chairman, became known to millions of Americans through the 52 days of televised public hearings held by the committee.[P] The public hearings covered the committee's investigation of the Watergate break-in and cover-up, and 62 witnesses were heard. The public's interest was particularly intense from mid-May to early August 1973, when many of the most important and powerful figures in the Nixon administration testified. Perhaps the most dramatic moment of all came on the afternoon of July 16, 1973 when Alexander Butterfield, former personal aide to the President, revealed the existence of taping devices in the White House. On these tapes, Nixon came to be the most damaging witness of all against himself.

In the summer of 1974 the Ervin committee published its final report, a 1,250-page volume, documenting in great detail the committee's findings on the Watergate break-in and cover-up, other illegal and improper campaign practices and financing, and setting forth 35 recommendations aimed at preventing abuses of government power.[30] Two important committee proposals were for the creation of a permanent office of special prosecutor, with fixed terms of five years, and for the creation of a Federal Election Commission. On September 30, 1974 the Select Committee went out of business, having cost the taxpayers $2 million.

Office of the Special Prosecutor

The second institution to get involved in Watergate was a new one to the

---

[P]The seven members of the Watergate Committee were Senators Ervin, chairman; Howard H. Baker, Jr., R-Tennessee, vice-chairman; Herman E. Talmadge, D-Georgia; Daniel K. Inouye, D-Hawaii; Joseph M. Montoya, D-New Mexico; Edward J. Gurney, R-Florida; and Lowell P. Weiker, Jr., R-Connecticut. Chief counsel and staff director was Professor Samuel Dash of the Georgetown University Law School; Dash was assisted by Minority Counsel Fred Thompson, former assistant United States attorney in Nashville, Tennessee, and Deputy Chief Counsel Rufus Edmisten.

American scene—the Office of the Special Prosecutor. It was created in May 1973 by congressional demand during the Senate confirmation hearings of Attorney General-Designate Elliot Richardson, and was given a $2.8 million annual budget, and an initial staff of 90. The first Special Prosecutor was Harvard Law Professor Archibald Cox, former Solicitor General during the Kennedy administration. In testimony before the Senate, Richardson publicly pledged that only the Attorney General would have the authority to fire the Special Prosecutor, and then only for what Richardson called "extraordinary improprieties."[31]

The Special Prosecutor organized a staff of attorneys, investigators, and supporting personnel, which during the first year included the Watergate Task Force, Campaign Contributions Task Force, Dirty Tricks Task Force, I.T.T. Task Force, and Counsel to the Special Prosecutor. A number of the investigations by the Special Prosecutor paralleled those by the Ervin Committee; Cox, however, had the authority to follow through to criminal prosecutions.

In October 1973 Nixon, disturbed by reports that Cox was looking into his acquisition of San Clemente, and by Cox's determined efforts to obtain White House tapes, provoked a confrontation, offering him a compromise release of tape transcripts, which he knew Cox would not accept. The "Saturday Night Massacre" followed on October 18, with both Richardson and Deputy Attorney General William Ruckelshaus resigning rather than following Nixon's order to fire Cox; Solicitor General Bork, as Acting Attorney General, finally fired him. Cox had served as Special Prosecutor from May 25 to October 20, 1973.

On November 5, 1973 in the wake of congressional demands for Nixon's impeachment, Leon Jaworski of Houston, Texas became Special Prosecutor. Jaworski served in that office until he resigned on October 25, 1974. During his tenure, indictments were brought against a number of corporate contributors and former members of the Nixon administration. Jaworski resigned three weeks after the opening of the cover-up trial of Mitchell, Haldeman, Ehrlichman, and LaRue—all were found guilty on January 1, 1975. Action by Jaworski's office led to the unanimous Supreme Court ruling on July 24, 1974 that Nixon must provide "forthwith" the tapes and documents relating to 64 conversations subpoenaed by Jaworski in April. Sixteen days later Nixon resigned and Gerald Ford was sworn in as President.

The day after Jaworski stepped down, Henry S. Ruth, Jr. of Bethesda, Maryland took over, faced with such issues as the question of public right of access to the Nixon White House tapes and documents; the filing of a report with Congress on the Nixon investigation; continued investigations into alleged misuse of government agencies and other unethical activities; future trials and appeals.

House Judiciary Committee

The uproar over the firing of Cox in the fall of 1973 resulted in the House of Representatives voting on November 15, 367-51, that $1 million be put at the disposal of the House Judiciary Committee to determine whether impeachment proceedings should begin. On February 6, 1974 the House voted, 410-4, to have the committee chaired by Peter Rodino, Jr., D-New Jersey, take up the question of whether grounds for impeachment existed.

Over the spring of 1974 the Rodino Committee (composed of 21 Democrats and 17 Republicans) sought through subpoena to get the White House to release tapes the committee wanted to listen to as part of its inquiry. Nixon's response to the pressure came on April 29 with his release of partial transcripts of 46 taped meetings and telephone conversations, edited by the White House.

Proceeding (under pressure) without the tapes necessary to prove Nixon's role in Watergate, on July 19, the committee's Special Counsel John Doar announced the case for impeachment, which he and his staff had been piecing together since the first of the year, and five days later the final televised debate on impeachment began. On July 28 Article I—covering alleged obstruction of justice—was passed by the committee, 27-11. Two days later Article II, accusing Nixon of repeatedly failing to uphold the law, passed 28-10; Article III, charging him with defiance of the committee's subpoenas, passed narrowly, while two other articles were rejected. With the disclosures by the White House a few days later that Nixon had in fact tried to obstruct the FBI's investigation, all ten Republicans who had held out against impeachment announced they were switching their votes. The committee thus unanimously recommended impeachment. On August 22, 1974, with Gerald Ford now President, the House voted, 412-3, to accept the Judiciary Committee's 528-page report,[32] which stated the unanimous committee view that Richard Nixon should have been removed from office for obstruction of justice.

April 7 and the Nixon Campaign

As the presidential campaigns of 1972 proceeded, controversy mounted over the FCRP's unwillingness to reveal the sources of money behind President Nixon's reelection drive raised before the FECA became effective. The controversy became an important campaign issue, only partially and temporarily resolved a week before election day.

A number of presidential challengers had followed the examples set by George McGovern and Paul McCloskey, and voluntarily made public the names of their pre-April 7 contributors. When some candidates, including President Nixon, refused to do the same, the media and Common Cause, a citizens' lobby, made an issue of their refusal. Leading Democrats assailed Nixon's "secret slush fund,"[q] but the FCRP continued to ignore pressures for voluntary

---

[q]The FCRP's first filing under the new law on June 10, 1972 revealed approximately $10.2 million in cash on hand as of April 7, 1972. When all the disclosures were made public,

disclosure, pursuant to a policy decision made on March 12 at a joint meeting of officials of the CRP, FCRP, and the White House. CRP officials claimed McGovern's and other candidates' disclosures were probably unreliable, did not seriously challenge any of them at the time, but later claimed this was established when the Comptroller General referred several McGovern committees to the Attorney General for "apparent violations" of the law. No McGovern committees were ever prosecuted.

After waiting some 60 days for a reply to a letter to John Mitchell, in September 1972 Common Cause took action against the FCRP.[r] A suit was filed charging the FCRP with violating the Federal Corrupt Practices Act of 1925 (FCPA) by failing to file the required reports for all of 1971 and early 1972.[33] The legal issues were complex because the suit was brought under the FCPA, which had been repealed when the FECA came into effect on April 7, 1972. While the FECA set down a far more stringent code of financial conduct than the FCPA, it was marred by one serious failure: the new law did not phase out reports required by the repealed FCPA. The old law required filings by any organized committee "which accepts contributions or makes expenditures for the purpose of influencing or attempting to influence the election of candidates or presidential and vice-presidential electors" in two or more states; it did not apply to committees organized solely for prenomination activities as the CRP committees in existence prior to April 7 claimed to be. Reports were required between the first and tenth days of March, June, July, on January 1, and several other times prior to election day. Thus, the last filing under the old law was required on March 10 for the period ending February 29, and it was questionable whether any contributions received between March 1 through April 6 were subject to any disclosure. This uncertainty was exploited by the FCRP, as it was by other federal candidates able to raise early money. Nixon's zealous fund raisers waged an intensive drive up to the last days before the new law went

---

the FCRP acknowledged collecting $19.9 million in undisclosed contributions before April 7, the details of which were not fully made public until September, 1973.

[r]Common Cause, attaining more than 300,000 members, grew out of the Urban Coalition Action Council. It became Common Cause in August, 1970, and granted members voting rights in April 1971. Before the Watergate events unfolded, its membership was about 200,000. Watergate caused a rise in membership, presumably reflecting public concern about reforming politics. Common Cause has been effective in seeking public disclosure of campaign funding, and in setting up its own monitoring system to prod enforcement of the FECA. The lobby group has also taken on battles for congressional reform, voting rights, the Equal Rights Amendment, public employment, ending of SST funding, and abuse of the congressional franking privilege. The staff consists of full-time lobbyists and researchers who issue a monthly newsletter from Washington. When necessary, Common Cause takes legal action as in the case of Nixon's campaign financing. Another successful case resulted in an out-of-court settlement, forcing national party campaign committees to stop "earmarking" of funds contributed for specific candidates, but laundered through party committees. Common Cause also successfully sued the Internal Revenue Service for its failure to carry out legislative intent for the $1 checkoff law in 1972.

into effect. Common Cause argued that under the General Savings Statute, the FCRP had to disclose everything in both periods because there was nothing in the new law that expressed any intention to bar the enforcement of the FCPA prior to April 7.

The FCRP considered all this moot, taking the position that President Nixon was not a candidate for reelection during the period prior to April 7, but rather was seeking the Republican nomination. It claimed the committee and its affiliated committees in existence prior to April 7, were, according to their charters, organized for the purpose of assisting solely in the renomination of the President, so they were not subject to disclosure requirements of the FCPA. Because that law applied only to presidential electors, and hence to the raising of funds to influence their election, the FCRP argued that it did not have to start reporting until after the candidate was formally nominated (or until after the new law took effect on April 7). This had been the practice in the prenomination periods for other incumbent presidents, such as Eisenhower in 1956 and Johnson in 1964. The suit challenged this view by quoting FCRP literature, which solicited funds for a "campaign" against the Democrats; by pointing out that the Nixon committee refused to file preprimary reports under the new law because, it said, its candidate was not running in the primaries (it did file the required periodic reports); and in depositions extracting the concessions from FCRP's officers that the money was raised, "for the purpose of assisting in the renomination and reelection of President Richard Nixon as candidate for the office of President."

Attorneys for the FCRP argued that public disclosure of contributors, the heart of the new law and the process President Nixon earlier said would restore public confidence in electoral honesty, was a violation of the rights of privacy and freedom of anonymous association. Disclosure, they held, would betray the promise of anonymity made to the contributors and invade their privacy. They contended that disclosure could be made by the individual contributors if they wished, but the committee would not violate its agreement of privacy by making such disclosures. FCRP lawyers sought to dismiss the suit, but Federal District Court Judge Joseph E. Waddy refused.

Legal proceedings, including the taking of depositions, delayed the trial for a while but it was finally set for November 1, 1972. Common Cause lawyers claimed delay past the election was the singular goal of the defendants, that Common Cause only responded to the other side's attempts to delay, and that Common Cause sought immediate disclosure. When it became apparent that there would be a trial prior to the election, with the potential for substantial publicity, the FCRP (after polling the major affected contributors for their concurrence) offered to name on November 1 the Nixon contributors of $100 or more for the period from January 1, 1971 through March 9, 1972. This still left the crucial period of March 10, 1972 through April 6, 1972, the heaviest period of undisclosed contributions to the FCRP, to be litigated in 1973.

Common Cause agreed to the partial disclosure and an additional delay in the trial of the suit until after the election because its lawyers felt it could not complete the trial and all appeals to force full disclosure before the election.

The agreement contained advantages and disadvantages for both sides. Common Cause won limited disclosure of Nixon contributors, assuming that they would not be able to accomplish full disclosure, including appeals, in the remaining week before the election. The FCRP was able to maintain its legal position without a trial or court ruling, and its officials would not be distracted from fund raising in the last week of the campaign. Moreover, FCRP officials would not have to take the witness stand before the election, and receive the attendant publicity, although Stans and others were prepared to testify if necessary.

As part of the agreement, the FCRP also consented to deliver all its records of preelection finance, covering expenditures and contributions, including the March 10 through April 6 period, to the court for safekeeping. Only the lawyers in the case were given access to the records.

When the FCRP report was released a few days before the election, it revealed the names of 1,573 persons who had given $5.4 million to the President's reelection drive through March 9, 1972. Included were two of the largest individual contributions in American history: $2 million from W. Clement Stone, Chicago insurance magnate; and $1 million from Richard Mellon Scaife, an heir to the Mellon fortune.

The case continued on until March 1973, when Maurice Stans called John Gardner to suggest a private meeting in the office of a Common Cause attorney. The meeting, at which various alternatives were discussed, did not lead to an immediate settlement; Gardner came away feeling Stans was only willing to disclose the names of those who gave less than $5,000; and of those giving more, only those contributors who agreed to have their names published. Stans claims he offered simply to reveal all information contributors would agree to his releasing, whether donors gave over or under $5,000.

Common Cause announced that there were "enormous gaps" in the records the FCRP had deposited with the court in November, and asked the court to order the FCRP to deliver all the data immediately. The gaps were expenditure records, which were claimed by FCRP to have been left out due to a misunderstanding on the part of the treasurer, and then voluntarily provided. On the day Common Cause filed the motion, April 23, 1973, the FCRP deposited three more cartons of records with the courts, saying they had just been found. Common Cause attorneys concluded that it took the threat of a contempt citation to make the FCRP produce the required records, but FCRP denies any lack of good faith.

Subsequent to the Common Cause motion filed in April, the Rose Mary Woods list[S] of contributors was made available. It was one of the documents

---

[S]A list of some 2,000 names known as "Rose Mary's Baby," with contributions made

Common Cause sought by subpoena after a deposition of Hugh Sloan surfaced the fact that a list existed, which contained a code identifying cash contributors. Sloan recalled that a copy had been sent to Rose Mary Woods at the White House. Following a meeting and a number of phone calls, the list—which has subsequently created a host of problems for some corporations—was delivered voluntarily on June 7, 1973 by Leonard Garment, a counselor to the President.

On July 25, 1973 Judge Waddy approved an FCRP offer to terminate the litigation by filing a public report, covering the FCRP's campaign finances between January 1, 1971 and April 7, 1972, without any finding that it was obligated to do so. The end of the struggle came on September 28, 1973, when FCRP filed a public list of donors and the amounts of donations to the FCRP prior to April 7, 1972, as well as expenditure listings. The report revealed that Nixon committees raised $11.4 million in the month before the new law took effect. Almost half of that total came in the last two days—on April 5 and 6, $2.3 million and $3 million were received, respectively—some of it unsolicited. The total for the entire 15-month period was $19.9 million.

Common Cause later challenged the completeness of the September 28 report for failure to include information prior to April 7, 1972 on contributions and expenditures of 50 state committees and the Republican National Committee; on pledges made to defendant committees, the RNC, and the 50 state committees; and on transactions of the National Committee for Revenue Sharing, the Asian Committee, and certain Delaware and Illinois committees. These requests were answered by the FCRP, which claimed never to have been responsible for providing information on the 50 state committees, the Republican National Committee, and the National Committee for Revenue Sharing, either under the FCPA or pursuant to any order of the Court, and never having in their custody possession or control of the records sought by Common Cause. The FCRP claimed the Republican National Finance Committee (RNFC) was totally independent; it was in fact regularly filing its own reports under the FCPA. According to the FCRP, the state committees operated independently, except where funds were transferred when needed for primaries or other purposes. The National Committee for Revenue Sharing was an issue committee not concerned with the reelection of the president. Also, according to the FCRP, there never was an Asian Committee prior to April 7, 1972, and all monies transferred from the Delaware and Illinois committees were reflected in the ledgers and included in the report. As to pledges made before April 7 and fulfilled later, the FCRP claimed it had no records on September 28, 1973 aside from those made available to Common Cause.

The consolidated report of September 28 was an accounting for the 450

---

before April 7 totalling almost $20 million, that had been sent to Miss Woods in May 1972 by Maurice Stans for possible use as a mailing list for White House greetings and party invitations.

committees with which the FCRP was associated, and for which it had records. Common Cause never claimed to have found an inaccuracy in the reporting for these committees, but continued to claim that FCRP should be responsible for reporting for the additional committees.

On June 28, 1974 Judge Waddy finally dismissed the Common Cause suit as moot, saying that Common Cause had subjected the President's backers to some harrassment, and ruled that recent higher court opinions cut the ground from under the law suit.[34] In doing so, Judge Waddy unsealed and made public information that the CRP had turned over to the court and that Common Cause reviewed in its search for more hidden funds while auditing the September 28 report with the court's approval. Common Cause claimed almost $2 million in additional undisclosed funds were discovered in this way and should have been included in the September 28 report, but FCRP attorneys denied this. With the dismissal, a number of campaign documents were unsealed, including an "ABCD List" of prospects for money raisers (a list that showed $250,000 in additional contributions from 15 individuals but that the FCRP denies were its responsibility), and the "Alpha-Four"—a four-column alphabetical list that showed an additional $750,000 in unreported funds, for which FCRP again denied responsibility on grounds that these were funds contributed elsewhere, not under FCRP control. Another $825,000 appeared as "quota reports"— money Common Cause claimed was raised by Nixon operatives and sent to various state committees claimed by FCRP as not under its jurisdiction or control.

Common Cause charged that in compiling its September 28, 1973 report, the FCRP had made inadequate use of a number of lists they supplied to Common Cause during discovery proceedings. The source of the lists was a voluminous card file compiled by Hugh Sloan for the FCRP after April 7th, which incorporated pre-April 7 information from 12 ledgers he maintained on an ongoing basis, both before and after April 7; all of these were turned over to the Court and were available to Common Cause.

The claim of Common Cause that the $2 million in previously undisclosed contributions from the lists and files should have been included in the September 28 report was never endorsed by Judge Waddy. The FCRP took the position that the so-called "secret contributions" attributed by Common Cause were in fact contributions made to other lawful committees for which all required reports were filed and over which the FCRP had no control; examples were contributions made to the RNC and some state committees.

The lists Common Cause cited were used for different purposes and give insight into the Nixon campaign:

1. The *ABCD List* was prepared and used to assist the state and local solicitation of contributions. It contained information from the card file and from the daily ledger.

2. The *Eight Category List* isolated contributors into various geographic

areas based not only on the size of their contributions but also on their donated services to the reelection effort; it did not contain amounts of money contributed.

3. The *Alpha Four Column List* lists individuals and the amounts contributed, including contributions made to the RNC. This was for the purpose of identifying individuals who contributed both to the Nixon effort and to the general Republican reelection effort during the 1972 campaign. But the RNC was regularly reporting its contributions.

4. The *Rose Mary Woods List* was considered by FCRP to be a casual and inaccurate[t] account of contributions received before April 7, and the information it showed was available from the card files and ledgers. It showed, in code, the cash contributions.

5. The *Steven Bull List* was a combined list of contributors and workers, containing no money amounts.

6. The *Quota Lists,* which were not prepared until after April 7, contained aggregate amounts of contributions by states and had no names or amounts for individual contributions.

All of these lists were drawn up later from the card files and ledgers used by the campaign.

Although the Common Cause suit against the FCRP was eventually dismissed as moot, it made a valuable contribution to public disclosure by eliciting more information on the early financing of a presidential campaign than had ever before been available. Throughout the proceedings, Common Cause and the media generally credited the suit with forcing disclosure; the FCRP persistently maintained that bargaining took place, that offers to disclose were voluntarily made, and then sanctioned by the court without prejudice or findings of fault. The Court never reached the procedural position where it was called upon to find fault. By making offers voluntarily, the FCRP produced most of what Common Cause sought. At the end, the facts were in the public domain, events overtook the suit, and the wearied judge dismissed it. Because President Nixon's campaign organization was centrally controlled down to the state and local levels, nearly all source and spending data for the Nixon campaign, pre- and postnomination, have now been disclosed. A possible exception, not part of the suit, could include monies that might have gone into funds controlled by Nixon's friend Bebe Rebozo without the knowledge of the FCRP.

Enforcement of Corrupt Practices Act

Ralph Nader and Public Citizen, Inc. brought suit in Washington, D.C.

---

[t]"Inaccurate" may not convey the correct meaning. In effect, the list was a "cumulative" credit of an individual's financial efforts. In addition to contributions to the FCRP and associated committees, contributions to the RNC or other committees were included on a subjective and selective, but not necessarily complete, basis.

district court, first in February 1972, seeking to compel Attorney General
John Mitchell and others to enforce the disclosure provisions of the Federal
Corrupt Practices Act. The suit alleged that voters had been deprived of relevant information (relating to campaign funding) on which to support candidates,
through the nonenforcement of the law.

In a subsequent (January 1973) continuation of the suit against then
Attorney General Richard Kleindienst, Federal District Judge William B. Bryant
agreed that "injury" had in fact occurred to voters, and that the law was drawn
up with the purpose in mind of providing such information to the voters before
an election. He held, nonetheless, that the Attorney General had the discretion
of when or when not to prosecute, and that the court could not intervene in
this discretionary process. Judge Bryant pointed out that the prerogative of
enforcing criminal law was vested by the Constitution in the executive arm of
the government, not in the courts. He ruled further that since a new law had
replaced the old act, and since the election in question was now over, the information was now moot, and he dismissed the suit on the grounds of failure to
state a claim upon which relief could be granted.

The dismissal was affirmed on April 4, 1974 by the Court of Appeals in an
opinion by Judge J. Skelly Wright.[35] The Court of Appeals agreed that plaintiffs
had suffered injury, but disagreed about the Attorney General's discretion, holding that exercise of such discretion is indeed subject to review. The Court of
Appeals held, however, that no relief under the old statute would be meaningful
in light of its repeal and replacement by the 1971 Act, and that the case was
essentially moot.

4

Spending in the 1972 Elections

The 1972 elections were a watershed event in the history of American political campaigns, not only because of the amounts of money spent in the presidential campaigns and the ways in which some of the monies were raised, handled, and disbursed, but also because a major revision in federal laws regulating political finance took effect in mid-campaign, on April 7, 1972.

By broadening the coverage of required disclosure, the Federal Election Campaign Act (FECA) changed the data base of information concerning the financing of federal campaigns. Because so much more is known about sources of funds and categories of expenditure in 1972 than for any previous election, comparison with data from earlier years is perilous. That problem notwithstanding, the massive amounts of data enable journalists and scholars to study and report campaign practices with greater detail and certainty than ever before.

Three supervisory officers—the Comptroller General, the Clerk of the House, and the Secretary of the Senate—received reports of income and outgo from candidates for federal office and political committees supporting them, causing considerable overlap and duplication. Of 4,744 separate political committees registered under the FECA, more than 1,000 filed with two or all three of the supervisory officers. The problem confronting the Citizens' Research Foundation (CRF) in this book has been to distinguish the discrete information from the overlapping in order to present as clear and as comprehensive a picture as possible. The massive amounts of data produced by the FECA have been extremely difficult to analyze and present in readily understandable and nonduplicative ways.

Total Spending

Candidates and political parties spent some $425 million on political activity at all levels in 1972; this figure is an upward revision from an earlier CRF estimate of $400 million used throughout 1972. This total has been arrived at from a variety of sources: the information filed under the FECA of 1971 and under the Federal Corrupt Practices Act (FCPA) prior to April 7;

This chapter was co-authored by Caroline D. Jones.

voluntary disclosures by some of the 1972 presidential contenders; the disclosures made in law suits, investigations, and prosecutions involving the Committee to Re-Elect the President (CRP) and certain Democratic presidential
campaigns; supplementary state presidential primary information not filed
under FECA; information concerning nonfederal candidates and committees
filed in 12 states with disclosure laws; and interviews. Projections round out
the inevitable gaps.

The 1972 total contrasts with reported expenditures in 1968 of $300
million—a 42 percent increase due to additional information and an actual rise
in spending, beyond the factor of inflation. The 1968 total itself was something of a quantum jump over previous totals. In 1952 the first presidential
election for which total political costs were calculated, it was estimated that
$140 million was spent on elective and party politics in all levels of government,
about one-third the total 20 years later. Table 4-1 shows the comparative
spending figures for 1952-72.

Table 4-1
Total Political Spending in Presidential Election Years, 1952-72

1952	$140,000,000
1956	155,000,000
1960	175,000,000
1964	200,000,000
1968	300,000,000
1972	425,000,000

Source: For 1952-68, Herbert E. Alexander, *Financing the 1968 Election*
(Lexington, Mass.: Lexington Books, D.C. Heath and Company, 1971), pp. 1-4,
derived in part from Alexander Heard, *The Costs of Democracy* (Chapel Hill,
N.C.: The University of North Carolina Press, 1960), pp. 7-8.

The 1972 spending fell into four major areas:

1. $138 million to elect a President, including prenomination campaigns and
   minor party candidates
2. $98 million to nominate candidates and elect a Congress, including labor,
   business, professional, party, and miscellaneous committee contributions
   to candidates for Congress, as well as such committees' fixed expenditures
   not disbursed to candidates but spent to maintain and operate such
   committees
3. $95 million to nominate candidates and elect governors, other statewide
   officials, and state legislators, and to campaign for and against state ballot
   issues and constitutional amendments
4. $95 million to nominate candidates and elect the hundreds of thousands
   of county and local public officials

The two major parties were fairly evenly divided in their spending of the
$137 million, which includes the prenomination as well as the general election
expenditures of presidential candidates—$69.2 million was disbursed by the
Republicans, $67.3 million by the Democrats. A major difference, of course,
was that Republican spending was concentrated almost exclusively on the
reelection of the President (less than two percent of their expenditures are
accountable to the primary campaigns of either McCloskey or Ashbrook),
while nearly half (49 percent) of the Democratic spending occurred before
George McGovern finally got the nomination in the summer of 1972. In the
postnomination period, the ratio shifts drastically in favor of the Republicans
(67-33), as shown in Table 4-2. The Republicans enjoyed a greater edge in
this respect than in any of the past general election campaigns of presidential
candidates where ratios have been calculated, in spite of McGovern's high
spending compared with other recent Democratic nominees: Humphrey,
Johnson, Kennedy, and Stevenson. In 1968 the ratio of major party expenditures (excluding the spending in the independent Wallace campaign) was
65-35 in favor of the Republicans.

Table 4-2
Ratios of National-level Direct Spending in Presidential Campaigns,
General Elections, 1956-72

	1956[a]	1960	1964	1968	1972
Republicans	59	49	63	55 (65)	67
Democrats	41	51	37	29 (35)	33
Wallace	--	--	--	16	--

[a]Derived from Heard, *Costs,* p. 20 and *1956 General Election Campaigns,* Report to the
Senate Committee on Rules and Administration, Subcommittee on Privileges and
Elections, 85th Cong., 1st sess. (1957), exhibit 4, p. 41. Deficits in 1956 are listed in
this report as bills unpaid as of November 30, 1956. Heard's figures for Republicans
and Democrats are for the full calendar year 1956, but labor figures are for January 1 -
November 30, 1956. Heard's ratio has been revised to include deficits.

Data on the expenditures of national-level committees primarily concerned with the presidential general election are available from 1912.[a] The
figures in Table 4-3 include spending by presidential candidate and party committees. Although there were some unusual years, the rise in expenditures was

[a]For a historical account of presidential campaign financing, see Herbert E. Alexander,
"Financing Presidential Campaigns," in Arthur M. Schlesinger, Jr., ed., *History of American
Presidential Elections,* 1789-1968 (N.Y.: Chelsea House Publishing in Association with
McGraw-Hill Book Co., 1971), vol. IV, pp. 3869-97.

Table 4-3

Direct Campaign Expenditures by National-level Presidential and Party Committees, General Elections, 1912-72

(In Millions)

1912	$ 2.9[a]	1932	$ 5.1	1952	$ 11.6
1916	4.7	1936	14.1	1956	12.9
1920	6.9	1940	6.2	1960	19.9
1924	5.4[a]	1944	5.0	1964	24.8
1928	11.6	1948	6.2[a]	1968	44.2[a]
				1972	103.7

Source: Citizens' Research Foundation.

Note: Data for 1912-44 include transfers to states. Total for 1948 includes only the direct expenditures of the national party committees. For 1952-68, data do not include transfers to states, but do include the national senatorial and congressional committees of both parties. For 1972, for comparative purposes, data do not include state and local level information, except for the presidential candidates. The Nixon component includes all spending for his reelection.

[a]Totals include significant minor party spending.

gradual from 1912 to 1952. Since 1956 the rise had been even more rapid than the big increases in overall political costs, with 1972 occupying a unique position.

Calculations of the cost per vote for the presidency since 1912 show a variable pattern for more than 40 years, and then a steady rise since the mid-1950s, culminating in an enormous leap for 1968. From 1912 to 1956, the cost per vote ranged from a little more than ten cents (in the wartime election of 1944) to around 31 cents (in the intense 1928 and 1936 elections); but after each rise, there was an almost comparable drop so that in 1912 the cost per vote was just over 19 cents and in 1956 it was just under 21 cents. By 1960 the cost per vote had risen to almost 29 cents and in 1964 it set a record at more than 35 cents. But for 1968 the record was shattered as the cost per vote jumped to 60 cents.

The 60-cent figure for 1968 includes Wallace spending beginning in February, which would normally be the prenomination period. But the American Independent Party had no convention, so no distinction can be made between primary and general election costs. If the Wallace component is excluded from the calculation, the 1968 cost per vote was still close to 51 cents.

Cost per vote in 1972 is difficult to calculate because the Nixon reelection campaign was geared from the start to the general election. The McCloskey and Ashbrook candidacies posed only minor nuisances in Nixon's quest for nomination. If one considers the full Nixon spending in 1971 and 1972, then adds in the McGovern general election campaign and national party spending oriented toward the presidential elections, following the criteria used in the historical data presented above, $103.7 million was spent for general election purposes in 1972. With 76,025,000 voters in the presidential elections, some $1.36 per vote is indicated. If the Nixon expenditures before his nomination are excluded, the 1972 cost per vote would still be more than $1.00.

There are several reasons for the extraordinary cost of the 1972 Presidential campaigns. The scientific and technological advances, which contributed to increased campaign costs in the 1960s, particularly in the areas of travel, polling, computers, and broadcasting, continued on into 1972. One intangible component of the rising costs is the role of the President. For many reasons, including the increased role of the United States in the world during the last decades, the power potential which the President holds, a growing view of the President as the initiator as well as executor of the nation's policies, and the direct impact of federal policy on more people, the presidency is more important today then previously, and therefore the stakes for achieving it are greater. The major unique causes of the high presidential costs in 1972 were the large number of prenomination contests in the Democratic Party, and, of course, the notable ability of the Nixon campaign to raise and spend money.

In most presidential election years, the candidate of one party is fairly certain of winning nomination and there is little major opposition. In 1964 this was true for the Democrats, who had an incumbent President; in 1960 the Republicans had the Vice-President, who was heir apparent; and in 1956 the Republicans had an enormously popular President. In 1968 there was real uncertainty and major contests in both parties for the presidential nomination. The 1972 presidential campaigns reached the record-breaking total of $138 million, in spite of the fact that one of the candidates was an incumbent President. The costs of future presidential campaigns cannot be expected to reach such high levels if the legal limitations and the government funding laws remain in force.

What follows is a new concept in presentation of political costs, differing in marked respects from 1968 and previous years in the Alexander and Heard studies, when the Federal Corrupt Practices Act (FCPA) permitted use of the classification of national-level political committees, that is, those operating in two or more states and reporting under the law. The FECA of 1971 changed the definition of a political committee to a monetary test: committees now were required to disclose if they raised or spent in excess of $1,000 on behalf of candidates for federal office, regardless of whether they were national, state, or local in scope, regardless of whether they were located in Washington, D.C. or Peoria, or operated in only one state.

With much overlap in the filings with the three supervisory officers, it became imperative to isolate the discrete presidential, senatorial, House, and other categories, and to eliminate the duplications that result when a single party, labor, business, professional, dairy, or miscellaneous political committee supported candidates for President, Senate, and House, and thus filed disclosure statements with all three supervisory officers. When the supervisory officers then compiled, as they were required by law to do, summaries of amounts raised and spent per candidate, by party, and by primary or general election, the utility of each compilation was diminished by the extent of the overlap.[1]   Scholars have commented on the need for assimilating the new information derived from the 1971 Act, reconciling it, and developing better conceptual frameworks.[b] Thus, we present for 1972 an aggregative, component by component building of data into a true picture of political costs, based on all relevant information contained in the three official summaries, CRF[2] and Common Cause[c] compilations.

Most dollar figures in this analysis are not gross but net amounts, or what we call direct expenditures. For example, when a dairy political committee supported financially candidates for President and Senate and House—usually candidates in both political parties—the amounts given (or more accurately, transferred), say to Nixon, were spent on goods and services by the CRP, and hence became part of presidential spending. To avoid double counting of transfers from one reporting committee to another reporting committee, wherein the money is raised by the dairy committee and reported as a receipt, then listed by it as an expenditure, then listed as a receipt by CRP and listed as an expenditure by CRP, we have adjusted for transfers of funds to the extent possible. Total receipts and gross expenditures are sometimes given in the following for clarity or emphasis, but most figures are net amounts, termed conveniently as direct expenditures (for staff, fixed costs, etc.), after transfers to candidates actually spending the money have been subtracted.

This mode of analysis is feasible because:

1. Unlike the situation under the FCPA, now the assumption can be made that all candidates and political committees active on their behalf are reporting. From the point of view of expenditures, it is important to know where money transferred around from one committee to another finally lands and gets spent for the candidate. Of the millions of dollars contributed before the FECA of 1971 by labor, business, party, or other committees to candidates for Congress, for example, only a portion was actually reported under federal law as having been spent by congressional candidates, because intrastate committees were not required to file. Now it is possible to calculate with some greater degree of accuracy how much it costs to elect a Congress or a President.

---

[b]For a discussion of the need for new modes of analysis in view of new forms of data available under the FECA of 1971, see Jeffrey M. Berry, "Electoral Economics: Getting & Spending," *Polity*, vol. VII, no. 1 (Fall 1974) 121-29.

[c]*1972 Congressional Campaign Finances*, Common Cause, Campaign Finance Monitoring Project (Washington, D.C.: 1974), 10 regional volumes; *1972 Federal Campaign Finances, Interest Groups & Political Parties,* Common Cause, Campaign Finance Monitoring Project (Washington, D.C.: 1974), 3 volumes. Although there were some discrepancies in component parts and totals among the Common Cause, Secretary of the Senate, and Clerk of the House reports, the totals were within close ranges, and our analysis averaged and rounded off dollar amounts in cases in which no superior compilation was available. In instances of major disagreement—which occurred especially as between GAO and the other two supervisory offices—original filings were used.

2. Gross receipts and expenditures for any given committee are available with reasonable levels of accuracy in the annual compilations of the three supervisory officers, and in the various Common Cause and CRF compilations. The advent of the FECA brought too many reporting committees to deal with individually in the 1972 version of the Alexander studies. Where only net amounts are given in this analysis, the researcher can get grosses for any given committee from other publications, thus obviating the need to present in this study lists comparable to those in previous works.[d]

Presidential Campaign Expenditures

Information about spending in the 1972 presidential contests is more comprehensive than in the past for several reasons. Some of the candidates in the prenomination period, spurred on by the new law and seeing a strategic campaign advantage, voluntarily disclosed some of their pre-April 7 political contributions and expenditures. Senator George McGovern and Representative Paul N. McCloskey, Jr. made full disclosures of their central campaign contributions; McGovern's campaign, however, had broad grass-roots support with many state and local committees not controlled by the national campaign, effectively excluding some data from the disclosure. In varying scope and for varying times, partial disclosures were also made by Hubert Humphrey, John Lindsay, Edmund Muskie, and George Wallace.

The other candidates, Nixon among them, flatly refused to make voluntary disclosure, although some data have been collected by CRF in presidential primary states requiring disclosure, or through interviews and other sources. Common Cause sued in the U.S. District Court to force disclosure of the pre-April 7 receipts and expenditures of the Nixon campaign—a suit finally declared moot in the fall of 1973, when the Finance Committee to Re-Elect the President (FCRP) put its receipts and spending on the public record. The Senate Watergate Committee, the Office of the Special Prosecutor, investigative reporters, and others unearthed still more data.

More is known also about spending on the presidential campaigns by numerous state and local committees; if they raised or spent in excess of $1,000, and spent only a portion of that on federal campaigns, they were required under the law to report their financial activity to the appropriate federal supervisory agencies; some such committees filed and some did not, but of those that did, some $19.5 million can be accounted for.

---

[d]For example, tables such as 4-13, 4-14, 4-15, 4-16, 4-17, 4-19, in Herbert E. Alexander, *Financing the 1968 Election*, (Lexington, Mass.: Lexington Books, D.C. Heath and Company, 1971),pp. 117-29.

The Democrats and Republicans together spent $136.5 million on all
aspects of their presidential campaigns.

Republicans

Spun out from the central Finance Committee to Re-Elect the President
and much more tightly controlled than the state and local McGovern committees, were state FCRPs in all 50 states, plus Radio, TV, and Media CRPs.
There was also a Democrats for Nixon committee at the national level, plus
14 state or regional affiliated committees. Beyond this there were in 1972
a miscellany of state and local Nixon committees particularly in southern
California, which were not part of the CRP network, also committees supporting Vice-President Agnew, and a small number of ethnic or heritage committees.

The Nixon-Agnew committees raised $62.7 million, as follows:

FCRP and satellites	$60.2 million
Democrats for Nixon and 14 affiliates	$ 2.4 million

In addition, the Republican Party at the national level, including Senate and
House campaign committees, raised $9.3 million, for a grand Republican national
total of $72 million raised. These amounts, unsurpassed in political annals, give
some notion of the magnitude and clout of the Republican apparatus in 1972,
the financial equivalent of a middle-sized corporation.

Nixon and Republican spending ran apace, as shown in Table 4-4.

Although officials of the Republican National Committee (RNC) often said
that they felt excluded from the Nixon reelection effort by virtue of the establishment of the Committee to Re-Elect the President, they reported direct
spending (without duplication caused by transfers of funds) by the RNC and its
affiliates of $6 million on activities mostly related to the presidential race, com-
pared with $4.7 million by the Democratic National Committee and affiliates —
and not including spending by the Capitol Hill campaign committees.

One component of spending in the Republican presidential race was the
Campaign Liquidation Trust, an organization set up early in 1974 with a transfer
of surplus funds from the FCRP when it ceased operating, amounting to $3.6
million. In December 1972 the FCRP surplus had been $5 million. The trust
was to cover such obligations as the legal debts that were being incurred from
Watergate-related expenses, as well as a sum ($775,000) set aside in anticipation
of a settlement of the civil suit for damages brought by the Democratic National
Committee — a payment made in the summer of 1974.

The only Republican outlays at the presidential level that were not related

Table 4-4

Republican Spending in 1972 Presidential Campaigns

FCRP and satellite committees (media plus 50 states)		$56,100,000	
Democrats for Nixon (national plus 14 state and regional)		2,400,000	
Mis. laneous state, local, and ethnic Nixon and Agnew committees, and miscellaneous cash disbursements		1,300,000	
Campaign Liquidation Trust:[a]			
Listed debts (principally legal)	$560,000		
Future legal bills	500,000		
DNC settlement	775,000		
Other expenditures	284,780		
Total CLT		2,100,000[b]	
Total Nixon-Agnew			$62,000,000
Other Republican candidates:			
Ashbrook		740,000	
McCloskey		550,000	
Total other candidates			1,290,000
Total Republican presidential			$63,290,000
Republican National Committee and affiliates presidential spending			6,000,000
Republican total: Presidential and national committee			$69,290,000

[a]Successor committee to FCRP.

[b]More than $3.5 million was turned over to the CLT by FCRP; some balance may remain when all litigation is concluded.

to former President Nixon were the expenditures of his rival from the left, Paul McCloskey, who spent about $550,000 on his unsuccessful presidential campaign, and his rival from the right, John Ashbrook of Ohio, who spent about $740,000 in an equally unsuccessful bid.

Democrats

To win the Democratic presidential nomination, Senator George McGovern spent $12 million. (See Table 4-5.) His rivals for that nomination, some 17 other candidates in the fray at some time during 1971 or 1972, had primary

Table 4-5
Democratic Spending in 1972 Presidential Campaigns

McGovern Pre-April 7 spending (1971, early 1972 primaries) voluntarily disclosed	$ 2,500,000	
Primary campaign reported under FECA	9,300,000	
Total prenomination[a]		$12,000,000
McGovern postnomination central and satellite committees[a]	18,600,000	
State and local McGovern, Eagleton, and Shriver committees	11,200,000	
Total general election		$30,000,000
Other Democratic candidates: Presidential	20,725,000	
Vice-Presidential	328,000	
Total other candidates		$21,053,000
Total Democratic presidential		$62,853,000
Democratic National Committee and affiliates presidential spending		4,482,000
Democratic total: Presidential and national committee		$67,335,000

[a]Adjusted for loan repayments and cost-of-stock refunds.

spending, convention expenditures, and other prenomination costs totalling $20.7 million more. In addition, four avowed vice-presidential candidates spent another $328,000. This total of $33 million in 1971-72 compares with the $25 million expended in Democratic presidential prenomination costs in 1967-68.

Once nominated, some $30 million was spent on McGovern's behalf in the general election period: by the central McGovern committee (McGovern, Inc.) and its satellite committees, by state and local affiliates and autonomous committees, and by committees organized to support the vice-presidential campaigns of Senator Thomas Eagleton and Sargent Shriver.

About $4.5 million was spent by the Democratic National Committee and its satellite committees; all but about $200,000 of that was spent after April 7. (See Table 4-6.) This money includes costs of the telethon staged by the Democrats on the eve of the nominating convention, and a variety of other political activities. These figures do not include national nominating convention costs. It has been customary, however, to add national party costs,

Table 4-6
Spending by Democratic National-level Committees, 1972

Democratic National Committee	$2,293,463
DNC telethon	1,761,110[a]
DNC '72	22,228
DNC Service Corporation	210,000
Pre-April 7	195,000
Total	$4,481,791

[a]Although the stated objective was fund raising to pay off preexisting debts, the telethon advertised the party to a vast national office and was therefore relevant to the 1972 campaign.

as shown in Table 4-6, to the presidential candidates' overall costs because traditionally most of the spending is concentrated after the national convention.

The Democratic telethon costs were high in 1972, and the net proceeds were used to pay off a portion of the debts left over from the 1968 campaigns. Added to that were 1972 debts of about $172,000, making 1972 national party and presidential-related expenditures about $4.7 million.

Minor Parties

Ten minor parties had candidates running for President in 1972 and eight reported spending in excess of $1.2 million. (See Table 4-7.) The most extensive effort was that of the American Independent Party (entered in some states as the American Party), spending some $710,000 on the election effort of the Schmitz-Anderson slate.

Table 4-7
Presidential and Other Spending in 1972 by Minor Parties

American Independent Party (Schmitz)	$ 710,000
Communist Party (Hall)	173,600
Socialist Workers Party (Jenness)	118,000
Socialist Labor Party (Fisher)	114,000
Christian National Crusade Party	93,000
People's Party (Spock)	40,539
Prohibition Party (Munn)	37,000
Libertarian Party (Hospers)	17,000
Conservative Party	6,000
Flying Tigers Party (Meads)	977
Independent Candidates:	
Harry Britton	358
Warren Owens	232
Total	$1,210,706

Presidential Spending: 1968 and 1972

Although caution must be taken in approaching comparisons made between different components of the spending in 1968 and 1972, some conclusions do seem warranted.

The 1972-related presidential bill, for pre- and postnomination, and including minor parties, was $137.9 million, recapitulated as follows:

Republican presidential	$ 63,290,000
National-level committees	6,000,000
Democratic presidential	62,853,000
National-level committees	4,500,000
Minor party, candidates & committees	1,211,000
Total	$137,854,000

Four years previously, about $100 million was spent in electing a President. The Republican bill in 1968, prenomination and general election, amounted to $45 million; $20 million of that was spent in the primaries. In 1972 the amount spent on the primaries was negligible, with only two rivals challenging the incumbent President, but the total presidential bill was $69 million.

The Democratic costs in 1968, prenomination and general election, were $37 million; $25 million of that was spent in the primaries. In the general election, $12 million was spent. In 1972, $33 million was spent in the prenomination period and $30 million in the general election period.

Thus, in both years the Republicans outspent the Democrats in the general election by about two to one. But in 1972 the amounts they were splitting by that ratio were about twice as large as they had been four years earlier.

Senate Contests

The Republicans and Democrats, plus some minor party and independent candidates, spent a total of $35.5 million on the 33 senatorial races in 1972, which saw the Democrats gain a net of two seats. (See Table 4-8.)

Almost all of the spending was by the campaign committees of the individual contenders; only $500,000 was spent directly by the major parties' senatorial campaign committees, the rest of their funds being passed on to the candidates for them to spend. Overall, the Republicans outspent the Democrats by nearly $6 million.

Some $8.1 million was spent in the primary campaigns for Senate nominations, $26.4 million in the general elections.

Table 4-8
1972 Senate Expenditures

Personal-Candidate Committees

	Primary	General Election	Total
Democratic	$3,700,000	$10,600,000	$14,300,000
Republican	4,400,000	15,400,000	19,800,000
Other	---	400,000	400,000
Total	$8,100,000	$26,400,000	$34,500,000
Pre-April 7 spending			1,000,000

Party Senatorial Committees[a]

Democratic Senatorial Campaign Committee	132,000
National Republican Senatorial Committee	340,000
Pre-April 7 spending	30,000
Total Party Senatorial Committees	500,000
Total	$36,000,000

[a]Directly spent, including allowances for radio and television facilities allowances, but not including transfers of funds made to candidates' campaigns.

House Contests

A total of $54.7 million was spent in 1972 on campaigns for the House of Representatives. Of this, $11.2 million was spent during the primary stages of the campaigns. (See Table 4-9.)

Democrats outspent the Republicans by nearly $5 million but much of that was accounted for in primary expenditures. In the general elections, expenditures in the individual campaigns were much closer—$20.2 million for the Democrats to $18.8 million for the Republicans. Added to that are the direct expenditures of the congressional campaign committees, not including amounts they contributed to candidates. The Republicans had a slight edge in spending in the general election, but, as noted, the Democrats far outspent Republicans in the prenomination campaigns.

Beyond the financial support that a congressional candidate might have gotten from either his own campaign structure or that tied to the national party committees, there were also a number of committees formed to generate support for certain types of candidates or for certain general goals. Categorized in these "nonparty" committees were such groups as the Committee for Twelve, which organized support for 12 liberal Democratic House candidates. In all, these committees, which filed with the appropriate federal officers, spent directly nearly $600,000 on the 1972 congressional elections. The differences between

Table 4-9
1972 House Expenditures

Personal-Candidate Committees

	Primary	*General Election*	*Total*
Democratic	$ 7,700,000	$20,200,000	$27,900,000
Republican	2,500,000	18,800,000	21,300,000
Other	---	1,000,000	1,000,000
Not allocated	1,000,000	---	1,000,000
Total	$11,200,000	$40,000,000	$51,200,000
Pre-April 7 spending			1,200,000

Party House Committees[a]

Democratic Congressional Campaign Committee	38,000
Democratic National Congressional Committee	194,000
	232,000
National Republican Congressional Committee	1,955,000
Republican Candidates Conference	42,000
	1,997,000
Pre-April 7 spending	70,000
Total Party House Committees	2,300,000
Total	$54,700,000

[a]Directly spent, including allowances for radio and television facilities but not including transfers of funds made to candidates' campaigns. Also, for Senate-House joint committees, see "Total Congressional Spending," below.

their gross and net expenditures were amounts contributed to and spent by candidates.

Such committees in support of Democratic congressional candidates spent directly about $358,000 in 1972, while their Republican counterparts spent directly a sum calculated at $227,000. (See Table 4-10.)

Total Congressional Spending

When all known funds spent on congressional races in 1972 are assembled, the Democrats are estimated to have spent $43 million, the Republicans $43.5 million. Another $1.4 million was spent on the campaigns of minor party candidates or independents. A final $2 million remains as pre-April 7 and "unallocated," listed in the official records but not positively identified.

Table 4-10

Spending by Nonparty but Partisan-identified Committees on Congressional Races

Democratic	Gross	Direct
Candidates '72 (House)	$ 7,000	$ 7,000
Committee for Twelve (House)	190,000	25,000
Committee to Elect Democrats (House)	12,000	12,000
DSG Campaign Fund (House)	252,000	62,000
National Committee for the Reelection of a Democratic Majority (joint)	792,000	155,000
Nineteen Seventy-Two Campaign Fund (Senate)	211,000	97,000
Democratic total	$1,464,000	$358,000
Republican	**Gross**	**Direct**
Congressional Victory Committee (joint)	$ 63,000	$ 19,000
Congressmen for '72 (Senate)	5,000	— —
Legislators for '72 (Senate)	6,000	— —
Midwest Republican Group (joint)	9,000	3,000
Republican 12 Committee for Defense (House)	27,000	6,000
Senators for '72 (Senate)	61,000	60,000
National Federation of Republican Women	70,000	70,000
Negroes for a Republican Victory	58,000	58,000
Women's National Republican Campaign Committee	11,000	11,000
Republican total	$ 310,000	$227,000

Table 4-11 recapitulates congressional- and Senate-related costs in 1972, covering both pre- and postnomination, and pre- and post-April 7 spending.

Special Interest and Ideological Groups

The continuing political interest of both organized labor and the business world was apparent in 1972. Spending by labor alone, in fact, was roughly equivalent in amount to spending by business, professional, health, and dairy committees combined. (See Table 4-12.)

Although labor was badly split over the candidacy of George McGovern, greatly eroding the usually solid Democratic support by union political action committees, labor's reported gross disbursements continued to rise—up from $7.1 million in 1968 to $8.5 million in 1972. However, the increase was almost

Table 4-11

House- and Senate-related Costs in 1972: A Summary

Democratic				
Senate	$14,300,000			
	132,000			
		$14,432,000		
House	27,900,000			
	232,000			
		28,132,000		
Joint[a]		72,000		
Party-related		358,000		
Total, Democratic congressional			in excess of	$43,000,000
Republican				
Senate	$19,800,000			
	340,000			
		$20,140,000		
House	21,300,000			
	1,997,000			
		23,297,000		
Joint[b]		0		
Party-related		227,000		
Total, Republican congressional			in excess of	$43,500,000
Other				1,400,000
Not allocated and pre-April 7			in excess of	2,200,000
Total congressional-related spending				$90,200,000

[a]Democratic Congressional Dinner Committee.

[b]The Republican Congressional Boosters Club, the Financial Advisory Committee, and the Congressional Gala had no direct expenditures.

entirely due to more comprehensive reporting requirements: (1) the previously unreported AFL-CIO spending from dues money for COPE staff and fixed operational costs; and (2) the first time filings of scores of state and local union political committees.

Business and professional groups, including those with special interests in the health field and in the dairy industry, were equally active—their reported gross disbursements in 1972 totalled just over $8 million, a figure not including the illegal corporate contributions.

The bulk of the above expenditure totals by both labor and the business-professional groups was reported under the provisions of the FECA of 1971;

Table 4-12
Spending in 1972

Labor Spending	Adjusted Gross	Direct Expenditures	Transfers
Reported under Corrupt Practices Act	$ 320,000	$ 170,000	$ 150,000
Reported under FECA	7,350,000	1,280,000	6,070,000
COPE-related spending by AFL-CIO[a]	810,000	810,000	---
Total	$8,480,000	$2,260,000	$6,220,000

Other Special Interest Spending	Adjusted Gross	Direct Expenditures	Transfers
Reported under CPA	$ 260,000	$ 170,000	$ 90,000
Reported under FECA			
Business/Professional	3,450,000	350,000[b]	3,100,000
Dairy	1,600,000	100,000	1,500,000
Education[c]	1,020,000	120,000	900,000
Health-related	1,310,000	110,000	1,200,000
Rural-related[d]	400,000	50,000	350,000
Total	$8,040,000	$ 900,000	$7,140,000

[a]Disclosed in 1972 for the first time, in compliance with GAO directive.

[b]Corporate committees had minimal direct spending; this is largely attributable to associations with ongoing operations.

[c]All education committees are included in this category, regardless of affiliation.

[d]Includes rural electric co-ops, agriculture committees, other than dairy, etc.

some reports, amounting to far smaller expenditures, were filed in the first months of 1972 under the old Corrupt Practices Act. The totals reflect adjusted amounts combining pre- and post-April 7 to cover the entire calendar year.

In order to put the following tables in perspective and relate them to other published material, it is necessary to make certain specifications:

1. Amended reports have been incorporated in the data presented, for sometimes substantive changes, additions, and corrections were made to the 1972 data. For example, N.Y. State United Teachers' VOTE/COPE ($567,000) in 1974 back-reported for 1972.

2. Adjusted gross figures below involve two types of adjustment. The first represent transfers between reporting affiliates; for example, dairy's C-TAPE $1,773,000 in expenditures were all transfers to TAPE, hence excluded from the adjusted gross. Second are "wash items"; for example, AMPAC (medical) reported $845,000 receipts, $881,000 expenditures, but $550,000/ $340,000, respectively, represented notes redeemed or purchased. The House gross spending total for other-than-single-candidate committees is $63,806,000;

the similar Senate total is $51,770,000. These unadjusted figures are meaning-less because they included such transfers of funds; GAO shows direct expendi-tures of special interest committees exceeding transfers by an improbable 50 percent, in contrast with the more realistic ratios below.

3. Direct expenditures include, but are not limited to, salaries, rent, opera-tions, fund raising, and so on. Some candidate-related items are inextricably included; for example, salaries pay special interest committee workers who give candidates advice.

4. The transfer column refers, in large measure, to funds transferred to federal candidates and campaign committees, but there were also significant transfers to state candidates and to nonreporting committees. For example, ABC (education) transferred $233,000 to the nonreporting California Teachers Association; labor groups in general transferred extensively (several hundred thousand dollars) to nonreporting affiliates. In the interest of consistency, all such items are included as transfers; because they are not duplicate reported they are not subtracted from the gross.

Based on computations within these parameters, the special interest break-down is shown in Table 4-12.

In addition to these two major groupings, a number of other special interests reported their spending to one or more of the supervisory offices in 1972—largely groups of an ideological nature, such as the Americans for Democratic Action on the left or its opposite on the right, Americans for Constitutional Action, or with an interest in a particular cause, such as the Campaign Fund for the Environment. (See Table 4-13.)

The total raised and spent by all these special interests—$19 million—is impressive. Of this amount, almost $14.5 million was given to candidates, party, or campaign committees to spend as they saw fit. The direct spending of all special interest groups comes to just under $5 million, as follows:

Labor	$2,260,000
Bus/Prof/Dairy & Agriculture	900,000
Ideological	1,700,000
Total	$4,860,000

State and Local Party Committees

A number of the official state party committees of both the major parties reported 1972 political expenditures to the General Accounting Office (GAO)

Table 4-13
Ideological Spending in 1972

	Adjusted Gross	Direct Expenditures	Transfers
American Conservative Union	$ 209,000[a]	$ 209,000	$ —
Americans for Constitutional Action	126,000	119,000	7,000
Americans for Democratic Action	75,000	75,000	—
Campaign Fund for the Environment	14,000	9,000	5,000
Committee for Responsible Youth Politics	20,000	8,000	12,000
Concerned Seniors for Better Government	39,000	—	39,000
Congressional Action Fund	102,000	65,000	37,000
Congressional Alliance '72	21,000	21,000	—
Conservative Victory Fund	379,000[a]	259,000	120,000
Council for a Livable World	166,000	135,000	31,000
League of Conservation Voters and LCV-CF	92,000[a]	30,000	62,000
National Committee for An Effective Congress	670,000[a]	266,000	404,000
One Percent Fund	9,000[a]	9,000	—
Set the Date	6,000	6,000	—
United Congressional Appeal	52,000	20,000	32,000
Universities National Anti-War Fund	8,000	3,000	5,000
Vote for Peace	110,000	37,000	73,000
Women for Peace	71,000	71,000	—
Young America's Campaign Committee	71,000[a]	71,000	—
Totals	$2,240,000	$1,413,000	$827,000
Reported under FECA	$2,240,000	$1,413,000	$827,000
Reported under CPA	408,000	287,000	121,000
Totals	$2,648,000	$1,700,000	$948,000

[a]The gross figures used here are taken from the House compilation, the transfers from Common Cause. The Senate publication gives somewhat different figures, where noted, but the final totals are almost identical.

or to the other supervisory offices, as did certain county committees — some 26 Democratic state committees and 36 Republican committees.[e]

[e]These are listed in Office of Federal Elections, U.S. General Accounting Office, *Report of 1972 Presidential Campaign Receipts and Expenditures* (Washington, D.C.: U.S. Government Printing Office, 1974) pp. 6-8, 61-66, with additional listings in *The Annual Statistical Report of Contributions and Expenditures Made During the 1972 Election Campaigns for the U.S. House of Representatives*, Part II, by W. Pat Jennings, as Clerk of the House of Representatives and Supervisory Officer (Washington, D.C.: U.S. Government Printing Office, June 1974) pp. 161-73, and *The Annual Statistical Report of Receipts and Expenditures Made in Connection with Elections for the U.S. Senate in 1972*, prepared under the direction of Francis R. Valeo, Secretary of the Senate, Supervisory Officer for Senate Elections (Washington, D.C.: U.S. Government Printing Office, October 1974) pp. 35-77.

Together these committees accounted for nearly $20 million in 1972 politi-cal expenditures, with Republican expenditures almost three times as large as those of their Democratic counterparts. (See Table 4-14.) These figures reflect compliance by ten more Republican than Democratic committees, so a compari-son of dollar amounts would be unfair. In any case, the amounts given are gross expenditure totals. Since the amounts spent by these Republican or Democratic committees on behalf of candidates for federal office are normally five to ten percent of the gross, and it is impossible to separate presidential from senatorial from congressional, the exact extent of their involvement in federal campaigns is unknown. Some 90 to 95 percent of these grosses went for state or local campaigns, or for party-ticket (from White House to courthouse) activities.

Table 4-14
Spending by State and Local Party Committees in 1972

Democratic	
State central committees	$ 3,500,000
County and ad hoc committees	1,700,000
Total	$ 5,200,000
Republican	
State central committees	$ 8,000,000
County and ad hoc committees	6,300,000
Total	$14,300,000

Individual Expenditures

A total of $98,060 in independent expenditures by 21 individuals was re-ported under Section 305 of the FECA of 1971 with respect to the 1972 presi-dential elections.

If all the various components, including a reasonable allocation of state and local party committee spending, are added together, the net spending accounted for in the 1972 federal campaigns was on the order of $250 million. This figure reflects all data filed under the Federal Corrupt Practices Act and the Federal Election Campaign Act, as well as that unreported in presidential campaigns in 1971 and early 1972 but disclosed in law suits or in interviews for this study. When reports were filed with two or more of the supervisory offices, they were counted only once in this calculation. Every effort was made to adjust for such items as transfers of funds, loan repayments, refunds, and purchase and redemp-tion of certificates of deposit, to avoid duplicate counting. Presidential cam-paigns are counted from 1971 through early 1975 when filings continued to be made, reporting disposition of debts or surpluses.

5 The Prenomination Campaigns

The Prenomination Campaigns

The 1972 pre-nomination campaigns were uniquely related to the issue of political finance. First, the Federal Election Campaign Act of 1971 (FECA) took effect in the middle of the primary season, causing different effects on different candidates. Those who had dropped out before April 7 were not technically covered by the new law; however, several asked the General Accounting Office (GAO) whether they were required to file under the new law. Although no longer campaigning, these candidates still had committees engaged in raising money to erase debts. The GAO's interpretation was that while the law did not specifically require filing for activities prior to April 7, in view of the fact that these committees would be competing for funds with active candidates at a time when the latter were required to file, it was considered in the spirit of the law for the inactive candidates to file accounts of the retirement of their debts. Some did and some did not.

Second, there was a controversial time gap. Between March 1, 1972, when filings for the last reporting period were due in accordance with the Federal Corrupt Practices Act (FCPA) of 1925, and April 7, when the new law took effect, candidates could raise and spend in secret at least part of their campaign funds. Fund raisers told individuals who contributed between March 1 and April 7 that they would not have to be identified nor reveal the amount they contributed. There were also instances of prepayment; not only President Nixon, but other candidates took advantage of the pre-April 7 "grace period" to collect funds from sources that they did not want to reveal and to spend them secretly.

Third, in part because of the April 7 demarcation, the topic of campaign financing itself became a major campaign issue. Senator McGovern and Congressman McCloskey raised the issue by voluntarily disclosing the names of all contributors to their campaigns and challenging rivals to do the same. After a good deal of press and public attention, many major candidates did so, but not before the issue had caused some damage to some candidates, notably Senator Muskie. Four candidates—Nixon, Ashbrook, Jackson, and Mills— steadfastly refused to disclose voluntarily their sources of funds, saying they would do only what the law required. Both Jackson and Mills had money,

---

This chapter was co-authored by Eugenia Grohman.

though demonstrating little popular support, and speculation was rampant about which wealthy individuals or special interests were supporting their candidacies. For Nixon, on whose behalf millions were raised and spent before April 7, the issue of the source and use of those funds continued to stay alive, ultimately becoming an important Watergate topic.

Strict comparability among the data available on the many Democratic prenomination campaigns is lacking. George McGovern, Hubert Humphrey, Edmund Muskie, John Lindsay, and George Wallace, for example, voluntarily disclosed information on contributors, dating in Wallace's case all the way back to 1969, and their campaigns were later covered by the FECA. Birch Bayh and Fred Harris, to take other examples, were in and out of the 1972 race before the FECA passed and even before voluntary disclosure became an issue; for their campaigns and others, interviews provided comprehensive data. For other candidates who did not voluntarily disclose, but who were still active when the FECA took effect, a mixture of hard and soft data is available. In spite of the differences in sources of data and amount of detail available for different campaigns, the total amounts raised and spent by all the prenomination candidates have been carefully determined.

Total spending by the 18 Democratic presidential candidates combined, from announcement or preannouncement to and including costs at the Democratic Convention, was a little more than $32.7 million. Senator McGovern's $12 million spent led the list. His nearest rival in money was Edmund Muskie, who spent about $7 million. Including these two, six candidates spent $1 million or more and 12 others spent a total of more than $4 million as shown in Table 5-1.

Table 5-1
Prenomination Spending by Democrats, 1971-72

George McGovern	$12,000,000
Edmund Muskie	7,000,000
Hubert Humphrey	4,700,000
George Wallace	2,400,000
Henry Jackson	1,500,000
John Lindsay	1,000,000
Terry Sanford	850,000
Wilbur Mills	730,000
Birch Bayh	710,000
Eugene McCarthy	475,000
Fred Harris	330,000
Shirley Chisholm	300,000
Vance Hartke	260,000
Sam Yorty	250,000
Harold Hughes	200,000
Patsy Mink	15,000
Wayne Hays	3,000
Edward Coll	2,000
Total	$32,725,000

In addition, four avowed vice-presidential candidates spent almost one-third of a million dollars:

Stanley Arnold	$124,000
Mike Gravel	100,000
Endicott Peabody	100,000
Patrick Lucey	4,000
Total	$328,000

Combining the presidential and vice-presidential prenomination totals, a little more than $33 million was spent by Democratic candidates in 1971-72.

On the Republican side (excluding Nixon), as noted previously, the total cost was $1,290,000: $550,000 for Congressman Paul McCloskey and $740,000 for Congressman John Ashbrook.

George McGovern's total of $12 million was more than that of any of the five major 1968 contenders, when McCarthy had spent $11 million; Nixon, more than $10 million; Kennedy, $9 million; Rockefeller, $8 million; and Humphrey, $4 million.

There are five major reasons for the prenomination cost differences between 1972 and 1968. Most important, the Democrats had a highly competitive contest for the nomination, with numerous candidates, which led to the unprecedented $33 million total in prenomination spending. The Republican total ($21 million with Nixon and $1.3 million without) is distorted by Nixon's spending throughout, directed at the November election and not at renomination.

The state of the economy in 1971-72 was not as favorable as it had been in 1967-68, which severely affected fund raising. The 1968 campaign had come at the end of a major economic boom, particularly on Wall Street, and much money was available for politics (as for everything else). The 1972 campaign came as the country was slowly moving out of a recession, and money for politics was scarcer. Yet, the polarizations that McGovern crystallized, first against other Democrats, then vis-à-vis Nixon, aroused emotions on all sides, and triggered massive contributions for him and for Nixon, while other candidates lagged far behind.

The competition of millionaire candidates such as John Kennedy in 1960, Nelson Rockefeller in 1964, and both Robert Kennedy and Nelson Rockefeller in 1968 tended to push total costs up, as their poorer rivals tried to match their resources. Yet, costs in 1972 pushed upwards without millionaires raising the ante.

Democratic candidates in 1972 could go into debt to the extent that they had four years earlier. Many providers of goods and services, particularly airlines, telephone companies, and auto-rental companies, had been left with huge unpaid bills after 1968—many still unpaid as 1972 approached—and were sure

not to let it happen again. Payment in advance became an important requirement for most candidates, and there were also frequent demands for deposits
before telephones were installed. Therefore, any candidate who did not have
the cash could not install the telephones or buy the airline tickets, and almost
every Democratic candidate at some time in 1971 or 1972 had to cut back or
do without because of cash flow problems.

The credit problem also was affected by the FECA of 1971. It provided
that within 90 days after enactment, or by May 8, 1972, the Civil Aeronautics
Board, the Federal Communications Commission, and the Interstate Commerce
Commission issue regulations on the extension of credit to political candidates
and any person or committee seeking credit on behalf of candidates for nomination or election to federal office. The regulations issued by the three agencies
differed because of problems peculiar to the various industries regulated, but
they generally required filing within 20 days written copies of credit agreements
detailing deposits, bonds, collateral, or other means of security agreed on to
insure payment of the debt. The extension of credit could not exceed the
amount of the security, although the FCC and CAB permitted unsecured extension of credit if the account was maintained on a current billing basis and no
bills remained unpaid more than 14 days after submission. Vendors could
refuse to extend credit, but extension of credit had to be on a reasonable and
nondiscriminatory basis. Prepayment of specific bills was sanctioned.

In 1968 there were significant differences between costs incurred and actual
expenditures for several candidates because of debts that were settled for less
than their full amount. For example, if a campaign purchased buttons costing
$100,000 but failed to pay the bill and then later settled for $75,000, there would
be a 25 percent difference between the campaign's committed cost and the real
expenditures. Because less credit was extended to candidates in 1972, and because
of the credit regulations, there was a much smaller difference between incurred
costs and actual expenditures in 1972.

Democratic Limits

Of unique importance to total 1972 costs was the agreement among major
Democratic candidates to limit their prenomination media spending. The limitations both preceded and were more stringent than the spending limitations of
the FECA.

Former Democratic National Committee (DNC) Chairman Lawrence F.
O'Brien initiated the agreement in order to try to keep candidate rivalries from
tearing the party apart and draining off excessive funds that then would not be
available for the general election. Early in February 1971 O'Brien hosted a
dinner party for various Democratic congressional leaders and potential presidential candidates. They agreed to consider a proposal to limit spending and to

meet for a second time. The second meeting, in December 1971 resulted in an agreement by five candidates to limit broadcast, print, and billboard spending in the primary states to five cents per registered voter.[a] This agreement limited television and radio spending to less than $3 million for each candidate for the 23 primary states and the District of Columbia. In addition, each candidate would have a bonus pool of $142,000 that could be divided among three or more states (a maximum of $47,333 extra for any one state).

Attending the meeting and agreeing to the limit were Senators Jackson, Muskie, Humphrey, and McGovern; Mayor Lindsay agreed when he became a candidate on December 28. Other announced candidates—Chisholm, Hartke, McCarthy, Wallace, and Yorty—never agreed to the limits but did not exceed them. Mills, who never formally announced his candidacy, did not sign the agreement and his broadcast spending in New Hampshire was well above the limits. In late February 1972 a further money agreement was concluded among the same five candidates. They agreed to limit their spending in the nonprimary states to three cents per registered voter for radio, television, newspaper advertising, billboards, and direct mail. This would limit each candidate to a total of $736,000 in the nonprimary states.

In spite of predictions that the agreements would be broken when the campaign heated up, and even in the bitter and close California primary battle—notwithstanding loud charges to the contrary—the limits were not exceeded.

The voluntary limits affected methods of paying advertising agencies. Prior to 1972 most political campaigns, like most commercial advertisers, paid their agencies a standard fee of 15 percent of the cost of broadcast time purchased. A campaign would pay its agency the gross cost of the broadcast time, and the agency would pay the broadcaster the net cost (gross cost minus 15 percent, the agency commission). This way the gross cost of the time purchased would be the figure used in determining a candidate's expenditures for broadcasting. To avoid having 15 percent of a candidate's limited broadcasting expenditures "wasted" on agency commissions instead of actual time costs, many campaigns in 1972 changed to a system of paying their agencies a flat fee. This way the agency fee would not be counted as media expenditure.[b]

The Democrats' agreement to limit spending in the prenomination period was unprecedented; it presaged other voluntary agreements by some candidates for other offices in the 1974 elections, and the FECA Amendments of 1974, which set overall spending limits on campaigns for federal office.

---

[a]See Appendix F.

[b]As noted elsewhere, the GAO amended its regulations to cover such flat fees.

Voluntary Disclosure

A portion of the receipts of certain of the candidates was revealed in voluntary disclosures. Table 5-2 summarizes the number of individual contributions of $500 or more and the total amounts of these contributions as disclosed voluntarily by six of the candidates. While most of the disclosures were originally for contributions of $1,000 or more, the Citizens' Research Foundation (CRF) was able to get additional data on $500 to $999 gifts as well.

Table 5-2
Number of Individual Contributions and Total Contributions of $500 or More Voluntarily Disclosed by Six Presidential Candidates, 1972

Candidate	Number of Contributions Listed	Total Amount of Contributions Listed
Paul N. McCloskey, Jr. (R)	110	$ 352,987
Hubert H. Humphrey (D)	149	780,491
John V. Lindsay (D)	74	361,600
George S. McGovern (D)	247	727,528[a]
Edmund S. Muskie (D)	846	1,588,645[b]
George C. Wallace (D)	39	98,807
Totals	1,465	$3,910,058

[a]Includes $135,000 in loans, of which $47,200 had been repaid at the time of disclosure.
[b]Includes one $5,500 loan.

The date of each voluntary disclosure, along with the period covered, is shown in Table 5-3. All candidates except McGovern and McCloskey cut off disclosure before April 7, so gaps remain.

In addition, the early Nixon data were disclosed involuntarily after long and protracted public debate surrounding the Common Cause suit. Several disclosures were actually made, finally covering the entire period from January 1, 1971 to April 7, 1972. Along with previously court-sealed FCRP records and the Rose Mary Woods lists, the disclosures unearthed most if not all of the Nixon campaign finance information.

The Democrats

The 1972 Democratic campaign differed from all previous prenomination contests of any party. The number of candidates alone made the race unique.

Table 5-3
Date and Period of Voluntary Disclosures

Candidate	Date Candidacy Announced	Date of Voluntary Disclosure	Period Covered by Disclosure
Paul N. McCloskey, Jr. (R)	July 9, 1971	March 1, 1972	July 12, 1971 - February 29, 1972[a]
Hubert H. Humphrey (D)	January 10, 1972	March 14, 1972	October 1, 1971 - March 10, 1972
John V. Lindsay (D)	December 28, 1971	March 7, 1972	Mid-December, 1971 - March 1, 1972
George S. McGovern (D)	January 18, 1971	February 28, 1972	January 18, 1971 - February 1, 1972
		March 27, 1972	Before January 18, 1971
		March 29, 1972	February 1, 1972 - March 10, 1972
		August 20, 1972	March 11, 1972 - April 6, 1972
Edmund S. Muskie (D)	January 4, 1972	March 27, 1972	November 1, 1970 - January 31, 1972
George C. Wallace (D)	January 13, 1972	March 29, 1972	March, 1969 - March 14, 1972

[a]Contributions through April 4, 1972 were made available and are included.

Fifteen candidates announced for one or more of the primaries, three others carried out major preannouncement or unannounced campaigns, several others were reported to be "seriously considering making the race," and Senator Edward M. Kennedy was an ever-present noncandidate.

Although signing an affidavit declaring his noncandidacy in order to keep off the primary ballots in several states, Edward Kennedy's presence was felt during most of the prenomination period, even as late as the covention, with a consistent first or second rating in the polls. After Muskie weakened and the party became more and more polarized between McGovern liberals and Humphrey centrists, Kennedy was seen as the one person who had equal appeal among the supporters of both.

The contest was also longer than most preconvention contests. Senator George McGovern set a record by formally announcing his candidacy in January 1971, but several other candidates were active even earlier. When the Democratic National Convention opened in July, 1972, there were still eight men and two women vying for the nomination. The second day of the convention saw Humphrey, Muskie, McCarthy, Mills and Mink withdraw; Wallace, Jackson, Chisholm, Sanford and McGovern were nominated, with McGovern winning on the first ballot.

There were several reasons for the record number of Democratic presidential candidates. The 1968 example of an unknown candidate, Eugene McCarthy, catching fire for a time was fresh in everyone's mind. Senators Bayh, Proxmire, Harris, Hughes, Hartke, and Jackson all hoped they could generate enough excitement to win one or two primaries. Many perceived the vulnerability of the front runner, Muskie; if Muskie were to falter, they wanted to be in a position to pick up the banner. Some were not serious contenders for the presidency, but wanted to make a political point or demonstrate political power, to dramatize issues, or be in the running for Vice-President.

The overhaul of the Democratic prenomination process spurred interest and hope. This process actually started before the divisive 1968 convention when the Commission on the Democratic Selection of Presidential Nominees surveyed the delegate selection process and presented its findings in Chicago. The convention adopted resolutions mandating certain reforms and the creation of a formal party committee on delegate selection. With the party selection process to be opened up, many candidacies were to be encouraged.

Other Democratic Candidates

Various political and public figures were mentioned, or mentioned themselves, in connection with the Democratic presidential race throughout 1971. The list included Lester Maddox, former Georgia Governor and candidate for ten days in 1968; former Attorney General Ramsey Clark, who enjoyed a brief boomlet in 1969; R. Sargent Shriver, later to become McGovern's running mate; Senator Walter Mondale of Minnesota; John Gardner, chairman of Common Cause, a Republican; and Ralph Nader, consumer advocate who has endeavored to stay out of partisan politics. None of these possibilities went from the stage of being on a list to the stage of "active consideration."

Two men, Senator William Proxmire and Representative William Anderson, reached beyond the rumor stage and both said financial concerns affected their presidential decisions. Proxmire, from Wisconsin, was probably better known nationally than some other Senators whose presidential considerings went further than his. A well-informed and persistent critic of government spending, particularly of waste in the Defense Department, Proxmire (like others in 1972) considered running as a way to dramatize the issue of priorities in national policy. In early September Proxmire was reported to be preparing a late October or early November announcement of candidacy (unless there were unforeseen financial or political setbacks), to have $100,000 in pledges, and to be raising money in California. Proxmire had travelled to New Hampshire to explore possible support. On November 6 he announced that he would not run. Proxmire said that if he had decided to run, financing would have been a problem because he had been critical of the defense and aerospace industries, had opposed the SST and Lockheed guarantee, and had sponsored truth in lending, fair credit, and billing legislation, which brought opposition of bankers, particularly since he was second-ranking Democrat on the Committee on Banking.

William Anderson was a congressman from Tennesee who received a good deal of national publicity in early 1971 over his rapid conversion from moderation to vocal opposition to the Vietnam War. On a trip to South Vietnam, he had discovered and been deeply shocked by the tiger cages for war prisoners. In mid-June Anderson traveled to New Hampshire saying he was not an active candidate but was not ruling out a presidential race. As a former commander of the atomic submarine Nautilus, Anderson was well known in Portsmouth. After several trips, no campaign was undertaken. In 1972, Anderson was defeated for reelection to the House.

Conclusion

It is interesting to consider which, if any, of the cost factors unique to 1972 may be operative in future prenomination campaigns. Clearly, the biggest determinant of the size of the prenomination bill is whether there is a major battle in one or both of the major parties. While it is common for only the "out" party to have a real nomination contest, 1968 was the shattering exception, and there is no way of knowing when, if ever, another "in" party will find itself having major disagreements over its nominee. On the other hand, it would also be possible for an "out" party to happen to agree on its nominee. Also, the impact of reforms in the delegate-selection process within the parties will continue to have an influential role in future prenomination contests.

The absence of a millionaire candidate in 1972 was a novelty for recent American presidential contests. Since the FECA sets limits on the amounts candidates and their immediate families can spend on their own campaigns, however, millionaire candidates will not make as much difference in future years. To the extent that the money available for politics varies with the state of the economy, it is not possible to predict which future campaign years will be affected by a booming economy and which by a sagging economy. Nor is it certain what effect Watergate and government funding will have on private giving in future years. The FECA limitations on contributions will surely affect fund raising for almost all future candidates.

Lack of commercial credit for presidential candidates is one factor here to stay. It seems likely that more providers of political goods and services than those covered in the three industries will not return to their credit practices of earlier years, having been so badly burned in 1968, and the regulations having proved in 1972 that they could demand and get advance or at least immediate payment. Candidates may still borrow some from individuals, but the FECA Amendments limit individual loans, and the time of million-dollar debts to creditors or lenders may be over for presidential candidates.

Whether the Democrat's agreement to limit spending in the primary states is a harbinger of similar voluntary cooperation in future years on other matters is unknown. No candidates complained about the agreement, possibly because the limits were only slightly less than any candidate would have wanted to spend or could raise. Nevertheless, the agreement was an unprecedented step that worked and did lower Democrats' spending somewhat. Whether or not the Democrats, or Republicans, will be that cooperative if and when they are less afraid of financial disaster, or in a two-man race, remains to be seen.

Because of all the above factors, it is impossible to predict the costs of future prenomination campaigns on the basis of the 1972 experience. Given a mix of 1968 economic conditions and the number of candidates in 1972, it seems possible that a hard-fought contest in one party could easily cost $30-$40 million again. Futhermore the subsidies provided by the FECA Amendments may attract an even larger number of candidates in the future.

The 1972 prenomination campaigns had one additional, only partly antici-pated cost, though not a cost to the candidates. After Robert Kennedy's assassination during the 1968 campaign, a system was begun under which the Secret Service would provide protection to all major presidential candidates, as determined by a special bipartisan committee. Beginning in June 1968 the protection service cost $5.45 million, almost all of which was expended in the

general election period. In 1972, because of the number of candidates and
because the protection service was begun early in the year, the total budgeted
for this was $62.3 million. Five candidates—Muskie, Humphrey, McGovern,
Jackson, and Wallace—were protected beginning March 20, 1972. When
Wallace was shot, Nixon ordered protection also for Senator Kennedy and
for two additional candidates—Chisholm and Mills. Protection required at
least 34 agents for each candidate on shifts around the clock. Presumably,
the cost figure does not include Secret Service protection of the President,
since that is provided in any case.

McGovern

Senator George McGovern of South Dakota ran the longest and most
expensive Democratic prenomination campaign of 1972. He broke precedent
by formally announcing his candidacy 18 months before the nominating convention, on January 18, 1971. Twelve million dollars later, he won the Democratic presidential nomination on the first ballot of the convention.

After his two-week long candidacy in 1968, McGovern had virtually disappeared from public presidential speculation, which was then dominated by
Senators Kennedy and Muskie. However, he chaired the Democratic Party's
Commission on Delegate Selection, which changed the selection process to one
more amenable to his kind of candidacy. When McGovern resigned the chairmanship in 1970, he and his aides knew the details of the new process and how
to use it better than anyone else. Most of the other candidates failed to take
full advantage of the selection procedures in 1972.

The McGovern campaign encompassed three strategies, covering the
primary states, the nonprimary states, and campaign financing. McGovern
believed the nomination would be decided in the primaries, and that the convention could not deny the nomination to the winner of the primaries. The
strategy for the primaries was two-fold: to concentrate on a few contests and
to depend more on grass-roots organization than on media or leadership endorsements. McGovern's financing strategy was similar to his political support—
build from the ground up. Some very large contributors and lenders provided
seed money, but the campaign's steady buildup of income from small contributors began to provide a healthy base for covering routine costs of national
headquarters' costs, and it sustained the campaign in the darkest preprimary
days when the polls measured his popularity at only three to six percent.

McGovern's January 1971 announcement resulted in part from his campaign financing strategy. It was coupled with the mailing of a seven-page letter
to 300,000 potential supporters,[1] explaining the reasons for his candidacy and
asking for help. The returns from this mailing helped McGovern to build a
lean but well-organized campaign operation. The development of a strong

field staff and the building of a nationwide grass-roots organization were given priority over a large Washington staff. By year's end, the campaign had about 25 paid staff in Washington and 35 in the field, perhaps the largest staff of any candidate. There were active McGovern organizations in every state, more than 300 campus groups, and local organizations operating in key states. McGovern's grass-roots operation during 1971 contrasted favorably with all other candidates except Wallace. While others sought large contributors and endorsements by prominent political figures, McGovern used loans primarily for seed money and built a grass-roots political and finance organization.

Voluntary Disclosure. McGovern publicly raised the issue of voluntary disclosure in the New Hampshire primary campaign. On February 28, 1972 he released a list of his larger contributors[c] from the campaign's beginning to February 1, 1972 (he had disclosed his personal finances a week earlier), and challenged his rivals, particularly front-runner Muskie, to do the same. Actually, Republican McCloskey had technically been the first candidate to disclose when his campaign manager, responding to a question raised at a February 24 press conference, read a list of McCloskey's top 50 contributors and amounts. At that time, McGovern's campaign manager promised a full disclosure at a later press conference.

Initially, all the other Democrats ignored the issue or flatly refused to disclose. But the issue caught on, slowly in New Hampshire and then more rapidly in Florida. Lindsay was the first Democrat to respond, disclosing on March 7. Humphrey's attitude changed when he saw disclosure developing into a good issue for McGovern and a difficult one for Muskie. The pressure on Muskie continued to build, particularly after his poor showing in Florida, and he finally disclosed on March 27. Two days later Wallace became the sixth and last candidate to disclose. McGovern benefitted from the disclosure issue both directly, as the first and most vocal supporter of voluntary disclosure, and indirectly, because of the harm the issue caused Muskie.

Muskie's disclosure covered the period beginning November 1, 1970, and he charged that McGovern's disclosure did not cover the preannouncement period. Muskie also implied that the uncovered period might have some very large or questionable contributions. This implication, along with other factors, prompted McGovern to release a list of the 44 contributors and one lender who had given before his January 1971 formal announcement. This was followed by two subsequent releases listing contributors from February 1, 1972 to April 6, 1972, covering the entire pre-FECA period. McGovern was the only candidate to update contributor data after the original disclosure.

Throughout 1972 McGovern's staff statements of the campaign's total cost

---

[c]Most major contributors were consulted before McGovern's disclosure.

were $7 million while the actual cost appears to have been closer to $12 million. The gap between the staff's estimate (since revised upward to $8.5 million) and the actual total costs most likely resulted from headquarter's unawareness of widespread local fund raising, borrowing, and spending. The main national committees alone raised about $7 million: less than $2 million in the pre-April 7 period and about $4.7 million according to FECA filings. But state and local McGovern committee FECA filings show additional receipts of $5.7 million, so the total reported receipts are more than $12 million (although this figure includes grosses, not net amounts, of concerts and other fund-raising events). The figure is also confused by millions of dollars in possibly double counted loans. In addition, it includes the costs of delegate campaigns in the states, and outstanding debts of perhaps $1.4 million, some of which were loans paid off in the general election period. The exact size of the prenomination debt cannot be pinpointed or the final disposition of all outstanding loans traced. Uncertainties about the conversion of some loans to contributions, the transfer of some debts to general election committees, and the various methods of listing debts and loans, remain. But that $12 million was spent is certain.

Costs. While the total cost of the McGovern prenomination campaign can be estimated at $12 million, expenditure details, especially in the pre-April 7 period, are sparse. Throughout 1972 press attention was on the amount and source of campaign income, with little interest in the total or the categorical costs. Candidates were not under public pressure to reveal the details of their expenditures and none did so.

The only hard expenditure figure is that for media time, compiled by the FCC. The McGovern campaign spent a total of $1,175,464 for all nonnetwork radio and television time,[d] twice that spent by his chief rival, Humphrey ($517,342), and more than Humphrey and Muskie ($541,623) spent combined ($1,058,965).

The FCC does not provide a state-by-state breakdown of the total, but data on McGovern media spending in the primary states account for more than 95 percent of the total. The primary state list in Table 5-4 compares these approximate broadcast expenditures figures with the limits in the Democrats' spending agreement. This listing shows the shape and strategy of the McGovern campaign. The media contingency pool was used in two key states: New Hampshire, where the campaign wanted an impressive first primary showing at

---

[d]Federal Election Campaign Act of 1973, appendix A, *Hearings* before the Subcommittee on Commerce, U.S. Senate, 93rd Cong., 1st sess. (1973). Hereafter referred to as FCC, *Survey 1972*. See p. 7. McGovern also spent a little money on media in 1971, which presumably is not covered in the FECA compilation. In mid-November, the campaign bought five minutes on 47 stations, at a cost of about $25,000 for both time and production.

Table 5-4

Broadcast Spending by McGovern Compared with Limits in Democrats' Spending Agreement

State	McGovern Expenditure	Democrats' Limit (plus up to $47,333 extra to be used in up to three states)
N.H.	$ 65,000	$ 18,000
Fla.	28,000	133,000
Ill.	(negligible)	254,000
Wisc.	95,500	117,000
Mass.	77,000	124,000
Pa.	13,800	257,000
Ohio	125,000	185,000
Neb.	27,000	33,000
Mich.	61,000	
Md.	(negligible)	76,000
Ore.	26,000	46,000
R.I.	7,800	22,000
Calif.	460,000	413,000
N.J.	57,000	151,000
N.M.	15,400	20,000
S.D.	(unknown; negligible)	17,000
N.Y.	66,000	353,000

(Total: $1,124,500)

a time when it was receiving little free media exposure, and California, a state particularly amenable to heavy media spending and the most important primary of the year. Media spending in the other states is indicative of the campaign's judgment of their strategic importance and the value of radio and television in each particular state. Florida, Illinois, Michigan, Maryland, and Rhode Island were not strategically important, nor was South Dakota, where McGovern was unopposed. Wisconsin, Massachusetts, Nebraska, Oregon, and New Jersey were more important, with slightly different emphases on the role of media. Although Pennsylvania and Ohio were both last-minute additions to the McGovern primary schedule, media were used differently in both states; in Pennsylvania the campaign was geared to local organization while in Ohio there was an intensive statewide media campaign. New Mexico's small population caused the campaign spending to approach the limit, but represented little expense. In New York McGovern faced only weak and disorganized opposition, which did not lend itself to a media campaign. Furthermore, the nature of the New York ballot, with voters choosing different delegates in each congressional district, and the delegates not identified by candidate preference, was not media oriented.

Presidential primaries are usually characterized by a frantic doing, redoing, and shuffling of media material. McGovern's media campaign was not; it was set up in advance and held to unwaveringly throughout. Yet, McGovern's media production costs were $300,000, about what would be expected for his $1.1 million for media time. As much as half of this cost was for cutting the hundreds of copies of spot announcements, a very expensive portion of production costs.

The campaign experimented with telephone press conferences by leading supporters, as a low-cost alternative to extensive travel by surrogate speakers. Simple, inexpensive devices were used by the candidate and others to telephone groups of reporters gathered in local McGovern headquarters across the country. Newspaper and radio reporters used this service extensively, and on occasion television film provided by headquarters was used on news broadcasts with the recorded voice of McGovern.

Some general conclusions about the campaign's expenditures can be inferred from the campaign's style and strategy. Personnel costs were high once the campaign began to rely on field staff for local organizing. Even if canvassers and volunteers were paid only token expense money, the total adds up astronomically when the volunteers number 10,000 (as in Wisconsin) or 50,000 (the goal for California). The campaign's unequalled effort in the nonprimary states also involved paid field staff. However, the national headquarters had a relatively lean Washington staff. The major exception was the large number of unpaid volunteers needed to handle the large volume of mail contributions. At least $1 million was spent for direct mail. The national headquarters building in Washington, D.C. was narrow, shabby and overcrowded. It had 4,000 square feet and rented for $1,200 per month. A year's prepayment brought the actual cost down to $950 per month.

The campaign economized on travel costs. Charter airplanes were used only for short-hopping campaign blitzes within a state. McGovern and his staff used commercial flights for all other trips, with the candidate flying first class and the staff going tourist. These savings in travel costs were offset somewhat by the sheer number of primaries in which the candidate was active (14). Attention to the nonprimary states and emphasis on local organizing necessitated extensive travel by both McGovern and the field staff.

For the period before April 7, 1972 total costs of the national campaign can be deduced from McGovern's voluntary disclosures and his first filings under FECA. The national campaign had income of $1,840,356 and there were unpaid loans of $87,800 for a total of at least $1,928,156. Since the major Washington committees reported less than $3,000 on hand as of April 7, the campaign must have spent the $1.9 million prior to that date. The first FECA filings reported debts of $173,666 as of April 7; subtracting the $87,800 in outstanding loans already accounted for, leaves other debts of $85,866. Therefore, the national campaign had costs of almost $2 million for the pre-FECA period. This figure does not include money raised and spent in this period by local and state committees.

Most of the costs can be roughly detailed. From the campaign's beginning through mid-December 1971, spending totalled about $1 million. Less than $30,000 of this was spent in the period before McGovern's formal announcement on January 18, 1971: $19,613 was received in contributions and McGovern borrowed an additional $10,000 during that time. Costs of about $1 million for a year works out to an average of $83,000 per month. Unlike other campaigns (such as Muskie's) that spent at that rate in 1971, much of McGovern's money went to political organizing in the field rather than plush offices and large support staffs in Washington. This resulted in McGovern receiving more for the early money spent than did other campaigns.

McGovern spending in the first four primaries was more than three-quarters of the approximately $1 million in costs for the pre-FECA months of 1972.

In New Hampshire McGovern forces admitted spending $161,000; 40 percent of the total ($65,000) was for radio and television. This was one of the two states in which the campaign used the allowable $47,333 media bonus. However, it is known that some large McGovern contributors who were helping out in New Hampshire paid some bills directly, thus increasing the total to be spent in New Hampshire.

In Florida McGovern spent less than $100,000, with $28,000 for radio and television. Late in the campaign the Florida television budget had been raised from $7,000 to $16,000 and the radio budget from $10,000 to $12,000. It was reported that a high campaign official personally carried $10,000 to Florida to buy television time during the final week. The campaign also mailed 170,000 pieces of literature to Democrats in Miami, St. Petersburg, and Fort Lauderdale during the final week.

The cost of McGovern's limited effort in Illinois was reported to be about $80,000. No money was spent on television, and only about $3,000 for radio. Twenty volunteer headquarters operated in the state. The heaviest spending was for telephoning, direct mail, and printed material. Salaries and travel were minor costs. Reports show $160,000 was actually raised in the state, of which $45,000 was sent to New Hampshire and some to D.C. However, questions arise from the FECA reports of the Illinois committee on the amount raised and spent in the state.

The reports showed $103 on hand as of April 7, which was two and one half weeks after the primary, and $88,000 raised and spent after that date. Therefore, either the campaign actually cost more than twice as much as claimed, or the $88,000 was spent on activity separate from the primary. For example, McGovern supporters organized and successfully carried out a challenge to the Illinois delegation to the Democratic Convention. This means almost $250,000 was raised in the state, $80,000 for the primary, $80,000 sent to other states, and $88,000 for the challenge.

Wisconsin's April 4 primary was a financial and political high point of the McGovern campaign; it cost $440,000. The Wisconsin McGovern committee reported only $21,728 spent after April 7, presumably for bills in connection with the primary and therefore included in the overall reported cost. Radio and television costs account for 22 percent ($95,500) of the total. The campaign spent considerable money on political organizing, which had begun in the state about a year before the primary. This included storefront headquarters in every sizable town in the state and brought out 10,000 canvassers on the last weekend before the primary.

The Wisconsin campaign's careful political and media planning did not extend to the financial side of the operation. The state McGovern committee was cited by the GAO because its records were virtually incomprehensible. As of late 1973 state campaign officials were still trying to straighten out the books.

The costs of these four pre-FECA primaries total $770,000, leaving about $250,000 in nonprimary costs for the pre-April 7 period of 1972. This averages about $80,000 per month, the same figure as calculated for 1971. This seems unlikely, since campaign activity was more intense in 1972; however, more staff members worked directly in the primary states after the first of the year and their salaries and expenses were included in the state costs. The two biggest non-primary state efforts in this period were in Arizona and Iowa, with each costing less than $10,000.

For the period after April 7, the McGovern campaign had costs of at least $10 million. After accounting for transfers among committees, Washington headquarters raised just over $4.7 million and the 35 states with reporting committees raised just over $5.7 million. The major movement in money transfers was from Washington to the states, so the amount spent directly by headquarters was just over $3.1 million while the 35 states directly spent almost $7 million. Against this apparent surplus of more than $300,000 must be balanced the reported national committee debts of $350,000 and reported state committee debts of $975,000 for an overall debt of about $1 million. This brings total post-April 7 costs to a least $11 million, but two other factors have to be considered. First, state committee debts were generally understated, some debts were "transferred" to Washington and not reported, some were assumed by successor general election committees, and some loans were not listed as debts. Therefore, debts were higher than reported although the actual amount is uncertain. Second, more than one-half of all reported loans, which totalled $2.5 million, were repaid during the prenomination period. This amount, close to $1.5 million, should be subtracted from both calculated income and expenditures to avoid double counting. Loans show up as income when received and as expenditures when repaid and so inflate both figures if repaid. Accordingly, in the post-April 7 period the campaign's adjusted spending was about $9 million ($10.5 million spent less loan repayments), with a net debt of $1 million, for a total cost of at least $10 million.

Of the 13 active primary campaigns post-April 7, all the states except

South Dakota had one or more committees that reported. The committees in these 12 states reported total expenditures of $6.4 million, about 92 percent of the almost $7 million reported by all committees in 35 states. In dealing with these totals and the individual state figures, three factors should be kept in mind: (1) while all state expenditures are assumed to be for that state's primary, the total cost could be understated if there was additional spending by the Washington committees; (2) if the state committees received loans and repaid them, both receipts and expenditures could be overstated; (3) the large debt in California makes a difference both in the overall and the California expenditure and cost figures. Adding the California debt of $740,000 to the overall figures brings the post-April 7 costs of these 12 primary states to $7.2 million and the costs of all 35 reporting states to $7.7 million.

The first two post-April 7 primaries were in Massachusetts, a key state in McGovern's strategy where his campaign had long been active, and in Pennsylvania, a late addition to his schedule. The Massachusetts committees reported spending $316,000. In addition to the $77,000 broadcast expenditure previously noted, the McGovern campaign spent $12,000 for newspaper ads and $3,000 on local committee costs in Massachusetts. Almost $233,000 was raised in the state, including $2,500 on hand as of April 7, and the remaining $120,000 was transferred in from Washington. Apparently all of it was not needed because Massachusetts sent more than $32,000 back to D.C. and also sent $5,000 to Ohio. Local organizing was emphasized with 35 offices around the state and about 3,000 canvassers working during the last preprimary weekend. Radio and television accounted for only 24 percent ($77,000) of the reported expenses. Because of pre-April 7 spending, it is likely that the total cost of McGovern's Massachusetts effort is more than the reported post-April 7 expenditures of $316,000.

The Pennsylvania campaign was shorter and more limited, and pre-April 7 spending was not significant. The FECA filings show total spending of $182,000 of which $164,000 was raised in-state (including $25,000 in loans). Radio and television played a minor role in the Pennsylvania campaign, with less than eight percent of the total ($13,800) spent for broadcast media. Last-minute funds were used to import and distribute 500,000 pieces of literature in the 30 districts in which McGovern delegates were running.

McGovern's next effort was in Ohio, also a late addition to his primary schedule. Unlike Pennsylvania, radio and television played a major role: 54 percent ($125,000) of the $231,400 in expenditures reported by 21 committees. Of the total, $151,000 was raised in the state.

In Nebraska expenditures of $146,400 were reported by four state committees, although as much as $180,000 may have been spent. While radio and television expenditures were only 18 percent of the known total ($27,000) the amount was 82 percent of the Democratic limit for the state. Only $41,100 was raised in the state; New Jersey sent $2,000 and $99,300 came from Washington.

Michigan had one committee that filed under the FECA. The committee had $2,126 on hand, it raised $120,163 directly, and $100,000 was transferred from Washington, for a total of $222,289. Its reported expenditures were the same, although the disposition of $23,341 in loans is unknown. The committee spent 27 percent of the total ($61,000) for radio and television.

Six Maryland committees raised more than they spent. The committees reported a total income of $88,912, direct expenditures of $75,968, and $13,000 was sent to Washington. There was virtually no media spending. The campaign decided to buy $4,000 worth of last-minute television time in response to enthusiastic crowd reactions. But the assassination attempt on George Wallace caused the cancellation of virtually all radio and television political advertising for the last day.

In Oregon total expenditures of $159,200 were reported by the one committee filing under the FECA.[e] Radio and television accounted for only about 16 percent ($26,000) of the total. The committee reported total income of $166,300: $1,000 on hand, $68,300 in direct receipts, $97,000 transferred in from D.C., and $6,000 transferred in from other state committees.

The Rhode Island campaign reported expenses of $24,400 of which broadcast media accounted for about 32 percent ($7,800). One committee reported $13,007 in direct receipts and $12,456 transferred in from D.C. Against this, the committee spent $24,423 and sent $1,000 to New Jersey. The committee also had $1,500 in debts.

The California effort was the longest and most expensive of the McGovern campaign. The total cost of the year-long effort was at least $4,174,500—more than 50 percent of the cost of all other primary campaigns and 35 percent of the total cost of McGovern's drive for the nomination. For the post-April 7 period, reports show expenditures of $3,312,600 and a debt of $739,900 for a cost of $4,052,500; adding reported pre-April 7 costs of $122,000 gives a total of $4,174,500. Important expenses such as radio and television production, advance, and the candidate's traveling party (including room, board, and transportation), were paid directly from Washington and are not reflected in this cost figure. Loans were a major factor in the California campaign and the income and expenditure figures may be distorted due to repayment of some loans.

The California press noted the state seemed overrun with McGovern committees, with attempts to count the number proving futile. Organized and staffed mostly by amateurs, California committees emphasized the grass-roots character of the campaign. A detailed analysis was made of some 70 committees operating in California; the committees' reports made reference to transfers

---

[e]Eight committees filing with the Oregon State Elections Division showed a total of $138,077 receipts and $136,018 expenditures; some of this may be additional to the amounts reflected in the FECA filing.

from other groups not reporting under the FECA, presumably because their operations were too small. The first committees were organized in 1971; most of the committees began reporting as of April 7, 1972, but others were formed after that date.

A definite structure existed in spite of the general impression of ad hoc groups organizing spontaneously across the state. The linchpin of the operation was the Central Control Fund, based in Los Angeles. Several major satellite committees were: McGovern '72 (Los Angeles), McGovern for President—Northern California (San Francisco), McGovern for President—Southern California (Los Angeles), Californians for McGovern (Los Angeles), and the McGovern Concert Committee, a fund-raising committee that turned its net receipts over to the Central Control Fund. These six closely coordinated committees received over 80 percent of the total California receipts. The 70-odd minor committees accounted for less than 20 percent of the total; financially, they were clearly not a major factor in the campaign.

Orbiting around the professional central organization were scores of mini-committees composed largely of students who wished to attend the Miami Beach Convention. The students also rang doorbells, passed out literature, and achieved a visibility that made them a potent asset. In addition to city and county committees, there were ethnic committees, such as Black Californians for McGovern, El Pueblo con McGovern, Comite pro Communidad Mexico-Americano pro McGovern.

The financial picture in California is confused by extensive transferring of funds. The six major committees had gross receipts of $3,766,000; subtracting the $757,500 transferred in from national committees gives gross in-state receipts of just over $3 million. After accounting for intercommittee transfers, the net receipts of the six committees come to about $2.1 million. Expenditure figures reveal the same pattern of extensive transferring. The six committees had gross expenditures of $3,851,000; subtracting $150,000 sent back to D.C. gives an in-state figure of about $3.7 million. After the intercommittee transfers are discounted, the expenditure figure is about $2.6 million. These net, direct expenditures of the six major committees and their debts, totalling $725,800 of the $739,900 total state debt, accounted for 83 percent of the total post-April 7 California campaign cost. The 70-odd committees accounted for only 17 percent of the total California expenditures.

The six major committees were dissimilar, as seen in Table 5-5 by their receipts and expenditure figures, adjusted for transfers. This list shows that four of the six were really operating committees, and that the Central Control Fund (CCF) was the main one. The CCF accounted for more than 60 percent of both the expenditures and the debts of all California committees. The other two committees functioned primarily as fund-raising groups; most of their funds were transferred to the four operating committees.

Table 5-5
Receipts and Expenditures of Six Major McGovern Committees

Committee	Adjusted Receipts	Adjusted Expenditures	(Debt)
Central Control Fund	$1,120,400	$2,033,300	($466,300)
McGovern '72 Committee	398,000	57,900	(218,800)
McGovern for President–No. Calif.	257,800	298,800	(7,500)
McGovern for President–So. Calif.	6,300	110,000	0
Californians for McGovern	107,600	121,200	(33,200)
McGovern Concert Committee	198,300	2,800	0

Table 5-6 gives a rough categorical breakdown of McGovern's budget for California. Some of the items are vague and do not conform to standard expense categories. The budget of $3.2 million was exceeded and does not include many local costs calculated for the California campaign.

McGovern's massive California campaign, like New Hampshire, placed heavy and almost equal emphasis on local organizing efforts and on media. The campaign spent the full amount for radio and television, including the available bonus: $460,333. This amounted to 11 percent of the total California cost. The California radio and television expenditures represented 42 percent of McGovern's media spending in all the primary states (and 39 percent of the total prenomination radio and television spending). It included $50,000 for a three-week TV feed operation, which was a new and very successful technique that combined news film and state-of-the-art video tape technology. The operation was so successful that Humphrey's media director sent telegrams to about 50 television stations in the state threatening to call for an FCC investigation if the tapes were used without being identified as "McGovern tape." The McGovern campaign responded by including a suggestion that the station use a disclaimer, such as "This film was furnished by volunteers for McGovern." The tape production and distribution reportedly cost about $2,000 per day. In addition, a high-level campaign strategy meeting reportedly decided to spend $50,000 on billboard space in minority communities to familiarize blacks and Mexican-Americans with McGovern's name and face.

The original goal of the local organizing effort was to contact each of California's five million Democratic voters twice. The effort began in April with a million-piece introductory mailing and the installation of a statewide telephone bank. The campaign reportedly also had a computerized list of 175,000 Jewish households for which one special mailing was done. During

Table 5-6
McGovern's California Budget

Electronic media	$ 450,000
Media production	20,000
Media buying (both Hall & Levine and Guggenheim)	40,000
Print media	50,000
Literature	500,000
TV feed operation	50,000
Telephones (not including NTA banks)	50,000
Polling	35,000
Staff salaries	200,000
Transportation, staff	25,000
Housing, staff	10,000
Field expenses for organizers (rent, printing, etc.)	75,000
Auto rental	35,000
Speakers, transportation, room and board	25,000
Northern California separately raised and spent	200,000
Black and Chicano campaign special funds	200,000
Locally raised and spent (rent, supplies, etc.)	150,000
Student effort (absentee ballot campaign, etc.)	75,000
Direct voter contact: includes preparation and distribution of lists and kits for NTA, volunteer phone work, volunteer door-to-door canvassing, computer letters, telegrams and get out the vote (GOTV) efforts. Rough breakdown:	1,000,000

Printouts and kit preparation	$200,000
Preparation of tape	100,000
Telephoning	250,000
Letters	250,000
Grams	100,000
Administration	50,000
Election day	50,000

Total	$3,190,000

the first two weekends in May, the campaign had more than 10,000 canvassers on the streets. By June 1 more than 200 storefront headquarters were operating.

The goal of ten million contacts was not reached, but the campaign must have set a new record for direct voter contact in California. McGovern's state campaign manager estimated that 70 percent of all registered Democrats, about 3.5 million people, were called or visited and an additional 20 percent, one million, received a McGovern mailing. The cost of this effort was at least $1 million and might have been much more. The local organizing effort included all the costs of the "direct voter contact" category and probably at least some of the costs of the "field expenses," "literature," "student effort," "locally raised and spent," "black and Chicano campaign special funds," and "northern California separately raised and spent" categories.

McGovern had three other primary victories on June 6, but they were hardly noticed because of the California victory. The most expensive was in New Jersey, where 13 committees reported expenditures of $296,500, including $2,000 sent to Nebraska. However, the committees' income was $336,800, of which $70,300 was transferred from D.C. and $1,000 from Rhode Island, and included $73,000 in loans. About $57,000 was spent for media. Three New Mexico committees received $45,591, including $29,000 transferred from Washington. They spent $43,845 directly and sent $600 to Washington. Media accounted for 35 percent ($15,400) of the total spent. No South Dakota McGovern committees filed under the FECA because that campaign was funded directly from Washington. Costs were minimal since McGovern was unopposed in his home state.

The New York campaign was McGovern's second most expensive primary effort, costing, with various New York committees operating long before the primary date, more than $1.4 million. But it was anticlimatic after California, receiving relatively little attention because McGovern had little opposition and because voting was on delegate slates rather than on candidate preferences. New York also had the second largest number of active committees, with 50 of them filing.[f] The total expenditures reported (accounting for transfers) by all the committees was $1,443,375. One major committee and several smaller ones were fully operational in 1971, so the reported expenditures do not reflect the total cost. Unlike other states, New York ended up with a considerable surplus—$215,000.

Two major committees—McGovern for President/New York (McG/NY) and Business and Professional Men and Women for McGovern (B&PM&W)— accounted for 70 percent of the total expenditures while 48 minor committees accounted for the rest. Funds were transferred more extensively among committees in New York than in California. For example, the two major committees reported gross receipts of $1.7 million, but after transfers (and a short-term repaid bank loan) are accounted for, their net in-state receipts were only a little more than half that amount, $860,850. The 48 minor committees also had extensive transferring, with gross reported receipts of more than $800,000 and actual net receipts of $339,400. Expenditures follow the same pattern: for the two major committees, reported expenditures were more than $1.5 million while actual expenditures were a little more than $1 million; for the minor committees, actual expenditures were $437,600.

---

[f]A committee called McGovern for President–New York Special Committee, which listed a D.C. address during the spring, has been judged to be a national committee and its receipts and expenditures are not included in the following analysis. The committee raised a total of almost $500,000. Less than $125,000 was spent directly, the rest being transferred with large amounts going to other national committees and to California.

The two major New York committees had significant role differences, one focusing primarily on fund raising, the other on operations. (Some of the expenditures were national in character, with only incidental benefit in New York.) The B&PM&W raised $569,500 and received an additional $22,800 in transfers from national and New York committees. Of this $592,300 in income, the committee directly spent only $238,300, while $3,000 was sent to Washington and almost $350,000 was transferred to other New York committees. The committee had a balance of about $1,200 and a short-term $150,000 bank loan, which was repaid, thus cancelling out as both income and expenditure. The McG/NY committee directly raised only $292,800 but spent more than twice as much, $592,900, also transferring $171,800 to other New York committees. Then $165,500 was transferred in from other committees ($115,200 from B&PM&W) and $477,700 from national committees. The committee ended with a $171,300 surplus.

The 48 minor committees directly raised $339,400 and spent $437,600. The funds of the local groups mainly went toward renting and operating storefront headquarters. These committees also ended up with a surplus of $42,500.

Radio and television accounted for a mere five percent ($66,000) of the more than $1.4 million spent for New York's campaign. This was the smallest percentage spent for broadcast media in a major state. The reason for this minimal broadcast effort is the nature of the New York primary: delegate candidates on the ballot were not identified as supporting a candidate, so there was no way to run a campaign for "McGovern delegates." An enormous local canvassing and literature effort, costing $400,000, was waged to identify the McGovern delegates. The primary states accounted for just under $8.1 million, or 67 percent of the campaign's total costs.

Active efforts were waged in all nonprimary states but two: South Carolina because its delegate selection process began too early and Maine because it was Muskie's home state. McGovern won delegates in all but three such states— Maine, Arkansas, and Washington—with campaigns ranging in cost from $200 in Vermont (for a statewide WATS line) to more than $100,000 in Connecticut. The total cost of the nonprimary states' campaign was probably $500,000.

The McGovern campaign boasted that the nonprimary state campaigns spent a mere $90,000 to win 300 delegates, an impressive cost of only $300 per delegate, but a deceptive figure because it included only some expenses paid for directly by the national headquarters, such as salaries and expenses of the assistant director and five regional directors, some salaries and expenses for about 20 workers for two-to-five weeks each in a given state, and some media, telephone, and local headquarters costs. Not included were the salary and expenses of the director of the operation and the people who worked in both primary and nonprimary states. These workers moved as the McGovern schedule of important caucuses, conventions, and elections required.

However, the big uncounted cost of the nonprimary state operation was for the amounts spent locally. In 17 nonprimary states, 31 McGovern committees reporting under the FECA aggregated expenditures of $346,400.[g] Most of these committees and expenses were directly related to the delegate selection process. This figure includes only post-April 7 expenditures while some states' delegate selection processes began before then, so there were probably some pre-April 7 expenditures not included in the reported total. Adding the two known figures and the unreported and uncounted local and national costs brings the total to at least $500,000.

The McGovern campaign actually won 376 committed delegates in the nonprimary states,[2] which gives a per-delegate cost figure of about $1,200. This is four times higher than the campaign's figure, but still only about one-seventh the direct cost (excluding national headquarters spending) of more than $8,350 per delegate won in the primary states ($8,085,000 for 967 delegates).

Sources. McGovern voluntarily disclosed for the entire pre-FECA period, but the income data is not precise. Loans were a major factor in financing McGovern's campaign. Some loans were repaid from other prenomination income, inflating both the total income figure and the loan percentage. Some were repaid from postnomination income, inflating those figures.

The McGovern prenomination campaign raised a total of $12.3 million, including loans (adjusted for repayments and renewed loans). The sources of $11.7 million are known. The remaining $600,000 is from transfers from nonlateral and nonreporting committees whose sources of income are not known.

Large contributions and loans accounted for about the same income as did small contributions: 49 percent ($5.7 million) came from contributions and loans of $500 or more, while 51 percent (just under $6 million) came from contributions of up to $500. The big contributions and loans category included: 23 percent ($2.6 million) in loans,[h] 13 percent (almost $1.3 million) in contributions of $5,000 or more, and almost 13 percent ($1.2 million) in contributions of from $500 to $4,999. This covers the full $11.7 million.

McGovern's financing shows a very large difference in the distribution of receipts for the pre- and post-FECA periods, $1.9 million (or 17 percent) received before April 7 and the $9.8 million (83 percent) received after April 7. Before April 7, 63 percent of the campaign's income came from under-$500 contributions; after April 7, it was 48 percent. For the pre-April 7 period, statistics support a pattern of top- and bottom-heavy campaign financing, with

---

[g]The remaining nonprimary eleven states and four territories did not have committees that reported under the FECA.

[h]Virtually all loans were large, starting at about $10,000.

loans playing a major role in providing seed money for large mailings. Of post-April 7 money raised, under-$500 contributions accounted for more than 48 percent ($4.7 million) of the total raised; almost 41 percent (just under $4 million) came from small contributions of $100 or less and less than eight percent ($754,000) came from contributions of $100 to $500.[i] This breakdown provides some support to the importance of the small contributor fueling McGovern's campaign: of the $4.7 million raised from relatively small contributions (under $500), 84 percent came from truly small contributions of $100 or less.

In the prenomination period, McGovern had four early large contributors or lenders who accounted for significant contributions and whose loans kept the direct mail drive solvent. They were: Max Palevsky, the computer executive who sold his interests to Xerox, who gave $148,875 pre-April 7 and loaned $225,000 in the prenomination period (also giving $9,825 to McCloskey during this period); Miles Rubin, chairman of Optical Systems Corp., of Los Angeles, who gave $37,400 and was owed $110,000 at the time of the convention (who also gave $2,000 to Muskie and, with his wife, $4,600 to McCloskey—both pre-April 7 gifts); Henry Kimelman, the campaign's fund-raising chairman, who gave $30,307 and loaned an aggregate of $230,000—all repaid; and another early contributor who gave more substantial support later in the McGovern campaign, Montgomery, Alabama attorney Morris Dees. Dees gave $2,422 pre-April 7; he gave $20,000 and loaned $190,000 post-April 7; he also served as coordinator of McGovern's direct mail drives. Another loan, for $40,000, came from Stewart Mott in the fall 1971 and was repaid in full. Mott became the campaign's most generous supporter after April 7, but in the pre-FECA period he gave only $5,000 to McGovern while giving $6,000 to McCloskey and $6,000 to Lindsay. Mott's $5,000 donation, made in December 1970, helped launch the direct mail effort.[j]

---

[i]This pattern of many $100-and-under contributors and heavy support from big (over-$500) contributors with a relatively small number of givers in the middle range ($100-$500) is similar to the pattern of contributions to Eugene McCarthy's campaign in 1968, when there were thousands of small contributors, 25 very big ($10,000-and-over) contributors and very few in the $100-$1,000 range.

[j]About a year earlier, Mott had loaned McGovern $35,000 needed to pay for network time for a nationwide television program about Vietnam; this amount is not included in his McGovern total. In 1972 Mott sponsored a number of meetings aimed at bringing together the Democratic campaigns of McGovern, McCarthy, Lindsay, and Chisholm, to avoid conflict on issues of common concern, which could cause mutual detriment during the primaries. He spent more than $1,000 in this activity, but not on any one candidate. On October 9, 1972 Stewart Mott publicized a statement Richard Nixon had made four years earlier in a speech on that day: "Those who have had a chance for four years, and could not produce peace, should not be given another chance." Mott's efforts, focusing on a day of commemoration of the statement and costing over $50,000 were (although a benefit to the McGovern campaign) entirely his own project.

McGovern emerged as the strongest liberal candidate by April, and Mott contributed $95,000 more to his campaign, bringing his total gift to $100,000. Then in April Mott dramatically announced that he would contribute $50,000 on the first of each month for the next five months, for a total of $350,000. The full pledge was dependent upon McGovern's winning the nomination; if he did not do so, the $50,000 per month payments would stop after July 1. Since McGovern did win the nomination and since some August income was used for prenomination costs, Mott's prenomination contributions to McGovern totalled $250,000. Mott also spent directly about $50,000 for pro-McGovern newspaper ads in Ohio and Pennsylvania and other activities on behalf of the campaign—some in connection with his one-person anti-Muskie effort in the early spring. Mott also loaned the campaign an aggregate of $200,000 in the prenomination period; some of the loans were made from a New York City office Mott offered to the campaign. The lending operation included a kiting scheme for the New York primary, designed to provide money to the campaign in advance of its deposit. Mott's combined pre- and postnomination contributions to McGovern were $400,000.

McGovern's three early big contributors continued to play major financial roles in the post-April 7 and general election periods. Palevsky gave $319,365 and loaned $230,000; Rubin gave $70,600 more for a year's total of $108,000 (and total loans of $192,852); Kimelman gave $52,227 more and loaned $200,000 for total contributions of $82,534 (and total aggregated loans of $430,000). Rubin and Kimelman, along with Dees, gave up their business activities for long periods in order to devote themselves fully to the campaign.

These three contributors were members of an exclusive organization called the Woonsocket Club, named after the small South Dakota home town of Eleanor Stegeberg McGovern, where the Senator first met his wife. It was the McGovern campaign's counterpart to Johnson's President Club in 1964 and to Nixon's RN Associates in 1968. Membership in the Club took a contribution of $25,000 or more. However, several McGovern supporters who did not give $25,000, but were reportedly members of the club because of the importance of their support, included Coretta (Mrs. Martin Luther) King, Julian Bond, Rev. Jesse Jackson, and Caesar Chavez. For their contributions, members were given a gold lapel pin and the opportunity to attend exclusive gatherings. For this group, McGovern waived the campaign's standing rule that the candidate would not appear while funds were being raised. The club was organized by finance chairman Kimelman and was co-chaired by Mrs. Charles (Marjorie C.) Benton, of Chicago, who with her husband contributed $23,015, and Harold Willens, the Los Angeles businessman long active in peace activity, who gave $26,325 (and loaned $22,500). The Woonsocket Club was organized early but the campaign managed to avoid publicity about it for a long time; the club did not surface publicly until the time of the California primary. As of early June there were reported to be about 35 members. Two celebrity members were brother and sister Warren Beatty and Shirley MacLaine, whose memberships resulted from their personal contributions of time (more than money) and from their successful fund-raising efforts.

Fund Raising. The McGovern campaign successfully used all of the standard political fund-raising techniques—personal solicitations; large, low-priced dinners; small, high-priced dinners; a computerized direct mail operation; and a series of concerts.

The key to direct mail success is the quality of the mailing list. The McGovern campaign benefitted enormously from the candidate himself, who took the name, address, and zip code of virtually every well-wisher. The campaign list began with 130,000 South Dakota names, plus a basic national list of 50,000 names added throughout 1969-70. In May 1970 McGovern joined five other senators in a television show opposing President Nixon's Cambodian policy. The show ended with an appeal for funds to pay for the television time, and more than 30,000 people responded with more than $500,000. Questions arose over who could use this 30,000-name list, but McGovern effectively answered the question by simply using it. Also in 1970 McGovern was asked to sign the cover letter for "Campaign '70," an effort on behalf of liberal Democratic senatorial candidates. McGovern agreed to do so in exchange for adding another 43,000 names to the list; this gave his campaign a total of 253,000 names.

As McGovern was preparing to formally announce his candidacy in January 1971, he consulted with mail order expert and millionaire Morris Dees about a letter of announcement outlining his positions on many issues, and appealing to the 253,000 people on his list for funds for his campaign. The letter and appeal, which cost about $30,000, were sent a few days before the January 18 announcement. About $300,000 was received from about 15,000 contributors.

The 15,000 responders to the first mailing were asked for the names of friends; they sent in 20,000 names. Immediately after these 15,000 givers were thanked for their contributions they were asked to give again by joining the $10 per month club, "only 33 cents a day." With mailing lists from SANE, an antiwar organization, *The New Republic,* and other organizations and magazines, the McGovern list grew, and many contributors gave often.

Throughout 1971 and early 1972 there were periodic stories about the success of McGovern's direct mail operation. By early August 1971 the campaign had sent 360,000 mailings and received about half a million dollars from 35,000 contributors. This ten percent response rate was considered unbelievable in the direct mail business, where a three percent response is considered excellent. The Muskie campaign had recently done a mass mailing that only paid for itself.

Several other mass mailings went out during 1971. The costs of the mailings averaged about 16 cents a piece, with every mailing returning much more than its cost.

Major press and public attention was finally focused on McGovern's un-predecented direct mail effort when he voluntarily disclosed on February 28, 1972, covering back to February 1. By then, $780,000 of the campaign's $1,255,900 in income had been received by mail from more than 40,000 con-tributors. The direct mail total included $264,251 from more than 6,000 Presidential Club members who gave $10 per month.

The campaign's goal was to raise $4 million from 100,000 small contribu-tors. By the convention, the campaign had raised $4.7 million from 110,000 contributors. (Many of these contributors had given as many as four times and there were 9,000 members of the $10 per month Presidential Club by then.) The $4.7 million in direct mail receipts was 75 percent of the total $6.4 million raised by the Washington headquarters—the almost $2 million received before April 7 and the $4.4 million covered in the GAO reports of the national com-mittees. Unfortunately, the statistics for small contributors are not compatible with other reported data. Campaign officials claimed that about $3.8 million (of the $4.7 million) came from small contributors; however, even if "small" includes all contributions under $500, the reported total to the national head-quarters was $3.2 million. This includes more than $1.2 million before April 7 and almost $2 million after that date. The direct mail claims may have been exaggerated, the definition of "small contributor" was perhaps different, or something else may have caused this discrepancy.

The mailing lists were also used for special, limited appeals. After McGovern's April 4 Wisconsin victory, telegram-type letters were sent to 70,000 previous supporters. After McGovern's Massachusetts victory, real telegrams were sent to 3,100 people who had given $50 or more in response to earlier mail appeals. The wires cost $1.30 each and arrived on April 26, the day after the primary. The wires asked contributors to make a special effort—loan or contribution— for Ohio. Contributions totalling more than $100,000 were received from 58 per-cent of the telegram recipients; less than one percent of them specified that their money was a loan. The lists were also used in the nonprimary states, as a starting point to find supporters and begin building grass-roots organizations.

Five concerts, organized and produced by Warren Beatty, reportedly raised a total of $1 million. The two largest concerts were the first, in California, and the last, in New York. The April 15 Los Angeles concert starred Barbra Streisand, James Taylor, Carole King, and Quincy Jones, and the ushers in the $100 per seat section included Beatty, Shirley MacLaine, Jack Nicholson, Julie Christie, James Earl Jones, and about two dozen other movie stars. There were 16,000 in the audience and the concert reportedly netted $300,000.

The New York concert in June, "Together for McGovern," brought together three famous acts that had split up: Peter, Paul, and Mary; Simon and Garfunkel; and Nichols and May. There were 19,500 people in the audience and a gross take of about $450,000. The Maidson Square Garden concert was followed by a dinner for performers and large contributors at the Four Seasons restaurant.

Picnics were held at the Hickory Hill home of Ethel Kennedy and on lawns across the country. Volunteers called thousands of Democrats to solicit funds. Literature tables were placed around Manhattan to seek contributions from passers-by. Several hundred thousand dollars were raised by the sale of specially prepared works of art, many of them donated by the artists.

The campaign's more ordinary fund-raising events included an August 1971, $2.50-per-plate luncheon for 250 people in Green Bay, Wisconsin; a $35-per-plate roast beef dinner for 1,800 at the San Francisco Hilton in early June 1972; and an exclusive party for about 40 people at the New York Park Avenue apartment of Mr. and Mrs. Jack Kaplan in early May 1972, where $963,000 in checks and pledges was reported publicly as received. (This was an exaggeration since some of the money counted to inflate the report had been given much earlier.)

More unusual events included a February 16, New York dinner featuring a special musical revue by Alan Jay Lerner, where $110,000 was raised from the sale of more than 1,000 tickets at $60 to $100 each. Eleven days later, a "public dinner" featuring the same show raised $50,000. In Philadelphia, in late May, McGovern supporters organized a 50-hour tennis marathon—at which tennis star Arthur Ashe appeared—to raise $5,000 ($100 per hour) for the New Jersey and California primaries.

Responding to one fund-raising idea, more than 1,000 people paid $10 each to see the candidate's house in the District of Columbia, causing a traffic problem for blocks in all directions. They also met Eleanor McGovern, and many bought McGovern sweatshirts, at $5 each. They could also participate in an auction featuring such items as: a week at a home on Cape Cod; tennis lessons from Allie Ritzenberg; hamburgers with Redskins' great Ray Schoenke; and woodcuts by Israeli artist Yankel Ginzburg.

Flow. The McGovern prenomination campaign raised virtually all the money that was wanted or needed, but the flow of contributions was not smooth nor at times equal to the campaign's immediate costs. Big loans were sometimes an absolute necessity if the campaign was to meet a planned expenditure.

In mid-1971 McGovern's base of small contributors and the few large contributors provided sufficient income to meet necessary costs. By mid-December McGovern reportedly boasted that the campaign had raised $1.2 million, spent $1 million, never been in debt, and could raise its second million within six weeks. Actually, it took four months to raise the second million, making McGovern's total pre-April 7 income just under $2 million. This was a difficult time for the campaign; as activity and expense increased, money did not. The campaign took out newspaper ads asking for money around April 9, hoping to capitalize on the Wisconsin results. The increased flow of contributions fell behind the campaign's expanding schedule of primaries and expenditures, and in mid-April the campaign was $184,000 in debt.

After McGovern's Massachusetts and Pennsylvania showings on April 25, contributions surged. A daily record of $110,000 in mail returns was received shortly after the Massachusetts primary. May was a good month, ending with a new record of $235,743 in mail receipts for May 30-31. But the California campaign's appetite was bigger than income, and loans, including Mott's $100,000 one, were needed.

McGovern's California victory did not result in an upsurge of contributions. His winning margin was only five percent and a formal challenge to his newly won 271 delegates was begun almost immediately. That California challenge cast a shadow over the remaining month-and-a-half of the prenomination period, both politically and financially. Large contributors were invited to the convention where the "one for four" repayment program was organized; about $1.3 million in loans and close to $200,000 in contribution pledges were received during convention week.

Muskie

Edmund Muskie formally announced his candidacy for the Democratic presidential nomination on January 4, 1972. Not quite four months later, the one-time acknowledged Democratic front-runner withdrew from further primaries although he did not formally give up his candidacy until the eve of the Democratic Convention. Muskie's formal campaign for the presidency cost approximately $7 million.

In a sense Muskie was an unannounced candidate for almost four years. In the wake of Humphrey's 1968 defeat, Muskie, his running mate, became a leading party spokesman. He gained particular stature with a nationally televised speech made for the Democrats on the eve of the 1970 congressional elections, in which he took the role of the reasonable man in contrast to the harsh rhetoric that had been offered by both Nixon and Agnew in a Republican broadcast preceding his. The Muskie telecast cost $25,000, most of it as a loan from W. Averell Harriman, later repaid. And the speech gave Muskie a favorable start on his 1972 goal.

Serious fund-raising efforts for Muskie date from November 1969, while he was still pondering whether or not to seek the presidency. He authorized a friend, Matthew Lifflander, a New York lawyer then working for the Hertz Corporation, to scout for early funds. Within a month Lifflander reported receiving pledges totalling $125,000 from six sources, in individual amounts ranging up to $25,000. These pledges were honored in 1970. Encouraged by this, Muskie authorized another fund-raising effort in Washington, D.C., organized by attorney Milton Semer.

These early fund-raising efforts were aided by an easy race for Senate reelection in November 1970; about half of the $200,000 raised for Muskie's reelection was channeled into the presidential effort.

The announced campaign began with plans for a major fund-raising drive
in early 1972. The need for early money was dictated by the strategy that
Muskie should actively contest all 23 primaries. For Muskie, this strategy
meant staging four major primary campaigns in a period of about six weeks—
New Hampshire, Florida, and Illinois in March, and Wisconsin in early April.
None of his opponents planned for more than two primaries during the period
from March 7 to April 4. Muskie also had a Washington headquarters operation
that was the most costly of any Democratic candidate. Cutbacks were made
from time to time, and just two weeks before the New Hampshire primary,
some staff members were let go, some took pay cuts, and some became unpaid
volunteers.

Voluntary Disclosures. The matter of voluntary disclosure became a particularly divisive issue among members of the Muskie campaign staff when, in
early 1972, Muskie publicly refused to disclose the names of his contributors.
He had adopted a policy of nondisclosure more than a year earlier following a
controversy over the source and intent of funds going into the Muskie Election
Committee (MEC).

The MEC was successor to a Muskie for Vice President Committee that had
continued to deal with 1968 campaign bills; it had been formed in February
1970, and a balance of $7,630 from the vice-presidential account transferred
to it. When disclosures of the MEC's receipts and expenditures were later made,
questions arose as to whether it was operating solely on behalf of his Senate reelection, as Muskie staff aides had claimed, or whether it also included presidential campaign activity. On the one hand, contributions had been received
from the Democratic Senatorial Campaign Committee, for example, which gives
only to senatorial campaigns. At the same time, such expenses were listed as
flights on Northwest Airlines, which did not fly to Maine, and all but one of the
nearly 100 individuals who had contributed $500 or more came from outside
Maine. The report seemed to reflect deliberate commingling of senatorial and
presidential campaigns funds to obscure clarity, but was a first if fumbling effort
at voluntary disclosure.

When the names of the contributors to the MEC became known, conservative columnist Kevin Phillips used the occasion to attack Muskie for being
financed by "celluloid sex."[3] The charge stemmed from the fact that some of
his major contributors were motion picture executives. This alarmed some contributors who were concerned about the effects of such a charge on their
businesses, and led the Muskie campaign to adopt the policy of nondisclosure.
Muskie, did, however, disclose his personal finances; the February 1971 report
showed his net worth at $153,141.

In mid-January 1972 Muskie fueled the growing controversy over voluntary
disclosure, when a reporter asked him why he would not disclose the names of
contributors to his campaign. Muskie's response, that if he did, he'd be out of

the race, started what became a major issue in his campaign. McGovern capitalized on the statement by announcing he would voluntarily disclose the names of all contributors to his campaign and challenged all presidential candidates to do the same. Paul McCloskey had already disclosed, and the challenge was picked up first by John Lindsay. Nixon, Henry Jackson, and Muskie said they would not disclose, while Hubert Humphrey and George Wallace effectively avoided the issue for a time. Humphrey then decided to disclose, sensing the potential damage to Muskie. The spotlight went to Muskie and stayed focused on him, in spite of his urgings that the press also look to other candidates, particularly Nixon. But the pressure only increased, since the Democrats and the press could do little about Nixon, and front-runner Muskie was running on the slogan, "Trust Muskie."

The issue badly split the Muskie staff, diverting its energies at the height of the primary campaigns. The political and media advisers tended to support disclosure. The latter group was particularly sensitive to an ad campaign being mounted at that time by Stewart Mott, a vigorous Muskie foe, on the issue of disclosure; the Mott ads, appearing in newspapers around the country, also revived the old "celluloid sex" charges. Mott spent $39,000 on the anti-Muskie activities.

Most of Muskie's financial advisers, however, tended to reject disclosure. They argued that there had been either an assumed or explicit promise of anonymity to some donors, and that it would be a betrayal to reveal names. They argued further that in the case of some contributors, particularly Republicans and those with government contracts, there could be fear of retaliation by the Nixon administration. Moreover, the MEC disclosure had soured some on the value of disclosure, as suspicion continued about its completeness. Dissension in the Muskie camp between the pro- and anti-disclosure groups grew to such a point that for a period of about two weeks in late March, shortly before the important Wisconsin primary, other campaign activity was seriously affected.

Muskie finally announced that he would disclose on March 27. The disclosure covered $2,027,840 in receipts from 13,982 contributors for the 15-month period from November 1, 1970, when the MEC disclosure ended, to January 31, 1972. Allegations regarding its completeness and honesty began within hours and continued after Muskie's candidacy. These allegations resulted, in part, from the campaign's own earlier boasts that nondisclosure was necessary to protect Republican contributors, yet no known Republicans were on the list. Muskie's disclosure contained several major limitations: the March 27 report was the only one the campaign made, so contributors in the February 1 to April 6 period were never revealed; the disclosures covered the Washington headquarters accounts, so contributions made directly to state committees, of which there were many, were not included; and loans were not included, except one, unexplained, for $5,500.

Because of the limitations, it is possible that the alleged missing contributions were made to state committees, or after February 1, or involved loans. But it is also possible that the Muskie campaign, as was charged, engaged in adjusting the records before the disclosure was made. Two major dissembling schemes were charged. One was that money was taken from the national accounts about to be disclosed and sent to state committees, which then treated it not as transfers of funds but as original, direct contributions from individuals. The campaign was known to have had committees in Rhode Island, for example, a state without any reporting laws, where it was claimed that contributions were concealed. The other alleged scheme was to convert some contributions into loans for the purpose of disclosure and then reconvert them back into contributions after the disclosure. Muskie campaign officials denied both charges, but claimed that in some cases they had received money without knowing whether it was meant to be a loan or a contribution.

One campaign official said that all large donors who had been promised confidentiality were personally contacted and their permission asked, but that even the "five or six" who refused were disclosed. Another official said that no names were left out, but that amounts of contributions were reduced. Yet, another official referred to the two weeks between the announced decision to disclose and the actual disclosure as a "mad period of renegotiation," implying that those negotiations involved changes. Long after the campaign, a prominent fund raiser said that he had given his personal pledge to "three or four" people not to disclose their names, that he had done it on his own without consulting Muskie, and that he simply would not violate that pledge.

Several anti-Nixon, establishment Republicans contributed to Muskie, but wanted to maintain their Republican ties, so sought to have their names taken off his list. Among the explanations of how this was accomplished was that the contributions were simply treated as cash and not reported. Several campaign officials claimed that some Republican money was actually returned, while one said that suggestions to return the money were discussed at the staff level but rejected. Others implied that perhaps $200,000 was not reported because it was going to be returned when the campaign received promised replacement contributions. It was not returned because the replacement contributions evaporated in the face of Muskie's poor showing in the April 4 Wisconsin primary. A final suggestion was that, because of disclosure, some Republican pledges were not honored.

The only certain ending to Muskie's voluntary disclosure is that the $2 million disclosed did not cover all the money the Muskie campaign received in the pre-FECA period. Whether there was deliberate manipulation of money and records prior to the published disclosure will probably never be known, nor the precise amount of the undisclosed income. Muskie may have wanted to fully disclose his sources of income, but became compromised by his fund raisers and contributors.

Costs. Of the total of approximately $7 million spent on the Muskie campaign, an estimated $5 to $5.5 million was spent by the central committees in Washington, with $1.5 to $2 million spent by the various state and local committees.

Over $500,000 was spent on media time and another $200,000 on media production. Some $2.5 million was spent on the Washington headquarters operation, and $100,000 was spent on direct mail.

The FCC compilation of primary radio and television spending[4] shows Muskie spent a total of $541,623 for media time in 1972, more than the Humphrey total ($517,342) and not quite half as much as McGovern ($1,175,464). The FCC total for Muskie included $332,573 for television, all but $28,025 for nonnetwork time, and $209,050 for radio, all but $2,900 for nonnetwork time. The $28,025 for television network time was for Muskie's ten-minute announcement speech on January 4. The reported cost at the time was $32,000, but this included the cost of editing nine minutes out of the Glen Campbell show, for which the campaign had to pay, to get the ten-minute prime time slot at the end of that show.

Virtually all the nonnetwork media total of $486,000 can be accounted for by states: an estimated $65,000 in New Hampshire; $165,000 in Florida; about $60,000 for television in Illinois; $128,000 in Wisconsin; $25,000 in Massachusetts; and $50,000 in Pennsylvania. Of the first four figures, all except Illinois represent more than the base amount in the Democrats' voluntary spending limit agreement, although only Muskie's New Hampshire spending hit the upper limit of the base amount plus the $47,333 bonus. However, the agreement specified that the bonus could be used in no more than three states, so if Muskie had remained in primary competition he would have been unable to use the bonus in any remaining primary state. This might not have been significant, since the only major media state remaining was California, in which the difference between the $413,000 base and a $460,333 possible maximum might not have been important. On the other hand, the Muskie campaign wasted a $47,333 bonus in order to spend only $11,000 above the base of $117,000 in Wisconsin. Although Wisconsin was "do or die," the full bonus was not spent.

Of the estimated $200,000 for media production costs, some $150,000 went to Robert Squier, Muskie's media consultant, who had been selected on the basis of his production of Muskie's 1970 election-eve speech. However, Squier left the campaign after the Wisconsin primary so the $150,000 does not include media production costs for Massachusetts and Pennsylvania, nor production costs for media other than radio and television. In addition, some non-

Squier production costs for the Florida and Wisconsin primaries were incurred when a major argument over Squier's work developed into a major conflict.

The Muskie direct mail campaign spent $99,113 for six mailings between May 1971 and January 1972, covering a total of 819,516 pieces.[k] The gross yield was about $200,000,[l] not counting the mail costs.

The $2.5 million spent at the Muskie headquarters in Washington can be accounted for chronologically: at least $70,000 in 1970, some $1.2 million in 1971, and about $1.3 million in 1972. The Muskie headquarters was one of the most expensively staffed of any of the Democratic contenders. The first office opened in early 1970, with six staffers. In August the staff grew to 12 with 10 summer interns, a figure consistent with the $8,000 per month cost reported at the time. Using the $8,000 per month figure for June-December and presuming somewhat lower costs for the first five months of the year, total 1970 office costs were in the $70,000-$85,000 range.

In 1971 the campaign cost about $90,000 per month, which included $40,000 for staff and almost as much for travel. The campaign's most consistently used budget figure for 1971 was $1.5 million. As Muskie's political and fund-raising problems emerged in the spring and early summer, budget estimates were reduced in stages to $1 million. By fall, headquarters costs were up to $100,000 per month and they continued to rise during the last few months of the year. Using an average of $100,000 per month for the year gives a $1.2 million cost for 1971. This is consistent with other data, detailed below. Field operations began in September, so most 1971 costs were for national headquarters.

From January 1972 through April and the end of Muskie's active campaign, the Washington costs were $300,000 per month; the staff alone accounted for about $100,000 per month. For the two-month inactive phase of the campaign, from late April through the convention in late June, headquarters costs neared $100,000 bringing the 1972 total to $1.3 million. While these costs are inflated because of the primary-related expenses that were paid from Washington accounts, the Muskie campaign had perhaps the most expensive headquarters operation among Democrats in prenomination history.

Muskie's travel expenses included the costs of an Electra jet, purchased from Northwest Airlines by a friend and leased to the campaign.[m] Some of the costs of campaign travel were later reimbursed by the press and Secret Service who travelled on the plane.

---

[k]For data returns, see Appendix G.

[l]Revealed after Muskie's withdrawal from active campaigning in "Muskie: 'It Couldn't Be Done Without the Money,'"*National Journal,* May 13, 1972, p. 805.

[m]The charter service, which reportedly owned only this one plane, was a subsidiary of the Pierce Life Insurance Company, owned by Joseph Albritton. Albritton, a wealthy Texas Democrat, is one of those who others claimed was a major Muskie contributor but campaign officials have denied he gave money.

The New Hampshire primary cost about $225,000. The spending was heavily concentrated near the end of the campaign; two-thirds of the total was spent in the four weeks before the primary. More than half of the New Hampshire total was for radio and television; of the $65,333 ceiling allowed by the Democrats' voluntary limit, Muskie spent $64,990. During the last two weeks, most television money went for time on Boston stations, chosen because of their deep penetration into populous southern New Hampshire. Boston's much higher cost—about $1,440 for a 30-second television spot compared with $48 on a New Hampshire station—meant that with spending limited, the campaign had to choose between five to six weeks of television with only a few spots a week, or a saturation two-week campaign. The latter was chosen. The radio campaign lasted three weeks.

Other New Hampshire costs included:

Print media	$25,000-$30,000
Literature and buttons	25,000- 30,000
Telephones	25,000- 30,000
Staff	25,000
Mileage and other expenses	5,000
Election Day (drivers, coffee, etc.)	3,000- 4,000
Key punching and labelling	3,000- 4,000
Rent	6,000
Office machinery & furniture	2,000

Added to the $65,000 television-radio spending, these New Hampshire costs total almost 90 percent of the $225,000 spent. Virtually all money came from Washington, and no significant amounts were raised locally. A *New York Times* survey of campaign spending[5] quoted a $290,000 cost estimate of a campaign official, with further costs attributable to New Hampshire—for candidate travel and other costs included in headquarters totals—bringing the total to $350,000. In view of the large gap between the campaign's known total cost and the available detailed data, these higher figures are more probable, but they cannot be verified.

Records filed under Florida law show a total of $250,181 spent by Muskie committees in that state's primary. However, Muskie's state manager said the total spending was about $300,000, while the national campaign treasurer said Florida cost $436,000. Including headquarters costs attributable to that state, the figure could reach $525,000.[6] Some reports and at least one Muskie campaign official have placed the total cost of the Florida primary in the $650,000-$750,000 range. These latter figures seem extraordinarily high and would mean that up to twice as much was spent from Washington as was reported spent in Florida.

Media spending in Florida was between $150,000 and $165,000. The campaign paid Amtrack $5,852 for a whistle-stop train trip from Miami to Jacksonville, the first and only such trip for Muskie and the first in Florida since FDR's campaign in 1932. Related costs brought the "Sunshine Special" total to about $40,000.

Total spending in the Illinois primary was about $220,000; a cutback was made during the last ten days from the original budget of $260,000 after the campaign judged that Illinois seemed safely won. Among the expenditures that are known are the following:

Television (ten days maximum; less in Chicago)	$ 60,000
Mail	30,000
Billboards	5,000
Staff payroll	30,000
Field staff	20,000
Total	$145,000

Muskie spent close to $600,000 on the Wisconsin primary. The centrally controlled campaign received a total of $338,000, about $90,000 of which was raised locally while the rest came from Washington. Direct spending by the central campaign totalled $340,000. A $20,000 deposit for telephones was paid directly from Washington, as were $26,000 in bills outstanding at the end of the campaign. An additional $134,000 was reported spent by local campaign committees. The salary, living and travel expenses of the state campaign manager, amounting to $20,000, were paid from Washington during the six months he was in Wisconsin. Some direct mail for Wisconsin, costing between $30,000 and $40,000, and $3,000 in expenses for advancemen, were also funded by the national campaign.

Television and radio cost $128,002, with $6,000 in local media production. One newspaper insert cost $9,000. Some $25,000 went for literature and buttons. Aside from media, the largest expenditure was $70,000 for telephones. This included a 75-telephone bank in Milwaukee for one month and smaller telephone banks in other cities. Staff salaries in Wisconsin were running $5,000 per week by the end of the campaign. The total salary cost, not including the campaign manager, may have been as high as $50,000. An additional $2,000 was paid in per diem expenses to organizers in the last week of the campaign.

After Wisconsin Muskie campaign expenses were cut back sharply. The remaining efforts were financed mainly from funds raised within the primary states. About $75,000 was spent in Massachusetts, of which some $18,000 came from Washington. Media spending in Massachusetts, all of it during the last three weeks of the campaign, came to $25,000. No salaries were paid.

Certain other costs were picked up by the Muskie delegate slate, which included practically all prominent Democratic office holders in the state; they provided the use of their staffs, telephones, and other facilities. Even some direct expenditures on Muskie's behalf were paid in this way. For example, the Muskie slate in the 9th Congressional District spent $350 on newspaper ads and distributed 30,000 flyers during the last week of the campaign to try to counter the McGovern surge.

Muskie's Pennsylvania campaign cost $176,050 according to reports filed under state law, with $15,000 reported from national headquarters. Operatives have said, however, that $60,000 of national money was sent in, and debts remained afterwards. The campaign spent $30,000 between January and April, with the remainder spent in the final four weeks. Most money went for advertising and printing. The campaign in Pennsylvania shifted from television to radio for financial reasons: television spending was $20,000, radio at least $30,000. Campaign literature included 102 different sample ballots. The field operation cost about $36,000. State reports show $1,500 paid to each of 14 coordinators a week before the election—presumably part of an all-out election day effort, for which $35,000 was known to have been spent in Pittsburgh alone.

Although Muskie withdrew from active competition two days after the April 25 Massachusetts and Pennsylvania primaries, some money had already been spent in a few other primary states: $105,637 in Ohio, $16,500 in Oregon, and $200,000 in California, where Muskie workers had been active for some ten months before. Additional indirect expenditures were made on Muskie's behalf. Senator John Tunney, for example, spent $13,000 on a Quayle poll in December 1971 to test California reaction to a Muskie endorsement, and shortly thereafter did in fact endorse Muskie, giving his campaign a big boost.

Spending was light in the nonprimary states, since the strategy had aimed at the primaries. Muskie spent about $10,000 in Iowa and slightly more in Arizona, $3,000 in Kansas, $5,000 in Missouri, $2,000 in Nevada, and $2,000 in Oklahoma. Overall spending by the national campaign in the nonprimary states was estimated at not much above $50,000.

Some $100,000 was spent at the National Convention in Miami, including $16,000 for hotel expenses and an estimated $11,000 for telephones. The campaign also paid travel costs to bring some supporters to Miami.

Sources. The Muskie campaign raised about $7 million in contributions and loans. However, because of the gap in his disclosure reports—between the voluntary disclosure that ended on January 31, 1972, and the beginning of the FECA on April 7—the sources of about one-half of the total are unknown. About $2 million was covered by the incomplete voluntary disclosures, some $1 million was raised in the April 7 to postconvention period, and $200,000 was raised after the campaign to reduce or eliminate debt. The remaining money was raised, either nationally or locally, during the February 1 to April 6 period, or consisted of loans later converted to gifts.

Muskie's voluntary disclosure for 1972, covering the 15 months from November 1, 1970 to January 31, 1972, listed 13,982 contributors who gave a total of $2,027,840. This represents more than one-quarter of the total the campaign raised, and includes most of the campaign's most successful fund-raising period, giving the best picture available of the sources of Muskie's campaign financing.

According to these voluntary disclosure figures, contributions of $500 or more accounted for 78 percent of the total ($1,588,645) and came from just six percent of the contributors (846). At the $1,000-and-over level, the number of contributors was 493, and the amount accounted for is a very high 69 percent ($1,406,505). The $5,000-and-over category accounted for 41 percent of the income ($840,454) from 96 givers. Finally, at the level of $10,000 and over, 29 known contributors accounted for 23 percent of the total ($475,993).

Muskie's FECA reports, reflected in the GAO's published listings, cover a little more than $1 million in receipts. A full 33 percent of the income (almost $350,000) came from loans (excluding one that was repaid during this period), and two lenders accounted for 30 percent ($324,000). An additional 26 percent of the post-FECA income came from $500-and-over contributors, of which five percent ($56,424) was from contributions of $10,000 and over and another seven percent ($62,653) from those in the $5,000 to $9,999 range. Refunds and miscellaneous income accounted for at least ten percent of the income and transfers (from nonreporting committees) accounted for about five percent. At the most, 15 percent of the income in this period came from contributions of under $100 and seven percent came from those in the $100 to $500 range.

The early fund-raising efforts by Matthew Lifflander produced a pledge of $25,000 from Arnold Picker, chairman of the Executive Committee of United Artists, who with his wife and nephew over the following two years would give Muskie a total of $79,893. The Pickers also loaned the campaign $183,000 and later forgave the loans, bringing their total contribution to over $262,000. They were Muskie's largest individual contributors by a wide margin.

The next largest listed contributor was Joseph Wilson of Rochester, New York, former Xerox chairman, who gave $50,000. However, Cornelius Dutcher, president of Steam Powers System, of La Jolla, California, who is listed for a $25,000 contribution on the voluntary disclosure, said that his total Muskie contribution was "more than $100,000." That would make Dutcher Muskie's second largest contributor. Immediately after Muskie withdrew from active campaigning, Dutcher took Muskie's San Diego money, most of which he probably provided, and turned it over to the California McGovern campaign.[n]

---

[n]Dutcher's total direct McGovern contributions were $49,000.

Mr. and Mrs. Joseph Filner of New York gave Muskie at least $71,000 and possibly $95,000. Although the data available make the total uncertain, they were still Muskie's third largest contributors. Mr. Filner is president of Noblemet International Company, metal traders.

Walter Koziol, president of Charmglow Products of Antioch, gave Muskie $26,000 prior to April 7 and $10,400 to the Wisconsin campaign, for a total of $36,400. Chicago attorney Harold L. Perlman was listed for $32,500 in Muskie's voluntary disclosure and an additional post-April 7 $2,500 in FECA reports, as well as a $1,000 loan after April 7.

Other Muskie contributors in the $20,000 or more category include Mr. and Mrs. Alexander P. Hixon of Pasadena, California, who are listed at $28,900; Irving Harris of Highland Park, Illinois, a stockbroker, who gave $25,424; and David Carley of Madison, Wisconsin, an Inland Steel executive who gave and loaned a total of $50,000.

Confusion and controversy surround Carley's political and financial involvement in the Muskie campaign.[7] A former gubernatorial candidate, Carley was originally chosen to head Muskie's Wisconsin campaign. Later, the campaign named a co-chairman, Richard Cudahy, heir to the meat-packing company and a former state party chairman. Unfortunately for Muskie, Carley and Cudahy were not political friends. Then the trouble was compounded when the national campaign sent in an "outside" campaign manager, Harold Ickes, an experienced political operative (and son of Roosevelt's famous Secretary of the Interior) who is Cudahy's cousin.

At this point Carley started asking publicly what had happended to the $50,000 he said he had given the campaign. The financial reports filed under state law in Wisconsin listed a $5,000 contribution and a $44,000 loan. Muskie's voluntary disclosure, however, had shown a $20,000 contribution from Carley, suggesting either a $29,000 loan or a $20,000 national gift in addition to the $49,000 given and loaned in Wisconsin.

Norman Cousins, editor of *World Magazine* in 1972 (formerly of *Saturday Review*) is listed for a $15,000 contribution. Clark Clifford, former Secretary of Defense, gave a pre-April 7 contribution of $10,000. The politically active Dunfey family from New England (who are hotel owners) were also Muskie contributors: each of the five brothers—Gerald, John, Robert, Walter, and William—gave $3,000 for a total family gift of $15,000. Joseph Sinay of Los Angeles, chairman of RB Industries and also an active fund raiser, is listed for $12,000 but is known to have given in the $30,000 range. James Goodbody, a Chevy Chase, Maryland stockbroker who worked as an unpaid volunteer with the Muskie National Finance Committee, is listed with his wife for a $10,100 contribution. Texas oilman J.R. Parten gave $13,000; he also gave $42,000 to McGovern. Texas realtor, Chester J. Reed, gave $10,000.

In his voluntary disclosures, Muskie listed only one loan—a small one of $5,500—but in the FECA reports, loans make up about one-third of the income.

These include the Pickers' $183,000 and $115,000 from Angelo G. Geocaris, a Chicago attorney, who was Muskie's chief Illinois fund raiser.

The Geocaris debt was a key point in negotiations surrounding Muskie's Illinois delegates after his withdrawal. The McGovern campaign said it would assume that debt in exchange for the delegates, but Muskie and Senator Adlai Stevenson, his Illinois chairman, would not release the delegates. In early October a letter signed by Muskie and Stevenson asked Illinois supporters for money to pay off the debt, explaining that they were not having a fund-raising event because they did not want to compete with McGovern and Dan Walker, the Democratic gubernatorial candidate in Illinois. The letter referred to a $135,000 debt of which $60,000 had been given to the national committees; the result of the fund-raising letter is not known, but the national campaign listed a $115,000 outstanding debt to Geocaris.

Three primary states provide interesting glimpses of locally raised income after April 7. In Massachusetts at least $100,000 was raised, of which about one-half was sent out of the state and about one-half spent on the state campaign. During the Pennsylvania primary, stories were published about Governor Shapp's vigorous efforts to pressure state employees into raising money for Muskie. Stories included claims of quotas set for employees of the state departments to buy $100 tickets to fund-raising dinners. In all, three fund-raising dinners (at prices from $30 per person to $100 per person) raised $200,000, about one-half of Shapp's goal. But all the money did not go to the Muskie campaign. Earlier, Shapp had said he wanted to raise at least $200,000 primarily to help Muskie, with any residue to be used to reduce the state party committee's debt. Financial reports of the Shapp-organized "Campaign '72 Committee" show $124,025 given to the main state Muskie committee, and $50,000 to the state party committee. (Later, the "Campaign '72 Committee" also gave $8,000 to the McGovern campaign.) The $124,025 given to the Muskie campaign from these dinners represented 70 percent of the total reported spent by the campaign and comprised most of the money raised locally.

For Ohio, one detail is illustrative. Almost one-quarter of the total $105,637 reported spent came from the UAW Voluntary Committee Action Program. The UAW's $24,995 came in equal contributions of $4,999 to each of five Muskie committees; with the under-$5,000 contributions the UAW avoided the new FECA requirement to report gifts over that total within 48 hours.[o]

The only other primary state that locally raised significant amounts of money was California: all of the estimated $200,000 spent by Muskie's committee came from within the state. In addition, California was a major

---

[o]The UAW's Ohio contributions were about two-thirds of all the labor money Muskie received. Business and professional groups gave even less than labor—a total of about $5,000 on the record.

exporter of money to the national campaign before 1972. In 1972 there was an agreement to let money raised remain in the state for use in the primary.

Fund Raising. Muskie's major fund raisers were Arnold Picker, Sumner Redstone, a Boston theatre executive, and Berl Bernhard, a Washington attorney who was also the national campaign manager.

Picker and Redstone directed the campaign's fund-raising efforts throughout 1971. Redstone was the key person for the more than $100,000 raised in his home state of Massachusetts. Bernhard took on fund-raising duties late in 1971, when money was needed for the upcoming rush of primary campaigning. In December 1971 and January-February 1972 Bernhard was credited with a major role in raising $1.5 million.

One effort to be aimed at middle-level givers in 1971 was cancelled after some embarassing premature publicity. At a mid-April meeting, Bernhard discussed plans for "Muskie-Century '71," a program aimed at $100 contributors. Following the meeting, one of those in attendance, Washington lawyer Robert H. Neiman, wrote an unauthorized letter to 75-80 friends enlisting their support. In candid terms he discussed the need for input somewhere between the large contributors ("older businessmen who are generally short on useful ideas") and the small "idealistic money" (which "does not carry with it . . . either lasting assistance to the campaign or significant perspective . . ."). A copy of the letter reached the *Washington Star*, embarrassed campaign officials disavowed it, and the project was scrapped.[8]

One other fund raiser who received a good deal of press attention was William King, a Los Angeles lawyer who was a long-time Nixon supporter and Republican fund raiser. He became disenchanted with Nixon, however, and in November 1971 switched his efforts to the Muskie campaign. The timing of King's switch announcement was delayed, ironically, because he was one of the organizers of a $500-per-plate Republican dinner in Los Angles on November 9—one of 20 such events held around the country that day to kick off the Republicans' 1972 fund raising and the Nixon reelection effort.

The high-price dinner was a successful technique for Muskie; he raised close to $1 million over an eight-month period at ten such affairs. The first of these was in September 1971. Muskie raised $150,000 during a California trip then, at least some of which came from a $250-per-person dinner with some Hollywood stars attending. Later, Stanley Goldstein of Providence, Rhode Island organized a $500-per-couple affair that netted at least $23,000.

In late November a $100-per-person clambake was held in Maine. Two months later the most successful fund-raising event in Maine's history occurred. About 700 people attended a $150-per-person dinner (with a private reception for $1000 contributors) that raised $150,000.

In early January, following Muskie's formal announcement, more than $50,000 was raised at a dinner in New York City. In late February Muskie returned to California for two dinners, one in Los Angeles and one in San Francisco. Close to 500 attended each dinner, priced at $250 per person, which together grossed $230,000. On March 1-2 dinners were held in New York and Boston at $500 to $1,000 per plate, which reportedly raised $150,000 and $60,000, respectively.

On April 17 Muskie's by-then disintegrating campaign got a lift from an unexpectedly successful $125-per-person dinner in Washington, D.C. (with the usual private cocktail party for $1,000 contributors), co-chaired by Averell Harriman and Eunice Shriver. The organizers had hoped at least 500 would attend, but 1,200, including six governors, nine senators, and 21 representatives, did so, and the affair raised more than $150,000. Three days later dinners were also held in Pennsylvania and Massachusetts.

Muskie was unresponsive to the special pleadings of potential or actual very large contributors. The only favor any contributor is known to have received was access to the candidate. A story is told that fund raiser and contributor Joseph Sinay asked for an audience with Muskie at the convention to tell him he opposed Muskie's participation in the challenge to McGovern's California delegates; he got his audience, after waiting about 12 hours on Sunday, and said his piece—which was ignored.

Two instances of corporate contributions to the Muskie campaign were disclosed after the Senate Watergate Committee's investigation of the 1972 campaigns.[P] Diamond International Corporation's vice president, Ray Dubrowin, made a $1,000 contribution that was drawn on the corporate account. Both Dubrowin and Diamond International were found guilty and fined. However, the Hertz Corporation was not prosecuted for contributions it allegedly made to the Muskie campaign. Apparently the former president of Hertz International Division (who was a volunteer in the Washington, D.C. Muskie campaign office) arranged for assistance in the renting of cars to designated Muskie campaign workers. The plan that was followed involved waiving deposits and holding accumulated bills until after the primaries. Initially, the services allegedly were provided by Hertz with the intent of writing off the bills as uncollectible. However, the controller of Herts Corp. refused to do this, and settlement of the bill then went through a complicated process. The Hertz Corp. hired outside lawyers who, it was alleged, subsequently made contributions in similar or identical sums to the Muskie campaign. Their contributions were claimed to total the amount owed (and paid) to the Hertz Corp. for rental expenses, although several of the lawyers denied this.

[P]See Senate Select Committee on Presidential Campaign Activities, *Final Report*, No. 93-981, 93rd Cong., 2d sess., June 1974 (Washington, D.C.: U.S. Government Printing Office, 1974) pp. 465, 473-81. See also **Corporate Prosecutions** (at Chapter 13 below) for a fuller account of the Diamond International Corp. contribution.

Debts. During 1971 and through the Wisconsin primary, Muskie campaign debts were generally paid off within 30 days. At that point, however, with Muskie's candidacy evaporating, debts began to build up and after the convention totalled about $350,000, including $200,000 owed to creditors and $150,000 to lenders. (This did not include the Picker loans, which were never carried as debts.)

There are conflicting accounts about the role played by the Muskie debt after Eagleton had left the McGovern ticket and a replacement was being sought. Even before the convention, there were reports that Muskie would agree to be the vice-presidential candidate if McGovern would assume responsibility for the debts, and these were revived in the wake of the Eagleton departure. Theodore White in *The Making of the President 1972* says that Muskie turned down the McGovern offer of the vice-presidential spot "for family reasons."[9]

By December 1972 the debt of the national Muskie committee had been reduced to $115,000. At this point the campaign offered to pay off the remaining bills at 25 cents on the dollar, except for creditors of less than $200, who would be paid in full.

Also paid in full were bills owed to federally regulated business, such as airlines and telephone companies. In early 1973 the total debt of all reporting Muskie committees was still about $340,000.

After Muskie's withdrawal, one fund raiser estimated that perhaps 25 percent of his financial supporters gave enthusiastically to McGovern; 25 percent gave token amounts but only because they were Democrats; 25 percent gave to Nixon; and 25 percent sat out the general election.

Humphrey

Minnesota Senator Hubert H. Humphrey entered the 1972 Democratic presidential contest in the fall of 1971, and his formal announcement came on January 10, 1972. Humphrey's nine-month campaign cost about $4.7 million, of which more than $900,000 was still owed more than three years after the campaign ended. Most of the debts were outstanding loans from individuals, and in late 1975 the campaign offered to settle those debts for three or four cents on the dollar.

Humphrey's candidacy was related to the successes and failures of other candidates. During 1969 and 1970 Humphrey was virtually ignored in presidential speculation, which centered around Kennedy and Muskie. By 1971 Chappaquiddick had seriously dimmed Kennedy's star, Muskie was having trouble getting his campaign launched, and Humphrey had regained attention and a favorable position by his convincing victory in the 1970 Minnesota Senate race.[q]

---

[q]He defeated popular Republican Congressman Clark MacGregor (later to become chairman of the CRP) by more than 200,000 votes for the seat given up by Eugene McCarthy.

During the fall of 1971 Humphrey travelled extensively (15,000 miles in one week in October), speaking at party functions on behalf of Democratic candidates and proving his campaigning abilities and popularity with the rank and file. Humphrey's original strategy was based on the assumption that the early primaries would be inconclusive and that all the candidates would be bloodied by the battles. He hoped to enter and do well in the late primaries, principally California, and then face a National Convention battle with Kennedy, who would have avoided all the primaries. When Muskie's campaign floundered and in the absence of any other strong centrist candidate, Humphrey first revised his strategy to include the mid-spring primaries in his stronghold in the Midwest and then abandoned it entirely and decided to enter almost all the primaries, beginning in Florida.

After impressive showings in Florida and Wisconsin, Humphrey won four primaries (Pennsylvania, Ohio, Indiana, and West Virginia) between April 25 and May 9. But on May 16 he lost in two: he ran third in Michigan with only 16 percent of the vote, and he ran second in Maryland, 12 points behind Wallace and five points ahead of McGovern. Humphrey's last chance for the nomination hinged on California and he undertook an aggressive, hard-hitting campaign. He came within five percentage points of McGovern, after having been 15 to 20 points behind in the polls a few weeks earlier. After his California loss, Humphrey worked on rounding up delegates in the nonprimary states and on developing support for a delegate challenge to McGovern's California victory. When he lost that challenge on a floor vote on the first day of the convention, Humphrey formally withdrew as a candidate, and his name was not placed in nomination.

Money played an important role in Humphrey's campaign, but not in the way he anticipated. By August 1971 Humphrey was reported to have received unsolicited pledges totalling $4 million, but the figure was grossly exaggerated. In January 1972 the campaign claimed it was starting with a well-financed organization, prepared to campaign in strategic primaries and to spend up to $5 million. However, Humphrey found that not all of these pledges were redeemable: the campaign found it difficult to raise about $3.5 million; had to borrow almost $1.5 million, of which only $251,000 was paid back during the campaign; received at least $75,000 in services paid for by others; and suffered from insufficient funds for most of the prenomination period.

Voluntary Disclosure, FECA Reports, and the Watergate Committee's Report. Humphrey was not the main target when McGovern raised the voluntary disclosure issue late in the New Hampshire campaign, and little initial pressure was on him to disclose. At first he refused, planning to wait until other candidates did so, but changed his mind when disclosure became a hot issue. On March 14 Humphrey became the fourth candidate to disclose, covering the period from October 1, 1971 through March 10, 1972.

However, Humphrey's disclosure was not a complete record of his pre-April 7 finances. First, contributions received prior to October 1 were not included; the Watergate Committee's *Report* shows one $35,000 gift in early 1971, raising questions about other pre-October 1 contributions. Second, Humphrey never updated his disclosure, so there is no information for the March 10-April 6 period, except for one $25,000 contribution that turned up in a GAO inquiry. Third, a total of $109,000 of Humphrey's own money was not included. Fourth, contributions of $276,000 realized from the sale of donated stock in January 1972 were apparently not included. Fifth, at least $25,000 spent for campaign services by noncampaign sources was not reported. Finally, at least $231,000 in pre-April 7 loans were not disclosed until later.

Unlike Humphrey's dozens of dummy committees in 1968, his 1972 post-April 7 campaign had only one major committee: the Committee for the Nomination of Hubert H. Humphrey, Inc. Most of the big givers apparently shunned the gift-tax escape hatch of many committees, permitting a simplified structure in the campaign organization.

While the single-committee structure would seem to be ideal for straight-forward reporting, the Humphrey organization managed to obscure the facts. Perhaps an honest effort was made to comply with the reporting law, but the computer-printed data from the Committee for the Nomination were so garbled with internal contradictions that some questions may never be resolved. In a letter to the GAO accompanying the September 1972 report, the commit-tee treasurer stated that corrections had been incorporated in the report to minimize the work required to revise earlier data. The letter also stressed that all this work was being done by Humphrey's staff at his own expense. This did not help, however, because the corrections were not identified as such and the work referred to never materialized. Because of this, many of the figures in this section represent logical deductions and estimates, derived from confused and contradictory reports, rather than straight reproductions of the campaign's reports.

During the Watergate investigations, the financing of Humphrey's presi-dential campaign came under further scrutiny.[10] The committee's report raised questions about nine matters: (1) an illegal corporate contribution-in-kind of $25,000 from a dairy cooperative, AMPI; (2) an illegal corporate contribution of $1,000 from Minnesota Mining and Manufacturing (3M); (3) the receipt of $276,000 from three contributions in apparent violation of the then-operative Federal Corrupt Practices Act (FCPA), prohibiting contributions of more than $5,000 to any one committee, with at least two of these contributions not covered in Humphrey's voluntary disclosures; (4) receipt of two contributions totalling $109,000 by Humphrey to his own campaign, which were not covered in the voluntary disclosure; (5) the receipt of a $100,000 loan also in violation of the FCPA, which was also not covered in the voluntary disclosure (repaid prior to April 7); (6) the use of a trust account maintained by the law firm of Jack Chestnut, Humphrey's campaign manager, to pay campaign expenses;

(7) the use of the 1970 Humphrey for Senate Committee for activity in connection with the presidential campaign; (8) the receipt of $48,000 in contributions made in the names of others; and (9) the destruction of pre-April 7 financial records of the Humphrey campaign.

Chestnut invoked the Fifth Amendment (against self-incrimination) in declining to answer questions about illegal corporate contributions or any other aspects of Humphrey's campaign finances. Late in 1974 he was indicted on one count in connection with an illegal $12,000 AMPI contribution to Humphrey's 1970 Senate campaign, which he had attempted to conceal as payment to a New York advertising firm handling publicity for Humphrey's 1968 and 1970 campaigns. His argument to dismiss the indictment on the grounds that the AMPI payment was an expenditure rather than a contribution was rejected by the judge. Chestnut was tried in New York in the spring of 1975; after a four-day trial and almost two hours of deliberation, the jury found him guilty. Humphrey himself was the first witness called by the prosecution. He said he had sought dairy aid in 1970, but denied knowing of illegal donations. Humphrey was also asked by Senator Ervin to be interviewed by the committee staff with regard to illegal AMPI contributions; he responded by saying he had no knowledge of illegal contributions and so would not inconvenience a staff member with a meeting. Humphrey said he came "close to quitting public life"[11] as a result of the revelations.

The AMPI contribution was made by using corporate funds to pay for $25,000 worth of computer services from a political firm working in Humphrey's campaign. The firm, Valentine, Sherman and Associates (VSA), had been formed in 1969 by two former Humphrey aides, Jack Valentine and Norman Sherman. This $25,000 was part of a total of $137,000 in corporate funds paid by AMPI to VSA in 1971-72 for services to Democratic candidates in several states; the Watergate Committee found some evidence that AMPI intended more than $25,000 to be for Humphrey's presidential campaign, and the committee also concluded that Sherman knew the money came from corporate funds and was illegal.[r] This $25,000 has to be added to the cost of Humphrey's campaign.[s]

The illegal gift from 3M resulted from use of corporate funds to reimburse ten company officials for their $100-per-person tickets to a Humphrey affair in Minneapolis, on April 13, 1972.

The Watergate Committee also uncovered the activities of Jackson & Co., a limited partnership set up to process stock sales for the purpose of making

---

[r]On August 12, 1974 Sherman pleaded guilty in U.S. District Court in St. Paul to "aiding and abetting" $82,000 in illegal donations of corporate dairy money. The charge stated that $50,000 had been for Humphrey's campaign. It is unknown why the figures developed by the Watergate Committee and those in the Sherman indictment are different. See "HHH Ex-Aide Pleads Guilty," *Washington Post*, August 13, 1974. Also see pp. 495-97, 520-21.

[s]The Humphrey campaign also received $17,225 in legal gifts from the political trusts of the three major dairy associations.

contributions to Humphrey's campaign. In December 1971 Jackson & Co. received substantial numbers of shares in Archer-David-Midland Company stock, the firm headed by Dwayne Andreas, the soybean millionaire; these shares were sold in January 1972, and the net profits of $362,046.30 were contributed to the Humphrey campaign. This total represented about $86,000 from Andreas; about $86,000 from Doris Hastings, a Florida friend of the Andreas family; about $104,000 from Sandra A. McMurtrie, Andreas's daughter; and about $86,000 from a blind trust set up for Humphrey, whose trustee was Andreas. The committee noted that the first three of these contributions were apparently in violation of the FCPA since they were in excess of $5,000 and made to a single political committee. Humphrey's gift of $86,000 and a later one of $23,000 in cash from the blind trust were not violations of the FCPA, because the law did not limit a presidential candidate's gift to his own campaign. The FECA, which took effect two months later, limited such gifts to $50,000, and the trust paid the appropriate gift taxes on Humphrey's gift.

The names of Humphrey, Hastings, and McMurtrie do not appear on Humphrey's voluntary disclosure, although the December 1971 gift of stock to Jackson & Co., and the January 1972 sale and subsequent contribution to the campaign were in the October 1, 1971-March 10, 1972 period purportedly covered by the disclosure. Andreas is listed in the disclosure, but for $75,000, and because the other gifts of stock are not included it is likely that Andreas' was also excluded and that the $75,000 listed is in addition to the $86,000 realized from ADM stock. This brings to at least $385,000 the total of non-reported pre-April 7 income to Humphrey's campaign, and the total of Andreas' gifts to $161,000.

A $100,000 loan from Paul Thatcher, the committee treasurer, was also a technical violation of the FCPA, because loans were included in the definition of contributions. As noted, this loan was repaid prior to April 7, so it does not affect the campaign's total income. However, the nondisclosure of the loan and its repayment was misleading. The trust account of the law firm of Chestnut, Brooks and Burkhard was used to pay campaign expenses—in particular, $25,000 of a VSA bill to the campaign. The money was part of the $100,000 Thatcher check deposited to the trust account on January 11; on January 31 a personal check for $100,000 went to Thatcher from the trust account as a loan repayment.

The Watergate Committee *Report* noted there were several active committees and bank accounts in the pre-April 7 campaign, whose existence was denied or at least not admitted to by Chestnut. In addition, the 1970 Humphrey for Senator Committee account was continued actively into 1972. It was this committee that received pre-October 1, 1971 money from Humphrey's friend S. Harrison Dogole—$10,000 on May 21, and $25,000 on July 26. This $35,000 was in addition to Dogole's $50,000 in the voluntary disclosure and $6,000 after

April 7, bringing his total contributions in this period to $91,000. This adds $35,000 more to Humphrey's known income. It also raises questions as to whether there were other unreported contributions in the pre-October 1, 1971 period.

Another notable contribution was that of John L. Loeb, Sr., who became the first person found guilty under the FECA for $48,000 he contributed to Humphrey in the names of others. Finally, the report observed that Chestnut had destroyed all the campaign's pre-April 7 financial records. While the destruction of those records was not illegal, one could not help but speculate as to why Chestnut or the campaign did not want those records made public.

Although Humphrey publicly answered most of the charges against him in a detailed memorandum,[12] the facts about Jackson & Company are not complete, and the relationships with Andreas and others and the actions of Chestnut have not been investigated with the same detail given to the CRP financing. It was not until late in its investigation that the Watergate Committee publicized information about Humphrey and other Democrats, and then the disclosures came from Republican minority members. None of the investigations of Special Prosecutor Leon Jaworski, the GAO, or the Justice Department seem to have dealt extensively with some of the questions raised.

In addition, an October 1973 GAO audit of Humphrey's campaign cited the Committee for the Nomination of Hubert H. Humphrey, Inc. for four major failures. The first involved the committee's failure to disclose $456,732 in income and $420,236 in expenditures for up to one year: the money was received and spent during the April 7, 1972-February 28, 1973 period but was not reported until amendments were filed on June 22, July 31, and August 8, 1973, after the audit had commenced. The audit reports noted that some of the late-reported contributions were substantial, including one of $35,000, two of $25,000, one of $15,000, and three of $5,000.

Second, GAO cited failure to document more than one-third of $680,000 in expenditures picked as a sample, including about $47,000 in payments to individuals. Because of the lack of documentation for these expenditures, the GAO requested supporting information for a sample of ten expenditures totalling $106,000. The committee produced documentation for only six of the ten, and one of the six clearly showed a less-than-complete report: a listed payment of $6,779 to one person turned out to be 68 separate checks for $99.99 each, which the recipient confirmed were actually used to hire 68 people for election-day work for Humphrey in Indiana's May 7 primary. Since the FECA requires separate documentation for any expenditure of $100 or more, the fact that the checks were for $99.99 and were made out to one person rather than the 68 actual recipients of the money suggests an attempt to hide the expenditure.

The third matter cited by the GAO audit concerned six apparent corporate contributions (totalling $1,900) to two California affiliates of the committee; the committee produced statements that in three of the cases individuals had reimbursed the corporation, and in the other three cases the committee returned the contributions as soon as the audit revealed their source. In spite of these answers, the GAO referred these matters to the Attorney General.

Finally, GAO noted the apparent failure of various individuals to pay gift taxes on contributions of more than $3,000 (or $6,000 if from a wife and husband) to the campaign's one committee. This issue was also noted by the Senate Watergate Committee, with reference to the $276,000 in stock profits from three individuals. The GAO's report said there was a total of about $1,047,000 from individuals (or couples) in amounts greater than $3,000 (or $6,000).

The GAO report noted that the committee went "to considerable expense and trouble to make its reports more complete and accurate and to obtain or restore basic records essential for proper accounting, reporting, and disclosure under the terms of the FECA of 1971."[13] However, since these efforts occurred after the audit began, the results were not timely as required by law and also raised questions about the intent of the committee. The GAO agreed with the committee that many of the problems occurred because of inadequate information to the central committee from the state and local affiliates and because of errors and defects in the computerized record-keeping system. However, the GAO stated that the undisclosed income and expenditures and the lack of documentation for expenditures were serious matters and referred them, along with the question of corporate contributions, to the Attorney General for appropriate action. The GAO also sent a copy of its report to the IRS with reference to the gift tax question. As of mid 1975, no action was taken by either the Attorney General or the IRS.

Costs. There is very little independent information available on the costs of Humphrey's campaign, although it is clear that all of the $4.7 million raised (in contributions and loans) was spent. Probably $1.9 million was spent before April 7 and $2.8 million after that date. Since the Committee for the Nomination had virtually no cash on hand as of April 7, money raised must have been spent prior to that date. For the pre-FECA period, Humphrey's voluntary disclosure, which detailed contributions between October 1, 1971 and March 10, 1972, totalled only $838,715, less than one-half of the costs now believed to have been incurred by the campaign before April 7. Humphrey's FECA reports revealed $231,000 in loans and $125,000 owed to commercial creditors from the pre-April 7 period, adding $356,000 to the costs. Then, two years later, the Watergate Committee's investigation uncovered the $445,000 in income noted above from the three contributors, from the trust fund, from AMPI, and from Dogole. Since Humphrey never updated his voluntary disclosure, there is no information for the March 10-April 6 period; based on the prior five-month record of $1.6 million in contributions, loans, and debts, it can be estimated that the campaign must have raised and spent at least $300,000 during that month, bringing Humphrey's total pre-April 7 costs to about $1.9 million.

Post-April 7, the campaign's reports indicate about $2,750,000 in expenditures, including about $100,000 that was transferred in from labor committees and spent. In addition, at least $50,000 in direct expenditures by labor committees on Humphrey's behalf can be identified, which brings the total post-April 7 cost to about $2.8 million and the total campaign cost to $4.7 million.

Broadcast spending, compiled by the FCC,[14] shows a total of $517,342: $343,067 for television, of which only $28,215 was for network time and the rest for nonnetwork time, and $174,275 for radio time, all nonnetwork. Humphrey filings account for about $450,000 of the $517,000 FCC total, showing nearly one-half of the broadcast expenditures—$234,800—were made in California. The only other primary states in which significant amounts were spent for radio and television were Florida, where at least $81,000 was spent, and Wisconsin, where about $57,000 was spent. No data has been compiled for travel, staff, headquarters, or other cost categories. According to campaign officials, the top staff, including the campaign director, the campaign manager, and the treasurer, were volunteers. Some paid their own expenses while others were reimbursed for their expenses.

For the pre-April 7 period, few details exist on the more than $1.9 million presumed spent. The campaign had costs of up to $300,000 in Florida and about $91,000 in Wisconsin, which were the two primaries in which Humphrey was active before the FECA took effect. There are no data to support other campaign costs of more than $1.5 million in the pre-April 7 period, particularly since the campaign had no Washington office nor a major staff operation until January 1972, most of the top staff were unpaid, there was no radio or television spending outside of the primaries, and the campaign lacked an extensive field staff in the nonprimary states.

In Florida Humphrey's three-pronged effort included a media campaign, vigorous personal campaigning, and a computerized mail and telephone campaign. The media campaign included $50,900 for television, $30,100 for radio, $6,400 for newspaper advertising, and $14,700 for outdoor advertising. Press reports just before the Florida primary noted the campaign was adding $5,000 to the television budget.

The Florida computer drive reportedly cost at least $100,000 and was carried out by Valentine, Sherman & Associates. Lists of the 1.6 million registered Democrats in the state's 16 largest counties were purchased, and these names and addresses, by precincts, were put in a computer with data from telephone books; this gave the campaign a working telephone list of about 800,000 Democratic households. If there had been enough time—four or five months—all of these households could have been polled and/or contacted in some way. In the last three weeks about 150,000 houses were called by computer, receiving a recorded message from Humphrey. In addition to the telephoning, about 200,000 letters were sent, 100,000 to teachers, pharmacists, Jews, senior citizens, and to those in "space-oriented counties" and 100,000 to blacks. The cost of this effort, added to the VSA project and media costs, totalled more than $250,000 in Florida.

In Wisconsin $58,000 of the $91,000 total reported spent under the state's campaign laws went for media; $31,400 for television, $25,800 for radio, and $1,300 for newspaper advertising. No other costs for the Wisconsin primary were calculated.

The Pennsylvania primary was key to Humphrey's developing campaign, and it had been budgeted for $250,000; however, financial difficulties limited Humphrey's spending, and it is believed only a little more than $100,000 was spent. But a more costly and effective campaign was possible because of an effort on Humphrey's behalf by labor. In a manner reminiscent of the successful pro-Humphrey, anti-Wallace effort of organized labor late in the 1968 general election campaign, the Pennsylvania unions mounted an effort that clearly made a major difference in the election result. Most of the $50,000 spent directly by labor on Humphrey's behalf in 1972 came from the national, state, and local steelworkers unions in Pennsylvania; further, a significant amount of the labor effort was in "in-kind" services that are not recorded as direct spending. The total dollar value of labor's direct and indirect contributions to Humphrey's Pennsylvania campaign cannot be calculated, but as detailed below, the statistics are impressive.

Of 1.6 million union members in Pennsylvania, 75 percent are Democrats. Humphrey's close relationship with the state's labor movement was established early: 50 of 131 Humphrey delegate-candidates (including three who were technically uncommitted) were union members and in each of the state's 67 counties there was a labor chairman as well as a campaign chairman for Humphrey. The director of the state's labor committee on political education organized 15,000 union members as "volunteers in politics," or "VIPs." Thousands of workers reportedly worked directly on the election. A total of 2.6 million "official Humphrey sample ballot" cards were prepared and distributed by various union locals, 500,000 of them by Philadelphia area unions alone. In addition, 500,000 pieces of Humphrey literature were distributed. The state labor organization placed the names of about 500,000 registered Democrats on computer lists and an unknown number of letters, signed by appropriate local union leaders, were written and sent by computer to the names on the lists. A week before the primary, at least 100,000 telephone calls were made (the goal was 400,000); in Philadelphia at least 60,000 calls were made to union members from a bank of 50 phones. There was a list of 52,000 people who had worked for former mayor Tate of Philadelphia, and they were systematically called. Major efforts, via telephone, mailing and other political organizing methods were also directed toward Jews, blacks, and senior citizens.

The media effort in Pennsylvania was minor. The campaign claimed only

$18,400 was spent, $3,900 on television, $12,700 on radio, and $1,800 on newspaper ads. Television consisted mainly of four half-hour call-in shows; much of the radio money was spent on black stations.

The Ohio and Indiana campaigns costs were about $175,000 and $100,000 respectively. Media played a minor role in both; only about $21,000 was spent on radio, television, and newspapers in Ohio and $6,000 in Indiana. The Humphrey campaign credited the closeness of the Ohio vote to McGovern's wider use of the media: because of this, and because of the last-minute nature of the effort in Nebraska, the Humphrey campaign spent relatively more on media in Nebraska than in Ohio and Indiana. It was still a modest amount, $12,000. In West Virginia about $9,000 was spent on media. The total costs of the Nebraska and West Virginia campaign are not known, nor is the total media, or any other figure, known for the Michigan campaign. In Maryland Humphrey was reported to have spent $23,000, which seems low since $10,200 was spent for media. (Some media was cancelled after the Wallace shooting.)

One of the least expensive uses of media in the Humphrey campaign was the call-in show, in which the candidate answered questions from viewers who could telephone directly to the studio. In seven primaries before Oregon (Pennsylvania through Maryland), 17 half-hour and two one-hour shows were shown over 26 stations at a total cost of only $208,000—$183,000 for time and $25,000 for production. The shows used a seven-second delay mechanism on the telephones so that obscene, drunk, or totally inarticulate callers could be screened out. Humphrey was considered effective on these shows, and they were a boon to the money-starved campaign.

California was the keystone to Humphrey's primary strategy and the campaign there was activated when he first considered running. Between May and November of 1971, Humphrey took seven trips to California, and a Humphrey committee was announced in the state in November. Six months later the campaign ran into trouble. Original strategy called for a heavy media campaign, for spending the full $460,000 allowed by the Democratic candidates' agreement, but the money was not there. Eugene Wyman had raised most of the budgeted amount, but more than $250,000 had been sent to Washington to meet urgent obligations. By June 1 less than one week before the election, the campaign had been able to raise and commit only $161,400: $97,000 for television, $39,400 for radio, and $25,000 for a special election-eve television show. An additional $50,000 was received for media on June 1, and the remainder came in later. Humphrey spent a total of only $234,800 for radio and television, about one-half as much as had been planned, as the agreement allowed, and as McGovern was spending.[t] The campaign actually raised $42,000 more for media than was spent, but it arrived too late to be used

---

[t]Humphrey's lack of money for paid television was one reason he pressed so hard for the free exposure of candidate debates.

effectively. The campaign had difficulty planning a media program; it switched from one media plan to another, and Humphrey was off the air throughout the state for one crucial day. The special election-eve telecast used the effective question-and-answer format with the candidate. The show cost $25,000 and was carried on about a dozen commercial stations and more than 30 cable outlets. In total, the Humphrey campaign claims to have spent no more than $500,000 on the California primary.

During the postprimary, preconvention phase, the major effort was the political and legal challenge to the California result. The legal work for that challenge was done by a friendly law firm, which did not get paid for the work. No salaries were paid to anyone who worked at the convention. The campaign did charter a plane to Miami and paid the staff's hotel bills.

These identifiable costs of just under $1 million in primary spending represent only 35 percent of Humphrey's presumed total expenditures after April 7. Even assuming costs of $300,000 for the other three primaries (Nebraska, West Virginia, and Michigan), which would be quite high, Humphrey's total primary spending would be only about $1.3 million, still less than 50 percent of his total costs in this period. Including the pre-April 7 state campaigns, Humphrey's primary spending was less than $1.7 million, 36 percent of his total costs of about $4.7 million. By comparison, McGovern, the only other candidate to go the whole primary route, used about 67 percent of his much higher expenditures for the primaries. For a candidate as badly strapped for money as Humphrey was, it is surprising that so little was apparently used for critical primary spending.

Sources. The Humphrey campaign is estimated to have raised a total of about $5 million. This includes $1,487,600 in loans, of which $251,000 was reported repaid during the campaign. Adjusting for the loan repayments, the campaign's net receipts were a little more than $4.7 million: $839,000 in voluntarily disclosed contributions for October 1, 1971 to March 10, 1972; $741,000 in undisclosed loans and contributions for that period; a $35,000 contribution before October 1, 1971; $300,000 in contributions for March 10 to April 6; and $2,815,000 received after April 7, as reconstructed from Humphrey's FECA reports.

The gross loan figure of almost $1.5 million represented more than 30 percent of income. Even adjusting for the loan repayments, Humphrey still received more than 25 percent of his net income from loans, of which about $925,000 remained outstanding three years after the campaign. It is perhaps a measure of the loyalty of Humphrey's major financial supporters that he alone of all the candidates could borrow so heavily, but it is also a measure of political weakness or of an inadequate fund-raising operation that the campaign found it necessary to borrow almost one-third of its income and then could not raise sufficient funds to repay more than a tiny fraction of those loans.

In addition to the loans, which were for large amounts, Humphrey depended heavily on large contributors. Of the total net income (deducting loan repayments), three-quarters, $3,524,541, came from known contributions and loans of $5,000 and over. This included: $643,541 from 37 contributors listed in the October 1-March 10 voluntary disclosure; the $741,000 in undisclosed contributions and in loans from that period; $35,000 from one contributor before October 1; one $25,000 contribution known in the otherwise missing March 10-April 6 period; $1,027,000 from 45 contributors in the post-April 7 period (some of whom also gave in the earlier period); about $156,000 from seven labor and several dairy and other groups in the latter period; and $840,000 in post-April 7 lenders (some of whom were also contributors) and one bank loan of $57,000.

At the level of $500-and-over contributions, 82 percent—$3,878,000—of the campaign's income is accounted for. For the post-April 7 period, income details reinforce the top-heaviness of Humphrey's financing: 90 percent of that $2.8 million came from $500-and-over contributions and 95 percent from over-$100 contributions.

Only five percent of Humphrey's post-April 7 financing came from $100-and-under contributors, and since a significant portion of even that small amount is specified to be $100 tickets, the truly small giver contributed little to the campaign. This is ironic for a candidate who considers himself a man of the people and who campaigned as a champion of the working person.

At the top of the scale, some 18 persons (counting husband and wife as one) each gave or loaned $50,000 or more, accounting for more than 60 percent of the campaign's known total income: $1,574,100 in contributions and $1,330,000 (subtracting one known repayment) in loans.

Humphrey's strongest supporter, Joseph Cole, gave a total of $687,000 to the campaign. Cole, a Cleveland manufacturing and distributing company executive, was also Humphrey's finance chairman, a major fund raiser, and an especially valuable source during one particularly tight moment of the campaign. Cole loaned $220,000 in early April; $100,000 of this was repaid in late April. He then made outright contributions of $52,000 in May and June, and during the same period, loaned an additional $415,000. Overall, Cole's loans totalled $635,000.

The second largest contributor, including loans, was Meshulam Riklis, who gave and loaned $675,000 to Humphrey's campaign.[u] An Israeli immigrant, Riklis began his business career in Minneapolis and went on to head Glen-Alden Corporation and Rapid-American Corporation, the latter a diversified manufacturing and retailing firm. Riklis gave a total of $125,000 and lent $550,000.

---

[u]One contribution, for $25,000, dated March 24, was revealed in a letter from Riklis' attorney to GAO on September 12, 1973, and is the only one known in the March 10-April 6 period.

The campaign's third largest reported contributor—the campaign's largest known contributor at the time—was Walter T. Duncan, who "gave" on credit and drew heavily on the resources and reliability of Humphrey's largest supporter (Cole) and other members of the Humphrey Committee to do so. A Bryan, Texas, man who later proved an embarrassment also to the Nixon administration, Duncan was reported to have given $300,000 to Humphrey— $100,000 in early May and $200,000 right after the California primary in June.

The fourth largest contribution came from Dwayne Andreas, discussed above, who gave $161,000. Fifth was S. Harrison Dogole, a Philadelphia friend of Humphrey, president of Globe Security Systems, Inc., who gave $56,000 and loaned $75,000 for total support of $131,000.

Sixth on the list was Humphrey himself, whose gifts of cash and stock from his blind trust totalled $109,000. Next was Sandra McMurtrie, Andreas' daughter, whose gift of stock netted the campaign $104,000.

Six of the other 18 largest supporters were contributors only, while the remaining five were both contributors and lenders. The six contributors and their gifts were:

Mr. and Mrs. Leonard Davis	$100,000
Doris Hastings	86,000
Clarence Quigley	80,100
Lawrence and Barbara Weinberg	66,000
John Factor	60,000
John and Frances Loeb	50,000

Leonard Davis of New York, founder and director of Colonial Penn Life Company, gave $50,000 pre- and $50,000 post-April 7. Clarence Quigley, an investor, president of Rowser's International, is a Minneapolis friend of Humphrey; Doris Hastings is the Florida friend of Andreas whose contribution to Humphrey was in the form of stock in Andreas' company. John Factor is the reformed underworld figure, "Jake the Barber," who loaned Humphrey $240,000 in 1968. (His late wife contributed an additional $100,000 in 1968). Factor's much more modest 1972 support included $35,000 given before April 7, and $25,000 after that date. Barbara Weinberg of Beverly Hills gave $50,500 post-April 7. Her husband, Lawrence, chairman of Larwin Mortgage investors, gave $15,500 post-April 7, and also supported McGovern and Yorty with smaller contributions. John Loeb of New York, another long-time Humphrey supporter, attained the dubious distinction of being the first individual to be charged with violating the FECA because $48,000 of his and his wife's gifts were made in the names of others.

The five who both gave and loaned at least $50,000 each are shown in Table 5-7. Kahn, a San Diego land developer, gave $25,000 pre-April 7 and made his loan in early June. Schwartz, a Beverly Hills banker, executive

Table 5-7
Contributors Who Gave and/or Loaned $50,000 or More to the
Humphrey Campaign

	Contribution	Loan	Total
Irvin J. Kahn	$50,000	$50,000	$100,000
Daniel Schwartz	47,000	50,000	97,000
Eugene V. Klein	31,000	50,000	81,000
Gilbert Lehrman	17,500	50,000	67,500
Paul Thatcher	25,000	25,000	50,000

vice-president of the National General Corp., and an associate of Frank Sinatra,
gave $35,000 pre-April 7, $12,000 post-April 7, and his loan came in mid-May.
Klein, television executive and chairman of the board of National General Corp.,
also of Beverly Hills, gave $10,000 pre-April 7 and five contributions totalling
$21,000 on May 1; he loaned $50,000 in mid-May. Lehrman, president of a
wholesale food distribution company, of Harrisburg, Pennsylvania, gave
$12,500 before April 7, $5,000 between then and April 21, and made his loan
on April 28. Paul Thatcher of Minneapolis, president of First Interoceanic
Corp., was the campaign treasurer; he made his contribution early and his loan
came in late April. (As mentioned above, Thatcher lent and was repaid $100,000
before April 7.)

Some of Humphrey's largest contributors and lenders from 1968 were
absent from the list of 1972 supporters or gave much less.[15] In 1968, Humphrey
was the Democratic nominee, whereas in 1972 he was only a candidate and
never the front-runner for the nomination. Lew Wasserman, the head of Music
Corporation of America and a long-time Humphrey supporter, loaned $240,000
in 1968, none of which was repaid, and gave an additional $54,096; his name
does not show up on any of Humphrey's 1972 contributor or lender lists.
Other familiar names missing in 1972 were Arthur Krim, Robert E. Short, Arnold
Picker, Arthur Houghton, and Robert Dowling. Two 1968 lenders of $100,000
each, Patrick O'Connor (not repaid) and Jeno Paulucci (repaid) gave less in 1972;
O'Connor gave $30,000 pre-April 7 and $864.65 on September 20, and Paulucci
gave $42,000 before April 7.

Other contributors or lenders of $25,000 or more in 1972 included: Lowell
Andreas, Minneapolis manufacturing company executive (brother of Dwayne),
who gave $30,000 ($25,000 pre-April 7 and $5,000 on June 2); Edward Daly of
California, chairman and chief executive officer of World Airways, Inc., who gave
$26,000 on April 19; Ben Fixman of Missouri, chairman of the board of Diversi-
fied Industries, Inc., who gave $35,000 and lent $1,000; Walter Shorenstein,
chairman of Milton Meyer & Co. Realtors, who gave $25,000 pre-April 7; the
late Eugene Wyman, a California attorney and a principal Humphrey fund raiser,
who gave $25,000 pre-April 7 and $2,000 on May 5; and Stanley Goldblum, of
Equity Funding fame, also a Californian, who loaned $25,000.

The big givers were concentrated geographically in a handful of states. Perhaps as much as 90 percent of Humphrey's big money came from New York, California, Minnesota, Ohio (Cole), Texas (Duncan), and Pennsylvania. A significant number of Humphrey's big contributors subsequently gave to Nixon: Duncan ($305,000, returned), Riklis ($188,000), Dwayne Andreas ($119,136.77 plus the controversial $25,000 pre-April 7 check), and Paulucci ($25,000).

Special interest funds were a sizeable source of income to the Humphrey campaign. The dairy industry distributed funds through three committees in 1971 and 1972, for a total $17,225: TAPE/CTAPE gave $12,500, SPACE gave $3,500, and ADEPT gave $1,225.[16] Labor and industry committees that made political contributions to Humphrey were:

TAPE—Trust for Agricultural Political Education
SPACE—Trust for Special Political Agricultural Community Education
ADEPT—Agricultural and Dairy Education Political Trust
EGA—Effective Government Association
TRW—TRW Good Government Fund
USA—United Steelworkers of American Voluntary Political Action Fund
COPE—Committee on Political Education, AFL-CIO
ILGWU—International Ladies Garment Workers Union
CWA—Communication Workers of America Committee on Political
    Education
SIU—Seafarers International Union
TPEL—Transportation Political Education League
ACRE—Action Committee for Rural Electrification

At least $25,000 in illegal corporate contributions from the Associated Milk Producers, Inc. (discussed above) was given to the campaign as computer services from VSA. (Humphrey had also received $10,500 from various dairy industry committees for his 1970 Senate campaign.) In the Wisconsin primary in 1972 Humphrey aired commercials reminding farmers that he was one of the senators who forced Nixon to raise milk support prices in 1971, an action that was later to become a target of political and legal charges of administration favors to the dairy contributors. Other group contributions included $500 from EGA, and $5,000 from TRW. From all these sources, the total for the presidential effort was $47,725.

A correlation exists between what the Humphrey committees reported as total contributions from labor—$121,558—and what can be extracted from the labor committees' reports—$156,952—but both figures are suspect because the itemizations are at variance. Sizeable contributions-in-kind, especially by USA in Pennsylvania, are not included in any Humphrey data. Labor also spent heavily on his behalf in the Pennsylvania primary—$41,699 by the Steelworkers alone. Labor's direct and indirect contributions to the Humphrey campaign were in excess of $170,000.

Almost every major union gave some support to the Humphrey campaign, though in some cases it was only a token amount. The Auto Workers made a small belated contribution to Humphrey; their larger support went to Muskie. National COPE gave $500 to the Friends of Humphrey in connection with a postconvention fund-raiser, but nothing earlier. California COPE gave about $40,000 for the United Labor Committee for Humphrey, which was an effective force in the California primary, and Indiana COPE gave $200. The ILGWU, a steady Humphrey supporter, contributed $4,500; CWA gave $8,200, SIU gave $10,000; and TPEL gave $14,400. The balance came from a dozen other unions, in amounts ranging from $100 to less than $5,000.

Another major category of funds was $36,370 from nonreporting Humphrey committees in existence before April 7: funds of the Humphrey '72 Finance Committee and the Humphrey for President Committee had cash on hand as of April 7, but not significant amounts. Local Democratic and miscellaneous committes, such as ACRE committees, together gave about $5,000.

Fund Raising. Humphrey's finance chairman and largest giver, Joseph Cole, was also a key fund raiser. Another key fund raiser, S. Harrison Dogole, was in charge of early campaign fund raising and was also a large contributor. The other two principal fund raisers were the late Eugene Wyman, one of the Democratic Party's most successful and powerful money figures, who gave $27,000, and Richard Maguire, a former party finance chairman. Maguire, who is not a wealthy man, apparently lent the campaign $60,000, reportedly a bank loan for which he put his home up as collateral; at least $40,000 was repaid.

The chief method followed by these fund raisers was simply to ask their and Humphrey's friends and former supporters for money. No funds were raised or fund-raising plans made in the summer and fall of 1971 when Humphrey was reassessing his role. The campaign may have been overconfident because of the direct and indirect offers of financial support Humphrey received before he entered the race. While this person-to-person method seems casual, it was not so in the Humphrey campaign. One of three people—Cole, Dogole, or Jack Chestnut, the campaign manager—was supposed to know about every fund-raising contact and to authorize the acceptance of campaign contributions.

Humphrey's success with person-to-person solicitation of large givers was notable, but it did not generate enough funds. Two reasons were given for Humphrey's money troubles. The first was that the left wing of the Democratic Party disintegrated early, leaving McGovern without competition for money, while Humphrey had to compete with Muskie and Jackson for "centrist" money. This argument, however, does not hold up: Muskie and Jackson faded only slightly later than, for example, Lindsay; Muskie probably kept as much money from McGovern as he did from Humphrey; Muskie was acceptable to many who would not support Humphrey; Jackson's money appeared to be unrelated to his success and not transferable; and McGovern did not pick up very much financial support from other left-of-center candidates as they folded.

The Humphrey campaign did make serious attempts to win over Muskie's contributors. In late March Eugene Wyman went to New York, raided Muskie supporters, and received $50,000-$100,000 in cash and commitments for more if Humphrey finished ahead of Muskie (presumably in Wisconsin's April 4 primary). Immediately after Muskie withdrew from primary competition, Wyman was quick to ask Muskie's supporters to switch: telegrams were sent to 330 California political activists asking for their help and counsel, while the telephone was used to reach others.

The second reason given for Humphrey's money troubles is more credible and revealing: that many felt McGovern was not a serious threat and the party would not nominate him.

The earliest known fund-raising event was an affair in Minneapolis in November 1971, hosted by S. Harrison Dogole. He reported receiving dependable pledges of up to $700,000, and there were others who wanted to wait and see how Humphrey would do in Florida. On March 6, 1972 a meeting at the home of Marquette National Bank President Carl Pohlad in Minneapolis reportedly raised in excess of $50,000. Although none of those attending the meeting appear on Humphrey's voluntarily disclosed list of contributors, the "receipts" may have been pledges, or even contributions unrecorded until after March 10. Further, those contributors were given tickets to an April 13, $100-per-plate dinner, which they were to try to sell. After that dinner the press reported $100,000 or more raised from 1,200 who had attended.

The mid-April period was a time of major fund-raising efforts. Two days after the one in Minneapolis, an Ohio dinner at $50 per person or $75 per couple drew 800 people. A Pittsburgh dinner drew 1,100 people at $100 per plate and is known to have had net receipts of almost $100,000.

By late April it was clear that the campaign's success with large contributors and a few big fund-raising events was not enough. A direct mail appeal, an expanded series of high-priced celebrity and other events, and the organization of state finance committees to raise local funds in each primary state were planned. The direct mail effort was apparently pushed neither very hard nor very successfully. Some events did occur, although success diminished as Humphrey's prospects faded. Local fund-raising efforts in primary states were successful.

Flow and Debts. The flow of money to Humphrey's campaign closely paralleled his electoral performance. His early money came from long-time friends and supporters (although some waited for the Florida results). After Florida, Humphrey reportedly asked Wyman for $50,000, which was raised in one day. However, Humphrey's Florida showing was not impressive enough to loosen the floodgates and his Wisconsin showing three weeks later had a discouraging effect. This mid-April period was during one of the campaign's worst financial binds, with debts of almost $700,000 and little cash on hand. At this point Cole loaned $220,000 to the campaign; and there were also two other $50,000 loans and one $25,000 loan. But by May 1, after Humphrey's impressive Pennsylvania showing and Muskie's withdrawal, the money flow picked up dramatically; close to $300,000 was raised in ten days. Cole was repaid $100,000 of his loan, and $50,000 in other loans were also repaid.

During the next two weeks the Indiana, Ohio, Nebraska, and West Virginia results were generally positive, but not strong enough to bring in the amounts needed for the final push in California. The May 16 Michigan and Maryland results finally dried up the money flow. New money was not forthcoming, and some pledges that were made before those primaries were not honored. Although Humphrey was not an active candidate in either the Oregon or Rhode Island primaries one week later, McGovern's strong showings further hurt Humphrey financially by making McGovern's nomination look more likely.

Humphrey's fading hopes now depended completely on California, and the money needed for that state was not available. Large California contributors were particularly bitter because they had sent more than $500,000 out of the state for earlier primaries on the promise that this eastward money flow would be reversed for the California primary. Virtually the entire California campaign was financed by loans. Before that primary, the campaign's debt was about $725,000; afterwards, it was more than $1 million. After California, there was no chance that Humphrey could win the nomination, and he was barely able to keep from going deeper into debt.

By November the debt was still reported to be $1.2 million, with about $300,000 of that owed to commercial firms and the remainder to individual lenders. The campaign tried to repay those loans, but it is unlikely that Humphrey will ever raise enough money to do so. Those who could not afford, or did not want, to have their loans turned into contributions were repaid as money was available during the course of the campaign. The remaining lenders probably understood that their loans would be repaid only if Humphrey won the nomination. By early 1975 the combined depts still totalled more than $900,000 and the Committee for the Nomination disbanded. A new committee, the Triple HHH Dinner Committee, inherited the debt and sought to settle the loans for a few cents on the dollar.

Hubert Humphrey, the veteran of presidential and vice presidential campaigns in 1960, 1964, 1968, and 1972, spoke out after his last experience about political fund raising and primary elections. Deploring the low turnout in presidential primaries and the tourist attractions they have become, he favored either a national primary on one day, or a regional series of primaries within time zones. Humphrey spoke emphatically on the subject of campaign financing, calling it "a curse." In an interview published in 1974 by the *New York*

Times,[17] Humphrey expressed feelings of desperation and frustration caused by having to "grovel" for cash he needed just to be heard on the radio or television. He also deplored the fact that most potential contributors of significant sums seemed to be either scared to give, because they would be listed and feared the results, or were in some kind of trouble and expected to be helped in return for their gifts.

Political Switch-Hitters: Walter Duncan and Walter Dilbeck

One of the most interesting noncontributors in 1972 was Texas financier Walter T. Duncan, who "gave" $300,000 to the Humphrey campaign, $305,000 to the Nixon campaign, and may have helped the Hartke campaign as well. Plagued by financial difficulties, Duncan never actually provided the money to either Humphrey or Nixon, and later requested that his IOU to Nixon be returned, which it was.

Duncan was relatively unknown in Texas political or financial circles, and the extent of his wealth from real estate, oil interests, and an automobile agency was also unknown. While mystery continues to surround the political and financial activities of Duncan, it appears that he was introduced into the world of high political finance by his partner and friend, Walter Dilbeck, an Evansville, Indiana businessman, who gave more than $100,000 to the Hartke campaign. When Hartke withdrew from the presidential race he became the national co-chairman of the Humphrey campaign and reportedly suggested Dilbeck as a potential donor. Humphrey fund raisers then called Dilbeck, who reported that he and Duncan had contributed to Hartke as "a stalking horse for Humphrey" in the New Hampshire primary, which Humphrey had not entered.[18] Dilbeck then put the Humphrey aides in contact with Duncan. According to some, Senator Hartke himself was instrumental in arranging Duncan's gift to Humphrey. Hartke had introduced the two men in Humphrey's office some 18 months earlier, and, in March, had become Humphrey's national co-chairman.

Duncan explained that he was "cash poor" but that he would make a sizeable contribution if credit could be arranged. He was directed to the District of Columbia National Bank by Humphrey advisers. The bank refused the unknown Duncan a loan but agreed to lend $100,000 to Joseph Cole, a Cleveland manufacturer and key Humphrey fund raiser, who in turn would lend it to Duncan, who in turn would "give" it to the campaign. Making the transaction even more difficult to follow, Cole arranged with Max M. Kampelman, a long-time Humphrey supporter, S. Harrison Dogole of Philadelphia, campaign treasurer Paul Thatcher, and Minneapolis businessman John Morrison for each of them to accept $20,000 of the loan if Duncan defaulted.

As the California primary approached, the Humphrey campaign was in debt and again turned to Duncan. This time, True Davis, board chairman of the National Bank of Washington (later alleged to be the source of some apparently incorrect press stories about Senator Thomas Eagleton), arranged for a $200,000 loan at his bank, executed on June 5. The campaign's June 10, 1972 report to the General Accounting Office reflected only that Duncan had contributed $300,000 on May 9, 1972.

Another prominent 1972 financial figure, Dwayne Andreas, board chairman of Archer Daniels Midland Co., proved central in the latter transaction. The $200,000 Duncan loan was secured by 10,000 shares of Andreas' company stock which was valued at the time at more than $400,000.

Dilbeck persuaded Duncan to give to the Nixon cause. At Dilbeck's invitation, the Finance Committee to Re-Elect the President (FCRP) chairman Maurice Stans met with Dilbeck and Duncan, and a short time later Duncan gave the Nixon campaign a one-year noninterest bearing note for $305,000, designedly more than he had given to Humphrey. The Nixon committee discounted the note with its bank, the First National Bank of Washington by borrowing against it the full amount, less interest to maturity. The bank accepted the $305,000 note after reviewing a Duncan financial statement, which he provided. Under the arrangement, the FCRP was liable on the obligation to the bank if Duncan failed to repay it; the FCRP had several similar arrangements with the bank on notes given by other contributors.

In order to make such impressive political contributions in spite of his financial limitations, Duncan thus in effect had borrowed heavily from banks. He asserted he had been promised nothing in exchange for his generosity. As time elapsed, he was unable to pay the loans. Four days after the $200,000 Humphrey gift was made, a 220-acre parcel of land Duncan owned was sold at public auction because he defaulted on a $2.6 million loan secured by the property. Duncan was subsequently sued in a variety of courts for failures to repay this and other loans[19] on certain pieces of real estate. In December the National Bank of Washington sued Duncan for repayment of the $200,000 loan secured by the Andreas stock. Andreas, Duncan, and the bank later worked out an agreement for Andreas to buy the note from the bank and secure it with some other parcels of Texas land owned by Duncan. Cole and the other guarantors of the $100,000 loan themselves began repayment.

On January 30, 1973 it was revealed that Duncan was being investigated by a federal strike force on organized crime for his dealings with the financial empire of Texan Frank W. Sharp. The Sharp holdings, including the Sharpstown State Bank and National Bankers Life Insurance Co., collapsed in 1971. This led to a scandal that included as principals Texas Governor Preston Smith and U.S. Assistant Attorney General Will Wilson, who later resigned under pressure. The federal strike force reportedly investigated whether Duncan actually gave the donations himself or was acting for others.

When Stans learned of Duncan's financial troubles, he arranged for an expert evaluation of Duncan's properties. The report showed that Duncan had borrowed to the hilt and had little or no equity in his various holdings. Stans had the FCRP pay off the obligation to the bank and returned the note to Duncan—thus negating the Duncan "gift" at a cost of almost $11,000 in interest (paid to the bank on the loan) to the Nixon treasury.

On March 21 Duncan and five others were indicted for conspiring to make false statements to get a $3.15 million loan in another transaction. A few days earlier Duncan's friend, Dilbeck, even though he had given no publicly reported contribution to FCRP, was rewarded with a dinner invitation to the White House for Nixon backers.

Underlining the complexity of the Duncan transaction, the August 9, 1973 GAO report (on contributions to both major parties by Walter T. Duncan) observed that both the amounts of his pledges and the methods of securing them "were influenced substantially by banking interests and by the amounts which could be borrowed from banks on the basis of signatures, guarantees or collateral either obtained by or provided directly by committee officials." The GAO asked the Justice and Treasury departments to investigate further and to clarify the actions and intentions of Duncan, the Humphrey and Nixon fund raisers, and the banks involved and to see if tax or other laws had been violated. No known action resulted from that request.

Walter Dilbeck is a flamboyant Indiana real estate developer and World War II hero who came to public attention during his short-lived association with Spiro Agnew following the former Vice-President's resignation.[20]

Dilbeck first met Agnew at Palm Springs, where a film project based on Dilbeck's war career was being discussed (he won the DSC and four Purple Hearts for heroism in Germany where he almost single-handedly killed 68 German soldiers).[21] Dilbeck was a Republican who had supported Ronald Reagan's candidacy in 1968, but was unorthodox in his political giving. He contributed at least $105,000 to Democratic Senator Vance Hartke's 1972 presidential effort in the New Hampshire primary, saying he thought Hartke "would make a good President."[22] (His role in the Hartke campaign is examined below.) But one of his most unusual roles in the area of campaign finance came later when tried to get big backers for McGovern during the general election campaign.

Dilbeck has claimed to have attempted to convince Walter Duncan, H. Ross Perot, the computer software millionaire, and perhaps others to contribute to the McGovern campaign because of his belief that the Democratic candidate was turning to Castro's Cuba for money. Dilbeck said later that he wanted to raise money for McGovern—who was then behind two-to-one in the polls—to help maintain the two-party system with American money. Although he did not want McGovern to win the election, he felt a credible showing would be healthy for the system. Dilbeck was unsuccessful in his efforts, made without McGovern's consent.

Hartke

Senator Vance Hartke of Indiana was a presidential candidate for twelve weeks in 1972, from January 3 to March 26. He campaigned actively only in the New Hampshire primary, in which he received less than three percent of the vote. Hartke's candidacy was perhaps the most enigmatic of the year, and few political observers even attempted to suggest a reason for it.

The financial side of Hartke's campaign was as murky as its political rationale, with widely conflicting reports of both its costs and sources of funds. One of the senator's aides said that the campaign cost a little more than $100,000; an analysis of the available information on identifiable presidential campaign costs and income indicates that almost $175,000 was spent; and an analysis of all the committees operating on Hartke's behalf in 1972 and their late-claimed (1973) debts suggests that Senator Hartke had about $260,000 in political costs in 1972.[v] These data raise questions about both the purpose of Hartke's presidential candidacy and his use of it as a fund-raising device.

Much of the hard data on the campaign's costs came from Walter J. Dilbeck, who had been a friend of Hartke since boyhood. (As noted above, Dilbeck, a business associate of Walter T. Duncan, supported Ronald Reagan in 1968 and later in 1972 played a major role in the Humphrey-Duncan story). According to Dilbeck, his involvement with the Hartke campaign began with a telephone call from Martha (Mrs. Vance) Hartke, reporting on the desperate situation in New Hampshire. Dilbeck claims he went to New Hampshire and found many bills and no money to pay them and so took out a personal loan from a New York bank for $60,000, which he deposited in a Manchester, New Hampshire bank. He then returned to Indianapolis, and received a frantic telephone call: 70 volunteers from Indiana colleges had been stranded at the Evansville airport for two days with no money to get to New Hampshire to help Hartke. Dilbeck spent about $3,000 to "bail them out" and also gave them food money for two weeks. He next went to Washington, D.C. and signed a 60-day note for $100,000. Since Dilbeck claims his financial involvement in the Harke campaign totalled about $105,000, the second must have been used in part to repay his earlier reported $60,000 loan.

Dilbeck provided a list of expenses for Hartke's New Hampshire campaign. The total on that list is $94,878 plus $10,000 for 15 months' interest on $100,000 at 8.5 percent for a total of $105,000. Two questions arise from this data. First, Dilbeck claimed the note was for two months, yet the list shows interest was paid for 15 months; the difference added about $9,000. Second, the list in fact totals not $94,878 but $89,778—perhaps simply an

---

[v]We are indebted to Robert Walters', "Rewards of Running," in the Washington *Star-News* of March 11, 1973, for some of the analyses of committee reports in this section; Walters obtained data in Indiana not otherwise available.

arithmetic error, or perhaps an additional $5,100 was spent but not listed. These discrepancies are not major, but they bring into question the accuracy of Dilbeck's information.

Dilbeck's list of New Hampshire expenses includes: $28,000 for advertising; $23,600 for hotels and meals; $10,000 for travel—including $45 for a speeding ticket for a volunteer; less than $7,700 for salaries and some volunteers' expenses; $4,400 for telephone; $4,300 for miscellaneous expenses, including medicine for volunteers and an unusual listing of $177 to "Olin Phumphrey 3/9/72—J. Inkenbrandt's Dogs;" $9,600 listed in payments to banks or bank officials, the purpose of which is not clear; and $12,250 in interest, covering the $100,000 already noted and another $2,250 listed as 90 days' interest on a bank loan to Dilbeck.

Whether this $100,000 represents the full cost of Hartke's New Hampshire campaign, or whether all of Dilbeck's expenses should be properly counted as Hartke's costs remains open because no other direct cost data are available for New Hampshire. Hartke's two New Hampshire committees—Hoosiers for Hartke and New Hampshire Volunteers for Hartke—were not in existence after April 7 and did not voluntarily disclose, so there is no way of knowing whether they received and spent money in addition to Dilbeck's or whether his money went through those committees. There is also no direct information on the national or non-New Hampshire costs of Hartke's campaign; the $175,000 total for the campaign has been inferred from income data. There is, however, information from Indiana filings (see below).

Three different claims about the source of money for Hartke's campaign were made, and committee reports suggest still other sources. While Dilbeck's claim appears to be substantiated by his list of expenses, two other reports are credible. One report, from a Hartke staff member, is that the campaign was financed by a personal loan on Hartke's house; this may be substantiated by filings showing bank loan payments in Indiana (Dilbeck's loans were with N.Y. and D.C. banks). The other report is that Hartke received money from Walter Duncan; this cannot be substantiated, but is possible.

In addition to the two non-reporting New Hampshire committees, three other committees active on Hartke's behalf in 1972 did report some or all of their financing, in either Indiana or Washington, D.C. One was a Draft Hartke Committee, based in Indianapolis, which operated from December 16, 1971 to April 6, 1972, and filed reports in Indiana. The committee raised $22,100, most of it from a January dinner in Indianapolis. There is no record of a balance at the time of the committee's demise, so the $22,000 must have been spent by April 6, although it is not known whether this money was used for Hartke's New Hampshire effort or for some other aspect of his campaign.

The second committee and the only one to file under the FECA was the Hartke Presidential Campaign Deficit Committee. This committee raised $34,777 during 1972, virtually all of it at a December dinner. It reported spending $27,375 during 1972 and had $2,508 in debts for an unencumbered balance at the end of the year of $4,894. But since the campaign was claiming debts well into 1973, one can assume that the money reported as a balance was used for some of the debts. However, the committee filed a termination report in 1974, showing $8,000 in debts, which would bring the committee's total expenditure beyond its reported income of $35,000.

Because this committee filed under the FECA, its sources were reported, and they were not Dilbeck, Duncan, or a loan on Hartke's house. Almost one-half of the committee's money, $15,375, came from labor and other committees.[W] Seven contributors gave $500 or more (for a total of $5,000) and 82 gave $100 to $500 (for a total of $12,925); many of these large contributors were officials of unions, trade organizations, and businesses that are affected by Hartke's Senate subcommittees. Only $1,227 came from small contributions of less than $100.

These two Hartke committees' funds and Dilbeck's contribution account for about $157,000 in income, but one other committee expended funds on behalf of Hartke's presidential campaign. The Volunteers for Hartke was the principal committee for Hartke's 1970 Senate reelection campaign and the subsequent 1971 recount, and it filed financial reports with the Secretary of the Senate. The committee began 1972 with $13,000 on hand and raised $32,200 during the year for a total available of just over $45,000. In March 1973 the committee claimed it still owed $10,000 for the costs of the recount, but it had spent at least $15,800 during 1972 for bills seemingly connected to Hartke's presidential campaign; it is not known what the other $19,000 was used for. (This committee also reported $10,000 in spending for political expenses that appear to be unrelated to the 1970 campaign, the recount, or the presidential effort.) The $15,800 brings the identified spending on behalf of Hartke's presidential effort to $173,000.

Then, in the February 28, 1973 reports of the Deficit and Volunteer Committees, new deficits appeared totalling almost $57,800. (Interestingly, two previously announced fund-raising events were expected to raise $60,000.) If these debts are added to the known spending of $173,000, it would mean a campaign cost of $231,000. Furthermore, the $10,000 in general political spending and the unidentified $19,000 of the Volunteers' Committee mean that Hartke had a total of $260,000 in political costs (expenditures plus alleged debts) for 1972. Since neither Hartke nor any knowledgeable political observer has claimed that his presidential campaign cost even one-half that much, it suggests that Hartke ". . . turned a short-lived, obscure and ill-fated

---

[W]It includes $11,375 from labor committees. However, the reports of the labor committees for 1972 show that they gave Hartke $23,300. Presumably, the missing $11,925 was given before April 7, and it is possible that it is not accounted for in any of Hartke's other reported income sources.

campaign . . . into an on-going and highly successful fund-raising operation," by using an alleged debt from his presidential campaign to raise money for his continuing political activities.[23]

Wallace

Governor George C. Wallace ran for President in 1964 and 1968 as well as in 1972 and, in some ways, he never ceased being a candidate. It is difficult to date the beginning of his 1972 candidacy and to price the cost of that campaign. Counting from January 13, 1972, when Wallace formally announced he was entering the Florida primary, the campaign lasted six months (until the Democratic Convention) and cost $2.4 million. But looking at all of Wallace's political activities beginning right after the 1968 election, except those related to his 1970 gubernatorial campaign,[x] one can calculate a 3 1/2-year effort costing more than $3.6 million.

Wallace's political headquarters in Montgomery, Alabama, was never closed; the mailing address was simply changed from P.O. Box 1968 to P.O. Box 1972. The campaign newsletter, *The Wallace Stand,* continued its monthly publication. Wallace was in a difficult financial position from late 1968 through 1970 because the death of his wife Lurleen (who had been elected Governor of Alabama in 1966 because state law prohibited Wallace from succeeding himself) left him with neither income nor access to the Governor's political power in the state. Wallace lived on campaign contributions in 1968; in 1969 he paid himself $14,000 as editor of *The Wallace Stand*; in 1970 he supplemented his editorial salary with $11,000 in speeches and royalties. Wallace's financial straits ended after 1970, when his reelection as Governor gave him the salary, the mansion, and the political power he had enjoyed from 1962 to 1968.

By the spring of 1971 contributions were reportedly "pouring in" to the Montgomery headquarters, and Wallace was carrying out an active schedule of out-of-state appearances. In May 1971 he said it was too early to start talking about a 1972 presidential campaign, but threatened to run again as a third-party candidate unless Nixon turned to the right. In early June Wallace said he was assessing his position; by early August he said he had decided to run in 1972. In mid-summer Wallace reportedly had a full-time staff of 30, with 15 of them on the road. Throughout the summer and fall there were many "appreciation dinners" for Wallace, mostly at $25 and $50 per plate, and his campaign was well under way. However, it was not clear whether Wallace was planning to run as a Democrat in the primaries, as in 1964, or as a third-party independent in the general election, as in 1968.

---

[x]Wallace's gubernatorial campaign was expensive partly because $400,000 in Nixon funds was reportedly being directed to assist Wallace's primary opponent, Governor Albert Brewer, who lost to Wallace in a run-off.

Early in January 1972 Wallace confirmed that he would run in the Florida Democratic primary, but made no definite statement about his plans for the rest of the year. The speculation was that Wallace would again run as a third-party candidate after first confusing the Democratic battle in the Florida primary, in which he was favored. After being challenged by Democratic National Committee chairman Larry O'Brien, Wallace publicly promised that his delegates would accept the Democratic Party's loyalty oath not to support the nominee of any other party.[y] O'Brien then agreed to give Wallace equal treatment at the convention (for housing, telephones, etc.), and Wallace's full participation as a Democrat—at least through the convention—was set for the long primary season.

During this period there was considerable speculation that President Nixon had arranged to drop a federal tax investigation of Gerald Wallace, the Governor's brother, if Wallace agreed not to run in 1972 on a third party ticket. The agreement allegedly was made in 1971 while the two were closeted alone during an airplane ride over Alabama; it was supposed to have been undertaken because the White House was fearful of another independent Wallace candidacy in 1972. It is known that the White House took an active interest in the Wallace tax investigation.[z]

There was an uncertain, on-again, off-again quality to the 1972 effort. Wallace spent a full two months campaigning for the Florida primary; he shocked the experts, and was himself surprised, by his smashing win over the ten other candidates (six of whom campaigned actively), carrying 42 percent of the vote. In contrast to the long, all-out effort in Florida, Wallace spent only one week in Wisconsin. He minimized the importance of Wisconsin—saying he expected to do well in Maryland and Michigan—but expanded his effort there at the last minute. Again the results were a surprise when Wallace ran second to McGovern. After changing his mind several times, he made a few trips to Pennsylvania and ran a last-minute effort there. The result again surprised observers, as Wallace edged out both Muskie and McGovern for second place to Humphrey.

Indiana was Wallace's first two-man race and he narrowly lost to Humphrey by five percentage points. In the same-day Alabama primary, he won most of the convention delegates elected. Two days later Wallace won the Tennessee primary with 68 percent of the vote after having been the only major candidate to campaign actively in the state. Two days after that Wallace decisively defeated Governor Sanford and Representative Chisholm in the hard-fought North

---

[y]Wallace himself did not accept O'Brien's challenge to make a similar pledge and, as late as April 1972, said he had made no commitment not to run as a third-party candidate. It was not until mid-June, a month after he was shot, that Wallace flatly stated there would be no third-party effort.

[z]See, for example, Steven Brill, "George Wallace Is Even Worse Than You Think He Is," *New York*, March 17, 1975, pp. 36-46.

Carolina primary. In West Virginia a few days later, Wallace suffered his only major defeat of the primary circuit, losing to Humphrey by a little more than 2-1 in the two-man race.

Wallace was leading in the polls in Maryland and Michigan when he was shot on the day before those primaries. He won an impressive 51 percent of the vote in Michigan over three active and three inactive candidates, receiving almost twice as many votes as the second-place McGovern. In Maryland Wallace won with 39 percent of the vote, 12 percent more than Humphrey, who ran ahead of McGovern. Even from his hospital bed, Wallace continued to make surprising primary showings. In Oregon, without campaigning at all, he ran 30 percentage points behind McGovern, but he was second in the field of eleven. In New Mexico, also without any personal campaigning, he ran a strong second, less than four percentage points behind McGovern. Wallace had not been entered in the California primary, but a write-in effort was started on his behalf after he was shot; he received five percent of the votes cast.

By the end of the primary season, Wallace had been on the ballot in 14 states; he had actively campaigned in nine primaries, winning five and placing second in four. He had won more primaries and more votes than any other Democratic candidate, but he had won surprisingly few delegates. Only in Texas, where a strong caucus effort yielded 42 delegates, more than any other candidate won there, did his delegate strength come close to his electoral strength. By late June, he had only 377 delegates, and his total at the convention was 386. If Wallace had run a Texas kind of operation in other places, he might have had 600 or more delegates. His campaign director claimed that lack of both money and manpower had contributed to this result. But Wallace's 42 Texas delegates had come from a campaign costing $8,000—and it would have cost little more to file delegate candidates in more of the primary states and to relate Wallace's personal campaign to those delegates.

Wallace joined four other Democratic presidential candidates (and McCloskey) in voluntarily disclosing his campaign's contributors for most of the pre-April 7 period. However, the form of Wallace's disclosure was such as to render it much less useful or informative than that of any other candidate. One copy of a 1,047-page computer printout was made available to the press during a three-hour plane flight from Tennessee to Wisconsin. The campaign did not release the full list, about 30,000 names, or a list of large contributors; most of the names on the printout included only initials and last names, and no addresses or other information, making it difficult to clearly identify the donors. The printout covered $924,000 received over a three-year period, from March 1969 to March 14, 1972, but no breakdown of amounts received for each of the three years or for any specific time periods was given. (The March 14-April 6 period was never covered by either voluntary discolsure or the FECA.) Money received in subscriptions to *The Wallace Stand*, or the profit from that operation, was not included in the voluntary disclosure.

The Wallace campaign reported total post-April 7 expenditures of $1.6 million. Although there was no official reporting of the campaign's debt, the campaign was not particularly secretive about it—some $225,000 in early 1973 (down from about $260,000 owed at the end of the convention). In the pre-April 7 period, Wallace was active in two primaries, Florida and Wisconsin, spending about $200,000 in Florida and $100,000 in Wisconsin. As of early January 1972 the cost of Wallace's Montgomery headquarters and related expenses were reported to be $100,000 per month. Using this figure for the three months before the FECA took effect gives a total of $300,000 for headquarters operation, added to the $300,000 for primaries in this period. This brings the total cost of the Wallace campaign during 1972 to about $2.4 million.

For the pre-1972 period the costs of the Wallace campaign can be deduced from its known income. Wallace's 1968 presidential campaign had ended with a $900,000 surplus. Campaign contributions beginning in March 1969, covered in Wallace's voluntary disclosure, total $924,000. Since Wallace's first FECA filing showed very little cash on hand as of April 6, it can be assumed that virtually all of the money received prior to that date was also spent before that date. Adding this $924,000 to the 1968 surplus of $900,000 gives a total of $1,824,000 available in the post-1968, pre-April 7, 1972, period. Of this, $600,000 is known to have been spent in 1972, on the Florida and Wisconsin primaries and for headquarters costs; this leaves $1,224,000 in expenditures for 1969-71. Adding this to the 1972 costs of a little more than $2.4 million gives a total 3 1/2-year Wallace campaign cost of at least $3.6 million.

The $1.2 million spent in 1969-71 went for headquarters, staff, and candidate travel costs, but no details are known. According to the FCC report, the 1972 campaign spent $432,246 on broadcasting, all nonnetwork, $308,526 on television, $123,645 on radio, and $75 on cable television.[24]

The Wallace campaign had no formal budgets, but each primary was expected to cost $100,000-$150,000. The first one, Florida, was Wallace's most expensive and its $200,000 cost was less than the campaign was prepared to spend; Wallace was believed to be so far ahead that a little more than a week before the primary the campaign cut back on television, radio, billboards, and newspaper ads. Wallace's Florida campaign used print materials heavily; at least two million pieces, including special interest "newspapers" for labor, for youth, for the elderly, and even a Wallace *Hoy* in Spanish for Cuban-Americans. Wallace's Wisconsin campaign was mostly a last-minute effort and it relied more heavily on media than most Wallace campaigns: 75 percent of the $100,000 total cost went for media.

For the six-week period from the Wisconsin primary through May 15 (the day Wallace was shot), which included the campaigns in Pennsylvania, Indiana, Alabama, Tennessee, North Carolina, Maryland and Michigan, Wallace reported spending little more than $650,000. Allowing about $150,000 for headquarters cost leaves only $500,000 for the seven primaries, which seems low, but the available state-by-state data fail to provide a better figure. Possibly the campaign incurred significantly higher costs during this period, going into debt, with the actual expenditures made and reported at a later time. The costs thus would become part of the reported postconvention debt. This explanation is supported by the fact that campaign income from April 7 to May 15 was also about $600,000 while amost $1 million was received after May 15. Since the campaign's costs in the post-May 15 period were much less than in the earlier period, it is likely that much of the $1 million received after May 15 was used to pay costs incurred before that date. This also seems likely because the Wallace campaign admittedly had money troubles in the spring and was $100,000 in debt early in May. The only known expenditures in those seven primary campaigns are for media: the campaign spent $45,300 in Alabama (more than half of it for newspapers), and about $20,000 in all the other six states together.[aa]

Wallace had not planned a major effort for the three primaries in which he was entered after May 15, and the campaigns were mostly local. For the last-minute California campaign, Wallace's national headquarters reportedly spent $90,000 to show a film on how to write-in for Wallace. However, the campaign's records show only $10,500 for television in California, leaving it unclear how the remaining money was spent. After Wallace was shot, there was a 50 percent increase in the amount of mail, including contributions, received in Montgomery. Staff was added at the headquarters office to cope with the deluge.

After the Democratic National Convention, at which Wallace spoke in a brief, postconvalescent appearance, the campaign did not fold completely, but it was significantly cut back. The Montgomery headquarters was moved from a $1,500-per-month to a $1,000-per-month office while the number of employees was cut from 105 to ten. All cars and trucks were returned and the number of telephones was sharply decreased. The campaign was further cut back in late 1972-early 1973 after a fund-raising mailing in the fall made no dent in the debt and barely raised enough to keep the headquarters going; two issues of *The Wallace Stand* were missed and the staff was cut to six (the campaign director and five secretaries). Meanwhile, the campaign's mailing address had been changed to P.O. Box 1976. Wallace's financial campaign in 1972 was not as solid as in 1968, and was subject to wide vicissitudes.

Sources and Fund Raising. Details on Wallace's campaign income are available for $2.5 million of the $3.6 million received: this includes $1.6 million covered in FECA reports and the $924,000 covered in Wallace's voluntary disclosure. The $900,000 left over from 1968 and the $225,000 remaining debt

---

[aa]In Michigan Wallace spent $8,100 on radio and television and the state Democratic party spent about $10,000 on anti-Wallace commercials. Such state party activity violated party rules.

are not covered in this breakdown. Of the $924,000 voluntarily disclosed, some
$197,000 came from "dinners and rallies."

Wallace did not do as well with grass-roots financial support as he had in
1968 (when only seven percent of the money raised came from contributions
of $500 or more), yet he out-distanced all of his 1972 Democratic rivals but
McGovern in small contributions: about 13 percent ($328,800) of the $2.5
million came from contributions and loans of $500 or more; only five percent
($130,400) came from contributions of $5,000 or more.

The campaign's largest contributor was Dwight Coffman of Washington
Court House, Ohio, vice-president and director of Visador Company, who gave
$19,000 ($10,000 before April 7 and $9,000 after). Family and business
associates of the late Leander Perez, the segregationist political boss of
Plaquemines Parish, Louisiana, also gave $19,000; $5,000 each came from two
sons and a daughter of Perez, and $4,000 from business associates, all in New
Orleans. In February 1973 Wallace asked 50 contributors to help raise $5,000
each to wipe out the $225,000 campaign debt. Wallace was particularly con-
cerned because he always insisted on paying off all debts in full.

Wallace's fund-raising operation was one of the most sophisticated and also
one of the folksiest in 1972. On the sophisticated side were computerized
mailing lists: in 1968 the campaign had used as many as 600 staff and volunteers to handle the mail and money, but in 1972 the operation was handled by
computer. The mailing lists included the names of those who contributed in
1968 and a reported 250,000 subscribers to *The Wallace Stand*. In the fall of
1971 the campaign designed a combination questionnaire and fund-raising
appeal, headed "Governor Wallace Wants Your Opinion," which was mailed to
the entire list, asking recipients to distribute it widely. The poll-appeal also
ran as ads in 71 newspapers in major metropolitan markets, all paid for by
local Wallace supporters, and in many weekly newspapers, some run for free.
By December the campaign claimed a total of seven million copies of the poll-
appeal had been mailed, with almost one million returned. The amount of
money received was greater than the mailing cost. The poll results were analyzed
geographically and used by the campaign to pick key issues in different primary
states (e.g., busing in Florida and high taxes in Wisconsin).

Another fund-raising method was a petition tied to precinct-level organizing.
Volunteer "official fund raisers" were signed up at Wallace rallies and given a
petition, headed by a one-paragraph pledge of support for Wallace and a declaration of principles, with space for 85 names, addresses, and the amount contributed. Each "official fund raiser" was expected to collect signatures and money
from among his friends, co-workers, or neighbors. Every petition was numbered,
staff members kept in touch with the "official fund raisers," and each petition
and the money accompanying it was picked up within three weeks. Every signer-

contributor received a written acknowledgement from the Montgomery head-quarters. In mid-May, a campaign official said the petitions were producing 10,000 names a day, although not all of the signers also contributed.

The campaign's fund raising was augmented by the sale of campaign materials and the famous Wallace rallies. Wallace's campaign was the only one to sell all campaign material—from a small five cent button to a $35.00 red Wallace blazer—and to make money from such sales. Any item that did not sell well was quickly dropped from the collection. Campaign materials were not sent free even to state or local Wallace committees, but were sold, invariably for profit.

Wallace rallies were also money makers, and their unvarying style and spirit were a unique mixture of jingoism, evangelism, populism, and hucksterism hardly practiced any longer in American politics. The routine was always the same. An hour before rally time, local volunteers appeared in the lobby, opening up trays of campaign trinkets and merchandise for sale. There were varieties of bumper stickers, George Wallace watches selling for $16.50, buttons at ten cents each, straw hats at $2.00, toy footballs, a paperback biography. A customer buying more than a dollar's worth of material got a free autographed picture of Wallace. On the stage, guitarist Billy Grammer and his trio played. Warmup shill George Mangum, a Baptist minister, preached that this was a people's campaign and the candidate needed money to buy TV time. Volunteers with buckets passed through the audience taking up collections. This provided time for local enter-tainers to do their thing. Once the fund raising was completed, Mangum roared: "Ladies and gentlemen, the next President of the U.S.," and Wallace spoke.[25]

The Wallace campaign also relied very successfully on one of the most com-mon political fund-raising methods, dinners. Unlike those of other candidates, however, Wallace's dinners were usually relatively low-cost affairs, with guests paying $25 or $50 per plate. There were many such dinners in mid- and late-1971, but few details are available. A $25-per-plate dinner in Houston on December 6, 1971 reportedly grossed $65,000—which would mean that 2,600 persons had attended if all paid the stated price. On January 2, 1972 it was claimed that seven recent dinners had grossed $300,000 and that a total of 30 were planned. Only one high-priced dinner was publicized—a $1,500-per-person, $2,500-per-couple affair in Montgomery; it was held at the Governor's mansion in late March and a local newspaper reported that 57 state officials and business-men attended although 100 had been expected.

One of the largest events was "Wallace's Woodstock," a country-fair style, fried chicken and corn-on-the-cob picnic-jamboree, on June 12, in Lakeland, Florida, at the 43-acre Old Plantation Music Park of Tammy Wynette and George Jones. Nearly 11,000 people paid $5 each and were entertained by country and western stars. The affair's organizer said he had gotten the idea for the event from George McGovern's star-studded Hollywood rally, and that there would have been 10,000 more people if a planned telephone hookup from Wallace's bedside to the jamboree site had been completed. Instead, George Wallace, Jr. briefly addressed the crowd to report on his father's condition.

Curiously, the flow of money to Wallace's campaign did not follow the rises and falls in the candidate's political fortunes, as is usually the case. After Wallace's smashing victory in Florida and surprising second-place showing in Wisconsin, one might have expected an outpouring of contributions. Yet, one reason for Wallace's later reversed decision not to campaign in Pennsylvania's late April primary was the need to determine priorities and the implication was that money as well as the candidate's time was limited. By May the campaign was admittedly in financial straits, running as much as $100,000 in the red, and this was after Wallace's surprising second-place showing in the Pennsylvania primary. In early May Wallace ran very close in the Indiana primary, then scored decisive victories in Tennessee and North Carolina, and still money was tight, even though Wallace was spending less than most of the other candidates in the primaries. By mid-May the polls were predicting two more Wallace victories—in the Michigan and Maryland primaries—and yet the campaign had only raised about $600,000 since April 7 and had probably incurred debts of more than $200,000 in addition. After May the outlook for Wallace's political fortunes nose-dived: the attempt on his life had left him politically and physically immobilized with less than 400 delegates and virtually no primaries or other opportunities to win significantly more; yet, the campaign raised almost $1 million in the next 3 1/2 months. More than $300,000 came in the last two weeks of May, after the shooting. Furthermore, two-thirds of Wallace's meager total of post-April 7 big contributions had been received by May 15 so that almost all of the $1 million came from small contributions. This pattern of financial support for Wallace again demonstrates the nature of his candidacy as a protest and a symbol; a cause, rather than a more ordinary political campaign tied to electoral success.[bb]

In June 1973 the Wallace campaign committee in Montgomery hired the direct mail company of Richard A. Viguerie (which had handled Ashbrook's presidential effort) to develop "the largest, most sophisticated mailing list" for a possible Wallace run in the 1976 presidential race. Between August 1973 and September 1974 the Viguerie company was paid nearly $800,000. Spending reports filed with GAO by the Wallace committee covering the period between January 1 and May 31, 1974 showed total receipts of $758,334 and expenditures of $640,835. Of that, Viguerie was paid $396,407 for printing, mailing fees, postage, computer processing, programming, raw computer time,

---

[bb]For "an in-depth account of Wallace's spectacular rise through the maze of Alabama politics . . .," [from jacket] see Marshall Frady, *Wallace* (New York; Cleveland: The New American Library, Inc. in association with the World Publishing Company, 1968).

and other expenses. By September 1974 three mailings had already been done for Wallace.[26] By December the campaign had raised more than $2 million, most of it used to develop the mailing list of three million potential backers, and more than nine million pieces of campaign literature had been mailed by Wallace headquarters.[27]

Scandal. Wallace's 1968 campaign was plagued with charges of kickbacks from contractors to the Alabama state government and other illegal and unethical fiscal activities. Some of those charges were not settled until well into the 1972 political season, and new charges, although many fewer than four years earlier, arose. Several of Wallace's top aides from 1968 were indicted in 1971, but all of them had broken with Wallace by 1969 and Wallace himself was never implicated in the scandals. In February 1972 several Alabama Air National Guard officials were indicted for illegal political fund raising in connection with Wallace's 1970 gubernatorial campaign. One month later Alabama's state highway director resigned abruptly amid reports that he and other top state officials were being pressured to contribute to Wallace's presidential campaign and that he had refused. His resignation came two days after the $1,500-per-person dinner at the Governor's mansion, to which it was alleged that state officials and businessmen expecting state contracts had been told to come and bring $1,500. No formal charges of indictments resulted from the 1972 campaign.

Jackson

Senator Henry Jackson's presidential campaign was a long and expensive one. It lasted 18 months—from early in 1971 through the balloting at the Democratic National Convention—and cost $1.5 million. The cost can be fairly well determined only because of the work of the Senate Watergate Committee, since most of Jackson's fund raising and spending occurred prior to April 7 and he consistently refused to voluntarily disclose—the only prominent Democrat active in the pre-FECA period who did not disclose.

Jackson began with an exploratory effort in January 1971, reportedly financed by $150,000 from friends,[cc] focusing early plans on the New Hampshire and Florida primaries. Because Jackson was not well known nationally, his strategy was to win one primary (or come very close) and build on a state-by-state basis as McCarthy had done in 1968 and as McGovern would also do in 1972. But the Jackson campaign proceeded on another level as well—going nationwide in making Jackson's formal announcement of candidacy. The campaign spent

---

[cc]This publicly claimed $150,000 never surfaced in the records of the pre-April 7 period, noted below.

$65,000 to televise the event on a limited national schedule designed to reach 70-80 percent of the population.

After preliminary probings, Jackson formally withdrew from the New Hampshire primary. Instead, he concentrated heavily on Florida for a full two-and-one-half months before the March 14 primary. His 14 percent, third-place finish, winning no delegates, was a blow from which his campaign never recovered: not quite bad enough to kill the campaign, but barely good enough to keep it alive. Jackson's effort for the April 4 Wisconsin primary seemed hopeless and suffered from lack of money. His last day of campaigning in the state was spent in Republican areas, actively seeking crossover votes. After a fifth place, eight percent showing, he decided to concentrate on the May 2 Ohio primary, although his name was also on the ballot in several other states. He ran a distant third in Ohio, with only eight percent of the vote again, and dropped out of participation in the primaries. Jackson said that he could not continue actively without going into debt, which he would not do; he also believed that it did not pay to put forth the large effort being made in the primaries. Jackson persisted as a candidate, however, believing he might be an acceptable compromise to a deadlocked convention, and his name was placed in nomination in Miami.[dd]

Although Florida was a devastating blow, and Ohio the final one, to Jackson's presidential bid, it was probably over long before: Humphrey's candidacy hurt Jackson badly and Wallace's decision to run as a Democrat was fatal. Humphrey and Jackson were not perceived as far apart on the issues, and Humphrey was much better known with a wide popular following in the party; many of Jackson's union and party supporters either preferred Humphrey in any case or preferred him after Jackson's standing in the public opinion polls stayed under five percent after almost a year of campaigning. On the other side, Jackson simply could not compete with Wallace's image and appeal as an outsider, however close their views might be. Jackson's strategy had been devised on the assumption that neither Humphrey nor Wallace would be in the primary races; with both in, Jackson never really had a chance.

Voluntary Disclosure; Involuntary Disclosure. Voluntary disclosure became a significant issue during the Florida campaign, with attention focused primarily on Muskie and Humphrey, the two major candidates who had not disclosed. However, after both did disclose, after Jackson's third-place showing (ahead of Muskie), and after the high cost of Jackson's Florida campaign became apparent, Jackson became the main focus of press and voter pressure to disclose his contributors. During the Wisconsin campaign, Jackson was the only active

---

[dd]His total of 534 votes on the first ballot (before the switches to McGovern began) included a high proportion of votes for Humphrey and other candidates who had withdrawn from the contest in the face of McGovern's almost certain first-ballot victory.

candidate who had not disclosed, and the issue was often, and hostilely, raised at his campaign appearances. When the state's five-day preelection financial reports showed that $215,144 of Jackson's reported Wisconsin receipts of $219,953 had come from two blind Seattle committees, both at the same address, the pressure on Jackson intensified. He did not relent, however, and his staff later admitted that the disclosure issue had hurt in Wisconsin. Further, unlike most other Democratic candidates, including those who ended their campaigns before voluntary disclosure became an issue or who also refused to voluntarily disclose during their campaigns, Jackson maintained his silence even after the campaign was over.

Having made commitments to some contributors that he would not reveal their names, Jackson had three choices, once disclosure became an issue: (1) he could break his word and disclose; (2) he could disclose a partial list; (3) he could refuse. Jackson believed the first choice was dishonorable, and he was publicly contemptuous of those candidates who had promised contributors anonymity and then broke their promise. He believed that partial disclosure, which his staff alleged other campaigns were doing, was misrepresentation, and he would not be a party to it. That left silence as the only honorable alternative, as Jackson saw it.[ee]

In a Wisconsin campaign appearance, Jackson denied a questioner's charge that he was being financed by defense contractors and went on to say:

> And I will not reveal who my contributors are because some are in business and can be retaliated against, and a number of contributors work for the federal government, in policy positions. Do you think the Nixon Administration would keep them on if I did?[28]

So Jackson kept his silence and could never shake off the charges that his campaign was supported by defense contractors, or a few very wealthy people, or some other questionable or special interest sources. It was not until two years later, when the Watergate Committee's investigation forced involuntary disclosure by the Jackson campaign, that those charges were, in part, laid to rest and, in part, proved.

The Watergate Committee received and examined the bank records of eight Jackson committees, all in Washington, D.C. or the state of Washington, all of which went out of business before the effective date of the FECA. The treasurer or trustee for all of the bank accounts was Stanley Golub, who was the treasurer throughout the Jackson campaign. The records covered the period beginning on June 1, 1971, although four of the eight committees showed balances on hand or earlier deposits, totalling $81,000, going back to December 1969.

[ee]*The New York Times,* in an editorial, said Jackson had a "higher obligation to the voters whose confidence he seeks" than to the contributors to whom he had promised silence, but Jackson never measured the issue in those terms.

The importance of this involuntary disclosure cannot be overemphasized: it accounted for $1,134,123 of Jackson's income, 76 percent of the total. The only pre-April 7 data otherwise available was a mere $121,689 (eight percent) raised or received directly in Florida. Without the Watergate Committee's data, and with the continued silence of Jackson and his staff, the cost of the Jackson campaign could only have been estimated and most of his contributors would never have been known.

Costs. The cost of Jackson's campaign has been calculated from three sources: the Watergate Committee's data and financial reports filed under Florida state law for the pre-April 7 period, and the campaign's FECA reports, for the post-April 7 period. Because the Watergate Committee's investigation was primarily concerned with contributions, the expenditures of the Jackson campaign for the period and committees covered by that investigation have been deduced from income data. That data covered $1,134,123 received before April 7; subtracting from this the $162,609 reported as cash on hand by all Jackson committees as of April 7 leaves $971,514 spent before that date. In addition, reports filed in Florida show $121,689 raised or received directly in the state (and not covered by the Senate Committee) and the Florida committee's FECA reports showed no cash on hand as of April 7. This brings total pre-April 7 spending to $1,093,203. For the post-April 7 period, the FECA reports show $395,947 spent and $7,976 in debts for a total campaign cost of $1,497,126.[ff]

The only known categorical cost is for radio and television. The FCC report shows $240,149 for television (all nonnetwork) and $50,520 for radio (all nonnetwork), for a 1972 total of $290,679. Unlike most other campaigns, Jackson's known radio and television spending does not tally closely with the FCC figures. Jackson spent the limit of $180,000 in Florida, about $109,000 in Wisconsin, and perhaps $22,000 in Ohio, for a known total of about $211,000. This leaves almost $80,000 in radio and television costs that cannot be tracked down. Another known cost, however, is that of Jackson's televised candidacy announcement in November 1971, which reportedly was $65,000. This brings Jackson's total radio and television spending to about $356,000, almost one-quarter of his campaign's total cost. The Jackson campaign believed that heavy media was necessary because Jackson was not well known. There were no disagreements between fund raisers and staff over this spending.

The staff costs of the Jackson campaign are not known, but were probably lower than for other campaigns because many of the top staff were volunteers.

[ff] Jackson has an inviolate rule against either borrowing or going into debt, and only three states—Florida, Ohio, and Alabama—ended up with small debts. The national campaign bailed out Florida before April 7 and was expected to eventually take care of Ohio ($7,000) and Alabama ($900) debts.

One aide said that there were limits on per diem and other expenses for staff and volunteers; for example, "only the Senator could fly first class." The campaign sent seed money to states to get them started; the amounts ranged from $1,000 to $5,000 and included money for telephone deposits, which telephone companies were requiring of political campaigns in 1972. After the startup money, every state campaign was supposed to be self-financed, but this proved to be an unrealistic expectation.

Chronologically, there is a little more information on the costs of Jackson's campaign. For 1971 the only direct information on costs is the $65,000 reportedly spent for Jackson's announcement. For the first three months of 1972, Jackson was active in two primaries: Florida, in which he spent at least $500,000 and Wisconsin, in which $183,000 was reported spent. Adding these three known costs totals $748,000, which leaves only about $345,000 for all headquarters and nonprimary states costs for a little more than ten months— June 1, 1971 to April 6, 1972,[gg] which is an average of $34,500 per month. This is low for a presidential campaign, but it could well be correct since many of the top Jackson staff were volunteers and the campaign had small headquarters and field staffs. A different analysis by the Watergate Committee of the headquarters bank account showed $217,000 spent from October 27, 1971 to April 5, 1972, which works out to a little more than $40,000 per month (not including startup money sent to the states). This suggests average costs of about $26,000 per month from June 1 to the end of October, and it is logical that the campaign's costs were relatively lower in the earlier months.

The Florida primary had been picked as Jackson's major strategic battleground and the campaign accorded it highest financial priority. Estimates of the total cost ranged from $400,000 (by a staff member right after the campaign) to "close to $750,000" (by a staff member almost a year later) and the $500,000 figure used throughout this analysis should be considered a conservative, minimum figure.

Jackson's largest cost in Florida was for radio and television; his $179,780 spent came within $553 of the Democrats' agreed limit for the state—the base $133,000 plus the $47,333 bonus allowed in up to three states. The media campaign began in January (a month ahead of all the other candidates) with five-minute spots on eight television stations, covering the state. These were mostly supplanted in mid-February by one-minute and 30-second spots. For radio, the campaign purchased commuter driving time. Reportedly, $12,000 was added to the television budget for the last two weeks of the Florida campaign.

There was also big spending for other media. Jackson's Florida reports showed $53, 284 for newspaper advertising all of which was probably for

---

[gg]This also assumes that Jackson had no costs in the early, January-June 1971, exploratory phase of his campaign, as the records of the Watergate Committee also seem to indicate.

1.9 million copies of an eight-page tabloid distributed as a supplement in Sunday newspapers. Jackson also used billboards in Florida, the only presidential candidate to do so. The billboards went up in January, a total of 500 in 11 metropolitan areas. The billboards caused some puzzlement at first because some said "Scoop for President" and many Floridians had no idea who, or what, "Scoop" was.

In addition to the heavy media campaign in Florida, Jackson carried out a heavy schedule of personal appearances, often campaigning from eight in the morning to midnight. He travelled to each of Florida's 12 congressional districts at least once and visited many towns that no other candidates went to.

Although the Florida primary was the strategic key to Jackson's candidacy, the campaign did not buy everything it was offered there; two specific cases of rejected proposals are known. Some ideas for direct mail were proposed for both political and fund-raising purposes and it was argued that they would pay for themselves. However, a test run showed that this was not so, and the staff decided to have only a very limited direct mail campaign aimed at specific urban and suburban target counties that they believed had a large proportion of Jackson supporters. But the targeting was rough, and even these limited mailings did not pay for themselves. The campaign consulting firm of Valentine, Sherman, and Associates (which would later work for Humphrey) proposed a $100,000 2 1/2-month statewide telephone canvass to identify Jackson supporters in order to maximize his vote. According to a staff member, the campaign turned it down for two reasons: "We did not have the $100,000 and we did not yet have the voters to identify because many of them did not recognize Jackson yet."

Jackson's Wisconsin campaign was a dispirited effort after his disappointing Florida showing. His filings under state law reported $183,336 spent, with no evidence to suggest any more was spent. Again media was the biggest item, accounting for 70 percent of the reported total. Radio and television spending was $109,023 (just under 60 percent) and newspaper advertising was $18,805 (just over ten percent).

For the post-April 7 period, 17 Jackson committees reported costs of $403,923 (including $7,976 in unpaid bills) in FECA filings. The main Washington, D.C. committee accounted for almost two-thirds of the total. Committees in five states reported expenditures of more than $100,000: Wisconsin, $25,000—most of which is probably included in the primary total noted above; Ohio, $33,000 spent and $7,000 in debts; Nebraska, $21,000; Washington, $15,500; and Oregon, $14,000.

Although Jackson made Ohio his main target after his weak Wisconsin showing, the campaign said it spent only $50,000 in Ohio, of which $22,000 was for media. The difference between $50,000 and the $33,000 reported by the Ohio Jackson committee was probably for media, spent directly from the Washington, D.C. committee.

Jackson dropped out of the primaries after Ohio, and the campaign's major expenses during the rest of the preconvention period were for travel, headquarters staff, and overhead. The Watergate Committee analyzed the main committee's bank records and concluded that the Jackson convention operation cost $138,500. This is disputed by Jackson staffers, but they used different definitions of convention expenses; they claim Jackson did not have that much money available by the time of the convention. All debts were paid off when the campaign terminated.

Lack of money hurt the Jackson campaign, particularly in Ohio, the only state in which Jackson ran and Wallace did not; with more money Jackson might have been able to take advantage of that fact. But one of the campaign's top advisers acknowledged that by Ohio Jackson had already been proven so weak that money could not have made a significant difference: Jackson had enough money to wage major campaigns in the early primaries and failed. As this adviser succinctly summarized the whole Jackson campaign: "[I] do not think that we lost for lack of money; we lost for lack of votes."

Sources. The Jackson campaign is known to have raised $1,493,330: $1,255,812 before April 7 and $237,518 after the FECA took effect. As noted above, all information on the sources of $1,134,123 of the pre-April 7 money—76 percent of the total—comes from the Watergate Committee. There is almost no information on the $121,689 raised in Florida before April 7 and the rest of the information comes from the campaign's FECA reports.

None of Jackson's big pre-April 7 contributors also gave in the post-April 7 period and all of his biggest contributions came in the earlier period. Since the campaign effectively collapsed before the FECA took effect, it might be argued that the collapse of his major financial support was to be expected, and that there was no particular significance in the difference between his pre- and post-April 7 contributors. However, because Jackson would never reveal who his contributors were and because of his own statements regarding them, it must be concluded that they did not want to be known and that their large gifts in the pre-April 7 period were made on the assumption that they never would be known.

Of the more than $1.1 million covered in the Watergate Committee's data, almost one-half of the money came from contributors who also gave to Nixon.[hh] The largest of these joint contributors, and Jackson's biggest contributor by far, was Leon Hess, chairman of the board of Amerada Hess Oil Company. Hess gave $225,000 to Jackson, only slightly less than the $250,000 he gave Nixon. Hess disguised both his Jackson and Nixon contributions by

---

[hh]We are indebted to James R. Polk, who examined the Watergate Committee's material (see "Hess Donations to Jackson in 1972 Disguised," *Washington Star*, August 7, 1974), for parts of this discussion of Jackson's contributors.

making them in the names of other persons, a practice that became illegal on April 7.[ii] One of these other persons was a Florida widow who knew nothing about and presumably could not afford "her" $9,000 contributions to Jackson and Nixon; her connection was apparently her accountant, also Hess's personal accountant, who had ten relatives or friends listed as Jackson contributors who were actually conduits for Hess's money.

Hess had reportedly met with Jackson some time in 1971 and agreed to contribute ten percent of the campaign's cost; his $225,000 turned out to be 15 percent of the cost. This was probably because the campaign's budget was reduced when Jackson withdrew from the primaries, although Hess might have given more if Jackson had done better, stayed in, and therefore had higher costs.

Jackson's second largest contributor, who gave $100,000, was also a Nixon giver, as well as a major Humphrey supporter—Meshulam Riklis. This very large Jackson contribution was actually the smallest of Riklis's known presidential contributions in 1972: he gave $125,000 to Humphrey and loaned an additional $550,000 (probably never repaid) and gave $188,000 to Nixon.

Jackson's third and fourth largest contributions were in cash: Walter R. Davis, an oil operator from Midland, Texas, gave $50,000 and Dwayne Andreas, the Minneapolis soybean tycoon, gave $25,000. Davis had been a 1968 Nixon contributor and had also given to a White House-backed operation for Republican senators in 1970, while Andreas was secretly supporting Nixon and Jackson at the same time in 1971-72. Andreas, like Riklis, was also a Humphrey supporter: in addition to his $25,000 to Jackson, Andreas gave $161,000 to Humphrey and $144,000 to Nixon, of which $25,000 became famous when it turned up in the hands of one of the Watergate burglars.

These four contributors—Hess, Riklis, Davis, and Andreas—accounted for more than one-third of the Jackson's pre-April 7 income. Three of them were also contributing to Nixon, all gave only before the FECA took effect, and three of the four further hid their contributions either by disguise or by giving in cash.

The $75,000 from Davis and Andreas was part of a total of $166,000 in pre-April 7 cash contributions to the national Jackson campaign, more than one-half of which came from people connected to the oil industry. These contributors included, in addition to Davis: E. Edmund Miller, president of Time Oil, who gave $15,000; Claude Wild, Jr., former Gulf Oil Corporation vice-president, who gave $10,000; and Edwin W. Pauley, chairman of Pauley Petroleum, Inc., who gave $10,000. All three of these men were also secretly contributing to Nixon. As discussed later, the Claude Wild gift was made with illegal corporate funds.

[ii]Both the Office of the Special Prosecutor and the Internal Revenue Service were reported to be investigating the Hess contributions.

Other cash contributors included: J. Peter Grace, chairman of W.R. Grace
& Co., $10,000; Fred J. Russell, former Under Secretary of the Interior in the
Nixon administration, $5,000; J.D. Coleman, of Saratoga, Wyoming, $5,000;
Ben Sonnenberg, a New York City public relations executive, $5,000; and B.L.
Perkins, of Boise, Idaho, $5,000.

In addition to the Jackson contributors who also gave to Nixon in large
amounts or in cash (Hess, Riklis, Andreas, Miller, and Wild), there were others
who gave to both Nixon and Jackson in 1972. They and their contributions
to Jackson were: Milledge A. Hart, III, president of Electronic Data Systems
Corporation, $10,000; C.R. Smith, chairman of American Airlines, $11,000
($3,000-post April 7); Justin Dart, head of the drug store chain, $5,000; John
Loeb, the New York stockbroker (who later was indicted for contributions to
Humphrey made in the names of others), $5,000; Nathan Lipson, an Atlanta
carpet manufacturer, $5,000; Charles E. Smith, a Washington, D.C., building
developer, $10,000 (half before, half after April 7); Samuel Rothberg of
Illinois, a leader in the Jewish community, $5,000; C. Douglas Dillon, former
Treasury Secretary, $2,000; Robert O. Anderson, chairman of Atlantic Rich-
field, $2,000; and Edward E. Carlson, president of United Air Lines, $1,000.
Almost all of these people gave more to Nixon than to Jackson; one exception
was C.R. Smith, who gave only a token contribution to Nixon.[jj]

The campaign was admittedly hurt by Jackson's refusal to disclose and
by the rumors of where his money was coming from. The two widespread
rumors that Jackson's money was coming primarily from Jews and from
Boeing and other defense industry executives were exaggerations. Yet, Jackson must have feared the truth of a third rumor—that some of his money was
coming from Republicans—enough to continue to take the heat of all the
rumors rather than disclose.

Two other rumors led to one of the year's most bizarre political "offers"
and to a probably too-strong reaction to an incident during the Wisconsin campaign. On November 12, 1971, M.T. Mehdi, secretary-general of The Action
Committee on American-Arab Relations, wrote to Jackson:[29]

> The Arab Americans and American Arabists, viewing you as a serious
> man . . . have decided to offer you the opportunity to wage your
> campaign for nomination as a freer man and with a greater possibility
> to succeed.
>
> More specifically, we are offering you our financial support.

[jj]In addition to all of these known joint Jackson-Nixon contributors, there were two
known instances of Democrats who worked for Jackson and later supported Nixon. One
was W. John Kenney, treasurer of the D.C. Citizens for Jackson, who was later listed in an
advertisement of Democrats for Nixon. The other was C. Farris Bryant, the former Governor of Florida, who was chairman of Jackson's finance committee in that state and then was
also involved in Democrats for Nixon.

Presently, there are pledges ranging from $800,000 to $1 million.... Furthermore, I am happy to advise you that we are ready to offer you at least twice as much financial support as the Jewish funds you are seeking and you can realistically expect.

Asked about the offer, Mehdi said: "While it is true that this is not done in public, in reality this is done, so why should we be so hypocritical?" What he was doing in making the offer, Mehdi said, was "as American as apple pie. We are looking for one great, strong politician to stand on his feet and say, 'To hell with Israel.'" While people who know Jackson might have simply dismissed this as a shocking insult to his integrity and convictions, for others it probably increased the speculation about Jewish support for Jackson's campaign. After the campaign, one official said that "not that much" was raised from the Jewish community—which the record now confirms—but that the fund raisers did not want to discourage the rumors during the campaign because they were trying to raise from Jews. The campaign did receive, unsolicited, a $1,000 contribution from an Israeli, which was returned because it was thought to be "improper;" it was also illegal.

The Wisconsin incident concerned a Boeing employee named Rodney W. Scheyer. In Wisconsin on company business and company salary, he spent time working for the Jackson campaign and also used $299.52 in company-advanced travelers checks to pay for some Jackson newspaper ads. He happened to be around one day when Jackson was making an appearance nearby and offered rides in his car to anyone who wanted to go. The car was filled with press people, one of whom asked him who he was and what he was doing in Wisconsin. This triggered front-page stories of Boeing employees working for Jackson on company time, which is illegal; of using Boeing money for the campaign, which is also illegal; and of Scheyer's having been sent to work for Jackson with company knowledge. The stories were probably overreactions to one case, but Jackson was vulnerable to that kind of story because of his campaign's extreme secretiveness.

The Florida filings show receipts of $149,537 by eight Jackson committees, of which $27,848 was transferred in from Washington, D.C. and the state of Washington. Of the remaining $121,689, $55,985 came from a Miami dinner committee and an additional $65,704 was raised in (or sent directly to) Florida. The campaign had hoped to raise the money needed for the Florida campaign within the state, but this proved to be a naive expectation; most political observers believe that Florida is an import state[kk] for all presidential candidates

---

[kk]One that cannot support a primary campaign internally, as distinct from a self-sufficient state (for example, New Jersey) and export states (for example, New York and California) which can support their own campaigns and still send money elsewhere.

(except, perhaps, Wallace). Even Jackson's strong position regarding Israel did not produce much money from southern Florida's large Jewish population.

For the $237,000 in income covered by the FECA reports, more than one-half came from 90 contributions of $500 or more; almost one-third of the total came from just nine contributors who gave $5,000 or more. The two largest contributions (but small compared to the pre-FECA givers) were for $10,000 each. They came from Julius Goldman, listed as a Sherman Oaks, California egg producer, and L.B. DeLong, an American in the import-export business living in The Netherlands. In the $100-$500 range, there were only 126 contributions that accounted for about $22,000. Less than one-fifth of the total, only about $40,000, came from contributions of less than $100.

A 1973 audit of the main campaign committee uncovered the fact that in May 1972 one contributor, Leo Harvey of Los Angeles, had used the by-then illegal device of contributing through other persons. The GAO concluded that $3,000 listed from him, $3,000 from his wife, $3,000 from his secretary, and $1,000 from his bookkeeper were all, in fact, from him ($4,000 was returned in June 1972). The matter was referred to the Justice Department, which later informed GAO that the matter had been investigated and no prosecution was contemplated.

Fund Raising. There were only five or six staff involved in fund raising in the Jackson campaign. Victor Carter, a Jewish Los Angeles businessman, was named finance chairman early in the campaign, but he was not the only and may not even have been the major campaign fund raiser, particularly since he went on a 90-day cruise during the campaign. Another major figure in fund raising was William Reed, an executive of Simpson Timber Company in the state of Washington. Reed, who had been a major figure in Jackson's Senate campaigns, was a former Republican national committeeman whose Republican financial connections fueled the rumors that Jackson was receiving significant contributions from Republicans—rumors that turned out to be true, although Reed's role in the Republican fund raising was never clear. Also associated with fund raising on a high level was Henry Feuerstein, a young Bostonian who allegedly reported directly to Jackson and not to any of the finance chairmen or campaign staff.

Fund raising in the Jackson campaign appears to have been unsystematic and highly situational. There were four major events and a few half-hearted mass fund-raising attempts. A total of only about 50,000 letters were mailed during the entire campaign; it is believed that the mailings did not pay for themselves. The rest of the fund raising was done at small gatherings, usually with the candidate, and by personal appeal. Money was often solicited for a specific need. For example, a half-hour film of Jackson prepared for use in the Wisconsin primary was considered so good that the campaign wanted to use it in Florida; so various people telephoned to ask for money specifically for

Florida media time for the film. The campaign did buy 18-22 half-hours, although it is not known how much of the cost of that time was raised in those telephone calls.

The major fund-raising events included at least three in Seattle and the Miami dinner, all before the FECA took effect. The first event, on November 15, 1971, was a $1,000-per-person dinner in Seattle at which Jackson informally announced his candidacy. One report said the affair netted $140,000 and another stated that $175,000 had been raised. On February 21, 1972 there was a $100-per-person reception in Seattle, the "Sunday with Jackson" reception whose receipts were sent in one lump sum to Wisconsin. That reception raised $107,624 from 1,216 individuals, according to a high campaign official. However, another staff person said that a "couple hundred" people had attended the $1,000-per-person affair and a "couple thousand" had attended the $100-per-person affair, and several staff people said that two Seattle events had raised about $400,000. If the $400,000 figure is correct, then either there was one more event or the attendance and money figures reported at the time of the two known events were way off. All that can be stated with certainty is that there were at least two major fund raising events in Seattle and they probably grossed at least $285,000 and may have raised as much as $400,000.

The one major, non-Seattle fund-raising event was a $100-per-person dinner at the Diplomat Hotel in Miami on February 12, 1972. Staff estimated that 700 people attended for a gross of $65,000-$70,000; as noted above, the Miami dinner committee filing under Florida state law reported receipts of $55,985. The dinner was preceded by a cocktail party for those who had bought books of ten tickets.

Some Jackson staff members believed that dinners were not worth the time and effort—a feeling shared by many people in many campaigns. For whatever reason, there were no other dinners after the Miami one, and the Seattle reception nine days later was the campaign's last major fund-raising event.

Lindsay

The presidential campaign of New York Mayor John V. Lindsay lasted 14 weeks, from December 28, 1971 to April 4, 1972, and cost about $1 million. Lindsay became active in late summer 1971, shortly after he switched his party affiliation from Republican to Democratic. However, he had been a potential presidential candidate for several years, and almost every move he made was considered by some observers to be related to a future candidacy.

In 1968 Lindsay had been active at the Republican National Convention, hoping to win either the presidential nomination, in the unlikely event that

Reagan and Rockefeller would deadlock Nixon, or the vice-presidential nomination on the unlikely possibility that Nixon would need a liberal running mate; most important, he was sounding out delegates about a future Lindsay candidacy.[30]

Speculation that Lindsay would switch to the Democratic Party had existed since 1968. His first clear actions came in the 1970 elections, when he endorsed Rockefeller's Democratic opponent, Arthur Goldberg, in the New York gubernatorial race and lent staff and gave financial support to various Democratic candidates in New York state and congressional contests. Lindsay formally became a Democrat on August 11, 1971; his presidential campaign began shortly thereafter.

The strategy for winning the nomination was based on the belief that McGovern was not a viable candidate—that the Democratic left would be without a candidate and Lindsay could fill the void. The strategy included two of the first three primaries (Florida and Wisconsin) and the first nonprimary state (Arizona), which Lindsay hoped would establish him as the strongest liberal Democratic candidate. Florida was chosen for the big leap into active campaigning; although not expecting to win there, the hope was for an impressive first-race showing. That strategy was short-circuited when Lindsay ran fifth in the field of seven active primary candidates. His 6.5 percent of the vote was only 0.4 percent ahead of McGovern's vote and Lindsay had out-spent the supposedly weaker candidate many times over.

Against contrary advice, Lindsay went on to Wisconsin, where his campaign was hampered by a late start, lack of money, and staff and voter reaction to his undistinguished Florida showing. On election night, as it became apparent that McGovern would win and that Lindsay was running behind the other five active candidates, he withdrew. He had been a presidential candidate for less than 100 days.

When Lindsay formally announced in late December, his campaign was reported to have a budget of $1 million, including the Florida and Wisconsin primaries. The components were $400,000 for Florida; $300,000 for Wisconsin; and the remaining $300,000 for headquarters costs, for a major effort in the Arizona caucuses in January, and for the beginning stages of other primary campaigns.

The Lindsay campaign actually spent $500,000 in Florida, $100,000 more than was budgeted, and about $234,000 (expenditure and debts) in Wisconsin, about $100,000 less than was budgeted. The remaining costs are less certain, but the estimates are: for headquarters, at least $100,000; for Arizona, at least $50,000; for Massachusetts and California, about $50,000; and for broadcast production, $94,000. This minimum total of $1 million does not include $100,000 spent for polling costs (discussed below); and probably does not include the costs prior to Linday's formal announcement.

The $94,000 cost for broadcast production was based on projections for a full campaign through the convention, but the campaign ended up spending only $247,000 for media, including billboards in Arizona. Of these time costs, about $17,000 was spent in Arizona, $160,000 in Florida, and about $70,000 in Wisconsin. The $94,000 amount included only the production costs for the central effort; additional sums were spent in various states for local productions. A little more than $30,000 was paid as a fee to Garth Associates for their work in the media effort.

The campaign did only one mailing, which was handled by Lindsay's wife Mary, at a cost of $1,800 for 20,000 pieces. No details are available on the headquarters' costs. The campaign did two or three polls in Florida and Wisconsin, whose cost is not known, and there is a dispute about a reported $100,000 poll done in September 1971.

The poll reportedly covered ten states and was focused more on issues and attitudes than on actual candidate preferences. According to one official, the poll did not cost $100,000 and, furthermore, was paid for by J. Irwin Miller and made available to Bayh, Muskie, and others, as well as to Lindsay. However, other sources confirm the $100,000 cost and insist the Lindsay campaign paid for it.

Chronologically, the campaign had four cost periods: preannouncement, Arizona, Florida, and Wisconsin. There is scanty information on the costs in the first period, between Lindsay's Democratic conversion in August and his presidential announcement in December. However, with no paid staff and a very minimal office operation, costs were fairly low. The only significant preannouncement expenses were for travel by Lindsay and his aides, and for entertainment, such as a rented yacht at the September meeting of Democratic governors and state chairmen.

Some critics charged that Lindsay used city employees for campaign jobs and activities. Some members of his mayoral staff did campaign with him but either resigned or claimed they were taking vacation days.

Lindsay's Arizona campaign combined a media blitz with a very effective local organizing effort to identify his supporters and get them to the precinct caucuses. At the time, estimates of the campaign's cost ranged up to $100,000. The only hard figure known is that the media campaign cost $25,000, of which $17,000 was spent to buy 42 television spots and 691 radio commercials. Lindsay was the only candidate to use billboards in the state, spending $5,000 on them.

Lindsay's Florida campaign was an all-out effort that cost about $500,000. The campaign did not file the required record of all expenditures, but instead filed a record of all bank deposits. The only cost that is definitely known is $160,000 for broadcast time. This was close to the $180,000 limit in the Democrats' spending agreement—the basic $133,000 for Florida plus the $47,000 bonus allowed each candidate in no more than three states.

Only a few isolated statistics are known for the massive, nonmedia part of Lindsay's Florida campaign. One month before the primary, the campaign installed 240 telephones for canvassing purposes; by the end of the campaign, about 300 telephones were being used and more than 300,000 calls had been made. There were about 30 paid staff in the state and additional young volunteers, some of whom received expense money. A dozen Lindsay storefront offices were organized in black communities alone. For a Tampa rock festival starring Richie Havens, the Lindsay campaign had buses at area high schools to provide free transporation to the concert. The last weekend before the primary, the campaign printed 300,000 special leaflets for distribution to every black community in the state.

After Florida, one-third of the staff became volunteers and the campaign had trouble recruiting more volunteers. The campaign reported expenditures of $208,470 in Wisconsin, probably close to the actual total spent. The campaign raised $50,000 locally (more than it had in Florida), of which more than half were loans. Out-of-state money was transferred in and spent by reporting Wisconsin committees. A debt of at least $25,800, which is not included in the reported expenditures, would bring total Wisconsin costs to at least $234,000.

In Wisconsin the campaign's media budget originally was $165,000; this meant Lindsay was planning to use the second of his three $47,000 media bonuses in Wisconsin (otherwise the spending limit would have been $118,000). However, about ten days before the primary, the planned television spots were postponed because the campaign ran out of money. In their place, several live, half-hour, call-in shows were substituted at a cost of $15,000. But money was later found, and the media budget was raised to $70,000—for six days of intensive radio and television spots—all of which was spent.

In the preannouncement period, travel money came from several of New York's John V. Lindsay (JVL) associations, which had been formed in Lindsay's first term as mayor and had become very important as his political and fundraising arm after his reelection when he was not a functioning member of any political party.

In late 1971 several of Lindsay's critics began raising questions about the JVL associations, asking whether they had filed the financial statements required under New York law; who the associations' contributors were; and whether and why their war chests, estimated at between $250,000 and $500,000, were going to be used for Lindsay's presidential campaign. The first issue became a big one in New York when it was revealed that the associations had not filed certain reports. In late November, the state attorney general said he would investigate the matter.

The associations at first claimed they were civic, not political, organizations and therefore not required to file. However, as the issue grew, the associations agreed to file, but still maintained that they were not required to do so. The agreement stipulated that the five associations, one for each of New York City's boroughs, would file reports by the end of the year (1971) covering their receipts and expenditures for 1969, 1970, and 1971.

The filings revealed that the associations' war chests were a fraction of their rumored sizes. For all three years (1969-71), total receipts of all five associations were less than $200,000. The associations' total 1971 receipts were $94,981 and their combined balance, at the end of the year, was only $37,618.35.

Contributors to the JVL associations were mostly city officials, state legislators, business concerns, and trade unions. The largest individual contributions were $500 from a few city commissioners and from the Negro Benevolent Association of the Department of Sanitation. There were many $100 contributions. The biggest money maker was the Brooklyn Association's 1,200-page banquet journal, which grossed about $100,000 with most of the money coming from advertisements by companies and organizations doing business with the city. The journal had not been distributed nor many of the ads paid for by the year's end, and the associations did not report this income from the journal.

The associations' expenditures for 1971 were about $100,000, of which Lindsay's travel expenses were only a part. Although the JVL associations played a major role in Linday's mayoral reelection of 1969 and supported him for President in 1972, they faded away in the waning days of his mayoralty.[31]

The campaign did not have a fund-raising staff. The campaign's treasurer, Fergus Reid, a New York stockbroker, was in charge of both income and outgo. Mrs. Lindsay's mailing brought in $30,000, and there were several fund-raising events in New York, but the campaign relied primarily on a few very large contributors.

While Lindsay was campaigning in Florida, McGovern raised the issue of voluntary disclosure. Responding almost immediately, on March 7, Lindsay was the third candidate (after McCloskey and McGovern) to disclose sources of his campaign's financing. For the period covered by his voluntary disclosure (mid-December to March 1), a total of 1,010 contributors gave $489,804 to the campaign.[ll] Just over 70 percent of the total, $350,105, came from 46 contributors who gave $1,000 or more; however, six of the 46 accounted for $290,000, or just under 60 percent of the total reported. Even this statistic is somewhat misleading, since one family accounted for $225,000—almost 50 percent of the money raised in that period.

[ll]$10,000 in cash was raised for Lindsay's presidential campaign by a city Highway Department official who solicited the money from two contractors who later got a $1.7 million job to supply the city with asphalt; this was the subject of a Senate Watergate Committee inquiry (Senate Select Committee on Presidential Campaign Activities, *Final Report,* No. 93-981, 93rd Cong., 2d sess., June 1974 (Washington, D.C.: U.S. Government Printing Office, 1974), pp. 558-63.) Lindsay's top campaign aide, Richard Aurelio, claimed the cash had been properly recorded and reported fully to the New York secretary of state, although a review of the finance records by the Senate staff contradicted this.

The family giving so much was that of J. Irwin Miller, board chairman of the Cummins Engine Company of Columbus, Indiana, an active supporter of liberal Republicans[mm] and a long-time friend and supporter of John Lindsay. In this period it was disclosed voluntarily that Miller gave $78,000, his wife, Xenia, gave $78,000, and his sister Clementine Tangeman gave $75,000; later it was acknowledged by the Millers that Mr. and Mrs. J. Irwin Miller together gave Linday's campaign $269,167. Another very large contributor was Arthur Houghton, the president of Steuben Glass, who gave $50,000; Elisha Walker, an independent New York investor, gave $10,000; and Stewart Mott, who also gave to McCloskey and McGovern, gave $6,000. Although all these contributors, except Mott, are Republicans, Lindsay in fact had lost some of his largest GOP financial supporters from the past when he became a Democrat. For example, John Hay Whitney, former publisher of the New York *Herald Tribune,* who has given to many of Lindsay's other campaigns, gave $5,000 to McCloskey but did not give to Lindsay in 1972.

For the four-week period (March 17-April 4) between Lindsay's voluntary disclosure and his withdrawal from the race, the only information available on the campaign's sources comes from the financial reports filed for the Wisconsin primary. The reports list total contributions of $91,116; of this, $37,000 came from four New York committees and $20,000 from six Washington, D.C. committees for which no individual contributors are known. Three large gifts came from Wisconsin individuals. Dr. Henry Goldberg, a Milwaukee surgeon, and a former intern at Brooklyn (New York) Hospital, gave $10,000 and loaned $10,000; Robert Kritzik, a Milwaukee industrialist, loaned $10,000, which was never repaid; and Attorney Bronson La Follette loaned $12,050, $6,000 of which was not repaid. Adding these contributions to the out-of-state committee money accounts for $83,000 of the total; the remaining $8,116 came from smaller contributors.

Disagreement arose in both Wisconsin and New York over the fact that the real sources of $57,000 of Lindsay's reported Wisconsin receipts were masked by the New York and D.C. committees. The D.C. committees in particular, with names like White House Improvement Committee, Washington Better Candidate Committee, Smithsonian Businessmen's Action Committee, Cherry Blossom Committee, Reflecting Pool Committee, Union Station Good Government Committee—and addresses at the railroad station—were fronts for anonymous large contributors. In fact, the New York and D.C. committees were conduits for additional contributions from the J. Irwin Miller family.

All of the campaign's fund-raising events took place in New York City. A series of $25-a-person dinners and other affairs were held in the late fall and winter of 1971, with one in Manhattan reportedly attended by 1,200 supporters.

[mm]In 1972, he and his wife also gave $5,500 and his sister $6,000 to McCloskey.

There was also a major event in Queens on February 11, which reportedly drew 1,300 people who paid from $50 to $125 to attend.

The biggest event was a January film premiere at Radio City Music Hall. There were reports that 5,000 of the theater's 6,000 seats were sold, at $80 to $100 each, but these figures conflict with later reports that gross receipts were $250,000 and the net was $150,000. If true, the gross figure would indicate that fewer than 5,000 tickets were sold, and the net figure would indicate that the campaign had to pay a large amount to the theater for the event. Apparently, many free tickets were distributed to fill the house. Charges of political arm twisting and violation of the intent (though not the letter) of the city charter were made with regard to this event. The charter prohibits political contributions from city employees and it was alleged that this was circumvented by high officials whose spouses and friends bought tickets.

The Lindsay campaign provided no information on contributors in the post-campaign period, which is significant because the campaign had a sizable debt. Lindsay withdrew from the presidential race as the votes were being counted in Wisconsin, and virtually no other costs were incurred after April 4. The campaign was about $200,000 in debt and new bills kept coming in. On the day of the Wisconsin primary, for example, it was reported that bills totalling $30,000 arrived from Florida, mostly from hotels. Two weeks later Lindsay was named in a $1,000 suit for a Wisconsin hotel bill. On April 17, 1973 Lindsay was sued in New York state court for a little more than $31,000 owed to David Garth, a close adviser and the man who had handled all of Lindsay's media since 1969. Garth explained that his suit did not reflect any change in his relationship with the Mayor, but that it was the only way he would be able to get his money.

At its peak the debt was at least $250,000. Except for the $26,000 owed to three lenders in Wisconsin, all of the money owed was to commercial firms. In February 1973 it was reported that the debt was still $200,000, but that the campaign did not consider the Wisconsin loans their responsibility.

A last, and reportedly successful, fund raiser was held for Lindsay at Lincoln Center's New York State Theater on December 15, 1973. The dinner-dance, held to pay off the remaining campaign debt, was described as being more like a victory party than a farewell gathering.[32] More than 1,000 guests paid $100 to $500 a ticket, and the gala grossed about $200,000, handling most of the "legitimate claims" against the campaign. Some hotel, car rental, and other bills were being contested as not legitimate, such as one car rental bill that was found in the name of a McGovern campaign worker, according to Lindsay officials. By fall 1974 the debt was less than $100,000, with the treasury containing more than $70,000. The "illegitimate bills" were still being resolved, with the remainder expected to be cleared up by the end of the year.

The FECA took effect three days after Lindsay withdrew. Since he was no longer a candidate, his committees were not required to file under the new law. Lindsay officials asked the GAO if their interpretation was correct and were told that although technically correct, such an interpretation was not in keeping with the spirit of the law. Lindsay and his advisers chose not to file.

Sanford

Terry Sanford, the president of Duke University and former governor of North Carolina, announced his presidential candidacy the day after the New Hampshire primary and stayed in the race through the first ballot at the Democratic National Convention. Many observers believed that the liberal southerner was really running for vice-president or to establish himself for a cabinet post.[nn]

Sanford's major primary effort was in his home state of North Carolina, where he sought to stem the challenge of George Wallace. Although unsuccessful against the well-organized, well-financed Wallace campaign there (he lost in the May 7 North Carolina primary by more than 100,000 votes) he continued a national effort to woo delegates up to and during the convention, where he received 78 votes.

The Sanford campaign is known to have cost about $850,000. A categorical breakdown, supplied by the campaign, accounts for almost 80 percent of the total:

Media	$ 96,800
Telephone	52,500
Salaries & fees	56,000
Travel	171,000
Rent, supplies, & services	95,500
Printing & postage	101,500
Research	19,000
Convention	70,000
Total	$662,300

Since Sanford was active in only one primary and had several national committees operating from that state, it is difficult to separate the primary from national spending. Reports filed with the North Carolina secretary of state ten days before the primary indicate expenditures by two state committees—the Sanford for President Committee and the Sanford Carolina Campaign Committee —totalling $379,403. However, the campaign claimed only about $200,000 of this should be counted as directly spent on the North Carolina primary, with the remainder related to the national campaign.

[nn]In response to such speculation, Sanford said, "I'd rather be president of Duke than Vice President, and unemployed rather than a Cabinet member."

Spending for television, radio, and newspaper advertising in North Carolina was reported at $142,536, with $31,000 of that going to Robert Drew Associates of New York City before the primary, on television production costs. The FCC report shows that Sanford spending for radio and television time was $94,796—$50,397 for television and $44,399 for radio, all of it nonnetwork.

The only other states that reported Sanford spending were Virginia, $5,500, and California, $2,000. The main Washington, D.C. committee reported direct expenditures of $218,000; this was presumably all for the national, delegate-hunting operation. Additional national-level expenditures were made with $175,000 from another North Carolina committee.

The two North Carolina committees reported preprimary receipts totalling $388,737 (including $55,000 transferred in). The committees also listed loans totalling $600,000: $300,000 was a March 17, 1972 loan from Anne R. Forsyth of Winston Salem, North Carolina—a tobacco and textile heiress and friend of Sanford—and another $300,000 was reported as "other loan or loans received prior to 4/7/72." In fact, both amounts were loaned by Forsyth, as well as $100,000 more loaned in June. Forsyth, who contributed $1,000 with her husband, Dr. H. Frank Forsyth, had offered to loan the campaign enough money to get started, but as of May 31, 1975 she had forgiven the entire $700,000 amount loaned to the 1972 committees. The total contribution of $701,000 is the largest amount any candidate except Richard Nixon received from an individual in 1972. By the time the loan was forgiven, it was no longer subject to gift tax—the IRS had considered it appropriately as a loan, untaxable, when made.

Two other large contributions were received:[oo] $10,000 from Joseph Cole of Cleveland and $5,000 from W.R. Davis of Midland, Texas. Cole was Hubert Humphrey's largest backer in 1972, contributing $52,000 and loaning a total of $635,000. Since Cole was obviously and publicly supporting Humphrey for the nomination, his gift to Sanford surprised some, but he was an old friend helping out. Davis was Henry Jackson's third-largest contributor, giving $50,000 in cash before April 7. Gifts such as these suggested efforts were being made to try to stop Wallace, since Sanford's campaign was pitched in that direction.

Probably because of its one financial mainstay, Anne Forsyth, the Sanford campaign had only a small fund-raising operation. There were no dinners or other major events. All of the large contributions were raised through personal solicitation.

Ambiguities in reporting transfers were fairly common for many 1972 committees, but in the case of the Sanford committees, transfers from state to national committees and back again proved particularly bewildering for those seeking to trace funds and account for costs. On March 25, for example, the

---

[oo]These were apparently received before April 7 by the Sanford Carolina Campaign Committee. The totals were included in the committee's FECA reports, but the individual contributors were not; the committee's North Carolina state reports, however, did list these pre-April 7 donors.

North Carolina Sanford for President Committee sent $100,000 to the Washington-based national committee, which was then hurriedly getting underway. By one month later, April 24, the national committee had sent $125,000 back into North Carolina. In spite of the complex criss-crossing of funds in the Sanford campaign, a GAO audit found only $50,000 in transferred money that had been reported improperly—that sum had been noted in a telegram to the GAO, then inadvertently left off the following formal report, and was finally disclosed in an amended report.

The GAO's audit report on the campaign, however, was critical with respect to one of the North Carolina committees, indicating that the Sanford committee had made a "number of errors": reporting of contributions and expenditures not supported by records; failure to itemize gifts of more than $100 in some cases, double reporting of expenditures; and failure to itemize some $19,000 in expenditures of over $100 each.

The GAO audit also found fault with a Sanford committee practice of estimating amounts received and spent, and noted three expenditures of approximately $875 that were "completely fictitious." The report stated that the treasurer of the committee in question had acknowledged making up the false expenditure figures in an effort to show a balanced budget: the treasurer, a student, attributed other errors to his own inexperience and confusion in coping with large amounts of paperwork in addition to other responsibilities in the campaign.

There is no evidence that any of the Sanford committees engaged in deliberate misreporting as a means of evading the law. Nor was the situation a case of confusion resulting from real or dummy committees operating out of the same headquarters; each of four Sanford committees was in a different location. Analysis of the committees indicates that the individuals involved kept meticulous account of their financial operation, but that they simply did not comply with the reporting format.

Although there was no evidence of fraudulent intent and the amounts of money involved were relatively small, the GAO recommended referral of the matter to the United States Attorney General for apparent violation both of the FECA (for inaccurate record keeping and reporting) and of criminal sections of Title 18 of the U.S. Code (for willful false statements), and also recommended that the United States Attorney General bring the matter to the attention of the attorney general of North Carolina; no action was taken by either. The auditors never questioned certain other inconsistencies and errors in the receipts, expenditures and transfers sections of the Sanford campaign's FECA reports.

Mills

Representative Wilbur Mills never formally announced his candidacy for the presidency yet was involved in speculation and maneuvering of almost a year's duration. His name was entered in two major primary contests, and he was involved in a vigorous effort to woo delegates right up to and at the Democratic National Convention. The campaign on his behalf cost about $730,000. In spite of Mills' contention that he was not really a candidate, it is difficult to believe that a campaign of such length and cost would have been possible without his consent, encouragement, and assistance.

Reports of a Mills candidacy surfaced early in 1971, and Mills travelled widely throughout that spring and summer. He attended the mid-July meeting of prospective Democratic candidates arranged by Party Chairman Larry O'Brien, but did not join the agreement to limit broadcast spending. A Draft-Mills committee was organized in June 1971, and a small headquarters opened in Washington. This was followed in the early fall by a "spontaneous" outpouring of 50 endorsements for Mills from fellow members of the House of Representatives. In mid-February 1972, when asked by election officials in Nebraska and Wisconsin, Mills did not sign an affidavit of noncandidacy for the primaries in those states.

By the end of January the Draft Mills for President Committee was running a very active and expensive write-in campaign in New Hampshire. The campaign was largely a media effort—heavy broadcasting, substantial direct mail, telephoning, and paid workers—with very little political organizing. Except for a "non-campaign visit" to speak to the state legislature in mid-February, Mills spent only three hours in the state, the day before the primary; instead, chartered plane-loads of New Hampshire leaders were flown to Washington to meet and eat with Mills. Mills received 3,500 votes in the primary, only 4.1 percent of the total.

During April a larger campaign was waged in Massachusetts. Mills did some active campaigning, but received only 3.1 percent of the vote. There was no active campaign by or for Mills in any other primaries, but an aggressive, well-financed search for delegates was carried on virtually until McGovern's nomination was insured.

Disclosure: The Watergate Committee. Wilbur Mills consistently refused to disclose voluntarily the sources of his campaign's income for the period before the FECA took effect. During the Watergate Committee's investigation, the chairman of the Draft Mills Committee said that about $200,000 had been raised between July 1971 and February 1972: this, added to the almost $300,000 in receipts reported under the FECA, led the Senate Watergate Committee to conclude that the campaign raised a total of almost $500,000.[33] But this calculation omits the February-March period, during which the campaign presumably raised most of the money for the hard-fought contest in New Hampshire, which is estimated to have cost about $200,000. This would make the campaign's income (and expenditures) at least $700,000; this figure is, in fact, low according to the CRF analysis of costs.

The investigation of the Mills campaign by the Watergate Committee—which admittedly was not "an exhaustive investigation" due to staffing and time limitations[34] —concentrated on contributions and services to the campaign from corporate sources, particularly the dairy industry. The investigation uncovered about $185,000 in legal and illegal dairy contributions, which is 38 percent of the campaign's income revenue. This included three instances of dairy cooperatives' corporate spending for the benefit of the Mills campaign.

1. Staff members of the Associated Milk Producers, Inc. (AMPI), worked on the Mills campaign while their salaries and living expenses were paid by AMPI; the committee estimated the value of this as "at least $25,000."

2. A $9,291.53 bill for 110,000 "Mills for President" bumper stickers was sent to and paid by AMPI.

3. An October 1971 rally in Iowa, ostensibly to celebrate the state-designated "Cooperative Month," was demonstrably conceived, initiated, and organized by officials in the dairy industry as a device to promote Mills' presidential candidacy. The Watergate Committee determined that Mid-America Dairymen, Inc. donated $15,000 in corporate funds toward the cost of the rally and that AMPI used at least $30,000 of its corporate funds.[35]

In all three cases, the value of the services or goods—totalling at least $80,000—has to be included in the real cost of the Mills campaign.

In addition to these instances of use of corporate funds, the Watergate Committee found four definite and one questionable case of direct, illegal corporate contributions to the Mills campaign. The first two were $5,000 cash contributions, one in August 1971, and another in November 1971, for which the giver was reimbursed from laundered AMPI corporate funds. The third was a $15,000 cash contribution from Gulf Oil Corporation. The lobbyist who handled this transaction, Claude C. Wild, Jr., (Gulf Oil vice-president), and the Gulf Oil Corporation were convicted and fined in November, 1973, for also making illegal contributions to the Finance Committee to Re-Elect the President. On November 29, 1973 Gulf Oil requested that the $15,000 contribution be returned and in December 1973 Mills repaid the money from his personal account. In the fourth case Minnesota Mining and Manufacturing Company (3M) and its chief executive officer, Harry Heltzer, were also convicted and fined for corporate contributions to the CRP, which came from the same source as a $1,000 contribution to Mills. The questionable case involved $40,000 in contributions from AMPI officials, directors, and employees who were solicited by top AMPI officials in a checkoff system authorizing payroll deductions as contributions to Mills. The contributions admittedly were made; the question was raised whether the contributors were later reimbursed from AMPI corporate funds, which officials denied. It should be noted that any illegal direct or indirect campaign contributions from the dairy industry were in addition to $55,600 in legal contributions to Mills from the political trust funds of the dairy industry.

In November 1974 Harold S. Nelson and David L. Parr, the two top AMPI officials during 1972, were convicted, fined, and sentenced to jail for making illegal corporate contributions. They were the first corporate officials to be given jail sentences, rather than fines alone, for the illegal use of corporate funds in political campaigns. At the time of sentencing, both men were also being sued by AMPI for their activities when employed by the co-op. Parr also had ties to Jake Jacobsen, a Texas lawyer who was a prosecution witness in the trial of John Connally regarding dairy funds and who arranged a $5,000 contribution to Mills from an unknown source, which was channelled to the Mills campaign through Parr.[36]

Costs. In late January 1972 the Mills committee was asked about reports of a $500,000 budget, which the campaign would neither confirm nor deny. There are no other references to budgets, but the campaign had no financial problems. Political decisions were not affected by costs, nor by the availability of money; the campaign appeared to do and spend whatever it wanted. An analysis of that spending shows that the campaign had direct expenditures of about $560,000; to this must be added $90,000 in debts (which were later paid) and at least $80,000 in goods and services from corporate sources, for a total campaign cost of at least $730,000.

For the period before September 1971, when Mills was travelling extensively, there is no information on costs. However, since there was no campaign office or staff before June, the main costs would have been for the travel, and most of that may have been free since Mills accepted free rides in various company-owned airplanes for his trips. Mills said that he never accepted fees for his speeches but expected those who invited him to pay expenses. The monetary value of reimbursed expenses and free transporation is not known. At the end of July, Representative James Burke of Massachusetts, one of Mills' most enthusiastic supporters and a fellow member of the Ways and Means Committee, boasted that the campaign had cost only $200 so far, for bumper stickers and postage.

The Draft Mills Committee began with a two-room office in Washington; at its largest, the staff numbered five. According to a committee official, headquarters costs averaged about $3,500 per month, for a total cost of not more than $25,000 for the six and one-half months the committee was in existence prior to the New Hampshire campaign.

The Draft Mills Committee's big endeavor was the New Hampshire primary, which the committee coordinator said cost $150,000. Of this total, $120,300 went for media and direct mail; $62,700 for television time, $22,000 for radio time, $15,600 for newspaper space, and $20,000 for direct mail. Details of the remaining $30,000 in costs are not known, but presumably they were for staff, travel, and office expenses. The phone drive was costly because, unlike most New Hampshire campaigns, Mills had to pay his "volunteer" workers. Reportedly, some worked for pay for Mills to sustain themselves, volunteering free for McGovern in off hours. One omission from this list of expenses is media production costs; given the $100,300 in time and space costs, at least $50,000 must have been spent to create and produce the newspaper, radio, and television material. This would bring the New Hampshire total to a minimum of $200,000, and probably substantially more was spent. In addition, the campaign had some significant in-kind contributions in the form of unpaid professional volunteers from Washington; at least four people who were registered lobbyists for industries and trade associations that were closely involved with Mills' Ways and Means Committee were reported campaigning in New Hampshire.

As noted earlier, Mills did not sign the Democratic agreement to limit broadcast spending, and his campaign's $84,700 for radio and television was well above the $65,000 New Hampshire limit, which was honored by all the other candidates. The campaign claimed that the higher spending was justified because Mills was a write-in candidate and was not campaigning personally, but aides said that he would abide by the agreement in all other primaries.

The Draft Mills Committee ceased operations before the FECA took effect on April 7. From late March to April 25 the campaign's attention and resources were concentrated on the Massachusetts primary, and there were one major and two minor Massachusetts committees reporting under the FECA. The formal Washington, D.C. "Mills for President" committee was not really active until after April 25, and none of its reported expenditures is believed to have been for the Massachusetts campaign.

The main Massachusetts committee reported costs of $143,000, two small committees spent about $7,000 for a total Massachusetts cost of about $150,000. The main committee had $36,000 on hand as of April 7 and receipts of $26,000; it spent the entire $62,000 and incurred a debt of $81,000. The Massachusetts campaign relied heavily on media and virtually the entire debt was owed to the campaign's advertising agency in Tennessee.

The Mills for President Committee, D.C., had no cash on hand as of April 7; it received and spent $266,000 and ended the year with a debt of $9,000. The $275,000 in costs were mainly for travel and expenses, presumably to woo delegates. The committee had a staff of 10 to 14 persons. Since there were no media expenses during this time, all the other expenses would have been for office rent, telephone, salaries, etc. Adding the postprimary costs of $275,000 to the New Hampshire costs of $200,000, the Massachusetts costs of $150,000, the preprimary costs of $25,000, and the $80,000 in in-kind goods and services gives a total cost of at least $730,000 for the entire Mills campaign.

Sources and Flow. Mills' aides and supporters were always quick to point out that questions of financing played no role in the campaign, that had Mills chosen to run seriously there would have been more than enough money. The campaign did not have any formal fund-raising organization; one high campaign official insisted that money just arrived spontaneously. Only one fund-raising event is known, and campaign officials denied that it was a fund raiser. The event was an appreciation rally for Mills in Arkansas in late August 1971. It was reported that big contributors bought many tickets to be given to state employees, although people were also asked for contributions at the rally.

For the presumed $261,000 raised before April 7 (counting the preprimary costs of $25,000, the New Hampshire costs of $200,000, and the $36,000 in cash on hand of the Massachusetts committee), the only information on its source comes from the Watergate Committee's investigation. That shows the $10,000 in laundered AMPI money, the $40,000 raised from AMPI staff and officers, the $15,000 from Gulf Oil Corporation, and $1,500 from TAPE, the AMPI political trust fund; this means that 25 percent of Mills's known pre-April 7 income came from dairy and oil interests, and more than one-third of that was illegally given. Furthermore, it was during this same period that the campaign received the benefit of the $80,000 in direct corporate spending. This means that 43 percent of the campaign's total pre-April 7 costs were paid for from dairy and Gulf Oil sources, and 31 percent of this $341,000 total was illegal corporate money.

The campaign's filings under the FECA cover $299,000 in income. Apart from the debt, the largest amount of money came from large contributors; a total of $128,150 came from 84 contributors who gave at least $500 each. Nine gave $5,000 or more; four of them were from Arkansas and each contributed $6,000. In the $100-$500 range, $14,010 was raised from 69 contributors. Less than $40,000 came from small contributions of $100 or less.

Included among the large contributions were gifts totalling $6,000 from ten presidents and one member of the board of eleven breweries. One of the company presidents, Robert A. Schmidt of Olympia Brewing Company, said: "Being in the brewing industry, you have to play both sides of the street. If they don't know that you contribute, the next thing you know, you might get an extra tax you don't like."[37] However, Henry King, president of the U.S. Brewers Association and the man who coordinated the contributions, said that he had not asked for the contributions on that basis and did not believe that such modest support from the beer industry would affect anyone in Congress.

Documents in the Watergate Committee files revealed that the two largest contributors, giving a combined total of $100,000, were associates of H. Ross Perot: Milledge A. Hart, III, president of Perot's company, Electronic Data Systems Corp., gave $51,000, and Mervin L. Stauffer, a personal assistant to Perot, gave $49,000. This money was never publicly disclosed by Mills' campaign, nor were contributions from truckers totalling at least $10,000, nor other gifts of up to $5,000 each from a Washington representative of an oil company and from lumber and tobacco interests.[38] Mills' campaign manager, Joseph Johnson, invoked the Fifth Amendment and declined to comply with requests from the Watergate Committee to discuss these matters. Mills also refused to discuss the information with the committee staff and was never invited to testify before the committee itself, although Senator Ervin tried. It was also reported but never substantiated that Mrs. Rose Kennedy gave a portion of Mills' funds for the New Hampshire primary.[39]

Mills was unique among the candidates in that he received significant financial support from national-level business and professional committees, which normally do not contribute very much to prenomination candidates.[pp] He received $54,100 from the political trust funds of the three major dairy industry groups in 1972: $25,000 from TAPE, $16,600 from ADEPT, and $12,500 from SPACE. Counting these legal and all the legal and illegal dairy contributions before April 7 totals $185,600: a full 25 percent of Mills' total campaign costs were paid directly or indirectly by the dairy industry.

Mills also received $3,000 from business committees, including $2,000 from Life Underwriters PAC, and from professional and trade groups' political action committees, including $2,500 from two medical committees; and $4,000 from organized labor, all of it from the Seafarers International Union.

Of the remaining $54,000 covered in the FECA reports, $21,000 was transferred from other committees, mostly other Mills committees that dissolved before April 7; about $17,000 came from miscellaneous receipts, including refunds. The final $17,000 was a loan to pay for a projected telephone setup at the Miami Convention, but the plan was dropped and most of the money refunded to the lender, Joseph W. Riddell, who had been a staff member of Mills' Ways and Means Committee more than ten years earlier.

The campaign's one loan and its debt appear to have resulted from a temporary problem in the flow of money to the campaign, rather than in any general difficulty in raising money. The Washington Mills for President Committee had no money on hand as of May 19, when it was set up. Two weeks later it had collected only $11,000 while picking up the Massachusetts committee's debt of $81,000 and $9,000 of its own debt. But the money began to come in during the summer of 1972: the fact that the campaign was over had seemingly little effect on donations. By November a total of more than $75,000 had been raised since the July convention. Of the $54,100 contributed by dairy industry committees after April 7, $14,100 was given after McGovern had won the Democratic nomination. Many of the postcampaign contributions came from officials in insurance companies and other businesses affected by Mills' Ways and Means Committee.

Bayh

Senator Birch Bayh of Indiana conducted a full-blown and efficient

---

[pp]Mills attracted some contributions, no matter how well he did in the Presidential race, because he was chairman of the House Ways and Means Committee. See Robert Walters, "The Scandal of Wilbur D. Mills," *Washingtonian*, November 1974, pp. 92-95, 184-85. See also a study of "Wilbur D. Mills 1972 Campaign Support" released April 2, 1974 by the Tax Reform and Research Group (Washington, D.C.), and Walter Shapiro, "Wilbur Mills: The Ways and Means of Conning the Press," *Washington Monthly*, December 1974, pp. 4-13.

campaign that spent $710,000 in a little more than a year. By the time he withdrew in mid-October 1971, most observers were convinced that he would not have been a major factor in the 1972 presidential race. There was speculation about the sources of his financing and on his reasons for running in a race in which he was viewed as an underdog at best.

Bayh was not well known nationally until 1969, when he successfully led the fights against Senate confirmation of Supreme Court nominees G. Harrold Carswell and Clement F. Haynesworth, Jr. Speculation centered on whether Bayh was running seriously for President, gaining visibility for his senatorial reelection, or acting as a "stand-in" for his close friend, Senator Ted Kennedy. By late summer Bayh's campaign slowed down, supporting rumors about money troubles. Unexpectedly, in early October Bayh's wife Marvella underwent major surgery, and he announced that he was withdrawing from the presidential race to be with her during her recovery.

The Bayh campaign had a budget of about $6 million for the whole prenomination period, including the convention. The budget for 1971 originally was $1.6 million, but the campaign had incurred costs of only $660,000 from January to mid-October. Expenses for 1970 had been $50,000, bringing the total expenditures for the campaign to $710,000.

The largest expenditure was for staff—35 at the Washington headquarters and 15 in the field—with payroll costs of $35,000 per month. Another major cost item for the campaign was travel. Bayh carried out a heavy schedule that was meticulously planned and executed with an impressive amount of advance work and heavy entertaining of political leaders and potential delegates.

One of the campaign's unique operations was the "Birch Bayh radio network." The candidate's statements and speeches were taped, sent to the Washington headquarters, and then fed over leased wires to the networks and to hundreds of radio stations.

During the campaign, the source of Bayh's income was the subject of much speculation. The campaign was over long before the FECA took effect, before any primaries might have made it subject to state disclosure laws, and before Senator McGovern and others made voluntary disclosure a campaign issue. The pressure for Bayh to reveal his sources of funds came mostly from the curious and from people active in other presidential campaigns. (Only one committee, Citizens for Birch Bayh, reported to the GAO: for the period April 7 to December 31, 1972, it reported receipts of $7,737 and expenditures of $22,368.)

After Bayh withdrew, the campaign did disclose to the authors the sources of almost all its income. Bayh had virtually no small contributors and 25 or 30 large contributors, of whom six were very large givers:

Milton Gilbert, chairman Gilbert Flexi-Van Corp.	$240,000 (includes $50,000 given in 1970 and $60,000 after Bayh withdrew)

Milan Panic, chairman & president International Chemical & Nuclear Corp.	$120,000	(includes $80,000 after Bayh withdrew and a $20,000 contribution-in-kind)
Charles C. Bassine, chairman exec. comm., director Arlen Realty & Development (N.Y.C.)		
Arthur G. Cohen, chairman, Arlen Realty (Bassine's son-in-law)	$100,000	combined donation
Joseph Kanter, Cincinnati banker and community developer	$ 50,000+	
Miklos Sperling, Indiana industrialist and engineer	$ 20,000	

Gilbert's contribution covered over one-third of the campaign's total income, while the six big contributors together provided more than three-fourths of the total income. Additionally, Panic provided use of an airplane, worth perhaps another $20,000.

One fund-raising dinner in Chicago raised $50,000 in April 1971. Rumors were heard of heavy labor contributions to Bayh—who had received at least $70,000 from organized labor for his 1968 Senate race—but it is unusual for unions to contribute to a presidential candidate before nomination, and unlikely that they contributed much to Bayh in the early, preprimary period.

The campaign's money flow did not run into trouble until mid-summer 1971. In a curious incident, the Bayh campaign did not have enough money to meet the payroll one week—and borrowed the money from the McGovern campaign. The loan was repaid within a few days. A Bayh staff member later said that the campaign really had been temporarily broke, because several donors had reneged on promised contributions. For example, $25,000 pledged by Stanley Goldblum, chairman and president of Equity Funding Corporation of America, was not available in cash when needed, although a gift of Equity Funding stock was mentioned as forthcoming.

The campaign did not borrow at any other time, but when Bayh withdrew, $230,000 was owed to commercial firms. This debt was not real, since the campaign had checks in hand totalling $405,000. However, the campaign only cashed one of these checks, for $5,000, because they had been solicited and given before the news of Marvella Bayh's illness and Bayh's decision to withdraw. After the withdrawal Gilbert gave $60,000 and Panic gave $80,000 toward the $230,000 debt. There were several other postwithdrawal contributions, and within a few weeks the debt had been reduced to about $65,000. The remaining debt was eventually paid off.

McCarthy

Former Minnesota Senator Eugene McCarthy waged active campaigns only in the Illinois primary and the Minnesota caucus-convention process, but his probing and actual candidacy stretched over a full year and probably cost $475,000.

McCarthy was first reported considering the Democratic race in July 1971; some commentators related his interest to the withdrawal of Senator Harold Hughes, since many of Hughes's supporters had been McCarthy supporters in 1968. By October a Washington campaign headquarters was operating at a cost of at least $5,000 per month. McCarthy announced his candidacy for the Massachusetts primary in mid-December[qq] and a month later made a more formal announcement. Financial considerations did not play any role in McCarthy's decision to enter the 1972 race or in his choice of battle sites. He did not plan a major national campaign, as he had done in 1968 at a cost of about $11 million, and was confident that he could raise the needed funds for a limited campaign. The purpose of McCarthy's 1972 minicampaign was, allegedly, "to keep the other guys honest," to get the others to adopt his platform, and to test whether some interest still remained for his candidacy. McCarthy chose Illinois for his major primary contest because it would be a two-man race, a clear choice for voters between him and Muskie. After losing the March 21 primary by almost 2-1, McCarthy's campaign became little more than the candidate's travelling, but McCarthy did not formally withdraw until the Democratic National Convention.

More than 90 percent of McCarthy's expenditures occurred before the FECA took effect, and pressure developed from the press and other candidates for McCarthy to voluntarily disclose his financial supporters. He refused. After the campaign, an aide gave two reasons for the refusal. One was that no candidate had released "an honest list," but as soon as they did, so would McCarthy. The other reason was: "It was embarrassing; we did not want to say (publicly) that we were not getting a dime," because if people do not think you have money they will not take you seriously. In fact, most of McCarthy's money came from large contributors.

More than two-thirds of the estimated $475,000 total cost of McCarthy's campaign was spent for the Illinois primary and on the effort to win delegates in the February 22 Minnesota precinct caucuses. The Illinois effort cost about $260,000 and the Minnesota effort cost about $70,000. The only other large expense was for the operation of the national headquarters, including the costs of McCarthy's travel, which totalled about $105,000. The remaining $40,000 of the estimated total cost was spent on limited campaign efforts in other states;[rr]

[qq]He hoped to win a majority of votes at an early 1972 caucus of liberal Democrats in the state, but he ran a very weak third (behind McGovern and Chisholm) and essentially abandoned his plan for Massachusetts.

[rr]McCarthy's name was actually on the ballot in 12 primary states.

the two largest known expenses were about $15,000 in California and at least $10,000 in Wisconsin.

The largest expense in Illinois was for campaign advertising: at least $100,000 for television and $45,000 for radio (including about $10,000 in production costs); at least $35,000 for newspaper advertising; and $5,000 for printing and materials. Other known costs included $5,000 for direct mail and $5,000 for polling. The rest of the approximately $50,000 spent by the national campaign organization covered the fees of the advertising agency that handled the media, the campaign office (plush hotel suites), travel, and political organization. An additional $10,000 was spent by the local McCarthy group; it went for storefront headquarters, food and expense money for volunteers, and some limited radio advertising. The $70,000 cost of the Minnesota campaign included $60,000 spent by the national campaign and $10,000 by the state McCarthy organization.

National campaign headquarters' costs ranged between $5,000 and $10,000 per month for most of the year (July 1971 to July 1972) of its operation. This included about $2,500 for travel (reportedly for two airplane tickets), about $2,500 for telephones, $300 for rent, and a maximum of $4,000 for salaries and staff expenses during the busiest months of the campaign. For the post-April 7 period the McCarthy campaign reported expenditures of $35,000. Since this was after the Illinois and Minnesota efforts, almost all of this money would have been for the national office expenses, indicating a monthly cost of about $8,750. Using this figure as an average for the eight months the headquarters was operating before April 7 gives a figure of $70,000, for a total campaign headquarters cost of $105,000.

Since almost all of McCarthy's funds were raised and spent before April 7, and since he did not voluntarily disclose, there is very little hard information on the financial sources. The FECA filing shows $10,000 in "cash on hand" as of April 7 and $25,300 received after that date. Of that $25,300, almost one-half came from two contributions: $6,500 from Dr. and Mrs. Martin Peretz (who gave at least $114,000 in 1968) and $8,000 from Mr. and Mrs. Stanley Sheinbaum. There was $3,000 from three other contributions of $500 or more; one gift of $100-$500; and $3,000 was transferred in from other committees. The report contains no information on contributions of less than $100.

Most of the estimated $440,000 pre-April 7 expenditures is believed to have come from large contributors, most of whom had been big contributors to McCarthy's 1968 campaign.[ss] However, the amounts they gave in 1972 were generally lower.

[ss] Stewart Mott, who gave $210,000 in 1968, gave only $5,000 in 1972, partly because he insisted on public disclosure and McCarthy would not disclose.

In addition to simply asking former big contributors for support,[tt] the McCarthy campaign employed two other fund-raising methods—mass mailings, and small gatherings such as cocktail parties and receptions. There were three mailings, all to people on 1968 lists. The first mailing of 100,000 letters was timed to coincide with McCarthy's announcement of candidacy. Although not especially successful, the mailings did produce about $15,000 above their cost. Cocktail parties and other small fund-raising gatherings were built into the travel schedule. It is reported that McCarthy "hit" five homes in Minneapolis in one evening and raised $15,000, but there were no major fund-raising events as in 1968.

McCarthy began his candidate explorations in July 1971 with no money on hand, and reportedly paid for the operation of the Washington headquarters out of his own pocket in the first months. Apparently the campaign had enough money; there were no debts and the only known loan was one of $10,000 during the Illinois campaign that was repaid during the campaign. Some of the money spent in states other than Illinois and Minnesota was raised in each state.

Harris

Senator Fred Harris of Oklahoma formally announced his candidacy for the 1972 Democratic presidential nomination on September 24, 1971. He withdrew from the race six weeks later, making his official campaign the shortest in 1972. His preannouncement campaign was also short; Harris had been "considering" only since mid-July. The three-and-a-half month presidential venture cost $330,000.

Lack of money was the official reason Harris withdrew, but there were others. Harris' campaign was rent by internal divisions over whether to run a "populist" campaign or a more conventional one. These divisions were a manifestation of a power struggle among the staff that began before Harris' announcement and never ended, making it virtually impossible to run an effective campaign. The original plan was to have a small, enthusiastic staff of nonprofessionals—no expensive media or campaign management consultants—to go on the road, take the case to the people, and make a virtue of spending little. But other advisors wanted a conventional media campaign, limousines instead of buses, and jets rather than commercial flights.

There was very little planning for fund raising, but Harris had one financial angel, Herbert Allen, Jr., a Wall Street broker who was a personal friend. Allen, who had given Humphrey $56,000 in the 1968 general election, was Harris' major backer. The campaign raised about $65,000 in Oklahoma and about $100,000 in

---

[tt]One major McCarthy supporter from 1968 reportedly made some of these fund-raising calls while actually acting as a McGovern campaign treasurer.

New York; the latter presumably through Allen. One reception in Oklahoma in early August raised $28,000. Allen contributed about $25,000 and raised about $75,000 from his friends.

Allen's desire was for Harris to maintain the populist image, not wasting money on frills, and to make an all-or-nothing effort in the Florida primary. He became disenchanted when Harris deemphasized issues like tax reform and moved to causes such as the breaking up of General Motors, although some staff viewed the breaking up of large corporations as a logical extension of Harris' stand on tax reform. Allen's disenchantment grew when the campaign spent $35,000 to rent a 727 airplane; the money could have supported the Florida campaign for a month or more.

Faced with pressing debts and severe lack of funds, Harris made a dramatic trip to California the weekend before he withdrew from the race in an effort to raise funds. He claimed to have received pledges for future contributions, but did not get the cash needed for current expenses. Consequently, he dropped out. After Harris withdrew, one supporter tried to get 10,000 people to give $5 a month; this idea of eliciting many small donations, which worked so well for McGovern, came too late, and lacked both a practical plan for implementation and a sure base of support.

Chisholm

Representative Shirley Chisholm, the first black and the first woman ever to run a determined campaign for President, announced her candidacy on January 25, 1972. Although finances were lean, she stayed in the contest until the Democratic National Convention six months later, where she was one of five candidates whose names were placed in nomination. The preannouncement phase of the Chisholm effort was also about six months long, although it did not begin in earnest until her early October announcement of intention to run in at least four primaries. The entire cost of the campaign was about $300,000.[uu]

Chisholm's name appeared on the ballot in 12 states; she campaigned actively in six of them and in one nonprimary state. Four delegates from New York, her home state, were pledged to her; her highest vote was 7.5 percent of the total in North Carolina, which gave her 18 delegates; she received 152 delegate votes on the first ballot at the convention.

Chisholm ran primarily as a symbol and spokeswoman. But she ran without the wholehearted support of many black leaders and groups. She did not attend the Black Political Convention that was held in Gary, Indiana in

---

[uu]See Shirley Chisholm, *The Good Fight* (New York: Harper & Row, Publishers, 1973), p. 45.

September 1971, to determine the best strategy for maximizing black influence in the 1972 election. Feeling that Chisholm's activities preempted the development of any other black strategy, many blacks responded with anger and resentment, negatively affecting her campaign throughout 1972.

Money was not a factor in Chisholm's decision to run, but it did affect the timing of her formal announcement, the choice of states she ran in, and the amount of time she spent in each.[40] Rather than establish a central finance structure, the campaign allowed each state to raise and spend its own funds with the national office paying for travel and some personal expenses. The candidate would stay in the state only as long as the local organization could afford to pay her way. There was no money for political professionals.

Since each state was politically and financially independent, the Chisholm national headquarters was a more limited operation than that of most other presidential candidates. The financial and political functions of the national campaign were separate. The main organizational and financial efforts were in Brooklyn, New York and Los Angeles, California, with no Washington, D.C.-based central committee; however, a national campaign headquarters was established in the Dodge House (a hotel near the Capitol), with a small staff including administrative assistant and political adviser Thad Garrett.[vv] Other committees in Massachusetts, Minnesota, Colorado, and Wisconsin operated independently.

The decentralization created more of a grass-roots image, but resulted in a lack of control that was taken advantage of repeatedly. In one case tickets were sold to a rally where the candidate was supposedly the featured speaker, only there was no rally, no speech, and a hustler disappeared with the ticket proceeds. Several other bogus fund-raising events were held and the receipts were never given to any campaign committees. Another problem especially common to underfinanced, losing campaigns was that the bills run up by individuals falsely claiming to be "with the campaign" kept arriving at the national office because no one was locally responsible. For example, in 1971 the campaign received bills for hotel suites at the September National Black Political Convention, which neither Chisholm nor anyone connected with her campaign had attended.

In October 1971 Chisholm said that $100,000 was the minimum needed for her effort; a month later she raised the figure to $300,000 and challenged her supporters to raise $250,000 by the end of the year. Three major (New York, California and Massachusetts) and several small Chisholm committees filed under the FECA, and unlike all other candidates' committees, they listed all receipts and expenditures from their dates of inception (January and February 1972)

[vv]Although some news stories refer to Garrett as the campaign manager, Chisholm was the only, and unofficial, campaign manager, assisted by her husband, who quit his regular job to be her full-time financial adviser.

rather than from the April 7 effective date of the FECA; therefore, they showed no cash on hand. The committees showed total expenditures of just under $96,000, and Congresswoman Chisholm's personal report indicated expenditures of $19,000. An additional unreported $60,000 may be accounted for in pre-announcement spending, according to Chisholm aides.

Adding the unreported $60,000 to the committee and candidate expenditures gives a total cost of $175,000 as of the election. However, the termination report submitted to GAO by the New York committee for the period November 16, 1971 through December 16, 1973 gave an updated accounting. Total individual contributions of $77,230, plus $39,200 contributions by groups, and $2,189 bank interest and telephone refund, totalled $118,620 in receipts for the 1972 campaign. Expenditures totalled $118,677 leaving a deficit of $57.09, which the campaign found impossible to reconcile. A total $1,588 was spent for media, $110,751 for personal services, salaries and reimbursed expenses, and $6,337 for transfers out. The candidate made a major contribution to the campaign, paying out-of-pocket expenses of $32,600, and was reimbursed for only $14,974. Adding the candidate's $17,625 expenditures that were not reimbursed to the updated total $176,826 in committees' reported expenditures, plus the unreported $60,000, brings the total accounted for campaign expense to $254,451. The remainder, up to the $300,000 total, remains obscured, and the money was probably spent in the states.

The Shirley Chisholm for President Committee (Brooklyn, New York) reported expenditures of $40,500. This money went for the operation of the Washington headquarters, including rent and staff salaries; campaign materials (in limited quantities, to establish a standard and provide uniformity throughout the country); travel expenses, including two or three advance people who operated out of Washington, D.C. (all travel was by commercial airlines); and at the Democratic Convention. There were no national media expenses; radio and newspaper advertising was paid for by the state committees. The Florida campaign cost about $15,000, and most of that money came from the national head-quarters. The national campaign also spent $10,000 at the Democratic National Convention. Since the known convention and Florida campaign costs exceed one-half of the reported expenditures of the New York committee, leaving less than $20,000 for all office, salary, non-Florida travel, and materials costs, it is likely that some or all of the $60,000 noted above went for the New York office expenses.

The Massachusetts committee reported expenditures of $16,507, presumably all spent locally on Chisholm's campaign. The California committee's reported receipts of $38,441, and expenditures of $36,057 were presumably used in-state. The California committee's termination report of September 8, 1972 indicated that excess funds would go to the Democratic Party of California. However, as shown in a GAO audit report of November 1974, the committee's Los Angeles bank accounts were closed out by paying about $3,100 to the committee's treasurer, Sara Brown Palevsky, who had loaned $10,000. The balance of the loan was forgiven but never reported as such. The GAO report also disclosed that several organizations affiliated with but independent of the Shirley Chisholm for President Committee, L.A., failed to register and report receipts and expenditures, and provided the main California committee with inadequate financial information.[41] The GAO report was forwarded to the Attorney General for further investigation and whatever action he should deem appropriate regarding the committee's failure to register and report under FECA requirements.

Although the campaign claimed to be run on the pennies, nickels, and dimes of hundreds of thousands of people, it was not without its large contributors. Almost one-half of the receipts reported to GAO came from 17 contributions. These included: $2,000 from Joan Palevsky; $10,000 from Max Palevsky; a $10,000 loan and $400 contribution from Sara Palevsky; $5,000 each from entertainer Flip Wilson and Betsy Babcock, a New York housewife; $2,100 from Stewart Mott; more than $1,000 from actor Sidney Poitier; and $1,000 from the Black Panthers, raised at an Oakland, California party. In addition, $25,236 came from 106 contributions of $100 to $500; and the total over-$100 contributions was $50,964. About $26,266 of the total reported income came from contributions of $100 or less, although another $5,000 in receipts from small nonreporting Chisholm committees may also have come from small contributors. It is also possible that a significant portion of the $60,000 reportedly received before Chisholm's announcement came from small contributions.

The campaign had a few fund-raising rock concerts that were modestly successful. Fund-raising events included celebrity-sponsored cocktail parties, of which the two most prominent were one in California given by Flip Wilson and Diahann Carroll and one in New York sponsored by Harry Belafonte and Lena Horne. A similar event was a $25-per-family outing sponsored by Jane Hart (wife of Michigan Senator Philip Hart) at her Frederick, Maryland farm. A planned "Dollars for Chisholm" drive never materialized because money was lacking for a computerized finance operation.

Three alleged illegal corporate contributions to the New York committee, which appeared as front page news during the campaign, totalled $686. The contributions came from one-person corporations and were openly included in the committee's financial report to GAO. Two of the contributions—one for $100, the other for $200—were returned when the FECA violation was made clear to the committee. The third—for $386—was from White Plains Manor, Inc., where a group of Hispanic-American women had raised the funds in a benefit affair for the Chisholm campaign. The Comptroller General referred the alleged violations to the Justice Department in September 1973. Chisholm publically fought the referral and her campaign was cleared of the charges in April 1974.

Yorty

Los Angeles Mayor Sam Yorty was active only in the New Hampshire primary, although his formal candidacy lasted from mid-November 1971 to the day after the California primary in June 1972. The campaign probably cost about $250,000; $25,000 was still owed at the end of 1972, and all but $7,000 was paid back in 1973.

Yorty's support for United States involvement in Vietnam separated him from the liberal Democrats, and his dislike of government control of the economy separated him from Senator Jackson, whom many considered his main competition. Late in April 1971 Yorty went to New Hampshire to test the waters. His reception there was chilly, but because of the enthusiastic support of William Loeb, the right-wing publisher of the *Manchester Union-Leader,* it was presumed Yorty could get significant support (about 15 percent of the vote). Yorty ran a vigorous campaign in New Hampshire and came in third, but he received only 6.1 percent of the vote. He did not campaign in Florida and ran last in the field of 11, getting only 0.2 percent of the vote. On the day after the Florida primary Yorty announced his withdrawal as an active candidate, but said he would continue as a California favorite son.

Yorty optimistically began his New Hampshire effort with a budget of $250,000, but the campaign cost only $120,000. The media budget began at $100,000 for radio and television; actual costs were $4,000 for radio only. The cause of the reductions was never officially stated, but it was reported that Yorty depended on Loeb, who presumably could not raise the money. The campaign's advertising agency, which had turned down other candidates in favor of Yorty, spent only $15,000 (for billboards and radio time) after expecting a $100,000 job. Media expenses were: $10,700 for billboards, including the space and the production costs; $4,000 for radio; about $15,000 for an eight-page tabloid supplement in the *Union-Leader*; and about $3,500 for other newspaper ads.

The remaining $90,000 spent in New Hampshire covered five headquarters around the state, staff, travel, campaign materials, and the Yortymobile—a large house trailer that had been fitted out with a conference room inside and a back platform that made it look like a whistle-stop train. The Yortymobile was in use as the candidate's main means of travel and campaigning from mid-December through the March primary.

No information is available on costs from the campaign's beginning through April 7 for other than the New Hampshire primary. Given the limited nature of Yorty's effort, however, it is unlikely that those costs were more than $25,000. From April 7 to June 7 the Yorty campaign spent $103,000. During that period the campaign headquarters consisted of an office manager, a secretary, and an answering service; most expenditures were for travel and personal services. The Yorty for President Committee reported receipts of $124,523, expenditures of

$117,846 and transfers to committees of $11,550, for the period from April 7 to December 31, 1972.

During his 15 years as Mayor of Los Angeles, Yorty had had semiannual fund-raising dinners, and the tickets specified that the money was a gift to Yorty. This device allowed Yorty to use the money any way he wished, although he claimed the funds were used for "voter education." Information is available on two dinners in 1971, but it is not clear whether all the proceeds went to Yorty's presidential campaign. The first was in April, before Yorty's scouting trip to New Hampshire; it was mostly $100 per plate, with some tickets at $15 per plate, and netted about $30,000. The second was in late October, shortly before Yorty's formal announcement of candidacy; tickets were $25-$100 per plate and the total raised was $150,000. During 1972, there were several fund-raising events specifically for the campaign, including a dinner-dance at the Hollywood Palladium and a champagne-and-hotdog reception.

Yorty's FECA reports cover the sources of $113,000 of his campaign's costs: $10,000 for New Hampshire bills; $88,000 for the ongoing campaign; and the $25,000 debt. The campaign had no very large contributors: $25,900 came from 30 contributors of $500 or more; $13,610 from 62 contributors of $100-$500. Contributions of under $100 accounted for $22,000, just under 20 percent of the $113,000 total covered in the report. All of the reported contributors were Californians, many of whom had been appointed to city posts or were doing business with the Los Angeles city government.

The entire debt was a loan owed to K. Sam Moldave, now a print shop owner, from Encino, California. Moldave, who made most of his money in the air freight business, was approached by a friend of Yorty. Moldave agreed to lend Yorty $25,000 at five percent interest, although he borrowed the amount at 7.5 percent interest. His contribution was to be the 2.5 percent difference in the interest after the loan was paid back. But Yorty did not pay back the debt, and Moldave went to court. He only got $10,000 back, and settled the remaining amount ($15,000) for $7,500, thus "contributing" $7,500. Legal fees ate up much of the final settlement.

Hughes

Former Iowa Senator Harold Hughes was one of the earliest active candidates, with a Washington office opened in the summer of 1970. Unlike most of the other early entrants, Hughes' campaign was an exploratory effort, mainly financed by a few individuals, to determine whether or not he should become a full-dress candidate. A little more than a year and $200,000 later, he became the first candidate to withdraw—in July 1971—more than six months before the first primary and a year before the Democratic National Convention.

When starting his campaign in 1970, Hughes said that if he could not muster sufficient support and money he would get out. Few candidates begin with commitments or even promises of enough money to go all the way. Most want enough to get started, and with a few successes gain new financial backers and more money. But Hughes and his staff were looking at the long haul, and the important question for Hughes was the ability to raise the necessary money; perceived money problems was one factor in Hughes' eventual decision not to run, but was probably not the major factor. Hughes was concerned that being a candidate colored everything he did in the Senate, particularly in the area of drug abuse, that every move would be termed political. In addition, Hughes apparently disliked certain kinds of campaigning and personal fund raising; he also commented that the "track was filled" and that there were "personal considerations," which it was rumored centered on his interest in extrasensory perceptions and beliefs. The nonmonetary reasons may have kept Hughes out even if he and his staff believed that they could raise the money—a generous late offer of $100,000 per month did not change Hughes' mind and probably forced him to make the decision final. In any case, the campaign never attracted expanding support.

The campaign was run under a committee called The District of Columbia Committee for Better Government, through which all income and expenditures were handled. The Hughes campaign did not have formal or operating budgets, although there was a projection that about $300,000 would be needed for 1971. This meant average costs of about $25,000 per month, which is just slightly more than the campaign was actually spending when it ended. The expenses had grown from a very modest $6,000 per month near the beginning, in mid-1970. Table 5-8, a breakdown of the five categories of monthly expenses, shows the growth of the campaign and some changes between categories over its year-long duration.

As expected in this kind of preprimary campaign, staff costs were the biggest expense category, comprising one-half or more of the total costs. These costs covered between six and nine people at the Washington headquarters. There were also about 20 interns who were paid modest stipends by their universities or other sponsoring institutions or by the campaign. Salaries ranged from

Table 5-8
Hughes' Campaign Expenses

Expense Category	Monthly Cost/Early	Monthly Cost/Late
Staff	$3,500	$12,000-$14,000
Travel	1,000	3,000
Telephone	500	2,000- 3,000
Postage	500	2,000
Office (rent, machinery, supplies, etc.)	750	1,500

$7,000 per year for secretaries to $23,000 per year for the top political advisers. From 5 to 15 staff worked in Iowa, as a volunteer support group for fund raising, mailings, and arranging and advancing some of the Senator's trips.

No money was spent outside of Washington and Iowa, except in Ohio, where local supporters raised and spent a little money for materials on Hughes' behalf. After Hughes withdrew, no more money was spent. Later, when Hughes endorsed and did some campaigning for Muskie, his expenses were covered by the Muskie campaign. However, the staff received a rarity in political campaigns: severance pay. Hughes withdrew and the campaign ended on July 18, but the staff was paid through September 1. This move was indicative of the suddenness of Hughes' withdrawal, his concern for the staff, and the fact that the campaign could financially afford to be considerate.

The Hughes campaign did not make a major effort to raise money. Hughes did not want money raised under the assumption that he was a full-scale candidate, and the staff seemed satisfied that enough money came in to cover ongoing expenses.

Virtually all of the money was raised by personal contact. No dinners, parties, or other fund-raising affairs were arranged. There were three or four mailings, one to a list of 60,000, but they were newsletters primarily aimed at developing political support and only incidentally at raising money and failed to even pay for themselves. The campaign received no in-kind contributions.

Hughes was not personally involved in fund raising and did not ask for money directly. But he knew virtually all of those who gave to his exploratory effort; many had supported his earlier campaigns for the Senate or for governor. The three main sources of funds were: Iowans; people in the peace movement; and individuals attracted to Hughes as a political leader.

The two principal fund raisers were Iowans who had performed the same role in other Hughes campaigns; they were William Knapp and Joseph Rosenfield, neither of whom were active in presidential politics before 1972 or after Hughes withdrew. They were also major contributors to his campaign. Knapp set up a program in Iowa for contributors to give $100 (or more) per month; this program probably accounted for one-half or more of the total raised. Nearly 90 percent of the money raised came from Iowa. (Some Hughes money, not more than $5,000, was left over from his 1968 Senate campaign.)

The only non-Iowan active in the financial end of the Hughes campaign was Robert Pirie, a Massachusetts lawyer who had worked in the 1968 McCarthy campaign. Pirie worked on fund raising for several months, until personal and political differences with the staff ended his participation in the campaign. All of the people who gave understood that Hughes' effort was a preliminary one, leaving no hard feelings when he withdrew.

Decisions on his first campaign travels were often made on whether those issuing the invitation would pay the travel costs. Hughes' rule to his staff was to stay in the black: don't spend money you don't have. The campaign followed this rule most of the time. After Hughes began his minicampaign it was receiving nearly $15,000 per month, enough to cover most expenses, and this inflow continued until the day Hughes withdrew. Several times there was insufficient cash on hand to meet the payroll, and campaign supporters would personally borrow several thousand dollars; these loans were repaid with the first money subsequently received. When Hughes withdrew, there was enough cash on hand to pay all outstanding bills in full and the six-weeks' severance pay to the staff. The year's first completed campaign was over with a financial balance sheet reading zero.

Patsy Mink

Hawaii's Democratic Representative Patsy Mink was one of the two female Representatives who sought the presidency. In September 1971 she was asked to run by a small group of liberal, antiwar Democrats from Portland, Oregon, headed by the state's former chairman for Senator Harold Hughes. The group wanted a woman to run for President and felt that Shirley Chisholm was not sufficiently opposed to the war. Mink agreed to campaign for the Oregon primary and to pay her own travel expenses if the Portland group could get a nominating petition signed by the required 4,000 Democratic voters, and would assist in her campaign. She spent more time campaigning in Oregon than any other presidential candidate, but received only 6,397 votes, 1.6 percent of the total.[ww] Her campaign ended with the Oregon primary on May 23, 1972.

The Mink campaign cost just under $15,000. The Oregon Patsy Mink for President Committee spent $10,032, including $1,117 of in-kind contributions. The committee raised just under $8,000: this included four cash contributions of $500 or more, totalling $2,487, and twelve cash contributions of $100-$500, totalling $2,251. The committee also received $2,280 in loans, of which only $150 was repaid. (The committee's FECA filing showed only $3,700 in expenditures; presumably, the majority of the campaign's income and expenses occurred before April 7.) In addition, Mink personally spent $4,330 on her campaign. There was also a Patsy Mink for President Committee in Honolulu that raised $340 and spent $533.

Wayne L. Hays

One unique candidacy was that of Ohio Congressman Wayne L. Hays. Hays is chairman of the House Administration Committee, which has jurisdiction over

---

[ww]George McGovern was the only other Democratic candidate to campaign in Oregon in 1972, although five names were on the ballot.

election legislation. Hays' run for the Democratic nomination was based on Ohio's congressional district basis of selecting national convention delegates; candidates for delegate to the Democratic Convention from his district ran pledged to Hays. The strategy seemed designed to give him bargaining power at the convention by control of several delegates. Hays reported late under the FECA that he had raised and spent almost $3,000, of which $1,621 was contributed by the United Steelworkers of America. One could argue that this money was spent in delegate selection rather than in serious candidacy, but Hays' public statements insisted on the latter interpretation.

Edward Coll

Edward Coll entered the New Hampshire primary to gain attention for his ideas on social reform. The 32-year-old social worker and activist from Hartford, Connecticut, was not constitutionally eligible for the presidency, nor had he a realistic political base of support.

After a two-month campaign, Coll received 231 votes, .3 percent of the total vote. He spent less than $2,000 on the campaign, most of it his own money. Coll believed the money was well spent because it achieved the involvement of a number of New Hampshire residents in social action programs, and inquiries were received from all over the country about his activities. The money went mostly for media: a flyer, one or two newspaper ads, bumper stickers, and some radio tapes. All of Coll's workers were volunteers who paid their own expenses.

The Democratic Vice-Presidential Candidates

Five candidates "ran" for the Democratic vice-presidential nomination in 1972, four of whom were nominated at the Miami Convention. Three of the five were announced candidates before the convention and spent significant amounts of money on their campaigns.

Three men sought to change the manner in which the vice-presidential candidate is chosen. One was Endicott Peabody, a former Massachusetts Governor, who announced his candidacy on December 27, 1971.[xx] Peabody's name was on the ballot in New Hampshire, the only state with a vice-presidential primary. He received 95.2 percent support of those who voted for Vice President (45 percent of the Democrats who voted for President); the remaining 4.8 percent wrote in Spiro Agnew. He attempted to run in five states, but could not get on the ballot. He took his case to court in Pennsylvania and was eventually rebuffed,

---

[xx]Peabody's efforts did not end with his 1972 campaign. See, for example, Endicott Peabody, "For a Grassroots Vice-Presidency," The New York Times, January 25, 1974.

five to two, by the state Supreme Court. He campaigned in 40 states and appeared at 17 state conventions, saying the "overriding issue" was simply that he was running for Vice-President.

Peabody's campaign cost at least $100,000; for the post-April 7 period, the campaign cost over $70,000. Receipts included 19 contributions in excess of $500, totalling $15,800; 13 contributions of $100-$500, totalling $8,900; $10,000 in contributions of under $100; and $13,500 from nonreporting committees. The campaign received a $10,243 loan from Mrs. Mary Peabody, the candidate's mother, $4,000 in loans from other relatives, and a $2,500 bank note; $13,493 was still owed by the Peabody for Vice President Committee-D.C. after the campaign. GAO figures covering April 7 to December 31, 1972, show $59,178 in total receipts, $18,575 transfers from committees, total expenditures of $74,063, and $6,148 transfers to committees.

Stanley Arnold, a wealthy New York marketing expert, also undertook a campaign he hoped would influence the manner in which the vice-presidential candidate is chosen. He announced his candidacy in a May 14, 1972 television speech. Arnold's name was placed in nomination at the Democratic National Convention, and he received 87 delegate votes. The campaign had four committees and was considered by the candidate to be a serious, continuing effort to reform the method of choosing vice-presidential candidates. Arnold claimed to have raised $150,000, only $2,000 of which he said came from members of his family, but his FECA reports show total income and expenditures of $124,000. Of the total, about $85,000 went for media advertising for his announcement (of which $33,375 was for production costs): full-page and half-page newspaper ads were run in 39 cities on May 12 and quarter-page ads ran two days later; his 15-minute appearance was carried on television stations in 39 cities. Of the $124,000 raised, $117,000 was cash on hand on April 7 and some observers believed the money came not from 30 friends but from Arnold himself and his family; this was denied by Arnold. Later GAO reports on the campaign transactions show receipts of $571 from Volunteers for Stanley Arnold, $10,678 from Citizens for Stanley Arnold, and $20,000 transfers from other committees.

Alaska Senator Mike Gravel, who also sought to change the way vice-presidents are selected, had received a good deal of publicity in 1971 from reading portions of the "Pentagon Papers" into the official record of a subcommittee. He announced his candidacy for the vice-presidency on July 6, 1972, and said he, too, was challenging the traditional method of selecting the vice-presidential nominee. His campaign cost close to $100,000. At the time of his announcement, Gravel said that $50,000 had been raised for his campaign—and this in the face of outstanding debts of $68,000 from his 1968 Senate race and about $50,000 for legal fees in connection with the "Pentagon Papers" episode. However, Gravel's FECA reports show that he raised only $15,055: $7,500 from six contributions of $500 or more; $7,500 from 32 contributions of $100-$500; and $55 from contributions of less than $100. Gravel lent his campaign

$19,800 and the campaign had additional debts of $39,953, with a balance of only $3,022, at the end. A GAO audit report of September 30, 1974, of The Friends of Mike Gravel Committee revealed receipts of $86,847 and expenditures of $86,817 for the period June 26, 1972, through December 31, 1973.

One unannounced and not nominated vice-presidential candidate was Wisconsin Governor Pat Lucey. His "campaign" was the traditional one of a politician who is, in fact, being seriously considered by the presidential nominee; it was reported that Lucey was one of the last several names to be crossed off McGovern's list of possible running mates. The size of his FECA reported expenditures shows the low-key nature of this effort: his campaign cost $4,349, of which $4,054 came from a Friends of Pat Lucey Committee in Wisconsin.

The last of the five vice-presidential candidates was Frances ("Sissy") Farenthold, a liberal Texas legislator whose one-day candidacy arose quite spontaneously at the convention. Little was spent on her campaign although women's groups at the Democratic Convention actively supported her.

Others were considered unannounced vice-presidential candidates, including: Senator Birch Bayh, Governor John Gilligan, Senator Fred Harris, and Senator Harold Hughes. Others were mentioned: Governor Reubin Askew, Senator Adlai E. Stevenson, III, Senator Ernest Hollings, Senator Walter F. Mondale, Senator Gaylord Nelson, Senator John Tunney, and a Mississippian, Charles G. Hamilton, who billed himself as "the leading candidate for Vice President."

The Republicans

The Republican's prenomination contest was a classic pattern leading to incumbent victory. Like Presidents Eisenhower in 1956 and Johnson in 1964, President Nixon had only minor opposition to his renomination and stayed carefully out of the battle. The two primary opponents, Rep. John Ashbrook and especially Rep. Paul McClosky, received early attention because Nixon's weakness in 1971 made a repeat of the dramatic upset of President Johnson seem possible. But Nixon's adept use of the media and his foreign policy coups did much to neutralize this opposition.

Throughout 1971, in the judgment of many political experts, Nixon was fairly weak for an incumbent President. In public opinion polls of three-way races (with Wallace as a third-party candidate), Nixon had about 43 percent. This was the same percentage by which he had won in 1968, but is considered low for an incumbent President. Other polls, asking how well people judged he was doing his job, consistently showed him at around 50 percent, also low for an incumbent. Many believed that Nixon's Vietnamization program was still a question mark among the people, and the economy was an especially weak point for him. Because media and political experts had drastically

underestimated the strength of the antiwar, anti-Johnson, and McCarthy movements in 1967 and early 1968 and were afraid of making the same mistake
again, they gave close attention to McCloskey's developing campaign in 1971
and early 1972.

It is difficult to describe financing in the Republican prenomination period.
McCloskey revealed contributions and expenditures from his entrance into the
race in mid-1971 until he withdrew, so information on that campaign is plentiful.
But Ashbrook did not voluntarily disclose his campaign's finances, and his two
major efforts in New Hampshire and Florida took place before the FECA went
into effect. Nixon's year-and-a-half campaign is difficult to separate into distinct
prenomination and general election periods. The Nixon pre-April 7 effort raised
money actually spent in the general election period, and some expenditures made
in the preconvention period were for goods and services to be delivered in the
postconvention period.

Though beginning the campaign from a position of weakness, Nixon and
the Committee to Re-Elect the President (CRP) managed to dissolve Republican
opposition by the end of the first primary. With aggressive fund raising and
astute political management, the CRP blocked all challenges to the President's
renomination.

Nixon

Richard M. Nixon conceded rather than formally announced his candidacy
for the Republican nomination for President. On January 7, 1972 he approved
leaving his name on the New Hampshire primary ballot, but also formally
announced he would not campaign in the primaries. Moreover, it was decided
not to use stand-in or favorite son candidates in the primaries (as President
Johnson had done in 1964), so that local organizations would get used to working for just one candidate. Nixon's reelection campaign had in fact begun almost
a year earlier, and the carefully planned strategy was in full operation by the
time his name was entered in the first primary.

Late in December, 1970 Special Assistant to the President Harry S. Flemming
left the White House staff. He soon opened an office within a block of the
White House, coincidentally in the same building as the D.C. offices of both
Nixon's old law firm (Nixon, Mudge, Rose, Guthrie, Alexander & Mitchell) and the
late Murray Chotiner, an old political friend of Nixon. Hugh Sloan followed from
the White House in late March. The Nixon campaign went public on May 11, 1971,
with its committee comprised mainly of former White House staffers, including
Jeb Stuart Magruder, Herbert L. Porter, Robert Odle, Flemming, and Sloan.

The Committee to Re-Elect the President, initially called the Committee
for the Re-Election of the President (CRP), was the major organizational force of
the Nixon campaign. Its operation became a most extreme example of candidate-

oriented campaign organization, whose intent and effort is wholly directed toward one candidate's election without reference to others on the ticket. Accordingly, the CRP directed the campaign, with Republican National Committee (RNC) personnel openly joining the effort after Nixon's nomination at the Republican Convention.

Before then, the RNC was in the ambiguous position of maintaining neutrality while actually supporting the Republican administration in its newsletters and publicity. The RNC computer system was pilot tested to devise the extensive direct mail program used by the Nixon campaign after his renomination. Although most of the direct mail campaign was carried out in the general election period, the costs of planning and preparing it were borne by the RNC at a time when Nixon was not the only Republican candidate, although the committee was later reimbursed. The RNC even began in late 1971 to recruit volunteers to work in getting out the vote in the general election, one year away.

Realistically, it is impossible for a national party committee to carry out its legitimate functions in support of an incumbent President without violating, or appearing to violate, its role of neutrality among party candidates. In 1971 and early 1972 the RNC was no more neutral nor less biased than the DNC had been in 1964. It is impossible to calculate how much of the RNC activities in 1971 and early 1972 benefited the Nixon campaign, or whether reimbursements fully covered such activities. While the relationships between the CRP and the RNC were at best tenuous at the political level even after Nixon's nomination, the relationships among the finance staffs were cordial and cooperative. The Republican Party had ongoing interests in electing senators and representatives as well as a President and was more concerned with the future of the party in 1974 and 1976, whereas the CRP goal was wholly to reelect Nixon, focusing only on 1972.

The Committee to Re-elect the President.   The CRP was originally established as a "citizens' group" (Citizens for the Re-Election of the President) by its then chairman, Francis Dale, a Cincinnati publisher, who in mid-1973 severed his association with the organization.[yy] Embittered by Watergate revelations, Dale felt he and the others who originally formed the CRP had been deceived; he said he was sickened to have his name associated with the organization.[42]   In September

---

[yy]The original CRP members represented the business-political orientation of the Nixon campaign: Dale; Frank Borman, ex-astronaut, and Eastern Airlines executive; Max M. Fisher, Marathon Oil executive, one of George Romney's chief fund raisers in 1968 and later one of Nixon's large contributors in 1972; Rita E. Hauser, long-time party activist and member of the United States delegation to the United Nations; John Erick Jonsson, honorary chairman and director of Texas Instruments and former Dallas mayor; Robert H. Volk, president of Unionamerica; Thomas W. Pappas, Boston importer; and Donald Schollander, former Olympic swimmer and college administrator.

1971 the CRP was reconstituted as the Committee for the Re-Election of the President, to manage the political aspects of the campaign; the citizens' organization was dissolved shortly thereafter.

On October 1, 1971 the Finance Committee for the Re-Election of President Nixon was created with Sloan as its chairman to handle finances. On February 15, 1972 it was dissolved, and the next day the Finance Committee for the Re-Election of the President was formed with Maurice Stans resigning as Secretary of Commerce to become the committee chairman while Sloan became treasurer. On April 7 this committee was in turn dissolved and was replaced by the Finance Committe to Re-Elect the President (FCRP). Stans and Sloan continued in their earlier positions.

On March 1 Mitchell had resigned as Attorney General and in April he became the campaign director of CRP. On June 30, 1972, he resigned from the post, and Clark MacGregor, assistant to the president for congressional relations, was appointed his successor.

In the course of 1972 the early amateur image of the CRP was rapidly transformed to that of a highly professional campaign organization. The staff, which numbered about 30 at the beginning, was headed by second echelon officials, many of whom had come directly from the White House. Watergate disclosures later revealed two memos from Gordon C. Strachan to his superior, White House Chief of Staff H.R. Haldeman, revealing that Haldeman directed the establishment of the CRP, and the campaign to reelect Nixon.[zz] Dated September 29, 1971, the first of these memos stated that Dale was to be the official spokesman and that Attorney General John Mitchell was not to be publically connected with the campaign. The memo further stated that both Mitchell and Magruder were in a "minor situation" and that any involvement by the Attorney General was to be denied. Actually, Mitchell was closely involved in all major decisions. The second memo, dated October 7, 1971, stated that any citizens' organization "will be merely a division of the Committee for the Re-Election of the President instead of an independent unit. . . ." These revelations illuminated the extent of White House direction of activities, particularly after Mitchell resigned in the post-DNC break-in period after July 1972. Mitchell had stayed in the Cabinet

---

[zz]Gordon Strachan testified before the Senate Watergate Committee that he regularly prepared "Political Matters Memoranda" for Haldeman—28 in all—and that he destroyed memorandum number 18 after the Watergate break-in. The memoranda covered the whole range of issues involved in running the 1972 campaign, and generally represented a summary of CRP press releases and surrogates' speeches and activities on the President's behalf. Haldeman would normally relay the information, but not the memos, to the President. After reviewing them, Haldeman would note appropriate actions and Strachan would contact CRP personnel to implement Haldeman's instructions. See Senate Select Committee on Presidential Campaign Activities, *Final Report*, pp. 18-20, or U.S., Congress, House, Judiciary Committee *Hearings*, "Summary of Information," 93rd Cong., 2d sess., July 19, 1974 (Washington, D.C.: U.S. Government Printing Office, 1974), pp. 25ff; summaries are given of "The Organization of the White House and its Relationship to the CRP."

in 1971, giving advice to campaign managers preparatory to taking over actively in early March 1972. By that time, the staff numbered about 100.

At the outset, the CRP was to be a think tank operation to plan for the campaign, to research primary state requirements and delegate selection procedures, and not to focus on campaigning. This related to a strategy calling for Nixon's posture to be that of President, not an active candidate, with no campaigning until the Miami Beach Convention. Republican opponents were ignored. The campaign staff would build a grass-roots network and direct mail operation, surrogates would campaign for the President, and various campaign officials would carry the attacks against Nixon's opponents. The theme of the campaign, "Re-Elect the President," was chosen to emphasize not Nixon but the office of the presidency.

Throughout 1971 Nixon had followed this "nonpolitical" strategy, refusing to discuss politics while carrying out well-publicized actions as President. Although United States troop withdrawals from Vietnam were continued during the first half of the year, many political observers believed support for the President was eroding, and public opinion polls seemed to confirm this. Then came two dramatic actions: the breakthrough in United States-China relations and a broad new economic program, including wage and price controls. A few months later, in one week in November exactly one year before the 1972 election, there were the Phase II guidelines, a new Secretary of Agriculture, more troop withdrawals from Vietnam, and a large political fund-raising dinner. Except for the establishment of the CRP and the dinner, 1971 ended with Nixon having made no direct political moves toward reelection, but having completely dominated the year's political developments.

One innovation in Nixon's reelection effort was the creation of the campaign's own advertising agency, rather than following the usual practice of buying the services of an established commercial agency. Dubbed the "November Group," it was incorporated January 25, 1972. Headed by Peter Dailey, president of a Los Angeles advertising firm, the in-house agency was established to create and produce the campaign's advertising and to purchase all media time and space. The New York-based agency was developed to keep more direct control over the advertising and the political loyalty of the people creating the work. When the November Group was organized it was expected the advertising effort would cost a total of $15 million for the whole campaign, almost all for the postnomination period; the November Group actually spent only half that much in all of 1972.

Advantages of Incumbency. An incumbent President can request, and is always granted, television and radio time whenever he decides he has an important message. These presidential appearances do not cost the campaign or the White House any money. During his first 40 months in office prior to his May, 1972, Moscow trip, Nixon made 32 special prime time appearances. These blocks of time—which do not include press conferences, interviews, or regular news coverage—were used to make announcements, deliver addresses, or report on recent events. A half-hour program, broadcast simultaneously on all three networks during prime time, could cost $250,000 (in addition to the cost of producing the program)—if the time could be purchased.

During the three weeks immediately preceding the New Hampshire and Florida primaries, the three national television networks carried a total of 41 hours and 44 minutes of special programs on Nixon's trip to China. Nixon's Moscow trip also occurred at an opportune time; he arrived in Moscow one day before the Oregon primary. His meetings with Russian leaders were well publicized while the McGovern-Humphrey battle in California was in full swing. Nixon returned home on the day after the second Humphrey-McGovern debate; he arrived at the Capitol by helicopter at the prime time hour of 9 p.m. and, with a background of floodlights and television cameras, walked into a joint session of Congress for a presidential report on the summit meeting. It was grand theater and extraordinarily effective politics, all staged as presidential business and at no cost to the campaign. Clearly, such televised travels were worth far more politically than any number of personal campaign appearances would have been.

Increasing opposition has arisen to these presidential "nonpartisan" appearances in recent years, and there have been increased efforts to equalize this media exposure. In 1970 CBS initiated its "Loyal Opposition" series to provide the Democrats with increased air time to answer presidential appearances. The Republicans then objected, invoking the doctrine of equal time to demand time to respond, which was granted by the FCC. The courts subsequently reversed the FCC decision, but the move caused CBS to discontinue its "Loyal Opposition" series. The 1972 campaign saw several complaints filed with the FCC by the Democratic National Committee for equal time to answer presidential appearances; these complaints were usually rejected. Since 1972 the opposition has regularly received time to answer.

Costs. From its inception, the Nixon campaign was focused primarily on the general election period. The President's renomination was assumed and his primary challengers were viewed as minor annoyances on the way to a tough race in the fall. This orientation makes it difficult to separate the campaign and its financing into clear prenomination and postnomination periods. Therefore, all general headquarters and overhead expenses are counted herein in the time period in which they occurred. This method overstates spending in the prenomination period and understates the cost of the general election campaign, since most of the earlier spending was directed to the November election. Using this method, the Nixon campaign spent a minimum of $20 million from early 1971 until the end of the Republican National Convention in August 1972—or approximately the amount it raised for prenomination purposes before April 7.

As noted, money was not solicited for a particular primary or even for the nomination contest, but for Nixon's reelection. While this is usual procedure for an incumbent President, major fund raising probably never began so early. The early effort was casual until late 1971 when new legislation appeared imminent, creating urgency in early 1972 to take advantage of the nondisclosure provisions of the law then in effect.

The Nixon campaign steadfastly refused at the time to reveal more information about its financing than was required by law: candidate disclosure was not required by New Hampshire law; it was by Florida law. Both campaigns occurred before the FECA took effect, requiring full disclosure thereafter.

The Nixon campaign spent about $250,000 in New Hampshire against two opponents and about $175,000 in Florida against one opponent. Both campaigns were low key, using little television and concentrating more on radio (spending about $32,000 for radio), mass mailings; and organizing local groups. The primaries were viewed as testing grounds for the general election and various headquarters workers were sent to Florida for on-the-job training. In one memorandum to H.R. Haldeman, dated February 16, 1972, Gordon Strachan wrote that extensive direct mail campaigns were proceeding as planned, costing $75,000 in New Hampshire and $100,000 in Florida, along with a $25,000 telephone campaign in New Hampshire. Also noted was a telephone poll in Florida, cost unknown. About $37,000 was spent on radio and television in New Hampshire, and in Florida.

The amounts spent in the New Hampshire and Florida primaries are not wholly significant because of the free media coverage the campaign received in addition to coverage of presidential diplomacy. For example, four days before the New Hampshire voting a troupe of 18 celebrities toured the state on behalf of Nixon. The troupe included New York's Nelson Rockefeller and three other governors, four United States senators, five representatives, two cabinet secretaries, one of the country's Equal Employment Opportunities Commissioners, baseball star Joe Torre, and singer Lainie Kazan. Among them, the celebrities visited 12 kaffeeklatches, 11 high schools, seven plants and offices, four newspapers, four campaign headquarters, three colleges, one nursing home, one housing project, one country club, and one grade school. They also made five street tours and gave two news conferences. This media exposure was inexpensive because it appeared in news stories, costing the campaign only the travel involved. Six days later, the Nixon "all-star" troupe to Florida included Governor Ronald Reagan, Senator Barry Goldwater, Interior Secretary Rogers Morton, comedian Red Skelton, and the current Miss USA. Also during the New Hampshire primary, Transportation Secretary John Volpe made the "surprise announcement" of an Airport Development Aid Program grant of $121,000 for the Manchester airport. This is yet another advantage of an incumbent running for reelection—announcements of government programs timed for maximum impact.

After the Florida primary, Nixon was virtually unopposed for the Republican nomination. McCloskey withdrew after getting 20 percent of the New Hampshire vote and Ashbrook became inactive, except for a token effort in California, after getting less than ten percent of the vote in both New Hampshire and Florida. In Wisconsin, a major Nixon advertising campaign on 29 radio and 12 television stations was cancelled a few days after the Florida results; only $18,000 of $143,000 planned was spent. Other Nixon expenditures in Wisconsin were similarly cut back. The Maryland CRP budget was about $46,500. The Oregon figures show that $100,000 was raised and expended in Nixon's primary effort.

If all the primary states and convention states are combined, perhaps as much as $5 million was spent by the national campaign in lining up pro-Nixon delegates and establishing state organizations.

A consolidated report filed with the Clerk of the House on September 28, 1973, covering all receipts and expenditures by the FCRP and its affiliated committees (for the period of January 1, 1971, through April 6, 1972) showed overall total contributions of $19,914,000 received during that period. This included total contributions of $18,444,000; miscellaneous receipts and refunds of $127,000; transfers of $716,000 from Herbert Kalmbach's 1968 trust funds; and $653,000 of deposited contributions originally received in cash. Expenditures of $9,739,000 left bank balances of $10,201,000 as cash on hand on April 7, when the FECA became effective. The CRP spent about $3.1 million on its staff and headquarters and on getting state CRP's started in the year before April 7. Prepayments of about $6 million were made, of which almost $5 million was disbursed on April 5 and 6. On these days, the Reuben Donnelley Corporation was prepaid $2.5 million for political mailings; Walter Weintz $1 million for fund-raising mailings in the next few months; and the November Group received $925,000 for media production costs.

Ashbrook

Representative John Ashbrook of Ohio was nationally little known, but well known in conservative circles when he challenged Richard Nixon's renomination, articulating right-wing positions. He announced his presidential candidacy on December 27, 1971, and stayed in the race through all the primaries. Ashbrook probably spent about $500,000 while his campaign's total costs were about $740,000. The discrepancy between expenditures and costs resulted from an agreement between Ashbrook and the conservative direct mail entrepreneur Richard A. Viguerie (see below).

Until late 1971 it appeared that no conservative candidate would challenge Nixon. Then Ashbrook announced his candidacy, saying that his campaign would be a focal point for conservative dissatisfaction, but that he would drop out if Nixon signalled more attention to conservatives. A fund-raising letter in early January asked potential supporters to inform the President that they were "suspending support" because of broken 1968 promises.

The signal did not come, and Ashbrook stayed in the race until the end, though active only in the New Hampshire, Florida, and California primaries. He received less than ten percent of the vote in his three efforts—9.6 percent in New Hampshire, 8.8 percent in Florida, and 9.9 percent in California—and was not taken seriously after his initial poor showing in New Hampshire.

Ashbrook was still in the most active phase of his campaign when voluntary disclosure became an issue in late February. In spite of prodding by McCloskey and the press, he refused to disclose. Therefore, financial data for the pre-April 7 period is very sketchy, but the total spent is estimated at about $160,000. Data for the post-April 7 period includes almost $340,000 in expenditures and a $240,000 "debt" to Viguerie, bringing Ashbrook's total costs to almost three-quarters of a million dollars.

At the time of his announcement, Ashbrook talked of a combined budget of $150,000 for New Hampshire and Florida, which was later raised to $175,000. In mid-February, Ashbrook's campaign reportedly set a goal of $300,000 for New Hampshire, and an early March report speculated that his Florida effort would cost about $450,000. In fact, Ashbrook stated that he spent only $32,000 in New Hampshire and $6,000 in Florida. Reports estimated that pro-rated costs for national headquarters, media production, and travel attributable to those primaries and probably not included in the candidate's statements would bring Ashbrook's total costs for the two primaries to $60,000.[43] Ashbrook did little local organizing in New Hampshire and none in Florida; virtually all expenditures were for travel, printing, postage, and media. There was one significant in-kind contribution in Florida: a pilot donated his services and airplane for the candidate's travel, and the campaign paid only for the gasoline.

No information exists on the costs of Ashbrook's national campaign operation, either before or during the New Hampshire and Florida primaries. Published reports of the returns from the campaign's first direct mail solicitation, plus the above information and data on the campaign's first FECA report, strongly suggest that at least $100,000 was spent on the direct mail effort in the pre-April 7 period.

For the post-April 7 period, Ashbrook's only primary campaign effort was in California. A San Francisco committee reported income and expenditures of about $35,000; little is known of additional money from the national committee spent for the California campaign.

Excluding the California committee's expenditures, FECA reports and GAO audit information show Ashbrook spent about $240,000 from April 7 to the end of 1972. Almost 75 percent of the total, or $176,000, went to Richard A. Viguerie Company, Inc. The campaign still owed Viguerie an additional $306,000 by the end of 1972, which was then "written off" by the company. Viguerie undertook a series of mailings in 1973 that raised $66,000, which reduced the debt to $240,000 and raised Ashbrook's actual expenditures to about

$500,000. The $500,000 includes about $160,000 spent before April 7, 1972; $35,000 spent by the California committee, presumably for that state's primary; $240,000 spent by the national campaign between April 7 and the end of the year; and the $66,000 raised by Viguerie in 1973 and applied to the Ashbrook debt. The remaining debt makes the overall cost of Ashbrook's campaign $740,000, of which $482,000 was paid or owed to Richard A. Viguerie, Inc. A GAO audit in 1974 revealed the details of the Ashbrook-Viguerie arrangement, and cited the Ashbrook committee for failure to properly disclose its debts to GAO. It referred to the Attorney General the apparent violation of the law that prohibits corporate contributions; debt forgiveness is considered a contribution.

Viguerie learned he would not be hired by the Nixon campaign in late 1971, and he began discussions with Ashbrook's aides. Nixon operatives then tried to persuade Viguerie to work for Nixon instead of Ashbrook. But Ashbrook and Viguerie signed a contract on January 1, 1972, which provided that Viguerie was the campaign's exclusive consultant for all mailings and direct mail solicitations. Viguerie's company was responsible for preparing and sending all direct mail, using its own lists. Viguerie had been in the direct mail business for various conservative candidates and causes and had developed the most extensive conservative mailing lists available. The campaign agreed to reimburse the company for all its direct costs (to vendors and suppliers) and to pay a fee of four cents for each name used and two cents for each letter mailed. A special joint bank account was established to hold funds received from the mailings for disbursement. The bank account required the signatures of a representative of the company and of the campaign for withdrawals.

GAO's review showed as of April 7 the campaign owed the company $367,000 from the joint bank account. The company may not have been reimbursed at all, and the $367,000 debt may represent the total cost of the direct mail effort to that point. The company may also have received some of the money from the direct mail solicitations. Since Ashbrook did not voluntarily disclose his pre-April 7 finances, it is unknown whether Viguerie received money between January 1 and April 7. The reported income from a January mailing suggests that Viguerie received about $100,000 during that period. The debt was reduced to $306,000 by December 1972, when the company's books showed a credit entry for the full amount. As noted, the debt had not been paid, but written off, and an additional $66,000 was applied to it during 1973.

The GAO report cited two major problems: first, that the Ashbrook committee did not disclose the Viguerie debt on and after April 7, 1972, as the law required; and second, that by writing off the debt, the company may have made an illegal corporate contribution.[aaa]

[aaa]Viguerie states in a letter to the author dated December 18, 1974 that the elimination of the amount from the company's books "was done in accord with the firm position

Ashbrook's response was that the written contract was not controlling, that the company had agreed to take all the risks if the mailings did not cover the costs. Viguerie confirmed Ashbrook's response, telling GAO the written contract "appeared to be in error, and that in all dealings with political committees, his company assumed all risk and that had been his verbal agreement with Representative Ashbrook since the inception of the agreement."[44]

The Ashbrook committee then amended its FECA reports to reflect debts to Viguerie of $367,000 as of April 7, $306,000 as of December 31, 1972, and $240,000 as of December 31, 1973. The question of an illegal corporate contribution remains even if the alleged verbal agreement rather than the written contract applied. By assuming the risks, or costs of the mailings, the company would still be making a contribution to the campaign, although the company would attempt to recover as much of the amount as it could. The possible violation of the law was referred to the Attorney General in June 1974; no action had been taken at this writing.

The roots of the financial problems lay in the belief that the conservative dissatisfaction with Nixon would be translatable into support for Ashbrook and that Viguerie's admittedly excellent conservative mailing lists were all that was needed for that translation. Both assumptions proved wrong.

The Ashbrook campaign apparently raised almost all of its income from Viguerie's direct mail effort, with perhaps a little coming through personal solicitation or from personal friends. A list of five contributors of $1,000 to $2,000 was submitted to GAO on June 22, 1972. The campaign held no major dinners, and a GAO audit of the California Ashbrook for President Committee revealed only $1,100 proceeds from two fund-raising events.

Information is only available for the first mailing of early January 1972. The goal of $175,000 for the New Hampshire and Florida primaries was almost reached from the 200,000 people that responded. Ashbrook is believed to have spent just over $60,000 in direct campaigning and backup before April 7, and the campaign's total cash on hand as of that date was reported to be less than $5,000. It appears that about $100,000 of the reported receipts went to Viguerie's company for mailing costs. These cost data for the pre-April 7 direct mail effort support GAO's finding for the period after April 7 that the company received 76 percent of the income generated by the direct mail effort.

Of the approximately $500,000 raised by the Ashbrook campaign, source details are missing on almost $300,000: the estimated $160,000 raised and spent before April 7; $4,000 cash on hand as of April 7; $64,000 in post-April 7 receipts missing from the FECA reports; and the $66,000 raised in 1973. Details are known only for a little more than $200,000: the $266,000 raised after

---

of our accounting firm . . . to have such items reduced or eliminated from the books so that the financial statements fairly present the financial condition of the company," and that it "in no way affected the political committee's indebtedness to the company."

April 7 minus the missing $64,000. Almost $173,000, or 85 percent, came from contributions of under $100. Only ten percent, or $20,000, came from contributions of $500 or more. According to campaign aides, there were no contributions of more than $5,000 and only a few in the $1,000-$5,000 range.

McCloskey

The beginning of California Representative Paul McCloskey's presidential campaign is difficult to pinpoint. Rather than actively seek the office, McCloskey found himself gradually pushed into contention by the momentum created by his opposition to the Vietnam War. By late 1970 he had become an active antiwar spokesman. McCloskey suggested a "national dialogue to discuss impeachment" in a speech at Stanford University as early as February 1971. The speech received much comment, and by mid-April he had received 30,000 letters running 20-1 in favor of his stand. He also received $4,000 in unsolicited contributions and talked money with some of Eugene McCarthy's 1968 supporters. McCloskey said he would run if the people wanted him to, but that he had neither the background nor the training for the job and would run to influence policy rather than to "dump Nixon." The campaign eventually cost about $550,000.

McCloskey's first active solicitation of money was for a trip to Laos late in April 1971. On the eve of his departure, he raised more than $12,000 at two stops in New York City.[45] Of the ten people who contributed to McCloskey's trip, seven also later contributed to his campaign.

In mid-May McCloskey opened a national headquarters in Washington with a few local volunteers and a paid staff of four. The next few months saw the staff gradually expand as the political climate changed. On July 9 McCloskey formally announced his candidacy for the New Hampshire and California primaries and greatly expanded his staff. September reports of plans to spend $1-$2 million in California gave way to reports of serious money problems. Over $200,000 had been spent by October when a new campaign manager, Alvin Toffel, took over. He found expenses running at $60,000 a month and a debt of $80,000. Feeling that efforts were being wasted on a national campaign instead of concentrating on an initial primary, Toffel cut operating expenses, closed a San Francisco headquarters, and laid off staffers in various offices; this reduced the level of expenditure to $25,000 per month. This covered fund raising, accounting, candidate travel, and political organizing. The thrust of the effort was directed toward New Hampshire and a hoped for spillover effect on the Massachusetts primary.

The McCloskey campaign was never very large. Of the $350,000 that was spent subsequent to the reorganization, over $200,000 was spent on New Hampshire. Of this, close to $20,000 was spent for television and radio;[bbb] some

---

[bbb]A good portion of this was contributed near the end by Paul Newman and Joanne Woodward.

additional television time was generated as a result of complaints to the networks under the "fairness doctrine." A great portion of the balance was spent on direct mail appeals to generate funds for the New Hampshire operation. At its peak, about 14 paid staff members supplemented by an equal number of volunteers worked in the Washington headquarters, with all of them going to New Hampshire during the final days of the primary for door-to-door organizing. Headquarters expenses at the peak were about $40,000 a month, mostly for direct mail. The financial side showed few detailed budgets or expenditure records, but a tight rein was held because finances were so scarce. The campaign left a $30,000 debt, most of which was cleared up by the end of 1972.

McCloskey dropped out after the New Hampshire race, having received only 20 percent of the vote in that primary. Interestingly, the *Boston Globe's* state-wide poll published on that date showed his strength in Massachusetts at 39 percent, with the primary in that liberal state about a month away. But the deadline for filing to return to Congress from California was March 10 and McCloskey chose to discontinue the presidential race. His name, however, remained on the Republican ballot in 12 other states as a symbolic protest to the war.

After McCloskey withdrew on March 11, a deficit committee was established to raise money for the campaign's debts. McCloskey then ran a congressional campaign, which left a $60,000 debt. The total debt from both campaigns was not paid off completely until 1974, with about $7,500 carried over from the presidential effort.

The McCloskey campaign was technically the first to voluntarily disclose its sources of campaign funds. The occasion was a February 24, 1972 press conference for the seven New Hampshire campaign managers, hosted by the Washington Press Club. When asked by a reporter to disclose principal contributors, Alvin Toffel, McCloskey's manager, read off the top 50 givers and amounts, for which he received a standing ovation from the reporters. Nixon and Ashbrook representatives had already refused. Next, Frank Mankiewicz promised to make full disclosure of McGovern's contributors at a later press conference. Mankiewicz did so on February 28, at which time McGovern raised the issue publicly by challenging his opponents to make similar disclosures.

From the beginning, Norton Simon was the financial foundation of the McCloskey effort. Together with his wife, actress Jennifer Jones, Simon was the largest contributor, giving $106,770. Much of this was given at the beginning of the campaign, with other amounts coming at strategic times. For example, at the crucial point when Toffel was brought in as campaign manager, he went to Simon, who gave about $18,000 to tide things over until the reorganization.

There was little organized fund raising—no fund-raising dinners or other major efforts—but friends and supporters gave cocktail parties and held other events. A few traditional Republican supporters were among McCloskey's financial backers. One of these, John Hay Whitney of Whitney Communications, gave McCloskey $5,000, reportedly because he felt McCloskey's views should have a platform for discussion.[46]

Though the McCloskey campaign could not afford a professional mailing operation, Toffel organized one using volunteers and the Washington staff. Working at the Washington headquarters, volunteers prepared and folded material, stuffed and addressed the envelopes, and even coded the return envelopes. This effort raised $175,000—one-third of the $525,000 total receipts voluntarily disclosed. One mid-November full-page ad in *The New York Times*, which cost $7,800, raised more than $5,000 above its cost at a crucial time. The ad prompted then-Vice-President Spiro T. Agnew to call McCloskey a "Benedict Arnold." That statement prompted money to flow in better for a while. The list of contributors generated by this effort later provided the financial base for McCloskey to survive a tough congressional reelection primary in his home district in 1972.

Of the total raised, more than two-thirds, or $352,987, came from 109 individuals or couples who each contributed $500 or more. Many of McCloskey's large contributors, including the Simons, were from his home state of California; among the very large contributors ($10,000 and over), six were from California and three of the six were from McCloskey's home congressional district. A number of people who contributed to McCloskey also contributed to one or more Democratic contenders. Among them were: J. Irwin Miller, the chairman of Cummins Engines, and his wife gave $5,500 to McCloskey and $269,167 to John Lindsay; Attorney Victor H. Palmieri gave $11,500 to McCloskey, $1,000 to Muskie, and $2,500 to McGovern-Shriver (he also lent McGovern $25,000); industrialist Max Palevsky gave $9,825 to McCloskey, $319,365 to McGovern, and $10,000 to Shirley Chisholm; Paul Newman and Joanne Woodward gave $7,500 to McCloskey and $15,005 to McGovern; Steward R. Mott gave $6,000 to McCloskey, $407,747 to McGovern, and $6,000 to Lindsay; Alejandro Zaffaroni, a drug executive, gave $11,000 to McCloskey, $5,000 to Muskie, $206,753 to McGovern, and $5,000 to Shriver; and Miles Rubin, chairman of Optical Systems Corporation, gave $4,600 to McCloskey, $108,000 to McGovern, $2,000 to Muskie, and $2,500 to Shriver.

One of McCloskey's and McGovern's early contributors was Louis Wolfson, who served several months in jail for the illegal sale of securities. The McCloskey campaign's view in accepting his contribution of $5,000 was that Wolfson had paid his debt to society and was willing to have his contribution made public, so why not accept his money.

Though he discontinued active campaigning after the first primary, McCloskey attempted to have his name put into nomination at the Republican National Convention. He claimed that the rules were arranged to prohibit this and that he was excluded from the important morning platform hearings and shunted to the afternoon hearings. The convention refused to seat McCloskey's one pledged delegate, Tom Mayer of New Mexico, but another delegate cast the vote for him—the only vote cast against Nixon—thus preventing a unanimous nomination.

The Primaries

For presidential prenomination campaigns, comparisons of candidates' total spending are tenuous since every candidate enters with varying emphases a different number and combination of primaries. Major differences in the length and cost of the candidates' pre-primary efforts in 1971-72 also affect comparisons of total spending. Three candidates—Senators Bayh, Harris, and Hughes, who together spent almost $1.3 million—were in and out of the race long before the primaries began. Although some data are lacking, meaningful comparisons can be made of the role of money on a primary-by-primary basis.

Primaries were held in 23 states and the District of Columbia. Ten of these —Alabama, Arkansas, Tennessee, Oregon, Rhode Island, New Mexico, South Dakota, New Jersey, New York, and the District of Columbia—either were uncontested or did not involve major campaigns and so are excluded from this analysis. Five of the primaries—North Carolina, Nebraska, West Virginia, Michigan, and Maryland—did not provide enough hard data to warrant more than a brief comment although they involved interesting contests. The remaining nine primaries—New Hampshire, Florida, Illinois, Wisconsin, Massachusetts, Pennsylvania, Indiana, Ohio, and California—provide good case studies of the significance of spending differences. In addition, one nonprimary state campaign which was held before the primary season began, raised consciousness about money.

Arizona

Arizona's January 29 local voting to elect 500 state convention delegates, who in turn would elect the 25 National Convention delegates, followed serious campaigns by Muskie, McGovern, Lindsay, Jackson, and the state AFL-CIO, and a last-minute effort by Humphrey.

Front-runner Muskie's campaign, which did not cost more than $15,000, was based on the support and organization of Representative Morris K. Udall, 21 of 36 state Democratic legislators, and most of the county chairmen. Muskie's major opposition was the AFL-CIO, which ran a well-organized mail and telephone canvass effort to identify union members running as uncommitted delegates. McGovern ran a strong local canvassing and organizing effort, with a few days of radio ads, spending perhaps $10,000. Jackson did not have an identifiable slate of delegates, but spent about $12,000 on newspaper ads and

mailings to identify the uncommitted delegates leaning toward him. In contrast
to these inexpensive efforts, Lindsay spent at least $50,000 and possibly as much
as $100,000. About $30,000 of his total was for a media campaign, aimed
primarily at Mexican-Americans and blacks; it included at least $18,000 for 42
television spots and 692 radio commercials, and more than 70 billboards across
the state.

The election results, in numbers of state convention delegates, were: Muskie,
189; Lindsay, 118; McGovern, 102; uncommitted (mostly union), 85; Jackson, 2;
Humphrey, 2; Chisholm, 1; Hartke, 1. Critics immediately charged that Lindsay's
lavish spending, particularly his "media blitz," accounted for his unexpected
second-place showing. Certainly Lindsay, newly a Democrat, a new presidential
candidate, and a relatively unknown figure in Arizona would not have had a
chance without a major publicity effort. Muskie was well known and had the
backing of most party leaders. Jackson, also politically unknown, might have
done better with a media effort, but since he and Lindsay were not competing
for the same supporters it is not clear that Lindsay's campaign had any effect on
Jackson's weak showing. McGovern, though, was a direct competitor for liberal
support, and Lindsay's aggressive campaign must have drained McGovern support.
However, McGovern had been an announced candidate for a year and his supporters had been working long and hard. His effort was low key and most of his
supporters probably turned out, while the Lindsay media campaign essentially
reached those who otherwise would not have participated. Two pieces of evidence support this interpretation. First, McGovern had done almost as well in
the Iowa precinct elections a week earlier with no competition from any liberal
Democrat. Second, the Lindsay billboards were apparently the first knowledge
many voters had of the election. The turnout, over 35,000 voters, was a major
surprise after an almost total blackout by the state's major newspaper.

New Hampshire

New Hampshire's first-of-the-year presidential primary on March 7 [ccc]
featured five Democratic candidates: Muskie, McGovern, Hartke, Yorty, and
Coll; all but Coll ran serious campaigns. Representative Wilbur Mills ran a
serious write-in campaign. The election results, the radio/television and total
costs of each of the serious candidates, and their approximate cost per vote, in
order of finish, are given in Table 5-9.

These figures clearly demonstrate that spending alone—even heavy media
spending—could not make Yorty, Mills, or Hartke serious presidential candidates.
Further, the prevailing wisdom that the support of *Manchester Union-Leader*

[ccc] It was set for March 14, but when Florida set its primary on that date New Hampshire
moved its primary up a week to maintain its "first" status.

Table 5-9
Democratic Cost per Vote in the New Hampshire Primary

Candidate	Rounded Votes	Vote %	Radio-TV Cost	Estimated Total Cost	Approximate Cost/Vote
Muskie	40,500	48	$65,000	$225,000	$ 5.50
McGovern	31,800	38	65,000	161,000	5.00
Yorty	5,300	6	4,000	120,000	23.00
Mills	3,500	4	85,000	200,000	57.00
Hartke	2,400	3	30,000	100,000	42.00

Publisher William Loeb was worth a minimum of 15 percent of the vote proved a myth: Loeb supported Yorty.

The 1972 New Hampshire Democratic primary was essentially a two-man race. Muskie and McGovern did not start out as equals; they did spend equal amounts on radio and television, but ended with almost 40 percent difference in total spending. Muskie began as the leading contender: well known, from a neighboring state, supported by most of the party leaders. McGovern was seen as an underdog by political professionals and pollsters: an unknown midwesterner with little prominent local support. Muskie began organizing in the fall of 1971, spent little time in the state, and used his media money for expensive Boston time, which put him on the air for only two or three weeks. McGovern began organizing in the state in January 1971, and relied heavily on building local organizations. He concentrated much of his personal time and energy for several months and stretched his media money for several weeks by using it on local stations. The spirit of the McGovern campaign emerged when some dedicated youngsters worked for the Mills campaign in the morning for from $2.50 to $4.00 per hour, earning enough money for the day, and then worked free for McGovern in the afternoon and evening. Some large contributors to the McGovern campaign are known to have paid some bills directly while visiting in New Hampshire, but precise amounts are not available.

Muskie's spending edge probably did not give him an advantage, particularly in view of his political advantages. Certainly McGovern got more for his money than Muskie, but in view of his all-out campaign, more money probably would not have made much difference. Considering where they started, McGovern's claim to a "moral victory" seems justified, and spending differences had a negligible effect on the outcome.

On the Republican side, four candidates were on the ballot, three of them serious (Nixon, McCloskey, Ashbrook), and comedian Pat Paulsen. Table 5-10 figures show little more than the popularity of the President and the weakness of both the McCloskey and Ashbrook challenges to his renomination. The New Hampshire primary was the first and only one with a Republican contest.

Table 5-10
Republican Cost per Vote in the New Hampshire Primary

Candidate	Rounded Votes	Vote %	Estimated Total Cost	Approximate Cost/Vote
Nixon	77,400	69	$250,000	$2.00
McCloskey	22,700	20	200,000+	8.80
Ashbrook	10,800	10	50,000	4.60
Paulsen	1,100	1	(less than $10,000)	(7.00)

Florida

The March 14 Florida Democratic primary ballot featured 11 presidential candidates: five of them ran all-out campaigns (Humphrey, Wallace, Muskie, Jackson, and Lindsay), two ran limited campaigns (McGovern and Chisholm), and four did not campaign at all (McCarthy, Mills, Hartke, and Yorty). The costs and results for the active candidates, in order of finish, are given in Table 5-11.

Nationally, the Florida primary was viewed with intense interest, because it was the first clash between all the presumed and potential major candidates. Two well-financed new faces were on their first primary outing of 1972 (Lindsay and Jackson), joining Humphrey on his first outing in 1972. Locally, Floridians saw the presidential contest competing with "antibusing" and "equal education" referenda on the primary ballot, which affected the turnout and probably helped the campaign of Wallace, who was closely identified with antibusing.

Some candidates included Florida in their primary schedules before Wallace

Table 5-11
Cost per Vote in the Florida Primary

Candidate	Rounded Votes	Vote %	Radio-TV Cost	Estimated Total Cost	Approximate Cost/Vote
Wallace	516,000	41.5	$ 75,000	$200,000	$0.39
Humphrey	231,000	18.5	81,000	300,000	1.30
Jackson	168,000	13.5	180,000	500,000+	3.00
Muskie	110,000	9.0	165,000	500,000+	4.50
Lindsay	81,000	6.5	160,000	500,000	6.20
McGovern	75,000	6.0	28,000	89,000	1.20
Chisholm	45,000	3.5	——	15,000	0.33

decided to run as a Democrat in the primary. He entered as the front-runner, changing the race from a free-for-all to an embarrassing game of catch-up with Wallace, whose showing was spectacular, both in political and financial terms. He proved that all the influence of the national Democratic leadership could not touch his Florida constituency, and ten years of national prominence allowed him to prove this at a low cost and an amazingly low cost per vote.

Jackson spent at least two-and-one-half times more than Wallace and received one-third as many votes. At the same time, Jackson spent about 75 percent more than Humphrey and received about 25 percent fewer votes. On the liberal side of the ballot, Lindsay outspent McGovern more than five to one, but received only one-half of one percent more of the vote.

In the minicontest for the black vote, Lindsay lost to the extent that his enormous investment and his supposed political appeal did not result in a strong black vote. Chisholm also lost to the extent that she did not demonstrate that she could be a unifying vote getter among blacks, although her minimal financial investment gave her an impressive cost per vote. If there was a winner, it was Humphrey, who proved he still had the support of a sizable part of the black community. In the minicontest for the Jewish vote, Lindsay and Jackson were losers: they both believed that they could demonstrate strong appeal to Jewish voters, and neither made significant inroads into Humphrey's traditional strength.

The amount of money spent in Florida seemed to have a negligible effect on the outcome. With the possible exception of Chisholm, who might have done a little better with a more than shoestring operation, campaigns seemed little affected by insufficient funds, and the most lavish spenders got few results for their extravagance. The results showed that even large amounts of money could not compete with years of public exposure and regional popularity.

Illinois

The Illinois primary on March 21 was a two-man race between Muskie and McCarthy, who spent almost identical amounts on their campaigns. (See Table 5-12.) Muskie had an advantage because McCarthy was not regarded as a serious presidential candidate. McCarthy's disadvantage could not be overcome by spending, as Mills had learned in New Hampshire, and money's role was insignificant in the Illinois outcome.[ddd]

[ddd]Illinoisans' interest in the race is indicated by the fact that almost 250,000 more people voted in the state gubernatorial race than in the presidential contest.

Table 5-12
Campaign Costs of Muskie and McCarthy in the Illinois Primary

	Votes	Vote %	Radio-TV Cost	Estimated Total Cost
Muskie	747,000	63	$ 60,000[a]	$220,000
McCarthy	439,000	37	140,000	260,000

[a]TV only—radio unknown.

Wisconsin

Six active candidates ran in the April 4 Wisconsin Democratic presidential primary: Humphrey, Wallace, Muskie, McGovern, Jackson, and Lindsay. This was only one less than had run in Florida, but the total costs of almost $1.6 million were a full 25 percent less than had been spent in Florida. The Wisconsin statistics for the active candidates are given in Table 5-13.

Unlike Florida, the Wisconsin primary was viewed as nationally significant; the state's electorate reflected national patterns, and each candidate tried hard to win. McGovern's clear victory in a crowded field established him as a major contender for the nomination, while Muskie's ten percent showing after spending more than $500,000 was virtually a fatal blow to his campaign. Humphrey and Wallace benefitted from the $100,000 or so each spent in Wisconsin—an amount considered less than the critical minimum needed for a serious campaign in the state—and from their previous campaigns and years of prominence. Considering these advantages, and with Wisconsin bordering on Minnesota, Humphrey might have been expected to do better. Lindsay and Jackson spent relatively little for relatively unknown candidates. However, their showings were very weak and

Table 5-13
Cost per Vote in the Wisconsin Primary

Candidate	Votes	Vote %	Radio-TV Cost	Estimated Total Cost	Approximate Cost/Vote
McGovern	332,000	30	$ 95,500	$440,000	$1.40
Wallace	248,000	22	75,000	100,000	0.40
Humphrey	234,000	21	57,000	91,000	0.39
Muskie	116,000	10	128,000	520,000+	4.40
Jackson	88,000	8	109,000	183,000	2.10
Lindsay	78,000	7	70,000	234,000	3.00

there is no evidence that big spending—which both had tried in Florida—
would have made any difference.

The problem in interpreting the Wisconsin presidential race is that the state
has an open primary: every voter can request the primary ballot of either party,
regardless of the voter's own party registration or "independent" status. Thus,
Republicans, for whom no real contest existed, could cross over and vote in the
Democratic primary. These crossover voters might try to complicate the Demo-
cartic results or promote the nomination of a weak Democratic candidate for
Nixon's benefit. There were two examples of attempts to influence the crossover vote in 1972, an indirect one by Nixon's campaign and a direct one by
Lindsay's.

The Nixon campaign originally planned a major effort in Wisconsin, to
demonstrate his strength by out-polling all the Democratic candidates combined.
An $80,000 media campaign began two days after the New Hampshire primary.
Then, three days after Florida and Wallace's spectacular showing, this media
campaign was quietly cancelled. The public reason was to save money; the real
reason was the hope that many conservative Republicans would cross over for
Wallace. Wallace did get Republican crossover votes, but there is no way to
determine if the number was affected by this indirect encouragement. McGovern
also received some Republican votes, but neither his nor Wallace's crossover vote
appears to have significantly affected the election result.

The Lindsay effort was very direct. He had begun with a high media budget
(about $165,000), and then cut it to the bone (about $15,000) after his weak
Florida showing. Then, in the last week before the Wisconsin election, he reinstated a $70,000 intensive media campaign around the theme, "The Switch is On."
The theme was intended both to reach Democrats—to switch away from the
front-runners, Humphrey and McGovern—and to reach Republicans—to switch
parties and cross over to the recently switched Lindsay. This effort failed, and
when the rough vote count was clear on election night, Lindsay dropped out of
the presidential race.

Massachusetts

Of the nine candidates listed on the April 25 Massachusetts ballot, only four
(McGovern, Muskie, Mills, and Chisholm) had active campaigns, and only
McGovern's was an all-out effort. Two of the active candidates received fewer
votes than Wallace, who spent only one day in the state and whose "organization"
did very little, or Humphrey, on whose behalf nothing was done in the state.
(See Table 5-14.)

Winning a majority of the popular vote and all 102 delegates, McGovern's
Massachusetts victory was clearly a boost to his nomination drive. Every prominent Democrat in the state except Senator Kennedy ran as a Muskie delegate and

Table 5-14
Cost per Vote in the Massachusetts Primary

Candidate	Votes	Vote %	Radio-TV Costs	Estimated Total Cost	Approximate Cost/Vote
McGovern	255,000	52	$ 77,000	$316,000+	$ 1.24
Muskie	107,000	22	25,000	75,000	0.71
Humphrey	39,000	8	— —	(None)	— —
Wallace	37,000	7	— —	(Negligible)	— —
Chisholm	18,000	4	— —	16,500	0.91
Mills	15,000	3	100,000	150,000	10.00

lost to McGovern's "unknown" delegates. But in terms of his opposition, McGovern's showing demonstrated little more than the fact that he was a serious candidate who could win significant votes with a serious campaign.

Muskie's $75,000 investment has to be considered less than the minimum needed for a major presidential campaign in Massachusetts. He effectively abandoned the state in favor of Pennsylvania's same-day primary although he did not say so. The Humphrey and Wallace votes, in spite of virtually no costs or campaigning, demonstrated again the value of long public careers. Chisholm received only a slightly higher percentage of the black vote than McGovern. Mills added another chapter to the 1972 story that money alone cannot make a serious presidential candidacy, with his $57 per vote in New Hampshire and $10 per vote in Massachusetts.

Pennsylvania

All four major candidates (Humphrey, Wallace, McGovern, and Muskie) were on the April 25 ballot in Pennsylvania; all but Wallace ran major campaigns. Jackson was on the ballot but was not active. Because of the importance and nature of the delegate race, discussed below, the number of delegates won has been added to Table 5-15. The cost per vote has been dropped because it was uniformly low and not significantly different for the candidates.

Humphrey was the front-runner and the greatest threat to Muskie, whose presidential bid was reeling by this time. Pennsylvania was a last-minute addition to the primary schedules of both McGovern and Wallace; each was expected to draw on his own constituency but not to be a major factor in the outcome.

Humphrey won as expected; it was his first primary victory, and big enough (35 percent of the vote) to establish him as a leading candidate on the primary trail. Muskie's fourth-place showing was the final blow to his campaign; two days later he withdrew from active competition. As the figures below indicate, there were virtually no spending differences among three of the four major

Table 5-15
Campaign Costs in the Pennsylvania Primary

Candidate	Votes	Vote %	Delegates	Radio-TV Cost	Estimated Total Cost
Humphrey	477,000	35	57	$18,400	$125,000[a]
Wallace	288,000	21	2	Unknown	Probably less than $100,000
McGovern	277,000	20	37	13,800	182,000
Muskie	276,000	20	29	50,000	176,000+

[a]Includes $50,000 in known direct labor expenditures.

candidates and the results seemed unaffected by money. This was not true for Wallace, but his consistent pattern of results appears never to have been seriously affected by money.

Spending was low considering the size and population of Pennsylvania. In part this was because both Humphrey and Muskie were very short of money and because both McGovern and Wallace decided late to compete there and so had short campaigns. Radio and television spending was also low, due to the nature of the state's primary. The preferential race was a completely non-binding contest; all the delegates were elected in 50 separate district races. Each district race could have had as many as 15 delegate candidates—up to three per presidential candidate and some running uncommitted (although there were actually very few Wallace-pledged delegates and McGovern had delegates in only 30 of the 50 districts). Delegates were listed on the ballot either alphabetically or at random, not grouped according to presidential preference. In this situation, promotion of a candidate's name via radio and television is less important than identifying the names of delegate candidates in the local races; the main technique for this is literature, especially the old standby, sample ballots.

While both McGovern and Wallace had done much better than expected in the preferential race, Wallace demonstrated his campaign's disinterest or incompetence in translating popular candidate support into delegate strength, winning a mere two delegates. McGovern, on the other hand, showed how good he was at that chore, winning more delegates than Muskie with virtually the same popular vote, with none of Muskie's established party support, and having run delegates in only 60 percent of the districts.

Ohio

Five candidates were on the Ohio ballot on May 2, but the presidential race

turned out to be a race between Humphrey and McGovern. (See Table 5-16.)
Muskie had withdrawn by then, having spent a little more than $100,000 in
the state. Jackson's last-ditch emphasis on Ohio, made because Wallace was not
on the ballot, fizzled when his $50,000 investment returned eight percent of the
vote, and he withdrew from primary competition. And McCarthy's $200 one-
trip campaign could hardly be called serious.

McGovern's decision to make Ohio a major effort was made only three
weeks before the primary, but a statewide organization had been growing for
almost a year. Humphrey considered Ohio a key state from the moment he
decided to run in 1972, because of his long-time strength in the midwestern industrial states. Given that strength, plus McGovern's late entry and presumed
weakness among blue-collar workers, Humphrey was the clear favorite.

Ohio Congressman Wayne Hays, chairman of the House Administration
Committee, ran for President from his district and won five delegates to the
Democratic Convention. Though his committee helped draft the Federal Election Campaign Act of 1971, he filed a report on campaign receipts and expenditures to the GAO after the deadline. He received five convention votes
because of Ohio's complicated system of filing and running separately in each
congressional district.

Ohio was billed as a test of media spending, and after the election McGovern's
near-win was widely interpreted as a media triumph. However, in view of the
overall financial and political picture of the race, this interpretation must be
questioned.

Although McGovern spent almost six times more on radio and television
than Humphrey, with more than one-half of McGovern's expenditures going
for media while Humphrey was investing less than one-eighth of his money in
media, McGovern's total spending was not significantly more than Humphrey's.
Since media is more important for a new or unknown candidate in a short campaign, McGovern's media spending was essential to a serious campaign, barely

Table 5-16
Cost per Vote for Humphrey and McGovern in the Ohio Primary

Candidate	Votes	Vote %	Radio-TV Cost	Estimated Total Cost	Approximate Cost/Vote
Humphrey	461,000	41	$ 21,000	$175,000	$0.38
McGovern	439,000	39	125,000	231,000	0.53

Note: In the race for delegates, McGovern again out-organized his opponent; he won 61 in
the district races to 41 for Humphrey, although Humphrey also got 38 for winning the
popular vote statewide and so came out ahead, 79-61. This was part of the reason for
McGovern's extreme anger at McCarthy's campaign: had all of McCarthy's votes gone to
McGovern he would have won the statewide vote and 38 more delegates.

making up for Humphrey's political advantages. In view of those advantages and the two candidates' relatively equal spending, the Ohio result would have to be called a very weak victory for Humphrey and an unexpectedly strong showing for McGovern, in which money differences had little effect.

Indiana

The May 2 Indiana primary was a two-man race, the first of two between Humphrey and Wallace. (See Table 5-17.) Muskie, by then a noncandidate, won almost 12 percent of the vote. Humphrey and Wallace were equally matched in terms of public recognition. Their expenditures were roughly equal; radio and television spending was negligible and not a factor, with Humphrey spending $6,000 and Wallace probably less. With no recognition or financial advantage on either side, Humphrey's narrow win was a setback. Wallace's showing was again stronger than expected, although he continued to show weakness in winning delegates. In the district races, Wallace won only 21 delegates to 36 for Humphrey, who also got 19 more for winning statewide.

Spending comparisons between different years are rarely meaningful because of the number of candidates, the intensity of the race, and other factors that create totally different situations. Yet in 1972 the amounts spent by the serious Democratic candidates in New Hampshire, Wisconsin, Massachusetts, and Nebraska, were nearly the same as amounts spent in 1968. Indiana and California were the only two races in 1972 in which costs were significantly different from those four years earlier, and the Indiana differences were huge. In contrast to 1972s rather tame effort costing less than $150,000 per candidate, Robert Kennedy and Eugene McCarthy had spent $750,000 and $700,000 respectively in their first head-to-head contest in 1968.

Table 5-17
Cost per Vote for Humphrey and Wallace in the Indiana Primary

Candidate	Votes	Vote %	Estimated Total Cost	Approximate Cost/Vote
Humphrey	348,000	47	$100,000	$0.29
Wallace	309,000	42	$100,000–$150,000	0.40

North Carolina

The North Carolina primary on May 6 was basically a contest between Wallace and Sanford, although it was somewhat affected by Chisholm, who campaigned actively and received close to eight percent of the vote. Wallace spent no more than $200,000; Sanford spent at least $350,000 and possibly $400,000. Sanford's spending advantage, and in particular his media effort (at least $200,000) must be considered a fairly equal balance to Wallace's popular appeal. The result—409,000 (50 percent) for Wallace to 304,000 (37 percent) for Sanford—was a very clear win for Wallace. Although Sanford stayed in the race to the end, his inability to beat Wallace in his home state kept his national campaign from ever getting off the ground.

Nebraska

Eleven names appeared on the May 9 ballot, but the Nebraska primary was actually another Humphrey-McGovern contest. The McGovern campaign cost just under $150,000; the Humphrey campaign was in the range of $75,000 to $100,000. In view of McGovern's long campaign in the state, his spending edge, and Humphrey's late entrance, McGovern was considered the favorite. Mc-Govern's victory with 41 percent to 35 percent for Humphrey was not a strong showing in view of his advantages, and the Humphrey showing was certainly better than expected.

West Virginia

West Virginia, May 9, was the last race between Humphrey and Wallace, who were the only candidates on the ballot. Neither waged a big campaign in the state, and their spending was low and comparable. Humphrey won overwhelmingly—67 percent to 33 percent for Wallace—giving Wallace his only major primary defeat of the year. Spending had little effect on the outcome.

Michigan

The May 16 Michigan presidential ballot included seven names, but the race was actually one of two same-day Humphrey-McGovern-Wallace contests. All three waged major campaigns; both the Humphrey and Wallace campaigns were financially weak, spending less than the $222,000 spent by all McGovern committees. The result was a smashing 51 percent win for Wallace, a weak second for McGovern with 27 percent, and a dismal third for Humphrey with only 16 percent.[eee] McGovern's spending edge and his increased press exposure was

---

[eee]The effect, if any, of Wallace's serious wounding in an assassination attempt the day before is uncertain.

considered a fair balance to Humphrey's and Wallace's much longer public prominence, so the race can be viewed as roughly even. The outcome was a major blow to Humphrey, a less than impressive showing for McGovern, and a dramatic demonstration of Wallace's enormous appeal.

Maryland

Maryland was the site of another Humphrey-McGovern-Wallace confrontation on May 16. (See Table 5-18.) Wallace's win was less impressive than his same-day majority victory in Michigan, but it was still another demonstration of his strength.[fff] Humphrey out-polled McGovern for second place, but failed to show any real ability to cut into Wallace's large following. McGovern's third-place showing was not disastrous, but it was hardly a boost to his drive for the nomination. McGovern's spending edge had no effect on the outcome; overall, money seems to have played a minor role in this election.

Table 5-18
Campaign Costs of Wallace, Humphrey, and McGovern in the Maryland Primary

Candidate	Votes	Vote %	Radio-TV Cost	Estimated Total Cost
Wallace	219,000	39	(Negligible)	$20,000
Humphrey	150,000	27	$10,200	23,000
McGovern	123,000	22	(Negligible)	76,000

California

Eight names and slates of delegates were listed on the June 6 California primary ballot, but the race was the third and decisive Humphrey-McGovern contest.[ggg] (See Table 5-19.) The five percent vote margin was close compared to

---

[fff] A postelection survey conducted for the *Washington Post* indicated that "sympathy votes" for Wallace did not play a significant role in the outcome.

[ggg] Wallace had failed to organize and qualify a slate of delegates before the late-winter filing deadline. After his consistent strong showings on the primary trail and then the shooting, a last-minute write-in campaign was organized. It cost about $90,000 and Wallace received less than five percent of the vote (161,000 votes). California was also one of Chisholm's big efforts, but was still a campaign that cost less than $50,000; she also won less than five percent of the vote (155,000 votes).

Table 5-19

Cost per Vote for McGovern and Humphrey in the California Primary

Candidate	Votes	Vote %	Radio-TV Costs	Total Cost	Approximate Cost/Vote
McGovern	1,527,000	45	$460,000	$4,175,000	$2.73
Humphrey	1,352,000	40	235,000	500,000	0.37

their earlier head-to-head meetings, but in contrast to those earlier contests and to every other presidential primary in 1972, money played a decisive role in the outcome.

California was the linchpin of McGovern's strategy from the beginning, and his investment in the state represented a full one-third of his total prenomination costs. California was equally important to Humphrey, but he was unable to plan for it effectively and his investment in the state represented only 14 percent of his much smaller total prenomination costs.

In the California campaign, McGovern had almost every advantage over Humphrey. His state operation had been organized and growing for 18 months, while the Humphrey operation was one-half as long. Perhaps more critical was the fact that McGovern's operation had been built from the ground up and so had enormous numbers of grass-roots workers and supporters, while Humphrey's top-down structure lacked the volunteers to reach California's millions of voters.

During the final phase of the campaign (the three weeks after the Maryland and Michigan primaries), McGovern also had three major advantages. One was his almost 100 percent spending edge for media. This was particularly important because part of the campaign took place while President Nixon was visiting the Soviet Union, which so dominated the news that little else was heard; hence, paid time counted even more.

McGovern had another media advantage, shown in a special *New York Times* survey of the state's four largest media markets.[47] McGovern received considerably more coverage than Humphrey: 32 percent more newspaper space and 56 percent more television time on early-evening news programs. This was not because of pro-McGovern media bias, but because the McGovern campaign was much better organized and adept at creating good news stories and because McGovern was the phenomenon of 1972, the new political face. Finally, there was McGovern's enormous overall financial advantage.

Humphrey's only advantage was the long-time loyalty of his many supporters in the state, but he could not fully benefit from that advantage because his money-starved campaign could not reach and turn out all his potential supporters. Whether or not Humphrey's $500,000 was used to maximum benefit, the amount was insufficient for an all-out presidential primary in California in 1972. The key is not that McGovern spent more than Humphrey, but that Humphrey's financial resources were not enough for a fair challenge to McGovern. The possible significance of this in terms of the outcome is that public opinion polls showed Humphrey behind by 20 percentage points before the final push, and he gained support steadily to finish only five percentage points behind. It seems reasonable to suggest that had Humphrey adequately financed his campaign in California, the outcome could have been different.

California was the second state in 1972 where costs were significantly different than in 1968, although the 1968 costs were similar to those in the state's 1964 contested Republican primary. Table 5-20 shows costs for California's last three contested presidential primaries. California's winner-take-all primary has traditionally been the most expensive contest of the presidential prenomination season and often a politically decisive one. With the termination of the winner-take-all feature in 1976 (because of the Democratic Party's reforms), the state may play a somewhat lesser role in the finances and politics of prenomination campaigns.

Following the Democratic Convention, these primaries and activities at Miami Beach left the major defeated candidates with debts as follows:

Humphrey	$1,000,000
Muskie	350,000
Wallace	250,000
Mills	91,000
Chisholm	50,000

Only Humphrey's debt was on a comparable scale with his, McCarthy's, and Kennedy's 1968 post-convention debts.

Table 5-20
Costs of California Primaries: 1964, 1968, and 1972

	Radio-TV Costs	Estimated Total Costs
1972		
McGovern	$460,000	$4,175,000
Humphrey	235,000	500,000
1968		
Kennedy	680,000	2,500,000
McCarthy	210,000	1,000,000
1964		
Goldwater	n.a.	2,000,000
Rockefeller	n.a.	2,000,000+

6 Financing the Conventions

The Federal Election Campaign Act (FECA) brought the 1972 party conventions within the purview of federal disclosure statutes for the first time. While required to disclose only income and expenditures after April 7, 1972, both parties released complete financial statements covering the entire convention planning period. As with presidential candidate disclosures, filings were made by convention committees with the Comptroller General.

The Republican National Convention in 1972 cost $1,881,576, more than twice the amount of $796,263 paid for the 1968 convention.[a] Staged like a professional television production, the Republican Convention was notable for its minute-by-minute script and its elaborate rounds of parties, luaus, lunches, brunches, and teas. The Republicans, like the Democrats, used the occasion of the convention to conduct a number of auxiliary events, the costs and receipts of which are not reflected in the convention totals: these included a rock concert for the young, heritage group receptions for the ethnics, and a $500-a-plate gala for the large contributors. Taking advantage of the Miami Beach setting the GOP leased and borrowed for the convention a flotilla of yachts, which came to be known as Nixon's Navy.

The funds for the Republican celebration were provided as follows:

1972 convention program ads	$1,664,500
Governor's Committee of Florida	52,450
Balance from 1968 convention	139,000
Interest income	17,000
City of Miami Beach: Tourist Development Authority	100,000
Hotel room assessments	28,000
Total	$2,000,950

The Republicans made available a full listing of their convention expenditures, shown in Table 6-1. The approximately $100,000 balance of income over expenditures was being held to publish the proceedings, and the remainder to go toward the 1976 Republican Convention. One item of interest is the

---

[a]For comparisons with 1968, see Herbert E. Alexander, *Financing the 1968 Election* (Lexington, Mass.: Lexington Books, D.C. Heath and Company, 1971), pp. 73-78.

Table 6-1

Republican National Convention Expenditures, 1972

1.	Salaries (for office personnel in Washington, D.C. office at Republican National Committee; office of the vice chairman of the Committee on Arrangements; office in San Diego and Miami Beach and for special professional, consulting, and technical services)	$ 271,849.95
2.	Transportation (staff, officers of convention, arrangements committee chairmen)	130,179.45
3.	Subsistence (food, lodging, and gratuities)	214,978.48
4.	Office space	20,301.15
5.	Office furniture, equipment rental, and supplies	59,865.40
6.	Telephone, telegraph, postage, and express charges	88,159.21
7.	Printing (not including printing of tickets, platform, proceedings, and official program book)	16,768.55
8.	Manufacture of convention badges	15,546.58
9.	Printing of convention tickets	20,135.91
10.	Construction in Convention Hall	156,338.76
11.	Special lighting	10,339.32
12.	Ushering service and security	101,581.21
13.	Insurance	37,785.00
14.	Technical services (use of screens, films, prompting device and operation, makeup, architectural service, platform design, etc.)	168,044.08
15.	Signs	6,664.84
16.	Music (orchestra, director, arrangements)	32,055.41
17.	Convention Hall decorations	17,762.65
18.	Reporting services (including meetings of committee)	19,652.66
19.	Meetings on convention planning and meetings of convention committees except platform (see no. 20)	34,836.39
20.	All expenses related to development of platform (professional services, printing, travel, reporting meetings, etc.)	98,967.50
21.	Special events	10,505.00
22.	Site Committee expenses	13,122.85
23.	Expenditures connected with preparation and distribution of 1972 official convention program	220,230.43
24.	Convention supplies (gavels, vests for pages, special paper, kits for delegates)	7,709.95
25.	Miscellaneous	19,464.87
26.	San Diego settlement charges	88,730.14
	Total	$1,881,575.74

San Diego settlement charges of $88,730. Actually, the costs of the decision to switch the convention to Miami Beach following the disclosures in the I.T.T. case were even greater. The Republicans never actually received any money from I.T.T.; the promise of the San Diego money came from a city-formed group called the Civic Committee to Invite and Host the Republican National Convention in 1972, in which I.T.T. played a major role. San Diego was an expensive diversion, not only because of the adverse reaction to the I.T.T. disclosures, but also, since it was a new city for a national convention, an earlier start was taken to make arrangements than would have been the case in a city where the staff had previous experience, and travel expenses to and from Washington, D.C. were high.

The 1972 Democratic National Convention cost $1,719,368, as shown in Table 6-2. This does not include the sum of $431,005 in hotel room fees, which were deposited in advance by the Democratic National Committee (DNC), held as a trust fund, and subsequently refunded to delegates or candidates ($9,622) or passed on to the hotels ($421,383). When the hotel fee costs are considered together with other costs, as they were in the 1968 accounting,[1] the Democrats would appear to have spent about $400,000 more in 1972 than they had four years earlier. The Democrats' Miami Beach meeting, however, lacked the balloons, hoopla, confetti, bands, and "spontaneous demonstrations" of its Republican counterpart. Apart from hotel room fees, the Democratic financial sources were as follows:

1972 convention program advertising	$ 978,019
Convention promotion contributors	297,139
Discounted Miami Beach Tourist Development Authority note	69,388
Miscellaneous contributions	150,432
Write-off of cash due to Democratic National Committee (DNC subsidy)	369,421
Total	$1,864,399

The DNC subsidy of $369,421 was composed of two elements: the costs to the DNC of the reform commissions, $210,000; and convention costs of $155,000, divided into approximately $100,000 spent on salaries, $30,000 on travel, and $25,000 on telephones. However, the $369,421 subsidy includes about $100,000 in debts still owed at the beginning of 1975, which the DNC agreed to pay off.

Robert Strauss, then Democratic National Committee treasurer, instead of seeking cash support from Miami Beach authorities, negotiated for direct provision of goods and services. In place of cash, the city agreed to contribute $500,000 in the form of providing the air conditioning, the convention podium,

Table 6-2
Democratic National Convention Expenditures, 1972

1.	Salaries and wages	$ 269,862.34
2.	Convention programs	292,716.00
3.	Rent	630.00
4.	Equipment rental	42,877.38
5.	Telephone and telegraph	109,437.04
6.	Supplies	12,644.14
7.	Postage	554.00
8.	Professional services	83,821.08
9.	Printing and publications	66,176.49
10.	Travel	266,080.76
11.	Convention Hall	308,693.80
12.	Security	40,112.00
13.	Special projects	32,000.00
14.	Meetings and conferences	3,029.92
15.	Overhead reimbursements	149,756.83
16.	Miscellaneous	7,005.39
17.	Transfers to other reporting committees	30,800.00
18.	Transfers to nonreporting committees	3,207.50
	Total	$1,719,368.67

and VIP seating construction. The city also subsidized shuttle bus service and the hotels agreed to provide certain numbers of free rooms for convention staff before and during the convention.

Program Books

In 1972 the Democratic and Republican convention programs grossed $1 million and $1.6 million respectively on advertising. These figures are a quantum rise in revenues from the $274,500 gross that was raised by each party through these publications in 1968. The circumstances were different then because the 1968 modification of the 1966 Williams Amendment gave the program committees only a short time to solicit advertising from limited numbers of corporations. The two committees formed a joint committee in 1968 that solicited for both at the same time. In 1972 each went its own way. The 1968 federal tax amendment permitted the costs of such ads in political convention books to be deducted as a legitimate business expense, provided that the proceeds be used to defray convention costs, and that the amount paid for advertising be reasonable in light of the business the taxpayer may expect to receive directly from the advertising or as a result of the convention being held in the area in which the taxpayer has a principal place of business.

The 1972 revenue figures of $1 million and $1.6 million disclosed by the convention program committees concurred with a study undertaken by Citizens' Research Foundation (CRF), which further provided the following details. The Democratic program advertising was sold at a rate of $11,000 for a black-and-white ad and $12,500 for a color ad. Inside front and back cover ads cost up to $25,000.[b] The Republican program cost $10,000 for a black-and-white ad and $11,500 for a color ad.

Counting each company represented in a complete, partial, or multiple page ad as one, 281 companies advertised in either the Republican or Democratic convention books or in both. Ninety companies advertised in both the Republican and the Democratic books.

The Republican convention book contained 160 pages of advertising representing a total of 181 companies. The total includes 148 companies that advertised on one complete page each, 29 companies that advertised on a total of five partial pages, one company that advertised on one complete page and also on one partial page, and three companies that advertised on two pages each. Ninety-one companies advertised in the Republican convention book only.

In the Democratic convention book a total of 100 pages of advertising represented a total of 100 companies.[c] The total includes 87 companies that advertised on one complete page each, eight that advertised on a total of two partial pages, four companies that advertised on two pages each, and one that advertised on three pages.

Only nine companies advertised solely in the Democratic convention book. I.T.T. advertised as a corporation in both the Republican and Democratic books. However, in the Democratic book only, there were also two additional pages of advertising for I.T.T. (Sheraton Hotels and Motor Inns, and I.T.T. Community Development Corporation.)

The Republicans out-solicited the Democrats in 18 separate categories: finance/real estate, electronics, shipping, gas/oil, metal industry, trucking, defense, airlines, automotive, conglomerates, lumber/paper, banks,

---

[b]There were two editions of the Democratic program book, one a Miami Beach edition, the other a final version with more advertising. Income figures are for both editions, but company figures reflect the final edition, which received broader distribution. The Miami edition brought in more than $200,000 of the total revenues.

[c]The ad for Democratic Campaign Services, Inc., a materials and service spinoff of the DNC, has been counted as one company and included in this analysis.

contractors/engineering, tire, food industry, miscellaneous industry, and miscellaneous retail services. Their largest advantage was among conglomerates. The Democrats delivered more money in the following categories: insurance, brewers, railroads, communications/television, and the tobacco industry. Their largest advantage was in railroad advertising.

One convention funding proposal, made public by Jeb Magruder when he testified before the Senate Watergate Committee, was suggested by him as a reason for the Watergate break-in. Magruder said the effort was made to find evidence of a kickback scheme connected with the convention proposal, and to tie it to the Democrats or to then Democratic National Committee Chairman Lawrence F. O'Brien.[2] The proposal, suggested by Walter L. Scott, was to sell booths for $5,000 each at a business trade show to be held on the convention floors, which promised to bring each party up to $400,000 profit. Both parties were initially interested, but shied away when the I.T.T. incident surfaced, and companies were afraid to participate in any but already accepted methods, such as advertising in the convention books.

Other Costs

In assessing the total costs of the party nominating conventions, it is necessary to consider the resources expended by other public and private groups in political, lobbying, and social activities, as well as the amounts spent by the convention committees. Substantial sums were, of course, spent by candidates and the delegates individually.

Costs rarely considered would include those related to credential fights. Following the Democratic presidential primary in California, legal efforts were made regarding the California unit rule, and although some of the legal counsel was volunteered, there were inevitable court-related costs, in preparing and typing and delivering briefs, in court appearances, and at the convention itself. For another example, the uncommitted delegate slates led by Chicago Mayor Richard J. Daley spent thousands of dollars on such items as full page ads in newspapers in *The New York Times* in their unsuccessful effort to retain their seats at the convention against a credentials challenge. Some credential costs, of course, were part of candidate expenditures before and at the convention.

The Ripon Society, an organization of progressive Republicans, brought suit in 1971 charging unconstitutional allocation of seats to the 1972 Republican National Convention, and then to the 1976 convention. That suit and appeals cost Ripon $11,000 in expenses for about 1,600 hours of professional and paraprofessional time that would have cost about $100,000. The law firm donated all but out-of-pocket expenses, and Ripon applied to the District Court in 1974 for financial reimbursement from the Republican National Committee (RNC). Legal costs for the RNC defense in 1973-74 were in excess of $51,000, and are continuing into 1976.

Costs that need to be tallied in a full accounting of convention-related expenses would include the various Democratic and Republican reform activities, which are only partially reflected in the salaries and wages categories of convention costs. These were expensive, particularly for Democrats, growing out of the 1968 Chicago Convention, the McGovern and Fraser reform commissions, and for the participants in these activities. Costs of the Democratic reform effort are highlighted in Appendix H, revealing Steward R. Mott's political expenses in 1972, which include $66,000 contributed to the work of the Center for Political Reform, a private organization that focused on structural and procedural reform in the nominating and convention processes within the Democratic party. The center attracted contributions other than Mott's, mainly from Humphrey, Kennedy, and McGovern supporters, and over a 19-month period spent $131,600. In addition, a newsletter entitled *The Informed Delegate '72* was published in cooperation with the Center for Political Reform, and Mott's listing shows a $17,000 investment-loss deduction for his portion of the publication and distribution costs.

The national nominating conventions have traditionally had a special role for party and candidate contributors. The major financial backers are rewarded with special seating and lounges for past favors and the opportunity is not lost to take advantage of the excitement to obtain new pledges of financial support for the sponsoring party or candidate.

The 1972 conventions were no different from earlier ones, although probably fewer Democratic large contributors were actually delegates. The Republicans held a $500-per-ticket gala at the Fontainebleau Hotel. This event raised an estimated $600,000 net and was split three ways among the Nixon campaign and the Senate and House Republican drives. For their part, the Democrats used the occasion of their telethon to hold their "Festival with the Stars" during convention time, with tickets priced at $500 per couple; contributors were given the opportunity to meet the telethon stars. The net income from this event was applied to the retirement of the 1968-69 debt. Both parties again took special care in the seating and entertaining of contributors throughout their conventions. Some large contributors also gave their own parties, and their suites or yachts at Miami Beach were well supplied with food and drink.

In contrast to the large contributors were the poor delegates.[d] The Democrats clearly had good intentions to assist delegates or alternates unable to attend the National Convention by reason of financial hardship. The McGovern and Fraser reform commissions jointly invited any duly elected delegate or alternate experiencing personal financial difficulty to contact the state and national parties for relief, and urged the chairmen of those party committees

---

[d]Democratic delegate quota requirements brought changes to the composition of delegations. Discussion of Democratic reforms follows below.

to insure impartial financial assistance to help the needy meet minimum living and travel expenses. The DNC took steps to minimize expenses for those who qualified by insuring rooms for $5 to $12 per night, and cafeteria meals for about $1. Expressions of hope for financial help were not binding in 1972, and many state party committees were under financial strain, but some made special efforts to help. For example, the Wisconsin Democratic State Committee provided dollar assistance, and special fund raising in California brought in over $100,000 to help pay the way for some Chicanos, blacks, and others. In some states party help was suspect and in others it was withheld because the money would go mainly to McGovern supporters. The 1972 Democratic Convention resolved that the DNC should set aside each year at least eight percent of its gross annual income to defray the reasonable and necessary expenses of those needing help to get to future conventions; DNC Chairman Robert Strauss expressed concern and appointed a committee to study it. Only one state, North Dakota, made provision for any delegate who could not afford the trip to claim up to $300 against expenses from the state treasury.

Government funds are another resource connected with the national nominating conventions. Costs for the city of Miami Beach for the two conventions were reported to be at least $3 million, though the direct and indirect benefits to the city in publicity and taxation from increased spending are harder to measure. One federal government cost was a grant by the U.S. Law Enforcement Assistance Administration (LEAA) to the city of Miami Beach for training, equipment, and study of police procedures for the conventions. The LEAA provided $395,424 to match $178,313 in local funds for the project. The grant was used, among other things, for body armor, 2,000 plastic handcuffs, television equipment, and a study by Florida Atlantic University for future use by other police agencies. Another federal government cost was in the Secret Service protection given to various presidential candidates, including, of course, President Nixon's security.

Corporations and private interest groups were present through hospitality suites and working lobbyists. As has been their custom for many years, the automakers provided courtesy cars to each convention—in 1972 some 200 new cars were made available. The airlines had stewardesses greeting delegates in the convention hall at the Flying Donkey Lounge or Flying Elephant Lounge. The National Education Association had its hospitality suite and the American Bankers Association welcomed delegates at the Playboy Plaza. Belcher Oil loaned its yacht to Senator Edward Gurney, R-Fla., to entertain his fellow delegates; the Whitaker Corporation made its yacht available to Attorney General Richard Kleindienst and his guests.

Common Cause directed significant efforts toward influencing both conventions and spent $53,585, approximately $37,000 of that at the Democratic event. Common Cause Chairman John Gardner testified before both platform committees on issues of governmental and party openness and accountability.

Legislative specialists from Common Cause attended both conventions and lobbied delegates by mail and in person on issues such as open meetings, campaign finance, and the congressional seniority system.

The National Women's Political Caucus also organized for each convention to present views on platform issues of concern and credentials challenges against delegations with very few women.

Democratic Miniconventions

The Democrats held two "miniconventions" after their regular National Convention in July 1972—one by choice, the other thrust upon them. Together they cost the Democratic Party about $510,000.

First was the convention hastily convened at a Washington, D.C. hotel in August 1972 after Senator Eagleton had left the ticket, which met for the purpose of ratifying Sargent Shriver as the replacement choice for Democratic vice-presidential nominee. The delegates to this convention were the members of the Democratic National Committee. They quickly and almost unanimously endorsed the Shriver candidacy; the only official candidate, he received 2,936 delegate votes. Missouri cast all 73 votes for Eagleton in a gesture of support, while four of Oregon's 34 votes went to former Senator Wayne Morse.

The committee assembled in Washington consisted of 278 members, whose votes were cast according to each state's voting strength at the National Convention. The miniconvention featured a number of the party's leaders in a show of endorsement—Muskie, Kennedy, Jackson, Humphrey, and Eagleton. Television coverage of the convention, although obviously limited by size and by the question under consideration, was extensive—complete with anchor men in their booths and floor correspondents. Senator McGovern's speech included an appeal for small contributions. The total cost of this convention to the Democratic National Committee was about $10,000.

A far more extensive meeting of Democrats—one which cost an estimated $500,000—was the three-day conference in Kansas City in December 1974 on party organization and policy. The 1972 National Convention had passed a motion to hold the mid-term convention, the culmination of the reform movement that reached back to 1968. It had been postponed until after the 1974 congressional elections in an effort to avoid divisiveness and the possibility of adopting platforms some candidates might not be willing to accept.

Attended by 1,700 grass-roots delegates representative of the diversity of its constituencies and 338 ex-officio delegates consisting of Democratic governors and members of Congress, the miniconvention ratified the party's first charter, which had been drafted over a period of two years by the 167-member Democratic Charter Commission led by ex-governor Terry Sanford of North Carolina. This was the first comprehensive charter written by any political party in the nation's history—a document which institutionalized many of the procedural reforms that had provoked intense controversy during the previous six years and marked a major shift in internal power away from organized labor.

Ratification was achieved with a minimum of change, omitting extreme reforms and tempering some of Senator McGovern's major guidelines. In 12 articles the new charter provides a party structure encompassing such matters as convention delegate selection, party officers, and a judicial council to arbitrate disputes. The charter resolved the difficult procedural issues of minority representation, which had disrupted the Democratic National Conventions of 1948, 1964, and 1972 by insuring full participation in party affairs regardless of age, sex, race, religion, ethnic origin, or economic status, while disavowing the politically hazardous quota system in favor of affirmative action programs. Also resolved, tentatively at least, were certain problems of internal democracy and popular access to party decision making. Various councils were created, including a Judicial Council to review and approve state delegate selection plans and an Education and Training Council mandated to carry out organizational "nuts and bolts" instruction. A National Finance Council was created to coordinate fund-raising and spending activities and to attempt to broaden the financial base.

Party unity was the goal, but there was clear evidence of the strength of the liberals in the victory of the blacks, women, and Latinos on affirmative action, the warm welcome given George McGovern, and the cheers for every suggestion to assault big business.

Labor leaders and traditionalists such as Chicago Mayor Richard J. Daley were upset with what they considered the gains of the reform faction. But in reality, the reformers had lost much of what they had originally sought. Their concept of a highly centralized party based on the European political model was scrapped. In addition, their efforts to substitute strong language for the compromise version of the charter were overwhelmingly defeated.

Though the conference was originally barred from dealing with policy issues, the delegates split up into eight panels out of which came resolutions on such subjects as foreign trade, economic controls, conservation, national health insurance, taxation, antitrust legislation, and the quality of law enforcement.

Party Reform

Amidst the chaos and trauma of the 1968 Democratic Convention in Chicago, almost unnoticed in the fierce debate later that night on the Vietnam plank, the delegates passed resolutions calling for the creation of national commissions to study party rules and procedures for the 1972 convention. Between the two conventions, these commissions cost the Democratic Party a good deal of money—well over $500,000—and a lot of energy. They interjected the issue of reform into the campaign of most Democratic contenders for the presidential nomination in 1972 and made it possible for one of them, George McGovern, to use their rulings to his advantage. The number of women, minorities, and young people appearing on competing delegate slates became a significant issue.

The impetus toward reform grew out of the 1968 insurgent campaign of Minnesota Senator Eugene McCarthy. Then Governor of Iowa Harold E. Hughes (aided organizationally and financially by McCarthy campaigners) organized an ad hoc unsanctioned commission on delegate selection procedures to report to the 1968 convention. The Hughes Commission Report[3] charged a variety of evils in the process of delegate selection and provided the foundation for the creation of the official commissions.

In its first postelection meeting on January 14, 1969, the Democratic National Committee adopted several resolutions that directed the National Chairman, Senator Fred Harris of Oklahoma, to create the two reform commissions. Harris appointed Representative James G. O'Hara of Michigan Chairman of a 26-member rules commission, and Senator McGovern chairman of a 28-member delegate selection commission. Hughes was named vice-chairman of the delegate commission.

The McGovern-Fraser Commission

The McGovern Commission first met in March 1969; with a quickly assembled staff, the commission held 17 field hearings and several meetings across the country to draft a series of reform guidelines. The result, a 63-page report entitled *Mandate for Reform*, was published and submitted to the DNC.[4] Shortly before publication, the guidelines and a comprehensive "compliance letter" were sent by the commission to each of the 55 state and territorial parties. Included was a detailed analysis of each state's delegate selection procedures, and a listing of procedures that were in need of revision to bring the party into compliance with the guidelines. Each state party organized its own reform commission to make recommendations on implementing the guidelines, and the McGovern Commission staff worked directly with the state commissions and state party committees to achieve compliance. In May 1970 DNC counsel Joseph A. Califano issued a legal opinion that the McGovern guidelines were to be regarded as rules to be followed by state parties, not merely as recommendations to the 1972 convention.

McGovern resigned his chairmanship in January 1971, when he announced his presidential candidacy, and the task of overseeing implementation was left to his successor, Representative Donald M. Fraser of Minnesota.

In February 1971 the DNC approved reform plans presented by the McGovern-Fraser Commission and, in a critical decision, incorporated the guidelines into the official call to the 1972 convention. They disregarded a recommendation that the DNC's own membership be denied delegate status at the convention.

The O'Hara Commission

The O'Hara Commission concentrated on procedures for the convention and its committees. Its most publicized recommendation was to alter drastically the apportionment of delegates among states at the convention. At its February 1971 meeting the DNC rejected an O'Hara commission proposal that would have based delegate strength of the individual states on a formula counting the state's previous Democratic vote for President for 50 percent and its Electoral College or population strength for the other 50 percent. The DNC approved an executive committee compromise in the matter of apportionment based on a formula of 54 percent population, and 46 percent past Democratic vote in the last three presidential elections. Under this formula the nine most populous states would have a majority of the 3,016 delegate votes, whereas at the 1968 convention it would have taken at least 13 of the most populous states to combine for a majority (the rejected O'Hara proposal would have further reduced the nominating voice of the smaller states, permitting a majority vote from just eight states).

Legal Challenges

Legal challenges were filed against the DNC's apportionment ruling from both extremes. Lester Maddox, then Lt. Governor of Georgia, argued for apportionment based solely on population. Kenneth Bode of the Center for Political Reform and a one-time staff member of the McGovern Commission favored a one Democrat-one vote formula. Initially, before different judges in federal court in the District of Columbia, the Bode challenge succeeded and the Maddox suit was dismissed. On September 30, however, the U.S. Court of Appeals upheld the DNC's original formula—reversing the district court's decision in favor of Bode and thus upholding the negative ruling on the Maddox proposal—so the DNC formula was used at Miami in 1972.

Impact of Reforms

Debate continues over whether the McGovern-Fraser Commission reforms were responsible for determining the nominee of the 1972 convention—by virtue of his chairmanship of the commission, McGovern obviously had a familiarity with the recommendations and rulings. Clearly, the reforms had substantial impact on the politics and financing of the preconvention period in 1972.

In an increasing number of primaries, candidates were forced to contest delegate selections, and for the first time, candidates—from McGovern to Wallace—conducted extensive organizational drives in nonprimary states, beginning with precinct caucuses. One of the commission rulings was that in the nonprimary states at least 75 percent of a state's delegates were to be chosen at the local district level.[5] As many candidates spent large sums to organize across the nation, abundant popular participation characterized the delegate selection process. But while the reforms certainly opened participation in the process, the costs of conducting a national campaign were substantially increased by new state primaries and newly contested state conventions.

The full impact on candidate financing was never felt, since several of the 1972 candidates did not conduct a full effort in the nonprimary states, and others began their efforts late in the process. The McGovern campaign strategy realized the significance of the reforms and took full advantage by winning delegate votes that in other years would have been determined by the existing local party leadership.

Past conventions might be characterized by overwhelming participation of a majority of white males over the age of 30, many of whom had been delegates to prior conventions. In 1972 only 14.2 percent of the delegates to Miami had been delegates to previous conventions. Of the delegates to the 1968 convention, 13 percent were women, 5.5 percent were black, and four percent were under 30. The 1972 convention was comprised of 39.7 percent women, 15.2 percent blacks and other minorities, and 21.4 percent young people.

Reform of the delegate selection process continued at the Miami Beach convention with passage of a series of resolutions, including mandatory proportional representation. The convention also called for a new commission to review the existing guidelines. This commission was initially chaired by United Auto Workers President Leonard Woodcock and subsequently by Baltimore City Councilwoman Barbara Mikulski.

In March 1974 the DNC approved the recommendations of the Mikulski Commission, which asked replacement of the quota systems by affirmative action programs for women, minorities, and youth.

Spending on Reform

Between 1969 and 1972 the DNC provided some $520,000 ($210,000 in 1972 alone) to support the several reform commissions, with the bulk of the money going to the McGovern-Fraser Commission. Yet, the commissions were continually strapped for funds. As early as July 1969 the McGovern Commission initiated its own fund-raising efforts through direct mail and personal solicitations. Eventually, more than $64,000 was raised to support the work of the commission from individual party reform enthusiasts and from such organizations as the United Auto Workers. Senators McGovern and Hughes each made $7,500 personal loans to the commissions to see their work through some lean financial times, and part of these loans were never repaid.

The O'Hara and Fraser commissions met jointly before the 1972 convention to propose a new charter for the party, which provided for a reapportioned DNC and a regular national party policy conference to be held between national nominating conventions. At the Miami convention, the consideration of the new charter was postponed in the interests of party unity, but two resolutions were passed by the delegates that spoke to the essence of the charter recommendations— DNC apportionment and the holding of a 1974 miniconvention. Two other resolutions bearing on delegate selection were approved at Miami. One mandated the DNC to set aside a trust fund of eight percent of its income for financial assistance for 1976 delegates. DNC chairman Strauss did not comply with the ruling and raised a question as to whether the party rule conflicted with the 1974 Amendments. The 1974 law stated that public funds for conventions may not be used "to defray the expenses of any candidate or delegate"; in accepting the government subsidy the party is bound not to go elsewhere for private funds, in effect setting $2 million as the convention spending limit. Strauss announced that he would not comply with the 1972 eight percent rule on grounds it would be illegal. Attorneys were asked to seek a ruling on the possible conflict. Another ruling directed the DNC to explore the feasibility of holding the 1976 convention on a university campus to encourage participation by "delegates of modest means."

Republican Reforms

The Democrats did not have a monopoly on party reform during this period. The 1968 Miami Republican Convention had passed resolutions banning discrimination in the delegate selection process for reasons of race, religion, color, or national origin, and empowering the national chairman to appoint a subcommittee of the Republican National Committee (RNC) to study rules and procedures for possible changes. State parties were also mandated by the 1968 convention to "take positive action to achieve the broadest possible participation in party affairs."

In June 1969 National Chairman Rogers C.B. Morton appointed the D O Committee (for delegates and organization), composed of 16 national committee people. Chaired by Missouri National Committeeperson Rosemary Ginn, the D O Committee issued two separate reports in 1971, which offered recommendations in the areas of convention rules and delegate selection. Democrats were critical of the Republican reform effort in that each of the D O Committee's meetings was held in executive session.

The GOP rules recommendations were similar to the proposals of the O'Hara Commission, and included limiting demonstrations and favorite son nominations and determining the order of the roll by lot—but only for nominations. Also suggested was the creation of several additional committees to further study a variety of procedural areas.

The delegate selection report, which followed the rules recommendations, also was similar to the Democratic effort, but was advisory in tone and nature. State parties were urged to hold open meetings, to ban proxy voting, not to charge delegate assessments, not to select ex officio delegates, and to endeavor to have equal representation of men and women and young voters.

The D O Committee effort was financed by the RNC and undoubtedly was strongly influenced by the fact that the incumbent president was seeking renomination and took a great personal interest in the 1972 convention.

Future Conventions

A bipartisan committee was jointly appointed by the Democratic and Republican national chairmen in early 1974 to study methods of financing the major party's quadrennial conventions. No formal recommendations were made because the Republicans were generally against government funding of the national conventions while the Democrats were for it. Some early Republican support for government assistance dissipated when RNC leadership opposed any such help. On April 26, 1974 the RNC adopted a motion as being "strongly opposed to Federal financing of National Party Conventions and [in favor to] continue to explore other alternatives." Notice was sent to all members of Congress and governors, Republicans and Democrats alike. The Republican opposition to public financing of the conventions stemmed in part from its continuing battle with the Ripon Society's suit over delegate selection. Some fear that public financing could open the door to different court interpretations of challenges to party procedures in delegate selection than would be the case if the convention were privately financed. On the other hand, the Democrats argued that most private convention financing has traditionally been through corporate purchase of advertising in program books or corporate gifts to host committees. Since 48 percent of the corporate gifts were shared by the federal government in revenue loss due to the corporate tax rate, the government was thus paying half the costs in any case, and to avoid further corporate influence in politics, the government should assume the remaining costs. The Democrats undertook a survey of a sample of the corporations that advertised in the 1972 program book, and found corporate reluctance to participate in 1976.

The 94th Congress debated public financing of conventions as part of a bill to provide limited public financing of presidential election campaigns. The House version set a $2 million ceiling on spending for the conventions and set aside $2 million each for the Republican and Democratic national conventions. Minor parties would receive money for their nominating conventions based on their performance in the previous election. Parties could elect whether to use private or public money to finance their conventions, but the limit would remain at $2 million. Under the bill, the conventions would receive money from the presidential checkoff fund.

During debate in August 1974 Republicans tried to kill the convention provision with an amendment that was tentatively adopted on a 223-193 vote. Later, at a Democratic request, the House took a second vote and defeated the amendment on a 205-206 vote, with Speaker Carl Albert voting to break the tie. The conference committee then included government funding of conventions up to $2 million, on an optional basis. The Federal Election Campaign Act Amendments of 1974 also eliminated any income tax deduction for any amount paid for advertising in a convention program book. If the Republicans were to seek private financing, it will not be likely to include corporate purchase of such advertising.

The Republicans subsequently displayed a large measure of ambivalence on the public funding issue when they decided to accept government money, beginning with initial payments in 1975. Their ambivalence at the national level was echoed in certain states where new laws were passed calling for public funds to support state campaigns. In Rhode Island, where Republicans were heavily outvoted in the legislature, and the checkoff system began to turn up funds four to one in favor of the Democrats, the Republican State Committee filed a court suit charging discrimination—but still took what state monies they were allotted. In Minnesota, where they also trailed badly in designated checkoff funds, the Republicans appointed a committee to investigate the inequality and ways to correct it, but again took the public money available to them.

Funds for Delegates

The McGovern and Fraser reform commissions also urged the state parties to remove all costs and fees involved in the delegate selection process. Delegates to the 1972 Democratic National Convention "added a call to the 1976 convention requiring that state parties, in selecting and certifying delegates, undertake to assure that voters in the state have the opportunity to participate fully in party affairs regardless of economic status, as well as sex, race, age, color, national origin or creed."[6]

In a report made in mid-1974 by the Rule 29 Committee to the RNC, recommendations were made to try to involve the poor, elderly, young, or minority groups in party affairs. In the future, expense paid trips financed by the state committees or RNC were recommended for those delegates not able to afford the cost. If followed, the plan would require each state committee to submit to the RNC a positive action plan that would include means of paying for lodging at, and transportation to, future national conventions. However, at the end of 1974 the Rule 29 Committee failed to reiterate these recommendations, and it remains to be seen whether they will be implemented. At the later meeting, the committee called for restraint in convention costs, asking that salaries, living costs, decorations, programs, and arrangements be kept to a minimum. A subcommittee of the Convention Arrangements Committee would have responsibility for convention budget approval, expense review, and auditing. The Rule 29 Committee reaffirmed the position of the RNC in not approving federal financing for Republican National Conventions, expressing the view that federal money would ". . . inevitably lead to Federal domination of the nominative and elective processes, which would be inimical to the best interests of the American people."[7] The report also stated that no fees should be required or assessments made as a condition of serving as a delegate or alternate delegate. Furthermore, each state party organization would be required to demonstrate its positive actions by submitting to the RNC examples of materials produced and activities undertaken to open opportunities for participation in all party activities without discrimination and to educate the citizenry of the delegate selection process.[e]

State vs. National Rules on Delegate Selection

On January 15, 1975 the Supreme Court held that the rules of the national political party must prevail whenever they clash with state laws regarding the seating of delegates to the political conventions. This settled in favor of the national Republican and Democratic organizations a question that had divided recent conventions, in particular the 1972 Democratic convention, from which the case stemmed.

When the Illinois delegate slate headed by Chicago Mayor Richard J. Daley was challenged by a rival McGovern slate, the Daley forces obtained an order from a Chicago judge, Daniel A. Covelli, barring the McGovern slate from attending the convention or representing Illinois. The McGovern delegates disobeyed the order and were seated after winning a credentials fight on the convention floor. After the convention Daley's lawyers pressed for contempt

---

[e]"Proposed New Rules" of the Rule 29 Committee, December 20, 1974, pp. 3, 29. The unpublished report also included recommendations relating to the conduct of the 1976 presidential elections, discussed below.

citations against the McGovern backers. The McGovern forces then succeeded in getting a stay order from the Supreme Court against the lower court. Two-and-a-half years later, the high court ruled that, in effect, the McGovern slate had the right to be on the floor after being duly accredited by the national party.

Writing for the order, Justice William J. Brennan, Jr. held that "the convention serves the pervasive national interest in the selection of candidates for national office, and this national interest is greater than any interest of an individual state."[8] Brennan said that if each state were to dictate party convention membership, this could "seriously undercut or indeed destroy the effectiveness of the national party convention." Justice Lewis Potter, Jr. concurred in the unanimous decision that the national convention had the power to deny the seats to the Daley slate; he was the lone dissenter, however, in the parallel decision that the party also had the power to seat its own choice rather than leave a delegation vacant.

FEC Ruling on Convention Services

In April 1975 both the Democratic and the Republican National Committees sought an advisory opinion from the Federal Election Commission in the matter of services and facilities that cities have traditionally offered in making competitive bids for selection as the national convention site. Both parties argued that if they were compelled to count such free services as expenditures, the $2 million limitation on spending would be unrealistically low.

The FEC subsequently ruled that certain free services and facilities provided by state or local governments and municipal corporations could be accepted by the parties and not charged against the $2 million ceiling.[9] But those same services, the commission decided, are prohibited by the FECA if donated or leased by a corporation to state or local governments below the fair market value.

The FEC made two exceptions to the general corporate prohibition against free or discounted services provided to the party conventions. One of these would allow the national committees to accept such items as free hotel rooms and conference facilities in return for booking a certain number of room reservations. Reductions in standard rates or the use of certain facilities in return for the purchase of a certain minimum quantity of whatever product or service a corporation deals in would be considered "details of an overall purchase transaction" and part of the "ordinary course of business," so long as other conventions of similar size and duration received similar benefits. As such, they would not violate the prohibition of corporate contributions. However, audits may be used to check on the validity of such actions.

In addition, the FEC ruled that local corporations could contribute to civic associations, business leagues, and other such groups that were working to attract the political conventions to the city. But such contributions have two requirements: (1) the collecting group or agency must be nonprofit with no part of net earnings benefitting any private shareholder or individual; and (2) the group must have the encouragement of commerce as its primary objective in seeking a major party convention.

The commission left undefined what constitutes a local corporation, but the debate in the FEC's closed meetings apparently led to the general conclusion that the local distributor of a national firm could qualify if exercising local autonomy, and if profits went primarily to the local outlet. An airline with administrative offices in the convention city, for example, would probably not qualify since profits would probably be the same no matter where the convention was held. But the local outlet of a fast food chain probably would qualify since its business would increase during the convention. Further questions will likely be decided by the FEC on a case by case basis.

Challenge to FEC Fund Distribution

The FEC came under legal challenge in June 1975 for a question growing out of the Buckley-McCarthy suit. The two major parties had requested $1.8 million each for the 1976 conventions, with the first installment of $600,000 due to be paid out on July 1, 1975. The plaintiffs' attorneys said they intended to seek an injunction to bar the payments. The request for the court order was subsequently withdrawn after the FEC agreed that no certification of payment to the parties would be made without a seven-day public notice of their intended action. This precluded a possibly adverse ruling against government funding, which the commission sought to avoid.

I.T.T.

The I.T.T. affair dealt with questions basic to the concepts of government noninterference with business, and conversely with business noninterference or influence of government. In May 1971 the giant International Telephone and Telegraph Corporation pledged up to $400,000 to attract the 1972 Republican National Convention to San Diego, California, allegedly to encourage favorable treatment in an out-of-court settlement of three antitrust suits, which the Justice Department was bringing against I.T.T. Although testimony three years later revealed that President Nixon had directed then Deputy Attorney General Richard Kleindienst to delay the appeal of an antitrust ruling to the Supreme

Court,[f] it was never conclusively established that the Nixon administration's settlement of the suit was in return for the conglomerate's 1971 pledge to the Republican National Convention.

Richard W. McLaren, assistant attorney general in the Antitrust Division of the Justice Department, sought to break up conglomerates by testing if the Clayton Act could apply to company mergers. In 1969 McLaren filed suits against three pending mergers of I.T.T. with Canteen Corporation, Grinnell Manufacturing Company, and Hartford Fire Insurance Company.

Under the leadership of its president, Harold S. Geneen, I.T.T. had risen to ninth on the "*Fortune* 500" list of largest corporations in the United States, with 331 subsidiary corporations, and 708 sub-subsidiaries. The $1.5 billion acquisition of Hartford alone would be the largest merger in United States corporate history. Ultimately, McLaren settled for a negotiated settlement allowing I.T.T. to retain Hartford (with annual premiums in 1971 of approximately 26 percent of I.T.T.'s operating earnings), and part of Grinnell. I.T.T. was required to divest itself of Canteen Corporation, the fire protection division of Grinnell, Avis Rent-A-Car, I.T.T.-Levitt and Sons, and two small insurance companies.[g]

Late in 1971 Lawrence O'Brien, Democratic National Committee chairman, wrote to Attorney General John Mitchell demanding to know if an out-of-court settlement with I.T.T. was linked to the pledge of one of its subsidiaries, Sheraton Harbor Island Corporation, to underwrite the GOP National Convention in San Diego. The July 31, 1971 settlement came just eight days after the selection of the GOP convention site for 1972 in San Diego. Estimates of the financial support pledged by Sheraton ranged at the time from $200,000 to $400,000. While Atlas Hotels, San Diego's largest chain, pledged only $24,000, their available units to house people for the proposed convention numbered 1,325 to Sheraton's 1,150.

Later testimony in hearings revealed that top I.T.T. executives and Nixon administration officials had met repeatedly in secret during 1970 and 1971 on the antitrust suits and a consent agreement, and while the negotiations were going on, I.T.T. offered the money to underwrite the convention. It was shown that in 1970 Geneen had complained to Mitchell and White House Domestic Advisor John Ehrlichman about McLaren's efforts in the case. Ehrlichman sent memos to McLaren, pressuring him to go easier on I.T.T., and referred to an "understanding" the administration had with Geneen. Nixon became angry when McLaren would not comply, ordered him fired from the Justice

---

[f] Then Attorney General John Mitchell had publicly disqualified himself from any I.T.T.-related matters, having represented I.T.T. as a private lawyer. Kleindienst was ultimately responsible for handling suits against I.T.T.; but it was later revealed that Mitchell was involved in discussions with the President about, and in settlement of, the antitrust suits.

[g] This divestiture of subsidiaries with annual sales of $1 billion is the largest corporate divestiture ever to result from an antitrust suit.

Department, and ordered that he should never hold another government position. McLaren left Justice several months later, but was appointed to a federal judgeship in Chicago.

The I.T.T. storm broke publicly with a column by Jack Anderson on February 29, 1972. The nationally syndicated columnist announced he held evidence that settlement of the I.T.T. antitrust cases had been privately arranged by Attorney General John Mitchell and Dita Davis Beard, I.T.T.'s chief Washington lobbyist. A confidential memo written June 25, 1971 by Mrs. Beard to W.R. Merriam, vice-president and head of I.T.T.'s Washington office, spelled out a secret deal between the Justice Department and I.T.T. Spokesmen for I.T.T. immediately denied that the memo was genuine or that there was any deal to dispose of the antitrust cases. I.T.T. termed its convention offer a nonpartisan civic venture, and noting that its Sheraton subsidiary had several hotels in San Diego, said it benefitted only from its local business interests.

Anderson followed up publication of the memo by writing that Deputy Attorney General Richard Kleindienst had held several private meetings with an I.T.T. director, Felix Rohatyn,[h] before the antitrust settlement was reached. Anderson charged Kleindienst had lied when he stated in a public letter that the antitrust cases had been "handled and negotiated exclusively" by the Justice Department's Antitrust Division. Kleindienst responded to the charges by asking the Senate Judiciary Committee to reopen its recently concluded hearings on his nomination for Attorney General.

The Kleindienst hearings dragged on for four months, with conflicting testimony and resolved little. No link was established between I.T.T.'s convention pledge and the antitrust settlement. While circumstantial evidence from the testimony pointed to a link, all government and I.T.T. witnesses denied any connection. The hearings also failed to determine if the memo from Dita Beard was real or a forgery. On March 26, after a visit from E. Howard Hunt, who was disguised in a red wig obtained from the Central Intelligence Agency, Beard testified from a Denver hospital bed, suffering from a supposed heart condition. She acknowledged writing a memo to Merriam about I.T.T.'s convention pledge, in order to correct a false impression: a White House staffer had apparently called to inquire about a $600,000 "commitment." But she denied writing the incriminating portions of the memo Anderson published that linked the pledge to the antitrust settlement. Beard claimed the Anderson version had been forged by someone bent on destroying her. While FBI tests suggested that the disputed memo may have been typed at I.T.T.'s Washington office, I.T.T.'s privately hired experts said it could not have been prepared on the date indicated, and was a fraud. Beard suffered an apparent heart attack while answering

---

[h]Rohatyn was also a partner in the investment banking house of Lazard Frères, which was handling the details of the proposed I.T.T.-Hartford merger.

questions, and her doctor said she would not be able to testify for about six months. A few days later she taped a television show and subsequently signed herself out of the hospital. The Senate Judiciary Committee commissioned two experienced cardiologists to examine her, and they were unable to find any evidence of heart disease.

When the hearings closed on April 27, Kleindienst won an 11-4 vote of confidence from the Senate Judiciary Committee. The vote was largely along party lines, the majority finding no substance to Anderson's charges against Kleindienst. His nomination as Attorney General was subsequently confirmed by the Senate on June 8, in a 64-19 roll-call vote.

Watergate Prosecutor Archibald Cox later found evidence that Kleindienst had lied to the Senate Committee. On learning he would be indicted for perjury, Kleindienst admitted that President Nixon had called him on April 19, 1971, and ordered him to delay the appeal of the antitrust ruling to the Supreme Court. Kleindienst said he had then sent word that he would resign if the President persisted in the orders to drop the appeal. He received an extension to file the appeal and enable the President to reconsider his position. Nixon then changed his mind, the appeal was filed, and the case was eventually settled out of court. The Attorney General maintained, however, that he had not lied to the committee.

In late March, 1974 Kleindienst pleaded guilty to a misdemeanor charge in connection with his 1972 testimony to the Senate committee. He was convicted of making false and misleading statements under oath, having already resigned as Attorney General. Three of the four lawyers on the force investigating the I.T.T. affair resigned, reportedly because Kleindienst received such a light sentence.

The Kleindienst hearings also failed to answer the question of the size and nature of I.T.T.'s convention pledge. Geneen testified that I.T.T. had made a commitment of $100,000 in cash [10] and a guarantee to provide another $100,000 if matched by other San Diego firms. Rep. Bob Wilson, R-California, a close friend of Geneen, testified that I.T.T. would never have had to provide the funds, which would have been used to stimulate other San Diego money. San Diego Republicans said I.T.T. only pledged to stand good for any shortage that might develop in efforts to raise the city's $600,000 cash commitment. I.T.T.'s guarantee was simply a "backstop" for money that San Diego Republicans were sure could be raised locally.

Geneen told the House Judiciary Committee that I.T.T's convention subsidy was "a solid business expenditure" meant to promote a new Sheraton hotel in San Diego. The hotel was to serve as President Nixon's convention headquarters. If true that I.T.T.'s pledge was devoid of political considerations, the $100,000 donation was legal. Corporate contributions to political conventions are legal if the money is given to the (nominally bipartisan) host committee for the event. Such donations are legally regarded as promoting convention business and enjoy the tax deductible status of a business expense.

In fact, a law suit charging I.T.T. with violating the FECA restrictions on corporate gifts to political conventions was dismissed May 17, 1972 by a federal judge in Los Angeles. I.T.T. argued in court that it did not give the money to the Republicans but to a civic group, the San Diego Convention and Visitors' Bureau, to help attract the convention in hopes of getting bookings for the three Sheraton hotels in the city.

During a 1972 investigation of "insider trading" and other possible violations of securities laws in the I.T.T./Hartford merger, I.T.T. and the White House sought to prevent the Securities and Exchange Commission (SEC) from subpoenaing company memos and letters detailing these meetings. But on March 21, six White House and Justice Department memos and 13 memos and letters from I.T.T. regarding the antitrust settlement were delivered to the SEC. Then, in August and September when the Senate Judiciary Committee and the House Commerce Committee tried to obtain these memos, the White House and certain SEC officials tried to keep them from the committees. On October 6, SEC Chairman William Casey sent 34 boxes of documents to the Justice Department (where they were immune from subpoena) rather than to Congress. And the 13 politically sensitive documents were put into a safe in the Justice Department until after the November elections. On November 30, 1972 Casey was promoted to Under Secretary of State for economic affairs.

The White House released a "White Paper" January 9, 1974, dealing with the I.T.T. affair, intended to give the administration side of the story. The statement presented facts selectively and was designed to reassure the public by defending President Nixon's intervention in the I.T.T. and milk fund cases. Although denying that the administration made a quid pro quo deal with I.T.T., the paper acknowledged the existence of opportunities for bribery. Nixon admitted that he and Ehrlichman had told Kleindienst to drop the case, which, if taken to the Supreme Court, might seriously weaken major American companies.

The I.T.T. affair was partly responsible for the Republican decision to move the 1972 convention from San Diego to Miami Beach. Delays and rising costs in readying the San Diego convention hall were among the reasons officially given for the change. But without a doubt the stigma San Diego bore from the I.T.T. affair was a major reason for the shift.

The fallout continued, as the I.T.T. affair progressed into 1974, with an investigation by a congressional committee into the legality of the Hartford Insurance merger. Rep. J.J. Pickel, D-Texas, accused the Internal Revenue Service of playing a part in what he called a cover-up of government favors extended to I.T.T. IRS had established a ruling that insured the takeover of Hartford while allowing I.T.T. to make a profit of nearly $6 million.[i]

---

[i] IRS approved the stock transaction in only seven days. Many tax attorneys and two former IRS commissioners regarded the transaction as a device to avoid the loss entailed in an immediate, unconditional sale as required by law, by paying a "parking fee."

Watergate Special Prosecutor Leon Jaworski announced in May 1974 that his office had found no evidence that executives of I.T.T. had committed any criminal offenses in connection with the 1971 settlement. His office continued the investigation of the tax ruling and several other unanswered questions concerning the conglomerate.

Another person caught in I.T.T.'s tangled web was California Lieutenant Governor Ed Reinecke, convicted of perjury on three counts for testimony before the Senate committee conducting hearings on the nomination of Kleindienst for Attorney General. Reinecke was indicted on April 3, 1974 while running for the Republican nomination for Governor of California. He was decisively defeated in the June primary, but refused to resign as Lieutenant Governor. He was charged with lying when he testified that the only time he and Attorney General Mitchell discussed I.T.T.'s offer to help finance the 1972 Republican National Convention was on September 17, 1971, two months after the Justice Department had settled its antitrust cases against the company. The government contended that Reinecke informed Mitchell of a $400,000 pledge in a May 21, 1971 phone call, during negotiations for the antitrust case. Reinecke told prosecutors later that he had actually informed Mitchell about the I.T.T. offer in three phone calls in May and June. Reinecke's perjury trial opened on July 16, 1974. Less than three months later, on October 2, Reinecke resigned as Lieutenant Governor of California. He was sentenced on the same day by U.S. District Court Judge Barrington D. Parker to a suspended 18-month jail term, and was placed on one month's unsupervised probation. Reinecke maintained his innocence, and expected to appeal.

Documents made public for the first time by the House Judiciary Committee on July 20, 1974 showed the depth of involvement of the President and his top advisors in the controversial 1969-71 I.T.T. negotiations. They further showed that top advisors knew of I.T.T.'s proposed financial support as early as 1969, and seemingly established a link between the financial pledge and settlement of the antitrust cases implicating John Mitchell, the Justice Department, and the senior staff in the White House.

The $700,000 Misunderstanding

The greed of the Democrats in 1965 produced for bipartisan voter registration efforts in 1972 about $400,000 and additional amounts in 1973 and 1974.

The story of this windfall actually began in 1964, with the success of the Democratic Convention program book; ads cost $15,000 per page, and the party netted close to $1.5 million. With this financial success the financially hard-pressed Democrats produced another program book in 1965. It was entitled "Toward an Age of Greatness" and extolled the virtues of President Johnson's Great Society; ads were again $15,000 per page and the party netted about

$601,000. A controversy developed over the legality of allowing the business ads in such books to be considered as legitimate business expenses, since the books were partisan, were not considered as defensible as the traditionally accepted National Convention program books both parties published, and the distribution was limited. The Democrats finally decided to let the uproar subside before spending the money,[j] and the 1966 Williams Amendment eventually prohibited such deductions.[k]

The money was unused until 1968, when Humphrey's money-starved campaign tried to get it freed for voter registration efforts. The fund's trustee refused, saying the planned voter registration effort might still be considered partisan or a party purpose; privately, some believed that President Johnson still controlled the money and would not help Humphrey's campaign.[11] In any case, the money remained unused for more than three years.

Finally, in early 1972 lawyers arranged for the money to be given to the Voter Registration Fund, an organization created especially to distribute these funds for nonpartisan voter registration. In order to qualify for grants from the fund, an organization had to fulfull stringent conditions:

1. Be tax-exempt by IRS standards
2. Be nonpartisan, operating in five or more states, and its voter registration activities could not be confined to any one specific candidate, area, or election period
3. Guarantee that not more than 25 percent of its income came from the fund or any single organization.

Seven major grants were awarded in April 1972. Three of them were for registration activities among 18 to 25 year olds: $75,000 to the United States Youth Council's Frontlash program; $50,000 to The Student Vote; and $35,000 to the Youth Citizenship Fund. The other four major grants were to organizations working primarily among minorities: $75,000 to the A. Philip Randolph Education Fund; $60,000 to the Voter Education Project of Atlanta; $50,000 to the NAACP Special Contribution Fund; and $25,000 to the National Urban League. A $50,000 grant announced to the Citizen Voter Research Education Project, for registration activities among Mexican-Americans in the Southwest, was never made because the organization failed to obtain IRS tax-exempt status.

These grants, and several smaller ones, represented about one-half of the fund's available total. The exact amount of the original money was $601,000,

---

[j] See Herbert E. Alexander, *Financing the 1964 Election* (Princeton: Citizens' Research Foundation, 1966) pp. 99-104, for a detailed discussion of this issue.

[k] An exception was made for the 1968 conventions of both parties; see Alexander, *Financing the 1968 Election*, Lexington, Mass: Lexington Books, D.C. Heath and Company, 1971. pp. 75-76.

which was placed in interest-bearing certificates of deposit and earned over $100,000 in interest. The amount that was turned over to the Voter Registration Fund was $729,104.02.

7

The General Election Campaigns

The 1972 presidential election was only partially a referendum on Richard Nixon's first four years in office; it also turned on what the voters thought of his opponent. The McGovern proposals on tax reform and welfare plans upset many of his fellow Democrats almost as much as they did most Republicans. The issue was often simply "McGovernism"—one sharpened by the strategy of the Committee to Re-Elect the President (CRP) to remove Nixon from the rough-and-tumble of the campaign, while Agnew and others served as surrogates for the President. Nixon refused a public debate with McGovern, and avoided campaign tours until the end of September.

In both camps campaign finance was a major issue. The Watergate revelations about secret funds and "dirty tricks" were a problem for the Nixon campaign. So too were the disclosures stipulated by the court before the election, resulting from the Common Cause suit. The net effect of these problems, ironically, was that the financing of the Nixon campaign became the best-documented in the history of presidential elections.

Campaign funding was also a major aspect of the McGovern story. His direct mail appeal was the most successful of any presidential campaign on record, as was the overwhelming support by small givers, which pulled the campaign out of debt and into the black. The Watergate disclosures became a major issue in the Democratic campaign, as McGovern tried to keep pressure on Nixon to reveal the full story. Another major issue, which McGovern had stressed from the beginning of his presidential bid—an end to the Vietnam War—was severely struck by the election eve televised announcement by Nixon that an agreement to end the war in Vietnam would soon be concluded.

Nixon Expenditures

Republican presidential expenditures for 1971 through mid-1975, all related to Nixon's 1972 nomination and election, and the Watergate-dominated aftermath, cost at least $61.4 million, as shown in Table 7-1. Surplus funds of about $1.2 million remained in mid-1975 to pay off additional legal fees and other related expenses, with any balance committed to go to the Republican National Finance Committee (RNFC). This compares with about $42 million for McGovern—$30 million in the general election period, and another $12 million to get nominated. In 1960 Richard Nixon and John Kennedy together

271

Table 7-1

1971-72 Republican Presidential Expenditures of CRP and Related Organizations: Pre- and Postnomination

Expense Category	$ Millions
Advertising (broadcast, including production costs and fees)	$ 7.0
Direct mail to voters (not including fund raising)	5.8
Mass telephoning to voters	1.3
State organizations (primary elections, personnel, storefronts, locations, travel, voter contact, etc.)	15.9
Campaign materials	2.7
Press relations, publications, and literature	2.6
Headquarters (campaign, personnel, rent, telephone, travel, legal, etc.)	4.7
Travel and other expenses of President, Vice-President, surrogates, and advance men	3.9
Citizen group activities	1.9
Youth activities	1.0
Polling (including White House-directed surveys)	1.6
Convention expenses	.6
Election night	.2
Fund raising (direct mail—$4 million, and major events—$1 million)	5.0
Fund raising (national administration and gifts for contributors)	1.9
Legal fees	2.0
Democratic settlement	.8
Democrats for Nixon	2.4
Total[a]	$61.4

[a]Does not include $1.4 million in miscellaneous cash, some used for dirty tricks or hush money in 1972-73, and some used for political or other purposes in 1969-70-71, not directly related to the 1972 presidential election.

reported spending less than $20 million on their general election campaigns (not including prenomination expenses), although disclosure laws were much less comprehensive then.

Nixon's 1972 campaign sought to attain the first truly "professionalized" national effort in American politics. The well-funded CRP had dozens of employees earning annual salaries at the rate of $30,000 or more and scores who earned at the rate of $20,000 or more (many were on the payroll for short times, however). Its two leaders earned $60,000 per year, the same as Cabinet officers Mitchell and Stans had received from the government. More than $3 million was budgeted for salaries in the general election period, and the monthly payroll exceeded $400,000 by August. Approximately 35 White House aides left their positions to work on the campaign.[1] Positions more traditionally filled by volunteers and low-salaried workers were staffed by well-paid professionals. Expensive consultants were hired; for example, a public relations man was hired at $2,000 per month to advise H.R. Haldeman in his area of specialization. The fund-raising arm had a paid staff of 40, in contrast to the dozen or so who raised Nixon money in 1968, but this was accounted for in part by the system of computerized central bookkeeping that in 1972 accounted for all listed contributions of more than $100 received by the central Finance Committee to Re-Elect the President (FCRP) and by all state affiliates as well.

Matched against their 1968 expenditures, the Republicans spent more in most aspects of campaigning—with the major exception of political broadcasting.[a] This was mainly because of a major strategy decision made by campaign manager Clark MacGregor in July 1972 to sharply reduce broadcasting expenditures. Nixon then enjoyed a comfortable lead in the polls, and could rely on considerable media exposure simply by virtue of his incumbency. The strategy was to shift spending away from broadcasting—well below limits set by the Federal Election Campaign Act (FECA) of 1971—into other areas of the campaign judged potentially more profitable, notably direct mail, mass telephoning, and storefront operations. In 1968 the Nixon forces had spent $12.6 million on television and radio time in the general election; four years later the CRP spent $4.3 million on air time.

MacGregor and the CRP were impressed with McGovern's storefront operations in the primaries. On August 1, 1972 there were fewer than 100 Republican storefronts, each costing from $1,000 to $1,200 a month (compared with $800 per month for McGovern's). By October, 2,000 were in operation. But while this program functioned at the grass-roots level, it was a tightly controlled effort, part of a highly professionalized plan to select and reach target groups.

Apart from the traditional appeals to Republicans, the direct mail program was seen as the way to the hearts and minds of the traditionally Democratic ethnic voters. About 25 million computer letters and telegrams were mailed to voters in key states who were identified through canvassing or phoning. Some $5.8 million went into the direct mail program directly; another $1.3 million was spent on telephones for canvassing and telephone banks. Letters were frequently keyed specifically to the recipient's ethnic heritage, issue concerns, and other factors that could affect his choice on election day. Additional millions of dollars were spent on buying and computerizing lists of target voters for the massive door-to-door, telephone and mail efforts. Attitudes toward the Republican ticket and on specific issues were key punched and added to computer files on these voters, and the mail they received depended on their individual computer profiles.

---

[a]For a discussion of broadcast spending, see Chapter 8.

In some cases a mailing was followed by a telephone call or personal visit, and sometimes both, to determine presidential preference and issue salience. Voters decidedly favorable or unfavorable to Nixon were noted, and the undecideds were sent another letter keyed to the issues they said were most important. In many cases they were canvassed again and their views noted. In the first week of November those who expressed a preference for Nixon at any stage in the process were phoned again and sent a computergram, a telegram-like computer letter, urging them to be certain to vote on election day. The mailings to Democrats and independents were signed by John Connally or James Roosevelt, among others, and those to Republicans by Republican governors or senators.

A substantial part of these efforts was keyed to the 12 target states regarded as critically important to Nixon. The major emphasis was placed within these states, and $2 million budgeted to reach "peripheral urban ethnics." Twelve basic versions of a letter and hundreds of combinations were used, based on political geography and ethnic groups.

Other efforts directed toward ethnic groups included the trips of the Nixon daughters, Tricia Cox and Julie Eisenhower. Government money spent on preparation of their speeches and briefing papers, and for the printing and distribution of their speeches, was reimbursed by FCRP. Detroit oilman Max M. Fisher traveled coast-to-coast speaking to Jewish groups (as an unpaid volunteer with expenses paid), as did Rabbi Ronnie Greenwald (at a salary of $1,850 per month). Up to 60,000 retired Italian-Americans, living on Social Security, were the major objects of a large direct-mail vote drive. The Republican National Committee even sent representatives to Italy, which reportedly had the only European parliamentary group to endorse Nixon.[2] The Italians had endorsed American presidential candidates before, but never a Republican.

Fearing the McGovern appeal to young voters, the CRP spent $1 million for a Youth Division directed by Kenneth Reitz. This group had a staff of 100, a 1,500-member speaker's bureau, and branches in 47 states, with a separate college program in all 50 states.

In his testimony to the Senate Watergate Committee on June 6, 1973, Hugh Sloan, Jr. said that there were some 450 finance committees in operation at various times before the April 7, 1972 disclosure deadline. Before the disclosure date, the Common Cause civil suit later brought out, the Nixon campaign had already spent more than $10 million. About $3.1 million was expended on the salaries and other expenses of the Citizens Committee and CRP, while about $6 million was prespending on work ordered in advance of April 7. The CRP eventually reported $10.2 million cash on hand as of April 7, and handled another $1.7 million in secret cash funds (revealed by Sloan 14 months later to the Senate Watergate Committee); of the latter, some had been disbursed before April 7.

The FCRP spent large amounts in fund raising for the campaign. At least

$4 million was spent on direct mail appeals for money (exclusive of the direct mail aimed at votes), while about $1 million was expended on direct costs of fund-raising events, mainly the major dinner events, and some $1.9 million went into salaries, travel, general administration, and gifts to contributors. This comes to about $7 million for fund-raising costs (including expenses of the 50 state affiliates), more than ten percent of the total of $62.7 million that was raised; fund-raising costs for direct mail were about 50 percent, for dinner events about ten percent, and four percent for all other fund-raising efforts. More than $400,000 of the fund-raising total went for gifts, thank you souvenirs and other expressions of gratitude to large contributors.

Several minor programs were also well funded. Hawthorn Books, Inc., headed by one of Nixon's largest donors, W. Clement Stone, was paid $42,000 to publish 30,000 copies of a photo book with an introduction by Julie Eisenhower. Print advertising was placed in journals seldom used by past presidential candidates, and included $2,913 in *VFW* on "Draft Dodgers" and $6,665 in *Successful Farming.* Some $48,700 was spent on a Nixon trip to Atlanta, including confetti blowing machines.

Of special interest, the costs to the campaign for Nixon and Agnew, their staffs and committees, at the Republican Convention in Miami Beach totalled $627,279. Election night costs for a victory celebration were $151,918.

White House Support

Information was obtained covering expenditures termed "White House Support"—a set of CRP-paid expenses totalling $3,284,541 (subsumed under other categories in Table 7-1), and encompassing the campaign role of the President and the First Family, the Vice-President, the White House staff, and the supporting public relations operations. Complete lists are provided in Appendix I; a breakdown of the respective elements involved is given in Table 7-2.

Table 7-2
White House Support, 1972 Campaign

Presidential and first family travel	$1,419,034.57[a]
White House staff expenses	185,291.51
Vice-presidential travel and expenses	1,046,279.77
Public relations operations	633,935.80

[a]The FCRP received about $300,000 in press reimbursements for travel of journalists accompanying these travellers, charged at first-class ticket rates.

Nearly half of the First Family White House support involved travel and associated costs by the President and Mrs. Nixon, their two daughters and sons-in-law. A total of $208,671 went for air travel (as reimbursements largely for travel on the presidential plane, Air Force One), and $9,848 for other forms of travel. First Family hotel costs were $83,923. Other costs in their support reflect the impedimenta of a presidential campaign appearance: for example, advance men ($514,008), public address systems and other audio devices ($45,677), banners and signs ($6,083), lighting costs ($28,648), and receptions ($45,233). The sum of $304,725 is listed under the First Family account for "gifts"—presumably for the Nixons to present to various personages on campaign stops. The CRP was generous with these sorts of largesse; witness the $400,000 spent on gifts and other gratitudes under fund-raising costs.

The most prominent administration campaigner was Vice-President Agnew, whose spending under White House support totalled $1,046,279. A major item was his air travel which came to $293,082. Another large item, $243,889, was for surveys and polls; presumably these soundings were taken before the decision to retain Agnew on the ticket, and were charged to his support. Hotel bills for the vice-presidential appearances came to $126,282.

Counting White House support, the CRP spent nearly $2.5 million for the candidates' travels around the country. The McGovern campaign, by contrast, spent about $1.5 million net on the same kinds of expenditures. The difference was not in actual travel (McGovern's travel expenditures were actually higher than Nixon's, though gross costs were reduced by press and Secret Service reimbursement for travel on campaign planes and buses), but in the other niceties and necessities of the twentieth century campaign trail—audio services, consultants, tapes and filming, sophisticated telephone hookups, and advancing. In these areas, the Nixon camp outspent the McGovern camp, but travel for a President is necessarily expensive.

The question of the use of White House employees in support of the campaign was first raised by Representative Wright Patman's Banking and Currency Committee in the fall of 1972. Patman's investigators reported that a great number of White House personnel had been reimbursed by the CRP, but they had difficulty ascertaining the overlap in activities paid from tax funds and those reimbursed from political funds.[3] The partial list obtained by the investigators at that time showed a total of $37,049 reimbursed by CRP (mainly for travel) to such White House aides as Special Counsel Harry Dent and John Scali and the then director of the Office of Economic Opportunity (OEO), Donald Rumsfeld.

Evidence of further White House spending on government officials' travel during the 1972 campaign turned up after Nixon left office. Senator William Proxmire, D-Wisconsin, asked the General Accounting Office (GAO) to look into the matter of reimbursement of such travel by the FCRP, and in late October

1974 the GAO issued its report.[b] The White House refused the GAO access to flight logs of the presidential crew on Air Force One, but available records indicated the FCRP paid $98,936 for 32 trips. Records of the 89th Military Airlift Wing show 103 trips in 1972, 26 of which were made by Cabinet officers and reimbursed by their respective agencies, and 77 trips made by others in the administration, with 23 reimbursed by the FCRP for $50,355.

Dudley Chapman, President Ford's associate counsel, was accused by Jack Anderson of trying to conceal the fact that there had been a special White House fund, known as the "Subsidiary Account," saying that the fund belonged to the Republican National Committee (RNC) and CRP jointly.[4] Registration and filings for 1972-73-74 submitted to the GAO in October 1974 indicated a White House location for the account and White House officials as officers. In a covering letter it was called a "custodial and bookkeeping device to facilitate disbursements on behalf of the actual committees" (RNC and CRP). The GAO charged that failure to disclose the account's existence until two years after the campaign was over constituted a violation of the FECA of 1971, as did the failure to maintain complete and accurate records of its receipts. The filed reports showed receipts and expenditures of about $16,300. In October 1974 the GAO recommended that these apparent violations be brought to the attention of the Justice Department; no action has occurred at this writing.

Discussion of Nixon expenditures would be incomplete without mention of the use of secret cash—about $550,000 hush money paid to defendants in a criminal case, both before and after they were found guilty, and close to $800,000 that funded a wide range of dirty tricks and espionage, from $5,000 for the Fielding break-in in California to $10,000 for a vote-siphoning scheme in New Hampshire, all designed to be untraceable to the CRP or the White House in case anything went wrong. Most of this money was from trust funds of almost $2 million left over from the 1968 campaign, which were handled by Herbert Kalmbach from 1969 to 1972 under the direction of individuals in the White House; a balance of about $600,000 remaining of these funds was turned over by Kalmbach to FCRP in February 1972 and eventually included in its accountings. The FCRP funds used were provided by the finance managers at the direction of the political managers, without question. Some of the Kalmbach funds were spent in 1969-70-71, before the Nixon campaign got underway, and thus were only indirectly involved with the 1972 campaign, for example, the

---

[b]GAO report, October 23, 1974. At Senator Proxmire's request, the summary of trips and the Comptroller General's covering letter to Proxmire were printed in *Congressional Record,* April 13, 1973, S7399-S7401. See also Jack Anderson, "White House Fund Exposed," *Philadelphia Bulletin,* November 14, 1974.

$400,000 that went to George Wallace's opponent in 1970, and money used by the Plumbers. The funds totalling about $550,000 were collected and used by Kalmbach and Fred LaRue to pay to Watergate defendants and their counsel in 1972 and early 1973. Most of the Kalmbach trust and LaRue funds were raised as political funds, however eventually used.[c]

Nixon Sources of Funds

Overshadowed in the publicity about the financing of Nixon's reelection campaign was the overall amount raised on his behalf. About $62 million was contributed to Nixon in 1972 through the CRP and the Democrats for Nixon. Another $8 million was raised by the Republican National Committee, much of it used in direct or indirect support of the Nixon administration or campaign. The total was more than twice that reported in the 1968 general election.

While condemned for some of its financial practices, the 1972 Nixon campaign in other respects was a model of centrally controlled committees. Most money raised for Nixon went through the national campaign and was spent according to central authority. After April 7 state Committees for the Re-Election of the President kept contributions of $100 and under but sent larger ones to the Washington committee for recording and itemizing on fund reports as required by law. The only larger contributions some state affiliates received and retained were those distributed to the state committees permitting the donors to avoid the gift tax; in many states such out-of-state contributions so distributed constituted the bulk of the large contributions. In most such cases the money was then transferred to FCRP for its use, although the national headquarters also transferred large amounts back to state affiliates when budget requirements so demanded. Budgets of the affiliates were approved centrally.

One measure of the differences in style and strategy of the Nixon and McGovern fund-raising campaigns was in their first moves. A few days before McGovern formally announced his quest for the presidency in January 1971 he mailed a letter to a broad-based list of 300,000 voters, giving his reasons for seeking the presidency and asking for donations, large or small. The Nixon fund drive was launched with an approach to a carefully selected list of names whose potential to contribute had been assessed at $5,000 or more. The FCRP checked

---

[c]For discussion of secret funds and their use, see Chapter 3. The Plumbers, under direction of E. Howard Hunt, received $5,000 for the Fielding break-in, $10,000 for "bribe money" if caught during the Watergate break-in (apparently not offered), and $550,000 (including lawyers' fees) in hush money—over $275,000 of which went to Hunt. Dirty tricks expenses included $400,000 in 1970 for Wallace's gubernatorial opponent, and close to $400,000 to finance operations by Anthony Ulasewicz ($51,918), Donald Segretti ($45,000), Murray Chotiner ($32,080), Lyn Nofziger ($10,000), G. Gordon Liddy ($235,000), and Charles Colson ($10,000).

on major contributors to known institutions; new companies that had gone public in the previous four years were also researched, as were the *Fortune* 500. McGovern had to borrow the money to pay for his first direct mail appeal; the Nixon drive never needed to borrow funds throughout 1971 and 1972.

Although both Nixon and McGovern wound up with about the same number of contributors—close to 600,000—the Nixon list was dominated by large contributors. A relative handful of contributors, 154 in all, accounted for $21.3 million—one-third of the Nixon total.[5]

One analysis of these large contributors showed a fair number in the "Horatio Alger" tradition, men who rose from poor backgrounds to command vast fortunes. Among them were men such as John A. Mulcahy, a poor Irish immigrant in the 1920s, who rose to the presidency of a steel industry equipment supplier, then became a major stockholder of a drug firm in a merger. A heavy contributor in the 1970 congressional campaigns, he gave Nixon close to $625,000 in 1972—$598,559 pre-April 7, and $26,000 post-April 7—and reportedly had pledged even more. Anthony Rossi, Sicilian born, former bricklayer, tomato farmer, and cab driver, who founded Tropicana Products, contributed $103,000. Abe Plough, chairman of the drug firm that makes St. Joseph's aspirin, began his career in Memphis, Tennessee in 1908 as a door-to-door medicine oil salesman; his 1972 gift to Nixon was $56,002.

Nixon's largest contributor, W. Clement Stone, who reportedly was an avid reader of Horatio Alger books in his boyhood, began his insurance office with $100 and a rented desk. Chairman of the Combined Insurance Co. of America, Stone gave some $2.1 million in 1972. In 1968 his money accounted for seven percent of the cost of Nixon's primary and general election fights, four years later it equalled about four percent of Nixon's reelection spending. Stone's political contributions in the years 1968-72, virtually all to Republican candidates, amounted to more than $7 million, as shown in Appendix J.

The great American fortunes were also well represented on the list of large contributors to Nixon in 1972—DuPont, Firestone, Rockefeller, Whitney. The second largest contributor was Richard Mellon Scaife of Pittsburgh, an heir to the Mellon oil and banking fortune, who gave $1 million. As details of the Watergate scandal surfaced, Scaife repudiated Nixon, and in a newspaper he publishes in Pennsylvania (the Greensburg *Tribune-Review*) called editorially in May 1974 for Nixon's impeachment.[6]

John Mulcahy, mentioned above, was Nixon's third largest contributor, giving $624,559. Arthur Watson, United States ambassador to France, gave $303,000; United States ambassador to Luxembourg and Director of Alexander's Dept. Store Ruth Farkas (with her husband, George Farkas) contributed $300,000.

The sixth through tenth largest Nixon contributors were business executives: John J. Louis, Jr., chairman of Combined Communications Corporation, gave $283,360; John Rollins, chief executive officer of Rollins International Inc.

(truck leasing and shipping), gave $265,524; Roy Carver, chairman of Bandag, Inc. (tread rubber company), donated $263,324; Sam Schulman, chairman of the board of National General Corp. (insurance holding company), gave $262,575; and Daniel Terra, chairman and president of Lawter Chemicals, Inc., donated $255,000.

Both Stone and Scaife, along with a number of the other large contributors, presumably made their contributions on the assumption that the details would not be made public, since the gifts were made prior to the April 7 disclosure deadline.[d] (Stone gave $2 million before the deadline, $51,643 later.)

The disclosures revealed that FCRP fund raisers brought in some $20 million before the April 7 deadline, with $11.4 million raised in the month before the FECA took effect. Of this amount, they received $2.3 million on April 5 and $3 million on April 6, the two days before the law became applicable. The money that was to prove so instrumental in the unravelling of the Watergate scandal and link it to the White House—$89,000 in laundered Mexican checks that were cashed through the Miami bank account of Bernard Barker—arrived in the Washington, D.C. office of Hugh Sloan, FCRP treasurer, late on the evening of April 5.[7] The four checks, plus $11,000 in cash, came along with $600,000 more contributed by Texans, including $50,000 from Clint and John Murchison, owners of the Dallas Cowboys. Throughout the month of March and up to the disclosure deadline, a steady stream of business executives arrived at FCRP headquarters in Washington with contributions, some giving cash later revealed to be illegal corporate gifts. Howard Hughes gave $50,000 in cash pre-April 7 and contributed $100,000 post-April 7. Another $100,000, held by Charles G. "Bebe" Rebozo until 1973, was returned to Hughes. J. Paul Getty gave $75,000 in the pre-April 7 period for a campaign total of $125,000.

With the Democrats deeply divided in 1972, particularly after the McGovern nomination in July, Nixon fund raisers sought to reach out for contributions from groups not normally found in the Republican camp. Some Jewish large contributors, long a major source of Democratic support, were wooed in a variety of ways. Secretary of State Henry Kissinger, then Nixon's chief adviser on foreign policy, spoke to meetings of wealthy voters in Los Angeles and New York in August 1972, with a view to assuring them of Nixon's strong backing for Israel at a time when McGovern's stand in that area was under question. Although no fund raising was done at the meetings—a condition of Kissinger's agreeing to appear—those attending were later approached for contributions. One who helped to arrange the "Kissinger seminars" was Gustave Levy of New York City, a senior partner in Goldman, Sachs & Co., who gave $90,443

---

[d]The promise of confidentiality could have its variations. One oil man said he would give on conditions of anonymity to all but four individuals—Nixon, Stans, John Mitchell, and Rogers Morton—who had some say on oil policy and quotas. These four, however, had to know of his gift.

to Nixon—$70,443 of that pre-April 7. In 1968 Levy had split his known contributions between the Republicans and Democrats—giving $7,000 to Republicans, $3,000 to Democrats.

Bernard Lasker, another split contributor in 1968 ($8,500 to the Republicans, $1,000 to the Democrats), was chairman of a Nixon fund-raising dinner in September 1972. He solicited support from the New York Jewish community among others, which grossed an unexpected $1.7 million.

Detroit industrialist Max Fisher, who was chairman of Concerned Citizens for the Re-Election of the President, an effort aimed at gathering Jewish support for Nixon, contributed nearly $250,000 of his own. Fisher gave $125,000 in cash in a pre-April 7 gift, and $124,773 after the disclosure deadline, most of it actually in 1973. He was also a Nixon supporter in 1968, giving more than $100,000. A Nixon fund raiser, particularly within the Jewish community, in both 1968 and 1972, Fisher was formerly president of the United Jewish Appeal.

Another traditionally Democratic group to provide substantial financial support to Nixon in 1972 was organized labor. In one respect, labor's major contribution to Nixon may have been in the funds it witheld from McGovern (it was labor's intervention with dollars in the 1968 race that was instrumental in helping Humphrey close the wide polling gap that existed early in the campaign and, in the view of some observers, narrowly miss defeating Nixon). Nixon received a known $165,000 from the labor campaign chests in 1972, $100,000 of that from the Seafarers' Union in a controversial gift raising legal questions. The Teamsters Union also contributed to Nixon, but the exact amount is disputed. On the record, Teamsters and affiliates gave $19,550, but former Teamsters President James R. Hoffa alleged that much more was given.

Direct Mail Appeals

Although direct mail did not have the importance for the Nixon campaign that it had for McGovern, the reelection effort also made extensive use of direct mail appeals. With some 30 million pieces mailed, this technique brought in $9 million gross. Prior to July 1972 the appeals to small contributors were conducted chiefly by the Republican National Committee. The RNC raised $5.3 million through its sustaining membership program during this period, with an average gift being $20. A telephone drive during this time brought in more than $500,000, with the average contributor giving $30. Together, the direct mail drives by the RNC and CRP brought in $14.3 million; combined telephone drives raised $2.5 million.

Various claims were made regarding numbers of Republican contributors in 1972. The RNC had about 250,000 givers, and national and state affiliates of the CRP combined claimed 600,000 contributors. Eliminating duplications and repeat contributors, probably 600,000 gave some money to the RNC in its annual program, its combined Nixon mailings after his nomination, or to some level of the CRP or Democrats for Nixon.

Democrats for Nixon

The most heralded adjunct to the Committee to Re-Elect the President was the Democrats for Nixon. This committee was founded in August 1971 to raise money and generate support from leaders and rank-and-file Democrats across the country who were unhappy with George McGovern as the 1972 Democratic standard-bearer.

John Connally, its chairman, set a goal to raise $2 to $3 million from disgruntled Democrats, and about $2.4 million was expended. However, Connally acknowledged that Republican loans and contributions financed much of the committee's efforts, and the CRP paid directly for most of the advertising by Democrats for Nixon. But the group's real contribution was in publicizing support from many more prominent Democrats than this type of committee, which is formed in nearly every election, is usually able to boast. Based in Washington, D.C., Democrats for Nixon had 14 regional and state affiliates.

Democrats for Nixon leaders included committee treasurer Leonard H. Marks, former director of USIA in the Johnson administration; Humphrey financial backer, industrialist Jeno F. Paulucci; former Boston mayor John F. Collins; Wallace's 1972 Florida primary manager, H.G. France; Miami Mayor David Kennedy; Florida Governor Farris Bryant; Democratic contributor and IBM Chairman Thomas J. Watson, Jr.; John T. Connor and C.R. Smith, both secretaries of commerce in the Johnson administration; International Brotherhood of Teamsters President Frank Fitzsimmons; athletes Sam Huff and Mickey Mantle; entertainers Frank Sinatra, Charlton Heston, and Sammy Davis; sons of the former President, James and Elliot Roosevelt; and even the wives of the loyal Democratic mayors of Milwaukee and Detroit. The staff director was George Christian, President Johnson's former press secretary. One of the better publicized defections was by a group of influential Maryland Democrats, including Harry W. Rodgers, III, a major fund raiser; Phillip Goodman, former Mayor of Baltimore; Dale Hess, former majority leader of the Maryland House of Delegates; and Irvin Kovens, millionaire Baltimore political broker.

The financial and publicity roles of the committee were minor compared to its chief function in the campaign: to attack McGovern. The "negative" media broadcast and printed about McGovern were sponsored by Democrats for Nixon, and Connally served as chief spokesman. This allowed the distinction to be made that the Nixon campaign itself did not spend its advertising dollars to criticize McGovern, but rather, to emphasize the positive accomplishments of the President, while disenchanted Democrats were attacking McGovern.

Financing for Democrats for Nixon advertising came indirectly from the CRP. An August 16, 1972 newspaper ad ("Announcing: Democrats for Nixon") that ran in 94 papers in 19 states, and cost a total $180,932, was paid for with an August 9 loan of $180,000 from CRP. Democrats for Nixon would also get certifications from the CRP for media broadcasts, would receive advances from the CRP, and would then repay the loans when they could, but that was not always possible.

The first broadcast spot package featured not Nixon or Agnew, but, instead, Connally attacking McGovern on his national defense views while identifying Nixon with Roosevelt, Truman, Kennedy, and Johnson. These spots were produced and the time was purchased in cooperation with the November Group, the CRP in-house advertising agency.

A study of voter reaction to three 60-second television ads Democrats for Nixon sponsored was made by Thomas E. Patterson and Robert D. McClure, co-directors of the Center for Opinion Research at Syracuse University.[8] Their research indicated that among voters with a high exposure to television, the "changing-stands" ad may have contributed to their views about McGovern's leadership qualities, retarding the normal expected gain in popularity for McGovern. Even more effective, from the point of view of Democrats for Nixon, was the "military spending" ad that showed miniature soldiers, ships, and planes being swept off a board, while McGovern's plans to reduce military spending were read out. The ad closed with scenes of Nixon aboard a naval vessel, while "Hail to the Chief" was being played, and the voice-over talked of Nixon's desire to maintain military strength. This ad had the clear effect, the study indicates, of McGovern registering negatively, while Nixon registered positively. A third Democrats for Nixon spot, however, attacking McGovern for his welfare spending plans appeared to have had no effect on voters.

In their testing, the authors sought to distinguish between what they term "image" beliefs and "issue" beliefs—the former, perceptions about the candidate, the latter, stands on given issues. Their findings are contrary to the popular view that TV is the place to "sell" the candidate, not the issue. In brief, voters seemed to see what they wanted to see in the candidate, and the TV spots did little to change that—their "image" beliefs tend to be "summary judgments based on many and diverse exposures to a presidential candidate." The "issue" beliefs, however, are more straightforward, based on facts that a TV spot can present in a short span of time. The research indicated, for example, that among the voters most affected by the TV spots were "those with an interest in the information but an unwillingness to attend to alternative sources requiring greater effort (e.g., the newspaper)."[9]

A 30-minute Connally speech broadcast in mid-October 1972—a wide-ranging and harsh attack on McGovern—was generally regarded as the most successful Democrats for Nixon technique and perhaps the best television of the Nixon campaign. Initially viewed in prime time on both ABC and NBC networks and other stations at a cost of $167,800, the program was judged to be so successful that a few days later $73,800 was spent for a prime time CBS network broadcast. The Democrats for Nixon campaign may well have proved crucial to the continued disaffection of millions of Democrats through the fall of 1972 and to substantial crossover voting in November.

In its report for the period September 1 to October 16, 1972, required on the 15th day preceding the election, the Democrats for Nixon showed media expenses totalling $329,155.73. Some $32,563 of this was actually spent in August on newspaper advertising, and was not certified until September by the Bureau of Advertising (which handled placement of ads for both the Nixon and McGovern campaigns). Other newspaper spending in September by the group amounted to $176,778 for full-page black-and-white ads that ran on September 26, 27, or 28 in 120 papers of all sizes across the country—from *The New York Times* and *Chicago Tribune* to the *Red Wing* (Minnesota) *Eagle* and the *Logan* (West Virginia) *Banner.*

The Democrats for Nixon proved particularly effective in undercutting McGovern fund-raising opportunities shortly after his nomination, by being first to get to a number of previous Muskie and Humphrey supporters. In some instances calls to prominent Democrats came directly from the White House; some stories claim that Nixon personally was making calls in an effort to get potential contributors in the Jewish community. Just how much in contributions McGovern may have lost through such efforts is speculative, but in fact his campaign at that time was preoccupied with the Eagleton affair, while Connally's group was hard at work. Max Palevsky, who left the Miami Convention angered by McGovern's staff, reportedly was visited at about that time by a White House staffer with the suggestion of consideration for a job in the next administration. He refused to give, and later returned to McGovern with important financial support. Walter Shorenstein, San Francisco real estate developer and a strong Humphrey supporter, was contacted by Connally to join the organization but declined. Apparently some promises of consideration for appointments as ambassador were made to Democrats. A number of Democrats who gave to Nixon secretly before April 7 were surprised when they were asked to give again publicly during the campaign. Other supporters gave only late in the campaign.

A January 31, 1973 report filed by the FCRP disclosed contributions to Democrats for Nixon, including $5,773 on November 3 from Deputy Secretary of Defense William P. Clements, Jr., and $4,000 on October 30 from Teamsters' Union President Frank E. Fitzsimmons.

Republican National Committee

Although much of the spotlight focused on the Committee to Re-Elect the

President, the Republican National Committee also played a sizable financial role in the 1972 campaigns. At the Republican National Finance Committee meeting in Washington in January 1973, it was reported that activities under the RNFC aegis had brought in just over $8.5 million toward the 1972 Republican campaigns.[10] Combined with the money that was raised by the Nixon reelection forces, in 1971-72, the total money collected by the presidential campaign and the national Republican Party came to more than $70 million. Adding in the senatorial and House campaign committees, the gross Republican total raised at the national level was about $74 million.

The RNFC contribution in 1972 had two objectives: (1) financing the programs and activities of the national committee and its satellite committees, which had a budget of $6,862,637; and (2) helping the Nixon reelection effort with direct mail and telephone solicitations after Nixon's nomination (for which FCRP made reimbursements), and with generalized support of the Nixon administration before the National Convention.[11]

The RNFC successfully reached its full 1972 fund-raising goal for the national party headquarters by late July 1972. This was done through a mail and telephone campaign early in the year that appealed to the small contributors with whom the RNFC has had much success in recent years. The Republican National Sustaining Fund was initiated on the basis of $10 per year per contributor, but later was raised to $15 per year. The program produced $700,000 in its first year; ten years later, it reached its high point, bringing in $5,282,000. Combined with other fund raising—for example, a RN Associates drive (contributors of $1,000 or more) raised $1,448,960—the fund helped the RNFC to end the year with a cash balance of $523,537. (See Table 7-3.)

Table 7-3
Republican National Sustaining Fund, 1962-72

1962	$ 700,000	1969	$2,125,000
1963	1,100,000	1970	3,040,000
1964	2,369,000	1971	4,369,000
1965	1,700,000	1972	5,282,000
1966	3,300,000	1973	3,964,000
1967	3,500,000	1974	4,759,482
1968	2,400,000		

After the convention, RNC finance personnel joined in the direct mail and telephone solicitation programs of the FCRP. The FCRP was supplied with its list of contributors to both the Sustaining and the RN Associates programs; in return the names of all contributors to the Nixon reelection campaign were later received. Whether, in light of Watergate, this gave the RNC a "very valuable bank of names for the future," as claimed in its 1972 Annual Report,[12] is a matter for speculation in view of the RNC's financial difficulties of 1974.

Together, the direct mail programs of the RNFC and the FCRP raised a total of $14.3 million in 1972 ($9 million to Nixon, $5.3 million to the RNC), with a $5.5 million expenditure for mail costs. In addition, the RNFC allowed the Republican Congressional Committee use of its lists of active and inactive contributors twice in 1972.

In February 1972, after finding in a test that telephone solicitation through commercial organizations was only a break-even proposition, the committee started its own telephone program using its own paid callers (mainly college students). Making tens of thousands of calls, they got pledges of $1.7 million but received only $544,000 in cash at a cost of $160,000. After Nixon's nomination, more telephone solicitation brought the 1972 total received to $2.5 million, at a cost of about $500,000.

In 1969 the RNFC had established two new categories of contributors, which fell midway between the $15 sustaining membership and the $1,000-and-over RN Associates—the Republican Campaigner Program for annual contributions in the $100-to-$500 range, and the Republican Victory Associates for $500-to-$1,000 contributions. Using computer-personalized letters, the committee raised $2,347,848 from these groups in 1972, of which $944,507 was raised by the Campaigner Program.

In its interaction with other fund-raising organizations, the RNFC provided $400,000 to the Republican Senatorial Committee from the 1971 "Salute to the President" dinner, while keeping $236,845 of receipts from that affair toward its own budget needs. It waived participation in the 1972 annual $1,000-a-plate spring dinner, permitting the congressional and senatorial committees to divide the funds between themselves, and also made cash grants of $300,000 each to these sister committees. The RNFC also gave $50,000 to the Congressional Boosters Club during the fall of 1972.

A number of the key members of the RNFC staff were assigned to assist the reelection campaign after Nixon's nomination, with their salary expenses borne by the RNFC. In particular, staff people buttressed the direct mail and telephone solicitation programs of the FCRP. Robert P. Odell, Jr., Buckley M. Byers, and Mildred Bighinatti, all of the national committee staff, were assigned to work with the reelection group on individual solicitation, group, and ethnic fund raising.

Republicans claimed about 600,000 contributors in 1972 had responded to mail and telephone drives, and that through the combined efforts of the RNC and the FCRP some 40 million solicitation pieces were mailed. They raised $14 million by mail and $2.5 million by telephone, for a total of $16.5 million at an overall cost of about $6 million—$5.5 million for mailing and $500,000 for telephoning. Of the mail money raised, about $5 million came from RNC mailings at a cost of 22 to 23 cents per dollar raised, while about $9 million was raised by the FCRP at a cost of 40 to 50 cents per dollar. The telephone money cost both committees about 20 to 25 cents of each dollar raised. The effort extolled the school of fund raising, which holds that to add a new contributor to the list, one is justified in a break-even cost of the first contribution, on the grounds that once added, a contributor will likely continue to give year after year at a steadily decreasing cost of soliciting future gifts.

In 1973 the Republican National Committee could measure the impact of Watergate by a large decline in contributions it received compared to the previous "off year," 1971. The RNFC received approximately $5.4 million in 1973, and had to rapidly reduce its original goal in what RNFC Chairman David K. Wilson termed "the political environment in the last half of 1973."[13]

Many contributors were turned off, some complaining that the RNC had not supported Nixon enough, while others could not understand why the RNC had not disowned him. In 1973-74 the leadership pronouncements were calculated not to upset relations with the White House, while trying to explain Watergate. The clearest and most truthful statement, that the RNC played no role in Watergate or "dirty tricks," was made repeatedly, and the Senate Watergate Committee completely absolved the RNC of any wrongdoing.[14] George Bush, RNC chairman, also admitted publicly that many donors were troubled because the RNC had raised money to erase a claimed deficit from Nixon's 1968 campaign, only to find out later that Herbert Kalmbach had secreted a $1.7 million surplus. Whereas after the election the CRP offered its surplus funds to the Republican cause, it soon became obvious that any such transfers would be embarrassing and probably would draw the RNC into litigation regarding Watergate. In any case, the litigation-related costs consumed most of the CRP surplus.

By mid-July 1973 the staff of the national committee was reduced by 25 percent, the national chairman voluntarily took a ten percent salary decrease, and certain activities were eliminated or cut back. The RNC was able, through such cuts, to end the year $309,485 in the black.

Republican Aftermath

The Republican Party's reform vehicle, the Rule 29 Committee, approved in late 1974 a series of recommendations that were aimed at preventing future Watergate-type excesses that might arise from a campaign organization such as the Committee to Re-Elect the President. In effect, the recommendations sought to put campaign financing into the hands of the RNC and under greater control by the national chairman. The proposals are to be reviewed by the Republican leadership two years after their adoption by the full national committee.

The committee called for the national chairman, after each national convention, to name a seven-member Select Committee on Presidential Affairs. Headed by the national chairman, this committee would be charged with obtaining from the Republican presidential candidate a full plan of campaign expenditures and periodic financial reports, in order to insure that all expenditures comply with the law and are ethical. A member of the committee would be one of three "designated agents" who would have prior responsibility for reviewing and approving presidential campaign expenditures.

The adoption of this policy by the RNC will implement a provision that was in Senate bills during 1973 but was not adopted by the joint conference committee and did not become part of the FECA Amendments of 1974. That provision would have required that the national committee of a political party be responsible to certify every expenditure in excess of $1,000 for the party's presidential candidate in the general election period. While the national committee probably would be subservient to the wishes of the candidate and therefore would likely certify all bills so as to prevent a rupture with the candidate, it was considered desirable by party advocates to insure that the national committee play an important role in the candidate's campaign. Unlike the situation in 1972, with excessive control by the Committee to Re-Elect the President, the hope was to tie the candidate to the party in a responsible and responsive way.

The Rule 29 Committee also recommended that the RNC have confirmation power over the finance chairman and general counsel, and set new dates for the election of the national (in the committee's words) chair.

McGovern Expenditures

McGovern's biggest single block of expenses was for broadcasting, for unlike Nixon, he badly needed national exposure. With what amounted to less than half of the FCRP budget, McGovern outspent Nixon by some $2 million on broadcasting. In time, the need to justify further expense on political broadcasts came with evidence from polls and other barometers that broadcasts were having little influence on voters. However, broadcasts were undoubtedly helpful in stimulating contributors and keeping them involved.

When broadcast money ran short, additional money and travel time were expended seeking free television time. McGovern would cross the country, speaking at public events which the local media would cover. Typical stops were for a Labor Day parade in Barberton, Ohio, a union picnic near San Francisco, a Seattle rally, a supermarket visit in Dallas, and a farm-implement plant tour in Peoria, Illinois.[15]

Travel cost a good deal of money when it was by Boeing 727 jets that the campaign leased from United Air Lines. United charged close to $60,000 initially for modifications to the planes. It then charged during travel $5,050 per day per plane, $445 per operational hour or fraction thereof, and $350 for each departure. Food and beverage charges were additional. When a trip was made on Eastern Airlines chartered aircraft, a $45,000 deposit was required on the Friday before a week of travel; thereafter it was $8,000 a day when in operation, $2,500 a day on layovers, subject to a $45,000 a week minimum.[16] The press travelling with the campaign, as well as the Secret Service, reimbursed much of these travel costs. Nonetheless, in the final accounting of McGovern campaign expenditures, the gross cost of air charter was nearly $1.9 million, with the net cost to the McGovern campaign $755,473. Postelection, mostly in 1973, $330,000 in travel reimbursements were added to the favorable financial result of the campaign.

After the broadcasting expenditures ($6.2 million), the largest functional cost was for direct mail ($3.5 million), which was the McGovern campaign's most publicized fund-raising device.

An early spending priority of $1 million was budgeted to register an expected seven million new voters. The Washington, D.C. operation had 25 paid workers, plus many volunteers, with about 15 additional field workers making up "troubleshooting squads" giving expert advice to the state units. But shortages and strategic disagreements led to the resignation of the effort's chairman, Representative Frank Thompson, D-New Jersey, who accused campaign manager Gary Hart of commandeering $350,000 earmarked for voter registration for other purposes—and the goals were not met.

An accounting by expense category of general election costs was prepared by CRF from checkbook entries for five McGovern central committees and accounts,[e] and is presented in Table 7-4. Additional expenditures were made through other accounts and by numerous state and local committees. In all, at least $30 million was spent, so the $18.5 million total shown here is incomplete; loan repayments, totalling $2.6 million, though not counted as expenditures, would bring total outlays accounted for to $21.2 million. For example, direct mail costs are noted here at $3.1 million, whereas a McGovern headquarters summary as of October 26, 1972 showed $3.3 million in direct mail costs, and later bills brought the cost to at least $3.5 million.

The local and state committees for McGovern were only loosely controlled, so an exact accounting of how much they spent is difficult. While they raised money on their own, many received transfers from national headquarters. At one point in October, the McGovern central committee estimated that more than half the funds it was receiving were going out immediately to the states to be spent on telephones, store fronts, literature, and the like.[17]

During the closing stages, the McGovern campaign outspent the Nixon effort for a period of ten days, mostly for television and other media advertising. About two weeks before the election, when over $3 million was collected by the McGovern campaign from the mail, the two major campaign committees, McGovern for President, Inc. and McGovern for President D.C., reported

---

[e]The committees were the McGovern Transportation Committee, McGovern for President Inc. Committee, McGovern for President Inc. Operating Account, Direct Mail Account, and Escrow Account. The period covered was from July 17, 1972 through May 31, 1973.

Table 7-4

1972 Presidential Expenditures by Five Central McGovern Committees, General Election

Expense Category	Amount
1. Media—broadcasting	
A. TV and radio time	$ 5,035,000[a]
B. TV and radio production	793,000
2. Media—nonbroadcasting	
A. Newspapers and magazines	962,273
B. Telephone canvassing	96,160
3. Direct mail	3,135,334
4. Campaign materials	176,049
5. Crowd events	25,200
6. Personal services	
A. Staff payroll	914,401
B. Outside professional services and consultant fees	269,763
7. Office expenses	822,339
8. Air charter	
Net cost	755,473
(Gross cost—$1,898,795; press and secret service reimbursement—$1,143,322)	
9. Field campaign	
A. Transportation	286,485
B. Other expenses	431,378
10. Transfers	
A. To state McGovern committees	3,074,541
B. To other organizations (e.g., for voter registration)	1,498,610
C. Payment of preconvention debts	267,410
Total expenditures	18,543,416
Loan repayments	2,634,969[b]
Total disbursements	$21,178,385

Note: These figures cover the expenditures from national campaign headquarters in Washington, D.C. Additional expenditures were made by numerous state and local committees not closely controlled by McGovern headquarters during 1972.

[a] Total network and nonnetwork broadcast spending by McGovern is reported at $6,210,788 for the general election period (in Federal Election Campaign Act of 1973, appendix A, *Hearings* before the Subcommittee on Commerce, U.S. Senate, 93rd Cong., 1st sess. [1973]. Hereafter referred to as FCC *Survey, 1972.*)

[b] Loan repayments are not counted as expenditures in order to avoid double counting.

spending $5 million for ten days starting October 17. By October 26 cash on hand totalled $202,720, while net debts of $2.8 million were listed. Though comparisons are difficult because of different accounting procedures, the six major Nixon units reported spending about $4 million during the same period, ending with a cash balance of $3.7 million. McGovern spent about $2.8 million for television and other media, while Nixon reported spending $500,000 less. McGovern collected funds at a rate of $470,000 a day, totalling $4.7 million, while individual collections for the Nixon campaign were about $2.5 million, plus about $280,000 from 25 state Nixon units.

Repayments of Loans

More than ten percent of the general election fund disbursements in Table 7-4 were repayments of loans—$2.6 million of a total of $21.2 million—from 66 individuals or groups (the latter chiefly labor groups). By agreement with note holders, these loans were repaid at the rate of 25 cents on the dollar biweekly as money became available. One of the note terms specified that one out of every four dollars contributed to the national campaign (whether solicited by direct mail, TV and radio appeals, or given by large contributors) would be set aside on a weekly basis to repay loans. Beginning August 14, 1972 each note holder every 14 days received exactly the same percentage repayment, unless that note holder specifically waived his repayment. (Mostly the unions, expecting little or no repayment, had agreed to waive some part of their loan repayment.) The only discrepancies that occurred in the amounts repaid to individual note holders came about by the timing of when the loan was made. For example, since the first loan repayment was made on August 14, only a portion of the loans to be made on the "one-for-four" program had been made by that time. There was approximately $160,000 in escrow for loan repayments on that date. With approximately $1.5 million in loans, therefore, each note holder received a ten percent repayment, and each note holder was repaid on exactly the same pari passu basis. By mid-October note holders who had made their loans before the first August 14 repayment had received a total of 50 percent return. Subsequent note holders received between 30 percent and 50 percent, depending upon when they made their loans.

Two weeks before the general election, staff members were warned that because of money shortages, salaries would have to be cut. Some shortages and salary cuts were partially created by the necessity to meet contractual obligations by repaying outstanding loans to wealthy contributors, triggering charges that the rich got their money while "poor" campaign workers went without. It was also charged by at least one disgruntled lender that the loan repayments were biased in favor of those close to McGovern, while those less close got delays or even less money. Three of the 500 or more employees who worked on the campaign sued for their lost wages. These employees, brought to the campaign by Lawrence O'Brien, former chairman of the DNC and one of those not considered in McGovern's inner circle, filed charges before the Minimum Wage Board and eventually were repaid. Officials said that all employees were back-paid by spring 1973.

A GAO audit shortly before the election disclosed that McGovern was receiving $35 a day expenses from the campaign treasury, while his wife Eleanor received $25 per day; other amounts were paid out for personal entertaining costs and extra help in the McGovern home during the campaign. It was learned later that McGovern's daughter Mary received $2,400 from mailing list rentals in 1973 for a 1974 summer job in Washington where she helped compile, sort, and file records on the 1972 campaign for historical purposes; three other persons were also paid from these funds for the project.

After the election central headquarters and various state and local committees had surpluses. In mid-October 1972 finance chairman Henry Kimelman had warned all known committees that the national campaign could not accept responsibility for campaign debts. Numerous committees tapered off spending accordingly, and ended with surpluses. Some 60 such committees—angered by Kimelman's message or thinking national headquarters had closed down—sent more than $300,000 in surpluses directly to McGovern's Senate office. Kimelman was not informed of the existence of that money until 1974, when some was sent to assist McGovern's senatorial campaign in South Dakota, and was disclosed publicly. Meanwhile, central headquarters had a surplus because some lower level committees had sent in left-over money; also, well after the election some loans due to be repaid were converted to contributions.

When the pressure for funds was at its height in mid-October 1972, Kimelman suggested to his fellow campaign finance managers, Miles Rubin and Morris Dees (who were also large lenders at that time), that all three convert 50 percent of their loans to contributions. They agreed. On October 15 all note holders were advised of that fact and were asked to do the same. The idea was to put the burden on the other note holders to do at least as much as the finance managers were doing. In effect, it was a "how could others do less" approach, inasmuch as the three were devoting full time without remuneration or even expense reimbursement. Most of the note holders had been prepared to convert some part of their loans to contributions. For example, a personal friend of Kimelman had agreed to a contribution of $30,000 at the convention. After explaining the pressing need for up-front money, Kimelman was able to convince him to loan $100,000 to the one-for-four program. Kimelman gave his personal guarantee that at least $70,000 of the loan would be repaid. As a result of the October 15 letter, some note holders agreed to convert 50 percent to contributions, others 40 or 30 percent. In spite of the considerable pressure for funds, 25 percent of contributions after October 15 were escrowed. The original group of note holders who had been receiving repayments from the August 14 date had already received 50 percent, unless they waived their partial biweekly repayment.

After the election, the campaign had no cash on hand and liabilities of $300,000 for past due payroll, vendors obligations, excluding commitments for loan repayments. In early 1973 it was suggested to suppliers (mostly hotels, printers, auto rental companies, etc. who had already made money from the campaign) that they agree to a lesser settlement of their outstanding receivables. A small amount, approximately $35,000, was saved through suppliers agreeing to settle for an amount less than their total amount owed them. Notable among 37 companies that forgave debts of over $100 (for a total of over $70,000 owed) at a rate of about 50 cents on the dollar, were Xerox Corp. and IBM. Xerox wrote off $9,606 as uncollectable, and IBM wrote off $1,575.

In December, 1974, $170,000 of the headquarter's surplus was sent to help pay bills incurred in McGovern's 1974 campaign, bringing the total to $470,000 of 1972 presidential funds used for the senatorial campaign. After those payments, $153,114 still remained, although obligations to the presidential campaign continued to arise and bills continued to come in—some for legal and accounting fees connected with investigations of the Special Prosecutor's Office, the IRS, and GAO audits. By mid-1975 about two-thirds of the remaining funds had been used up.

McGovern Sources of Funds

Three days before George McGovern formally announced that he was seeking the presidency, some 300,000 letters went into the mail, timed to arrive on the day of his entry. The seven-page letter discussed in detail his reasons for seeking the nomination, and appealed for funds to help the cause. This type of fund raising was to characterize the McGovern solicitations, bringing his campaign significant portions of the money raised, and helping him to wage the most successful financial campaign in Democratic Party history. Hubert Humphrey, both in seeking his party's nomination and in the general election, had raised about $15 million (including loans) in 1968, and his combined debts of $7 million drained needed Democratic Party funds from McGovern's general election effort and contributed to the party's divisiveness in 1972. Although the McGovern general election campaign was launched with a reported $280,000 debt, it managed to end the race with the first Democratic presidential surplus since Franklin D. Roosevelt.

Through a variety of appeals, primarily direct mail, about 600,000 persons contributed to the McGovern campaigns. Because of the widely decentralized nature of the campaign with much spontaneous grass-roots activity not accounted for, the precise number is difficult to fix. McGovern's national finance chairman, Henry L. Kimelman, estimated the number of contributors at closer to one million, claiming more than 200,000 contributors in the preconvention period, if one counts ticket purchasers to concerts, which raises the total by 100,000 contributors (bringing in $700,000), and contributors to McGovern local committees.

In spite of the financial successes, however, there were many moments when only the interjection of borrowed money—loaned in some instances by a group of young millionaires—kept the effort afloat. Lack of funds for television commitments was a frequent concern.

In the period of almost 15 months between the announcement of his candidacy and the April 7, 1972 disclosure date of the FECA, McGovern reported contributions totalling just over $1.7 million. Approximately $650,000 came from direct mail. Some $300,000 was received in the final four weeks before the disclosure date. These figures were disclosed by McGovern voluntarily, but because of the decentralized nature of his campaign, more was actually raised and spent, and when loans are counted in, about $2 million had been raised. Disclosure of the pre-April 7 receipts of the Nixon campaign, however, were brought about by the Common Cause law suit, and a comparison of the fund-raising successes of the two would be rivals in the general election is illuminating, even if the McGovern figures are incomplete. (See Table 7-5.)

McGovern's major backers in the preprimary period were relatively few. Chief among them were: Kimelman, who in McGovern's voluntary disclosure was listed as having made contributions of $30,307, plus $27,800 in loans and a $7,200 repaid loan; Max Palevsky of Los Angeles, who gave $25,000; and Mr. and Mrs. Albrecht Saalfield of Shaker Heights, Ohio, $31,000. Saalfield was headmaster of the University School in Shaker Heights. Listed for only $5,000 (and a $40,000 repaid loan) was GM heir Stewart Mott of New York City,

Table 7-5
Pre-April 7, 1972 Receipts

(In Millions)

	Nixon	McGovern
January, 1971 to March 10, 1972	$ 8.5	$1.4
March 11 to April 6, 1972	11.4	.3
Totals	$19.9[a]	$1.7[b]

[a]With cash, $21 million.
[b]With states and loans, $2 million.

whose contributions to the candidate later totalled some $400,000, making him McGovern's largest backer in the combined campaigns.

During July and August campaign receipts totalled $5,020,234 with expenditures of $5,090,540. Cash on hand totalled $25,226, and McGovern for President, Inc., one of the two major committees, received $2,064,467 in loans to that time. Loans enabled McGovern to raise almost as much as Nixon in this period, except that McGovern was pledged to pay back some loans. Nixon committees received $5,979,440 in contributions for the same period, including $1,659,196 in the three week period August 10-August 31. In the prenomination period—from January 1971 through the July convention—McGovern raised approximately $12 million, with a third of that from direct mail. While the direct mail effort continued through the Eagleton crisis, many traditional wealthy Democratic contributors hung back. A survey of 35 such persons in early August, who had previously contributed a total of $1.2 million to the Humphrey and Muskie campaigns, found only three who were solidly behind McGovern and intending to contribute substantially to his campaign.[18] Fifteen of the 35, however, said they would give nothing or only a token amount to McGovern, while 17 were undecided. After the convention, with a number of former Humphrey and Muskie supporters expressing reservations about Mc-Govern, the Democrats for Nixon drive headed by John Connally adroitly moved in on these disaffected backers and successfully siphoned off money.

Some of McGovern's problems with large givers went back to January 5, 1970, and his first meeting with Democratic businessmen in a New York hotel. When asked his position on Israel by Meshulam Riklis, chairman of the board of Rapid-American corporation, McGovern answered that lasting peace could only be accomplished by a negotiated settlement worked out by the United Nations. This position, which was not acceptable to Zionists, cost McGovern the support of some of the Jewish community, even diverting unprecedented resources to Nixon.[19]

McGovern's financial problems in the general election began almost immediately, when the Eagleton affair brought the whole campaign to a near standstill for several weeks. Missouri Senator Thomas F. Eagleton's brief candidacy as McGovern's running-mate generated more than 100 contributions; about $12,000 had been put in a special account and 70 additional checks had not been cashed at the time he withdrew. All the money was returned to the donors when Eagleton withdrew due to public furor over the disclosure that he had been hospitalized for psychiatric treatment three times during the 1960s.

McGovern was able to compensate for loss of regular Democratic money with a combination of loans and donations, substantially from the small group of young millionaires (mostly having inherited wealth) who were sympathetic to the issues he was raising, particularly on Vietnam policy. One example was Alan Davis, then a 24-year-old, third-year law student at New York University, whose family's fortune was in the insurance business. Davis lent $100,000 to the

McGovern campaign, in an interesting way. At the Democratic Convention, Davis and his wife told Kimelman they thought it was of vital importance to elect McGovern President, and they wanted to lend $500,000. Before accepting, Kimelman met with Alan's father, Leonard Davis, a major Humphrey supporter, who stated his dislike of political loans, which he believed were often not repaid. So the loan was pared to $100,000, and was later converted in part to a contribution.

Morris Dees, then 35, the millionaire civil rights lawyer and a key strategist in the McGovern direct mail campaign, lent an aggregate of $190,000 of his own money, essentially to get and keep direct mail efforts moving. As with the others who loaned money, Dees' loans were largely paid back as the small contributions began to come in. Max Factor III of the cosmetics family, 26, made a $50,000 loan. Stewart Mott lent up to $200,000 at any given time. Professor Martin Peretz of Harvard, whose wife is a Singer Company heiress, lent the campaign $59,000.

The McGovern campaign's financial statement filed in early September disclosed that a total of $2 million in loans had been made in August. Even larger loans were to follow: in the September 1 to October 16 reporting period some $2.9 million in loans were added to the August total. This represented about one-third of the total McGovern campaign receipts listed during this period. The largest of all loans came in during this period, and again it was from young millionaires.

Nicholas and Daniel Noyes, brothers then in their twenties, loaned a total of $500,000. Nicholas was a student at Indiana University and a conscientious objector to the Vietnam War; his brother Daniel was a congressional intern. The Noyes were heirs to the Eli Lilly drug fortune, and their grandfather was a contributor to Nixon in both 1968 ($3,000) and 1972 ($5,000).

Most of the loans in the general election period were made under what was termed the one-to-four program described above. This loan pyramiding was very successful, providing seed money for mail, and permitting other loan repayments. The Noyes brothers, for example, were repaid $100,000 of their mid-September loan by the time of the filing of the October financial statement. Some $4.7 million in loans were made in this program, and by mid-1973 the loans were either repaid or, in many instances the lenders agreed to convert the balance into contributions.[f] The repayment program led to misunderstandings and bitterness among some noteholders, who felt that certain lenders were receiving favored treatment in the quick return of their money, while other returns were being delayed. At least one lender threatened suit to get his money but did not follow through.

One plan to keep money in a primary state and use it for local purposes was formulated in Massachusetts. Twenty–five percent of the money raised at a

---

[f]For examples of loan conversions and loan repayments see Appendix K.

Boston $1,000-per-couple cocktail party was earmarked for the Massachusetts Democratic State Committee where it would be used to help pay Senator Edward Kennedy's Senate campaign debts from 1970—arrangements made by Kennedy's brother-in-law, Stephen Smith.[20] Kennedy, however, said that he had been out on the campaign trail for McGovern and had seen what the needs were; accordingly, he asked that all the money—which came to $50,000 net—go to the McGovern campaign. Kennedy had also earlier made an appeal for McGovern funds in a four-page letter sent to past Democratic contributors.[21]

Although organized labor was badly split over the McGovern candidacy, he was able to turn to labor for some support at critical junctures in the campaign. Some $400,000 of the initial $2 million in loans to McGovern in August while the campaign was struggling to get underway came from the political action funds of several large labor unions. The campaign borrowed $200,000 from the United Automobile Workers (UAW), and $100,000 each from the treasuries of the Communication Workers of America and the Machinist Non-Partisan Political League. The UAW also made an outright contribution at that time of $75,000 over and above the loan, while three other unions—Oil, Chemical and Atomic Workers; Amalgamated Clothing Workers; and Meat Cutters and Butchers —gave a total of $62,500.[22]

The use of show business personalities became a familiar part of fund raising for the McGovern campaign; a number of successful concerts held during the preconvention period grossed close to $1 million and a number of celebrities worked nearly full time for the campaign.

In September New York City was the scene of a two-day Art for McGovern exhibition at which the sale of 79 works by artists such as Georgia O'Keefe, Willem De Kooning, Claes Oldenburg, Louise Nevelson, and Andy Warhol grossed nearly $100,000.[23] A cocktail party by Publishing People for McGovern at the Tavern-on-the-Green in Central Park sold more than 1,700 tickets at $7.50 (and drinks at $2 each); among those present were Joseph Heller, Roger Angell, Isaac Asimov, Budd Schulberg, Lois Gould, Sue Kauffman, and Gay Talese.[24]

In spite of the loans in August, direct mail, and fund-raising efforts by celebrities, the McGovern campaign in early September was, in the candidate's own words, "desperately short."[25] This was before the full response to post-nomination mail developed. Morris Dees was so confident that the response would come that at the height of the Eagleton affair in August, he raised his sights from $7 million to between $14 and $15 million (the final total achieved was $12 million plus some $3 million from television appeals and $1 million from newspaper coupons). In mid-October two days alone brought in 160,000 pieces of mail response. McGovern made appeals for money to every likely crowd.

The need for money to meet commitments was such that certain major contributors were asked to make cash loans in order that stock gifts could be used as soon as possible. A gift of stock might take weeks to clear and be converted into badly needed cash. So a cash loan was requested to help tide the campaign over, and then was repaid when the cash from the gift arrived. And to the same ends, Stewart Mott opened a special account at Irving Trust in New York City into which he deposited several hundred thousand dollars of marketable securities, against which the McGovern campaign could borrow. Even a delay of three to four days, Mott noted, could be crucial in some instances.[26]

In October the financial picture was brightened by additional money from Max Palevsky. The founder of Scientific Data Systems, Palevsky became Xerox Corporation's largest stockholder when he sold his company to the larger one. Palevsky was McGovern's largest contributor before the convention, giving more than $100,000, and lending $230,000, but had differed with McGovern's staff over its reorganization for the general election campaign and the need to improve issue development to reach the larger electorate more effectively. He abrubtly left Miami Beach just before McGovern's acceptance speech. Palevsky gave more money in October, by contributing $183,000 in stock to make possible the repayment of loans he had made during the California primary, but he did not participate further in any other way. His combined contributions totalling $319,365, pre- and postnomination, were second only to Stewart Mott's $407,747 to McGovern.

When Martin and Anne Peretz converted a $151,300 loan into a contribution in 1973, they became McGovern's third largest contributors, with a total of $275,000. Fourth was Dr. Alejandro Zaffaroni, the Uruguayan-born President of Alza Corporation, the drug research firm, of Atherton, California. His gifts of $206,752.76 from stock sales came during October; he also gave $5,000 to Sargent Shriver's campaign. The Noyes brothers also converted $400,000 of their original half-million dollar loans ($205,000 from Nicholas Noyes and $199,317 from Daniel Noyes) into contributions. Mott, the Peretzes, and Zaffaroni were all large donors to Eugene McCarthy's campaign for nomination in 1968.

Next among the largest McGovern contributors in 1972: Alan (director of Colonial Penn Group, Inc.) and Shane Davis of New York City gave $158,872; Richard Salomon, director Squibb Corp. (pharmaceuticals), donated $137,752; Joan Palevsky, former wife of Max Palevsky, contributed $118,617; and Miles Rubin, chairman of Optical Systems Corp. (cable television), gave $108,000.

One large contributor "gave" McGovern $100,000 in 1973. However, the gift, made long after the election was lost, had been covered by a loan from Stewart Mott during the campaign when the funds were needed. John Lewis, a criminal defense lawyer with the Legal Aid Society in New York, promised to repay Mott with money from a trust, which did not come due until July 9, 1973. The $100,000 repaid loan is not included above. As of mid-1975 all loans but one had been repaid or forgiven. Hugh Hefner of Playboy Enterprises lent $40,000 to the campaign, of which 60 percent was repaid. The $16,000 (40 percent) still "owed" represents an amount that the campaign believed was converted by agreement to a contribution. The matter has not been pursued by Hefner and so remains open.

In the fall of 1972 Stewart Mott spent additional money in support of the antiwar effort (and thus in tacit support of the McGovern candidacy). He set up a "Vote for Peace" committee, and lent it more than $90,000 in order to purchase network television time. On the prime time half-hour show, antiwar congressional candidates were given an opportunity to air their views. Mott subsequently reported that the public response to the program repaid him only a small fraction of his loan, leaving $75,000 cost to him. This was a rare program in which a network agreed to sell time to advocates on a controversial issue. Mott also donated $30,000 to congressional candidates who opposed the war in Vietnam.

Direct Mail Campaigns

The key to the financial success and to some extent the preconvention political success of the McGovern campaign was the massive direct mail drive begun in early 1971. During 1971, when McGovern was the choice of, at most, fewer than ten percent of Democrats in the national opinion polls, $600,000 was raised by this means. Between the New Hampshire primary in March 1972 and the convention that summer, an additional $2.4 million was raised through direct mail; that spring some three million pieces were mailed. Thus, McGovern raised some $3 million prenomination, at a cost of over $1 million. In the general election campaign, $12 million was brought in through direct mail, with 15 million pieces mailed, at a cost of about $3.5 million to the national headquarters accounts alone; some state groups mailed their own in competition.

This fund raising had its beginnings in South Dakota politics where McGovern was a compulsive list keeper while he criss-crossed the traditionally Republican state. As he moved into preliminary soundings of his presidential chances, a record was made of the name and address of persons McGovern and his aides met across the country, which his aide Jeff Smith then compiled into massive lists.

In May 1970 along with several other senators,[g] McGovern had organized a 30-minute television broadcast opposing the Cambodian invasion, which raised almost $500,000 from 50,000 viewers. These contributors were added to the McGovern lists. Also that year he signed a massive direct mail appeal for the 1970 Campaign Fund on behalf of some fellow Democratic senators, and gained more names for his lists.

When McGovern decided to announce his candidacy, he consulted with direct mail expert Morris Dees about an announcement letter that would go out on his mailing lists. Dees called in Thomas Collins from the New York mail firm of Rapp and Collins to discuss combining the announcement with a fund-raising

---

[g]Democrats Frank Church and Harold Hughes, and Republicans Mark Hatfield and Charles Goodell.

appeal. The direct mail strategy subsequently adopted proved the most successful effort at this approach in American political history—more than tripling the Goldwater effort of 1964. Dees, whose loans to the campaign were partially repaid, donated his services.

Collins wrote for McGovern's signature an extraordinary seven-page letter, which outlined his positions on all major issues, in addition to announcing his candidacy and appealing for funds. At a cost of some $40,000, the letter was mailed to 300,000 names from the 1970 television and Senate lists, McGovern's personal lists (40,000 names), the membership of SANE (an antiwar organization), and Department of Agriculture lists of South Dakota farmers (100,000 names).

To the amazement even of some in the McGovern campaign, the mailing grossed some $300,000 from 16,000 contributions. Collins explained later that the mailing was successful because of the emotional issue of Vietnam and the general alienation of many citizens. Collins claimed the letter set forth clear stands that people wanted to hear, using his knowledge of the psychology of response in addressing the issues.

Inspecting the replies from this first mailing, Dees generated new strategies to keep the money coming. Before the Wisconsin, Ohio, and California primaries, contributors were asked again for more gifts. Some contributors gave on a monthly basis. In the pre-California letter, it was noted that Stewart Mott had promised to match each contribution, dollar for dollar, up to a limited amount. McGovern signed off the letter, "Will you dig a little deeper as your investment in hope?" That letter was claimed to have netted $600,000, exceeding both expectations and Mott's matching agreement.

In McGovern's nomination acceptance speech, a Kimelman idea—the Million Member Club—was announced, a concept seeking one million McGovern contributors—a goal never reached. Dees inspired a mailing to prenomination contributors, offering them a sterling silver "F.M.B.M." pin (for McGovern before Miami). During the fall campaign, a mass mailing offered a "sweepstakes" ticket for dinner at the McGovern White House, an effort that Dees said he believed increased response by 50 percent.[h]

Two examples of mail drive response to selected lists are shown in Table 7-6.

---

[h]The "sweepstakes" offer prompted some observers to charge that this was in violation of federal antilottery laws. (Title 18, U.S.C. section 1302). The letter's postscript said McGovern would invite 250 people picked at random from among contributors to a "peoples dinner" at the White House. Challenger Representative Victor V. Veysey, R-California, said the postscript had the elements of a lottery: a prize, consideration, and the element of chance. Dees, originator of the letter, admitted that the word "contributors" was a mistake, and that only 300,000 of the three million letters went out before it was changed to "supporters." The Postal Service investigated the matter, and then dropped it after concluding that dinner at the White House had no monetary value and was thus not a lottery offer.

Table 7-6

Examples of Mail Drive Response to Selected Lists

New York Review of Books Actives
(MP08) Magazine (liberal—book reviews, intellectual, political)
F 71,931

% 1st week	0.78	$ 1st week	$14,729	Average contribution	$26.21
% 2nd week	2.46	$ 2nd week	50,697	Average contribution	28.61
% 3rd week	1.04	$ 3rd week	22,487	Average contribution	30.06
	4.28%		$87,913		$28.52

Estimated total % 5.7 (4,110)
Estimated total $117,217
$ return per name invested $1.63

I.F. Stone Reports
(MP07) Magazine (liberal political)
F 61,985

% 1st week	0.93	$ 1st week	$15,888	Average contribution	$27.54
% 2nd week	2.64	$ 2nd week	45,295	Average contribution	27.62
% 3rd week	1.06	$ 3rd week	16,350	Average contribution	27.41
	4.63%		$78,033		$27.09

Estimated total % 6.2 (3,841)
Estimated total $104,044
$ return per name invested $1.68

Good use was made of McGovern's financially responsive constituency; givers were drained repeatedly. For example, lists of nearly 100,000 donors were mailed in early August, bringing in $1 million at a cost of $20,000.

McGovern mailings averaged about 16 cents a piece, broken down as follows:

Postage	$0.080
Letter	0.015
Envelope	0.008
Return envelope	0.005
Mailing house fee	0.015
Lists and record keeping	0.030
Agency fee	0.010
Total	$0.163

One major appeal of McGovern fund raisers was for loans from wealthy individuals to put into the direct mail drive. This seed money made it possible to reach out continually to the many thousands of small contributors, who, in turn, helped repay the loans.

McGovern invariably appealed for funds at the conclusion of his television broadcasts, and some five-minute programs were essentially fund raisers. Such appeals generated an estimated $3 million from the viewers. Broadcasts were timed to coincide with direct mail appeals that were already on their way. The aim was to have the appeal arrive in the mail about the time of the broadcast, triggering mail response by the television sign-off appeal.

An example of how a McGovern television appearance could produce a flood of contributions can be seen by his October 10 half-hour speech on Vietnam. For the two previous weeks, contributions from direct mail appeals had run from $700,000 to $800,000 each week. By Friday, October 13, however, three days after the speech, $1.5 million had already been counted for that week, and bags of unopened mail had to be stacked over the weekend. Additional volunteers were called in, and by the following Friday a total of $3.6 million had been processed and banked in one five-day period, $3.1 million of that from direct mail.[27]

The fund appeals tagged on at the conclusion of the McGovern television broadcasts were the result of the finance office winning a major battle with the political counterparts and Guggenheim Associates. No one was particularly happy about using a fund appeal, but there was no possible way to continue to pay for the time the political people wanted without generating income from these broadcasts. The $3 million raised from this source was claimed to be more than the cost of the TV and radio time in which the fund appeals were used.

In a mailing of plastic phonograph records, the McGovern campaign netted $100,000 at a cost of $10,000. Late in October, with money badly needed, a highly profitable Western Union mailgram was sent to many contributors.

For their roles in the direct mail campaign, Dees and Collins have since been approached by numerous political candidates for help and advice. Such "magic" cannot easily be transferred to other candidates. McGovern got started early, he had lists of responsive contributors constantly replenished by television appeals, and the war in Vietnam dragged on, triggering emotions among many McGovern supporters.

Nixon's release of the White House transcripts in April 1974 added a footnote to the McGovern direct-mail campaign by revealing that the Postal Service, on White House orders, was monitoring the volume of the McGovern mail. In his September 15, 1972 meeting with John Dean and H.R. Haldeman, Nixon asked both men about watching the flow, at one point asking Haldeman: "Have you had your Post Office check yet?" Although the transcripts do not indicate whether Nixon ever received a report on McGovern's mail, apparently the monitoring of the mail had continued through the last two months of the campaign.[28]

It also should be noted that a number of McGovern supporters, large contributors among them, were on the White House enemies list.

In the intraparty fight that followed his defeat, McGovern's list of contributors became the object of some dispute between his supporters and regulars at the Democratic National Committee (DNC). Claiming the list was his possession, McGovern ordered it impounded. (The list is owned by McGovern for President, Inc.) The leadership of the DNC, however, claimed McGovern had promised one-time access to the list in return for his use of a committee mailing list. Kimelman pointed out that the list would be no good to the DNC unless it were used for purposes with which the McGovern forces basically agreed, and that they could not expect to raise "anti-McGovern" money with the list.[29] Nevertheless, the list was productive, and at one point in mid-1973 it was claimed that two-thirds of DNC mail response came from names on the McGovern list. Adding this to previous DNC and telethon lists has given the committee a major resource, although most McGovern supporters were not National Democratic Party enthusiasts. After 1972 McGovern sold lists to selected buyers for income to the McGovern for President Committee and its successor, partially finding its way, as noted, to his 1974 senatorial campaign.

The favorable attention given to McGovern's small gifts campaign stands in contrast to the adverse publicity attached to Nixon's fund raising—highlighted by the illegal corporate contributions and suspected or actual cases of favoritism. McGovern officials claim that those large donors who gave asked nothing in return, and no jobs were promised should McGovern be elected. The only known corporate gift to the campaign came to light as a result of widescale investigations triggered by Watergate. A small, undetermined portion of $16,040 in Greyhound Corporation money went to McGovern committees (the unknown balance went to Nixon committees), but corporate records were lost. The Greyhound gifts were made in the names of individuals, and thus went unnoticed; the corporation was found guilty in 1974 of reimbursing officers for their presidential gifts. The instances of forgiveness of debts by Xerox Corp. and IBM, noted above, were not regarded as corporate contributions. However, in its subsequent investigation of the McGovern campaign,[30] the Watergate Committee did not challenge the legality of these acts but did question the campaign's purpose in seeking to reduce the debts while sums being transferred to McGovern's senatorial committee exceeded the total owed the presidential campaign's creditors.

Considering the small financial staff, it is remarkable that the McGovern books and campaign fund filings were as well organized as they were; none of the referrals by the Comptroller General to the Attorney General relating to McGovern committees were pursued by the Justice Department. The intense scrutiny of all 1972 campaigns by investigative forces such as the Watergate

Committee and the GAO charged no illegal or unethical activities by the
McGovern campaign.

Democratic National Committee

The Democratic National Committee confronted a particularly challenging
set of problems in 1972—much more so than their rivals at the Republican
National Committee. The latter, while eclipsed by the CRP, at least had the
satisfaction of both beginning and ending 1972 in the black. The DNC, however, began the year with a $9.3 million debt left over mainly from the 1968
Humphrey campaign. The matter of how much Democratic money raised in
1972 was to go toward retiring that debt led to occasional bitterness between
the McGovern campaign and DNC officials.

While the McGovern for President Committee was raising a record $30 mil-
lion for the Democratic nominee's campaign, other traditional sources of regular
Democratic funds were being siphoned by Democrats for Nixon and the CRP.
In the face of these countertugs, the DNC was able to keep the operations of
the national headquarters in the black, and to channel funds raised from a controversial preconvention telethon toward retirement of the debt. By year's
end, DNC Treasurer Donald A. Petrie reported that the debt was down to
$4 million. Petrie noted: "This may not be the only time in history that the
[DNC] reduced its current debt during the course of a campaign, but it certainly has not happened very often."[31]

From the convention until the November election, excluding the telethon
money, the committee raised $500,000. An important fund-raising project was
the DNC Associates program organized by Petrie. The program had a regular
membership, requiring a monthly payment of $98 (or $1,176 per year)—the
Republicans had a comparable category, RN Associates, which included donors
of $1,000 or more on an annual basis. By election time the DNC had 143 mem-
bers of the associates program; their contributions were providing a regular
monthly income for the headquarters activities.

Another 1972 innovation was the creation of the DNC Services Corporation,
a company designed to conduct all the housekeeping and business functions of
the DNC, thereby insuring corporate insulation against personal liability for
members of the committee.

One of the most important developments was the massive increase of names
on donor lists. By the November election there were 80,000 names on the DNC
lists, with another 300,000 from telethon pledge lists, and the promise of some
600,000 names of McGovern campaign contributors. The McGovern list, regarded
as a gold mine by Democratic politicians eager to make use of it, was jealously
guarded by the McGovern campaign. The list was finally made available to the
DNC and other committees in 1973; its value decreased through heavy use.

Another source of income for the DNC could hardly have been anticipated: the $775,000 it received from the February 28, 1974 settlement of its civil damage suit against the Committee to Re-Elect the President. The suit for $6.4 million in damages had not been filed with any intent of raising Democratic money; in fact the award proved to be near a break-even proposition. It was a way seen to force disclosure of Watergate details.

The traditional shuffling of the DNC major officers had an interesting variation in 1972. Coming into the convention, the DNC treasurer was Robert Strauss. He stepped down from that post following McGovern's nomination, and the candidate's own nominee for the job, Donald A. Petrie, took over for the campaign. Strauss then formed the National Committee for the Re-Election of a Democratic Congress, and served as its chairman while it raised and spent about $800,000 to help Democratic candidates for the Senate and the House in the general election. Following McGovern's decisive defeat, Strauss came back to the DNC as its chairman, succeeding Jean Westwood, whom McGovern had chosen as chairwoman. Strauss' move to the chairmanship was an unusual one, for a national party committee treasurer has rarely become a chairman.

Democratic Telethons

To overcome the $9.3 million debt largely left over from Humphrey's 1968 campaign, the DNC turned to the telethon. Previously used mainly to benefit charities, the non-stop continuous telecast was effectively converted to political fund raising, but only after a wracking fight within the Democratic Party as to where the proceeds from the first telethon in the summer of 1972 should go. Questions were also raised about the fairness doctrine and the equal time issue.

The first telethon, held in Miami Beach on July 8-9, just before the convention opened, was a star-studded 19-hour show broadcast nationally over ABC-TV. John Y. Brown, board chairman of Kentucky Fried Chicken, organized and underwrote the affair by guaranteeing its costs jointly with several others. Six thousand telephones, manned by 12,000 volunteers, were set up in 32 regional centers across the country. Contributors could even charge their contributions on certain credit cards.

The goal was $5 million, and the final tabulation from 300,000 contributors showed a gross of $4,461,755. Several hundred thousand more dollars were raised at a $1,000-a-plate dinner held in Miami Beach in conjunction with the telethon. Production costs of the telethon were about $1.9 million. The net amount to the DNC was about $2 million, because some 15 percent of pledges were not honored. Thus, the costs of this type of fund raising proved to be very high, virtually a one-for-one basis.

The first telethon was also beset by both political and technical problems. Actor Warren Beatty, who had produced the McGovern galas that raised more

than $1 million, refused to produce this show because the funds to be raised
on the eve of the 1972 Democratic Convention were to be used to pay old
debts at a time when the nominee of the convention would need funds. Paul
Newman, Ben Gazzara, and Joey Bishop refused to participate. Governor
George Wallace's wife, Cornelia, backed out of her promise to sing after her
husband became too ill to tape his segment. Mayor Daley cancelled the
Chicago phone bank when his convention delegates were not seated by the
credentials committee. Once underway, the video transmissions were garbled
occasionally and audio lines crossed. A water main break disrupted the New
York City phone bank for eight hours.

DNC officials had negotiated a trust agreement requiring that the funds
raised by the telethon be spent to settle the party's debt and to pay production costs before they could be used for the 1972 campaign. Robert Strauss,
who was then committee treasurer, contended that without settling debts with
industries such as the airlines and telephone companies, the Democrats would
have difficulty operating in the oncoming fall campaign. Candidates across
the country, moreover, would benefit by having access to the mailing list of
those people who had contributed to the telethon.

Front-runner McGovern was not happy with this agreement, but finally
went along. However, Stewart Mott, a major McGovern contributor and co-
chairman of his finance committee, did not. Acting independently, Mott
threatened to go to court unless part of the proceeds were turned over to the
1972 presidential nominee. Mott argued that the telethon funds would be
raised largely on enthusiasm for McGovern's candidacy. He accused party
officials of deceiving the public to believe the telethon would collect money
for the 1972 campaign. He also contended the 1968 debts could be postponed until after the election, and that settling them before the campaign
would be of no advantage because the party's credit had already been
damaged. But Mott finally decided against going to court, and the telethon
proceeded under the trust agreement.

The 1968 debt of $9.3 million, reduced by telethon and other funds to $3.1
million by the fall of 1973, was divided into three categories, as follows: The
$3 million in personal loans was paid back at a rate of 20 cents on the dollar (to
which all note holders who did not convert their loan to a gift agreed) leaving
none outstanding. Government-regulated creditors such as airlines and telephone
companies were paid in full, reducing these debts from $3.1 million to $2.6 million. Other general creditors were paid 25 cents on the dollar, excepting small
creditors who were paid in full, reducing this category from $3.2 million to
$600,000. Payments were made after the November election.

Undaunted by the problems of the 1972 telethon, and with the Democratic
Party now more united as the Watergate scandals were surfacing, John Y. Brown
went ahead with another such production in September 1973, this time making
the loan guarantee himself. The broadcast, "American Goes Public," a

deliberately shortened seven-hour affair to gain prime time was seen nationally on NBC-TV, beginning at 7 P.M. eastern standard time. In preparation for the event, advance mailings were sent to 600,000 names from the lists of the previous year—those from McGovern, the DNC, and the 1972 telethon.

This telethon cost $2,273,237, including the mailings. The break-down of receipts and expenditures shown in Table 7-7 documents why the costs of running telethons are so high. From $5.4 million pledged, an actual $4.2 million was received. This left a net receipt of just over $1.9 million, which was distributed, under a previously agreed upon formula: one-third to the DNC for the debt retirement, and two-thirds to the state party committees. The amount received by an individual state was determined by the amount that state's contributors had given to the total, that is, if California contributors accounted for 20 percent of the total, the state committee would receive 20 percent of the state money. Connecticut, Hawaii, and Mississippi did not participate. Amounts earned by states ranged from $173,066 for California, to Wyoming's $486.

A third telethon was held in June 1974, in an atmosphere charged with the issues of honesty in government and the manner in which campaign funds were raised. A 21-hour show, "Answer America," was aired on CBS-TV and cost the Democrats $2.5 million. Its net was about $2.7 million, with the same formula of one-third to the DNC, two-thirds to the state committees, obtaining in the distribution of the funds. Brown was an organizer but not a loan guarantor in 1974.

It was an ironic note, with the telethon theme so strongly against corruption in government, that Senator Humphrey should play a prominent role in the broadcast only a few days after the Senate Watergate Committee had alleged violations in his 1972 presidential campaign. Answering the charges, Humphrey said it was a "smear job" by some minority members of the Watergate Committee, and there was nothing wrong with the way he gave money to his own campaign.

Two Westinghouse stations, KDKA-Pittsburgh and KPIX-San Francisco refused to carry the 1974 telethon. Defense of the broadcasting company's decision was made by Westinghouse President Donald H. McGannon:

> McGannon, who has been identified with the Democratic party in Connecticut, his home state, said that his company had been "continuingly concerned" about political fund-raising through television because of the serious fairness problems that arise and because television licensees might actually be in violation of Federal statutes when they carried political telethons.
>
> He said that since CBS would be paying the affiliated stations advertising compensation for only 5 1/2 hours of the 21-hour telethon, in effect the stations themselves would be donating to the party the remaining 15 1/2 hours. That "can be construed as a

contribution by a corporation," he pointed out, which is in violation of Federal law.

"Political telethons create further serious problems concerning balance and fairness because of political statements and arguments made during those programs intended to raise campaign funds," Mr. McGannon said. He said that the current situation was particularly critical because this . . . will be the Democrats' third [telethon] in two years, while the Republican party had not had any in that period.[32]

The committees formed for the first two telethons—Democratic National Telethon Committee (DNT) and Democratic National Telethon Committee II, Inc. (DNT II)—were audited by the GAO to determine whether they had properly

Table 7-7
1973 Telethon: Income and Expenses Through January 31, 1974

Income		
Cash contributions	$3,292,739	
Credit card charges	556,055	
DNC-direct mail contributions	400,000	$4,248,794
Less refunds and credit card charge backs		(33,579)
Net contributions		$4,215,215
Expenses		
Network time	810,377	
Production cost	426,119	
Regional cost (postage–mailing supplies)	116,018	
Advertising and public relations	164,227	
State reimbursements (NET)	284,773	
Direct mail cost	150,000	
Credit card and bank service charges	45,622	
General and administration		
Salaries	57,029	
Travel	68,257	
Telephone	20,517	
Interest	20,538	
Data processing	64,566	
Donor Receipts	26,651	
Misc. (legal fees, freights, etc.)	18,573	
Total expenses		$2,273,237
Net receipts		$1,941,978
Distribution to states		$1,100,000

complied with the law. The GAO reported in November 1974 that although there were certain minor discrepancies in the reports filed by DNT and DNT II —chiefly understatements of receipts and expenditures—the two committees had generally complied with FECA regulations, and that no further government action was recommended.[33]

The Republicans, determined to learn from Democratic telethon success, scheduled a regional pilot telethon for the West Coast to be held in August 1974. It was cancelled at the last minute—another Republican casualty of Watergate— due to President Nixon's resignation.

By the time of the Democrats' 1975 telethon, held on the July 26-27 weekend, provisions of the 1974 Amendments raised an issue for the newly created Federal Election Commission: would an individual who guaranteed or endorsed a bank loan to the DNC to absorb telethon production costs be subject to the new individual contribution limits? The FEC ruled that such individuals are included under the top ceiling imposed. Guaranteeing a loan under these circumstances would count against the $25,000 overall ceiling on individual contributions to federal candidates. Just what amount would be counted, however, was left unclear—if the loan was repaid could the lender then still contribute up to the $25,000 overall limit within a calendar year? In its ruling the FEC set no time limit on when a contribution value could be assigned. In so doing, it may have helped open debate on an area of the 1974 Amendments that will be of some controversy.

Fund Raising Abroad

The drives for funds were also carried overseas by both Nixon and McGovern, who sought support from the Americans living abroad. In Europe alone there were almost 1.5 million Americans, making up a sizable proportion of the absentee vote.

The CRP had 12 committees in Europe, and held Nixon dinners in Rome and Brussels, fund-raising auctions, and parties for visiting White House officials. Chairman of the European Republican Committee was Clement M. Brown, Jr., a resident of Paris. In mid-October 1972 he said that although a "modest" goal of $100,000 had been set, he was doubtful they would achieve 50 percent of that.[34] Ads that ran in European newspapers urging support for Nixon were paid for by the FCRP in Washington.

The McGovern people claimed volunteers at work in 42 foreign countries as "Americans Abroad for McGovern-Shriver." They held rallies in Jerusalem, Copenhagen, Brussels, Hong Kong, and New South Wales; a picnic in Berlin; a party at the Hard Rock Cafe in London; a registration drive at branches of McDonald's in Tokyo; an art sale (works donated by American artists) in Rome; and a reception-dinner for John Kenneth Galbraith in Paris. The fund-raising efforts in Europe produced an estimated $35,000-$45,000, perhaps nearly matching the Nixon effort there.

The defection to the Nixon camp of Angier Biddle Duke, former ambassador to Spain, was a blow to McGovern. His financial and social influence could have been of great help to the Democrats' foreign efforts.

Whereas Nixon supporters abroad tended to be representatives of established business, the American Chamber of Congress, and American Club members, the McGovern forces abroad tended to be young—under 30, and many were women.

FCRP Requests GAO Audits of
McGovern Campaign

An innovation in 1972 campaigning was the registering of formal complaints to the Comptroller General about alleged violation of law or requests for investigations by campaign managers against their opponents. On several occasions Republican National Chairman Robert Dole of Kansas, and Nixon Campaign Manager Clark MacGregor complained to the Office of Federal Elections (OFE) that the McGovern campaign had violated the law. Part of the motivation may have been a desire to offset some of the damaging Watergate revelations about the Nixon campaign.

The initial group of charges by Dole were partially dealt with in a 38-page GAO report released on October 6, which referred three of the 14 charges to the Attorney General. These pertained to improper records for a New York fund-raising rally, improper acceptance of contributions from foreign nationals, and inadequate identification of sponsors in a newspaper advertisement. The referrals—over the advice of OFE staff members that the matters were only "technical violations" not meriting such action—were reported to reflect concern by the GAO and its OFE director, Phillip S. Hughes, that the newly created office appear strictly nonpartisan.

A later Dole letter and several matters under continuing investigation led to a second major (18-page) GAO report on the McGovern campaign on October 31. In this instance the Comptroller General "concurred in the recommendation of OFE that none of the matters raised by Senator Dole or discovered in GAO's own audit be referred to the Attorney General at this time."[35] The findings were that the errors appeared generally to be the product of record keeping and reporting deficiencies, which were being corrected. The bookkeeping arm of the McGovern campaign was understaffed, in part because when money was available for hiring more personnel, political activities seemed more important than more bookkeepers.

Both Dole and MacGregor wrote to Hughes in the week before the election, citing additional alleged violations. On January 18, 1973 the GAO released its third general report on the McGovern campaign, again finding no matter for referral to the Justice Department.

In March 1973 CRP official DeVan L. Shumway wrote Hughes that information had come to his attention that "a very large number of the McGovern Campaign committees, perhaps all of them" were in violation of Section 302(e) of the FECA of 1971, which details the manner in which campaign committees are authorized to raise money. He asked that Hughes investigate the matter.[36] Hughes wrote Shumway in June 1973 saying the OFE's investigation indicated that there had been verbal understandings about such authorization, but no authorization in writing for most McGovern campaign committees. He told Shumway that his office was bringing the matter to the attention of the Attorney General for whatever action he deemed appropriate.

Although the McGovern campaign registered some complaints with the GAO regarding FCRP practices, the charges did not instigate, but rather pursued, faltering investigations of Watergate-related incidents.

Minor Parties and Candidates

As noted earlier, minor parties and candidates relating to the presidential elections or reporting with the GAO spent some $1.2 million. Of these, the Schmitz-Anderson ticket of the American Party spent the most, but others attracted attention as well.

Schmitz-Anderson

Lame-duck California Congressman John G. Schmitz was the 1972 standard-bearer for the American Party (AP), the American Independent Party (AIP), and other strongly conservative groups. Schmitz won the nomination after George Wallace was seriously wounded in an assassination attempt and would not in any case have run on that ticket. Both Schmitz and running-mate Thomas J. Anderson, columnist and publisher from Tennessee, belonged to the John Birch Society. Unlike Wallace, Schmitz actually joined the AP. He became disenchanted with the Republicans and particularly President Nixon, who he said "sold out" to Russia over Vietnam, and criticized the President for what he called "liberal" domestic policies.

Schmitz and Anderson spent over $700,000, and ended their efforts with a $7,500 surplus. Most of the campaign's time, effort, and money was spent in California, though committees were established and contributions were reported from at least eight different states. The ticket was on the ballot in 33 states. Approximately $200,000 was spent for communications, 80 percent of which was spent for television in California. Schmitz, Anderson, and the American

Party filed a $25.2 million suit against three major television networks, alleging they were being deprived of equal air time required by federal law.[37] The suit was dismissed. They also made wide use of radio talk shows. A modest sum was spent for travel, campaign kits and salaries, mostly in California. During its height, the campaign cost about $25,000 a week to run.

Most of the campaign's large contributors came from the West and Midwest, with some from the South. Only a few came from the East, but of those, the Guydosh family of Pennsylvania were the largest contributors, giving a total of $10,000. The Agnew family of Centralia, Washington, gave a total of $9,000; J.W. Scott, North Dakota, gave $6,000; and Dr. Thomas Parker, South Carolina, gave $6,710.

Roughly two-thirds of the total money raised came from small donors: 53 percent was from $100-and-under contributors; 11 percent was from $100-$500 contributors; and 26 percent was from $500-and-over contributors. Some transfers-in from other committees were also amounts raised in small donations.

Transfers provided some discrepancies in record keeping—transfers-in and transfers-out do not cross check. Some of the discrepancy can be explained. For example, the American Party of the U.S. (AP/US) received almost $10,000 in transfers of under $1,000 each from nonreporting state units. These groups had total receipts of under $1000 and were thus exempt from the reporting requirements. But AP/US also received funds of over $1,000 each from a number of state committees that did not report. Sometimes the transferred-in funds, as reported by AP/US, exceeded total receipts plus cash on hand, as reported by the committee in question.

The GAO audited the national and 24 state AP committees, and the national and a number of local Schmitz-Anderson committees. Amended reports on campaign funds were filed by AP committees and by the Schmitz-Anderson Committee correcting the discrepancies to the satisfaction of GAO.

Roughly $50,000 of the $131,289 in transfers were nonlateral, or, funds from nonreporting committees. Total adjusted receipts came to $702,300, minus total adjusted expenditures of $694,320, and left a surplus of about $7,500. The surplus funds were returned to state chapters of the American Party and American Independent Party.

Fund-raising functions were usually low-cost affairs. One such dinner took place in Topeka, Kansas, drawing 125 people at $25 a plate. Another, held in Pasadena, California, drew 400 people at $10 a plate.

Other Minor Parties

The second largest spender among the minor parties was the Communist Party, with its long-time general secretary, Gus Hall, as the presidential candidate; the Communist Party was on the ballot in 13 states and spent $173,000.

Late in the campaign, the party bought two five-minute periods on a national radio network, at a cost of $1,500, for a statement by Hall to 190 stations in those 13 states. Radio spots were also bought on a New York and a Long Island radio station.[38]

The Socialist Workers Party ticket was headed by Linda Jenness, who early in 1972 said the party was projecting a campaign budget of $500,000.[39] However, the party ultimately reported spending only $118,000 and was on the ballot in 23 states. In reports on campaign spending, the Socialist Workers refused to identify their contributors by name and address, and brought civil suits in a number of states to protect the contributors' right of privacy against fear of harassment. In 1975 a systematic campaign of harassment against party members by the FBI was subsequently disclosed.

The Socialist Labor Party, with presidential candidate Louis Fisher, was on the ballot in 12 states and reported spending $114,000; earlier hopes for a bigger budget of $200,000, which was planned to be spent on one big national TV spot, were disappointed.[40]

The People's Party was a remnant of the 1968 reform movement, known then as the Peace and Freedom Party; it was led by Dr. Benjamin Spock and was on the ballot in ten states, spending $40,539.

8

Specialized Expenditures

Broadcasting

A major element in campaign financing is spending on political broadcasting. Among political expenditures, political broadcasting costs are unique because comprehensive and detailed data are available. The Federal Communications Commission (FCC) provided invaluable information for analysis of political broadcasting in 1972, as it has in its biennial reports since 1960. In 1972 a new factor was present. The Federal Election Campaign Act (FECA) of 1971 set a limit on spending in the communications media for candidates for federal office and established a sublimit on spending on the electronic media. This chapter explores the ways this new law affected broadcast spending as compared with past years, in terms of various levels of candidacy.

Campaign Publicity

Table 8-1 gives a breakdown of total advertising expenditures for the Nixon and McGovern national-level general election campaigns, based on information provided by the two candidates' national campaign organizations. The broadcasting charges in this table are lower than the FCC figures used in the discussion of political broadcasting that follows, because the latter reflect all network and station charges, including those for broadcasts placed by state and local Nixon and McGovern committees not controlled by national-level headquarters. However, the figures for broadcasting costs in this table are closer to the related FCC totals than was the case in the 1968 election.[a] In 1972 the Nixon committee's report shows broadcasting costs that are 88 percent of the FCC reported total for Republican spending, and the McGovern committee's report shows broadcasting costs that are 77 percent of the FCC total. By comparison, in 1968 the Republican report showed broadcasting costs that were 65 percent of the FCC total and the Democratic report showed them as 62 percent of the total. This greater centralization of broadcasting expenditures in the hands of the national campaign organizations is no doubt due to the limitation provision of the FECA,

---

[a]See Herbert E. Alexander, *Financing the 1968 Election* (Lexington, Mass.: Lexington Books, D.C. Heath and Company, 1971), p. 12. This volume contains most data comparisons for 1968, 1964, and 1960 used herein. See especially pp. 92-105.

Table 8-1
National-level Nixon and McGovern Advertising Expenditures,
General Election, 1972

	McGovern	Nixon
Time and space		
TV		
Network	$2,251,088	$2,152,000
Regional spot	1,820,000	1,125,000
Radio		
Network	120,000	333,000
Regional spot	700,000	234,000
Ethnic radio and TV		14,000
Subtotal	4,891,088	3,858,000
Adjustment	− 80,000	
Newspapers	962,273	670,000
Total time and space	$5,773,361	$4,528,000
Production		
Radio and TV	792,596	n.a.
Newspapers	n.a.	n.a.
Total production	$ 792,596	$1,500,000
Agency fees	220,000	884,437
Totals	$6,785,957	$6,912,437

which required strict accounting of broadcasting expenditures and resulted in greater central control over all broadcast spending by candidates. According to the Act, a broadcaster could sell political advertising only when the candidate or his authorized agent gave written consent to contract for such time and certified that the charges incurred would not cause him to exceed his spending limit.

The Republican national campaign formalized control over all advertising expenditures through a system of distribution by quota of political scrip (Figure 8-1) to all local committees and groups. Each certificate authorized a maximum permitted expenditure on broadcasting. By means of this system, expenditures on political advertising by local campaign organizations were strictly controlled. The Democratic national campaign's methods for regulating expenditures by autonomous groups were less formal and permitted somewhat greater local spending.

While the FCC figures enable a complete analysis of gross time charges, the disclosures by the candidates' campaigns given in Table 8-1 are particularly

---

ADVERTISING CERTIFICATION   № 5 3 7 0 7

- - - - - *ONE HUNDRED DOLLARS* - - - - - **$100.00**

I hereby certify that expenditure of the amount shown on this certification for advertising detailed on the attached documents will not exceed the spending limitation
of Richard M. Nixon, candidate for the office of President of the United States of
America, in the general election of 1972, as specified under Section 104 of the
Campaign Communications Reform Act of 1971 Public Law 92-225.

Issued to: .... Date: ....

ONIY THE ORIGINAL GREEN COPY OF
THIS CERTIFICATION IS VALID IN THE
AMOUNT SHOWN ABOVE.

Loghene Washburn.

AUTHORIZED SIGNATOR

Figure 8-1. Nixon Campaign Media Expenditure Voucher

valuable as they relate production costs to time and space charges. The total
expenditures for the 1972 national Nixon campaign are less than two-thirds of
the reported total for 1968. While the reported total for media production costs
appears to have declined by 25 percent from 1968 (from $1.98 million to $1.5
million), this is only due to the exclusion from this total of the fixed costs of
the November Group, Inc., which was established by the Committee to Re-Elect
the President (CRP) in 1972 as an in-house agency to produce all advertising. If
its agency fees of $884,437 are added, media production costs rise to over 50
percent of time and space charges for the Nixon campaign. Including time and
space purchases, production and fixed costs, the November Group operation
cost about $7 million. As shown below, the campaign materials budget for the
Nixon campaign was separate; although the November Group designed the
materials, funds for printing and distribution were paid directly by CRP and
were not channelled through the November Group.

On the Democratic side, while total time and space costs rose by over $1
million from 1968, media production costs in fact declined to 15 percent of
time and space charges, from 25 percent in 1968. This decline in the proportion
of media production costs occurred because the agency that was organized for
the McGovern campaign, Guggenheim Productions, Inc., charged unusually low
rates on all production and distribution work, as shown in Appendix L.

Generally, however, the production costs of political advertising tend to be
high. Production costs in normal advertising agency commercial work run about

seven percent of time and space charges, but 20 to 50 percent production charges are not unusual in politics, because of the crash nature of campaigns, overtime, new issues cropping up, and the scrapping of undesirable spot announcements. For example, in Robert Kennedy's 1968 primary campaign, which was undertaken at very short notice, broadcast production costs were at least 50 percent of the broadcast time costs.

The Federal Election Campaign Act of 1971 and Broadcasting Costs

The FECA affected broadcasting in several significant ways, imposing the following limitations and restrictions in areas where none had existed. First, the law limited the amounts candidates for federal offices could spend on radio, television, cable television, newspapers, magazines, billboards, and automated telephone systems in any primary, runoff, special or general election to ten cents times the voting-age population of the geographical unit covered by the election, or $50,000, whichever was greater. Second, it restricted candidates to spend no more than 60 percent of their media expenditures on broadcast advertising. And third, it provided that the broadcast media could not charge candidates more than the lowest unit rate charged any other advertiser for the same class and amount of time or space for a period extending 45 days preceding a primary election or 60 days preceding a general or special election. At other times, rates could not exceed the charges made for comparable use for other purposes.

The provision of the FECA that limited broadcast expenditures varied in significance for the campaigns for different offices. For example, in the presidential general election, the limits on spending set by the law apparently did not directly determine the level of broadcast spending. Both Nixon and McGovern spent well under the $8.5 million limit set for presidential and vice-presidential candidates in the postnomination period.[1] For the Democrats, the $8.5 million limit was in any event much higher than they had ever spent on broadcasting in a presidential general election campaign, and the $6.2 million spent in the McGovern campaign was the highest Democratic total to date. While Republican spending in 1968 had been well over this limit ($12.6 million), in 1972 the much lower expenditure for broadcasting ($4.3 million) was more the result of a campaign strategy in which spending was diverted to other areas than of the constraints of the law. As a spokesman for the Nixon reelection committee stated, the campaign concentrated on an "extensive people to people program" rather than on air time.[2]

The FECA may have contributed indirectly to some shifts in spending for both Republicans and Democrats away from broadcasting to unregulated areas, such as direct mail operations, campaign consultants, computers, and pollsters.

The most striking increase was in the use of direct mail as a medium of communication. In some cases direct mailing was not employed merely as a substitute for broadcast communication, but was regarded as a superior means for reaching specially targeted groups with individualized messages. The Nixon campaign letters to ethnic blocs such as the eastern European groups are an example. Direct mailing has thus emerged as a medium of increased importance. Since the 1974 Amendments provide strict limitations on amounts individuals can contribute, candidates may be forced to an even greater use of mail solicitation for the many small contributions that are fast becoming a campaign necessity.

The spending limits may have had more direct impact in the other federally regulated races than on the presidential campaigns. The 1972 total broadcasting costs of $6.4 million for senatorial races are much lower than the 1970 total of $16 million, and even than the 1968 total of $10.4 million.[b] In most senatorial and House races the actual spending was much less than the allowed limit. In 34 senatorial races, four candidates appear to have overspent the general election limit. In one race, both overspent. Of the two races in which one candidate overspent, one won and one lost. In Senate primaries, two overspent, one winning and one losing. Nine House candidates appear to have exceeded the spending limit in the primary and general election each. Of these three were winners.[3] No prosecutions occurred.

While the broadcasting costs of House races did increase from 1970, from $6.1 million to $7.5 million, the increase is slight compared to the rise in spending in gubernatorial races.[4] Between 1968 and 1972 expenditures in gubernatorial races increased by 50 percent, from $6.2 million to $9.7 million. Expenditures for all other state and local offices increased to 40 percent of total broadcast costs in 1972,[5] while in 1968 their combined total with House races was 23 percent.[c]

Of more general importance in limiting expenditures was the FECA requirement that broadcasters charge political candidates the lowest unit cost for the same advertising time available to commercial advertisers. This provision affected spending in the anticipated sense that the cost-per-time segment dropped sharply. In one extreme case a radio station, which had charged $42 for a political spot before the law was enacted, now was obliged to charge at its

---

[b]See *Federal Election Campaign Act of 1973*, Appendix A, *Hearings* before the Subcommittee on Commerce, U.S. Senate, 93rd Cong. 1st Sess. (1973). Hereafter referred to as FCC, *Survey 1972*. See table 11, for 1972 totals, and "Broadcast Spending: Presidential, Senate Costs Drop," *Congressional Quarterly*, May 12, 1973, p. 1134. See also Paul A. Dawson and James E. Zinser, "Broadcast Expenditures and Electoral Outcomes in the 1970 Congressional Elections," *Public Opinion Quarterly*, XXXV, 3 (Fall 1971), 398-402.

[c]*Survey of Political Broadcasting, Primary and General Election Campaigns of 1968* (Washington, D.C.: Federal Communications Commission, August 1969), p. 1. Hereafter referred to as FCC, *Survey 1968*. The 1968 FCC Survey combined House and state and local races (excluding gubernatorial) in one category.

lowest unit rate of $4 for the same time spot. An unanticipated consequence was that as the profitability of political broadcasting declined, less time was made available by broadcasters for political use. Total broadcast spending, therefore, was kept down by a combination of a reduction in actual cost and a limited supply of available time.

The provisions of the FECA regarding the media were seen by some, chiefly the broadcasters themselves, as creating difficulties and hardships. Increased amounts of paperwork, for example, were inevitable with regard to the certification process; stations had to obtain not only certifications but also written authorization from candidates for their agents making the certification. Stations had to retain the certification in their public files for two years. Of particular concern to the broadcasters was the provision that broadcasters must sell candidates time at the lowest unit rate; they saw it as discriminatory because the print media was not similarly regulated. Others worried about the economic consequences of lowered rates. Broadcasters tried but were unsuccessful in having the lowest unit rate provision declared unconstitutional; they were successful (along with newspaper publishers) in the *ACLU* v. *Valeo* decision — described elsewhere — which declared unconstitutional the enforcement procedures for the media limitations, which placed responsibilities on media vendors, reinforced by criminal sanctions if violations occurred, with respect to time and space certifications by candidates.

The growth in overall broadcast spending by federal candidates in the 1972 campaign seems to have been slowed or reversed. It is too soon to draw a detailed picture of the FECA's impact. For example, it cannot be determined where stable or declining expenditures as compared to 1968 signify lowered costs or less time purchased or both. It is known that the lowest unit rates permitted more time to be purchased by candidates at costs similar to or less than in 1968 or 1970, in spite of inflation and price rises. On the other hand, it has not been determined to what extent the spending limits exercised a restraining effect on broadcast spending or if in fact candidates would have spent more if there had been a higher limit. Nonetheless, the fact that the amounts spent for broadcasting increased so sharply in gubernatorial and state and local categories, where the lowest unit charge applied but the expenditure limitations did not, suggests that the law must be considered to have had a real, if unmeasured, impact in limiting broadcast spending in federal campaigns.

Political Broadcasting: The FCC Report

The total spent on political broadcasting in 1972 between January 1 and November 7 as reported by the FCC—representing all network and station charges for both television and radio usage by candidates and supporters at all levels for both primaries and general election periods—was $59.6 million.[6]

This figure is only $.7 million greater than the total for 1968, or an increase of one percent, and it represents an interruption of the trend of sharply rising broadcasting expenditures from one presidential election year to the next. Between the 1960 and 1964 elections, and between the 1964 and 1968 elections, the increases were in the 70 percent range. Between 1964 and 1968 radio expenditures rose 93 percent and television 60 percent; between 1968 and 1972 radio expenditures rose by only seven percent (from $20.9 million to $22.4 million) while television expenditures declined by two percent, from $38 million to $37.2 million.[7] The decline of television expenditures occurred in the general election period (from $27 million in 1968 to $24.6 million in 1972), while spending on television in the primaries increased by $1.7 million (from $10.9 million in 1968 to $12.6 million in 1972).[8] While radio spending increased slightly in the general election period (to $13.5 million in 1972 from $13.3 million in 1968), the larger increase, as in 1968, was in the primaries ($8.8 million in 1972, compared with $7.6 million in 1968).[9]

The very slight increase in total political broadcasting costs is evidence of its relative decline in importance in campaign spending rather than of any slowing of the rate of increase of total campaign expenditures. Total political spending in 1972 rose to $425 million from $300 million in 1968. Political broadcasting costs thus declined to 14 percent of the total, from 19.6 percent in 1968, and were even lower than the estimated 17.3 percent of the total in 1964. Some of the reasons for this decline in the proportion spent on political broadcasting are the emergence in importance of nonbroadcast media of communication, such as direct mailing, and the regulations of the new law. Nonetheless, at 15 percent of the estimated total of expenditures, it remains as the largest identifiable cost in political campaigns.

The additional production and promotion costs incurred in connection with broadcasting raise this total considerably. If average production costs and agency fees of 25 percent, which, as indicated earlier, may be low, are added to the total broadcast expenditures of $59.6 million for 1972, the cost of broadcast advertising to candidates was approximately $75 million. To this figure must be added the cost of "tune-in" ads in newspapers and other promotional expenses. Thus, at least $80 million, about one-fifth of the estimated total of all political spending, is directly related to political broadcasting. If one were to add other allied costs—travel to the broadcast city, speech writing, and other such planning and preparation—then a total of 50 percent more than the $59.6 million total time costs would not be unreasonable, making broadcast-related expenses as much as $90 million for 1972.

Primary and General Election Costs

The total broadcast spending by Democrats in all contests in 1972 exceeded that by Republicans by $13.7 million, all accounted for by greater Democratic spending in the primaries. Combining primary and general election expenditures, the Democrats spent $34.4 million and the Republicans $20.8 million.[10] This is 93 percent of the total of broadcast expenditures. Other parties and independents spent $4.5 million, 88 percent of which was in state and local elections.[11] The Democratic and Republican totals differ considerably from 1968, when each party spent an equal total of $27.9 million. The 1972 gap is the result of, on the one hand, a $6.5 million, or 23 percent, increase in spending for the Democrats and, on the other, a $7.1 million, or 25 percent decline in total spending for the Republicans.

In 1972 total primary spending by all parties increased to $21.5 million from $18.5 million in 1968, making the primaries' share 36 percent of 1972 total political broadcasting spending, as opposed to 31 percent in 1968.[12] Total Democratic primary spending increased from $12.4 million in 1968 to $16.9 million in 1972, and the Republican total decreased from $5.4 million in 1968 to $3.2 million in 1972.[13] All other parties spent $1.4 million in the primaries, over 99 percent of which was in state and local elections.[14] Given in percentages of the total primary spending on broadcasting by all parties in 1972, the Democratic total is 79 percent, as opposed to 67 percent in 1968, and the Republican total is 15 percent, as opposed to 29 percent in 1968. As a share of its own broadcasting totals, Republican spending in primaries dropped to 15 percent from 19 percent in 1968, while Democratic spending increased to 49 percent of the party's total from 44 percent in 1968.

Thus, in 1972 the Democrats maintained the pattern of outspending the Republicans in the primaries, this time vastly, by $13.7 million. While in 1968 they had outspent them 2.5 times, in 1972 it was by more than five times. The disparity between the extremely low Republican presidential primary spending of $67,000 and the Democratic presidential primary total of $3.4 million does not alone account for the widened gap. Excluding the presidential primaries, the Democrats still exceeded Republican primary spending by four times ($13.5 million to $3.2 million.)[15] Spending totals in Democratic primaries continue to be much higher because in many states and localities with higher Democratic registration, winning the Democratic nomination is tantamount to winning the election, so the stakes are higher. In many elections Democratic candidates spend more in the primary, where competition is fiercer, than in the general election.

Total expenditures by the major parties for 1964, 1968, and 1972 are shown in Table 8-2. It should be noted that in 1972 the FCC report included for the first time figures on spending on cablecasting (CATV), and these are included in all television spending totals. However, most political time on CATV is given free of cost, which means nearly all of the spending total for television is for commercial television. In fact, the total spending in 1972 on CATV amounted to only $74,000.[16]

Table 8-2

Total Television and Radio Network and Station Charges for Political Broadcasting by Election and Major Party: 1964, 1968, and 1972

	(In Millions)					
	1964		1968		1972	
	Rep.	*Dem.*	*Rep.*	*Dem.*	*Rep.*	*Dem.*
Primary	$ 2.9	$ 6.8	$ 5.4	$12.4	$ 3.2	$16.9
General election	13.0	11.0	22.5	15.5	17.5	17.5
Totals	$15.9	$17.8	$27.9	$27.9	$20.8	$34.4

Sources: *Survey of Political Broadcasting, Primary and General Election Campaigns of 1964* (Federal Communications Commission, July, 1965), table 1; *Survey of Political Broadcasting, Primary and General Election Campaigns of 1968* (Washington: Federal Communications Commission, August, 1969), table 1. Publication hereafter cited as FCC, *Survey 1968; Survey 1972*, table 14.

Note: Totals in tables may not add due to rounding.

In all presidential elections, from 1952 to 1968, Republicans outspent Democrats in total general election spending on broadcasting. In 1972, however, the totals of the two parties for the general election period were the same, $17.5 million.[17] This closing of the gap, which in 1968 indicated 46 percent greater spending by the Republicans, was produced by a drop of $5 million in Republican spending and an increase of $2.1 million in Democratic spending. The proportional spending for radio and television in the general election for both Democrats and Republicans was approximately the same, 34 percent for radio and 66 percent for television.[18]

In the general elections a total of $38.1 million was spent by all candidates of all parties on broadcasting,[19] a decline of $2.3 million (six percent) from the 1968 total. This decline represents a reversal of sharply rising broadcasting expenditures in general elections since 1952, with an average rise between elections (until 1968) of 60 percent. Still, the 1972 total was over six times the amount spent in 1952, the year television first became a major expense item in national campaigns: television expenditures in 1972 were eight times the 1952 level, while radio expenditures had more than quadrupled in the 20 years. In the 1972 general election, the Democrats spent 34 percent of their total broadcast expenditures on radio, as compared with 32 percent in 1968, and Republicans spent 34 percent on radio, as compared with 33 percent in 1968. It should be noted that there was a levelling-off of the rapid rise in the share of radio expenditures over the course of the last several elections. Table 8-3 details the expenditures for broadcasting in the last six presidential year general elections (equivalent figures for the primary periods are not available for 1952-56-60).

Table 8-3

**Distribution of General Election Costs for Broadcasts by Party and Facility:
1952, 1956, 1960, 1964, 1968, and 1972**

			(In Millions)			
	1952	*1956*	*1960*	*1964*	*1968*	*1972*
Republicans	$3.5	$5.4	$ 7.6	$13.0	$22.5	$17.5
Democrats	2.6	4.1	6.2	11.0	15.4	17.5
Other	——	0.3	0.4	0.6	2.5	3.1
Totals	$6.1	$9.8	$14.2	$24.6	$40.4	$38.1
Television	$3.0	$6.6	$10.1	$17.5	$27.1	$24.6
Radio	3.1	3.2	4.1	7.1	13.3	13.5

Sources: 1952, Alexander Heard, *The Costs of Democracy* (Chapel Hill, N.C.: The University of North Carolina Press, 1960), p. 22; 1956-68, FCC, *Survey 1968*, table 3; 1972, FCC, *Survey 1972,* table 11.

The Presidential Campaigns

The total spent on broadcasting by all presidential and vice-presidential candidates in primary and general elections in 1972 was $14.3 million. The Democrats spent $9.7 million, the Republicans $4.4 million, and $300,000 was spent by other parties.[20] This is about half the $28.5 million spent on presidential campaigns in 1968. A significant difference, as well, in 1972 was the absence of a strong third-party candidate such as George Wallace had been in 1968, when $2 million was spent by minor parties. While in 1968 the totals spent on presidential campaigning represented about 48 percent of total political broadcasting costs, only about 24 percent was so spent in 1972. By comparison, the senatorial races were 11 percent of the total (18 percent in 1968), House races 13 percent (no comparable figures for 1968), and gubernatorial 17 percent, as opposed to 10.5 percent in 1968.

This precipitous drop in presidential broadcast spending represents, first, a decline in total presidential primary expenditures on broadcasting to $3.5 million in 1972,[21] from $8.2 million in 1968. This decline is disproportionately large in relation to the total decline in presidential broadcast spending, with presidential primary broadcast costs at 16 percent of the primary total for broadcasting in 1972 as opposed to 44 percent in 1968. Presidential general election broadcast costs dropped from $20.3 million in 1968 to $10.8 million in 1972.[22] In 1972, presidential general election broadcast costs were only 28 percent of the total general election broadcast spending, while in 1968 they were 50.2 percent. Table 8-4 details the presidential broadcast totals.

Table 8-4

Network and Station Charges for Presidential and Vice-Presidential Candidates by Party, Primary, and General Elections, 1972

(In Millions)

	Rep.	Dem.	Other
Primary			
Television	$0.03	$2.3	$0.002
Radio	0.03	1.1	0.003
Totals	$0.07	$3.4	$0.005
General Election			
Television	3.6	4.8	0.2
Radio	0.7	1.4	0.1
Totals	$4.3	$6.2	$0.3

Source: FCC *Survey 1972,* table 11.

Much of the actual decline is accounted for by a sharp drop in Republican presidential broadcast spending, from $15.6 million in 1968, to $4.4 million in 1972. While in 1968 Republicans spent over $3 million in the presidential primaries, in 1972 they spent only $70,000. This was due, of course, to the fact of an incumbent president, who faced only minor opposition from Representatives McCloskey and Ashbrook. In the general election the Republicans spent only $4.3 million, compared with $12.6 million in 1968.[23] Naturally, the division between primary and general election spending changed sharply. While in 1968 the Republicans spent 19 percent of total presidential broadcast spending in the primaries, it was only 1.5 percent in 1972.

While the Democratic spending total in the presidential primary and general election was higher than for the Republicans, it too declined since 1968, from $10.9 million to $9.7 million in 1972.[24] Although Democrats continued to outspend Republicans in the primaries ($4.8 million to $3 million in 1968 and $3.4 million to $70,000 in 1972), in the general election they also outspent the Republicans, $6.2 million to $4.3 million. This is a reversal of 1968 (and other presidential general elections) when the Republicans spent $12.6 million to the Democrats' $6.1 million. While Democratic presidential primary broadcast costs decreased by 29 percent from 1968, their general election costs increased by 1.7 percent.

The pattern of spending by facility differed for each major party. In 1968 both parties spent approximately 2.5 times as much on television as on radio. In 1972 the Democrats spent nearly three times as much, while the Republicans spent five times as much.[25] Television expenditures for the presidential contests declined to 30 percent of total television broadcast costs from 56 percent in

1968, and radio expenditures declined to 15 percent from 36 percent. The 1964, 1968, and 1972 costs by facility are compared in Table 8-5.

Table 8-5
Network and Station Charges for Presidential and Vice-Presidential
Candidates by Facility, Primary, and General Election: 1964, 1968,
and 1972

	(In Millions)		
	1964	*1968*	*1972*
Primary election			
Television	$ 1.2	$ 6.2	$ 2.3
Radio	0.6	2.0	1.2
Totals	$ 1.8	$ 8.2	$ 3.5
General election			
Television	$ 8.9	$14.6	$ 8.6
Radio	2.1	5.7	2.2
Totals	$11.0	$20.3	$10.8

Sources: FCC, *Survey 1964*, tables 1, 9A, 22A; *Survey 1968,* tables 1, 9, 20; *Survey 1972,* table 11.

The lower presidential campaign broadcast spending is due to several factors. As discussed earlier, the limit set by the 1972 election law was probably not significant. The broadcast media spending limit for presidential candidates in the general election was $8.5 million. Both McGovern and Nixon underspent this limit by comfortable margins; McGovern's broadcast spending was $6.2 million, and Nixon's was only $4.3 million. More significant in determining the lower spending was the Nixon strategy to communicate with and mobilize potential groups of voters by mail and telephone drives, and the McGovern problem in raising more money amid little evidence that McGovern's greater broadcast spending was influencing the electorate or the polls.

The Nixon broadcast strategy was shaped by the comfortable lead in the public opinion polls, which the President enjoyed following the conventions. Broadcasting did not begin until October; reliance before then was on the media exposure, which the candidate received as incumbent President. Programs and spot ads sought to emphasize the image of Nixon as a statesman and a President at work, above the battle of a political campaign.[26] When he appeared it was, for example, mostly in film clips of his trips to China and the Soviet Union.

The television and radio broadcasting for the Republicans was divided between two committees—Democrats for Nixon and The Committee for the Re-Election of the President. In fact, the budget for the Democrats for Nixon advertising accounted for more than half of the total Nixon broadcast spending (see Tables 8-1 and 8-3). The breakdown is given in Table 8-6.

Table 8-6
Broadcasting and Newspaper Budget for Nixon Advertising

Television		
Network	$1,270,000	
Local	935,000	
		$2,223,000
Newspapers	199,000	
		$ 199,000
Total		$2,422,000

Although the broadcasts for both committees were produced by the November Group, their appeals and messages were very different. The Democrats for Nixon ads were generally more hard-hitting and aggressive, directly attacking McGovern. For example, in what has been regarded by some as the most effective political ad of the campaign, a Democrats for Nixon spot showed a poster of McGovern spinning in 180 degree turns while a narrator recited contradictory McGovern positions.[27] The Democrats for Nixon ads were meant to appeal to "switch voters," traditionally Democratic voters who were possibly willing to cross party lines and vote for Nixon. These groups were primarily targeted as well by the Republican direct mail campaigns. The advertising placed by the CRP was more moderate, emphasizing mainly the President's accomplishments in his first administration. Nixon himself appeared live only in a series of radio addresses carried over the major radio networks; his few television programs were taped.

The McGovern strategy was very different. It was designed to get the candidate before the public on the broadcast media as often as possible. The effort was to try to overcome charges that he was a radical while keeping his populist image intact. The thrust of the McGovern advertising emphasized McGovern's human appeal, his concern for the people, and his responsiveness to them. The television campaign began with five-minute spots of unrehearsed footage taken during the primaries, showing McGovern talking with different groups of voters about the campaign issues.[28] On October 10 McGovern began a series of half hour "fireside chats," in which he covered such issues as the Vietnam war, the economy, and morality in government. Due to the method of purchasing time, his October 10 talk was seen by over 30 million people across the country, claimed to be the largest audience for a political broadcast in recent history.[29] At the end of each fireside chat an appeal for contributions was made. More than $3 million was received from broadcast appeals, which allowed still more time to be bought. McGovern also conducted a series of 60-minute television regional "talk-a-thons" (similar to Nixon's in 1968) in which voters called in questions on the air. Through these talk-a-thons the McGovern campaign sought to appeal to undecided Democratic voters and to highlight, by contrast, Nixon's electoral inactivity.[30] Until the last two weeks of the campaign, McGovern's ads did not aggressively attack Nixon. When such advertising did not seem to influence poll results, Lawrence O'Brien, McGovern's campaign manager, and others, brought pressure to produce several ads attacking Nixon. These were shown and were regarded as effective, if late.[31] Charles Guggenheim, McGovern's media consultant, did not feel comfortable producing such ads. Therefore Tony Schwartz, another veteran political advertising expert, was brought in for this purpose.

Both campaigns were affected in their programming by studies made by media experts in the last few years, which show that voters are more influenced by television news than political advertising. The use of documentary-style features of different sorts in both campaigns was a response to this.[32] For their half-hour telecasts, both campaigns bought time across the networks in selected cities only. In cities or regions where it was felt unnecessary or useless to spend broadcast money (e.g., the South for McGovern) time would not be bought. The preferred time for these broadcasts was in the 7:30 P.M. prime time slot, which ordinarily is local station time. However, the national network can preempt it for political advertising.[33]

Sustaining Time

Certain network interview and documentary programs are exempt from the "equal time" provisions of Section 315. In these categories, time can be provided to one candidate without obliging broadcasters to provide precisely equal time for other candidates. Some of these programs, such as "Meet the Press," are commercially sponsored. Others are simply donated by the broadcasters. In the latter case, the time provided is called "sustaining time." In the sustaining time category in the 1972 general election, the commercial television networks offered only one hour of free time,[34] down by more than 66 percent from 1968, 75 percent from 1964, and only two percent of the amount of time made available in 1960 when Section 315, the so-called equal time provision, was suspended. Commercial radio networks did considerably better in 1972 than television. In 1972 they offered 19 hours[35] of sustaining time, which is nonetheless 21 percent less than the 24 hours provided in 1968. On educational noncommercial television and radio networks, candidates in the general election received more sustaining time than they did on the commercial networks. A total of 35 hours was given candidates,[36] 15 hours more than the total for the commercial television and radio networks.

A comparison of commercial network sustaining time provided in the general election for the last five presidential election years is given in Table 8-7. (All of the time was for presidential or vice-presidential candidates or supporters.) Noncommercial network time is not included as FCC figures present only a combined television and radio total for it. FCC data also did not allow consideration of the amount of sustaining time used by the candidates themselves, as had been possible in 1968.

The major parties are normally the beneficiaries of the sustaining time, which is exempt from "equal time" requirements. It cannot be determined how the one hour of sustaining time granted by the commercial television networks was divided. However, on the commercial radio networks, Democrats received ten hours of sustaining time in the general election, Republicans seven hours, and minor parties two hours.[37] For the Democrats and Republicans these totals are nearly the same as for 1968. In 1968, however, minor parties received nearly seven hours of sustaining time, most of which was devoted to George Wallace's candidacy. The decline in sustaining time on commercial radio networks in 1972 reflects primarily a decline in sustaining time offered to minor party candidates, none of whom presented a strong challenge to the major party candidates. On the educational noncommercial television and radio networks Democrats received 16 hours, Republicans 16 hours, and other parties three hours.[38]

In the primaries, however, commercial television networks provided 21 hours of sustaining time to presidential candidates and their supporters.[39] This is 48 percent greater than the 1968 total of 13 1/2 hours. The Democrats received seven hours, while the Republicans received 14 hours. The inequality disappears, however, if the totals of sustaining time are combined with the totals of commercially sponsored free time. The Democratic total then is 38 hours

Table 8-7
Commercial Network Sustaining Time Provided to Candidates and Their Supporters, General Election: 1956, 1960, 1964, 1968, and 1972

(In Hours and Minutes)

Year	Total Time, All Parties and Candidates	
	Television[a]	Radio[b]
1972	1:00	19:00
1968	3:01	24:17
1964	4:28	21:14
1960	39:22	43:14
1956	29:38	32:23

Source: FCC, *Survey 1968*, table 4; FCC, *Survey 1972*, tables 22 and 23.

[a]Three networks.

[b]Seven networks in 1968 and 1972; four networks in all other years.

while the Republican is 36.[40] This is the inverse of the 1968 totals when the
Democrats received over twice as much sustaining time as the Republicans.
Radio networks provided 15 hours to the Republicans and 16 hours to the
Democrats,[41] while in 1968 they had given ten hours to the Republicans,
20 1/2 hours to the Democrats, and one hour to minor parties.

One widely used means of, in effect, gaining free time was the feeding
of tapes by the campaign organizations to local stations for use as news clips.
Both presidential campaigns spent several hundred thousand dollars to produce and distribute taped recordings of candidates and spokesmen to hundreds
of radio stations across the country for free rebroadcast during news programs.
Audio feeds, or actualities as they are sometimes called, are essentially anal-
agous to the printed press release still used for newspapers.

Radio stations, eager to use free and interesting material, would often take
two or three separate quotes per day from campaigns and alternate them
through their news broadcasts. Campaigns were able to replace the dry reading
of quotations by newscasters with the cheers and bands of the campaign
trail.

Two staff "radio reporters" accompanied McGovern in all his travels, taping
everything he said, and then selecting several quotable segments for transmission
to Washington headquarters. From there the feeds were telephoned to 16 regional centers and then telephoned to individual stations. Stations were also able to
phone McGovern and Nixon headquarters at special numbers in Washington to
receive the actualities.

In what may become more common practice in future campaigns, the
McGovern California primary effort even employed a video tape crew to travel
mornings with the candidate, and then reproduce video tape feeds for transport
to all California television stations the same afternoon.[42]

Equal Time, Access, and Fairness Issues

In previous campaigns broadcasters could influence the nature of political
communication by granting discounts on some kinds of time and not others. The
provision of the FECA that stipulated that broadcasters must supply time at the
lowest unit rate eliminated this possibility. Broadcasters were still able to influence, to some extent, the nature of a candidate's broadcasting, as they maintained discretion over the amounts of time, and in what lengths, they would make
it available. Some stations limit political broadcasting to 60-second spots; others
will sell only five-minute programs.[43] Frequently stations are reluctant to sell
time in segments of five minutes or more during evening prime time hours. During
the 1972 campaigns a conflict developed between the broadcasters and the presidential candidates over their half-hour political programs. Some local stations
refused to carry McGovern's first half-hour telecast because of its length. While

the networks were able to persuade a number of local affiliates to carry the subsequent half-hour programs, in some cities they never appeared as local stations continued to resist giving up the prime time slot (7:30 to 8:00 P.M.), which McGovern wanted to buy. Initially, the Westinghouse Broadcasting network refused to carry the Democrats for Nixon 30-minute programs in which John Connally spoke unless the candidate himself appeared. Westinghouse did this on the basis of its interpretation of the FCC's prime time access rule, which holds that political broadcasts made by surrogates for a candidate do not exempt a network from returning an equivalent amount of network time to the local stations. The program did appear, however, on local stations after consultation between network lawyers, FCC attorneys, and representatives of the Democrats for Nixon.[44]

The question of the length of political advertising segments has now emerged as a significant issue in discussion of further reform of political advertising. While the new law confronted in part the problem of financing, some critics maintain further changes are necessary to improve the quality of political communication in political advertising. It has been frequently maintained, for example, that 60-second, and shorter, spots are inappropriate for informing the public about a candidate, however effective they may be in selling commercial products. The application of commercial advertising methods of presentation have themselves been attacked for primarily communicating images and information not relevant to rational political choice. Any efforts to bring in these areas, however, clearly raise serious problems of censorship and governmental interference with the free flow of information.[d]

The provision of the law requiring that broadcasters provide "reasonable access" to candidates led to a large number of conflicts between stations and candidates over the amounts of time made available. In October 1972 there were 3,231 complaints and inquiries to the FCC—2,764 concerned candidates' rights and 467 involved the fairness doctrine. This was ten times more than the 310 complaints received in October 1968.[45] The potential for such conflicts is inherent in the vagueness of the concept of "reasonable access."

During the campaign the courts were called upon to rule on two appeals concerning the interpretation of the fairness doctrine. In one, the Supreme Court denied review of a lower court ruling, which held that networks need not make time available to the opposition to respond to broadcasts made by the President prior to his candidacy.[e] In the other (*CBS* v. *DNC, ABC* v. *DNC, FCC* v. *Business Executives' Move, Post-Newsweek Stations* v. *Business Executives' Move*), it ruled in May 1973 (on the basis of an appeal from an FCC ruling

---

[d]See, for example, "TV in Election Campaigns—A Call for Change", *U.S. News and World Reports*, November 27, 1972, pp. 84-88.

[e]For information regarding *Democratic National Committee* vs, *FCC*, see "Presidential Talks Not a Ticket for the Other Side", *Broadcasting*, October 16, 1972, p. 18.

made during the campaign) that broadcasters have an absolute right to refuse to sell time for advertisements dealing with political campaigns or controversial public issues. The case arose out of unsuccessful efforts by the Democratic National Committee and Business Executives Move for Vietnam Peace to buy network time to present their views.[46]

Once again in 1972 there was no repeal of Section 315 of the Federal Communications Act—the so-called "equal time provision"—which would have been necessary in order to allow 1960-style debates between the major party candidates. The Senate version of the FECA allowed for a repeal of Section 315 for presidential campaigns, but this was struck from the House's version of the bill. The White House had made it clear that whether the new equal-time amendment passed did not matter, as the President would not debate his Democratic challenger.[47] The extraordinary exposure of debates is normally more valuable to the underdog or less well-known candidate. Nixon clearly was the front-runner throughout the campaign, and thus felt nothing was to be gained by agreeing to debate.

Throughout the campaign, the Democrats sought to use Nixon's unwillingness to debate as a means of embarrassing the Republicans. McGovern made repeated public offers to pay for national television time for a series of debates (for which a repeal of Section 315 would not have been required). At one point Lawrence O'Brien held a press conference where three 1968 television tapes were played of Nixon encouraging the idea of debates between presidential candidates.[48] The White House remained adamant, however, insisting that a President makes policy every time he speaks and that political debates are not a good place to make policy.[49] As a possible alternative to a direct confrontation, ABC and CBS offered Nixon and McGovern, in the week before the election, time to present their opposing views in sequence on a series of separate video tapes. The McGovern campaign accepted the offer, but the Republicans turned it down.

An alternative form of joint appearance was arranged in the California Democratic primary between Hubert Humphrey and George McGovern. It was similar to the joint appearance of Eugene McCarthy and Robert Kennedy before the 1968 California primary on ABC's "Issues and Answers." A regularly scheduled news show such as "Issues and Answers" is normally excluded from coverage under the "equal-time" provision, making such an appearance possible if opponents do not challenge the appearance, as they sometimes have not. Three confrontations over national television, on each of the networks' news programs, were held. Although billed as debates, they were more joint question-answer sessions with newsmen.[50] Los Angeles Mayor Sam Yorty, another candidate in the Democratic primary, filed suit in U.S. District Court to force the network to include him, but was turned down.[51]

The suspension or repeal of the equal-time provision to allow debates in presidential campaigns remains a goal of many critics of political broadcasting. What is clear from past efforts is that if the question of suspension of Section 315 is considered anew every four years, the decision will be based largely on the political situation and advantage of the moment. If there is any hope of diminishing partisan and immediate-advantage considerations, the decision on changing Section 315 may have to be made for more than one election at a time, and probably well before an affected election.

Spots and Program Time

On television networks, presidential and vice-presidential candidates in the general election period spent slightly more for announcement time than for program time: $2.5 million for announcements and $2.4 million for programs.[52] This differs from 1968 when $4.6 million was spent on program time and $4.2 million on announcement time. On local television stations, however, over three times as much was spent on announcement time as on program time—$2.9 million and $900,000.[53] (There are no comparable figures for 1968.) By contrast, on network radio $311,000 was spent for programs as opposed to $163,000 for announcements.[54] This is also a reversal of 1968 network radio spending when $452,000 was spent on announcements and $240,000 on program time. On local radio stations, however, $1.7 million was spent on announcement time and only $40,000 on program time by the presidential candidates.[55]

The programming in network television time segments for both the Nixon and McGovern campaigns was obtained from campaign officials. The Nixon campaign data follow:

8 half-hour broadcasts, all prime time, also carried by some nonnetwork stations	$ 495,800
75 five-minute spots, 33 daytime, 42 prime time (cost includes time plus editing costs. Editing costs ran from nothing to $3,000 or $4,000.)	672,800
41 60-second spots, all prime time	1,162,000
Total	$2,330,600

Note: The first broadcasts were on September 18. Most of the broadcasts ran after October 2, building up to election eve.

The programming in network television time segments for the McGovern campaign was as follows:

9 half-hour broadcasts, all prime time	$ 647,827
49 five-minute spots, 10 daytime—$55,661, 39 prime time—$508,085	563,746

35 60-second spots, all prime time	1,036,299
Total net (including editing)	$2,247,872

Costs for the above were averaged by campaign staffers as follows:

Half hours	$64,783
Daytime, five minutes	5,566
Evening, five minutes	13,028
Prime time, 60 seconds	29,609

According to campaign officials, the October 25 broadcast was carried on two networks, so ten half hours were actually paid for.

The programming in network radio time segments for the Nixon campaign was as follows:

3 30-minute broadcasts, regional only	$ 25,400
2 25-minute broadcasts	18,700
43 15-minute broadcasts, mostly simulcast on three networks	264,100
8 10-minute broadcasts, mostly Clark MacGregor—morale building, morning commuting hours	45,600
1 five-minute broadcast	1,800
14 60-second broadcasts, mostly tune-in ads for TV broadcasts	2,000
30 30-second broadcasts, mostly tune-in ads for TV broadcasts	14,600
Total	$372,200

Samples of similar data for the McGovern campaign are presented in Appendix M.

As the breakdowns of network expenditures for Nixon and McGovern indicate, both candidates purchased spot and program time in almost similar fashion. Both spent the most on 60-second spots. For both the five-minute spots were the greatest number of units (a marked increase over other elections). The Nixon campaign made eight half-hour broadcasts while the McGovern campaign made nine. On network radio, the usage of broadcast time by the two parties differed much more sharply. The Democrats used network radio mainly for spots, while the Republicans' largest expenditure was for broadcasts of 15 minutes and over. It was on these broadcasts that Nixon read a series of position papers on various issues. Nixon spending on network radio was over four times as large as McGovern's ($363,000 to $82,000).[56] The program time purchased for these position papers accounts for the unusual preponderance given to program time spending in network radio spending totals.

In the presidential primaries $1.8 million was spent on announcement time on television and $500,000 on program time. On radio, $1.2 million was spent on announcements and $30,000 on programs. In the primaries, then, spending on announcements was six times as great as for program time.[57]

On nonnetwork broadcasting the difference in spending between program and spot time was much greater. On nonnetwork television, for primaries and general election, candidates at all levels spent $29 million on announcements and $3.2 million for program time, a ratio of 9 to 1, as compared with 6 to 1 in 1968.[f] On nonnetwork radio, the ratio of announcements to program time spending declined to 20 to 1, from 40 to 1 in 1968: $20.1 million was spent on announcements as opposed to $1 million on program time.[58]

The overall ratio of spending on announcements versus program time on both radio and television was 8 to 1 in 1972.[59] This is an interruption of the trend of increasing relative spending on announcements over the last decade. In 1970 it was nearly 20 to 1,[60] and in 1968 it was 10 to 1. The proportion is still greater, however, than the 6 to 1 in 1966 and the 4 to 1 ratio in 1964. In presidential broadcast spending for television and radio in primary and general elections, the overall ratio for announcement versus program time spending is much smaller, about 5 to 2 ($10.2 million to $4.2 million). The disproportions between announcement and program time spending tend to be much greater on local stations than on the networks, and on radio than on television.

States

Nonnetwork radio and television station charges for political broadcasting totalled $54.2 million in 1972,[61] an increase over the $49.3 million total in 1968. While total network and nonnetwork spending increased by one percent over 1968, nonnetwork spending increased by ten percent. Nonnetwork spending among Democrats in 1972 was $31.8 million, nearly double the Republican total of $18.1 million.[62] By comparison, in 1968 Republicans spent $22.1 million and the Democrats $24.7 million. The Democratic increase of 20 percent in nonnetwork spending was the same as for the total Democratic spending increase; however, the Republican decline of 18 percent was significantly smaller than their 25 percent decline in total broadcasting expenditures. The Democratic increases were incurred mainly in nonfederal campaigns, since presidential and senatorial broadcast spending declined in 1972, signifying an upsurge in Democratic spending and financing at the state and local levels.

---

[f]FCC, *Survey 1972*, table 16. For previous years see Alexander, *Financing the 1968 Election*, p. 103.

Republican and Democratic spending at the state level followed the overall
pattern of primary and general election spending as shown in Table 8-8.

Table 8-8
**Radio and Television Station Charges (Nonnetwork), Primary and
General Election, 1972**

| | *(In Millions)* | | |
	Primary	*General Election*	*Total*
Republican	$ 3.2	$14.9	$18.1
Democrat	16.8	14.9	31.8
Other	1.4	2.9	4.3
Totals	$21.4	$32.7	$54.2

Source: FCC *Survey 1972*, table 15.

Spending totals for all offices in primaries and general elections ranged from
a high in Texas, where $5.6 million was spent on all nonnetwork broadcasting to
a low of $82,000 in Wyoming. More than $2 million was spent in seven states:
California, Florida, Illinois, Louisiana, New York, North Carolina, Texas, and in
Puerto Rico, compared with nine states in 1968. At least $1 million was spent in
eight other states—Alabama, Georgia, Indiana, Ohio, Pennsylvania, Wisconsin,
Michigan, and Tennessee, compared with five in 1968.[63]

Democrats spent most in Texas ($4.3 million) and least in Wyoming
($20,000). Republicans spent most in Illinois ($1.9 million) and least in Vermont
($57,000). Something of a shift in Republican spending priorities is evident by
the fact that while in 1968 $7,000 was spent in Mississippi (its lowest total), over
$100,000 was spent there in 1972. Of the other ten states of the Old South,
spending increased by over $100,000 in five of these states, by lesser amounts in
two, and declined in three. Eight states ranked below Mississippi in Republican
spending in 1972, only one of them (Arkansas, $95,000) in the South.[64]

In the primaries Democrats spent more than $500,000 on radio in two states
(three states in 1968)—Texas ($1.3 million) and Florida ($762,000), while Republicans did not exceed that sum in any state.[65] For television, the highest Republican expenditure in the primaries was in Texas ($234,000). Democrats topped
that figure in 11 states: Alabama ($286,000), Arkansas ($279,000), California
($474,000), Florida ($881,000), Georgia ($464,000), Illinois ($426,000), Louisiana ($1.1 million), Missouri ($402,000), North Carolina ($1 million), Texas ($2.1
million), Wisconsin ($329,000).[66]

In the general election comparison of television expenditures by party shows
that the most spent by Democrats was $769,000 in Illinois. Republicans out-spent
this total only in that same state, where their total was $1.3 million.[67] The

pattern of disparities in radio expenditures was different. The Democrats' highest radio total was $363,000 in California. The Republicans spent more in two states, Illinois ($441,000) and New York ($398,000), and in Puerto Rico ($454,000).[68]

Conclusions

Certainly in terms of cost and the attention it received, political broadcasting was of prime importance in the 1972 campaign. Nevertheless, measured in terms of total political expenditures, its importance declined. While total expenditures increased by approximately $125 million over 1968, the expenditures for broadcasting remained nearly constant. This decline in relative importance was due to several factors. The FECA played a role through the controls it placed upon broadcast charges and the limits it set for spending by federal candidates. The limits may well have functioned directly to restrain spending and indirectly, by sending money into areas of unregulated expenditure. Limitations on the utility and the influence on the voters of broadcasting were also recognized. Both parties found that broadcasting, as a mass medium, does not allow candidates to address different groups within the public directly. Direct mailing and telephone contacts may well be more effective for these purposes.

The lessons of the role of broadcasting in the 1972 presidential campaign will probably not be lost on future candidates. In spite of the $10.8 million spent by the presidential candidates for political broadcasts in the general election, the public support indicated for them in public opinion polls changed only slightly from the conventions until Election Day. In winning one of the largest pluralities in presidential campaign history, Richard Nixon spent significantly less on political broadcasting than his Democratic opponent, George McGovern, and less than he had spent in the much closer 1968 election. McGovern's broadcast strategy was one of maximum exposure and wide use of the media, to help reshape unfavorable images of the Senator as a radical. Nixon's strategy was one of minimal exposure. Also striking, in terms of the role of broadcasting, was the dismal failure of "media candidates," such as John Lindsay and Wilbur Mills, who invested heavily in broadcasting, in several of the Democratic primaries.

None of these facts should suggest that television and radio broadcasting are of no real importance in determining the success or failure of a campaign or that candidates will in the future so regard them. Rather, it appears that increasingly it is understood that the power of the broadcast media as a tool of political communication is limited, and that the effectiveness and the extent of media usefulness will vary from one election and candidate to another. The large-scale use of the media in a campaign is not necessarily the most effective strategy, although its absence may be harmful. For an unknown candidate, there may be no better way to spend his money than on broadcasting; for one who is well-known, there may be danger of overexposure. The onset of regulation of broadcast spending, therefore, has coincided with (and may have contributed to) the beginning of a critical reevaluation of the role of broadcasting in political campaigning. Together they have at least temporarily brought to a halt a spiral of rising political broadcast spending, which only a few years ago seemed to be without end.

Campaign Materials

Both the Nixon and McGovern campaigns spent sizable sums on literature and materials, much of which was centrally produced and distributed.

The Nixon campaign printed and distributed more than 20,000 catalogues of its various materials and paraphernalia, and used centralized warehousing and distribution. The Nixon materials budget was $2.7 million, nearly twice the cost of a comparable program in 1968. This reflected the greater emphasis on storefronts and field organization, which stressed free handouts. Four warehouses each served up to 16 states, and each state was allocated quotas without cost and then charged for additional materials. More than 6,000 orders were filled, including storefront kits and airmail packages sent out for Agnew rallies. The printing and warehousing was handled by the Reuben H. Donnelley Corporation, and the design and supervision were directed by the November Group, the specially organized CRP advertising arm. The design costs were incurred within the November Group's budget, but printing, warehousing, and distribution costs were paid directly by CRP, and the funds for these were not channelled through the November Group.

The cash position and style of the McGovern campaign, and the early concentration on nomination, did not lead to such centralization as in the Nixon effort. Some literature was centrally purchased and distributed, but much nationally designed printed matter was distributed to the states in photo-ready mats, which were then prepared by local printers at local cost. This did not allow bulk buying but saved on shipping costs. Substantial literature and materials, however, were prepared, designed, and produced by the state committees. A significant proportion of that was locally produced with little control from even state-level committees.

A comparison of the central supplies of both campaigns, with references to the comparable 1968 Nixon campaign, is given in Table 8-9.

Production costs, warehousing, and distribution handled by the November Group brought the Nixon total up to the $2.7 million actually spent. Costs of literature and publications of CRP, along with the press office, cost an additional $2.6 million, as shown in Table 7-1.

Table 8-9
Campaign Supplies Costs, 1968 and 1972

| Item | Nixon | | | McGovern | |
	1972 Quantity[a]	1972 Cost	1968 Cost	Quantity	Cost
Buttons and tabs	25,000,000	$ 400,000	$ 300,000	10,804,100	$ 82,419
Bumper strips	16,000,000	$ 450,000	$ 300,000	5,320,000	$ 77,140
Posters	100,000	$ 100,000	$ 70,000	1,000,000	$ 46,000
Brochures	40,000,000	$ 300,000	$ 500,000	26,975,000	$161,694
T-shirts	10,000	$ 20,000	—		
Jewelry	10,000	$ 25,000	$ 50,000	Total	$367,253
Strawskimmers	40,000	$ 25,000	$ 30,000		
Balloons	300,000	$ 7,000	$ 70,000		
Floppy hats	10,000	$ 20,000	—		
Totals		$1,347,000	$1,320,000		

[a]Overall, the quantity of items purchased was greater in Nixon's 1968 campaign, although the cost was less. (See Alexander, *1968*, p. 82.)

Impact of Law in Professionalizing Politics

A major part of campaign spending in 1972 was devoted to the purchase of services of political consultants, some using sophisticated technology. It would be meaningless to estimate such expenditures for the 1972 presidential campaigns, because often staff members performed equivalent functions while on a campaign payroll rather than an outside consultant's firm.

Among the campaign consultant services available was that of the general campaign consultant who undertook to run a candidate's entire campaign. Most consultants concentrated on basic strategic decisions: what issues the candidate would stress, where and how the campaign would be run. Some firms specialized in assembling volunteer organizations for candidates. Others concentrated primarily on preparing and scheduling advertising on television and other media.

In addition to such organizations, other consultants specialized in particular aspects of campaigning. Some firms placed voters' names on computer tapes, along with information on their party or candidate preference, occupation, age, ethnic background, and other available data. Tapes were then used for direct mail appeals, for fund raising, and for reminders to vote on election day.

Some firms specialized in the use of automatic electronic equipment to make phone calls to thousands of voters, often with a recorded message from the candidate himself. Other firms hired callers who gave a message to the voter or sought his or her opinions.

Another form of specialization was polling. At the state and sometimes even the local level, professional pollsters were hired, and their polls used as an integral tool in shaping campaign strategy.

The proliferation of consulting firms points up the increasing professionalization of electoral politics. Some criticize this tendency to rely on profit-making firms with no base in the candidate's constituency, and that bypass established party organizations in the process. But few party organizations are geared to provide such services with the competence and reliability some of the professional consultants demonstrate.

Fees for consultant services are usually a flat amount per month, plus expenses. In addition, 15 percent commissions normally are paid on the amounts spent for media advertising, particularly for amounts spent on television and radio air time. The commission is a payment for the consultant's skill in scheduling and placing actual broadcasts.

When the Congress enacted the FECA limitations on expenditures in the communications media, the law clearly intended that advertising agency commissions, or their equivalents, be part of the expenditure limits. No doubt the Congress also intended a limit that was equitable among candidates, advertising agencies, and media. There seemed to be no basis for distinguishing among different billing practices for media usage (e.g., "gross" or "net" rates).

While the trade practice with respect to commissions is usually stated to be

15 percent of the gross amount, there are variations in some instances. Some candidates pay their agents on a fee rather than a commission basis. Others hire agents as members of their staffs.

After some complaints of unfairness in the application of commissions against media expenditure limitations, the Comptroller General, who had statutory responsibility under the 1971 law for drafting regulations for the communications media limitations,[g] concluded that Congress intended to include agents' commissions within the spending limitations, whether paid in the traditional manner as commissions, or paid as a fee, or paid as salary. He thus proposed a regulation that could apply whether the charge was billed as "gross" or "net." If the charge was gross, the 15 percent commission was included. If the charge was net, then 17.65 percent of the charge had to be added to the charge to arrive at the same result. If a candidate had an arrangement for paying other than commissions to an agent, he would be required to charge against his limitation only the lesser amount actually paid to the agent, effective upon his submission to the appropriate supervisory officer of a brief statement describing the alternative arrangements used. The candidate remained responsible for keeping track of his spending for the media and for allocating agents' commissions or their equivalent to each election campaign.

After receiving and evaluating comments on the proposed regulation, a final regulation was promulgated on August 31, 1972.[h] It provided that a flat fee covering primary campaigns as well as a general election period must be apportioned to each election limitation—primary, runoff, or general—on a reasonable basis. A flat fee also had to be apportioned on a reasonable basis between the 60 percent limitation on spending for the use of broadcasting stations and the overall limitation on spending for the use of communications media. A fee arrangement based on the dollar volume of media-use-purchased was to be expressed as a percentage and applied uniformly. If a separate fee, a reduced commission, or other cost basis were established for different election periods, the cost of each would apply to the corresponding limitation. The candidate's records were required for audit purposes to reflect accurately the basis of the allocation as well as the amounts allocated.

The amount of commissions or fees paid or allowed to sales representatives by the media could not be deducted in determining the amount to be charged against the candidate's spending limitation.

If a cash discount was given for prompt payment of the media charge, only the net amount paid to the media was chargeable against the spending limitation. However, if the cash discount was not earned because of a failure to make prompt payment, then the full amount paid to the media had to be charged to the limitation.

-----

[g]In part shared with the Federal Communications Commission.

[h]The date the regulation was published in the *Federal Register*, vol. 37, no. 170, p. 17802.

The impact of this regulation was felt particularly by the Nixon campaign, for its media campaign was operated by the November Group as an in-house agency. Since the FCRP transferred funds to the group, and the group paid salaries to its media experts, no agency commissions were involved. Accordingly, Lawrence F. O'Brien, national campaign chairman for McGovern, urged the GAO to undertake an audit.[69] Because of the importance of the issue, the GAO decided to audit both the November Group and Guggenheim Productions, which performed media and production work for the McGovern campaign. O'Brien's request also reflected a belief, which press reports mentioned at the time, that some of the funding for the political espionage and sabotage conducted by certain Nixon campaigners may have been funnelled through the November Group. However, the GAO found no misuse of November Group funds, and both it and Guggenheim Productions satisfied auditors that all reported income and expenses of both agencies were properly supportable business transactions.[70]

Later, however, in the course of another inquiry, the GAO learned of a newspaper ad placed by the November Group and paid for with campaign funds that were not reported by the Finance Committee to Re-Elect the President (FCRP). In this episode the White House demonstrated that it could use "dirty tricks" not only to cause trouble for Democratic presidential contenders but also to attempt to create the impression of public support for President Nixon's policies. On May 8, 1972 the President had announced that he had ordered the mining of North Vietnamese harbors to halt the flow of war materiel from the Soviet Union. The move provoked protest across the nation. This, in turn, alarmed the White House, where officials felt the mining decision could make or break the President. So White House and reelection committee staffers went into action.

On May 10, 1972 *The New York Times* ran an editorial criticizing the mining as "counter to the will and conscience of a large segment of the American people." A week later, an ad appeared in the *Times* entitled "The People vs. *The New York Times*," citing polls showing that anywhere from 59 to 76 percent of the public supported the President's action. The ad was signed by 14 persons and appeared to represent citizens rallying behind the President.

It was later discovered that the ad was spurious. It had been requested by CRP officials, written by the November Group, reviewed and edited by Charles W. Colson, former special counsel to the President, and paid for by FCRP with a cash payment of more than $4,000. The names of seven of the 14 persons who agreed to co-sponsor the ad were provided by the Nixon reelection committee. The other seven on the sponsors list were obtained by the November Group from among relatives and personal friends of its staff. For example, the woman designated in the ad as "coordinator" was a November Group secretary and the wife of one of its officials. She said she was not aware of any responsibility associated with being listed as coordinator. Those approached by the November Group were asked if they were willing to be named in an ad favoring the

President's decision to mine the harbors. None saw a copy of the ad until it appeared in the *Times*, and none helped pay for it.

After investigating the ad, the GAO referred the matter to the Justice Department for possible prosecution. The GAO found that the ad appeared to violate the statutory requirement that every ad concerning a candidate for federal office bear the names of the committee responsible for it and the committee's officers. Moreover, the FCRP had failed to report and keep records of the transaction, as required by law.

A crucial part of the media experience in the 1972 campaigns concerned the limitations on expenditures of communications media as set forth in Title 1 of the FECA. These limitations raised practical as well as constitutional questions, and the provisions led to full employment of media and campaign management consultants. A candidate needed a media plan to enable him to get the most impact for the limited dollars he could spend. Moreover, the candidate or his agent had to certify to a broadcaster or newspaper that each purchase would not cause him to exceed his limitation.[i] While this had a disciplining effect, by forcing the candidate to ask whether each expenditure was really necessary and whether it was the most effective way to spend scarce dollars, the experience in 1972 was that a considerable amount of unauthorized spending for the media occurred without certification.[71] This raised the question of whether the candidate should be held responsible for such unauthorized spending, and whether the broadcaster or newspaper should be required to police the advertisements. Many vendors understandably disliked having the burden of enforcement fall on the seller, making him criminally liable, rather than on the buyer or the candidate. This was illustrated by the *ACLU-Jennings* case.

The complexities arising from the need to authorize and certify advertising—to comply with the media limitations—led the Bureau of Advertising of the American Newspaper Publishers Association to set up a centralized system whereby political advertising could be disbursed to the daily newspapers.[72] The bureau established an escrow account in New York into which monies received from federal candidates were deposited, along with the required certifications. Blanket approval for advertisements was then sent to the newspapers chosen by a candidate.

Both The November Group, for Nixon, and Rapp & Collins, for McGovern, placed their ads through the bureau's system, and the papers were paid out of an escrow account at their general rates. The service was offered to the newspapers at no charge by the bureau, and had the approval of the Comptroller General.

Participating newspapers were told that they could accept no other advertising from any local group wanting to place an ad for one of the candidates

---

[i]For examples of candidate authorizations and certifications for media expenditures within the limits, see Appendix N.

without getting authorization from Nixon or McGovern themselves. They were also advised that in the case of a derogatory ad against a candidate, they needed either a certification from the logical beneficiary candidate or a statement from the advertiser that his expenditure was not authorized by any federal candidate. For any further form required by individual state laws, the papers were asked to contact the respective agencies directly.

The bureau made a formal tally of the newspaper dollars spent by the national campaign committees: this showed $759,000 spent by the CRP, and $748,000 by McGovern. The Republicans placed ads in some 793 papers across the country, whereas the Democrats concentrated their ads in the big cities in 17 key states. Additionally, about $250,000 was placed by certification for several state Nixon committees and some local McGovern committees. Most, but not all, the advertising was tune-in for broadcasts. No advertising was placed for Senate or House campaigns.

Abuse of the Congressional Franking Privilege

Possibly one indirect result of the limitations placed on media spending in the FECA was an increase in abuses of the congressional franking privilege. Many candidates seemed to turn to direct mail campaigning, and some incumbents took advantage of the then vague wording in the law dealing with the franking privilege,[j] which said only that congressmen may use the frank for correspondence "on official business."

In fiscal 1972 members of Congress sent 308.9 million pieces of franked mail. About 326 million pieces were sent in fiscal 1973, and an estimated 354 million pieces, at a cost of $35.7 million, were sent in 1974. Studies have shown that members of Congress send nearly twice as much franked mail in an election year than they do in a nonelection year.[k]

In 1968 the Postal Service stopped supervising the frank, and in 1971 Representative Morris E. Udall, chairman of the House Postal Service subcommittee, advised his colleagues in a memorandum that the Postal Service would be of no help in determining what was official mail. The service, he wrote, was trying

---

[j]Under Title 39, Section 3210 of the FECA Amendments of 1974, congressmen are now strictly prohibited from sending franked mail to solicit financial or political support. The Act also prohibits franking any mass mailing less than 28 days before a primary or general election in which the congressman is a candidate, with the exception of matter specifically requested, mailings to congressional colleagues and government officials, or news releases to the media.

[k]Common Cause monitored congressional mail sent out under the frank and on October 5, 1973, sued the Postmaster General and the Secretary of the Treasury in an effort to prevent abuse of the franking privilege.

to remain nonpolitical and had nothing to gain in trying to rule on when members of Congress—who would pass on its appropriations—might use the privilege.

Twelve lawsuits involving the franking privilege had been filed by 1972, but court decisions further clouded the interpretation of what was and was not frankable. Representative Frank Annunzio, D-Illinois, was taken to court by his Republican opponent after he had mailed some 134,000 questionnaires, under his frank, to residents of both his old district (which had been reapportioned out of existence) and his new one. The court ruled that the mailing to his old district was permissable, even though it was the first time in four terms that he sought to solicit constituent opinion through the mails. He was enjoined, however, from further mailings to the new district on grounds that these were obviously intended to enhance his changes of winning the election and thus were not "official business." Annunzio lost his appeal of the ruling.[73]

In a New Jersey case, Henry Helstoski, another four-term House Democrat, was enjoined from mailing materials under his frank, which had been printed at his own expense, including a questionnaire. The court allowed franking of materials published as official documents and not printed at Helstoski's own expense. The New Jersey ruling brought strong negative reaction on the House floor, with Helstoski complaining that the ruling had declared, in effect, "Congress, do not communicate with your constituents."[74] Representative Wayne Hays said the decision meant nothing, and he told members to ignore it.[75]

Even the best of intentions can sometimes bring about abuse of the franking privilege. Senator Alan Cranston, D-California, has been in the forefront of the campaign reform movement, and a supporter of the ballot proposition (now California law) that challengers should be allowed to spend more than incumbents to help erase that traditional edge. In 1973, following the Watergate revelations, Cranston wanted to raise his money through small contributions, eschewing large gifts. He used a direct mail campaign for his approach to the voters. After a number of test mailings (to lists ranging from subscription lists of magazines to voter registration lists) to determine which would bring the best returns, it was found that Cranston's own newsletter mailing list would be the best. This list of 285,000 names, stored in the Senate's computer memory banks, had been built up over the previous four years. At a $30,000 mailing cost to the campaign—the test mailings had gone out under Cranston's frank—Cranston raised $185,000 in pledges, most of which were paid.[76]

Postal Rates for Political Mail

A quiet, unpublicized battle has been fought in administrative hearings and legal memoranda over the question of reducing postal rates for political mail. The Republican and Democratic parties sought to cut the cost of political mail at least in half.

The battle was touched off in 1970 by an anticipated increase from four to five cents a piece in the rate of third-class bulk mail, which includes political mail. This was part of a general increase in postal rates, which was eventually approved by the Postal Rate Commission. The issue was initially raised by the then California secretary of state, now Governor, Edmund G. Brown, Jr. The Postal Rate Commission ruled in June 1971 that a change in status of political mail should be raised in a mail classification case, not in a postal rate case.

The Democratic and Republican national committees joined the controversy in 1972, concerned about the costs of the forthcoming election campaigns. In a complaint filed with the Postal Rate Commission, they argued that the five cent rate more than covered postal costs for political circulars and imposed a financial burden on candidates and so, ultimately, on the public (i.e., contributors). They asked the commission to do one of two things: either (1) authorize political mail to be sent at the same preferential third-class rate allowed nonprofit organizations, for example, religious, fraternal, labor, educational organizations, or (2) establish a separate category for political mail with a rate between that for nonprofit and for regular third-class bulk mail. However, their request was rejected and the five cent rate allowed to stand.

Changes proposed in the classification of mail early in 1973 gave the political parties a second chance to seek reduced rates. Since that time, they have been trying to overcome the opposition of the Postal Service. The parties argue that political fliers serve the public as much or more than mail from groups that already enjoy the nonprofit rate, and that reducing the cost of political mail would serve the pressing need to halt the cost of campaigning. In 1973 they asked the commission either to put political mail in the nonprofit class, costing 2.1 cents a piece, or make it a separate category costing 2.5 cents. The parties maintained that the latter rate, which would cover all "directly attributable" costs and part of overhead costs, would not be a "subsidized" rate. Political mailings in 1974 cost the regular third-class rate of 6.1 cents per piece for the first 250,000 pieces and 6.3 cents thereafter.

The Postal Service adamantly continued to oppose either change. It objected to the first plan on the ground that only Congress may add to the number of subsidized mailers and to the second on the ground that the new category would require other mailers to bear the rest of the overhead cost of political mail.

The Postal Rate Commission divided the case into three phases, and by early 1975 had moved slowly into the first phase and hearings on the changes proposed by the Postal Service. These should be followed by hearings on many proposals for changes in mail classification, including those by Republican and Democratic party representatives, and finally by proceedings looking toward long-range mail classification.

The Postal Service claims that the commission has no jurisdiction over the proposal to grant political parties the same preferential treatment as nonprofit organizations. The service would honor, however, a commission determination that political mail should be classified in a separate category.

If relief is to come to the political parties, observers feel that it will come from Congress and not the Postal Rate Commission. Those arguing for relief envision some arrangement similar to that granted by the FECA of 1971 to political candidates in the matter of buying radio or TV time; that law provides that political candidates cannot be charged more than the lowest unit rate offered to other advertisers. The Democratic National Committee expressed interest in pushing for congressional action in late 1974; with the new, heavily Democratic Congress that convened in January 1975, congressional movement could occur.

Private Public Opinion Polls

Public opinion polls were a vital part of political campaigning in 1972. Very few serious candidates for national or statewide office ventured onto the campaign trail without first hiring a professional pollster to sample the moods and preferences of the voting public. In polling, as in all other phases of campaign activity, costs rose. In the 1968 elections candidates at all levels spent about $6 million for professionally conducted polls.[77] For 1972 that figure increased to about $7.5 million—a 25 percent rise. Perhaps half the increase represented higher costs, and half, the increased use of pollsters by state and local candidates. Altogether, this calculation represents about 1,250 separate polls (some repeated in series for the same candidate), with an average cost of about $6,000. This latter figure is reasonable, considering that a statistically reliable poll must usually reach at least 500 interviewees, no matter how small the constituency being sampled. Costs are probably even held down somewhat by the significant competition between rival pollsters.

The total expenditure for Nixon polling, both pre- and postnomination, was $1.28 million;[1] the McGovern figure for the same periods approached $700,000. The $1.28 million was spent from December 1971 on, and represented in part a cooperative Republican effort, including some shared-cost polling and joint-purchase polling by candidates for Senate or Governor, and some payments by state committees. About 75 percent of this was spent on personal interviews; the remaining 25 percent on telephone polling. Political committees provided about $980,000 of the purely presidential polling costs,

---

[1] Earlier in 1971 David Derge, a political scientist who had been overall supervisor of opinion survey work done for Nixon in the 1968 race, received just under $172,000 from the Kalmbach fund for work he did during the Nixon first term in a variety of public opinion surveys and analyses that were directed by the White House. These were not considered election related. Other unspecified survey work was done for or paid for by the CRP so that the total is closer to $1.6 million, as shown in Table 7-1.

with about $750,000 of that recorded from April 7 on. About $380,000 of this was spent before the convention—$230,000 of that prior to the April 7 deadline for reporting expenditures; about $600,000 could be accounted for between convention and election; and the balance—including one $25,000 poll taken after the November election—went for issue-related polls that were commissioned by the White House.

The breakdown for McGovern for 1971 and 1972 shows about 35 percent spent before the convention and 65 percent after. The $700,000 included some peripheral services for poll-related phoning and printing of questionnaires, but the campaign absorbed some additional minor costs for telephoning and other poll-related items.

With the two major party nominees for President together spending almost $1 million on private polls during the period after the national party conventions, the ratio of spending was about the same here as in the campaign generally, two to one. This represents almost a 50 percent increase over corresponding 1968 figures. Both 1972 efforts were conducted by sophisticated pollsters; both played important roles in shaping campaign strategy and tactics.

Before the conventions, two-thirds of a total $1 million spent for polling by all major party candidates for President could be attributed to Nixon and McGovern. This million dollar figure represents no rise from the 1968 campaign. A major difference this time was the absence from the race of New York Governor Nelson Rockefeller, who had spent $250,000 on polls in the 1968 preconvention period. Interestingly, none of the 1972 candidates seem to have conducted surveys, as Rockefeller had done in 1964 and 1968, designed to prove that he would be stronger in the general election than his rivals within the party.

Information is scarce on the polling operations of the unsuccessful contenders for the Democratic nomination. Senator Edmund Muskie, Senator Hubert Humphrey, and former New York Mayor John Lindsay all employed professional pollsters. Governor George Wallace, who, as the American Independent Party candidate for President in 1968, had spent only $37,000 on polls, once again relied little upon them.

The Nixon polling operation in 1968 had been considered the longest, most costly, and most complex polling project in campaign history. In all respects, this was exceeded by the CRP's 1972 efforts, when polling was conducted by three organizations under the direction of Robert Teeter, a professional pollster on leave of absence from Market Opinion Research Company (MOR) of Detroit. Teeter worked full time for the Nixon campaign, coordinating the work, ordering surveys, and interpreting them. The polling was done by MOR; Opinion Research Corporation (ORC) of Princeton, New Jersey, which had a major part of the 1968 Nixon effort; and Decision Making Information (DMI) of Santa Ana, California.

Responsibility among these polling organizations was divided, for the most part, geographically. ORC, which did about 30 percent of the political polling, did some surveys commissioned independently by the White House, for which they were paid after the election so that others would not know of their work. In addition, the New Jersey organization was assigned those states where the other pollsters had little or no experience, did special polls of certain segments of the electorate, and also conducted national surveys. In all, ORC conducted survey work costing somewhat less than $500,000. About one-third of this was regular White House polling; the remainder, campaign polling. MOR, which conducted about half of the Nixon polling, concentrated on the East and the Midwest. In addition, the Detroit-based company conducted about half of the national surveys. DMI, which did perhaps 20 percent of the polling, worked mainly in the West and somewhat in the South.

Nixon pollsters conducted massive personal interview polls in 12 to 18 states three times in 1972. These were supplemented, late in the campaign, by phone polling in possible swing states. Other polls were conducted for the President, but none of these seems to have played a significant role in the campaign. Perhaps the most unusual was the so-called "Cohen Poll," conducted by a pro-Nixon rabbi, which attempted to ascertain feeling among Jewish voters in metropolitan areas by phone-polling all the Cohens in the telephone book. Insignificant sums of money were spent on such unscientific projects.

The results of the Nixon polling efforts shaped the conduct of the campaign. Although the President was, according to his pollsters, winning less than 50 percent of the voters at the beginning of 1972, his strength improved by spring, again after McGovern was nominated, and still more after the Eagleton affair; it rose steadily to a peak of 64 percent. At that point CRP strategists shifted from a program calling for an undifferentiated broadcast publicity campaign to more selective attempts to pinpoint campaign targets among certain segments of the electorate—notably young voters, regional voters (particularly in the South), and ethnics. After the resignation of John Mitchell, CRP leaders, now headed by Clark MacGregor, realized that with the polls heavily in their favor, they could afford to redirect their efforts away from the expensive electronic media. The goal now was to consolidate leads, to reinforce, and to activate organizationally. The decision was made to deemphasize television and radio and to concentrate the budget on a direct mail drive designed to keep those young, southern, and ethnic voters interested enough to turn out on election day. The opening of storefront centers and a heightened telephone campaign were other tactics used. Clearly, the CRP polling work, which amounted to less than two percent of the campaign's costs, had played a significant role in adding to Richard Nixon's landslide reelection.

In the prenomination period, starting late in 1971, Senator George McGovern's campaign employed an organization that had little experience in national campaigns—Cambridge Survey Research Company (CSR) of Cambridge, Massachusetts, headed by then 21-year-old Harvard senior Pat Caddell. CSR's preconvention work covered mainly primary states and a complete national survey at a cost of some $248,000. Later, the organization conducted the McGovern polling operation for the general election, concentrating on 25 key states with large electoral votes for evidence that McGovern had some chance to carry them. Some states were written off as unwinnable, and concentration was focused on the rest. National surveys were also conducted in July, September, and October. The Caddell group's surveys began, as did CRP's with personal interviews; phone polling was also used, especially in follow-ups of previously interviewed persons late in the campaign.

The CSR polls conducted for Senator McGovern during the primary period played a major role in his rise from an almost unknown candidate to the front-runner and finally the Democratic presidential nominee. He began in 1971 with little more than a five percent recognition factor. CSR polls conducted in states that had presidential primaries were designed to show how the candidate might come from far behind to win; they reportedly focused on how well McGovern was running against his opponents at any one time, on how firmly or weakly committed voters were to other candidates, and on the kind of issues that concerned them most. Obviously, many of the results of these surveys were useful, considering McGovern's surprisingly good showings in primaries in New Hampshire, Wisconsin, and Ohio.

The McGovern forces had the advantage of sophisticated polling at a small fraction of the total campaign costs. There was some state and candidate sharing of costs, though mostly the others tagged onto McGovern's polls. McGovern would have spent more on polling had the money been available, particularly for so-called "media focus surveys" that attempted to determine which media attract attentive audiences among critical segments of the electorate.

Both the Nixon and McGovern campaigns used the same polling organizations during the primaries as during the general election. In both cases the post-convention polling was a continuation of preconvention polling strategy. In the Nixon campaign preconvention polling was conducted more with an eye to the general election than to the primaries. Nixon pollsters did in-depth surveys of New Hampshire, Florida, and Wisconsin, prior to those presidential primaries. These showed Nixon far ahead of his opposition—as did the primary elections themselves, after which Nixon had no significant primary opposition.

Youth Registration

Throughout 1971 newspapers and popular journals were filled with accounts of the possible impact of ratification of the Twenty-sixth Amendment to the Constitution, which lowered the voting age to 18 in federal elections. Predictions ranged from the total demise of the Republican Party to a negligible impact on elections to posts from the White House to the courthouse.

Many Democrats saw the youth vote as the salvation of the party and each of the major candidates employed young people to initiate registration and campaign activities on college campuses and assembly lines. The eventual nominee, Senator George McGovern, viewed the youth vote as pivotal to his nomination and election.

Faced with early polls showing President Nixon trailing behind several Democrats among young voters, the Republican National Committee and the Committee to Re-Elect the President at first downplayed the effect of the youth vote and made no extensive plans for youth registration drives.

The 11.4 million potential young voters between 18 and 21 and another 13.7 million potential registrants between 21 and 25 who were ineligible to vote for President in 1968 also became registration targets for more than 35 nonpartisan national organizations. Groups experienced in registration such as Frontlash and the League of Women Voters added youth to their target groups. Existing student and youth organizations added the subject of registration to their agendas, and a variety of foundations funded new registration organizations such as the Student Vote and the Youth Citizenship Fund. To assist in realizing this massive registration potential and to break down procedural barriers to registration, Common Cause organized its Voting Rights Project under Connecticut Democratic activist Anne Wexler.

After the Miami convention, National Chairwoman Jean Westwood appointed Anne Wexler to head the Democratic National Committee registration operation, while McGovern strategists pointed to the youth vote as the key to victory and confidently predicted a McGovern majority of two or three to one among youth voters. The Democratic effort began with a $1 million budget; but as fund raising failed to keep up with needs after the convention, the national registration staff could afford to employ only about 60 full-time workers, and spent less than $700,000. The Democrats concentrated on college campuses and on black and Spanish-speaking and union-member voters of all ages, and claimed credit for nearly three million registrants. In most localities, young Democratic registrants outnumbered young Republican-affiliated first-time voters by margins of three to one. It was estimated that the Democratic effort registered some six to eight million voters of a total 13 million new registrants.

Spurred by postconvention polls, which now showed Nixon holding a substantial margin over McGovern among unregistered young voters, the CRP shifted from its 1971 posture of indifference toward the youth vote to adoption of a vigorous computerized registration program aimed at youth and older voters. Concentrating on suburban residents, working youth and ethnic "heritage groups," the Republican effort cost more than $3 million dollars, much of which was spent on computer lists and mailings in key states. Republican estimates of their registration successes were approximately equal to Democratic claims. In contrast to the Democrats' reliance on handwritten 3 X 5 cards used on large campuses and in urban ghettoes, the Republican effort was eased by massive computer lists and a selective registration of only those voters who seemed likely, after a telephone interview or personal visit, to vote Republican, at least in the presidential election.

Postelection surveys revealed that the great investment of dollars and rhetoric by both sides had minimal impact on the presidential election. While voters tend to claim that they voted for the winner, it is possible to conclude that the youth vote was actually split between Nixon and McGovern. A Census Bureau study conducted in late November 1972 indicated that voting rates of the 21-24-year-old age group were 12 percent below the reported average of other age groups. The study rated the participation of the 18-21 age group at 15 percent below the total average. The newly enfranchised voters constituted only six percent of all who voted in 1972, and the fact that fewer than half of the new registrants voted caused a minimal drop in the median voting age from 46.7 to 44 years. However, the youth who did turn out voted solidly for liberal candidates for the Congress. A survey by the University of Michigan's Center for Political Studies showed that 67 percent of the 18-24 year olds voting cast their ballots for Democrats in House contests.

Legislative action to reform voter registration was spurred by the failure of 62 million eligible citizens to vote in 1972. With voter turnout at 77 million, only 55 percent of eligible voters had cast ballots, and this encouraged legislative action for new registration procedures. Claiming that low participation was primarily due to restrictive voter registration procedures, Senate Post Office Committee Chairman Gale McGee of Wyoming shepherded a mail voter registration bill to the Senate floor in 1973. The bill would have organized a federal voter registration administration in the Census Bureau, which in cooperation with the postal service, would distribute registration post cards to every American household at least every two years. The proposal would have covered only federal elections, but states adopting the federal standards would have received federal government grants.

The Nixon administration vigorously opposed the proposal, claiming that it violated states rights and constituted an invasion of privacy into the political affairs of all citizens by the federal government. A bipartisan coalition of senators led by James B. Allen of Alabama, Sam Ervin of North Carolina, and Hiram Fong of Hawaii made the same arguments and expressed fear that the bill would encourage widespread vote fraud. This group was able to defeat a similar bill in 1972 but as support grew for some sort of legislation in this area, the three Senators led a filibuster in April 1973. The month-long filibuster was ended on a third cloture vote of 67 to 32 on May 9, 1973. The bill passed the Senate by a vote of 57 to 37 but a year later the House voted to shelve it. If some such plan were enacted, the United States would no longer be the only mature democracy in the world that fails to provide for governmental responsibility to maintain current voter rolls.

9 The Impact of the New Federal Election Laws: Part II

Tax Incentives and Tax Checkoffs

The Revenue Act of 1971 provided the first effective tax legislation to deal with campaign financing—both in the form of tax incentives, which went into effect for contributions made after December 31, 1971, and tax checkoffs, the more controversial of the two measures, which did not take effect until January 1, 1973.

The tax credits and deductions had an easy passage, but the accompanying checkoff had a long and stormy history. The checkoff was a revised version of the Long Act of 1966-67, which had brought adverse reaction then, and an even greater controversy as formulated by Senator John Pastore in 1971. Public reaction in 1971 was generally more favorable than in 1966 because the Democratic debt and the Republican financial superiority were widely perceived as possibly restricting any Democratic presidential nominee to an inadequate campaign for want of dollars. In the course of Senate debates in 1966, 1967, and 1971, there were few Republicans voting in favor; none supported the checkoff in the final vote in 1967, and only two supported it in 1971. Democratic solidarity was notable in 1971 with only four defections in the Senate.

While the Revenue Act offered long-awaited reforms in federal election financing, a ruling by the Internal Revenue Service on the gift tax in 1972 ran directly counter to reform goals, by, in effect, sanctioning the proliferation of "dummy" committees created to help contributors avoid the gift tax. And a second tax avoidance scheme, contributing appreciated securities to avoid capital gains taxes, was allowed to continue through the election year and was not stopped until August 1973. While Congress was offering reform in the area of tax legislation and campaign finance, the IRS in the same election year was upholding the status quo.

Tax Checkoff

The first experiment in federal subsidy, the presidential campaign tax checkoff contained in the Revenue Act of 1971, did not apply to the 1972 elections and only became effective on January 1, 1973. Under the law a taxpayer may designate that $1 ($2 on joint returns) of his taxes shall go into the Presidential Election Campaign Fund. Under the 1974 Amendments the

353

dollars checked off are earmarked on Treasury books for automatic transferral to the Campaign Fund, without further congressional appropriation necessary.

Starting in 1976 the Democratic and Republican presidential nominees may, if they wish, and if the funds are there, receive as much as $20 million each from the federal monies, the amount set as the limit on presidential campaign spending in the general election. Acceptance is optional: a candidate who takes federal funds cannot privately raise money; a candidate who does not intend to participate may raise the same limited amount from private sources, plus a 20 percent addition if that money is used exclusively for fund-raising purposes.

Largely because of the way in which the first year's checkoff forms were devised, the initial response was discouraging to proponents of the law. In a controversial action, linked by some to Nixon's stated opposition, the Internal Revenue Service designed a half-page checkoff form, separate from the main 1040 income tax form. The special forms were not always readily available even when requested. A limited educational campaign about their use was launched by the Advertising Council but was not widely broadcast. With only about three percent of the taxpayers taking the trouble to submit the special form with their 1972 returns, the total money checked off came to about $4 million.

For the following year Senator Russell Long, D-Louisiana, the original sponsor of the tax checkoff, extracted a promise from the new Commissioner of Internal Revenue, Donald C. Alexander, that the checkoff form would be inserted on a redesigned front page of the 1040 form. Such a provision was signed into law in July 1973, included in debt ceiling legislation. The same law also eliminated the taxpayer's designation of the checkoff to a Republican or Democratic fund (included on the old form) and specified that all allocations would be made to the same general, nonpartisan fund from which allocations would be set by formula. Also included on the 1974 forms for 1973 income was an opportunity for the taxpayer to make a 1972 checkoff if he had not done so previously.

With the required taxpayer action simpler and in plain view, and during a period when Watergate revelations were being made, the response on the 1973 forms increased. Fifteen percent of the taxpayers checked off $17.5 million from their 1973 taxes, while another $8.4 million was added from the 1972 provision. By July 1, 1974 nearly $30 million had been collected toward the needs of the 1976 presidential campaigns.

Provisions for distribution of the federal election funds were changed in the 1974 Amendments to the FECA (Federal Election Campaign Act). As they now read, only the presidential candidate of the Democratic or Republican parties would receive public funds before the 1976 election, since no candidate of another party received 25 percent or more of the popular vote for President in 1972. A minor party candidate may receive payments before the election if he or another candidate of such party received between five and 25 percent of the previous presidential vote. If a new party emerges that had not been on the ballot four years before, the candidate of such party can qualify retroactively for a share of the funds if he receives five percent or more of the presidential vote in the current election.

The amount of money a minor party candidate may receive in public funds is determined by his share of the popular vote in relation to the average popular vote received by the Democratic and Republican candidates. The amount of money that a major party candidate may receive has been limited, for all practical purposes, to the $20 million ceiling set by the FECA Amendments of 1974. Both these amounts are tied in to the Cost of Living Index and will rise accordingly.

The 1974 Amendments also authorized two other uses for money raised through the checkoff system. Both the Republican and Democratic National Committees may receive funds, not to exceed $2 million, to help pay the costs of the national nominating conventions.[a] Candidates for presidential nomination may receive up to $5 million each in preconvention campaign expenses. To qualify for the money, a candidate must show that he has raised $5,000 in contributions of $250 or less in each of 20 states.

By mid-1975 four candidates for Democratic nomination had qualified for matching grants by meeting the 20 state requirement. Candidates who qualify may legally spend up to $10 million in the quest for the nomination, and half of this can be publicly financed. In addition a 20 percent overage for fundraising costs is permitted. Thus, a candidate can raise $7 million in private funds if $2 million is spent on fund raising, and the government will match $5 million, for a grand total of $12 million permitted to be spent.

Since it first went into effect, the tax checkoff has had its share of supporters and detractors—with the latter generally expressing more concern over the way the money is to be distributed than the fact that its source is tax dollars. A number of people and committees have been actively working to publicize the tax checkoff program to the taxpayers, particularly after the disastrous first year, and their work seems to be succeeding. For 1974 returns the IRS estimated some 24 percent checkoff response; an additional $32 million was provided for the fund. If the rate of checkoffs continues, some $90 million will be in the fund by April 15, 1976. Under present limitations on spending, but with the inflation factor, this would probably be enough money. Any excess funds will revert back to the general fund of the Treasury to be used as normal tax revenue. A fund for the 1980 campaign will then begin to be built through checkoffs on the 1977 returns, and continue through the next three years.

The limited success of the checkoff campaign can be attributed to a number of factors. Certainly the campaign abuses revealed by the Watergage affair played a role, and the ground was fallow even before that scandal escalated. A survey

---

[a]Although provision is made for funding of minor party conventions on a proportionate basis, none will qualify in 1976.

for the Twentieth Century Fund, conducted in December 1972 by National Opinion Research Center, indicated that 45.2 percent of those surveyed said they would participate in the checkoff if they knew how the system worked. At that point only a little more than a third had any knowledge of the plan, which then called for the separate and frequently unavailable tax form.[1] While the rise in checkoff response has been substantial, from four to 24 percent in three years, the 45 percent poll indication does not seem likely in the near future.

Efforts at informing the public followed after the low 1973 response. The bipartisan $1.00 Check-off Committee was formed to undertake an educational campaign and to induce taxpayers to support the plan. The committee urged major employers to encourage employee participation, and unions and other groups to encourage their members. A number of corporations mailed messages with their employees' W-2 forms asking cooperation. The AFL-CIO's Committee on Political Education also urged participation of union rank and file. Many tax accountants who handle individual taxpayer returns have helped to explain the checkoff plan to their clients. For example, H & R Block, one of the nation's largest income tax services (which in the first year had charged some clients 50 cents each to fill out the separate form), by 1975 undertook to explain to each taxpayer how the checkoff works; on some 35 percent of returns their clients agreed to check off. One of the most widespread misconceptions in the early years was that a checkoff meant the taxpayer was increasing his tax liability.

Concern over the tax checkoff plan has been aimed mainly at the matter of fund distribution—in particular, whether the manner of allocation of major as against minor party monies is constitutional. This concern has brought together two such disparate politicians as the Conservative Party's Senator James Buckley of New York and the former leader of the peace movement, Eugene McCarthy, who represent interests they feel suffer discrimination as a result of the new law. Others in 1974-75 expressed concern over the drain on the U.S. Treasury in times of economic hardship; the revenue losses, which the tax checkoff and tax incentives programs entail, have to be absorbed by other public finance measures.

A more pragmatic concern is whether the amounts available for presidential campaigns are realistic in light of known spending in the past. Both Nixon (at more than $60 million) and McGovern (in excess of $40 million) were well above the $20 million limit in 1972, and inflation has soared since then. How the candidates will be able to stay within the limits—even though tied to cost of living— poses some real problems.

One study[b] attempts to demonstrate that the tax checkoff method of

---

[b]Data compiled by David Adamany, secretary of revenue, State of Wisconsin.

generating funds for political campaigns involves families from a broader range of income levels than does any other method. The data for 1972 income show that only 1.0 percent of tax returns used the tax deduction and only 2.1 percent of tax returns used the tax credit methods, and that the people who use these two devices tend to be in the higher income brackets. Private contributions with no governmental subsidy were made by 12.4 percent of all United States families in 1972. Among families with incomes of less than $5,000, for example, the private contribution method produced a 3.7 percent participation rate, whereas the checkoff produced a 12 percent rate.

Tax Incentives

The Revenue Act of 1971 provided tax incentives for political contributions in two forms: (1) political contributors could take a tax credit against their federal income tax for 50 percent of their contributions, up to a maximum of $12.50 on a single return and $25 on a joint return (the 1974 Amendments to the FECA increased these amounts to $25 and $50 respectively); or alternatively, (2) contributors could claim a tax deduction for the full amount of contributions up to a maximum of $50 on a single return and $100 on a joint return. (The 1974 Amendments increased these amounts to $100 and $200 respectively.)

Eligible as contributions are gifts to candidates for election to any federal, state, or local elective office in any primary, general, or special election, and gifts to any committee, association, or organization operated exclusively for the purpose of influencing or attempting to influence the election of such candidates, for use to further such candidacy.

Contributions do not qualify for the tax incentive program if they are made to "political action committees" engaging in general, political, educational, or legislative activities. A campaign committee may be run in conjunction with a PAC, but contributions must come from individual taxpayers directly to the campaign committee in order to qualify.

The IRS estimated that the revenue loss in a presidential year from the tax incentive program and the checkoff opportunity would be close to $100 million. Data from the 1972 returns indicate that some $26.5 million was claimed in tax credits (on about 1.8 million returns), nearly $52.3 million in tax deductions (on close to one million returns), while an additional $2.6 million in revenue loss came from tax checkoffs (on 1.5 million returns), for a total of $81.4 million.[2] It is ironic that the tax incentive program, which cost nearly $80 million in revenue loss in 1972—and will likely cost at least that in 1976—should have passed Congress with little debate, while the checkoff system raised such controversy. The checkoff plan costs less in revenue loss, and is widely conceded to be the fairer of the two plans since there is equal participation by all who choose to checkoff. In the tax deduction, the amount of government revenue loss is determined by the taxpayer's income bracket.

Of course, more than just dollars are involved, and the checkoff has received much attention. Although tax incentives do not insure adequate funds, they do provide incentives to broaden the financial base, and are designed to encourage political giving. Opponents claim the tax incentives program benefits higher income citizens, and is a windfall to contributors who would have given anyway.

At the time of the passage, the tax incentive law was criticized by several groups for certain of its provisions. The Democratic Study Group (DSG) in the House of Representatives, for example, claimed that the program discriminated against minor parties, nonparty groups raising funds for candidates, and the candidates themselves.[3] The law restricted the circumstances under which credits or deductions could be claimed for gifts to minor parties or nonparty groups, while permitting major parties to raise tax deductible funds at any time and for any purpose. The DSG was further critical of the fact that the tax incentive provisions applied only to gifts to publicly announced candidates. It was noted that most candidates, especially incumbents, delay announcing candidacy as long as possible because of the FCC equal time requirement and other disadvantages to a congressman or senator who appears too early as a candidate. The DSG also warned about the haziness of the public announcement requirements, noting the abuses that were risked by bogus candidates. None of these fears were borne out.

Gift Tax

While the FECA went into effect on April 7, 1972, with the declared policy of achieving full disclosure of political funds, only 11 weeks later, on June 21, the Internal Revenue Service issued Ruling 75-355,[4] one of the most important events in the campaign year. This ruling effectively reaffirmed previous IRS policy that the provisions of the federal gift tax apply to political contributions, and the reaffirmation was made retroactive. This encouraged continuation of the practice of establishing multiple paper committees all founded for the same purpose: to permit a donor to avoid the tax on contributions in excess of the $3,000 allowable exclusion from the gift tax if the contributions were split among multiple political committees supporting the same candidate. The use of this device hindered full disclosure because multiple gifts to one candidate, even if fully and promptly disclosed by each committee, required studious aggregating to determine the total for an individual giver. The practice was used on a wide scale in political campaigns in the 1968 and previous elections, but was not challenged until the 1972 election.[5] Nixon's largest individual supporter, for example, was W. Clement Stone of Chicago, who contributed $2.1 million to the campaign, almost all of it in amounts of $3,000 or less, to literally hundreds of small committees set up to channel such money to the Nixon campaign. Stone had to pay no tax on these gifts.

The only limiting feature of the new IRS ruling was that it recognized a committee as a separate recipient only if at least one-third of its officers were different from those on other committees. This caused great searching for persons to agree to serve as officers of such committees. Tax lawyers began to study the question of just how many persons and committees were necessary to avoid gift tax liability.[6] The GAO, which under the FECA was charged with compiling and producing a coherent, alphabetical list of contributors, announced in August 1972 that it could not have its list ready by the November elections;[7] it did, however, publish a preliminary list in October 1972 and a final one in March 1974.

The effect of frustrating the disclosure objectives of the FECA was one that some observers felt had been deliberately sought for some time by fund raisers in the Nixon campaign.[c] Some 450 separate and secret fund-raising committees had been organized for Nixon under the direction of public relations executive Robert Bennett, son of Utah Senator Wallace Bennett and sometime employer of E. Howard Hunt. The committees bore such names as United Friends of a Balanced Society, Improved Society Support Group, and Better America Council. Most of these committees were quietly dissolved in the days before April 7;[8] funds were transferred and consolidated into readily controlled committees that would register under the new law—some 60 in all, to cover both national and state operations.

The IRS ruling also had the effect of a loss in government revenue amounting to millions of dollars. Richard Mellon Scaife of Pittsburgh, another large Nixon contributor, had given $1 million before April 7, by way of 330 or so separate committees and paid no tax; had the gift tax applied, he would have had to pay between $244,000 and $590,000 on his donation, depending on the extent of his other gifts through the years. In 1968 Mrs. John D. (Martha Baird) Rockefeller, Jr., had given a single committee, Rockefeller for President, a total of $1,482,625 to benefit Nelson Rockefeller's campaign and, it was later learned, had paid gift taxes of $854,483.[9]

The McGovern campaign also proliferated committees; some 350 were registered with the GAO under the new law.

Public Citizen, a Ralph Nader organization, brought suit against the IRS, its commissioner, and the Secretary of the Treasury, in September 1972. The lawsuit sought an injunction against unlawful withholding of records of communication between the White House, other agencies in the executive branch, and the IRS, and internal IRS memoranda. Senators Adlai E. Stevenson, III, D-Illinois, Hugh Scott, R-Pennsylvania, and Charles McC. Mathias, Jr., R-Maryland, led a simultaneous congressional effort, which included introducing a bill that would eliminate political contributions from the definition of "gifts" for the purposes of the gift tax.

---

[c]See, for example, Appendix O. Jerry Landauer, "How Political Donors Avoid Gift, Gains Taxes by Contributing Stock," *Wall Street Journal*, September 27, 1972.

Under the Freedom of Information Act, the Public Citizen suit sought to determine who requested the June ruling. The IRS conceded that the ruling did not originate in the customary way, but that it was drafted in the Office of the Chief Counsel of the Treasury Department instead of in the IRS. It was later shown that the White House requested the ruling as a direct benefit to the Committee to Re-Elect the President (CRP). Career IRS officials said they had not been notified of the ruling in advance.

Following the election, a public interest law firm, Tax Analysts and Advocates, later joined by the National Committee for an Effective Congress and two individuals, sought to have the IRS ruling set aside, filing suit in March 1973 in the U.S. District Court in the District of Columbia. The suit was premised on grounds that the IRS ruling was in direct conflict with a 1941 Supreme Court decision, which held that for the purpose of calculating the proper number of $3,000 exclusions from the gift tax, the eligible beneficiaries are the persons for whom the gifts are intended. The suit sought a permanent injunction requiring withdrawal of the ruling.

On June 8, 1974 District Court Judge June L. Green ruled in favor of Tax Analysts and Advocates et al., declaring the 1972 IRS ruling to be "null and void." Thus, future donors would have to pay the gift tax on all contributions in excess of $3,000 given to a single individual or candidate.

Judge Green based her opinion on the 1941 decision of the Supreme Court— *Helvering v. Hutchins*—in which a taxpayer had set up a single trust for the benefits of all of her seven children and yet took the allowable exclusions on each of them. The court held that the true test of applicability of the tax exclusion was who the beneficiaries really were.

The IRS argued before Judge Green that the *Helvering* case did not apply because political donations are not destined for the personal use of a candidate and therefore "he has not, in fact, received any legal benefit." Judge Green, however, took a different view: "It seems abundantly clear," she held, "that, win or lose, a candidate's 'personal' career is enhanced by his candidacy, and since his candidacy is financed by contributions . . . a contribution creates a legal benefit."[10]

Tax experts felt the broader significance of Judge Green's ruling was that it granted a public interest group, whose own tax treatment was not at issue, the standing in court to challenge the way the IRS enforces tax laws with regard to other taxpayers. Generally, courts have held that a citizen may take the IRS to court only to contest his own tax liability.

The question of applying the gift tax to political donations was brought home also in a 1971 legal case involving Edith M. Stern, a New Orleans philanthropist, who refused to pay gift taxes when she gave more than $16,000 to political candidates in Louisiana.[11] Disturbed by what she felt was her state's economic backwardness, Mrs. Stern said she was contributing to two reform slates "to protect my property and personal interests by promoting efficiency in government." She claimed her money was an economic investment, not a gift. A U.S. District Court upheld Mrs. Stern's contention that a contribution made as an economic investment is not liable to the gift tax. When the IRS took the case to the Court of Appeals, Mrs. Stern's position was reaffirmed there.

Mrs. Stern's gift, directed basically at procuring good government, was judged not taxable. This implies likely gift tax exemption for those more clearly investing their political contributions in return for "good government"–be they wealthy individuals or lobbyists for special interest groups seeking, at the least, personal access to government representatives, or "protection of property and personal interests." There would presumably be no need, then, for these contributors to avoid gift taxes by spreading their gifts among multiple committees organized to receive the money.

The irony of the Stern decision is that the courts authorized a tax break for the very type of political gifts that are most subject to criticism–those for which the donor stands to gain economically. The decision seemed to some observers to encourage the wealthy to seek a quid pro quo in return for their contributions, in order to justify them to the IRS.

The Justice Department did not appeal the Stern decision to the Supreme Court, fearing it would be upheld and therefore apply in all 50 states. The Stern decision is binding on gift taxes only in the six states of the Fifth Circuit (Alabama, Florida, Georgia, Louisiana, Mississippi, Texas). Elsewhere, the IRS was not bound to abide by the appellate court decision, and declared it would not; the IRS stated that in the case of political donations made as economic investments it would waive the gift tax in only six of the 50 states.

Finally, Congress enacted an exemption for political gifts made after May 7, 1974, in effect making the $3,000 gift tax limit no longer applicable to political contributions. Of course, the $1,000 contribution limit starting January 1, 1975 makes the gift tax question moot for federal campaigns (possibly excepting candidate contributions to their own campaigns, which are technically expenditures and hence are not considered gifts).

In the wake of the congressional action and Judge Green's ruling nullifying earlier IRS practice, the service began an investigation in 1975 into the circumvention of the gift tax by large contributors to the Nixon, McGovern, and other campaigns. The specific target of the IRS probe was the manner in which the hundreds of committees had been formed in order to permit large donors to escape the tax. It was reported that added revenue from the investigation could run as high as $10 million.

The IRS was seeking to determine whether the committees were legitimate–with separate identities, separate officers, and separate purposes–or whether in the great proliferation of 1972 committees, some may have been bogus. Those whose giving was under investigation included W. Clement Stone, Nixon's largest contributor, and Max Palevsky, a major McGovern supporter, along with hundreds of others. Many of the contributors were incensed that the IRS proceeded with this investigation three years after the event, in what appeared to them to be retroactive consideration of a practice that was common and traditional when it occurred.

Appreciated Property

When an individual sells a block of stock that has appreciated in value, a capital gains tax is levied on the increase. Until 1975 when a political committee was given that same block of stock as a contribution, neither the committee nor the donor had to pay tax. This encouraged contributions of appreciated property, such as stocks, and was used by both parties in their fund-raising appeals in 1972.

Both parties made their large donors aware of the advantages of such giving. Fund raisers for the Finance Committee to Re-Elect the President (FCRP) sent form letters to prospective donors, indicating that payment of the capital gains tax could be avoided and suggesting that such contributions could be fashioned to avoid a gift tax.[12]   A full year before the election, the McGovern National Finance Chairman, Henry L. Kimelman, sent to the members of the Finance Committee a legal opinion sanctioning untaxed giving, which he had obtained from Stanley S. Weithorn of Upham, Meeker & Weithorn, a New York law firm;[13] the covering memo is found in Appendix P.

Some contributors simply made gifts of stock outright. Others, such as General Motors heir, Stewart R. Mott, George McGovern's most generous backer, developed variations on the theme, ironically on the advice of his lawyers at another New York law firm—Mudge, Rose, Guthrie & Alexander—of which Richard Nixon had formerly been a partner. Mott gave the McGovern organization stock that had increased in value. The organization would sell it, return the purchase price (known as the "basis" in legal terms) to Mott, and keep the profit. Both Mott and the McGovern campaign would thus escape the capital gains tax, and he would get back the original sum of money he had invested. Following this procedure, Mott was listed in the GAO contributor printout for an aggregate of more than $715,000 in contributions to McGovern. But over $300,000 was returned as basis (listed as expenditures by McGovern committees, and inflating McGovern's total spending), and Mott's net gifts totalled $400,000.

In addition, campaign organizations receiving stock transfers would commonly divide the proceeds from the sale among a multitude of committees, allotting to each a maximum of $3,000; in this way the contributor would avoid the gift tax applicable to donations over $3,000, and the aggregate amount of the multiple contributions would be obscured.

The overall technique worked as follows: A wealthy person wishing to donate, say, $90,000 to a campaign would make a gift of stock that cost him

$10,000 but was currently worth $100,000—a not uncommon degree of appreciation in the early 1970s. The campaign central committee would sell the stock for $100,000, keep $3,000 for itself, give $3,000 to each of 29 satellite committees, and refund the remaining $10,000 to the donor. Neither the central committee nor the donor would have to pay capital gains on the $90,000 profit, and the central committee would not report a gift of either $100,000 or $90,000 because that would make the donor liable to the gift tax. Instead the committee and its 29 spin-off committees would each report a gift of $3,000. Anyone trying to discover the donor's total contribution would have to piece together 30 separate reports.

The IRS has traditionally based the capital gains exemption for political gifts on the assumption that political committees operate either at a loss or no gain—for the same reason appreciated securities have long been an accepted manner in which to donate to nonprofit organizations such as educational institutions.

This premise came under challenge, however, in the wake of financial practices disclosed by Watergate-related investigations by groups such as Public Citizen and Common Cause. In August 1973 IRS announced a new ruling under which it would tax the gains made by political campaign committees from sales of stock. In the case of the 1972 election, however, IRS said the tax would only apply on stock sales after October 3, 1972. This brought an angry denunciation from Representative Henry S. Reuss, D-Wisconsin, a leader in the fight to tax political stock gifts. He claimed that almost all of the 1972 stock gifts and sales by campaign committees occurred before October 3, and would have little effect on the millions of dollars collected in this manner.

The GAO asked the Nixon campaign to provide a list of stock gifts, and from April 7, 1972 until December 31, 1972 the FCRP compilation showed some $4.9 million donated in gifts of stock. However, adding in pre-April 7 gifts, Hugh W. Sloan, Jr., former treasurer of the FCRP, estimated appreciated stock valued at $18-$20 million had been received and sold. Congressman Reuss calculated the potential tax liability could have exceeded $5 million.[14]

In December 1974 Congress enacted as a rider to an unrelated bill a provision that reversed the IRS ruling on gifts of appreciated stock given and sold before October 3, 1972. Instead, the law was made to apply only to gifts on transfers made after May 7, 1974, in taxable years ending after that date. This provision removed from liability any gifts made to the Nixon, McGovern, or other campaigns in 1972, and saved those campaigns hundreds of thousands of dollars in potential taxes had the original IRS intent been followed. Both Republicans and Democrats favored the change in dates, but extensive lobbying on behalf of the bill was done by Henry Kimelman, McGovern's 1972 campaign treasurer. The McGovern campaign had a $368,000 surplus in mid-1974, but was reserving some funds to pay the new tax if it became necessary. Had the October 3, 1972 date become effective (Kimelman estimated), the tax would have been some $300,000.

The 1972 Campaign Liquidation Trust (successor to the FCRP) also benefitted from the elimination of the potential capital gains taxes. The October 3,
1972 cutoff would have cost an estimated $500,000 in taxes on $3.4 million
of the 1972 gifts sold after that date.

Taxing Political Committees

Over the years the Internal Revenue Service treated political committees
the same way as other tax-exempt organizations even though they were never
specifically listed in that category in the IRS Code. Under both Republican
and Democratic administrations, the traditional assumption behind the "hands-
off" policy was that political committees almost immediately spent all contributions they received and therefore, in practice, had no taxable income.

As legal observers have noted, it is difficult to find statutory or constitutional bases for this position.[15] Under the IRS Code of 1954, a political party's
income would seem taxable, and a Treasury regulation specifically precluded
from treatment as tax exempt those organizations engaged in "direct or indirect
participation or intervention in political campaigns on behalf of or in opposition
to any candidates for public office."[16]

The IRS assumption that political campaigns had no taxable income came
under particular challenge in 1972. The secret funds channeled to the Watergate defendants, totalling nearly a half million dollars, were from political contributions. Tax accountants and lawyers believe that someone clearly should
have had to pay taxes on these funds.[17] And Mitchell Rogovin, former IRS
chief counsel and later counsel for Common Cause, held that the IRS had
"neither constitutional nor statutory authority" for their premise that political
organizations always operate at a loss; he noted that the Justice Department
once argued to the contrary when—in 1967—the political entity in question was
the Communist Party of the United States.[18]

In April 1973 George P. Schultz, then Secretary of the Treasury, asked Congress to review the tax laws as they applied to political committees, urging that
whatever Congress did it should seek to "minimize the involvement of the IRS
in the political system." The GAO's Office of Federal Elections also requested
clarification of the IRS position, suggesting that traditional practice made it
difficult to audit the transactions to determine exactly what the contributor
gave, what the committee received, and to determine total amounts of contributions.

In August 1973 IRS announced plans to tax gifts of stock, but invited
Congress to legislate on the subject. In December of that year, while legislators
continued to debate the issues, the IRS announced three revenue rulings that
were designed to clarify the rules, and that would be applicable unless Congress
legislated differently. The new rulings provided that income tax returns for the

year 1972 were due from political parties by April 15, 1974 (the time was later extended);[19] that unexpended campaign contributions transferred to the United States government after a federal election could not be deducted from their taxes by contributors;[20] and that contributions received and spent in a campaign were not taxable, but that income generated from contributions through bank deposits, sales of appreciated securities, and so on, were.[21]

In the spring of 1974 the House Ways and Means Committee, from which tax legislation originates, decided tentatively to require political parties and campaign committees to pay income taxes for the first time. Also tentatively, the committee voted to require contributors to pay capital gains tax on gifts of appreciated securities; the IRS had proposed previously that political committees pay such tax. The committee asked IRS to postpone the effective date of the imposition of the tax.

The FECA Amendments in late 1974 amended the IRS Code by requiring the Secretary of the Treasury to exempt by regulation political committees having no gross taxable income. However, the December 1974 Tariff Amendments defined taxable income to include net investment income, but exempted most other forms of income such as contributions, membership dues or fees, and proceeds from fund-raising events and sales of campaign materials. Political committees showing no taxable income for the year would not have to file a return; those that did, however, would be required to file.

To summarize, all political organizations with taxable income in excess of $100 must file a tax return and pay any taxes due. IRS rulings specifically mention three kinds of income that are taxable to political organizations: (1) interest, (2) dividends, (3) net gains from the sale of appreciated property sold after May 7, 1974. The only other kind of income that is taxable to a political organization is business income which is obviously unrelated to politics (i.e., rental income). The law specifically allows each political organization a $100 exemption from these forms of income.

10 Sources of Funds

For more than two decades, two of the country's major public opinion research organizations have asked questions about political contributions of national samples of voters. Both the Gallup Poll and the Survey Research Center (SRC) show a large increase in the number of contributors during the 1950s. The number remained relatively steady in 1960 and 1964, fell off in the 1968 election, and in 1972 climbed back to about what it had been eight years earlier. Gallup did not include questions on political contributions in its 1968 and 1972 surveys. Table 10-1 shows solicitation and contribution data for each of the presidential years since 1952.

Applying these percentages to the adult, noninstitutionalized population gives an indication of the numbers of individuals who said they made a contribution at some level to some campaign. This shows:

  3 million individual givers in 1952
  8 million in 1956
10 million in 1960
12 million in 1964
  8.7 million in 1968
11.7 million in 1972

The increase from 1968 to 1972, apart from possible standard sampling variation, which could apply in any of the years, might be traceable to a greater effort by the Democrats, who were confronted with a huge national party debt and an unprecedented number of presidential primaries. The 1972 Democratic telethon may account for some of the increase. And 22 states and the District of Columbia had presidential primaries in 1972, a third more than in 1968, with more candidates contesting than in 1968. For the first time since the 1956 election, the surveys indicate, the Democrats had an edge over the Republicans both in contributions solicited and received from the general public.

Looking at levels of contributions to each party, Table 10-2 shows the percentages reported by Gallup and SRC as giving solely to each of the two major parties. (Contributors who gave to both parties are not reflected in these percentages.) The percentages represent averages of Gallup and SRC results when they differed for the same election year. An irony is apparent in that each party received contributions from the largest percentage of people in the same years its candidates received the smallest percentage of popular votes. Thus,

Table 10-1
Percentage of National Adult Population Solicited and Making Contributions

Year	Organization	Solicited by:			Contributed to:		
		Rep.	Dem.	Total[a]	Rep.	Dem.	Total[a]
1952	SRC				3	1	4
1956	Gallup	8	11	19	3	6	9
1956	SRC				5	5	10
1960	Gallup	9	8	15	4	4	9
1960	Gallup						12
1960	SRC				7	4	11
1964	Gallup				6	4	12
1964	SRC	8	4	15	6	4	11
1968	SRC	8	6	20[b]	3	3	8[c]
1972	SRC	9	13	30[d]	4	5	10[e]

Sources: Survey Research Center, University of Michigan; data direct from center or from Angus Campbell, Philip E. Converse, Warren E. Miller, Donald E. Stokes, *The American Voter* (New York: John Wiley and Sons, 1960), p. 91; Gallup data direct or from Roper Opinion Research Center, Williams College.

[a]The total percentage may add to a different total than the total of Democrats and Republicans because of individuals solicited by or contributing to both major parties, other parties, nonparty groups, or combinations of these.

[b]Includes 3.5 percent who were solicited by both major parties and 1 percent who were solicited by Wallace's American Independent Party (AIP).

[c]Includes 0.6 percent who contributed to Wallace's AIP.

[d]Includes 8 percent who were solicited by both parties.

[e]Includes contributors to American Independent Party.

Table 10-2
Percentages of Contributors Giving Solely to Each of Two Major Parties

	Contributed Only to:	
	Rep.	Dem.
1952	3	1
1956	4	5.5
1960	5.5	4
1964	6	4
1968	3	3
1972	4	5

Sources: Survey Research Center, University of Michigan; data direct from center or from Angus Campbell, Philip E. Converse, Warren E. Miller, Donald E. Stokes, *The American Voter*, p. 91; Gallup data direct or from Roper Opinion Research Center, Williams College.

the Democrats received contributions from five percent in 1956 and 1972, both years when Republican Presidents were reelected by landslide majorities. And the highest percentage of contributors to the Republican Party occurred in 1964, when that party's candidate was buried under a Democratic landslide. However, in each case the candidate of the losing party—Adlai Stevenson in 1956, Barry Goldwater in 1964, and George McGovern in 1972—was the object of enthusiastic support from large numbers of people on the basis of his perceived ideological positions on issues. These fervent supporters might well have been far more motivated to contribute when such candidates were running than they, or anyone else, would be when there was no such "ideological" candidate in the race. Thus, in 1968, when both major parties' nominees, Nixon and Humphrey, were considered to be at the "center" of their parties, contributions to both parties were far lower—accounting, perhaps, for the unusually low percentage of the population who contributed to either party in 1968. With the candidacies of men such as McGovern and Wallace who tend to represent ideological extremes, the parties could polarize, thus drawing more people into political involvement through campaign contributing, but losing centrists and independent voters.

Another long-term pattern that the survey figures suggest is that of a declining return on investment in a broad-based solicitation effort, as shown in Table 10-3. In 1956 about half of those who were asked to contribute actually did so, and in succeeding presidential elections through 1964, that percentage climbed to 77 percent. It then dropped sharply in 1968, and in 1972 was down to 33 percent. Both of the last two elections have often been cited for the disillusionment with candidates and the political process that was noted in large segments of the electorate; the voter turnout in 1972 was one of the lowest in years. Concurrently, the techniques of fund raising—through TV, sophisticated direct mail appeals, and other efforts—have increasingly sought to reach broader audiences, and may be reaching more persons but many less likely to contribute.

Table 10-3
Percentage of Individuals Solicited Who Contributed, 1956-72

Year	Percent
1956	50
1960	70
1964	77
1968	40
1972	33

Sources: Survey Research Center, University of Michigan; data direct from center or from Angus Campbell, Philip E. Converse, Warren E. Miller, Donald E. Stokes, *The American Voter,* p. 91; Gallup data direct or from Roper Opinion Research Center, Williams College.

Still, the percentage of those asked who did give something, even in 1972, compares favorably, for example, with the contribution levels among certain special interest groups to be considered later, where solicitation for major gifts is more systematic. That there is a reservoir of untapped potential for campaign funds is certainly suggested by other survey findings. From time to time Gallup has asked people if they would contribute $5 to a campaign fund of the party of their choice if they were asked. Throughout the 1940s and 1950s, approximately one-third of people surveyed said that they would be willing to contribute; in the 1960s the percentage so inclined rose to more than 40 percent. In 1972 the Twentieth Century Fund conducted a survey asking whether people would be willing to check off $1 of their taxes for use in a presidential campaign fund that would be set up by Congress; 45 percent said they would. Even with the enormous costs of today's presidential elections, only a small portion of this sort of potential would have to be realized to eliminate many of the financial problems of the parties.

Large Contributions

Information available about political contributors in the 1972 election is vastly greater than for any previous presidential election, chiefly because of the Federal Election Campaign Act's (FECA's) expanded coverage, but also for Watergate-related reasons.

In 1968, working with information from reports filed by 222 national-level committees with the Clerk of the House of Representatives, from the Secretary of the Senate, and from various other sources, Citizens' Research Foundation (CRF) established a data base of about 15,000 persons making a total of about 21,000 different contributions in sums of $500 or more.

In 1972, from April 7 on, the FECA required that the three supervisory officers receive such filings. In addition, contributions and loans by individuals made prior to April 7, 1972, including some 1971 gifts and loans for 1972 campaigns, were voluntarily disclosed by some of the presidential candidates.[1] Still more information resulted from the Common Cause suit against the FCRP, and from the publication of lists of contributors to the FCRP, which were in the possession of Rose Mary Woods, Nixon's personal secretary, again including 1971 data. Other individual contributions of $500 or more to Humphrey, Mills, Jackson, and others came to light during the Senate Watergate investigations and in newspaper disclosures. A listing by CRF of large contributions and committees in 12 states was also available.[a] Only contributions from individuals, not committee contributions or transfers of funds, are included in these tallies.

---

[a]*CRF Listing of: Political Contributors of $500 or More in 1972 to Candidates and Committees in Twelve States* (Princeton, N.J.: Citizens' Research Foundation, 1974). The states are California, Connecticut, Florida, Hawaii, Maryland, Massachusetts, New York, Ohio, Oregon, Pennsylvania, Texas, and Wisconsin.

The General Accounting Office (GAO), a major source for information about contributions to the presidential campaigns, had on file about 19,910 contributions of $500 or more to presidential or vice-presidential candidates. The GAO also had on file records of 3,476 large contributions to state or local candidates and parties, third parties, and others not categorized as Republican or Democratic gifts, and 6,157 to national-level Republican and Democratic committees.

CRF counted some 7,834 contributions of $500 or more to candidate committees filed with the Secretary of the Senate, and 4,904 additional contributions to party and miscellaneous committees. At least 10,166 additional large contributions were reported to the Clerk of the House by candidates, candidate committees, and miscellaneous committees not reporting to the Comptroller General or the Secretary of the Senate. From the voluntary disclosures, the Common Cause suit, and the Rose Mary Woods list, 4,342 pre-April 7 contributions of $500 or more emerged, and the Senate Watergate committee produced evidence of another 32 large contributions. There were 14,929 large contributions to candidates and committees in the 12 states that CRF studied. This makes a grand total of 71,750 contributions of $500 or more in the 1972 election, more than a three-fold increase over the CRF data base of 1968. No separate count of individual contributors was made for 1972 because the numbers were so great and the sources so diverse. But if one applies the same ratio of contributors to contributions as was found in 1968 when a separate count was kept, one could project some 51,230 individual contributors of $500 or more in the 1972 campaign (husbands and wives are counted as one). However, many of the large contributors in 1972 were recorded more than once because their gifts were made in sums of $3,000 or less to avoid the gift tax. Therefore, it is likely that the actual number of contributors who gave $500 or more in 1972 was fewer than 51,230; a reasonable estimate would be 50,000 such contributors.

In the analyses that follow, it is important to remember that the data normally do not include single contributions of less than $500, even if one individual made gifts that aggregated $500 or more.

Contributors of $10,000 or More

In 1972, because of the expansion of information sources and interest in the events of the year, CRF prepared a publication of contributors and lenders of $10,000 or more.[2] To compile this listing, both governmental and nongovernmental sources were examined. In some cases, if warranted, verified information received in interviews about contributions was added to officially filed listings of contributions. Where precise amounts could not be verified, minimal known amounts were given. Therefore, some contributions may have been larger than indicated.

Since the 1960 elections, CRF has kept count of very large contributors (those whose contributions aggregated $10,000 or more). In 1972, $51.3 million was raised from 1,254 individuals who each made aggregate gifts of $10,000 or more to candidates and/or committees of one or more parties. This is more than four times the amount recorded from contributors in this category in 1968 under less stringent reporting requirements. The average contribution rose from $28,745 in 1968 to $40,925 in 1972. As shown in Table 10-4, 1968 reflected a dramatic increase over previous election years in the numbers of contributors of $10,000 or more.

Table 10-4

Individuals Contributing $500 and Over, $10,000 and Over, and Amounts Given by Individuals Contributing $10,000 and Over

Year[a]	No. of Individuals Contributing $500 and Over	No. of Individuals Contributing $10,000 and Over	Amounts Given by Individuals Contributing $10,000 and Over
1952	9,500	110	$ 1,936,870
1956	8,100	111	2,300,000
1960	5,300	95	1,552,009
1964	10,000	130	2,161,905
1968	15,000	424	12,187,863+
1972	51,230[b]	1,254[c]	51,320,154

[a]The filings and lists that provided data about individual contributors of $500 or more were not the same for each of these six years. Data for 1952 and 1956 are from Alexander Heard, *The Costs of Democracy* (Chapel Hill: The University of North Carolina Press, 1960), p. 53, note 37. For subsequent years, see Alexander, *Financing the . . . Election.*

[b]As noted above in the text, this figure is derived from the same ratio used for the 1968 figure, when reporting conditions were somewhat different, and may be inflated.

[c]Includes individuals who contributed an aggregate of $10,000 or more to candidates and/or committees. Does not include: candidates who contributed to their own campaigns; loans; contributions that if combined with loans add to $10,000 or more; or returned contributions.

Sixty-four percent ($33,084,200) of the $51,320,154 contributed by very large donors came from those who gave to only one party (straight contributors). Of the remainder, 36 percent ($18,235,954) came from individuals who gave to two or more opposing parties (split contributors).

Some $14.3 million of the straight party gifts came from 82 individuals who gave an aggregate of $100,000 or more. Table 10-5 shows the distribution of the 1972 straight party contributors.

Gifts in the $100,000 or more category made up 48 percent ($11,081,142) of the total straight contributions ($23,336,120) to the Republican party or candidates, and 34 percent ($3,243,358) of the total straight Democratic

Table 10-5
1972 Straight Party Contributors of $10,000 or More

	Number of Contributors	Amount
$ 10,000-$24,999	582	$ 8,473,099.22[a]
$ 25,000-$49,999	176	5,803,485.66
$ 50,000-$99,999	71	4,483,114.72
$100,000 & over	82	14,324,500.31
Totals	911	$33,084,199.91

[a]This includes $207,397.65 from contributors who gave amounts of less than $10,000, which aggregated $10,000 or over (e.g., Republican−$6,000, miscellaneous−$4,000).

contributions ($9,393,414). The major beneficiary of large contributions was former President Nixon, who received $19.8 million in gifts from straight party contributions in the $10,000 and over category, with more than half of that sum (52 percent) in gifts made before the April 7 disclosure deadline. McGovern's straight party contributors in the $10,000 and over category gave him a total of $4.1 million (96 percent of it after April 7). Other major beneficiaries of gifts in this category include Humphrey ($973,465), Muskie ($913,838), Sanford ($711,000), and Bayh ($430,000) in his 1971 campaign. In all, 16 presidential candidates were recipients of straight party contributions in the $10,000 and over group—13 Democrats (McGovern, Muskie, Humphrey, Wallace, Jackson, Mills, Bayh, Hartke, McCarthy, Lindsay, Sanford, Yorty, and Chisholm), and three Republicans (Nixon, McCloskey, and Ashbrook); four Democratic (Shriver, Eagleton, Gravel, and Peabody) and one Republican (Agnew) vicepresidential candidates were also recipients in this category.

Split Contributors

Some $18.2 million came from individuals who split their aggregated $10,000-or-more gifts between or among the candidates and/or committees of different parties. The Republicans received $11.7 million of the $18.2 million amount; the Democrats received $6.2 million, with the remainder going either to minor parties or to business, professional, labor, or nonpartisan committees. There were 343 contributors with an aggregate gift of $10,000 or more in the split contribution category. Just over half of the split total, $9.9 million or 55 percent, came from 40 contributors whose aggregate giving was $100,000 or more.

The split contributors tended to divide their gifts between different levels—giving, for example, to a presidential candidate of one party and a senatorial candidate of another, or to a candidate of one party in the primary and a candidate of another in the general election; in most cases, the primary candidate had lost the nomination. Still there were exceptions to this, even at the presidential level. Appendix Q lists the 116 split contributions made to candidates or committees at the same level.

Ninety-one contributors in the very large gift category gave money both to Nixon and to one or more of the Democratic contenders for nomination. In 14 instances, contributors gave both to Nixon and McGovern; Nixon won in dollar amounts from these, but by a far smaller margin than in the general election—$213,445 to $191,746.

At the presidential level, the most frequent splits were between Nixon and Muskie and between Nixon and Jackson; there were 29 instances of each combination. Nixon and Humphrey figured in 27 splits. Nineteen of the split contributors gave to Nixon and two Democrats; three gave to Nixon and three Democrats; and one contributor, Charles E. Smith—a Washington, D.C. realtor—divided his contributions among no less than six presidential candidates: Nixon ($10,000), McGovern ($2,100), Jackson ($10,000), Humphrey ($3,000), Muskie ($5,000), and Hartke ($250).

A number of split contributions totalling $10,000 or more occurred at the congressional and state levels. Nine individuals split their contributions between rival senatorial candidates from the same state, and four did the same between House candidates. Four splits also occurred in state contests—two in Texas and two in California.

Lenders of $10,000 or More

Some 284 individuals made loans of $10,000 or more to candidates and/or committees of the major parties in 1972; two more individuals lent $10,000 or more to other parties or other committees. A total of $11.8 million was lent, $9.9 million to the Democrats by 202 lenders and $1.9 million to the Republicans by 82 lenders.

More than $4 million of the Democratic loans were to the McGovern campaign. This includes $566,617 in loans to McGovern, which were later converted to contributions. The largest of all converted loans were those by Anne Forsyth to Terry Sanford, totalling $700,000.

In addition, 45 individuals made loans that aggregated $10,000 or more to candidates of both parties, adding more than $2.7 million to the loan total. Most of this, $2.2 million, went to Democrats, with the McGovern campaign accounting for about $1.4 million of the "split loan" total. McGovern also had loans of $10,200 from this category converted. Adding together these straight and split lenders, McGovern received $5.4 million, of which nearly $600,000 was converted into gifts.

Summary of Contributors and Lenders of
$10,000 or More

In 1972 the count CRF kept of those individuals who either contributed or
lent in aggregates of $10,000 or more was 1,456 (1,254 straight and split con-
tributors plus 331 straight and split lenders, adjusting for 129 individuals who
fell into both $10,000 or more contributor and $10,000 or more lender categories). This number is three percent of all contributors of $500 or more, and a
fraction of one percent of the total number of contributors in 1972—probably
some 11.7 million givers at all levels.

The Republicans raised $35,084,262 from contributors of $10,000 or more,
while $2,343,478 was in loans of $10,000 or more. The comparable Democratic figures were $15,633,427 in contributions and $12,138,716 in loans.
Although the Democratic amounts are totals for all candidates and committees
on record, it is clear that the total large loans made to McGovern ($5,440,122),
particularly at the onset of his general election campaign, added largely to the
loan total.

Historically, the large individual contributor has played a major role in
presidential elections but never before 1972 was so much detail about the contributions of such persons available. The top 25 contributors in 1972 gave a
total of $11.6 million dollars to political candidates at the federal, state, or
local levels. The top ten contributors accounted for $7.4 million of that total
and are listed in Table 10-6.

Table 10-6
1972 Ten Largest Contributors

W. Clement and Jessie V. Stone	$2,141,665.94
Richard Mellon Scaife	1,068,000.00
Stewart Mott	830,339.50
Anne and Frank Forsyth	703,000.00
John A. and Naomi Mulcahy	681,558.97
Leon Hess	481,000.00
Meshulam Riklis	449,000.00
Max Palevsky	377,190.00
Martin and Anne Peretz	343,968.47
Dwayne Andreas	342,994.11

Note: Includes 1970-71 gifts to 1972 presidential campaigns.

Five of the top ten gave at least part of their political contributions to the
Finance Committee to Re-Elect the President (FCRP), although several also
supported Democratic centrist candidates such as Jackson and Humphrey. The

first two on the list, W. Clement (and Jessie V.) Stone and Richard Mellon Scaife, were for Nixon; the third, Stewart Mott, was for McGovern. The fourth, Anne (and Frank) Forsyth, gave most of their gifts to the candidacy of Terry Sanford.

Five of these donors—Mott, the Forsyths, Riklis, Palevsky, and the Peretzes—were also large lenders. With the exception of Riklis' $550,000 loan to the Humphrey campaign, none of these loans are still outstanding; all were either converted to gifts that are included in the contributions above, or were repaid.

Missing from this list of top givers, except for Richard Mellon Scaife, are the names of the great American fortunes—the Fords, Rockefellers, Whitneys, and Astors—whose support had been crucial in earlier political campaigns, particularly those of the Republicans. In 1972 they were replaced by donors such as W. Clement Stone or John Mulcahy who could boast of Horatio Alger-type success stories. On the Democratic side, the liberal millionaires Stewart Mott, Max Palevsky, and Martin Peretz are among the top ten, replacing the traditional Democratic supporters, such as the Lehmans, the Harrimans and others.

The Nixon campaign in 1972 numbered 153 individuals who made contributions of $50,000 or more, accounting for $19,801,585, or 33 percent of the campaign's total.

McGovern had 41 contributors in the $50,000 or more category, whose gifts and/or loans made up $7,118,282, or 25 percent of his campaign total. Twenty-seven McGovern supporters made outright gifts of $50,000 or more, while 30 lent the sum of $50,000 or more; 16 of the 57 both contributed and lent $50,000 or more, so the actual number of individuals is 41. Of McGovern's $7.1 million from contributors in this category, $3,296,464 was in gifts, $3,821,818 was in loans (the contribution figure, $3,296,464, includes loan amounts that were converted to contributions).

The Nixon campaign thus had about six times as much money as the McGovern campaign in outright gifts from very large contributors.

The Democratic presidential campaign counted five contributors who gave about $200,000 or more; Daniel Noyes, who gave just under that total ($199,317) is not included among the five. In contrast, the Committee to Re-Elect the President (CRP) had 21 contributors in the $200,000 and over category. The top Nixon and McGovern contributors are listed in Table 10-7.

Several of the very largest contributors gave to both Republican and Democratic presidential campaigns. Leon Hess, of Amerada Hess, who is in Nixon's Top 25 list (with a gift of $250,000), also gave $225,000 to the presidential primary campaign of Senator Henry Jackson. Meshulam Riklis, chairman of Rapid American Corporation, gave $188,000 to Nixon, and was also a major contributor to the primary campaigns of Jackson (with a $100,000 gift) and Hubert Humphrey (with a $125,000 contribution). Riklis also lent Humphrey $550,000 for his 1972 presidential bid.

Table 10-7
Top Nixon and McGovern Contributors

Nixon	Amount	McGovern[a]	Amount
W. Clement Stone	$2,051,643.45	Stewart R. Mott	$407,747.50
Richard Mellon Scaife	1,000,000.00	Max Palevsky[b]	319,365.00
John A. Mulcahy	624,558.97	Anne and Martin Peretz	275,016.44
Arthur Watson	303,000.00	Alejandro Zaffaroni	206,752.76
Ruth and George Farkas	300,000.00	Nicholas Noyes	205,000.00
John J. Louis, Jr.	283,360.22	Daniel Noyes	199,317.11
John Rollins	265,523.50	Alan and Shane Davis	158,872.25
Roy Carver	263,323.77	Richard Saloman	137,752.02
Sam Schulman	262,574.56	Joan Palevsky	118,616.86
Daniel Terra	255,000.00	Miles Rubin	108,000.00
Walter Annenberg	254,000.00	Bruce Allen	100,000.00
John Safer	251,000.00	John Lewis	100,000.00
Kent Smith	251,000.00	Henry Kimelman	82,533.99
Leon Hess	250,000.00	Albrecht Saalfield	82,000.00
Saul Steinberg	250,000.00	Diana and Salim Lewis	74,950.00
Jack Massey	249,999.96	Howard Metzenbaum	72,416.98
Max Fisher	249,773.05	Abner Levine	69,452.53
Ray Kroc	237,000.00	Alva Ted Bonda	67,454.73
Jack Dreyfus	231,000.00	Carol Bernstein	63,926.03
F.L. Cappeart	213,000.00	Robert Meyerhoff	63,486.52
Raymond Guest	200,000.00	Frank Lautenberg	57,955.48

[a]Includes loan amounts that were converted.

[b]Includes contributions from 1970.

Combined Contributions and Loans of
$10,000 or More

Forty-one persons made loans and contributions in the 1972 campaigns, which when added together came to $10,000 or more. The totals of the loans and contributions were divided very evenly, $234,304 in loans, $239,800 in contributions.

The Democrats received more than four times as much money as did the Republicans in this category—$377,169 to the Democrats, $94,435 to the Republicans. Fifty-two percent of the Democratic money and 43 percent of the Republican money came from contributions.

In addition, two individuals whose combined loans and contributions aggregated $10,000 or more split the money between the two parties. Of the total of $30,700 involved, the Republicans got $17,800; the Democrats received $11,900, with $1,000 from one of the individual's total going to a miscellaneous committee.

Candidates' Contributions and Loans of
$10,000 or More to their Own Campaigns

A total of 247 candidates either contributed directly to their own campaigns in 1972 or put up personal money to help pay off debts they incurred. Nearly $3.6 million was in contributions, $2.2 million in loans.

The former Postmaster General in the Nixon administration, Winston M. Blount, an Alabama millionaire, paid $325,000 on his own 1972 campaign debt for his unsuccessful race against Senator John J. Sparkman. Although the 1974 Amendments limit a Senate candidate to personal contributions of $35,000, as did the 1971 FECA, outstanding debts from the 1972 campaign were exempted so they could be paid off. Blount made his payments in the form of a $325,332 contribution to the Blount for Senate Campaign Committee to pay off his remaining 1972 debts, which included $35,000 owed to his brother William H. Blount.[3]

Overall, Democratic candidates contributed more to their own campaigns than did Republican candidates—$1.8 million Democratic candidate contributions to $1.2 million Republican candidate contributions (the latter includes Blount's $325,332). Table 10-8 shows the distribution of contributions for Republicans and Democrats.

The distribution of loans by candidates to their own campaigns shows much the same pattern, with the Democratic loan total amounting to $1,239,839, and the Republican loan total being $997,217.

Individual Contributions Returned

Ten of the very large contributors had some or all of their campaign gifts returned; the total returned from this group amounted to $1,268,000. The bulk

Table 10-8
Republican and Democratic Distribution of Contributions

	Republican	Democratic	Miscellaneous
Less than $10,000	$ 46,059.89	$ 100,734.50	$ 0.00
$10,000-$24,999	606,980.52	975,386.16	435,552.85
$25,000-$49,999	243,691.00	389,987.66	115,483.03
$50,000-$99,999	0.00	209,333.35	0.00
$100,000 and over	325,332.00	109,000.00	0.00
Totals	$1,222,062.41	$1,784,441.67	$551,035.88

of the returned money, $1,250,000, was returned by the FCRP. The McGovern campaign returned $14,000, and Jackson returned $4,000 in gifts from large contributors. (These returned amounts are not included in any of the totals or analyses above.)

Commentary

In 1972 political contributors of $10,000 or more gave $55,577,729. The components of this amount, as noted above, are: contributions of $10,000 or more to one or more parties (plus contributions of under $10,000 from lenders of $10,000 or more to one or more parties); contributions that when combined with loans added up to $10,000 or more to one or more parties; contributions by candidates to their own campaigns, either of $10,000 or more, or of less, which when added to loans totalled $10,000 or more, and also their under-$10,000 contributions to other candidates and committees. Not included are contributions that were returned.

The comparable loan figure is $17,177,196, which includes loans that were later converted, forgiven, or repaid. The components of this amount are: loans of $10,000 or more to one or more parties (plus loans of under $10,000 from contributors of $10,000 or more to one or more parties); loans that when combined with contributions added up to $10,000 or more to one or more parties; loans by candidates to their own campaigns, either of $10,000 or more, or of less, which when added to contributions totalled $10,000 or more, also their under-$10,000 loans to other candidates and committees.

In the future, because of the $25,000 overall limit on individual contributions to federal candidates contained in the 1974 Amendments, much of the money of over-$25,000 contributors will be excluded. Some state and local contributions not falling under the federal limits are included in the 1972 data, and will continue to aggregate above the $25,000 federal limit.

Extent of Large Contributions

The extent to which the large contributor dominated the funding of Richard Nixon's reelection campaign while playing a smaller role in that of George McGovern's campaign was dramatized in a study made for the Senate Watergate Committee by Alexander W. Keema.[4] The study considered what the impact would have been on the 1972 race had individual contributions been limited to $3,000. An even lower limit of $1,000 per campaign went into effect in 1975 as a result of the FECA Amendments of 1974.

Keema, an experienced auditor on loan from the auditing staff of the Office of Federal Elections at GAO, shows that the CRP would have lost just over half of its total contributions if gifts were limited to $3,000 from an individual to a candidate. According to the study, the CRP raised $63,400,000 (a somewhat higher figure than is used in this book), but only $30,657,000 of this came from contributors of $3,000 or less. Table 10-9 reproduces Keema's findings.[b]

In contrast, McGovern would have lost only $13,248,000 of his total individual contributions ($49,660,000) to his combined primary and general election campaigns, 27 percent of the total, (again a higher figure than used in this book). Available to McGovern, in fact, if a $3,000 limit per contributor had been in effect, would have been nearly $6 million more than Nixon would have had.

Hardest hit by such a limit, however, would have been Hubert Humphrey's 1972 presidential bid, in which 69 percent of his money came from contributors giving more than $3,000 each. Only $1,577,000 of the total of $5,049,000 raised for Humphrey, Keema's study shows, came from contributors who would qualify under the $3,000 limit. Edmund Muskie would have fared, proportionately, close to where McGovern did—33 percent of the total raised for him ($872,000 or $2,312,000) would have been lost.

McGovern did depend heavily on large contributors, however, for his "up front" money, which came in during the early stages of his primary campaign. The Keema study analyzed contributions and the impact of the $3,000 limit both before and after the April 7 disclosure date, which, in McGovern's case, could also serve to mark a time when he was just beginning to move up in the national polls (the Wisconsin primary, which McGovern won, was on April 14).

---

[b]Keema notes problems in using the data. The pre-April 7 figures for the Democratic candidates were compiled from contributions voluntarily disclosed by the candidates in the *CRF Listing of: Political Contributors of $500 or More Voluntarily Disclosed by 1972 Presidential Candidates.* The data do not include contributions of less than $500. The total receipts of candidates in the pre-April 7 period are thus necessarily understated while the percentage of receipts lost (in excess of $3,000) is somewhat overstated; the pre-April 7 figures for Nixon were taken from the FCRP filing with the Clerk of the House of Representatives on September 28, 1973. All figures from April 7 to December 31, 1972, for all candidates were taken from filings with the GAO.

A computer program was used to aggregate the multiple contributions made by many individuals to the numerous committees supporting each candidate (such multiple contributions were usually made to avoid gift taxes). Contributions were aggregated by matching names and addresses of contributors. Some contributions were not aggregated due to differences in street names, numbers, middle initials, etc. Such differences resulted in the treatment of some multiple contributions by the same individuals as contributions by different people. This distortion is reflected in the post-April 7 contributions of all candidates. Because of this type of distortion, the amount theoretically lost under a $3,000 contribution limit would be somewhat understated while the net amount available to the campaign would be overstated. However, since the computer failed to distinguish between contributions from individuals and those from a man and wife, all contributions were treated as though they were made by single individuals. This distortion tends to offset the incomplete aggregation problem. A sampling of the computer detail indicates that the total of post-April 7, 1972 contributions of $3,000 or less is somewhat overstated while the total of contributions in excess of $3,000 is somewhat understated.

Table 10-9
Impact of a $3,000 Limit on Contributions to Four Presidential Candidates, 1972

Period	Total Contributions Received	Amount That Would be Lost to Campaign (in Excess of $3,000)	Amount That Would be Available to Campaign (Amts. $3,000 or Less)	Percent of Contribution Lost Under $3,000 Limit
Richard M. Nixon:				
Pre-April 7, 1972	$19,940,000	$15,516,000	$ 4,424,000	78%
April 7-December 31, 1972	43,287,000	17,227,000	26,060,000	40
Totals	$63,227,000	$32,743,000	$30,484,000	52
George S. McGovern:				
Pre-April 7, 1972	$ 728,000	$ 454,000	$ 274,000	62
April 7-December 31, 1972	48,932,000	12,794,000	36,138,000	26
Totals	$49,660,000	$13,248,000	$36,412,000	27
Hubert H. Humphrey:				
Pre-April 7, 1972	$ 781,000	$ 538,000	$ 243,000	69
April 7-December 31, 1972	4,268,000	2,934,000	1,334,000	69
Totals	$ 5,049,000	$ 3,472,000	$ 1,577,000	69
Edmund S. Muskie:				
Pre-April 7, 1972	$ 1,589,000	$ 554,000	$ 1,035,000	35
April 7-December 31, 1972	723,000	318,000	405,000	44
Totals	$ 2,312,000	$ 872,000	$ 1,440,000	38%

Source: Table is from Alexander W. Keema, III, "Campaign Finance Reform: Limiting Campaign Contributions," *GAO Review* (Summer 1974), p. 56.

Some 62 percent of the McGovern money that came in before April 7 was from contributors who would exceed the $3,000 limit—$454,000 of a total $728,000.

The drive among large contributors for Nixon is now a familiar part of the Watergate story; Keema notes that some 78 percent of the CRP's pre-April 7 contributions were over the $3,000 level.

In evaluating his study findings, Keema points out that had there been a $3,000 limit in 1972, it might well have changed the outcome of some Democratic primaries. As it was, Muskie, the acknowledged front-runner early in 1972 with a national name, had a two-to-one money advantage over McGovern in the pre-April 7 period—a period when many political observers felt Muskie stumbled badly in the New Hampshire primary and then came in a disastrous fourth in the Florida primary. Had there been the $3,000 limit, however, Muskie, less dependent than the then relatively unknown McGovern on large contributors at that stage, would have had a five-to-one edge in funds over McGovern. With this kind of advantage Muskie could conceivably have cut some of the losses he was suffering then.[5]

The degree to which the CRP was counting on the large donor can be seen elsewhere. In the spring of 1971 White House aide Jack Gleason prepared a proposed budget for the 1972 campaign and transmitted it to Jeb Magruder. It set the needs at $40 million (half again as much was actually raised) and had a breakdown of projected sources of funds by size of contribution. More than 90 percent of the total needed was seen as coming from contributors over the $3,000 limit; some 56 percent in fact was projected as coming from contributors in the $100,000-plus category. Only $1,500,000, the Gleason figures indicated, could be expected from contributors in the under-$1,000 category, and another $1,250,000 would come in the $1,000-$5,000 range.[6]

The man seeking out the big contributors at this stage of the campaign was Herbert Kalmbach, who, as he travelled around the country meeting with potential contributors, suggested an amount to each, and used the aggregate— $13.4 million—as a "goal figure" he sought to produce. He succeeded in getting $10,658,000, with over $8.8 million of that contributed prior to the April 7 disclosure date.[c] Kalmbach's efforts with the individual large contributor amounted to a commitment for nearly one-third of the total CRP budget as it was then conceived; Kalmbach stated that he did not know until 1973 that some of the contributions had been illegal corporate gifts.

Had he been restrained by a $3,000 limit, however, Kalmbach would have

---

[c]The Watergate Committee *Report* contains a notable list of "Individuals Solicited by Herbert W. Kalmbach and Actual Contributions"; see Senate Select Committee on Presidential Campaign Activities, *Final Report*, No. 93-981, 93rd Cong., 2d Sess. (Washington, D.C.: U.S. Government Printing Office, June 1974), pp. 508-10.

been virtually out of business. According to Keema's figures, only two of his 67 individual contributors would have been under the limit in their pre-April 7 contributions—James Copley of La Jolla, California gave $500; Lebaron Willard of Baltimore, Maryland, Chairman of the Commercial Credit Co., gave $3,000. Both men, however, gave substantially more later in the campaign; Copley's total gift was $30,478, Willard's was $9,250. More importantly, had his 67 contributors been limited to $3,000, Kalmbach could have raised only $191,000 instead of $10,658,396—or less than a fiftieth of the actual total.

While the methodology used in Keema's study combines pre- and post-April 7 contributions, and thus distorts figures (especially for McGovern because it combines his pre- and postnomination contributions) the implications are certain: tremendous amounts of money would be lost to politics by the $3,000 cutoff initially being discussed as a contribution limit. The $1,000 limit enacted in the 1974 Amendments cuts even deeper. An analysis of just how deeply was prepared by Common Cause for use in arguing in favor of the Amendments in the suit brought against the law by Senators James Buckley, Eugene McCarthy, and others. Although the data are not directly comparable with the Keema analysis, the base being different, the findings are revealing. They indicate that had there been a $1,000 limit in 1972, Nixon would have raised $24,470,000 and McGovern $24,540,000. It would have eliminated $33,100,000 in contributions to Nixon and $13,225,000 in gifts to McGovern. Minor party committees, which raised $1,043,000 in 1972 in individual contributions would still have raised $977,000. Of course, the matching incentives in the presidential prenomination period and government allocations in the presidential general election period are intended to provide alternative sources to make up for the losses.

Keema's article also contains data illustrating the use and importance of loans to the four campaigns; these are shown in Table 10-10. Loans were included within the definition of contributions under the 1971 law, and are limited to $1,000 under the 1974 Amendments. In 1972, according to Keema, in excess of $9.6 million in loans was made at one time or another to the McGovern campaign—a higher figure than otherwise used in this book. Some lenders rolled over their loans, getting repaid, and lending again. Most lenders were also large contributors, and some converted loans, or portions of loans, to gifts. The Nixon campaign had no need of loans since contributed money was available, and contends that the Keema figures are in error. The FCRP states that it received no loans in 1972 from anyone; however, it did discount with banks certain notes received from contributors, totalling about $600,000. All such amounts were repaid in full except for the $305,000 from Walter Duncan, which the FCRP repaid when Duncan defaulted. In any case, either a $3,000 or $1,000 limitation considerably reduces the importance of loans as a factor in financing campaigns.

Table 10-10
Loans Made and Repaid to Four Presidential Candidates, 1972

Candidate	Total Contributions Received	Total Loans Received	Total Loans Repaid	Net Receipts Available to Campaign	Loans as Percent of Total Contributions
Richard M. Nixon	$63,227,000	$1,249,000	$ 589,000	$62,638,000	2%
George S. McGovern	49,660,000	9,633,000	5,209,000	44,451,000	19
Hubert H. Humphrey	5,049,000	1,533,000	464,000	4,585,000	30
Edmund S. Muskie	2,312,000	223,000	114,000	2,198,000	10

Source: Table is from Keema, "Campaign Finance Reform," p. 58.

Notes: The four candidates made widely varying use of loans to finance their campaigns. To the extent that these loans were repaid, the "Total Contributions Received" figures overstate the amounts that the candidates had available for normal campaign expenditures. Loans that were not repaid by the candidates' committees were generally forgiven and thus converted into ordinary contributions.

While the great majority of loans were made to political committees by individuals, a few loans were made between political committees.

Thus, the total loan figures may be slightly overstated.

The FCRP contends that the loan figures are in error, as explained in the text.

Thirteen Selected Groups

The Gore Committee in 1956 compared its lists of contributors against lists of officers and directors of 13 various trade associations and special-interest groups, and in succeeding presidential elections CRF has analyzed current lists of officers and directors of the same 13 selected groups against contributor lists. Appendix R presents the groups and the results of the 1972 analysis.

The individual officers and directors identified with these groups are assumed to contribute as individuals, not formally on behalf of the group. Table 10-11 shows a comparison of the last five presidential elections in total giving in large sums by members of these groups.

Table 10-11
Total Contributions of 13 Selected Groups: 1956, 1960, 1964, 1968, and 1972

Year	Republicans	Democrats	Miscellaneous	Total[a]
1972	$3,323,283+	$339,950+	$32,206	$3,695,440+
1968	1,132,982+	136,106	11,967	1,281,055+
1964	200,310	225,790	4,618	468,218
1960	425,710	62,225	2,500	493,465
1956	741,189	8,000	2,725	751,914

[a]Republican and Democratic columns do not equal the total amounts because some contributors belonged to more than one of the 13 groups, and duplicated amounts have been subtracted in the overall totals.

Some 31 percent of the officers and directors of these combined groups were reported as contributing in 1972—about three times the percentage for the population as a whole. From 1956 through 1968, with less disclosure than in 1972, the percentage of contributors recorded among the 13 groups did not exceed 18 percent. The highest level of participation in 1972 was among members of the Business Council, an elite group who own, finance, or manage the country's major enterprises; 80 percent (88 members of 112) made a contribution of $500 or more; they were also the highest in 1968 when, with the less comprehensive disclosure law, 58 percent made large contributions.

Business Council contributors since 1956 are shown in Table 10-12.

At the bottom of the 13 groups was the American Medical Association, for which, for the second straight presidential election, no gift of $500 or more from an officer or director was reported. Of course, these doctors may be contributing in smaller amounts or through groups such as AMPAC.

Over the last five presidential elections, members of the groups have tended to contribute heavily to Republican causes; only in 1964, as with a number of other traditionally Republican supporters, was the dollar total slightly larger for the Democrats than it was for the Republicans. In 1972, 90 percent of the

Table 10-12

Business Council Contributors and Partisan Contributions Among Active and Graduate Members: 1972, 1968, 1964, 1960, and 1956

Year	Number of Members	Number of Contributors	Number of Contributors and Amount of Contributions Rep.	Dem.	Miscellaneous
1972	118	93[a]	89 $1,014,123	23 $154,555	9 $11,742
1968	119	69[b]	67 280,913	5 83,000	9 3,300
1964	118	63[c]	36 87,100	33 135,450	
1960	124	80	73 241,060	7 35,140	
1956	161	73	68 268,499	4 4,000	

Source: 1956 data from Gore Committee *Report*, exhibit 22, pp. 86-88.

[a]Total members include 17 splits, 6 R & M, and 2 who gave to Republican, Democratic, and miscellaneous causes.

[b]Total members include three splits and 2 R & M (Rep. & Misc.).

[c]Total members include six split contributors, each counted twice, once in Republican column and once in Democratic column.

total went to the Republicans, and the bulk of it ($2,602,849 of $3,323,283) went to the Nixon campaign. McGovern, in contrast, got only $1,250, or less than one percent of the far smaller Democratic total.

The same heavy Republican preponderance holds as one goes down the list, looking at the giving patterns of each group in 1972. In ten of the groups, more than 80 percent of the money was contributed to the Republicans; the National Coal Association records no Democratic contributions, three others—the Chiefs of Foreign and Special Missions, the Manufacturing Chemists Association, and the National Association of Manufacturers—gave over 90 percent Republican.

The one real exception to this pattern in 1972 was the American Bar Association; the Democrats received more money than the Republicans, $33,473 to $28,450, a sharp turnabout from 1968 where the contributions of ABA officers and directors had split 80-20 for Republicans. It should be noted, however, that nearly half ($15,000) of the 1972 Democratic total was a contribution by one individual, E. Smythe Gambrell of Atlanta, Georgia, to his son's senatorial campaign. Of the Republican total $17,800 or 63 percent was donated to the Nixon reelection effort.

The reward of certain ambassadorial posts to large contributors has been common practice in United States politics, and thus one of the groups analyzed was the chiefs of foreign missions and special missions. In 1972 there were 116 such posts, 80 held by foreign service career officers, 36 held by others. From the entire group, there were 23 large contributors, 20 of whom were not career officers. The 23 gave a total of $1,117,964, 99 percent of which went to Republicans. The average individual contribution from this group was far larger than from any of the others—about $48,400 was the mean, compared with, for example, an average of $12,700 from the Business Council contributors. Other mean individual contribution figures above $2,000 are shown by the American Petroleum Institute ($9,400), National Association of Manufacturers ($4,160), and the U.S. Chamber of Commerce ($2,100). Six individuals in the chiefs of mission category, all of them already serving as ambassadors in 1972 by appointment of President Nixon, made contributions of $100,000 or more to the Nixon reelection campaign. These were: Walter H. Annenberg, Great Britain, $254,000; Arthur K. Watson, France, $303,000; Kingdon Gould, Jr., Luxembourg, $100,900; Vincent de Roulet, Jamaica, $103,000; Shelby Cullum Davis, Switzerland, $100,000; John P. Humes, Austria, $100,000.

Petroleum Groups

The alleged influence of the oil and gas interests on national policy is a perennial campaign issue that has taken on a new shade of concern since the energy crisis in the winter of 1973. The contribution patterns of officers and directors of five petroleum organizations were analyzed both in 1968 and 1972; the American Petroleum Institute was one of the 13 groups discussed above, plus four others—American Gas Association, National Petroleum Refiners Association, Independent National Gas Association of America (INGAA), and Independent Petroleum Association of America (IPAA).

Contributions from these organizations were more diversified and less Republican than a number of other groups examined. About 52 percent of their contributions, for example, went to the Nixon campaign, compared with some 70 percent to that cause from the 13 selected groups considered above. Figures in Table 10-13 show the percentage of Republican contributions in 1972 from each of five organizations. Some 30 percent of the total money, it should be noted, is represented by the contributions of one individual, Leon Hess, chairman of the Executive Committee of Amerada Hess Corporation, whose gift to the Nixon campaign of $250,000 was nearly matched by the $225,000 gift he made to the presidential prenomination campaign of Democratic Senator Henry Jackson.

The percentage who contributed to a political campaign in 1972 from among the officers and directors of these petroleum organizations was about

Table 10-13

Five Petroleum Organizations Contributors and Partisan Contributions Among Officers, Directors, and Honorary Directors, 1972

Organiz.	Total Contributions of Officers and Directors	Nos. of Contributors	Percent of Total		
			Republican	Democratic	Miscellaneous
American Petroleum Institute	$ 928,680	98	88%	12%	0.2%
American Gas Association	11,500	8	69	26	5.0
National Petroleum Refinery	503,357	19	54	46	0.3
INGAA	13,034	10	90	4	6.0
IPAA	218,697	76	55	45	0.0
Totals	$1,623,887[a]	199	73%[b]	27%[b]	0.3%[b]

[a]Some individuals are officials of more than one of the five groups. In these cases, the contributions are included in each individual group; however, the final total eliminates all contribution duplications.

[b]Fractional differences not adding to 100 percent are due to rounding.

that noted in the aforementioned 13 selected groups—31 percent, or 199 of 645 in the total group. Participation levels ranged from 50 percent for the American Petroleum Institute to 29 percent with IPAA, 28 with INGAA, 22 with the American Gas Association, and 16 percent among members of the National Petroleum Refiners Association.

In contrast, the National Coal Association was another of the 13 groups, and 26 percent or 11 of 42, of its officers and directors, contributed $18,300 to Republicans and no money to Democrats. In addition, one director lent $10,000 to a Republican.

Largest Defense and Industrial Companies

Analysis was also made of large contributions ($500 or more) by officers and directors of the 25 largest contractors for each of the following: the Defense Department, the Atomic Energy Commission, the National Aeronautics and Space Agency.[d] The three agencies are the federal government's largest buyers of military and other hardware. Defense alone spends more than $20 billion a year on weapons systems and equipment.

As a control group, large contributions from the officers and directors of the 25 largest industrial companies on the "*Fortune* 500" list were also studied. The composite of the four "top 25" lists totalled 72 companies because of duplications (General Electric, for example, appeared on all four lists; others were on two or three.) The total number of officers and directors of these companies was 2,159. Table 10-14 presents the groups and the results.

Table 10-14

Contributions from Officers and Directors of the 25 Largest Defense and Industrial Companies in Each of Four Groups, 1972

	Pentagon	*AEC*	*NASA*	*Fortune Industrial*
Total number of officers and directors	998	632	772	1,073
Number of individual contributors	364	184	236	402
Total contributions	$2,107,677	$674,535	$1,276,705	$1,757,251
Republican				
Number of contributors[a]	306	140	173	329
Amount of contributions	1,852,694	616,570	1,082,203	1,516,374
Democratic				
Number of contributors[a]	54	18	39	58
Amount of contributions	216,613	25,965	163,821	202,429
Miscellaneous				
Number of contributors[a]	57	52	52	55
Amount of contributions	38,370	32,001	30,681	38,449

Note: For each of the four groups, certain individuals were officials of more than one company within that group. They and their contributions have been counted only once.

[a]Due to the presence of individuals who gave to more than one party or cause, the number of Republican, Democratic, and miscellaneous contributors is larger than the total number of individual contributors given at the top of each column. The first total gives the actual number of individuals.

The study revealed 30 percent (641 persons) of these members of the top echelons of American business as large contributors. Their total contributions

---

[d]For an independent analysis of this data, see *Congressional Quarterly Weekly Report*, October 5, 1974, pp. 2668-74.

exceeded $3 million. Support for Republican candidates dominated. Of a total of $3,065,908 recorded in the study, $2,613,304—85 percent—went to GOP candidates or committees. The Democrats got $403,324, while $49,280 went elsewhere—to minor parties and political action groups.

Among the largest contributors in the business community was multimillionaire recluse Howard Hughes, president of Hughes Aircraft Corporation, with gifts of $197,000 to the Republicans and $3,000 to Democrats. His company was the tenth largest Pentagon contractor in fiscal 1972, with contracts totalling $688,132,000, and the twentieth largest NASA contractor ($22,029,000 in fiscal 1972). Not counted in his gift to the Republicans is $100,000 given to the Nixon campaign before the April 7, 1972 disclosure deadline—the now-famous $100,000 given to Charles G. (Bebe) Rebozo, who has said he kept the cash in a strongbox for three years and then returned it. In addition to Hughes, two other executives of his company gave $1,000 to the Republicans and $1,700 to the Democrats.

The analysis did not include corporate contributions, a category of funds that was found to have been illegally contributed in 1972. Only three of the 72 companies—Goodyear Tire & Rubber, Gulf Oil, and Northrop—are among those named for illegal contributions. For example, Gulf's gift of $100,000 to the CRP was subsequently returned. Other illegal Gulf money (also returned) went to the campaigns of Representative Wilbur Mills ($15,000) and Senator Henry Jackson ($10,000). Gulf's totals for this study's purposes were $14,900 to the Republicans and $10,625 to the Democrats—all from officers and directors of the company, and all perfectly legal, so far as is known.

A new focus is provided to the charge by some that certain segments of industry make bloc contributions in return for government contract favoritism. The contributions were broken down into three groups: officers of the company, those who are both officers and directors, and those from outside the company who sit on the board of directors. It is from this last group that the bulk of campaign contributions was made to both parties.

Some 66 percent of the total amounts contributed in 1972 came from outsider directors—a group of men (no women), many from the financial or legal world, who in most cases, because of position and wealth, are serving on a number of boards. They are more likely to be tapped in major fund drives. Forty-three percent of outside directors, for example, were contributors, compared with 23 percent of the insiders, who are more likely to be solely concerned with the company's well-being. It is difficult to ascertain the motives of the outsiders who contribute to any one particular candidate. A case in point would be John McCone, CIA director during the Kennedy and Johnson administrations. McCone was included in the study because of his directorships on the boards of Standard Oil of California and I.T.T. and his contribution of $14,000 to the Nixon campaign. However, McCone is also on the boards of Pacific Mutual Life Insurance and the United California Bank, companies not included in this study. Therefore, his interests must be considered diverse and cannot be attributed to any one company.

Interesting variations emerge among the three different groups of government contractors that were studied. The percentage of large contributors was
highest in the group of Pentagon contractors—37 percent of these officers and
directors made a large gift in 1972. For AEC and NASA contract firms, the
comparable figure is down to about 30 percent. The level is highest of all
among the officers and directors of the companies on the "500" list, where the
impact of government contracts could be more diffuse. Put another way, the
level of large contributions, particularly to Republican causes, from individuals
tied to defense contract firms is, from this evidence, below what it is for the
top-level business community as a whole.

Nor is there evidence of a direct correlation between the amount of business a company got from the defense agencies and the size of campaign contributions from the company's officials. Executives of Litton Industries, for
example, gave the largest amount ($281,709) to political campaigns, but Litton
ranked eleventh as a Defense Department contractor in fiscal 1972 ($616,299,000
in contracts). Lockheed Aircraft Corporation, by contrast, was the largest Pentagon contractor in 1972 ($1.7 billion), yet its officials contributed only $5,100 to
political campaigns that year, ranking it near the bottom.

A point worth emphasizing about the preponderance of Republican contributions from these executives is that these are not exclusively gifts to a presidential race, whose imbalance could be explained by business skittishness over
McGovern's economic proposals. It includes money to Senate and House races,
where the Democrats have been in long-time control. That control, and its accompanying influence over public policies leading to federal contracts, apparently had
little impact on the natural Republican proclivity of these businessmen. These
totals also include money for state races in ten states, where control at the state
level might have economic implications.

The Democratic money tended to be spread far more thinly than the Republican contributions, partly because of the greater demands from the various
presidential primary candidates. An example of the kind of financial edge Nixon
had is seen in the giving patterns of the 25 largest Pentagon contractors. The
former president got 81.9 percent of all Republican large gifts from these officers and directors, McGovern got only 3.4 percent of the far smaller Democratic
total. Table 10-15 shows the division of contributions from the Pentagon contractors to leading presidential contenders.

Analysis reveals that in the case of seven companies on the composite list,
there were no large political contributions of any kind by their officers or directors. Five of these companies were big AEC contractors, two were on the NASA
list. These companies were Reynolds Electrical Engineering Corporation, Holmes
& Marver, Inc., United Nuclear Corporation, Teledyne Isotopes, Inc., Lucius
Pitkin, Inc. (AEC contractors), and Grumman Aerospace Corporation and Federal Electric (NASA).

In contrast to these low political engagement boardrooms are 15 companies
where large gifts were made exclusively to Republican causes. On this list are

Table 10-15
Contributions to 1972 Presidential Contenders: Pentagon Contractors

Nixon	$1,516,922
McGovern	7,450
Lindsay	78,000
Muskie	12,125
Jackson	2,827
Sanford	1,000
Humphrey	700
Mills	500

more of the familiar names of American business, such as Boeing, Sperry Rand, Union Carbide, Dow, Goodyear, International Harvester, and Eastman Kodak. One contractor had officers and directors who contributed only to the Democrats—from the AEC list, it is the United Power Association, a cooperative formerly called the Rural Cooperative Power Association.

Interesting patterns were found in the contributions of officers of three companies, General Motors, Standard Oil of California, and Tenneco, Inc. Twenty-three of 37 GM officers each gave between $1,000 and $3,000 to the Nixon campaign. Thus 62 percent of officers checked gave to the single campaign. The contributions were made variously in the pre- and post-April 7 periods, but systematic solicitation seems to have occurred for so many to have given amounts in similar ranges to one campaign. The Standard Oil pattern showed 16 of 21 officers, or 76 percent, who gave to the Nixon campaign; all but two gave identical amounts, $500 each. Twenty-two of Tenneco's 26 officers, or 85 percent, made contributions to Nixon in individual sums of $150 to $1,250. No similar patterns existed among directors, as distinct from officers, of GM, Standard Oil, or Tenneco, or among officers or directors of the other companies studied.

The study examined the dates of the contributions made in light of the April 7, 1972 deadline, under the new law, after which names of contributors had to be disclosed. Some 56 percent of the money contributed to the Nixon campaign from the Defense Department contractors came in before the disclosure deadline. With the AEC group, 56 percent was pre-April 7; with NASA 45 percent; with the *Fortune* 500" list, 51 percent.

As has been noted, the fact of the new disclosure law makes it difficult to plot any true increases in large gifts from 1968 to 1972. An identical study in 1968 of large contributions was made from the same composite list; in that year the list totalled 70 companies, with 2,129 officers and directors. Of this number, 378—18 percent—made gifts of $500 or more that were on record under the then existing disclosure laws. From this, the Republicans received $1,250,284, compared with the $2,745,945 total in 1972; the Democrats got $216,200 in 1968, while four years later they reported raising $397,324 from these same kinds of sources. While these comparisons suggest that big business gave more in 1972 than in 1968, the wider scope of disclosure in 1972 is an unmeasurable factor.

Convention Program Books. The 1972 convention program books were examined for corporation ads bought by companies on the composite list discussed above—representing the major contractors for the Pentagon, the Atomic Energy Commission, and NASA, as well as the 25 largest companies on the *"Fortune 500"* list. The analysis shows that 15 of the 72 companies bought ads in both the Republican and Democratic books. The amounts spent on the ads by individual companies range from $10,000 to $23,000. Four companies—Continental Oil, Fairchild Industries, McDonnell Douglas, and North American Rockwell—bought ads only in the Republican Program book. I.T.T. bought ads only in the Democratic program book.

Campaign Contributions by the Very Rich

The dominant allegiance to the Republican party among persons with great fortunes—a fact of United States political history for decades—was never more apparent than in 1972. Analyzing the contribution patterns of the nation's centimillionaires—those with fortunes of $150 million or more—Republican money outnumbered Democratic money by better than ten-to-one as Table 10-16 indicates. The Republicans' advantage was even more marked than it had been in the 1968 election, when this particular category of contributors was also studied.[e]

Table 10-16
American Centimillionaires' Contributions in 1972 and 1968 Campaigns

	1972	*1968*
No. of Contributors	51	46
To Republicans	$5,550,896	$ 984,000
To Democrats	496,522	121,000
Miscellaneous	23,600	11,000
Totals	$6,071,018	$1,105,000

There were 66 centimillionaires on the *Fortune* list, each with a wealth of at least $150,000,000. Forty-six of them (70 percent) were recorded as political contributors in 1968, with total gifts of $1,105,000. Four years later, 63 of

---

[e]See Arthur M. Louis, "America's Centimillionaires," *Fortune*, May 1968, pp. 152-57, 192-96. The 1972 list is found in Appendix S.

those individuals were still living, and 51 of them—or 81 percent—made contributions to a political candidate or committee. The total of their contributions reported in 1972 was more than five-fold the reported 1968 gifts, when contribution disclosure laws were less stringent.

The largest single contributor in this group was Chicago insurance executive W. Clement Stone who gave a total of $2,141,666 in 1972, all but $8,412 of that to the Republicans. Stone's 1968 contributions were listed as $200,000 to the Nixon campaign in the 1968 analysis of centimillionaires. Subsequently, in 1973 it was disclosed by Stone that his contributions to Nixon's 1968 pre- and postnomination campaigns had been $2.8 million; only the $200,000 had been publicly disclosed. Of course, this revision would change the 1968 analysis of the centimillionaires, but the total still would not approach the $6.1 million figure for all centimillionaires in the 1972 analysis.

Twenty-four of the 51 contributors in 1972 gave only to Republicans, while five gave only to Democrats. Among the major Republican-only supporters were: Richard Mellon Scaife of Pittsburgh ($1,068,000); Mrs. Joan Whitney Payson, New York ($149,000); J. Paul Getty, Los Angeles ($128,000); the late Winthrop Rockefeller ($115,700); and Peter Kiewit of Omaha, Nebraska ($100,912).

The five contributing only to the Democrats were: former Senator William Benton ($32,250); Mrs. Iphigene Sulzberger of *The New York Times* family ($24,500); Daniel K. Ludwig, New York ($2,500); James S. Abercrombie, Houston, Texas ($1,000); and Jacob Blaustein, Baltimore, Maryland ($1,000).

Of the centimillionaires who gave, 17 made split contributions, giving to both Republican and Democratic sides, although often only a nominal amount to one side. However, the largest Democratic contributor, Leon Hess, who gave $228,500 to Democrats (accounting for more than half of the Democratic total) was the second-largest Republican contributor, giving $252,500.

New Rich of the 1970s

In 1973 *Fortune* compiled and published a list of 39 individuals who had amassed the bulk of their fortune since their 1968 list was put together;[f] this did not include persons who became wealthy entirely through inheritance. To be included one had to have in 1973 a fortune of at least $50 million.

Of the 39 individuals, 28, or 72 percent, contributed in 1972 to a political campaign or committee. Although the Republican contributions of this group in 1972 heavily outweigh the Democratic gifts, the advantage was not as overwhelming as it was with the older, more established wealth—about three-to-one

---

[f]Arthur M. Louis, "The New Rich of the Seventies," *Fortune*, September 1973, pp. 170-75, 230, 232, 236, 238, 242. The 1972 list is found in Appendix T.

Republican compared with ten-to-one on the earlier list. The Republicans received $1,118,754, the Democrats $321,865, while $4,000 fell in the miscellaneous category. Sixteen of these contributors gave only to the Republicans, two only to the Democrats.

The major Republican donors in this group include Roy J. Carver, Muscatine, Iowa ($300,971); Daniel J. Terra, Kenilworth, Illinois ($273,500); Henry S. McNeil, New Brunswick, New Jersey ($112,000); Edward J. Frey, Grand Rapids, Michigan ($108,000); and Anthony T. Rossi, Bradenton, Florida ($106,000).

The major Democratic contributors were Leonard Davis, New York ($232,500) and Arthur G. Cohen, also of New York, who gave $61,500[g] to the Democrats and $40,500 to the Republicans; Davis and Cohen together account for 91.3 percent of the Democratic total.

Of the new rich who gave, eight made split contributions to Republicans and Democrats.

Contributions by Family Groups

The 1972 political contributions by members of 12 prominent American families were analyzed by CRF, as they had been in the three previous presidential elections, and by the Gore Committee in 1956. These families were: The Duponts, Fields, Fords, Harrimans, Lehmans, Mellons, Olins, Pews, Reynolds, Rockefellers, Vanderbilts, and Whitneys. Considered in the study were only those carefully checked to be family members, including members by marriage. Husbands and wives were counted separately, and divorced spouses were not included. Table 10-17 presents the totals.

In an election campaign marked generally by increased numbers of contributors publicly disclosed it is noteworthy that numbers of contributors, but not size of contributions, declined among these families. In 1968, 122 members were recorded as making a gift to a political campaign or committee; four years later 88 were so recorded. But the total amount of support in 1972 was substantially greater—$3,691,746, compared with $2,766,136 in 1968. Table 10-18 shows the pattern of giving among the 12 families since the 1956 presidential election.

The family giving the most in 1972 was the Mellons, a fact attributable largely to the gift of one individual, Richard Mellon Scaife of Pittsburgh. His contribution of $1,068,000 to the Republicans makes up 83 percent of that family's total.

The vice-presidential nomination of Nelson Rockefeller in 1974 provoked

---

[g]Cohen made a $100,000 combined contribution with his father-in-law, Charles C. Bassine, to Bayh. We have attributed $50,000 of the contribution to Cohen.

Table 10-17

Contributions of 12 Prominent Families, 1972

Name	Number of Members Contributing[a]	Total Contributions	Contribution Breakdown		
			Republican	Democratic	Misc.
DuPont	85	$ 547,683.60	$ 505,233.60	$ 35,200	$ 7,250
Field	5	18,450	6,500	10,750	1,200
Ford	17	194,646.49	159,026.49	35,620	--
Harriman	3	57,269.56	43,500	13,769.56	--
Lehman	6[b]	40,400	4,000	31,400	5,000
Mellon	15	1,290,125	1,287,625	500	2,000
Olin	6	317,413	314,413	--	3,000
Pew	11[c]	281,623	277,623	4,000	--
Reynolds	3	21,125	3,000	18,125	--
Rockefeller	19	521,360	470,200	33,210	17,950
Vanderbilt	5	30,651.08	13,019.08	15,632	2,000
Whitney	8	371,000	369,000[d]	1,000	1,000
Totals	183	$3,691,746.73	$3,453,140.17	$199,206.56	$39,400

[a]In this analysis, husbands and wives were counted separately. Therefore, Mr. and Mrs. _____ would constitute two contributing family members.

[b]Lehman Brothers (Investment Banking Firm) was counted as one contributing member.

[c]Contributions from the estate of J.N. Pew, deceased, were included with contributions from Mary Ethel Pew, executrix of the estate.

[d]Total does not include a $250,000 contribution to Nixon, which was returned.

Table 10-18

Pattern of Giving Among 12 Prominent Families: 1956, 1960, 1964, 1968, and 1972

	1956	1960	1964	1968	1972
Republican	$1,040,526	$548,510	$445,280	$2,580,785	$3,453,140
Democratic	107,109	78,850	133,500	149,700	199,206
Miscellaneous	6,100	22,000	24,146	35,651	39,400
Totals	$1,153,735	$649,360	$602,926	$2,766,136	$3,691,746

an intensive investigation of the past political contributions of the former Governor of New York, as well as other members of the Rockefeller family. Appearing before the House Judiciary Committee in November 1974, Governor Rockefeller said that in his 18 years in public office, he and members of his family had spent more than $17 million on his various political campaigns; he noted that this kind of family spending had been necessary because "it's very difficult for a Rockefeller to raise money for a campaign. The reaction of most people is, 'Why should we give money to a Rockefeller'?"[7]

Earlier, in testimony he gave to the Senate Rules Committee on his nomination, Rockefeller submitted a summary of his own political contributions during the years 1957 through 1974, as shown in Table 10-19.[h] He said his political spending since 1957 totalled $3,265,374, which included $1,000,228 in his own presidential campaigns, $80,599 directly to his New York gubernatorial campaigns, and $1,031,627 to New York State Republican party and local committees and clubs.[i] In addition, his brothers and sister had supported Nelson's political activities with contributions totalling $2,850,000, and his stepmother, the late Martha Baird Rockefeller, added another $11 million or so. Adding in Winthrop Rockefeller's spending and family contributions to his campaigns in Arkansas, Nelson Rockefeller accounted for about $20 million spent on the Rockefellers' own campaigns.[j]

The 1972 contributions by the Rockefeller family were considerably less than they had been four years earlier, a change again traceable to one individual. In 1968 Mrs. John D. Rockefeller, Jr. contributed at least $1,482,625 to Nelson's presidential campaign, while Nelson Rockefeller himself made a known $356,000 contribution to his campaign. Counting the latter, the Rockefeller total in 1968 was $2,070,375. Four years later, the total money from the 19 members of the family who contributed was only about a quarter of that—$521,360. Nelson Rockefeller and his wife in 1972 contributed a total of $82,500 to the Republicans.

---

[h]For a year-by-year accounting, see Senate Committee on Rules and Administration, *Hearings* on the *Nomination of Nelson A. Rockefeller of New York to be Vice President of the United States*, 93rd Cong., 2d sess., September 23, 24, 25, and 26, and November 13, 14, 15, and 18, 1974 (Washington, D.C.: U.S. Government Printing Office, 1974) pp. 479-92. Also in House Committee on the Judiciary, *Hearings* on the *Nomination of Nelson A. Rockefeller to be Vice President of the United States*, 93rd Cong., 2d sess., November 21, 22, 25, 26, 27; December 2, 3, 4, and 5, 1974, Serial No. 45 (Washington, D.C.: U.S. Government Printing Office, 1974) pp. 43-57.

[i]The testimony confirmed that Nelson Rockefeller had contributed $200,000 to George Romney's presidential campaign of 1968, as indicated in Herbert E. Alexander, *Financing the 1968 Election* (Lexington, Mass.: Lexington Books, D.C. Heath and Company, 1971), p. 15.

[j]CRF data bearing on the Rockefeller family's political spending and giving was frequently cited in the press during the confirmation hearings. A close estimate of $25 million for the family giving and spending from 1952 to 1970 is found in Herbert E. Alexander, *Money in Politics*, (Washington, D.C.: Public Affairs Press, 1972), pp. 47-48, and is to be contrasted with the exaggerated estimate of $58 million for Nelson's and Winthrop's campaigns and $10 million additional for family contributions to other candidates and parties given in George Thayer *Who Shakes the Money Tree?* (N.Y.: Simon and Schuster, 1973), p. 163. Even counting in the costs of the Rockefeller townhouse operation in New York City, which handles both political and publicity activities, would not make up the difference between the imagined and the real.

Table 10-19

Summary of Political Contributions by Nelson A. Rockefeller, 1957-74

1.	Republican party national committees and clubs	$ 85,199
2.	New York State Republican party and local committees and clubs[a]	1,031,637
3.	Out-of-state Republican committees and clubs[a]	20,820
4.	Nelson Rockefeller presidential campaigns	1,000,228
5.	1968 Romney presidential campaign	200,000
6.	1972 Nixon presidential campaign	62,025
7.	Rockefeller team New York State campaign	80,599
8.	Winthrop Rockefeller team Arkansas campaigns	274,000
9.	Congressional, state, and local candidates in New York State[a]	411,966
10.	Congressional, state, and local candidates outside New York State	98,900
	Total (18 years)	$3,265,374

Source: *The New York Times,* November 14, 1974

[a]In Maine, Westchester County, and in New York City, in each of which locations he has a residence, Rockefeller gave a total of $404,370 during this period to various committees and candidates; this sum is a part of, not in addition to, the sums embraced by categories 2, 3, and 9.

The Rockefellers have been for decades one of the largest influences in the financing of certain Republican candidates and committees. Yet, some members, particularly younger ones, also contribute to the Democrats—in 1972 to the extent of $33,210. This was primarily from three members of the family, Sandra Ferry of Cambridge, Massachusetts who contributed $15,600 to the Democrats, and Mr. and Mrs. John D. "Jay" Rockefeller IV of West Virginia (she is the former Sharon Percy) who gave $9,610 to the Democrats, $3,000 to the Republicans. Other members of the Rockefeller family contributing to the Democrats in 1972, all from New York City, were Mr. and Mrs. John D. III, ($3,000), Abby Rockefeller ($1,000), Alida Davison Rockefeller ($1,000), Mr. and Mrs. David Rockefeller ($500), Richard G. Rockefeller ($2,500), and Jeremy Waletzky ($1,000).

The trend toward Democratic contributions in these formerly all-Republican family groups, observable since 1956, continued in 1972. In 1956, for example, the DuPont, Ford, Mellon, Olin, Pew, Rockefeller, and Whitney families were exclusively Republican contributors. By 1968 only the Olins and Pews continued to show up consistently as only Republican supporters (though the Vanderbilts and Whitneys were Republican-only in 1968) and in 1972 the Pews, too, defected from their historic Republicanism when Walter Crocker Pew of Philadelphia ($3,500) and George Thompson Pew of Haverford, Pennsylvania ($500) made Democratic contributions; in 1972 the Olins were the sole remaining family in the Republican-only category.

In the 1968 election there were only two families whose Democratic contributions exceeded Republican gifts—the Fields and the Lehmans—although giving from the Ford family was fairly evenly divided ($57,750 Republican, $52,000 Democratic). In 1972 four families gave more to the Democrats than to the Republicans—the Fields, the Lehmans, the Reynolds, and the Vanderbilts. The Ford family donations, meanwhile, swung heavily back into the Republican camp—$159,026 to $35,620.

A decline in total contributions was noted with three of the families—as already indicated, the Rockefellers, along with the Fields and the Lehmans, the two traditionally Democratic families in the group. The remaining nine families showed substantially larger contributions in 1972 over 1968.

Executive Club of New Jersey

One unusual instance of a fund-raising organization refusing for a time to divulge the names of contributors during the 1972 campaign—until challenged by the GAO—involved a group called the Executive Club of the Republican Party of New Jersey. Its membership was secret and New Jersey law did not require the names to be revealed. The club contributed at least $100,000 to President Nixon's reelection drive, spreading the money among 34 campaign committees to avoid the gift tax. When the contributions were reported on CRP and affiliated committee filings made with GAO, a search revealed the club had failed to register or to file a report listing receipts and expenditures. The club erroneously claimed to be exempt from the federal law requiring groups that raise over $1,000 for federal election campaigns to register and to identify all contributors of more than $100. The club's chairman, William B. Colsey III, claimed it was legally a private, not a political, organization, since fund raising was not its main purpose. He described the $100,000 as dues it had chosen to turn over to the President's campaign.

The Executive Club had been formed in 1971 to further Republicanism in New Jersey. Colsey described the club as providing a vehicle for informal communication by members with the Republican Governor, William Cahill, and the state administration in New Jersey. He said the club raised money solely by assessing its 149 members' annual dues of $1,000 and that the directors had decided to spend club funds on the presidential race. According to some sources, some club members hoped that President Nixon would consider Governor Cahill as a running mate if Vice-President Agnew was not renominated.

However, when press reports of the club's donations led to a challenge from the GAO, the club relented and did register and supply a list of individual contributors. The list showed that 86 wealthy business and professional men in New Jersey and adjacent states had paid $1,000 each to join the club. However, taking advantage of the April 7 enactment of the FECA, the club never reported the names of perhaps 63 other members who had paid their $1,000 dues before April 7.

The club was not charged with violating the law. GAO's concern was that similar clubs with a state or local orientation might spring up to evade the federal disclosure law. The incident pointed up the all-encompassing definition of a "political committee" in the FECA—one that catches any groups that participate even incidentally in campaigns for federal office.

Colsey, a Mt. Holly lawyer who worked closely with former New Jersey State Treasurer Joseph M. McCrane, Jr. in fund raising for former Governor William T. Cahill's 1969 campaign, was selected as chairman of the Executive Club in recognition of his success in raising state Republican funds. He was a major Nixon fund raiser in New Jersey in the 1972 campaign, and was rewarded for his success by appointments by Nixon, to the United States delegation on the United Nations Commission on International Law, and to the International Maritime Commission.[8]

But during Cahill's 1973 campaign, Colsey became an object of federal grand jury and state investigations into fund-raising practices during the 1969 Cahill campaign. He was forced to resign membership on the New Jersey State Republican Finance Committee early in 1973, and was subsequently indicted for his roles in a number of schemes involving his alleged offering of political favors in return for financial favors.[k] He was disbarred as a result of a zoning case in Gloucester Township for advising a client to make a $15,000 "political contribution" to insure the awarding of certain building permits, and for further disguising the bribe by reporting it as his own income and paying tax on it.[9] In

---

[k]During 1973 and 1974 Colsey was involved in a number of suits for alleged bribery, conspiracy, and kickbacks in which he worked closely with former State Treasurer Joseph McCrane, Jr., and Colsey's partner in Realty Associates Company, Bruce Mahon. In the case, State Attorney General George F. Kugler, Jr., began investigations in January 1973, which led to Colsey and Mahon being indicted on April 19 for alleged conspiracy to have $6 million in state funds, controlled by McCrane, illegally deposited in Trenton's Broad Street National Bank in return for the bank's purchase of $6 million in securities from a brokerage house that employed McCrane's brother. The alleged conspiracy was never carried out—an associate of the bank president told a state senator of the approach, according to one news account, which was never denied. He, in turn, reported what he knew to the State Attorney General's office. (See John McLaughlin, "State Senator Blew the Whistle on McCrane," New York *Daily News*, May 17, 1973.) On May 9, 1974 New Jersey Superior Court Judge George Y. Schoch refused to dismiss the indictment, which the defendants maintained was unconstitutional. On May 31 Schoch declared a mistrial and ordered the jurors and lawyers for the defense and the state not to disclose the reason. Reportedly a juror had heatedly accused the defendants of guilt during a recess. Judge Schoch rescheduled the trial for early 1975 since he wished to retain jurisdiction.

Another transaction, which was challenged in a civil suit on January 7, 1974, involved a state lease negotiation between Realty Associates (a Colsey and Mahon firm) and the Arnold Constable Building in Trenton. Under secret agreement the two men were receiving ten percent of the rent for office space, or $7,400 per month. The 15-year renewable lease could have brought $4 million had the monthly payments continued undiscovered.

May 1973 the GAO announced plans to audit the by then defunct Executive Club to determine whether filing errors in the club's report of campaign expenditures were "inadvertent or an attempt to mislead."[10]

Millionaires Club

An attempt by a group of millionaires to achieve political impact to influence reform died abortively in 1971, a victim of publicity and uncharitable interpretation.

At the onset of the presidential campaigns, a novel effort was made to organize the very rich into a lobby to press for governmental and political reform. The approach was to be direct. Meeting privately, 60 millionaires, all of them prominent campaign contributors to both political parties, agreed to ask various presidential candidates to consider supporting proposed reforms, while the millionaires considered their support of the candidates. Among the reforms were: abolition of the seniority rule for committee chairmen in the Congress, greater productivity from government, modernization of state and local government, and strict limitations on campaign spending. The millionaires decided to ask presidential candidates to come before them to make known their position on these questions. Although the prospective lobby included some Republicans, it was apparent it would focus on Democratic candidates.

The millionaires sought to keep the organizational meeting secret, but it drew considerable publicity and some unfavorable comment. *The New York Times* editorially accused the group of seeking to dictate reforms to presidential contenders with their checkbooks. The publicity nipped the new lobby in the bud. The millionaires disbanded quietly in the face of press accounts of their plans.

The moral of the story may be that when the rich use their money for political ends, they inevitably inspire deep suspicions, however lofty their intentions. The 1971 efforts may have presaged post-Watergate actions by numerous large contributors to seek election reforms that would relieve them of future excessive contributions. Many large contributors appeared happy to be let off the hook when low contributions limits were enacted.

11

Sources of Funds: A Computer Analysis of Contributions by Size, Region, and Date

Until recently most studies of political finance restricted their analyses to the large contributor, since information about other contributors was unavailable or incomplete and physically difficult to collect and handle. The new disclosure laws, however, make possible a much more systematic collection and processing of campaign finance information. During the 1972 presidential campaign, the General Accounting Office centralized the collection of records of all declared contributions made to presidential candidates in amounts in excess of $100 from April 7 forward. This information makes possible an extensive analysis of political contributions focusing on three major variables: size of contribution, geographic origin, and time of contribution.

The new data make it possible to answer for the first time many interesting questions about the structure of political finance. For example, we can now examine in detail the distribution of each candidate's contributions of more than $100 by the size of contribution. Also, we can now tell with accuracy how political contribution patterns vary on the basis of geography—which states dominate finance, which states give proportionately more and less on a per capita basis, and which states have unusual patterns of contributions. Furthermore, it is possible to examine when contributions were made—how fast money flowed and how these flows varied by geography and size of contribution.

To answer such questions we have conducted an extensive analysis of the structure of campaign finance, using the official data from the General Accounting Office, taken from a copy of its computer tape. (See Appendix U for a discussion of the methods used and the overall significance of the data). The conclusions drawn in this chapter are based on individual contributors who made a disclosed contribution of more than $100 to a presidential campaign committee after April 7, 1972 and before January 1, 1973. The contributions are aggregated for each contributor according to the method discussed in Appendix U.

Size of Contributions

The presidential candidates who disclosed contributions of more than $100

This chapter was co-authored by Clifford W. Brown, Jr.

403

to the General Accounting Office raised approximately $39 million from such contributions on or after April 7, 1972 and before December 31, 1972.

Table 11-1 provides the total dollar amounts received in contributions over $100, the number of contributors, and the mean contribution for selected candidates. This table indicates the impressive totals of Nixon and McGovern, but it also indicates decided differences in the mean contribution of the principal contenders, with Humphrey relying upon significantly larger-than-average contributions and Wallace relying upon relatively small contributions.

Table 11-1

Total Money Raised in Contributions Exceeding $100, April 7, 1972–December 31, 1972 *(Selected Candidates)*

	Number of Contributors	Total Dollars	Mean Aggregated Contribution per Contributor
Nixon	16,387	$23,857,651.09	$1,455.88
McGovern	11,166	11,687,208.13	1,046.67
Humphrey	636	1,704,225.88	2,679.60
Muskie	584	394,318.01	675.20
Jackson	164	179,288.70	1,093.22
Wallace	273	174,490.96	639.16
Mills	151	197,614.00	1,308.70
Hartke	81	17,275.00	213.27
Chisholm	26	31,844.65	1,224.79
Sanford	23	10,752.00	467.47
Mink	5	1,608.60	321.72
Yorty	91	77,900.00	856.04

These differences are illustrated much more extensively in Tables 11-2 through 11-7, which show the distribution of candidate dollars by size of contribution to the principal candidates for the primary and general election together. The most interesting conclusion that emerges from an examination of these figures is the great similarity between the post April 7 contribution patterns of Nixon and McGovern. While Nixon raised twice as much money as McGovern, the overall percentage distribution among categories is roughly similar from top to bottom.

The similarity of the distribution of contributors in Tables 11-2 and 11-3 is even more impressive. To be sure, there are some variations in these overall patterns. McGovern is stronger in the below-$1,000 category, with 22.0 percent of his money falling there compared with Nixon's 14.1 percent; Nixon is stronger

Table 11-2

Richard Nixon: Breakdown by Dollar Category of Aggregated Contributions
(National Totals, April 7-December 31, 1972)

Dollar Category	No. of Contributors	Percent of Total Contributors	Total Dollar Amount	Percent of Total Dollar Amount
$ 101 - $ 499	8,391	51.21%	$ 1,820,154.36	7.63%
500 - 999	2,865	17.48	1,544,264.30	6.47
1,000 - 1,999	3,019	18.42	3,206,966.22	13.44
2,000 - 2,999	794	4.85	1,750,280.07	7.34
3,000 - 3,999	420	2.56	1,286,177.14	5.39
4,000 - 4,999	93	0.57	393,655.72	1.65
5,000 - 5,999	230	1.40	1,173,011.11	4.92
6,000 - 6,999	107	0.65	654,904.06	2.75
7,000 - 7,999	78	0.48	569,846.96	2.39
8,000 - 8,999	17	0.10	138,597.83	0.58
9,000 - 9,999	28	0.17	259,316.29	1.09
10,000 - 19,999	193	1.18	2,471,030.37	10.36
20,000 - 29,999	62	0.38	1,491,607.81	6.25
30,000 - 39,999	14	0.09	490,208.51	2.05
40,000 - 49,999	19	0.12	856,514.07	3.59
50,000 - 59,999	16	0.10	859,528.77	3.60
60,000 - 69,999	5	0.03	319,554.40	1.34
70,000 - 79,999	4	0.02	305,745.75	1.28
80,000 - 89,999	4	0.02	342,813.64	1.44
90,000 - 99,999	8	0.05	760,432.62	3.19
100,000 +	20	0.12	3,163,041.09	13.26
Totals	16,387		$23,857,651.09	

in the $1,000 category, and relatively strong in the $50,000-$100,000 category. There are one or two other variations, but overall the pattern is quite similar: both candidates raised a lot of money in every category of contribution. Each showed depth from top to bottom. Each demonstrated a strong reliance on the $1,000 and $10,000 contribution, and neither showed a strong dependence (in this period) on the contribution exceeding $100,000. The ideological difference between the candidates, then, did not seem to manifest itself in these post-April 7 contribution patterns, since neither "fat cats" nor "small" donors contributed disproportionately to either candidate.

It should be noted that Nixon raised a large amount of money in the higher dollar categories before April 7, and that McGovern raised a large amount of

Table 11-3

George McGovern: Breakdown by Dollar Category of Aggregated Contributions
(National Totals, April 7-December 31, 1972)

Dollar Category	No. of Contributors	Percent of Total Contributors	Total Dollar Amount	Percent of Total Dollar Amount
$ 101 - $ 499	7,219	64.65%	$ 1,504,330.33	12.87%
500 - 999	1,843	16.51	1,061,568.74	9.08
1,000 - 1,999	1,236	11.07	1,428,621.34	12.22
2,000 - 2,999	314	2.81	718,087.19	6.14
3,000 - 3,999	152	1.36	489,023.25	4.18
4,000 - 4,999	54	0.48	231,869.25	1.98
5,000 - 5,999	96	0.86	496,784.11	4.25
6,000 - 6,999	43	0.39	267,433.38	2.29
7,000 - 7,999	21	0.19	152,357.54	1.30
8,000 - 8,999	12	0.11	99,632.26	0.85
9,000 - 9,999	21	0.19	194,637.60	1.67
10,000 - 19,999	92	0.82	1,153,815.50	9.87
20,000 - 29,999	24	0.21	575,186.30	4.92
30,000 - 39,999	17	0.15	590,255.35	5.05
40,000 - 49,999	6	0.05	267,882.10	2.29
50,000 - 59,999	2	0.02	109,086.51	0.93
60,000 - 69,999	1	0.01	60,500.00	0.52
70,000 - 79,999	2	0.02	150,375.62	1.29
80,000 - 89,999	1	0.01	84,108.25	0.72
90,000 - 99,999	2	0.02	187,355.25	1.60
100,000 +	8	0.07	1,864,298.26	15.95
Totals	11,166		$11,687,208.13	

money through loan financing throughout his campaigns. Some of these loans were converted to contributions during and after the campaigns; most of these conversions were not considered as contributions in this analysis unless they were reported as such by candidates or political committees during the 1972 period and recorded on the computer tapes used in this study. Thus, there is a small bias to this analysis, since the mean size of loans is substantially higher than the mean size of contributions. (See "Loans" below.)

When the Nixon and McGovern patterns are compared with those of other candidates, however, striking differences emerge. The totals are much lower, of course, and this fact alone would account for a less balanced pattern. Also, the other candidates were raising money for primary campaigns while the

Table 11-4

Hubert Humphrey: Breakdown by Dollar Category of Aggregated Contributions
(National Totals, April 7-December 31, 1972)

Dollar Category	No. of Contributors	Percent of Total Contributors	Total Dollar Amount	Percent of Total Dollar Amount
$ 101 - $ 499	245	38.52%	$ 61,139.77	3.59%
500 - 999	131	20.60	74,540.95	4.37
1,000 - 1,999	121	19.03	133,545.16	7.84
2,000 - 2,999	53	8.33	115,050.00	6.75
3,000 - 3,999	13	2.04	41,100.00	2.41
4,000 - 4,999	7	1.10	29,500.00	1.73
5,000 - 5,999	18	2.83	90,650.00	5.32
6,000 - 6,999	14	2.20	84,500.00	4.96
7,000 - 7,999	5	0.79	36,500.00	2.14
8,000 - 8,999	0	0.00	0.00	0.00
9,000 - 9,999	1	0.16	9,000.00	0.53
10,000 - 19,999	14	2.20	157,500.00	9.24
20,000 - 29,999	7	1.10	168,700.00	9.90
30,000 - 39,999	0	0.00	0.00	0.00
40,000 - 49,999	1	0.16	45,000.00	2.64
50,000 - 59,999	2	0.31	100,500.00	5.90
60,000 - 69,999	0	0.00	0.00	0.00
70,000 - 79,999	1	0.16	71,000.00	4.17
80,000 - 89,999	1	0.16	86,000.00	5.05
90,000 - 99,999	0	0.00	0.00	0.00
100,000 +	2	0.31	400,000.00	23.47
Totals	636		$1,704,225.88	

overwhelming bulk of both Nixon's and McGovern's money was raised for the
general election. The differences, however, are still very significant. Humphrey
is decidedly top heavy. (See Table 11-4.) Whereas Nixon raised only 46.4 percent of his money in contributions of $10,000 or more during this period and
McGovern only 43.1 percent, Humphrey raised 60.4 percent. Similarly, only
15.8 percent of Humphrey's money came in contributions of less than $2,000
while 27.5 percent of Nixon's and 34.2 percent of McGovern's money came in
this dollar range. Also, only 38.5 percent of Humphrey's contributors are
found in the less-than-$500 category, compared with 51.2 percent for Nixon
and 64.7 percent for McGovern. Furthermore, Humphrey's overall pattern is
much less uniform than the patterns of Nixon and McGovern. Four dollar categories lack any contributions and four more have only one. Although smaller

Table 11-5
Edmund Muskie: Breakdown by Dollar Category of Aggregated Contributions
(National Totals, April 7-December 31, 1972)

Dollar Category	No. of Contributors	Percent of Total Contributors	Total Dollar Amount	Percent of Total Dollar Amount
$ 101 - $ 499	375	64.21%	$ 71,804.45	18.21%
500 - 999	93	15.92	50,423.46	12.79
1,000 - 1,999	68	11.64	73,750.00	18.70
2,000 - 2,999	21	3.60	46,885.26	11.89
3,000 - 3,999	13	2.23	39,880.00	10.11
4,000 - 4,999	3	0.51	13,500.00	3.42
5,000 - 5,999	5	0.86	25,000.00	6.34
6,000 - 6,999	2	0.34	12,000.00	3.04
7,000 - 7,999	0	0.00	0.00	0.00
8,000 - 8,999	0	0.00	0.00	0.00
9,000 - 9,999	0	0.00	0.00	0.00
10,000 - 19,999	3	0.51	40,074.84	10.16
20,000 - 29,999	1	0.17	21,000.00	5.33
30,000 - 39,999	0	0.00	0.00	0.00
40,000 - 49,999	0	0.00	0.00	0.00
50,000 - 59,999	0	0.00	0.00	0.00
60,000 - 69,999	0	0.00	0.00	0.00
70,000 - 79,999	0	0.00	0.00	0.00
80,000 - 89,999	0	0.00	0.00	0.00
90,000 - 99,999	0	0.00	0.00	0.00
100,000 +	0	0.00	0.00	0.00
Totals	584		$394,318.01	

dollar totals would tend to create distributions of this nature, nevertheless the Humphrey pattern is still one of a financial effort that lacked depth.

Humphrey also raised a significant amount of money through loans, some of which were later converted to contributions, and some of which remained as debts after December 31, 1972.

If Humphrey's overall financial picture was top-heavy, the patterns of the rest of the Democratic hopefuls during their late primary season were quite the reverse. No contributions were reported in excess of $30,000, and only 11 contributions in excess of $10,000 were reported for the entire field. Wallace (who was a serious contender for five weeks during this time) raised 72.41 percent of his money in contributions of less than $3,000; Muskie (who was no longer a serious candidate), raised 61.59 percent in this category. Jackson raised most

Table 11-6
Henry Jackson: Breakdown by Dollar Category of Aggregated Contributions
(National Totals, April 7-December 31, 1972)

Dollar Category	No. of Contributors	Percent of Total Contributors	Total Dollar Amount	Percent of Total Dollar Amount
$ 101 - $ 499	76	46.34%	$ 17,235.10	9.61%
500 - 999	32	19.51	16,755.05	9.35
1,000 - 1,999	31	18.90	33,773.55	18.84
2,000 - 2,999	9	5.49	21,500.00	11.99
3,000 - 3,999	5	3.05	15,000.00	8.37
4,000 - 4,999	1	0.61	4,000.00	2.23
5,000 - 5,999	7	4.27	35,500.00	19.80
6,000 - 6,999	0	0.00	0.00	0.00
7,000 - 7,999	1	0.61	7,000.00	3.90
8,000 - 8,999	0	0.00	0.00	0.00
9,000 - 9,999	0	0.00	0.00	0.00
10,000 - 19,999	2	1.22	28,525.00	15.91
20,000 - 29,999	0	0.00	0.00	0.00
30,000 - 39,999	0	0.00	0.00	0.00
40,000 - 49,999	0	0.00	0.00	0.00
50,000 - 59,999	0	0.00	0.00	0.00
60,000 - 69,999	0	0.00	0.00	0.00
70,000 - 79,999	0	0.00	0.00	0.00
80,000 - 89,999	0	0.00	0.00	0.00
90,000 - 99,999	0	0.00	0.00	0.00
100,000 +	0	0.00	0.00	0.00
Totals	164		$179,288.70	

of his money in more middle-range amounts. (See Tables 11-5 through 11-7.) The fact that none of these candidates seemed to have much of a chance for the nomination by April 7 was presumably a decisive element in scaring away big money.

To put these contribution patterns in perspective, it is interesting to compare them to contributions made to the Republican and Democratic National Committees during the same period. (See Tables 11-8 and 11-9.) Although a few sizable contributions were made to these committees, approximately three quarters of the money raised by them in contributions over $100 came in contributions of less than $3,000. These figures show the extent of dependence of the 1972 national candidates on the large contributor when compared with the national parties.

Table 11-7

George Wallace: Breakdown by Dollar Category of Aggregated Contributions
(National Totals, April 7-December 31, 1972)

Dollar Category	No. of Contributors	Percent of Total Contributors	Total Dollar Amount	Percent of Total Dollar Amount
$ 101 - $ 499	156	57.14%	$ 29,052.43	16.65%
500 - 999	54	19.78	27,950.00	16.02
1,000 - 1,999	42	15.38	43,606.00	24.99
2,000 - 2,999	12	4.40	25,745.00	14.75
3,000 - 3,999	1	0.37	3,882.53	2.23
4,000 - 4,999	0	0.00	0.00	0.00
5,000 - 5,999	7	2.56	35,255.00	20.20
6,000 - 6,999	0	0.00	0.00	0.00
7,000 - 7,999	0	0.00	0.00	0.00
8,000 - 8,999	0	0.00	0.00	0.00
9,000 - 9,999	1	0.37	9,000.00	5.16
10,000 - 19,999	0	0.00	0.00	0.00
20,000 - 29,999	0	0.00	0.00	0.00
30,000 - 39,999	0	0.00	0.00	0.00
40,000 - 49,999	0	0.00	0.00	0.00
50,000 - 59,999	0	0.00	0.00	0.00
60,000 - 69,999	0	0.00	0.00	0.00
70,000 - 79,999	0	0.00	0.00	0.00
80,000 - 89,999	0	0.00	0.00	0.00
90,000 - 99,999	0	0.00	0.00	0.00
100,000 +	0	0.00	0.00	0.00
Totals	273		$174,490.96	

Geographic Distributions

A far more interesting set of statistics emerges from an examination of the geographic breakdowns of political contributions in 1972. It is now possible to see where the money comes from—what states and regions dominate American political finance, and what states and regions are more "backwards" in their support of candidates. First, political contributions to national candidates are highly concentrated in a few large states—and are much more concentrated than population, votes, personal income, or even bank deposits. Second, among these few large states, New York and California hold massive preponderance. Third, the larger contributions are significantly more concentrated than the smaller contributions. Fourth, McGovern's contributions in 1972 were much

Table 11-8

Republican National Committee: Breakdown by Dollar Category of Aggregated Contributions

(National Totals, April 7-December 31, 1972)

Dollar Category	No. of Contributors	Percent of Total Contributors	Total Dollar Amount	Percent of Total Dollar Amount
$ 101 - $ 499	753	46.63%	$ 168,197.37	15.38%
500 - 999	447	27.68	233,370.13	21.35
1,000 - 1,999	323	20.00	336,968.56	30.82
2,000 - 2,999	45	2.79	94,138.16	8.61
3,000 - 3,999	17	1.05	52,000.00	4.76
4,000 - 4,999	1	0.06	4,000.00	0.37
5,000 - 5,999	13	0.80	65,500.00	5.99
6,000 - 6,999	5	0.31	30,599.36	2.80
7,000 - 7,999	1	0.06	7,500.00	0.69
8,000 - 8,999	0	0.00	0.00	0.00
9,000 - 9,999	3	0.19	27,000.00	2.47
10,000 - 19,999	7	0.43	74,000.00	6.77
20,000 - 29,999	0	0.00	0.00	0.00
30,000 - 39,999	0	0.00	0.00	0.00
40,000 - 49,999	0	0.00	0.00	0.00
50,000 - 59,999	0	0.00	0.00	0.00
60,000 - 69,999	0	0.00	0.00	0.00
70,000 - 79,999	0	0.00	0.00	0.00
80,000 - 89,999	0	0.00	0.00	0.00
90,000 - 99,999	0	0.00	0.00	0.00
100,000 +	0	0.00	0.00	0.00
Totals	1,615		$1,093,273.58	

more concentrated than Nixon's and his largest states (aside from New York, California, and Illinois) were different than Nixon's largest states. Fifth, the contributions made to other candidates, while differing in geographic distribution from the contributions to the principal contenders, were still concentrated in a handful of states. Finally, contribution patterns vary widely by region.

Concentration in the Big States

Nixon and McGovern. The financial receipts of both Nixon and McGovern were dominated by New York and California, and the role played by these two

Table 11-9

Democratic National Committee: Breakdown by Dollar Category of Aggregated Contributions

(National Totals, April 7-December 31, 1972)

Dollar Category	No. of Contributors	Percent of Total Contributors	Total Dollar Amount	Percent of Total Dollar Amount
$ 101 - $ 499	775	59.07%	$177,303.94	20.73%
500 - 999	302	23.02	184,949.12	21.62
1,000 - 1,999	177	13.49	204,150.51	23.86
2,000 - 2,999	31	2.36	65,432.25	7.65
3,000 - 3,999	4	0.30	12,000.00	1.40
4,000 - 4,999	3	0.23	12,768.88	1.49
5,000 - 5,999	5	0.38	25,632.00	3.00
6,000 - 6,999	3	0.23	19,002.00	2.22
7,000 - 7,999	1	0.08	7,288.00	0.85
8,000 - 8,999	1	0.08	8,000.00	0.94
9,000 - 9,999	1	0.08	9,000.00	1.05
10,000 - 19,999	8	0.61	87,734.62	10.26
20,000 - 29,999	0	0.00	0.00	0.00
30,000 - 39,999	0	0.00	0.00	0.00
40,000 - 49,999	1	0.08	42,200.00	4.93
50,000 - 59,999	0	0.00	0.00	0.00
60,000 - 69,999	0	0.00	0.00	0.00
70,000 - 79,999	0	0.00	0.00	0.00
80,000 - 89,999	0	0.00	0.00	0.00
90,000 - 99,999	0	0.00	0.00	0.00
100,000 +	0	0.00	0.00	0.00
Totals	1,312		$855,461.32	

states is phenomenal. Approximately 50 percent of McGovern's money and nearly 40 percent of his contributors came from these two states. Nearly 30 percent of Nixon's money and about a quarter of his contributors also came from New York and California. In terms of total contributions, large contributions, contributions of less than $10,000, and contributions of more than $100, but less than $500, these states dominated the McGovern campaign. In all but the smallest category, they comfortably led the Nixon totals. (See Tables 11-10 and 11-11.) Illinois also played a significant role in the financial campaigns of both Nixon and McGovern, contributing approximately six to seven percent of the money and donors in each campaign. These three states, of course, contain the leading financial centers of the nation.

Table 11-10
Geographic Distribution of McGovern's Money

	Total Dollars	Percent	Dollars Contributed >$100<$10,000	Percent	Total Contributors	Percent	Number of Contributions >$100<$500	Percent
Alabama	$ 26,022.12	0.22%	$ 6,022	0.09%	22	0.20%	17	0.24%
Alaska	4,612.50	0.04	4,613	0.06	14	0.13	10	0.14
Arizona	29,333.25	0.25	29,333	0.44	51	0.46	39	0.54
Arkansas	10,038.75	0.09	10,039	0.15	25	0.22	16	0.22
California	2,220,869.02	19.00	1,263,116	19.01	2,096	18.77	1,368	18.94
Colorado	59,557.07	0.51	24,057	0.36	73	0.65	53	0.73
Connecticut	547,051.85	4.68	322,936	4.86	426	3.82	247	3.42
Delaware	9,690.25	0.08	9,690	0.14	30	0.27	24	0.33
D.C.	302,928.64	2.59	246,928	3.71	393	3.52	237	3.28
Florida	167,141.47	1.43	117,041	1.76	219	1.96	146	2.02
Georgia	18,940.50	0.16	18,940	0.28	47	0.42	35	0.48
Hawaii	11,235.91	0.10	11,236	0.16	38	0.34	31	0.42
Idaho	2,884.23	0.02	2,884	0.04	13	0.12	11	0.15
Illinois	709,500.23	6.07	432,397	6.50	741	6.64	474	6.56
Indiana	427,567.94	3.66	39,959	0.60	71	0.64	55	0.76
Iowa	17,527.05	0.15	17,527	0.26	46	0.41	33	0.46
Kansas	50,834.36	0.43	16,834	0.25	42	0.38	32	0.44
Kentucky	22,463.75	0.19	22,464	0.33	42	0.38	26	0.36
Louisiana	17,710.90	0.15	17,711	0.26	35	0.31	26	0.36
Maine	12,544.28	0.11	12,544	0.18	20	0.18	12	0.17
Maryland	273,206.32	2.34	189,602	2.85	312	2.79	211	2.92
Massachusetts	638,094.33	5.46	445,659	6.70	706	6.32	459	6.36
Michigan	229,784.14	1.97	190,778	2.87	410	3.67	285	3.95
Minnesota	56,495.20	0.48	56,495	0.85	139	1.24	94	1.30
Mississippi	12,550.75	0.11	12,551	0.18	15	0.13	5	0.07
Missouri	50,476.25	0.43	50,476	0.75	125	1.12	95	1.32
Montana	13,135.40	0.11	13,135	0.19	25	0.22	23	0.32
Nebraska	68,537.44	0.59	42,135	0.63	50	0.45	30	0.42

(cont.)

Table 11-10 (cont.)

	Total Dollars	Percent	Dollars Contributed >$100<$10,000	Percent	Total Contributors	Percent	Number of Contributions >$100<$500	Percent
Nevada	$ 34,029.50	0.29%	$ 4,030	0.06%	11	0.10%	6	0.08%
New Hampshire	51,478.50	0.44	51,478	0.77	60	0.54	33	0.46
New Jersey	446,638.38	3.82	281,189	4.23	515	4.61	352	4.87
New Mexico	27,181.31	0.23	27,181	0.40	46	0.41	28	0.39
New York	3,609,776.58	30.89	1,638,026	24.65	2,299	20.59	1,325	18.35
North Carolina	60,262.64	0.52	45,263	0.68	67	0.60	45	0.62
North Dakota	1,150.00	0.01	1,150	0.01	7	0.06	7	0.10
Ohio	332,010.08	2.84	184,815	2.78	377	3.38	257	3.56
Oklahoma	14,283.30	0.12	14,283	0.21	29	0.26	20	0.28
Oregon	66,577.50	0.57	31,977	0.48	65	0.58	47	0.65
Pennsylvania	241,238.88	2.06	241,239	3.63	493	4.42	336	4.65
Rhode Island	20,252.57	0.17	20,253	0.30	36	0.32	29	0.40
South Carolina	5,404.50	0.05	5,405	0.08	16	0.14	14	0.19
South Dakota	18,776.26	0.16	18,776	0.28	48	0.43	35	0.48
Tennessee	12,143.00	0.10	12,143	0.18	34	0.30	23	0.32
Texas	231,488.93	1.98	114,214	1.71	161	1.44	92	1.27
Utah	96,584.75	0.83	12,476	0.18	28	0.25	16	0.22
Vermont	40,413.75	0.35	40,414	0.60	61	0.55	37	0.51
Virginia	80,605.00	0.69	70,605	1.06	157	1.41	108	1.50
Washington	57,090.28	0.49	57,090	0.85	135	1.21	111	1.54
West Virginia	12,797.50	0.11	12,798	0.19	17	0.15	14	0.19
Wisconsin	87,708.42	0.75	52,708	0.79	133	1.19	94	1.30
Wyoming	4,550.00	0.04	4,550	0.06	6	0.05	3	0.04
Guam	654.00	0.01	654	0.00	2	0.02	2	—
Virgin Islands	50,955.15	0.44	2,100	0.03	7	0.06	4	0.06
Puerto Rico	5,780.00	0.05	5,780	0.08	7	0.06	3	0.04
Foreign	66,643.45	0.57	66,643	1.00	123	1.10	84	1.16
Totals	$11,687,208.13		$6,644,342		11,166		7,219	

Table 11-11

Geographic Distribution of Nixon's Money

	Total Dollars	Percent	Dollars Contributed >$100<$10,000	Percent	Total Contributors	Percent	Number of Contributions >$100<$500	Percent
Alabama	$ 123,358.91	0.52%	$ 67,197	0.53%	134	0.82%	88	1.05%
Alaska	42,218.25	0.18	32,218	0.25	69	0.42	46	0.55
Arizona	162,791.94	0.68	93,209	0.73	121	0.74	55	0.66
Arkansas	76,920.36	0.32	47,920	0.37	108	0.66	68	0.81
California	3,334,979.55	13.98	2,015,097	15.75	2,585	15.77	1,340	15.97
Colorado	270,010.04	1.13	158,710	1.24	388	2.37	319	3.80
Connecticut	539,231.19	2.26	224,620	1.76	273	1.67	112	1.33
Delaware	226,412.30	0.95	94,337	0.74	93	0.57	29	0.35
D.C.	502,351.58	2.11	371,788	2.91	425	2.59	425	2.51
Florida	1,231,029.80	5.16	743,906	5.81	854	5.21	854	4.91
Georgia	318,514.52	1.34	191,514	1.50	203	1.24	203	1.18
Hawaii	172,577.15	0.72	134,577	1.05	126	0.77	126	0.54
Idaho	18,015.00	0.08	18,015	0.14	31	0.19	31	0.19
Illinois	1,831,704.82	7.68	743,436	5.81	936	5.72	936	5.51
Indiana	138,925.32	0.58	118,925	0.93	243	1.48	243	1.70
Iowa	403,992.36	1.69	87,021	0.68	141	0.86	141	0.91
Kansas	124,469.78	0.52	102,168	0.80	156	0.95	156	1.06
Kentucky	77,794.00	0.33	36,794	0.29	60	0.37	60	0.46
Louisiana	123,189.00	0.52	107,689	0.84	180	1.10	180	1.19
Maine	46,610.01	0.20	31,610	0.25	57	0.35	57	0.35
Maryland	547,936.46	2.30	500,936	3.92	621	3.79	621	3.18
Massachusetts	340,292.83	1.43	330,293	2.58	451	2.75	451	2.71
Michigan	767,152.61	3.22	397,504	3.11	532	3.25	532	3.48
Minnesota	500,880.74	2.10	228,464	1.79	238	1.45	238	1.22
Mississippi	290,817.68	1.22	83,817	0.66	138	0.84	138	0.97
Missouri	246,008.16	1.03	192,617	1.51	263	1.60	263	1.78
Montana	14,072.00	0.06	14,072	0.11	20	0.12	20	0.12
Nebraska	102,224.58	0.43	92,225	0.72	124	0.76	124	0.63

(cont.)

Table 11-11 (cont.)

	Total Dollars	Percent	Dollars Contributed >$100<$10,000	Percent	Total Contributors	Percent	Number of Contributions >$100<$500	Percent
Nevada	$ 141,356.00	0.59%	$ 53,856	0.42%	50	0.31%	50	0.20%
New Hampshire	12,916.00	0.05	12,916	0.10	30	0.18	30	0.26
New Jersey	534,937.56	2.24	320,615	2.51	418	2.55	418	2.43
New Mexico	61,469.27	0.26	51,469	0.41	66	0.40	66	0.45
New York	3,586,327.89	15.03	1,550,271	12.12	1,446	8.82	1,446	6.48
North Carolina	145,211.86	0.61	119,712	0.94	196	1.20	196	1.42
North Dakota	6,473.66	0.03	6,474	0.05	14	0.09	14	0.12
Ohio	465,114.01	1.95	337,582	2.64	438	2.67	438	2.87
Oklahoma	276,852.36	1.16	153,591	1.20	210	1.28	210	1.53
Oregon	233,476.26	0.98	145,243	1.14	251	1.53	251	1.98
Pennsylvania	1,519,864.56	6.37	663,642	5.19	829	5.06	829	4.36
Rhode Island	47,253.92	0.20	47,254	0.37	53	0.32	53	0.36
South Carolina	57,281.00	0.24	57,281	0.45	109	0.67	109	0.89
South Dakota	6,912.00	0.03	6,912	0.05	18	0.11	18	0.14
Tennessee	256,396.89	1.07	95,811	0.75	148	0.90	148	1.10
Texas	2,261,862.28	9.48	943,456	7.37	1,145	6.99	1,145	6.91
Utah	77,301.77	0.32	32,802	0.26	29	0.18	29	0.35
Vermont	10,260.00	0.04	10,260	0.08	23	0.14	23	0.14
Virginia	523,237.38	2.19	311,374	2.43	489	2.98	489	3.35
Washington	164,119.92	0.69	149,119	1.17	216	1.32	216	1.37
West Virginia	17,636.00	0.07	17,636	0.14	47	0.29	47	0.38
Wisconsin	646,629.63	2.71	322,686	2.52	464	2.83	464	3.27
Wyoming	55,550.00	0.23	12,550	0.10	16	0.10	16	0.10
Guam	—	—	—	—	—	—	—	—
Virgin Islands	3,050.00	0.01	—	—	8	0.05	8	0.07
Puerto Rico	47,000.00	0.20	20,750	0.16	16	0.10	16	0.03
Foreign	124,679.93	0.52	90,179	0.70	88	0.54	88	1.05
Totals	$23,857,651.09		$12,794,120		16,387		14,673	

The remaining important states in the 1972 financial campaigns differed dramatically by candidate. McGovern's next largest states were Massachusetts, Connecticut, and New Jersey with respect to total dollars raised and dollars raised in amounts less than $10,000. Pennsylvania replaced Connecticut in fifth place in terms of total contributors, and ran fourth behind Massachusetts in terms of dollars raised in amounts less than $2,000. With respect to small contributions, Michigan and Ohio ran ahead of Connecticut, but Massachusetts, New Jersey, and Pennsylvania still remained among the top six. Although some states are ahead of others in some categories, Table 11-10 shows how highly concentrated McGovern's money was. Some 52 percent of his total money came from the states that lie between Boston and Washington, D.C. These states, together with Illinois and California account for over 75 percent of his money. Another nine percent of his total came from the remaining states in the Midwest and the rest of the country contributed about 15 percent.

McGovern's total number of contributors—as opposed to total money— were spread a bit more widely, but they were still very concentrated. About 47 percent came from the states between Boston and the District of Columbia, and another 25 percent were located in Illinois and California.

Nixon's geographic base was somewhat broader. (See Table 11-11.) He raised only 33 percent of his money in the states from Boston to the District of Columbia. Significantly he collected approximately 15 percent in Florida and Texas combined. The Midwest, including Illinois, accounted for 16 percent of the total (a figure not substantially different from McGovern's). These percentages, together with California's 14 percent, total approximately 78 percent of his money.

The degree to which Nixon's and McGovern's contributions were concentrated in a few states is illustrated in Tables 11-12 and 11-13. Table 11-12 presents the states that, when combined, amounted to 50 percent and 75 percent of the candidates' money raised, broken down by size of contribution. (Thus, 50 percent of Nixon's total money was raised in five states, 75 percent in 14 states; 50 percent of money raised in contributions of less than $10,000 was raised in six states, etc.). Table 11-13 provides a measure of concentration for some political and economic statistics for comparative purposes.

The total dollar contributions of both Nixon and McGovern are more concentrated than population, total vote, personal income, and even bank deposits. All ranges of McGovern's contributions are more concentrated than these comparative indexes, and all but the smallest dollar category for Nixon are more concentrated than every index except the nation's bank deposits. These statistics also show that: (1) McGovern's money at all levels was significantly more concentrated in a few states than Nixon's was; (2) the smaller the contribution of each candidate, the less concentrated those contributions were; and (3) the distribution of Nixon's smaller contributions approximated the national distribution of population, total vote, and personal income, while McGovern's decidedly did not.

Table 11-12
Numbers of States from Which Nixon and McGovern Received 50 and 75 Percent
of the Dollar Category

Dollar Category	Number of States from Which Nixon Received 50 Percent of the Dollar Category	Number of States from Which Nixon Received 75 Percent of the Dollar Category	Number of States from Which McGovern Received 50 Percent of the Dollar Category	Number of States from Which McGovern Received 75 Percent of the Dollar Category
Total dollars	5	14	3	8
<$10,000	6	14	3	9
<$2,000	7	15	4	10
$100>$500	8	18	4	11

Table 11-13
Numbers of States by Percentage of Population, Vote, Income, and
Bank Deposits

Factors[a]	Number of States That Make Up 50 Percent of the Respective Category	Number of States That Make Up 75 Percent of the Respective Category
Population	9	20
Total vote	8	19
Personal income	8	17
Bank deposits	6	17

[a]The distribution of population was based on the 1970 census report. The total vote and candidate vote (employed in other tables) came from the U.S. Congress, Clerk of the House, *Statistics of the Presidential and Congressional Election of November 7, 1972,* reprinted in the *Statistical Abstract of the United States, 1974* (Washington, D.C.: U.S. Government Printing Office, 1974). The distribution of personal income reflects the "current income from all sources during calendar year 1970" appearing in the *Statistical Abstract of the United States*, 1974, p. 380. The distribution of Bank Deposits was based on the total deposits of insured commercial banks, 1972, from the U.S. Federal Deposit Insurance Corporation, *Assets and Liabilities; Commercial and Mutual Savings Banks,* reprinted in the *Statistical Abstract of the United States, 1973.*

These indexes were selected to provide some rough basis of comparison for the contribution statistics. Personal income and bank deposits were added to the political indexes to provide a measure of the normal distribution of spending power and of national wealth. Bank deposits were selected as an index because they are concentrated in the nation's financial centers where large political contributions normally are thought to be concentrated.

These statistics illustrate the fact that Nixon had a much wider geographic financial base than McGovern did—especially among smaller contributors, but they also illustrate that campaign laws that limit the size of contributions will tend to broaden the geographic base of American political finance and reduce to some extent the overwhelming role played by the large states, especially the large financial centers. The McGovern figures show that such limitations will also tend to widen the geographic financial base of candidates who have primarily a regional appeal.

The Other Candidates.   The financial bases of the other presidential hopefuls were even more restricted than the bases of the two major contestants. Humphrey, for example, received approximately 85 percent of his money from six states: New York, California, Texas, Minnesota, Pennsylvania, and Ohio. (See Humphrey, Table 11-14.) Although the actual contributors were more widespread than the money was, still 85 percent of them were located in ten states. Muskie's geographic pattern resembled Humphrey's, and 90 percent of his money came from nine states: New York, Pennsylvania, D.C., Florida, California, Ohio, Maine, Massachusetts, and Illinois. (See Muskie, Table 11-14.) Eighty-four percent of his contributors were located in ten states. Aside from the favorite son states of Minnesota and Maine, most of Humphrey's principal states appear in Muskie's column as well. Money for these centrist regulars came from the large industrial states with the surprising exceptions of Michigan and Illinois where neither candidate did very well. Hardly any money was raised during this period by either of these candidates in middle-range or small states (except in their home states and in the capital region of Maryland, D.C., and Virginia). Also noteworthy is the fact that Muskie did remarkably poorly in California compared to the patterns of other serious contenders.

Henry Jackson's contribution patterns also reflected a high degree of concentration in a few states. (Eighty-four percent of his money came from California, Massachusetts, Ohio, D.C., New Jersey, Washington, Nebraska, and from Americans living overseas.) The presence of Massachusetts, Ohio, and Nebraska reflect, in part, serious primary campaigns waged by Jackson in these states. (See Jackson, Table 11-14.) It is important also to notice that during this period Jackson did quite poorly in New York: he did not raise money after April 7 the way Humphrey, Muskie, and the two principal contenders did. This is somewhat surprising in light of his traditional support within the Jewish community. Quite possibly, Jackson raised significant funds in New York before April 7.

George Wallace, not surprisingly, raised most of his money in the South and in a few states where he actively contested a primary. Eighty-eight percent of his money came from nine states; 83 percent of his contributors were located in ten states. His principal states were: Louisiana, Alabama, Texas, Florida, Michigan, Tennessee, Ohio, Indiana, Missouri, and (with respect to *contributors*),

Table 11-14
Geographic Distribution of Selected Candidates' Post-April 7 Contributors and Aggregated Contributions in Amounts Over $100

State	Number of Contributors	Percent of Contributors	Total Dollars	Percent of Total Dollars
		Humphrey		
Alabama	2	0.26%	$ 5,200.00	0.31%
Arizona	3	0.39	4,150.00	0.24
California	134	17.29	347,136.26	20.37
Colorado	4	0.52	2,650.00	0.16
Connecticut	4	0.52	1,150.00	0.07
D.C.	44	5.68	31,520.48	1.85
Florida	58	7.48	42,640.16	2.50
Georgia	7	0.90	8,400.00	0.49
Illinois	7	0.90	15,250.00	0.89
Indiana	2	0.26	1,300.00	0.08
Iowa	3	0.39	526.00	0.03
Kentucky	1	0.13	500.00	0.03
Louisiana	1	0.13	5,000.00	0.29
Maryland	43	5.55	47,992.00	2.82
Massachusetts	5	0.65	4,500.00	0.26
Michigan	20	2.58	13,550.00	0.80
Minnesota	72	9.29	170,780.30	10.02
Mississippi	2	0.26	700.00	0.04
Missouri	17	2.19	18,700.00	1.10
Montana	3	0.39	1,500.00	0.09
Nevada	3	0.39	4,500.00	0.26
New Jersey	5	0.65	4,500.00	0.26
New York	72	9.29	475,250.00	27.89
North Carolina	1	0.13	165.00	0.01
Ohio	24	3.10	68,127.42	4.00
Oklahoma	3	0.39	7,000.00	0.41
Oregon	1	0.13	1,000.00	0.06
Pennsylvania	56	7.23	90,750.00	5.32
Rhode Island	5	0.65	4,500.00	0.26
South Carolina	2	0.26	1,000.00	0.06
Tennessee	1	0.13	1,000.00	0.06
Texas	5	0.65	303,168.61	17.79
Virginia	19	2.45	11,755.00	0.69
West Virginia	2	0.26	1,650.00	0.10
Wisconsin	2	0.26	1,014.65	0.06
Puerto Rico	1	0.13	200.00	0.01
Foreign	2	0.26	5,500.00	0.32
Totals	636		$1,704,225.88	
		Muskie		
Arizona	1	0.17%	$ 1,000.00	0.25%
California	39	6.68	33,739.50	8.56

Table 11-14 (cont.)

State	Number of Contributors	Percent of Contributors	Total Dollars	Percent of Total Dollars
Colorado	17	2.91%	$ 3,497.50	0.89%
Connecticut	16	2.74	8,228.09	2.09
Delaware	2	0.34	325.00	0.08
D.C.	75	12.84	39,899.12	10.12
Florida	6	1.03	35,500.00	9.00
Illinois	14	2.38	21,074.84	5.34
Indiana	4	0.68	1,250.00	0.32
Kentucky	1	0.17	500.00	0.13
Maine	35	5.99	24,475.00	6.21
Maryland	24	4.11	9,295.37	2.36
Massachusetts	36	6.16	21,448.00	5.44
Michigan	8	1.37	1,986.00	0.50
Missouri	1	0.17	250.00	0.06
Nevada	3	0.51	765.00	0.19
New Hampshire	4	0.68	2,400.00	0.61
New Jersey	2	0.34	375.00	0.10
New Mexico	6	1.03	2,100.00	0.53
New York	96	16.44	90,806.50	23.03
Ohio	36	6.16	32,300.00	8.19
Oklahoma	6	1.03	1,386.00	0.35
Pennsylvania	83	14.21	41,930.01	10.63
Rhode Island	1	0.17	250.00	0.06
Texas	48	8.22	12,337.08	3.13
Virginia	19	3.25	6,200.00	1.57
Wisconsin	1	0.17	1,000.00	0.25
Totals	584		$ 394,318.01	

Jackson

State	Number of Contributors	Percent of Contributors	Total Dollars	Percent of Total Dollars
Alabama	1	0.61%	$ 400.00	0.22%
California	27	16.56	39,350.00	21.95
D.C.	10	6.13	16,930.00	9.44
Florida	4	2.45	1,625.00	0.91
Georgia	2	1.23	6,673.55	3.72
Maryland	3	1.84	4,000.00	2.23
Massachusetts	24	14.72	33,595.00	18.74
Michigan	2	1.23	2,200.00	1.23
Nebraska	10	6.13	7,861.00	4.38
New Jersey	2	1.23	16,470.00	9.19
New Mexico	6	3.68	2,450.00	1.37
New York	9	5.52	1,000.00	0.56
North Carolina	2	1.23	1,700.00	0.95
Ohio	27	16.56	18,130.05	10.11
Oklahoma	1	0.61	1,000.00	0.56
Pennsylvania	3	1.84	2,500.00	1.39
Rhode Island	2	1.23	500.00	0.28
Tennessee	1	0.61	875.00	0.49

(cont.)

Table 11–14 (cont.)

State	Number of Contributors	Percent of Contributors	Total Dollars	Percent of Total Dollars
Texas	1	0.61%	$ 250.00	0.14%
Virginia	1	0.61	500.00	0.28
Washington	23	14.11	9,279.10	5.18
Wisconsin	2	1.23	2,000.00	1.12
Totals	163		$ 169,288.70	

Wallace

State	Number of Contributors	Percent of Contributors	Total Dollars	Percent of Total Dollars
Alabama	72	26.37%	$ 31,318.68	17.95%
Arkansas	2	0.73	610.00	0.35
California	5	1.83	2,100.00	1.20
Florida	26	9.52	14,314.00	8.20
Georgia	6	2.20	5,488.03	3.15
Hawaii	1	0.37	500.00	0.29
Illinois	2	0.73	277.50	0.16
Indiana	12	4.40	10,235.00	5.87
Kansas	1	0.37	300.00	0.17
Kentucky	1	0.37	300.00	0.17
Louisiana	17	6.23	31,660.00	18.14
Michigan	28	10.26	12,244.65	7.02
Mississippi	5	1.83	875.00	0.50
Missouri	5	1.83	6,400.00	3.67
Nevada	1	0.37	300.00	0.17
North Carolina	3	1.10	901.51	0.52
Ohio	5	1.83	10,521.00	6.03
Oklahoma	2	0.73	1,200.00	0.69
Oregon	1	0.37	140.00	0.08
Pennsylvania	2	0.73	2,500.00	1.43
Tennessee	19	6.96	11,437.00	6.55
Texas	43	15.75	26,326.59	15.09
Utah	2	0.73	1,200.00	0.69
Virginia	1	0.37	500.00	0.29
Washington	2	0.73	384.00	0.22
Wisconsin	9	3.30	2,458.00	1.41
Totals	273		$ 174,490.96	

Mills

State	Number of Contributors	Percent of Contributors	Total Dollars	Percent of Total Dollars
Alaska	1	0.66%	$ 4,500.00	2.28%
Arkansas	22	14.57	74,400.00	37.65
California	4	2.65	3,500.00	1.77
Colorado	1	0.66	1,500.00	0.76

Table 11-14 (cont.)

State	Number of Contributors	Percent of Contributors	Total Dollars	Percent of Total Dollars
Connecticut	6	3.97%	$ 2,700.00	1.37%
D.C.	5	3.31	7,900.00	4.00
Florida	3	1.99	1,500.00	0.76
Illinois	5	3.31	4,800.00	2.43
Maine	1	0.66	150.00	0.08
Maryland	2	1.32	700.00	0.35
Massachusetts	14	9.27	5,450.00	2.76
Michigan	3	1.99	2,000.00	1.01
Minnesota	2	1.32	2,000.00	1.01
Missouri	3	1.99	1,500.00	0.76
New Jersey	9	5.96	4,650.00	2.35
New York	39	25.83	41,550.00	21.03
Ohio	3	1.99	2,000.00	1.01
Pennsylvania	7	4.63	6,910.00	3.50
Tennessee	4	2.65	4,000.00	2.02
Texas	7	4.63	15,000.00	7.59
Virginia	5	3.31	9,204.00	4.66
Washington	1	0.66	500.00	0.25
Wisconsin	4	2.65	1,200.00	0.61
Totals	151		$ 197,614.00	

Hartke

State	Number of Contributors	Percent of Contributors	Total Dollars	Percent of Total Dollars
California	1	1.23%	$ 1,000.00	5.79%
D.C.	40	49.38	7,850.00	45.44
Florida	4	4.94	750.00	4.34
Illinois	5	6.17	1,875.00	10.85
Indiana	8	9.88	1,275.00	7.38
Maryland	6	7.41	900.00	5.21
New York	4	4.94	1,875.00	10.85
Ohio	4	4.94	500.00	2.89
Virginia	9	11.11	1,250.00	7.24
Totals	81		$ 17,275.00	

Chisholm

State	Number of Contributors	Percent of Contributors	Total Dollars	Percent of Total Dollars
California	10	38.46%	$ 24,355.00	76.38%
Idaho	1	3.85	1,000.00	3.14
Massachusetts	6	23.08	2,525.00	7.92
Montana	1	3.85	200.00	0.63
New York	7	26.92	2,804.65	8.80
Washington	1	3.85	1,000.00	3.14
Totals	26		$ 31,844.65	

(cont.)

Table 11-14 (cont.)

| | | Sanford | | |
State	Number of Contributors	Percent of Contributors	Total Dollars	Percent of Total Dollars
North Carolina	20	86.96%	$ 9,002.00	83.72%
South Carolina	1	4.35	1,000.00	9.30
Tennessee	1	4.35	250.00	2.33
Virginia	1	4.35	500.00	4.65
Totals	23		$ 10,752.00	

| | | Mink | | |
State	Number of Contributors	Percent of Contributors	Total Dollars	Percent of Total Dollars
Hawaii	2	40.00%	$ 700.00	43.52%
Oregon	3	60.00	908.60	56.48
Totals	5		$ 1,608.60	

| | | Yorty | | |
State	Number of Contributors	Percent of Contributors	Total Dollars	Percent of Total Dollars
California	91	100.00%	$ 77,900.00	100.00%
Totals	91		$ 77,900.00	

Wisconsin. (See Wallace, Table 11-14.) Hardly any money came from the Northeast: for this period, Wallace listed no contributions of more than $100 from New England, New York, New Jersey, Delaware, Maryland, or West Virginia. He had only two such contributions in Pennsylvania, and only one in Virginia. Aside from one contribution in Nevada, two in Utah, one in Kansas, and two in Oklahoma, Wallace received none in the plain and mountain states. In fact, the only states (aside from Alabama and Louisiana) where Wallace received a significant number of contributions over $100 were states in which there had been a serious nomination contest. He raised very little money in Mississippi, Georgia, and the Carolinas. It would appear that his efforts to raise money of significant size, if there were any such efforts, simply accompanied his primary activities in four states (Florida, Tennessee, Indiana, Michigan) and his caucus efforts in Texas. Most of the other minor candidates raised money in a handful of states. For example, Yorty raised all of his money during this time period in California; Chisholm raised 76 percent in the same state. Hartke received 45 percent of his money from the District of Columbia, Sanford 83 percent from North Carolina; Patsy Mink split her meagre receipts of more than $100 almost evenly between

Hawaii and Oregon. Wilbur Mills' money came from 23 states, but he raised 37 percent of it in Arkansas. (See Table 11-14.)

Regional Patterns of Contribution

The aggregated geographic totals give some indication of the impact of certain states on political finance, but they do not indicate the intrinsic significance of the amount of contributions in a given state. There may be a lot of campaign money raised in New York and California, but then there is a lot of money in New York and California to begin with. It is necessary, then, to examine the contribution patterns in each state on a relative basis to see the fascinating variations in campaign finance practices around the country.

One way to put the contributions into perspective is to compare the geographic distribution of these contributions with the geographic distribution of various political and economic factors. We have examined four categories of contributions: (1) total dollar amounts, (2) total number of contributors, (3) total dollars raised in amounts less than $10,000 (to eliminate the distortions of single large contributions in a given state), and (4) the total number of "small" contributions—contributions of more than $100 but less than $500. Each of these categories was compared to five political and economic indicators: (1) population, (2) total vote, (3) candidate vote (McGovern or Nixon), (4) personal income, and (5) bank deposits.[a] By comparing the national distribution of each of the four categories of contribution with the national distribution of each of the five political-economic factors, it is possible to see on a relative basis where states overcontributed and undercontributed to candidates when compared to national expectations of contributions based on the distribution of population, personal income, and so forth. Since the patterns vary markedly by candidate, it is appropriate to treat Nixon and McGovern separately.

McGovern's Regional Patterns

The Northeast (New England, New York, New Jersey, Pennsylvania, Delaware, Maryland, D.C., and West Virginia). As we said above, about half of McGovern's money came from this region of the country. In addition to its absolute importance, however, the region also was McGovern's strongest area on a relative basis. New Hampshire, Vermont, Massachusetts, Connecticut, New York, New Jersey, Maryland, and the District of Columbia were consistently above the national average in every category of contribution compared to every political and economic factor analyzed. (For example, see Figures 11-1 to 11-3).

---

[a]See Table 11-13 for an explanation of these indexes.

Rhode Island and Delaware were above average in some categories. Pennsylvania was below average in all categories, but only moderately so in most categories. Only Maine and West Virginia were substantially below average on a consistent basis. This indicates that the Northeast as a whole—not just the large states— gave strong backing to McGovern in comparison to the rest of the country. In fact, Illinois and California were the only other states in the country that gave McGovern a showing consistently as strong as the eight Northeastern states mentioned above. Figure 11-1, for example, illustrates the relative position of the various states when the distribution of McGovern's small contributions are compared to the distribution of the nation's population. (The numbers reflect the contributions as a percentage of population.) For example, McGovern's contributions in the $101-$499 range in New York State were actually 209 percent of what they would have been had these contributions been evenly distributed throughout the states on the basis of population. The Northeast stands out dramatically on this map. This pattern, of course, is consistent with the presumed "liberal" politics of the region.

The South (Virginia, North and South Carolina, Kentucky, Tennessee, Georgia, Florida, Alabama, Mississippi, Louisiana, Arkansas, Oklahoma, and Texas). This region was nearly a total disaster for McGovern, mitigated only slightly by modest performances in Florida and occasionally in Texas and Virginia (Washington, D.C. suburbs). For example, McGovern received only six contributions of more than $5,000 in the entire region outside Florida and Texas. The South's relative performance was clearly the nation's worst for McGovern. With respect to contributions in the $101-$499 range, no state in the region (except the two mentioned) contributed more than 25 percent of what it would have, had these contributions been evenly distributed nationwide on the basis of population. The pattern does not change much when the South's low level of personal income is controlled. Only one state (in addition to the two mentioned) contributed more than 30 percent of what it would have contributed had these small contributions been evenly distributed nationwide on the basis of personal income. The pattern is somewhat better when compared to the distribution of McGovern's vote—since his vote in the South was also very low (see Figure 11-2)—but even in this category, the region was his worst. The pattern is the same for total money raised (although Texas' percentage is better in this category), for total contributions, and for money raised in contributions of less than $10,000. (See, for example, Figure 11-3.) In this region, at any rate, political and fund-raising performances seem to have matched each other.

The Midwest (Ohio, Indiana, Illinois, Michigan, Wisconsin). Aside from Illinois, the states of this region are consistently below average with respect to almost every contribution category and every political-economic index. As

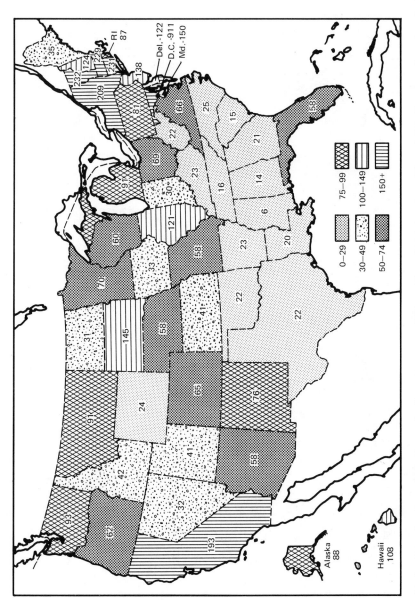

Figure 11-1. Distribution of McGovern's Contributors of More Than $100 but Less Than $500 Compared to the National Distribution of Population

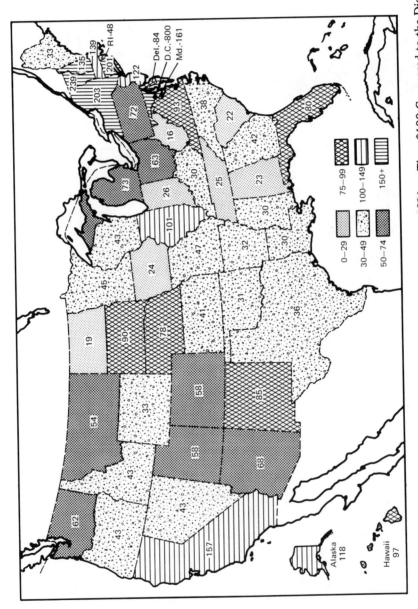

Figure 11-2. Distribution of the Number of McGovern's Total Contributors of More Than $100 Compared to the Distribution of McGovern's Vote

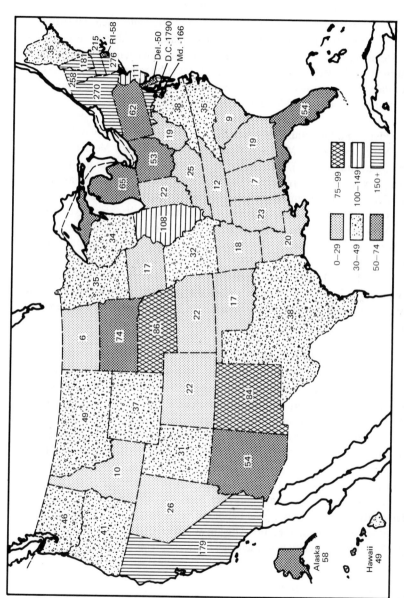

Figure 11-3. Distribution of McGovern's Contributions of More Than $100 but Less Than $10,000 Compared to the National Distribution of Total Votes Cast for All Candidates in the 1972 Presidential Election

Figures 11-1 to 11-3 illustrate, Indiana is only marginally better than the Deep South in most respects. (In terms of total dollars Indiana is above the nation's average because of the large amount of money contributed by two members of the Noyes family.) Ohio and Michigan are consistently better than the South, but usually far behind the principal states of the Northeast. (In this respect, Pennsylvania's patterns are more similar to those of Ohio and Michigan than to the patterns of most states in the Northeast.) Overall, the Midwest with its substantial Democratic populations and its unions must have been a severe disappointment to the McGovern fund raisers. (It must be remembered, however, that our data base consists of individual contributions and, hence, does not include money raised through unions or other groups.)

The Plains and Mountains (Minnesota, Iowa, Missouri, North and South Dakota, Nebraska, Kansas, Montana, Wyoming, Colorado, New Mexico, Idaho, Nevada, Utah, and Arizona). Generally, McGovern's performance in this region was on a par with his performance in the Midwest—below the national average, but significantly better than his performance in the South. There were, however, a few states in the region where he performed relatively well: his native South Dakota, Nebraska (where he fought a hard primary campaign), and New Mexico (for reasons that are not clear). Generally, his regional performance was better among the contributors of $101 to $499 than among large contributors: he received only 12 contributions of more than $5,000 in the whole region. In terms of total dollars raised his performance was generally poor in the plains and mountains, although some large contributions in Utah and Nevada interrupted the pattern.

The Pacific States (California, Oregon, Washington, Alaska, Hawaii). Led by California this region was McGovern's second best in the country. California's impressive absolute performance was matched by an equally impressive relative showing. McGovern's small contributions in California, for example, were 193 percent of what they would have been had they been distributed evenly throughout the country on the basis of population. Every size of contribution matched against every political and economic category showed California substantially above the national average in its performance for McGovern as shown in Figures 11-1 to 11-3. Alaska and Hawaii approximated the national average with respect to the total number of contributions and the total number of small contributions. They lagged behind in total money and money raised in contributions of less than $10,000. Oregon and Washington were generally below average—but not drastically below average in most categories.

Nixon's Regional Patterns

Nixon's patterns of contributions present a far more complex picture than

McGovern's do. For example, McGovern's strengths lay almost exclusively in the Northeast and California, while Nixon showed relative strength in some dollar categories throughout every region of the country. Also, McGovern's areas of strength and weakness were generally the same for every level of contribution: where he did well among smaller contributors he also did well among larger contributors. Nixon's performance, however, varied widely in this respect. In the Northeast, for example, he was strong relatively with respect to the larger contributions and weak relatively with respect to the smaller contributions. In the plains and mountain states the situation was the reverse, and so forth.

The Northeast. Nixon's relative performance in the Northeast presents an interesting pattern. In terms of total money raised, he performed very well in Connecticut, New York, Pennsylvania, Delaware, Maryland, and D.C. In each of these he comfortably raised more money than he would have raised had his total money been distributed nationwide on the basis of population, personal income, the total vote cast, and his own vote. New York dips slightly below the national average when Nixon's total contributions are examined on the basis of the nationwide distribution of bank deposits since New York has an exceptionally high percentage of the nation's bank deposits. With respect to money raised in aggregated amounts of less than $10,000, Nixon's performance in these same states is generally poorer, although still somewhat above the national average.

The rest of the states in the region are generally below average with respect to total contributions and money raised in amounts less than $10,000. Northern New England, Rhode Island, and West Virginia were all relatively poor regions for Nixon. (It should be noted that Nixon's poor performance in New Hampshire may have been due to the April 7 deadline.)

With respect to the total number of contributors, the region was just slightly below Nixon's national averages. The states mentioned above that gave him an above-average performance with respect to total money generally approximated the national average with respect to the total number of contributors. The New England states where he performed so poorly in the total dollar category were much stronger in the contributor category. As the size of the contribution diminished, the region became more homogenous. In the $101-$499 category the whole region is comfortably below the national average—except for Delaware, Maryland, and D.C.

The large urban and suburban states of the Northeast, then, provided a disproportionately large amount of Nixon's larger contributions, a roughly proportional amount of his middle-range contributions, and a disproportionately smaller number of contributions in the smallest dollar range studied. The rest of the region gave a smaller proportional amount of his large contributions, and a much larger proportional amount of his smaller contributions. (Figures 11-4, 11-5, 11-6, and 11-7 illustrate these trends and provide the actual numbers.)

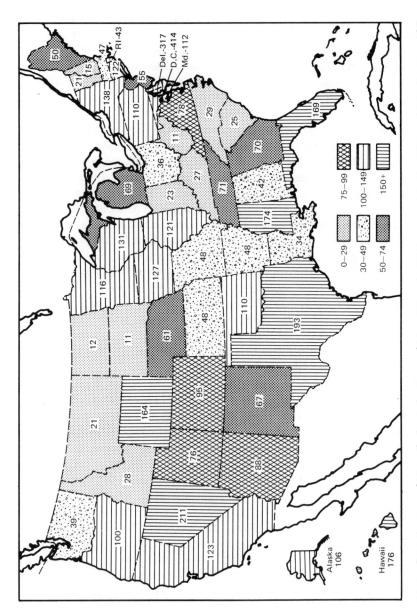

Figure 11-4. Distribution of Nixon's Contributions of More Than $100 Compared to the National Distribution of Personal Income, 1972

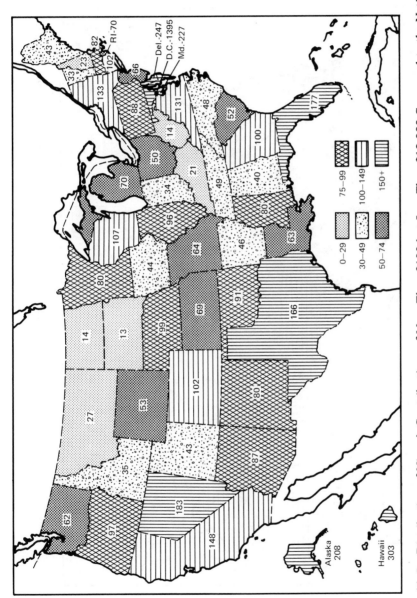

Figure 11-5. Distribution of Nixon's Contributions of More Than $100 but Less Than $10,000 Compared to the National Distribution of the Total Votes Cast for All Candidates in the 1972 Presidential Election

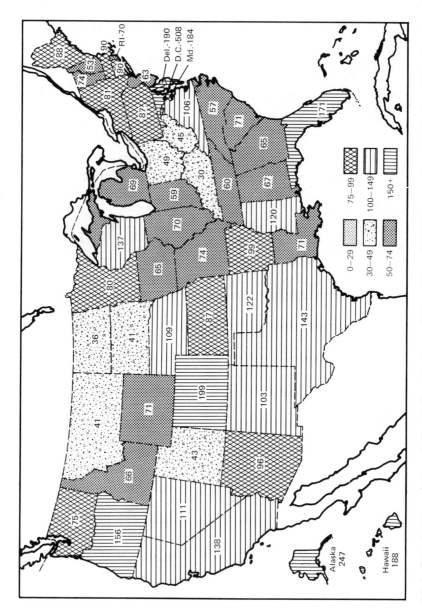

Figure 11-6. Distribution of Nixon's Total Contributors of More Than $100 Compared to the National Distribution of Personal Income, 1972

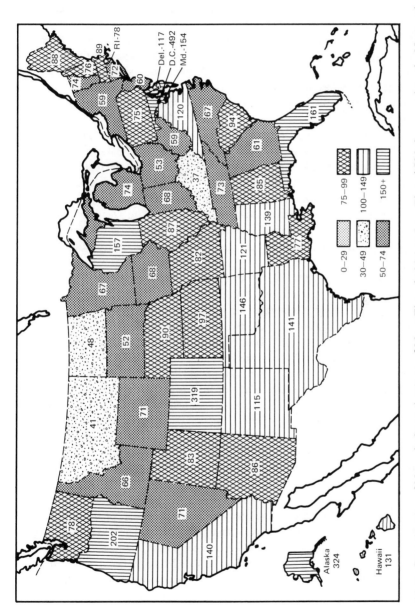

Figure 11-7. Distribution of Nixon's Contributions of More Than $100 but Less Than $500 Compared to the National Distribution of Personal Income, 1972

The South. The South presents a much less consistent picture than the Northeast. Texas, Florida, and Virginia (partly due to the Washington suburbs) consistently contributed above the national average in all categories from top to bottom. With respect to total money raised by Nixon, the rest of the region is comfortably behind the national distributions in all categories with the exception of the state of Mississippi where one large contribution (after the election, incidentally) raised the state to an above-average national standing. Most of the region is considerably below average in this category. The pattern is the same for money raised in amounts less than $10,000—in this category Mississippi is comfortably below the national average. Aside from Texas, Florida, and Virginia only Georgia approaches the national average for contributions of less than $10,000.

The South contributed a higher proportion of Nixon's smaller ($101-$499) contributions, and as a whole was marginally above the national average. Southern statistics are tricky because the national indexes for the region are generally low: the South has the nation's lowest per capita income and lowest percent of its population voting. The low base lines tend to inflate the relative figures. These indexes are balanced to some extent by Nixon's high vote margins that tend to deflate the relative figures. On the average, however, the South was Nixon's worst region for all but the smallest category of contributions.

The Midwest. Unlike the Northeast and the South, the Midwest presented a relatively consistent pattern irrespective of the size of contribution. Illinois and Wisconsin were very strong states for Nixon on a relative basis in almost every category of comparison. Of the two, Wisconsin was stronger. By contrast, Ohio and Indiana were very weak states for Nixon. One of the great mysteries of the 1972 financial campaign is why these two solidly Republican states made such a poor financial contribution to Nixon. Michigan lay somewhere in between the solid performances of Illinois and Wisconsin and the poor performance of Ohio and Indiana—but it was consistently below the national distribution in all categories.

The Plains and Mountains. This region presents a mixed pattern of contributions. Contributions of $101-$499 on a relative basis generally improve the further south one goes in the region. (See Figure 11-7.) The northern tier of states is substantially below the national averages for most political-economic indexes. The states in the central and southern parts of the regions tend to approach the national average. The one state that is consistently strong in this dollar category is Colorado. With the exception of Alaska and the District of Columbia, Colorado has the highest relative distribution of Nixon's contributions in this dollar range. This pattern is generally the same for his total contributions.

Total money and money raised in contributions of less than $10,000 present a different pattern. In these two categories the region as a whole is comfortably below the national average, with the northern states considerably below average and the southern states marginally below average. A few large contributions in Minnesota, Iowa, Wyoming, and Nevada raise these states above the national average with respect to total money raised, but in middle-range contributions the region does not do well at all.

The Pacific States. The Pacific was consistently Nixon's best region. California dominates the region and on a relative basis California was a very strong performer for Nixon in every range of contribution. The state was substantially above the national average from top to bottom in virtually all dollar categories. Alaska and Hawaii also performed substantially above the national average in virtually every dollar range. Oregon was less impressive than these three in terms of total dollars raised, but was very strong in terms of smaller contributions. Washington was the only state in the region that ranked consistently below the national average in all categories.

Conclusion

These 1972 geographic patterns of presidential finance show that contributions tend to reflect wider political support rather well. McGovern's money came almost exclusively from the two regions of American "liberalism," while Nixon's money came from his two traditional areas of support: the "Sun Belt," which gave a disproportionate amount of his smaller contributions, and the financial centers of the Northeast, Illinois, and California, which gave a disproportionate amount of his larger contributions. Tables 11-15 through 11-18 provide a state-by-state breakdown of the contributors and contributions on the basis of the size of aggregated contribution and show in detail the patterns of contribution for each state.

It is safe to conclude that the election of 1972 was a transitional year so far as political finance was concerned. Not only will new reforms alter these geographic distributions, but the imperatives of raising more money at lower levels will probably force fund raisers to examine more closely those states that have traditionally been "undercontributors." It is probable that the next few presidential campaigns will see geographic patterns of finance approximate more and more the relevant socioeconomic indexes of the country.

The Time Factor

The General Accounting Office (GAO) data for 1972 enables us to examine for the first time the dates when contributions were made to presidential

Table 11-15
Distribution of McGovern Contributors by Dollar Size of Aggregated Contributions and by State

	>$100<$500	$500-$999	$1,000-$1,999	$2,000-$4,999	$5,000-$9,999	$10,000-$99,999	$100,000+
Alabama	17	3	1	0	0	1	0
Alaska	10	2	2	0	0	0	0
Arizona	39	7	2	2	1	0	0
Arkansas	16	5	4	0	0	0	0
California	1,368	381	188	103	34	19	3
Colorado	53	14	4	0	0	2	3
Connecticut	247	76	58	23	16	5	1
Delaware	24	4	2	0	4	0	0
Florida	146	32	30	5	0	2	0
Georgia	35	6	5	1	0	0	0
Hawaii	31	6	1	0	0	0	0
Idaho	11	2	0	0	0	0	0
Illinois	474	111	101	32	14	9	0
Indiana	55	7	2	2	3	0	2
Iowa	33	10	2	1	0	0	0
Kansas	32	5	2	2	0	1	0
Kentucky	26	10	4	1	1	0	0
Louisiana	26	5	2	2	0	0	0
Maine	12	4	3	1	0	0	0
Maryland	211	40	42	11	5	3	0
Massachusetts	459	118	66	39	17	7	0
Michigan	285	67	44	9	3	2	0
Minnesota	94	31	12	2	0	0	0
Mississippi	5	5	3	2	0	0	0
Missouri	95	14	14	2	0	0	0
Montana	23	1	0	0	1	0	0
Nebraska	30	4	8	4	2	2	0
Nevada	6	3	1	0	0	1	0
New Hampshire	33	11	7	7	2	0	0

Table 11-15 (cont.)

	>$100<$500	$500-$999	$1,000-$1,999	$2,000-$4,999	$5,000-$9,999	$10,000-$99,999	$100,000+
New Jersey	352	74	47	25	8	9	0
New Mexico	28	7	8	3	0	0	0
New York	1,325	385	323	154	52	58	2
North Carolina	45	9	7	3	2	1	0
North Dakota	7	0	0	0	0	0	0
Ohio	257	59	41	9	4	7	0
Oklahoma	20	3	5	1	0	0	0
Oregon	47	9	4	2	1	2	0
Pennsylvania	336	86	51	16	4	0	0
Rhode Island	29	2	2	2	1	0	0
South Carolina	14	1	1	0	0	0	0
South Dakota	35	10	2	0	1	0	0
Tennessee	23	8	3	0	0	0	0
Texas	92	27	21	10	5	6	0
Utah	16	6	5	0	0	1	0
Vermont	37	14	6	3	1	0	0
Virginia	108	23	22	2	1	1	0
Washington	111	16	4	2	2	0	0
West Virginia	14	1	1	0	1	0	0
Wisconsin	94	21	13	3	0	2	0
Wyoming	3	2	0	1	0	0	0
D.C.	237	69	51	25	6	5	0
Virgin Islands	4	2	0	0	0	1	0
Guam	2	0	0	0	0	0	0
Puerto Rico	3	2	1	1	0	0	0
Foreign	84	23	8	7	1	0	0
Totals	7,219	1,843	1,236	520	193	147	8

Table 11-16
Distribution of Nixon Contributors by Dollar Size of Aggregated Contributions and by State

	>$100<$500	$500-$999	$1,000-$1,999	$2,000-$4,999	$5,000-$9,999	$10,000-$99,999	$100,000+
Alabama	88	20	17	4	2	3	0
Alaska	46	9	12	0	1	1	0
Arizona	55	25	29	2	6	4	0
Arkansas	68	30	8	0	1	1	1
California	1,340	448	474	198	78	46	1
Colorado	319	30	18	12	6	3	0
Connecticut	112	57	66	22	7	8	1
Delaware	29	13	21	18	3	9	0
Florida	412	151	169	68	36	17	1
Georgia	99	37	33	26	6	2	0
Hawaii	45	23	34	16	6	2	0
Idaho	16	7	6	2	0	0	0
Illinois	462	173	173	81	21	22	3
Indiana	143	49	41	7	1	2	0
Iowa	76	27	22	9	1	4	1
Kansas	89	20	28	16	1	2	0
Kentucky	39	8	7	4	1	1	0
Louisiana	100	29	38	10	2	1	0
Maine	29	16	6	5	0	1	0
Maryland	267	119	166	58	10	1	0
Massachusetts	227	100	81	30	12	1	0
Michigan	292	71	98	48	11	12	0
Minnesota	102	46	39	27	13	10	1
Mississippi	81	22	27	4	3	0	0
Missouri	149	42	42	23	5	2	0
Montana	10	5	4	0	1	0	0
Nebraska	53	27	32	9	2	1	0
Nevada	17	8	15	3	3	4	0
New Hampshire	22	3	4	1	0	0	0

Table 11-16 (cont.)

	>$100<$500	$500-$999	$1,000-$1,999	$2,000-$4,999	$5,000-$9,999	$10,000-$99,999	$100,000+
New Jersey	204	77	87	30	11	9	0
New Mexico	38	16	4	4	3	1	0
New York	544	276	317	184	72	47	6
North Carolina	119	31	27	14	3	2	0
North Dakota	10	2	2	0	0	0	0
Ohio	241	77	61	42	9	8	0
Oklahoma	128	31	28	12	7	4	0
Oregon	166	37	27	14	2	5	0
Pennsylvania	366	157	186	82	15	22	1
Rhode Island	30	6	13	1	3	0	0
South Carolina	75	15	14	2	3	0	0
South Dakota	12	4	2	0	0	0	0
Tennessee	92	16	30	4	4	1	1
Texas	580	185	217	90	39	31	3
Utah	14	4	2	5	2	2	0
Vermont	12	9	2	0	0	0	0
Virginia	281	90	76	26	7	9	0
Washington	115	49	31	17	3	1	0
West Virginia	32	9	6	0	0	0	0
Wisconsin	274	77	62	31	10	10	0
Wyoming	8	3	3	0	1	1	0
D.C.	211	65	88	32	21	8	0
Virgin Islands	6	0	2	0	0	0	0
Guam	—	—	—	—	—	—	—
Puerto Rico	3	4	3	4	1	1	0
Foreign	42	10	18	9	5	3	0
Totals	8,390	2,865	3,018	1,306	460	325	20

Table 11-17

Percentage Distribution of McGovern Contributions by Dollar Size of Aggregated Contributions and by State

	>$100<$500	$500-$999	$1,000-$1,999	$2,000-$4,999	$5,000-$9,999	$10,000-$99,999	$100,000+
Alabama	12.51%	6.79%	3.84%	0.00%	0.00%	76.86%	0.00%
Alaska	33.83	22.76	43.36	0.00	0.00	0.00	0.00
Arizona	26.85	13.47	8.01	18.75	32.92	0.00	0.00
Arkansas	31.40	28.75	39.85	0.00	0.00	0.00	0.00
California	13.75	10.12	9.93	13.59	9.48	21.26	21.87
Colorado	19.16	13.49	7.75	0.00	0.00	59.61	0.00
Connecticut	9.06	8.10	12.74	11.30	17.84	17.34	23.63
Delaware	46.90	28.33	24.77	0.00	0.00	0.00	0.00
Florida	18.62	10.38	19.09	7.78	14.15	29.97	0.00
Georgia	38.76	17.42	27.72	16.10	0.00	0.00	0.00
Hawaii	54.98	30.67	14.35	0.00	0.00	0.00	0.00
Idaho	64.46	35.54	0.00	0.00	0.00	0.00	0.00
Illinois	12.79	8.80	16.31	10.67	12.37	39.06	0.00
Indiana	2.44	0.85	0.47	1.40	4.19	0.00	90.65
Iowa	41.85	35.33	11.41	11.41	0.00	0.00	0.00
Kansas	12.86	6.24	4.18	9.84	0.00	66.88	0.00
Kentucky	22.44	25.15	19.02	8.90	24.48	0.00	0.00
Louisiana	37.55	14.45	14.12	33.88	0.00	0.00	0.00
Maine	19.44	21.97	27.50	31.09	0.00	0.00	0.00
Maryland	15.66	8.52	18.12	12.40	14.69	30.60	0.00
Massachusetts	14.40	10.35	11.71	16.80	16.58	30.16	0.00
Michigan	25.79	16.61	22.40	9.18	9.05	16.98	0.00
Minnesota	35.45	30.85	25.73	7.97	0.00	0.00	0.00
Mississippi	7.80	23.71	24.06	44.42	0.00	0.00	0.00
Missouri	38.29	16.12	32.14	13.44	0.00	0.00	0.00
Montana	31.41	3.88	0.00	0.00	64.71	0.00	0.00
Nebraska	10.24	2.93	13.61	14.29	20.40	38.52	0.00
Nevada	2.97	5.94	2.94	0.00	0.00	88.16	0.00

Table 11-17 (cont.)

	>$100<$500	$500-$999	$1,000-$1,999	$2,000-$4,999	$5,000-$9,999	$10,000-$99,999	$100,000+
New Hampshire	13.27%	12.38%	14.18%	39.97%	20.20%	0.00%	0.00%
New Jersey	16.13	9.57	12.35	15.89	9.02	37.04	0.00
New Mexico	20.73	14.62	32.96	31.69	0.00	0.00	0.00
New York	7.79	6.11	10.45	11.75	9.27	30.75	23.87
North Carolina	15.79	8.56	12.74	16.10	21.92	24.89	0.00
North Dakota	100.00	0.00	0.00	0.00	0.00	0.00	0.00
Ohio	15.28	10.76	14.21	7.34	8.08	44.33	0.00
Oklahoma	27.47	11.55	39.91	21.07	0.00	0.00	0.00
Oregon	13.02	8.60	6.05	9.85	10.51	51.97	0.00
Pennsylvania	28.54	20.34	24.83	16.49	9.89	0.00	0.00
Rhode Island	32.63	5.80	12.59	24.29	24.69	0.00	0.00
South Carolina	53.74	14.80	31.46	0.00	0.00	0.00	0.00
South Dakota	29.42	28.44	10.65	0.00	31.49	0.00	0.00
Tennessee	39.51	34.75	25.73	0.00	0.00	0.00	0.00
Texas	8.15	6.61	10.71	11.95	11.93	50.66	0.00
Utah	3.55	3.62	5.75	0.00	0.00	87.08	0.00
Vermont	21.87	22.76	17.82	25.18	12.37	0.00	0.00
Virginia	26.58	15.65	30.22	7.70	7.44	12.41	0.00
Washington	36.48	15.29	7.49	11.91	28.83	0.00	0.00
West Virginia	17.95	3.91	11.72	0.00	66.42	0.00	0.00
Wisconsin	22.09	12.68	16.22	9.11	0.00	39.90	0.00
Wyoming	12.09	21.98	0.00	65.93	0.00	0.00	0.00
D.C.	16.34	13.13	19.04	22.62	10.40	18.49	0.00
Virgin Islands	2.16	1.96	0.00	0.00	0.00	95.88	0.00
Guam	100.00	0.00	0.00	0.00	0.00	0.00	0.00
Puerto Rico	11.51	19.03	17.30	52.16	0.00	0.00	0.00
Foreign	29.25	20.44	12.45	27.30	10.57	0.00	0.00

Table 11-18
Percentage Distribution of Nixon Contributions by Dollar Size of Aggregated Contributions and by State

	>$100<$500	$500-$999	$1,000-$1,999	$2,000-$4,999	$5,000-$9,999	$10,000-$99,999	$100,000+
Alabama	15.14%	8.51%	13.78%	7.94%	9.09%	45.53%	0.00%
Alaska	23.97	11.61	28.90	0.00	11.84	23.69	0.00
Arizona	7.59	8.38	17.81	2.76	20.71	42.74	0.00
Arkansas	22.52	20.93	11.05	0.00	7.80	37.70	0.00
California	8.11	7.13	15.05	15.46	14.66	32.28	7.30
Colorado	19.99	6.73	7.48	11.65	12.92	41.22	0.00
Connecticut	4.71	5.62	12.88	10.13	8.32	31.94	26.41
Delaware	2.65	2.87	9.67	19.41	7.07	58.33	0.00
Florida	7.10	6.50	14.87	13.99	17.98	30.96	8.61
Georgia	6.08	6.08	11.01	23.00	13.95	39.87	0.00
Hawaii	7.67	7.01	20.71	24.05	18.54	22.02	0.00
Idaho	20.90	19.43	37.47	22.20	0.00	0.00	0.00
Illinois	5.52	5.24	10.22	12.63	6.87	27.65	31.86
Indiana	19.85	18.88	30.32	12.96	3.60	14.40	0.00
Iowa	4.35	3.34	6.13	6.19	1.49	20.32	58.19
Kansas	14.72	8.13	23.24	31.98	4.02	17.92	0.00
Kentucky	10.02	5.14	9.00	11.57	11.57	52.70	0.00
Louisiana	17.47	12.38	31.43	18.02	8.12	12.58	0.00
Maine	13.77	17.16	13.29	23.60	0.00	32.18	0.00
Maryland	10.60	12.08	32.03	27.08	9.63	8.58	0.00
Massachusetts	15.30	15.73	25.60	21.33	19.10	2.94	0.00
Michigan	8.15	4.90	13.32	16.22	9.23	48.18	0.00
Minnesota	4.81	4.82	8.00	14.17	13.82	31.05	23.34
Mississippi	5.37	4.04	9.77	3.27	6.38	0.00	71.18
Missouri	11.94	9.70	18.56	25.03	13.06	21.70	0.00
Montana	15.43	20.61	28.43	0.00	35.53	0.00	0.00
Nebraska	10.60	13.26	31.83	24.02	10.51	9.78	0.00
Nevada	3.08	3.54	10.97	6.37	14.15	61.90	0.00
New Hampshire	39.03	14.52	30.97	15.48	0.00	0.00	0.00

Table 11-18 (cont.)

	>$100<$500	$500-$999	$1,000-$1,999	$2,000-$4,999	$5,000-$9,999	$10,000-$99,999	$100,000+
New Jersey	8.71%	7.94%	17.01%	14.87%	11.40%	40.07%	0.00%
New Mexico	14.67	14.15	6.51	14.64	33.76	16.27	0.00
New York	3.42	4.10	9.39	13.80	12.51	36.62	20.16
North Carolina	17.27	10.99	19.83	21.61	12.74	17.56	0.00
North Dakota	39.27	15.45	45.29	0.00	0.00	0.00	0.00
Ohio	11.69	9.36	14.36	23.10	14.06	27.42	0.00
Oklahoma	10.76	6.28	10.73	12.73	14.98	44.52	0.00
Oregon	18.02	9.71	13.21	16.40	4.86	37.79	0.00
Pennsylvania	5.48	5.71	12.93	13.91	5.64	47.64	8.69
Rhode Island	13.47	6.35	27.51	6.86	45.81	0.00	0.00
South Carolina	26.50	13.36	26.62	6.98	26.54	0.00	0.00
South Dakota	42.13	28.94	28.94	0.00	0.00	0.00	0.00
Tennessee	7.03	3.22	12.32	3.95	10.84	18.37	44.26
Texas	5.94	4.44	10.20	10.80	10.33	33.46	24.82
Utah	4.14	2.59	2.59	19.54	13.58	57.57	0.00
Vermont	25.93	49.71	24.37	0.00	0.00	0.00	0.00
Virginia	11.81	8.77	15.88	13.97	9.08	40.49	0.00
Washington	15.62	16.68	19.92	27.06	11.58	9.14	0.00
West Virginia	37.85	28.12	34.02	0.00	0.00	0.00	0.00
Wisconsin	10.18	6.49	10.44	12.52	10.27	50.10	0.00
Wyoming	2.79	2.70	6.30	0.00	10.80	77.41	0.00
D.C.	9.29	6.82	18.60	16.12	23.17	25.99	0.00
Virgin Islands	34.43	0.00	65.57	0.00	0.00	0.00	0.00
Guam	—	—	—	—	—	—	—
Puerto Rico	1.60	4.26	6.38	21.28	10.64	55.85	0.00
Foreign	7.68	4.80	16.09	19.03	24.51	27.89	0.00

candidates. Figure 11-8 portrays the total weekly dollar flow into the Nixon and McGovern campaigns. (McGovern's loans are also portrayed because they were extensive. See "Loans" below.) The most obvious and most impressive dimension to this chart is the enormous surge of money to Nixon during the closing weeks of the campaign. Beginning in July his cash flow is represented by a curve that rises exponentially until election day—a curve with enormous surges in three of the last four weeks. One could speculate that this last-minute money represented "opportunity money" since the outcome of the election had been largely conceded by the middle of October.

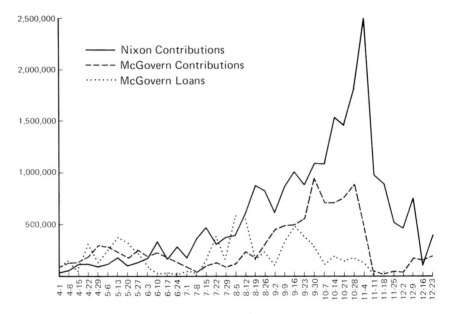

Figure 11-8. Weekly Receipts from Contributions of More Than $100 (*In Dollars*)

McGovern's incoming cash flow presents a much more varied and interesting picture. There was a modest inflow during the primary season—averaging around $200,000 per week. This total declined throughout June, reaching its low point in early July at the time of the Democratic National Convention. This decline, however, was offset in part by a surge of money to the Democratic National Committee at the time of the telethon. (See Figure 11-9.) After the convention McGovern's receipts continued at a relatively low level. It was almost September before McGovern's weekly intake from contributions equalled his primary season weeks. By this time Nixon's "take-off" had occurred. During September,

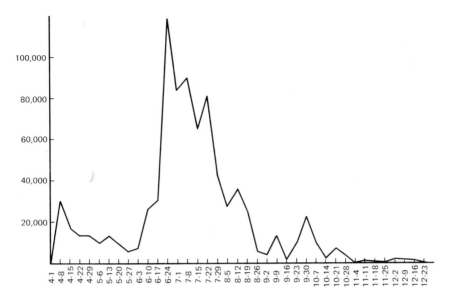

Figure 11-9. Weekly Receipts of Democratic National Committee from Contributions of More Than $100 (*In Dollars*)

McGovern held steadily on a plateau around $500,000 per week. In October he reached another plateau around $750,000. In no case did he reach a level of $1 million per week. Nixon, however, had receipts over the $1 million level during seven weeks—and during the last week of the campaign he broke through the $2 million mark.

McGovern enjoyed an extensive and well-organized loan program that supplemented his cash flows from contributions. During the primary season, during the Eagleton affair in early August, and during September, McGovern raised a substantial amount of money in loans, enough money to enable him to match Nixon's total income almost until the middle of October. (Of course, a fairly large amount of these were repaid out of contributions.)

The "smaller" contributions—the contributions larger than $100, yet smaller than $500, present a somewhat different picture. Figure 11-10 portrays their weekly flow for both candidates. (These contributions are not aggregated by donor—they represent the actual number of contributions.) Nixon's pattern is somewhat less exponential than the pattern of his total dollar receipts, although there was an incredible surge in the last three weeks. McGovern, on the other hand, repeated his summer dip, and experienced an enormous surge in September that was maintained until the end of October. He ran comfortably ahead of Nixon almost every week after Labor Day until the last week of the campaign.

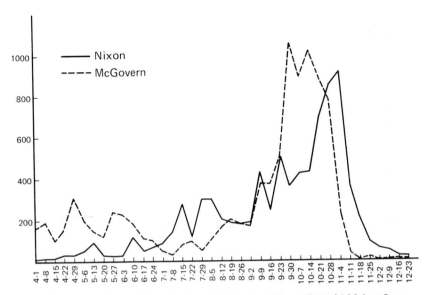

Figure 11-10. Total Weekly Contributions of More Than $100 but Less Than $500 (*By Number of Contributions*)

Figures 11-11 and 11-12 portray the total number of contributions and the number of contributions in the $1,000 range.

There are some geographic variations in the time flows of cash into the various campaigns. In the Nixon campaign most areas of the country followed the national pattern of reaching a maximum during the last week or two of the campaign. The one important exception to this national trend was California. Nixon's fund-raising efforts there peaked in early October and were generally in decline for the rest of the campaign. Although the total dollar amounts were impressive when compared to other states and regions, the trend there was decidedly downwards. The Nixon totals in New York, the Northeast generally, and the Midwest, however, surged strongly during the last weeks of the campaign. An exceptional surge occurred in the Deep South where the totals remained low until the middle of October—and then rose dramatically for the last two weeks of the campaign.

Overall, with these few exceptions, Nixon's regional time flows tended to conform very well to national totals. This is somewhat surprising since efforts at fund raising presumably differ by region and since there are widely differing aggregate patterns of contributions in the various regions of the country, as noted above. These graphs show dramatically that Nixon's political contributions ebbed and flowed generally in response to national, not local, forces.

McGovern's regional time flows of money are somewhat more erratic than

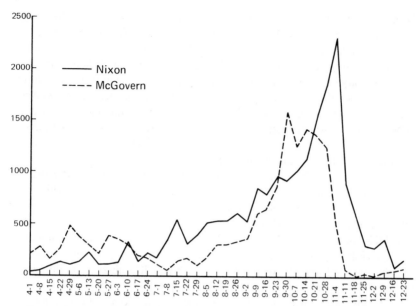

Figure 11-11. Total Weekly Contributions of More Than $100 (*By Number of Contributions*)

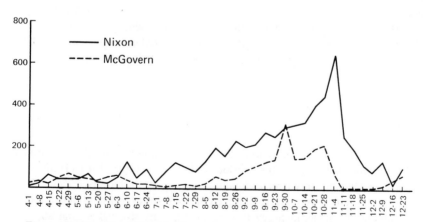

Figure 11-12. Total Weekly Contributions of More Than $999 but Less Than $2,000 (*By Number of Contributions*)

Nixon's and do not conform to the national totals as well as Nixon's do. In the preconvention period, New York dominated McGovern's financial situation even more dramatically than it did overall. His receipts from the other regions were modest during this period. Significantly, money raised in California during the late primary season was not substantially more than the money raised in the Midwest, despite the early June primary there. The region was far behind New York during most of this period. All regions experienced the mid-summer dip, but New York recovered first. New York's role in McGovern's financial picture until Labor Day was so crucial that it is not an exaggeration to say that New York carried the bulk of the campaign until September.

California money began to surge into the McGovern campaign after the beginning of September. Its weekly patterns were erratic with large swings in the size of receipts, but its totals during September and October were impressive. Still California and the Pacific region during this period did not equal the totals of the Mid-Atlantic states. New York, New Jersey, and Pennsylvania combined reached a cash flow of more than $200,000 per week in mid-September and sustained this level steadily for seven weeks, while California receipts fluctuated between $350,000 and $75,000 per week.

The contribution patterns from New England approximated the national totals with some significant early money, a mid-summer dip, and a September-October surge. The Midwest enjoyed a similar pattern, but the fall surge was much stronger than New England's. The rest of the country contributed so little to McGovern that its patterns are not statistically very significant. (See Figure 11-13.)

These McGovern figures show that the Eagleton affair probably had a very serious impact on the McGovern financial campaign. The mid-summer dip was reflected in all sizes of contribution and the entire financial picture remained quite bleak until after Labor Day. Nixon, on the other hand, began a solid growth in receipts during the mid-summer and kept building his weekly total through the end of the campaign. Both candidates relied tremendously on late contributions, but Nixon far out-distanced McGovern from the middle of October until the election.

Loans

McGovern and Humphrey were the two candidates who made extensive use of loan financing during the time period studied. (See Table 11-19.) Humphrey's loans were generally very large and came from just seven states (see Table 11-20). McGovern's loans were spread over much of the country. They included a significant number of smaller loans, even though the average size was around $6,700—considerably above the average of his contributions. Although McGovern's pattern of loans was much more erratic than the pattern of his contributions (see Table 11-21), the overall geographic distribution of loans roughly paralleled the

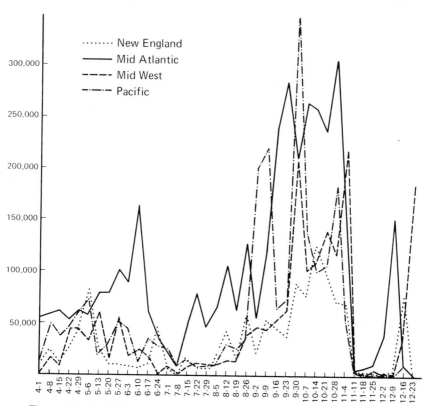

Figure 11-13. McGovern Weekly Receipts from Contributions of More Than $100 by Selected Region (*In Dollars*)

Table 11-19
Loans to Principal Candidates

Candidate/Committee	Number	Dollar Amount
Humphrey	40	$1,934,625.00
Muskie	84	217,500.00
McGovern	1,007	6,733,394.77
Wallace	4	16,000.00
Jackson	5	10,246.27
Miscellaneous Democrats	28	206,907.96
Nixon	11	103,500.00[a]
Democratic National Committee	6	1,663,100.00

[a]Derived from GAO listings but not actual loans according to the FCRP.

Table 11-20
Geographic Distribution of Loans of More Than $100 to Selected Candidates,
April 7, 1972 to December 31, 1972 (Percentage of Nationwide Total)

State	Nixon	McGovern	Muskie	Humphrey	Jackson	Wallace
Alabama		7.73			3.70	31.25
Arizona		0.74				
California	45.41	20.07	0.92	9.10		
Colorado	2.90					
Connecticut		3.40	5.75			
Delaware						
Florida		0.14	85.52			
Georgia						
Hawaii		0.13				
Idaho		0.01				
Illinois		9.61	1.38			
Indiana		6.72				
Iowa						
Kansas		0.02				
Kentucky		0.38				
Louisiana		0.02				
Maryland		1.71	5.29			
Massachusetts		9.55			4.88	
Michigan		0.25				
Minnesota		0.16		18.82		
Mississippi						31.25
Missouri		0.04		0.83		
Montana		0.38				
Nebraska		0.16			88.20	
New Hampshire		0.02				
New Jersey		2.24				
New Mexico		0.02				
New York	19.32	21.08		28.43		
North Carolina	0.97	1.88				
North Dakota		0.01				
Ohio		3.28		32.82		
Oklahoma		0.05				
Oregon		0.92				
Pennsylvania		0.39	1.15	3.64		
Rhode Island		0.04				
South Dakota						
Texas	24.15	0.76				37.50
Utah		0.33				
Virginia	7.25	0.01				
Washington		0.03				
Wisconsin		0.88				
D.C.		0.99		6.36	3.22	
Virgin Islands		5.73				
Foreign Countries		0.09				

overall geographic distribution of his total receipts from contributions. The
Northeast, Illinois, and California accounted for 69 percent of his loans. Table
11-21 shows that the loan patterns in California, Connecticut, Illinois, Maryland,

Table 11-21

Distribution of McGovern Aggregated Loans of More Than $100 by State and Dollar Range, April 7, 1972 to December 31, 1972

State	>$100<$500	$500-$999	$1,000-$1,999	$2,000-$4,999	$5,000-$9,999	$10,000-$99,999	$100,000+
Alabama	0.00	0.00	0.21	0.00	0.00	0.00	99.73
Arizona	0.00	0.00	0.00	0.00	100.00	0.00	0.00
California	0.50	0.38	0.82	2.31	4.07	53.92	38.00
Colorado	100.00	0.00	0.00	0.00	0.00	0.00	0.00
Connecticut	0.20	1.09	0.44	4.60	31.90	15.37	46.40
Delaware	100.00	0.00	0.00	0.00	0.00	0.00	0.00
Florida	8.22	16.95	51.28	23.55	0.00	0.00	0.00
Georgia	100.00	0.00	0.00	0.00	0.00	0.00	0.00
Hawaii	2.79	5.59	35.75	0.00	55.87	0.00	0.00
Idaho	33.33	66.67	0.00	0.00	0.00	0.00	0.00
Illinois	0.63	0.47	0.00	0.75	6.54	43.66	47.96
Indiana	0.00	0.00	0.00	0.66	0.00	0.00	99.34
Iowa	100.00	0.00	0.00	0.00	0.00	0.00	0.00
Kansas	100.00	0.00	0.00	0.00	0.00	0.00	0.00
Kentucky	1.75	0.00	0.00	0.00	0.00	98.25	0.00
Louisiana	29.82	0.00	70.18	0.00	0.00	0.00	0.00
Maryland	0.73	0.44	1.74	0.00	10.01	0.00	87.08
Massachusetts	0.07	0.14	0.00	0.78	0.00	49.50	49.50
Michigan	37.90	14.79	0.00	47.32	0.00	0.00	0.00
Minnesota	4.58	28.63	19.08	47.71	0.00	0.00	0.00
Missouri	4.92	33.07	62.01	0.00	0.00	0.00	0.00
Montana	0.00	3.10	0.00	0.00	0.00	96.90	0.00
Nebraska	2.18	0.00	20.48	30.92	46.42	0.00	0.00
New Hampshire	66.71	33.29	0.00	0.00	0.00	0.00	0.00
New Jersey	3.71	4.76	4.38	5.32	3.66	78.18	0.00
New Mexico	0.00	33.33	66.67	0.00	0.00	0.00	0.00
New York	0.52	0.11	0.49	2.35	5.08	38.70	52.74

(cont.)

Table 11-21 (cont.)

State	>$100<$500	$500-$999	$1,000-$1,999	$2,000-$4,999	$5,000-$9,999	$10,000-$99,999	$100,000+
North Carolina	0.21	0.00	0.00	2.38	0.00	97.42	0.00
North Dakota	100.00	0.00	0.00	0.00	0.00	0.00	0.00
Ohio	1.10	0.53	1.31	1.90	0.00	4.53	90.62
Oklahoma	26.69	14.66	0.00	58.65	0.00	0.00	0.00
Oregon	0.75	2.03	0.00	0.00	0.00	97.23	0.00
Pennsylvania	5.36	5.81	27.30	15.38	0.00	46.14	0.00
Rhode Island	0.00	50.00	50.00	0.00	0.00	0.00	0.00
South Dakota	100.00	0.00	0.00	0.00	0.00	0.00	0.00
Texas	2.04	0.00	0.00	0.00	0.00	97.96	0.00
Utah	0.00	75.00	25.00	0.00	0.00	0.00	0.00
Virginia	35.14	64.86	0.00	0.00	0.00	0.00	0.00
Washington	42.86	0.00	57.14	0.00	0.00	0.00	0.00
Wisconsin	2.77	1.68	9.24	23.53	11.76	51.01	0.00
D.C.	1.50	0.00	2.26	0.00	0.00	96.24	0.00
Virgin Islands	0.00	0.00	0.00	0.00	0.00	0.00	100.00
Foreign	0.00	0.00	0.00	0.00	100.00	0.00	0.00

Massachusetts, New Jersey, New York, Texas, and D.C. (together with a number of other states) were, not surprisingly, top-heavy, generally much more top-heavy than contribution patterns in these states. When these figures are considered in conjunction with McGovern's contributions, it is easy to see that his overall effort was, like Nixon's, significantly dependent on a relatively few wealthy backers. (GAO listings included items a casual reader would consider loans, but FCRP denies that any loans were received.)

12 Business and Labor in Politics

Business and the 1972 Election

The business community had reason to be alarmed by the image it projected as details of corporate contributions to the Nixon reelection campaign became known. In mid-1973, at the peak of the Watergate investigations, a Gallup survey found that business ranked last among eight institutions measured in terms of public confidence and respect; an Opinion Research Corporation survey also measured a sharp decline in the percentage of those strongly supporting business. The *Wall Street Journal*, *Business Week*, and other periodicals published articles about draining public confidence in business, coupled with the growing cynicism that part of what Watergate signified—spying, sabotage, "dirty tricks"—was connected to cash supplied by big business. Historian Arnold Toynbee declared that the decline in political morality in America was due to the face that it had sunk to the lowest level of American business morality.

Such blanket indictments were rejected publicly by business leaders; yet, there was clear concern in the nation's board rooms about a decline of public confidence. And many businessmen saw in the situation an opportunity for positive action. The 1972 political scandals increased public awareness of the need for election reform, and created an environment for socially responsible political activity by corporations.

In this atmosphere, Common Cause entered what was termed a "subtle dialogue" with officials of corporations such as Ford Motor Company to encourage them to bring pressure on Congress to create a public subsidy for federal election campaigns. In a Detroit speech on October 18, 1973, Henry Ford II called for a change in federal election laws to "minimize the opportunity for influence peddling and buying."[1] Only ten percent of citizens of voting age contributed to candidates or parties, Ford pointed out, and he called for public as well as private campaign financing on a "direct, systematic, and substantial basis."

Certain important segments of the business community, however, opposed the idea of public financing of elections while endorsing other reforms. The Chamber of Commerce of the United States, for example, said it was "opposed to any direct form of public financing or Government subsidizing of election campaigns or other expenses connected with elections to public office." In testimony presented before the Senate Subcommittee on Privileges and Elections in September 1973, the chamber argued that "Federal funds applied to

457

presidential and congressional campaigns, and perhaps later to state and local campaigns, would substantively change the extent of personal participation in politics." Such funding, the statement given on behalf of the chamber read, could "sound the death knell for voluntary action by the citizenry in contributing to the party of their choice."

At the same time, the chamber (which has a membership of more than 46,000 corporations, firms, and individuals) noted a national poll of its membership showing 93 percent of those surveyed favoring overall reform of the electoral process and 94 percent supporting public disclosure of contributions to and expenditures by all candidates for federal office. The survey indicated also that 76 percent favored voluntary funding of political campaigns, but nearly half believed individual contributions should be limited. More than 90 percent wanted stricter laws and penalties to curb violence and improper election practices. Seventy-four percent approval was given the idea of an independent agency to govern and enforce the Federal Election Campaign Act (FECA).[2]

Similar opposition to public financing was expressed by The Business Roundtable in a May 1974 statement on election reform prepared by a subcommittee of its Policy Committee, headed by David Packard. The statement also opposed putting limits on the amounts individuals could contribute as well as on campaign expenses; absolute ceilings, it argued, "would, by necessity, be arbitrary and unfair in effect." It did favor, however, limitations on cash contributions. At the same time, the group called campaign contributions "a legitimate form of political expression," endorsed the concept of indirect public support of campaign costs through increased tax incentives and the granting of free time to candidates by the media, and also called for creation of an independent election commission, and for a requirement that each candidate for federal office designate one central committee for the purpose of filing disclosure reports.[3]

A number of these steps were also embodied in a series of ten proposals issued in 1973 by the Public Affairs Council (PAC) "to insure vigorous and even-handed" enforcement of the election laws. The PAC, however, favored limitations on individual campaign contributions and expenditures, and urged Congress to support most of the general campaign finance reform measures that were subsequently enacted in the FECA Amendments of 1974.[4]

Many business leaders felt that the heart of the problem that was thrown into such sharp focus in 1972 was the massive private gift to a candidate. They noted particularly the strain on corporate morality when a political party in power aggressively solicited campaign funds from large corporations, which necessarily and constantly were dealing with governmental agencies and regulatory bodies.

The 1972 campaign, businessmen pointed out, had brought extraordinary pressures. It was the first campaign in memory, for example, in which solicitations were so widely made by so high a former government official as Maurice

Stans, who as Secretary of Commerce had close associations with many of the businessmen he was soliciting. One might have to hearken back to the days of Mark Hanna and his systematic assessment of corporations for funds in support of William McKinley for a historic parallel; it was the Hanna approach, in fact, that led to the Tillman Act of 1907, the first federal law to prohibit corporate contributions.[a] In the Stans-Kalmbach approach, the round sum of $100,000 was the most frequently mentioned figure, and both men acknowledged seeking donations of this size from corporation officials. In 1972 Stans told the *National Journal* that he was urging big corporate donors to contribute at least one percent of gross income, a low price to pay every four years, he felt, "to ensure that the executive branch is in the right hands."[5]

Much of this money was raised in perfectly legal fashions, some of which took advantage of loopholes in the tax law. There were various forms. One, for example, was a kind of "Bundles-for-Nixon" campaign where personal checks of individual executives were collected and presented in a single package. Some chief executives made their contributions on a matching basis with other employees or together with checks from other members of their own families.

The Disclosure Gap

The largest loophole, perhaps, was that provided by the gap between old and new laws, the period from February 29, 1972, expiration of the final reporting periods under the old law, and April 7 of that year, when the new Federal Election Campaign Act became effective. During that period of less than six weeks, the Finance Committee to Re-Elect the President (FCRP) raised more than it had in the previous 14 months—$11.4 million.

That these figures are known is due to their release by the FCRP under a court-stipulated agreement with Common Cause. The FCRP at first said that the list was destroyed; in a deposition from former FCRP Treasurer Hugh W. Sloan, Jr., however, it was disclosed that a copy of the list had been sent to President Nixon and was in the possession of his personal secretary, Rose Mary Woods. The list was later turned over to the Office of Special Prosecutor, the Justice Department, and the Senate Watergate committee.

In June 1973 a special staff under the direction of Thomas F. McBride, special assistant to Special Watergate Prosecutor Archibald Cox, was set up to investigate whether the FCRP used extortion or other illegal forms of fund

---

[a]For a history of attempts to regulate corporate involvement in federal elections from 1900-1972, plus examination of 1972 corporate practices, legislation, and other effects of 1972 practices, see *The Corporate Watergate* (Washington, D.C.: Investor Responsibility Research Center, Inc., [Special Report 1975-D], October 1975).

raising in 1972. Investigators accumulated allegations that Republican finance officials had drawn up a confidential list of corporations and individuals who were having problems with the government, and proceeded to solicit funds in late 1971 and early 1972 from that list.

Corporate contributions to political campaigns have been forbidden since the 1907 Act, and both individuals and corporations in violation can be charged with a crime. The law provides a $5,000 fine for corporations, with fines of up to $10,000 and jail terms for individuals. The Special Prosecutor's Office adopted a policy that those corporate officers who came forward voluntarily and early to disclose illegal political contributions would be considered to have "mitigating circumstances" in their cases, and they would be charged only with a misdemeanor (the 1907 law termed such violations a felony).

"Laundering" Money

A new term entered the American popular political lexicon in 1972—*laundering* of money: the practice of passing money received illegitimately through various individuals or enterprises, making it "clean" again, as well as conveniently difficult to trace. The practice is common in organized crime, and indeed the FBI saw parallels with its use there, and the manner in which it was handled in the movement of corporate funds donated to the Finance Committee to Re-Elect the President.

It was the Watergate burglary that first brought the laundering of money in politics to wide public attention. Several thousand dollars in $100 bills were in the possession of the Watergate burglars when they were caught on June 17, 1972. Government investigators traced the money to a $100,000 contribution to the Finance Committee to Re-Elect the President. The FBI established that the $100,000 came originally from the corporate bank account of the Gulf Resources & Chemical Company, a Texas-based conglomerate in Houston. Four days before the April 7 disclosure deadline, the money was transferred from the account by company President Robert H. Allen, a major Nixon fund raiser in Texas, to the bank account of a Gulf subsidiary in Mexico, Compania de Azufre Veracruz, S.A. (CASAVA). There is was used by a Mexico City attorney, Manuel Ogarrio, to negotiate four bank drafts totalling $89,000 and $11,000 in cash.[b] Ogarrio turned these over to CASAVA President Diaz de Leon, who the

---

[b]The money was apparently negotiated in the combination of bank drafts and cash because the $11,000 was all the cash that could be secured on somewhat short notice. April 4, 1972 was the Tuesday after Easter, and all banks in Mexico had been closed for the previous week, Holy Week. When Ogarrio and De Leon met that day, the attorney also received a check for $100,000 as payment for legal services he had earlier rendered CASAVA; thus, identical sums of $100,000 apparently changed hands, which may have helped further to cloud the money trail. Ogarrio later suggested to Allen that there might

next day (April 5) delivered the money to the Pennzoil Company offices in Houston. Later that evening, in a suitcase carried by Pennzoil Vice-President Roy J. Winchester, the money was flown to Washington in the Pennzoil company plane, along with $600,000 also raised for Nixon from Texas sources. The $700,000 total was turned over to FCRP treasurer Hugh Sloan. Sloan and Stans testified to the Watergate Committee that the four bank drafts for $89,000 were given to G. Gordon Liddy, then FCRP counsel, later convicted as a Watergate conspirator. The checks ended up in the Miami bank account of Bernard L. Barker, apprehended with four accomplices at the Watergate break-in. Also in the Barker account was a fifth check for $25,000 from Kenneth H. Dahlberg, a Nixon fund raiser from Minneapolis; Dahlberg had actually gotten the amount from Dwayne O. Andreas, also of Minneapolis, who previously had been a major supporter of Hubert Humphrey, and wished to keep secret his Nixon contribution.

The $100,000, which Robert Allen initially had transferred to Ogarrio was subsequently, on January 24, 1973, returned in a check drawn on the account of the Media Committee to Re-Elect the President.

Investigators for the House Banking and Currency Committee reported that the Pennzoil offices were a major collection point for Republican contributors from Texas, Mexico and surrounding areas, with Allen and Pennzoil President William Liedtke, Jr. as the principal fund raisers (Liedtke himself gave $23,349 to the Nixon effort pre-April 7, and $1,000 later). Part of the Texas money, it was disclosed, had been contributed by executives of three firms that had won a billion dollar contract to bring natural gas from the Soviet Union to the United States. The companies, all based in Houston, were Brown and Root, Inc., Texas Eastern Transmission Co., and Tenneco.

Business and Professional Committees

In 1972 some 200 business- or professional-related committees registered under the FECA of 1971. These business, corporate, trade, and professional association committees spent $6.8 million, with some 82 percent of that sum, $5.6 million, disbursed to presidential, senatorial, and congressional candidates. These figures exclude the dairy committees, which are treated separately, but include other agricultural groups such as cattlemen, citrus, rice, and soybean producer committees. Health industry committees are included as are education

---

be an additional fee for his trouble in handling the Watergate money, but there is no record of any such payment. See Senate Select Committee on Presidential Campaign Activities, *Final Report*, No. 93-981, 93rd Cong., 2d sess., June, 1974 (Washington, D.C.: U.S. Government Printing Office), pp. 514-22. It has been suggested by some that the $11,000 in cash was never produced by Ogarrio but was retained by him as a fee for laundering the money; no proof has surfaced.

committees, although the latter is an optional inclusion because some educational committees could be regarded as within the labor union category.

BIPAC. Included in the totals are the activities of such national-level business-oriented committees as the Business-Industry Political Action Committee (BIPAC), which was created in 1963 to "provide financial support to congressional candidates who support the principles of constitutional government." BIPAC was in part a response to the growing total of labor contributions from union members. In 1972 BIPAC spent $512,434 on political activities, with $428,100 going to the direct support of candidates or their personal committees.

AMPAC. Since 1961 the American Medical Association has sought through its political action committee (AMPAC) to further the goal of "minimizing government control over the medical profession," through direct support of candidates, as well as political education activities. In 1972 AMPAC received $845,166, mainly in membership contributions from medical personnel as well as other non-medical "friends of medicine" (such as pharmaceutical firms, which are reported to comprise 15 percent of the AMPAC membership, although the organization will not reveal its total membership).

Since it was first organized, AMPAC has spent at least $3 million on political activities, almost all of that in contributions to candidates. In 1972 the group spent $874,902 in all, and $853,051 went to candidates (total expenditures were up from $682,000 in 1968).

Whereas in 1968 BIPAC and AMPAC together accounted for 61 percent of the total expenditures of business committees (amounting to a little more than $2 million), four years later—with the two committees providing about the same total in dollars—their percentage of the total was down to about 20 percent.

Committees from certain types of industry or business were active in 1972. The political action committees of firms in the aerospace industry, five in all, spent $283,732 on political activities. Thirteen PACs from the construction industry spent $287,000, while 12 from savings and loan institutions spent $228,000. Nine committees in the communications industry—the political arms of such trade groups as the Recording Industry Association of America, National Cable Television Association, and the National Association of Broadcasters—had expenditures totalling $162,871.

A total of 87 political action committees were under the aegis of individual corporations. In the two years following the election, 22 of these corporate-related committees were terminated, some because of the adverse publicity generated by the TRW case. Lockheed Aircraft Corporation's Good Citizenship Program, which spent $77,343 in 1972, was the largest single firm to terminate its committee.

Meanwhile, 31 new corporate-related committees were started in the years 1973-74, for a net gain of nine. Thus, at the time of the 1974 congressional elections, 96 corporate committees were in operation. The corporations starting up political action committees ran the gamut of American industry—Coca Cola, Kennecott Copper, Georgia Pacific, Harrah's Club, Mellon Bank, and American Export Lines were among the newcomers to the ranks.

In 1972 the proportion of the various committees' funds that went to the Nixon campaign varied greatly. The Active Citizenship Fund of the Hughes Aircraft Company, for example, reported $147,396 in employee contributions, $23,877 (16 percent) of which was given to the Nixon reelection campaign, and $3,808 (2.6 percent) of which was given to McGovern. Hughes Aircraft established the program in 1964 as a payroll deduction plan; the program has successfully encouraged employees to voluntarily support the candidate or party of their choice. In 1972, 33.5 percent (10,126) of all Hughes Aircraft employees contributed, compared with 10,508 employees in 1970. Additional contributions in excess of $50,000 in 1972 were known by Hughes management to have been made by employees to other than the Active Citizenship Fund, bringing the Hughes effort to claim more than $200,000 for the year. The fund's expenditures were more than twice those of any other corporate committee in 1972. Its nearest competitors were the Good Government Club of General Telephone of California ($71,000) and the Political Awareness Fund of Union Oil of California ($70,175). A total of 2,854 Hughes employees registered as voters in 1972 through the fund's program, and 88 candidates for public office were featured at 42 "free time" rallies, attended by a total of 22,000 employees.

The Effective Government Association of Merrill, Lynch, Pierce, Fenner and Smith spent $70,725 on political activities in 1972, of which $15,500, 22 percent of the total, was earmarked for the Nixon campaign. In 1968, when the EGA won a measure of attention for contributions to congressmen on "relevant committees" at a time when Merrill Lynch was charged with illegal action by the SEC, it contributed $6,000 (of $46,000 raised from employees) to the Nixon campaign. The Better Government Association (later known as Responsible Government Association) organized by Gould, Inc. of St. Paul, Minnesota, spent $29,250 on political activities in 1972, two-thirds of which ($20,000) went to the Nixon campaign.

In all, $422,194 contributed by business and professional committees went to the Nixon reelection campaign. A summary of business and professional committee contributions to 1972 presidential candidates is contained in Table 12-1. A breakdown for each committee is in Appendix V. McGovern, in contrast, received only $21,197 from these committees. Wilbur Mills was given $8,100 toward his Democratic presidential nomination campaign, with about half of that coming from two political action groups in the financial sector— $2,000 from the committee of the National Association of Life Insurance Underwriters, and $2,000 from the Better Government Committee of Smith, Barney & Co.

Hubert Humphrey received $7,715 from such committees, $5,000 of that

Table 12-1
Total Business and Professional Committees' Contributions to 1972
Presidential Candidates

Nixon	$422,193.75
McGovern	21,197.05
Mills	8,100.00
Humphrey	7,715.00
Hartke	2,500.00
Jackson	1,000.00
Schmitz	343.00
Total	$463,048.80

from the Good Government Fund of Thompson Ramo Wooldridge, Inc. (TRW).
Vance Hartke got $2,500 political action money for his attempt at the 1972 pres-
idential nomination, Henry Jackson received $1,000, while the American Indepen-
dent Party candidate John G. Schmitz received $343 from the Hughes Active
Citizenship Fund. Lockheed Employees' Good Citizenship Program gave the largest business committee amounts to both Nixon ($50,000) and McGovern ($8,000).

Corporate Political Activity: The New Legislation

The Federal Election Campaign Act of 1971 contained two amendments
that appeared to contradict each other in reference to corporate and labor political committees and their activities. This contradiction had the effect of reducing
certain forms of corporate political activity in 1972 campaigns.

Corporations have been prohibited since 1907 from making money contributions to federal political campaigns, a prohibition later extended to cover goods
and services that are equivalents to cash. The amended Section 610 of the 1971
act stipulated that a corporation (or a labor union) could use corporate funds
(and union dues money) to establish and maintain a political action committee
to operate a separate segregated fund for direct political activity, provided the
money was voluntarily contributed.

On the other hand, the amendment to Section 611, which broadened and
redefined the long-standing prohibition against political contributions by government contractors, banned both direct and indirect contributions by corporations.
Were not the costs of administering the separate funds permitted to be collected
by 610 really indirect contributions of the corporation or labor union as defined
by 611? It appeared to many that the FECA, as amended, took away with one
hand what it gave with the other.

Efforts at resolving the dilemma were protracted, and the contradiction was
not, in fact, clarified until President Ford signed the new campaign reform legislation into law in October 1974. The issue was first raised legislatively in the

late spring of 1972 at a time when the Good Government Fund of TRW, Inc. was under court challenge by Common Cause, a case discussed below in greater detail. Two weeks after Common Cause filed suit, Rep. Samuel L. Devine (R–Ohio)–TRW, Inc. was home-based in Cleveland–introduced a bill to exempt corporations and unions from Section 611. Devine was a member of the House Administration Committee, which handles election laws. The House passed such a bill that fall in spite of strong opposition from Common Cause, and editorial objection from *The New York Times* and the *Washington Post*.[6] Among those lobbying strongly for the bill was organized labor.

Certain unions received federal government contracts to train workers, and labor may have feared that its political contributions would be threatened by a successful Common Cause suit against TRW. In any case, the measure passed the House in October 1972, by a 249-124 vote.

The House passed the Devine bill in the last weeks of its session but Senate Majority Leader Mike Mansfield (D–Montana) had said that no bills coming out of committee after September 15 would be considered for action in the Senate unless they were of an emergency nature. The Senate Rules and Administration Committee, however, decided to consider this bill with no hearings and no public notice, and with only a bare quorum present. Senator William Proxmire (D–Wisconsin) who had been serving in a watchdog capacity alert to special interest tax bills that the Senate Finance Committee had approved without hearings, enlisted the two Republican Senators from Vermont, George Aiken and Robert Stafford, to help guard against an effort to offer the Devine bill as a rider. This attempt was made by Senator Howard Cannon (D–Nevada) who offered it as an amendment to a completely unrelated bill for tariff-free imports of upholsterers' needles and pins. Proxmire threatened a filibuster, warning that he and others were "determined to oppose this amendment in every way we can for as long as necessary." Aiken, noting that a quorum was not present, said he was "sure every Senator would want the folks back home to know how he voted on it in a yea-and-nay vote." But with the campaign in full swing, the Senate was eager to adjourn and in no mood for a marathon speech that could be broken only by a two-thirds vote. Therefore, the supporters let the amendment die; however, Senator Cannon promised "we will be back here next year with similar legislation again."[7]

As in fact they were. When legislation was again on the agenda in the summer of 1973, this time with the complete story of Watergate and its attendant abuses emerging, the Senate passed and sent to the House Administration Subcommittee on Elections a bill providing for a revision of Section 611 "to permit corporations and labor organizations holding government contracts to establish, administer or solicit voluntary contributions to separate segregated funds, as permitted under Section 610."[c] This provision was retained in the

---

[c]As described by a newsletter of the U.S. Chamber of Commerce (undated).

law that finally went into effect on January 1, 1975. It clarified the discrepancy to the satisfaction of such organizations as the Public Affairs Council, the U.S. Chamber of Commerce, and the labor unions. The PAC generally praised the new law to its members, pointing out that, in the case of the contradiction that had worried many, "the roadblock is down" and that business should expect a "proliferation of corporate 610 committees" in future campaigns.[8] The U.S. Chamber of Commerce wrote that it was pleased that the reform bill "rectifies the ambiguity between Sections 610 and 611." It noted that under the law effective January 1, 1975, "any corporation or labor union, whether or not a government contractor, will be given explicit permissibility to establish and administer, and solicit contributions to, a separate segregated fund for the purpose of influencing the nomination or election of any person to federal office."[9]

PAC Survey of Political Fund Raising in 1972

In the fall of 1973 the Public Affairs Council conducted a survey among 430 companies that dealt with company involvement in the political arena—through encouragement of employee interest in politics, education in public affairs, fundraising programs, and corporate philanthropy. A total of 198 companies, or 41 percent, responded to the questionnaire sent to PAC's basic mailing list. The survey was essentially a repeat of one conducted in 1965.

One series of questions in the survey dealt with employee fund-raising programs in the 1972 election. Some 17 percent of the companies said that they had conducted a program to raise campaign funds for political parties and/or candidates among all of their employees. This represented a sharp decline in such programs—down from 39 percent—which had similar projects in the 1964 election. A higher proportion, however, had separate fund-raising programs aimed at just management people—an area that came under question in the confusion about the new requirements of the FECA of 1971. Forty-six percent of those replying said they had such programs in 1972. Survey evidence suggests, however, the impact of that confusion—28 percent of those replying said that the FECA caused them to either modify or suspend their management programs.

Ruling Requested by the NAM from Justice Department

Evidence of the dilemma felt by the business community in the matter of corporate political activity—particularly in light of the disposition of the TRW case—was the letter written by the general counsel of the National Association of Manufacturers (NAM) in the fall of 1972 seeking a Justice Department opinion on behalf of the NAM's member companies. Richard D. Godown, the NAM counsel, asked Henry Petersen, then Assistant Attorney General in charge of the Criminal Division of Justice, about the matter of a corporation serving as a "conduit" for voluntary political contributions.

Petersen replied, in an informal opinion, that when the "contributing employees drew their checks payable to the ultimate beneficiary" rather than to a corporate committee that this would not constitute a political committee as such required to register. "Under such circumstances, the role of the corporate committee is reduced to merely serving as a collection center and a messenger service."[10]

The 1974 Amendments did not affect the status or operation of wholly voluntary payroll deduction systems, in which each employee makes his or her own decision whether to participate and, if so, the amount to be paid in. All withheld amounts are sent to a bank, which sets up an individual account for each employee, under a trustee-type arrangement, and disbursements are made only when the employee so directs the bank trustee. The employee may, if he wishes to do so, have his payments returned to him at his request.

Such plans are not "political committees" and are not subject to the registration or reporting requirements applicable to political committees. The status of this system is the complete divorcement of the company—or its executives—from decisions regarding the specific candidates or parties to receive the money.

An individual who solicits and receives campaign contributions, or acts as an agent for each contributor, forwards the separate checks to candidates or committees, and is not thereby a political committee, only the equivalent of a fund raiser. This is limited to situations where the individual checks are forwarded. If the individual who solicited the funds commingles them, then he would seem to be acting on behalf of a political committee, and would have to register and report.

Communications Permitted by Section 610

Other language in the FECA of 1971 permitted activity not allowed before. Section 610, for example, allowed electioneering by corporations, specifically "communications by a corporation to its stockholders and their families on any subject" (the same right was given labor to reach its members). The first large corporation known publicly to have taken advantage of this section was Liggett and Meyers, Inc. In October 1972 the president of the company, M.E. Harrington, sent a letter to 45,000 stockholders strongly endorsing Richard Nixon's reelection and denouncing George McGovern. He criticized the Democratic candidate for his "misunderstanding of the business community," and suggested to the stockholders that were McGovern to be elected they might expect a

$16 billion tax increase on corporations, and as much as a 25 percent increase in corporate income taxes, "much of which would be used to support ill-conceived goals."

The absence of the word "employee" in the section permitting corporate communications was troubling to some businessmen. But the Public Affairs Council reported to its membership in early 1972 that according to a Senate staff member the term corporation was meant to include everyone within the corporate structure, including employees.[11] And the U.S. Chamber of Commerce cited a letter from the Justice Department stating that the wording "would not prohibit a corporation from conducting nonpartisan voter education programs among its employees."[12]

Who Is a Government Contractor?

One important question raised by the 611 amendment, and not clarified by the 1974 Act, is: "Who is a government contractor?" For example, in the meaning of the law was a physician rendering services under the Medicare Program to be considered a "government contractor?" How about a farmer participating in the Federal Price Support Program? In May 1972 the Justice Department gave an advisory opinion—"No" for the doctor, "Maybe, Maybe Not" for the farmer.[13]

Doctors participating in Medicare programs, the department said, were not government contractors within the legal definition; they were neither employed by the government, nor did they furnish it services. The beneficiaries of Medicare were the elderly patients, not the government.

The status of the farmer participating in the federal price support program was unclear, the Justice Department said, and the matter of defining his relationship was really up to the Agriculture Department. There the matter rested.

The TRW Case

One 1972 casualty of the prohibition on contributions by government contractors (Section 611 of the FECA of 1971) was the Good Government Fund of Thompson Ramo Wooldridge, Inc. (TRW), a defense contractor based in Cleveland, Ohio. TRW's fund had been established in 1964 as part of a program to provide employees an opportunity to contribute to political candidates or parties through voluntary payroll deductions. The program was available at 16 different plant locations, and funds were forwarded to headquarters in Cleveland for distribution. Participating employees had two options: to designate the candidates or party of their choice for a gift, or to make their contribution to the Good Government Fund. Gifts in the first category were forwarded to the designated candidates or parties within five days. Gifts in the Good Government Fund were apportioned by a disbursement committee to four categories of recipients: political parties at the local, state, and national levels; candidates; special fund-raising activities; and congressional campaign committees. These funds were distributed each year about equally between the Democratic and Republican candidates and parties. In 1964 the total from the TRW program, both designated and undesignated, was $87,000; four years later the fund increased to $117,372.

In 1972 the fund drew the criticism of Common Cause; on May 15 of that year Common Cause sued TRW, in U.S. District Court, District of Columbia, seeking to obtain enforcement of Section 611. Common Cause charged that the Good Government Fund, which was managed by senior corporate officials, distributed contributions to candidates "with regard to the potential benefits that can accrue to TRW, Inc.," including the benefits of "access, influence and political power."[14] This constituted, Common Cause alleged, a political contribution by a government contractor.

On August 8 TRW and Common Cause settled the suit. The Good Government Fund was disbanded and the balance of $17,527 remaining in the fund was returned to the contributors. TRW officials said they did not believe that the "undesignated" account was illegal, but rather than proceed with expensive litigation, they agreed to dissolve it. Up to that point in 1972, the fund had made three contributions totaling $5,600: a contribution of $5,000 to a committee supporting the presidential candidacy of Hubert Humphrey; $500 to a committee to elect a Democratic congressional candidate in California; and $100 to a Democratic candidate for state representative in Ohio.

Not affected by the suit was the other portion of the TRW program, a payroll checkoff plan that facilitated small individual contributions by employees. Common Cause chairman John Gardener said that his group favored such efforts "to broaden the base of financing of elections . . . so long as the distribution of contributions is made by the contributing employee free from influence by corporate officials."[15]

Corporate-oriented Solicitation by the FCRP

Operating through several programs, the FCRP engaged in a systematic solicitation of contributions from corporate executive and middle management salaried employees. One was known as the "corporate group solicitation program" (CGSP), an effort to generate funds by encouraging individual corporations to stimulate employees to contribute; it was designed to function similarly to local community chest fund raising from business employees. A second program was an industry-by-industry campaign, which concentrated on 60 major industries.

CGSP

The CGSP was aimed at people within the corporations who were thought most likely to contribute to a Republican presidential candidate. It was run by two vice-chairmen of the FCRP, Newell P. Weed, Jr. and Harold B. Scott.

The approach was to send a "bipartisan" appeal to the target group, with the exception that the return would be largely dominated by Republican contributions. In some instances, the plan was implemented within a firm on an outwardly bipartisan basis, but the chief officer of that firm sought a result "heavily weighted in favor of the President."[d] Weed and Scott were aiming for a large number of smaller donors, rather than a few major contributions, and anticipated "the law of numbers" would make the program successful. They projected an example of a firm with 500 employees contacted, with an 80 percent return in gifts averaging $100; nationwide, they calculated that such results could produce $20 million.[16]

An important aspect of the CGSP was the design to relieve a company of responsibility for filing political committee disclosure forms under the 1971 law. This was accomplished by having company employees make out their checks directly to the FCRP (or another candidate or committee), with the company or an officer collecting and mailing them together to the intended beneficiary. This meant there would be no public record of gifts as gathered by the company, but recipient committees presumably reported the contributions from the individual givers. The Justice Department, in September 1972, issued an informal opinion saying, in effect, that this practice was legal.[17]

The program ultimately reached 1,893 corporations, generating, according to Weed and Scott, a total of $2,791,134 in support for Nixon.[18] Central to the approach was an emphasis on insuring that the contributions derived from a corporate program would be identified by FCRP, while the company maintained its bipartisanship and avoided the necessity of registering as a political committee.

Some corporate officers objected when approached; they were disturbed at the idea of pressuring executives into giving to "the right man," no matter how subtle the suggestion. They were reassured by the FCRP that this was similar to programs used by many corporations in encouraging political contributions.

Industry-by-Industry Program

A second method of encouraging contributions by corporate employees from middle management on up was the industry-by-industry solicitation

---

[d]December 1972 Weed-Scott Report (p. 18), apparently directed to Stans, cited in Senate Select Committee, *Final Report*, pp. 544–46.

program directed by Buckley M. Byers. This was essentially an effort that covered many of the corporations in the CGSP, but its focus was on urging leading executives in some 60 industries to make solicitations within their own industry. As Byers put it in a memo to Stans in the fall of 1972, "[the industry leader] personally knows his counterparts who are the chief executive officers . . . [and] also knows what the specific problems of the industry are, what President Nixon has done to help his industry and also what the alternatives would be for the industry."[19]

Overall, the program was successful in spite of the fact that it was started fairly late in the campaign. An incomplete November 1972 report by Byers showed at least $7 million in contributions resulting from the program, with the largest industry contributors as follows:[20]

Pharmaceutical	$885,000
Petroleum Products	809,600
Investment Banking	690,812
Trucking	674,504
Textile	600,000
Carpet	375,000
Auto Manufacturers	353,900
Homebuilders	334,059
Insurance	319,000

The list did not include airline industry contributions, and also showed figures for other industries that were far below the actual aggregate amounts contributed,[21] since many contributions came in through solicitations made directly by FCRP to individual businessmen.

As in the CGSP, some corporate officers objected when approached with Byers' proposal, in this case resenting the idea that the industry rather than a specific company (especially one that relied heavily on receiving government contracts) should be recognized as the source of large contributions. While there is no evidence that participants in the industry-by-industry program were rewarded by the government, it is known that the FCRP received and forwarded industry problems to administration officials, without recommendation or follow-up, according to FCRP operatives. Byers even recommended "that many of our industry chairmen be asked to serve as appointed members of the Republican National Finance Committee" and saw his organizational nucleus as potentially "invaluable in the senatorial and congressional races in 1974, . . . 'the answer' in 1976."[22]

Business and Industry for the President: The
City Chairman's Guide

Another carefully orchestrated drive by FCRP for votes as well as funds from the business community was the formation of the Business and Industry Division of the Committee to Re-Elect the President (CRP), under the chairmanship of Donald M. Kendall, chairman and chief executive officer of Pepsico, Inc. This effort Kendall termed a "challenge" to business to "stand up for what it believes politically."[23] Nixon himself had asked Kendall if there were ways in which the business community might be organized for the campaign; his response was the Business and Industry project.

The blueprint for the effort was contained in the *City Chairman's Guide*— seemingly misnamed because it sounded as if it applied to city party chairmen, not businessmen. It was an inch-and-a-half thick, professionally packaged looseleaf notebook in white vinyl cover with blue and red printing, which contained step-by-step advice on how the business community was to be organized. In 25 sections—from Introduction and Objectives to Get Out the Vote and Check List—the guide carefully spelled out what was desired of the businessmen who volunteered. Advice was given on forming advisory councils, holding meetings, developing contact lists, approaching employees and stockholders, and public relations. One section contained two sample "nonpartisan speeches" and one sample "partisan speech." (The last opened up with "Let's talk turkey!" and went on to discuss the coming election as "a showdown on the free enterprise system.") The sample speech then discussed the speech-writers' view of the McGovern tax reform plan, and concluded that the proposals would have a "staggering effect . . . on your business, on your investment, on the economy, the job market, on our general national growth."[24] Guidelines were given for solicitation of both votes and dollars by corporate political action committees, partisan and nonpartisan varieties.

A separate kit for employee groups was also prepared for wider distribution as part of the "Support Your Candidate Program" of CRP. It contained sample letters, flyers, and pledge cards along with copies of the FECA and an interpretation of both the new law and the 1971 Amendments to the Internal Revenue Code.

Responsiveness Program

Beginning as early as the summer of 1971, the White House developed, and the CRP later implemented, a plan to use the resources of the federal government in aid of Nixon's reelection; the plan came to be called the Responsiveness Program, and it encompassed a number of ways in which federal agencies could use both the promise of federal monies and the threat of government action to solicit financial and other support. John Dean later testified that in 1971 H.R. Haldeman told him that officers in the White House "were being told the President's wish was to take maximum advantage of the incumbency."[25]

The program was designed and supervised to a large degree by former special assistant to the President, Frederick V. Malek, who in a December 23, 1971 memorandum to Haldeman said that one of the plan's basic objectives was "to 'politicize' the Executive Branch."[26]

Malek's responsibility, he noted to Haldeman, would be "effectively orchestrating the various White House support offices" in order that they might be able to inform their "constituent group of what the President has done to benefit them and to ensure that the President and the entire Administration is portrayed as favorably as possible to the group."[27]

> ... we have already initiated programs to derive greater political benefit from grants, communications, and personnel. Also ... we will soon be establishing firm White House control over the handling of key issues and constituent groups. These White House directed efforts will control the key Executive Branch operations having the highest potential political payoff. In addition, we should take action to ensure that the day-to-day Departmental operations are conducted as much as possible to support the President's re-election. Since it is impossible for the White House to directly control day-to-day activities, we must establish management procedures to ensure that the Departments systematically identify opportunities and utilize resources for maximum political benefit. [28]

To deal with the problem of what he termed "general insensitivity to political needs" within the various Departments, Malek proposed a series of briefings within each department and the formation of task forces "chaired by the Under-Secretary and containing the politically reliable Assistant Secretaries and sub-Agency Heads."[29]

Malek cautioned against the "substantial risk" in trying to pressure civil servants into partisan support, and said that it should be made to appear as if initiative had come from department heads, not the White House.[30] In a later memo to Haldeman, as the program took shape, he advised there be no written communication from the White House to the departments: "Also oral and written communication concerning the program within the Department would be structured to give the impression that the program was initiated by the Department Head without the knowledge of the White House."[31]

Jeb Stuart Magruder subsequently researched the question of the extent to which previous administrations had made similar efforts to use the advantage of incumbency and he found "nothing of the magnitude of the present administration's activities to use federal resources to ensure re-election."[32]

The record is now replete with instances of where the Responsiveness Program was at work in the 1972 campaign. In a June 7, 1972 memo to Haldeman, in fact, Malek cites a number of projects then underway.

He noted, for example, that Senator John Tower's office had requested that a $2.2 million migrant worker program grant be given to the "pro-

Administration Lower Rio Grande Valley Development Council" as opposed to an Office of Economic Opportunity (OEO) group which the Department of Labor had already judged to have the better proposal. In giving the grant to the former group, Malek said, "there would be a significant plus for the Administration, as OEO's negative voice would be silenced, and the Council's positive feelings towards the Administration could be stressed." Despite the Labor opinion on which of the two had the better proposal, the department deferred to Tower's choice.[33]

Another case involving the Labor Department, which dealt directly with campaign contributions, was the suggestion by an assistant secretary to the under secretary, who was directing Labor's contribution in the Responsiveness Program, that health and safety standards be delayed or toned down with a view to attracting donations from business. The strategy was outlined by George C. Guenter, then Assistant Secretary of Labor in charge of Occupational Safety and Health Administration (OSHA) to Under Secretary Laurence H. Silberman. Guenter pointed to the "great potential of OSHA as a sales point for fund raising," and suggested that no controversial worker health and safety standards be issued during the campaign. Silberman said he never responded to the memo; Guenter said he was only making a "statement of my views," but it was later reported that in the case of 14 different substances where more stringent exposure standards were requested by the National Institute of Occupational Safety and Health, only the one on asbestos led to new regulations being issued, and that came after petitions by the AFL-CIO.[34]

In a number of instances the Responsiveness Program sought to win the support of minority groups. A Chicano consulting firm, which had been active in support of the reelection campaign, received nearly $2 million in federal funds awarded outside normal procedural channels, another Chicano firm, which did not make a campaign contribution, lost its preferred status as a government contractor. In another instance, the Labor Department gave a $30,000 grant to a Chicano group with discussion of $6 million to follow; it was later disclosed that there had been no intention of awarding the $6 million, and that the $30,000 was for "neutralizing" the group until after the election.[35]

In another instance aimed at encouraging black voter support of the President, the Office of Minority Business Enterprise (OMBE) made a $75,000 grant to the Gate City Advertising and Public Relations, Inc. of Jacksonville, Florida, whose president, Woodrow Page, ran the Nixon campaign for black voters in that city. The application for the grant had gone first to the Committee to Re-Elect the President, then to the White House, until it finally got to OMBE. In another case, James Farmer, the former Assistant Secretary of HEW, received a grant from the Office of Education to fund a project in Washington; a Malek memorandum indicated that this was done with a view to giving Farmer time to work in the reelection effort and in particular to talk to key black leaders in an effort to gain their loyalties.[36]

The Watergate investigators found that a number of minority groups that had received Small Business Administration (SBA) contracts received letters urging them to contribute to the Nixon campaign; attached to the letter was a statement by the President about his support of these SBA contracts. The implication was that if the minorities wanted to keep receiving the SBA money they should contribute.

Evidence indicates that federal resources were employed to secure the support of older Americans. Seven governmental agencies that had senior citizen programs were each asked to produce an informational brochure, published at government expense, which was highly favorable to Nixon. The brochures were then released at periodic intervals during the campaign. Also in the area of seeking older voter support was the creation of the Federation of Experienced Americans (FEA) in March 1972 on White House initiative. The FEA then received nearly $2 million in grants—one from OEO for $400,000 as a planning grant, another for $1.5 million from the Labor Department to train and provide work for 350 elderly poor persons, all within the Spanish-speaking community. The FEA, viewed not surprisingly as "friendly to the Administration," received the favors, while other senior citizens groups, viewed as "enemies," were shorted.[37]

In another use of federal grants, the Department of Transportation awarded $7.6 million to the Dallas-Ft. Worth Regional Airport to help in the building of a shuttle transportation system at the hugh airfield. There were at the time specific congressional restraints on use of such funds on intraairport projects; Congress, in fact, had set down the restraints with the Dallas-Ft. Worth grant application pending, believing that it might open the door to a host of such proposals. The chairman of the Texas Airport Authority that benefitted from the grant was John Erik Jonsson, chairman of the Nixon reelection campaign in Texas. His $26,013 gift to Nixon was part of the $700,000 in Texas money flown to Washington on the Pennzoil company plane to make the April 7 disclosure deadline.

The Watergate Committee dismissed the claim that the Responsiveness Program was really little more than "politics as usual": "Certain of the activities described not only appear to contravene the fundamental notion that our Nation's citizens are entitled to equal treatment under the laws, but also raise questions as to the applicability of specific federal civil and criminal statutes." The committee rejected the proposition that the conduct of the Responsiveness Program should be viewed as "acceptable political practice." It went on to say that "the responsiveness concept involved the diverting of taxpayers' dollars from the primary goal of serving all the people to the political goal of re-electing the President. To condone such activity would display a limited understanding of the basic notion that the only acceptable governmental responsiveness is a responsiveness to the legitimate needs of the American people."[e]

---

[e]Senate Select Committee, *Final Report*, pp. 437–41. For an examination of the widespread placing of CRP workers and other Nixon administration choices in career and

Watergate Committee Questionnaire

In its efforts to gather evidence of illegal or improper activities in the 1972 campaign, the Senate Select Committee on Presidential Campaign Activities sent in the fall of 1973 a written questionnaire to about 700 individuals in three categories: (1) large contributors; (2) corporate officers; and (3) union executives.[38]

The names of the individual contributors were obtained from General Accounting Office (GAO) compilations of post-April 7 contributors who were listed as having given $3,000 to either a Democratic or Republican presidential candidate. All of the approximately 110 Republican contributors had given to the Nixon campaign, whereas the approximately 50 Democratic contributors had supported various candidates. (Contributors' spouses who had given $500 or more to a presidential candidate were also asked to fill out individual questionnaires for the committee.) The $3,000 figure was selected in part because of the anticipation that then proposed legislation would place that as the maximum an individual could give to a particular presidential candidate. Not included in this survey were the largest individual contributors and contributors of large amounts of cash who were interviewed extensively by committee personnel.

The corporate questionnaire was sent to officers from a selection of corporations on the "*Fortune* 500" list. The size and geographical distribution of the companies was taken into account, but no effort was made to create a scientific sample. Those known to have made a substantial contribution to a presidential candidate or who were under investigation were deleted from the list. (Questionnaires went to the chief executive officer, the chief fiscal officer, and the officer in charge of governmental relations in 136 different corporations.)

A third questionnaire was sent to top officials in 70 unions; selected were national and international unions, not locals, with a membership of at least 50,000. Of the more than 700 questionnaires sent, the committee received a response from officers and officials of every corporation and union canvassed, as well as from 80 percent of the unaffiliated individuals.

The corporate questionnaire appears to have been responsible for uncovering two illegal corporate contributions and evidence of a third offense. Subsequent to the survey, Diamond International Corp. and Carnation Co. both pleaded guilty to violations of Section 610 of the campaign finances act. The questionnaire to RCA officers disclosed a possible violation of Section 610 in connection with the activities of the Hertz Corp., an RCA subsidiary; at issue was an alleged Hertz rental, at special considerations, to campaign workers for Senator Edmund Muskie.[39]

---

noncareer government jobs, largely instrumented by Fred Malek, see Arthur Levine, "I Got My Job Through CREEP," *Washington Monthly*, November 1974, pp. 35-46.

Of the 334 people who responded to the corporate survey, 164 individuals from 112 different corporations made a contribution of $100 or more to a presidential candidate in 1972. The new disclosure law apparently had an effect on contributions; fewer people contributed larger amounts of money after April 7, 1972 than before that date. Corporate officers who responded gave a total of $1,896,322 to presidential races in 1972, and some two-thirds of that sum was given before April 7. Over 75 percent, $1,443,830, was given to the Nixon campaign.

Of the $452,492 contributed to Democratic candidates, 87 percent—all but $58,225—represents contributions by a husband and wife to the Lindsay campaign. Aside from this, the corporate executives contributed more than 25 times as much to Nixon as they did to all the Democratic candidates combined, and Nixon's contributions totalled more than 100 times the McGovern gifts.

The results from national and international union officials reveal a strong dominance of Democratic support, and no apparent illegal union activity. McGovern received a total of $678,782 from 19 separate unions; Nixon received $44,500 from six. Other Democratic candidates to receive union support in the survey were: Humphrey, $176,556 from 15 unions; Hartke, $14,250 from six unions; and Muskie, $5,736 from two unions.

In two cases the political action arms of the unions made significant loans to presidential candidates. The Communications Workers loaned $100,000 and the United Auto Workers loaned $200,000, both to the McGovern campaign. In both cases only part of the loan was repaid, and the large balance—$90,000 in the case of the Communication Workers, $140,000 with the UAW—was treated as a donation.

Project on Corporate Responsibility

The Project on Corporate Responsibility was split off from the center of the same name in an effort to secure tax-exempt status. The center was engaged in efforts aimed at improved business behavior in areas of public concern. Its activities in the matter of litigation and stockholder resolutions were formed as the separate project.

The project introduced stockholder resolutions on corporate fund disclosure for the 1973 annual meetings of General Motors, I.T.T., Eastman Kodak, and Union Oil of California. The resolutions called for publication in annual reports or elsewhere of complete statements of officers, contributors, contributions, and expenditures of political funds. They also asked for written reports to shareholders covering all policy communications to federal officials, as well as a listing of all memberships in business or trade associations engaged in efforts to influence federal legislation. None of the four were adopted.

The project brought a stockholders' suit in the U.S. Second Circuit Court against the New York Telephone Company, charging that corporate contributions to aid passage of a state transportation bond issue (later defeated) were illegal. The court directed that 30 officers and directors of New York Telephone were personally liable to repay the company treasury the $50,000 that had been contributed to the "Yes for Transportation Committee." The committee, which was backed by New York Governor Nelson Rockefeller, sought public approval of a $2.5 billion referendum, principally for roads.

New York Telephone appealed the decision in an action watched closely by other corporate contributors that had supported the referendum—including Gulf, Mobil, and Texaco. The company argued that the prohibition of corporate political gifts should not foreclose contributions to nonpartisan causes; it further noted that its 90,000 employees used New York roads and public transportation and therefore had a definite interest in improvement. The company won its appeal two-to-one in the Second Circuit in April 1974.

A.T.&T. Suits

American Telephone and Telegraph Company became involved, through several of its subsidiaries, in a number of suits that questioned the Bell System's participation in political campaigns. A stockholder suit involving the 1968 election was reinstated by the Third District Circuit Court of Appeals in November 1974.[40] This suit demanded that the American Telephone and Telegraph Company collect $1.5 million for services owed from the Democratic Convention in Chicago in 1968. The suit, filed by A.T.&T. stockholders in 1972, had been dismissed on grounds that collection procedures were within the discretion of the company's directors. The shareholders contended that the failure to collect the debt amounted to a political contribution that violated the ban of corporate campaign spending.

Also in November 1974 suit was brought against Southwestern Bell Telephone Company by an executive who had been dismissed and by the family of another who had committed suicide, charging that the company had maintained a secret political fund. A $29 million libel and slander suit was entered by the family of T.O. Gravitt, head of the Texas operation of Southwestern Bell, whose death in early November 1974 was ruled a suicide, and by James M. Ashley, a rate negotiator who worked under Gravitt and was dismissed soon after Gravitt's death.

The suit asked that the company make available to the plaintiffs records that they contended would show the existence of illegal political funds raised through employee contributions, as well as records that they alleged would show relationships between Southern Bell, Pacific Bell, other associated Bell

System companies, and A.T.&T. and the Nixon reelection committee.[f] The plaintiffs also charged that Southwestern Bell had a secret bugging system, which it used to get financial information about some of its largest customers. Mr. Gravitt was reported to have left a note that said "Watergate is a gnat compared to the Bell System" and also contained a list of documents and tape recordings that would support this charge.[41]

The investigation broadened when the former manager of Southern Bell Telephone Company in North Carolina, John J. Ryan, made charges of a similar nature. He claimed he administered a political slush fund to which company executives were expected to contribute; in a typical election year, the fund amounted to about $12,000 and usually went to congressional and gubernatorial candidates thought to be favorable to the interests of Southern Bell.[42]

The scandal spread into Kansas and Missouri when it was revealed that members of the state regulatory agencies had received gratuities from the phone company. Ashley, who had launched the case with his charges against Southwestern Bell in Texas, said that when he was assigned to the Bell System's St. Louis, Missouri office in 1970, he was one of 40 Bell executives in Missouri required to contribute $50 a month to political candidates designated by the company.[43]

In May 1975, another of A.T.&T.'s affiliates, the Chesapeake & Potomac Telephone Company of Maryland, announced it was conducting an internal audit, ordered by its parent firm, in search of possible political slush funds or kickback payments.[44] The audit had been asked in April 1975 by John D. de Butts, the A.T.&T. chairman.[45]

A.T.&T.'s involvement with the Nixon administration was suggested in evidence assembled by the House Judiciary Committee considering impeachment. A February 16, 1972 memo from Gordon Strachan to H.R. Haldeman notes that Charles McWhorter—a former aid to Vice-President Agnew—would "continue to travel at A.T.&T. expense" during the campaign. McWhorter, the memo noted, "has terminated his formal ties with the Vice President's office to protect against any suggestion of impropriety."[46]

Center on Corporate Responsibility

The Center on Corporate Responsibility was denied tax-exempt status in

---

[f]Apparently management practices of the 23 subsidiaries are very similar, and Bell executives often move from one subsidiary to another during their careers. (See Nicholas M. Horrock, "U.S. Investigating 2 A.T.&.T. Concerns," *The New York Times,* February 9, 1975.)

May 1973 by the Internal Revenue Service, following a suit by the Washington-based public interest group, which charged that an extraordinary two-and-a-half year delay on its application was politically motivated. Tax-exempt status would have allowed contributors to the center's work to deduct their donations. The center, which said it could not survive without such status, maintained that its educational and research efforts and litigation activities qualified it to receive tax exemption.

After the negative IRS ruling, the center sued to force disclosure of names of persons outside IRS who had discussed the center's application with the agency. Specifically named were some in the White House, in the offices of domestic affairs, presidential counsel, and domestic council, headed respectively at that time by John Ehrlichman, John W. Dean, III, and Kenneth Cole.

In its ruling, IRS noted that the center had many of the same directors as the Project on Corporate Responsibility, which earlier had been split off from the center in the attempt to gain exempt status. Activities of the latter group, such as proxy contests to elect corporation directors and to submit proposals for changes in company policies to stockholder meetings, could not be financed with tax-deductible funds, IRS ruled.

The New York Times editorialized that the IRS ruling could weaken or destroy other tax-exempt organizations (such as the League of Women Voters or the NAACP) with close ties to groups engaged in lobbying or in direct efforts to support social aims. It could create a dangerous imbalance between corporate and public interest, which could be construed as denying citizens equal protection under law, the paper said, since business could continue treating enormous expenditures on lobbying or proxy fights as "necessary and ordinary business expenses," which are deductible.[47]

On December 12, 1973 U.S. District Court Judge Charles R. Richey ruled in favor of the center's claim that the Nixon administration used political pressure on the IRS to deny the group tax-exempt status.[48] Failure of the administration to produce evidence needed in the case, and to comply with several court orders forced Judge Richey to rule that the IRS denial to the center for tax-exempt status had no legal basis.[49] The IRS subsequently wrote to the center granting them tax-exempt status.

Investor Responsibility Research Center Reports

Investor Responsibility Research Center, Inc. (IRRC) was organized to provide to its institutional investor subscribers (such as universities and foundations), research and information on corporate policies and practices,[g] for

---

[g]In 1974, 24 reports were published: "Analysis No. 1, Corporate Involvement in Electoral Politics," and 23 supplements setting forth the resolution proposed, in each case

guidance in their investment politics. In 1973 the center began publishing a series of reports on general corporate political activity and on a number of shareholder resolutions dealing with specific corporations and their involvement in electoral politics. Such companies as I.T.T., Northrop, Goodyear, and Gulf, which had figured in the post-Watergate investigations into illegal campaign contributions, were covered in IRRC reports, as were a number of other corporations.

IRRC reported, for example, on the case of Union Oil Company of California and the "Political Awareness Fund."[50]   The fund had registered with the General Accounting Office as an unaffiliated fund, but later, after GAO inquiry, admitted its association with Union Oil. The fund was more heavily tilted toward the Republican side than are most company committees. It reported contributions of $70,175 in 1972. Of 20 Senate candidates supported, 17 were Republicans, and nearly all were "conservative" judged by ADA and ACA ratings. Of 65 House candidates receiving support, 56 were Republicans. The donations were listed as follows:

Nixon for President	$20,700
Senate candidates	13,900
House candidates	23,150
Senate and local	6,925
Democratic Congressional Campaign Committee	5,500
Total	$70,175

The Political Awareness Fund (PAF) was later subjected to a GAO audit, which determined that from April 7, 1972 to August 31, 1973 expenditures of $74,850 were made by transferring funds to other political committees or candidates. The total transferred to committees supporting presidential candidates, $20,700, went to committees supporting the reelection of Richard Nixon. In the PAF and several other corporate and labor union political action committee

---

by a shareholder, at the annual meetings of 23 corporations. Those corporations, including some not described in the text, are: First National City Corporation; Chase Manhattan Corporation; Manufacturers Hanover Corporation; Goodyear Tire & Rubber Co.; E.I. Du Pont de Nemours & Co.; C.R. Bard, Inc.; General Electric Co.; Gulf Oil Corporation; Standard Oil Co. of California; Union Oil Co. of California; Phillips Petroleum Co.; Warner-Lambert Co.; Eastman Kodak Co.; Marathon Oil Co.; United States Steel Corporation; RCA Corporation; International Telephone & Telegraph Co.; Ford Motor Co.; Northrop Co.; Minnesota Mining & Manufacturing Co.; Xerox Corporation; J.C. Penney Company, Inc.; General Motors Corporation.

See also "Minding the Corporate Conscience 1974: A Survey of activist challenges to corporations in the areas of corporate responsibility, equal employment, South Africa, environment, energy, military production, consumer issues, and political contributions," *Economic Priorities Report*, vol. 5, no. 1 (1974), 22-27, 59 ff. and *The Corporate Watergate* (IRRC Special Report 1975-D).

audits, the GAO made a point worth recounting. In its financial reports, the PAF did not list the value of contributions-in-kind in the form of administrative support furnished by Union Oil Company to the PAF, because its officials believed the FECA exempted the company support from being considered as a contribution. The GAO conceded that the 1971 FECA amendment to Section 610 permitted the use of corporate or labor union funds to establish, administer, and solicit political contributions in a separate segregated fund, and gave Union Oil Company the legal right to establish and give administrative support to the PAF. However, the GAO argued that the definition of "contribution" relating to disclosure of political receipts and expenditures clearly included "anything of value" given to a political committee including contributions-in-kind, and did not contain any exception for committees established under Section 610 as amended. GAO therefore ruled that the amendment to Section 610 did not relieve political committees of the duty of reporting contributions-in-kind as receipts under disclosure provisions of FECA.

The PAF amended its reports to show an estimated $2,396 of contributions-in-kind had been received from the Union Oil Company. This estimated value consisted of administrative services such as computer time ($1,700), stationery and forms ($130), and postage ($566).

In other cases the GAO encountered reluctance on the parts of some companies to agree to amend their political action committee disclosures to include an itemization of the cost of company support for fear that such disclosure would show a violation of Section 611, which prohibited "direct or indirect" contributions by government contractors. This controversy was resolved by the 1974 FECA Amendments, which specifically exempt such supportive costs from disclosure.

The 1974 IRRC report on Union Oil recounts an incident that occurred in connection with the 1972 Nixon campaign. In response to a newspaper inquiry, Fred L. Hartley, president of Union Oil Co. of California, issued a statement on July 12, 1973, which said in part:

> On the afternoon of February 17, 1972, Mr. Maurice Stans and Mr. Leonard Firestone called on me in my office and told me they needed money for the campaign for the reelection of the president and would like me to give $100,000. I told them that I did not wish to personally make a contribution of such great magnitude and I pointed out to them it was illegal for a corporation to give a campaign contribution to a federal election. I further told the gentlemen I would not give a contribution until after April 7 since my personal support of the American political system is one I do not have to hide from anyone.

The statement described still another request made to Mr. Hartley in October 1972. On October 24, 1972 he transmitted a personal check for $3,000, made out to the Finance Committee to Re-Elect the President, to Mr. Firestone, who was then chairman of the California Finance Committee to Re-Elect the President. He later tried and failed to get the contribution returned.[51]

Another IRRC report cited the instance of Tennessee Eastman, a division of Eastman Kodak, which was brought to light by the Center on Corporate Responsibility, for having given misleading information on its funds.[h] The "Volunteers for Better Government" (VBG) registered with the GAO as an unaffiliated fund in Kingsport, Tennessee. Two of the three directors of VBG were Kodak employees, and the third was the local legal counsel for Kodak, Howard Wilson. Apparently Wilson was the only 1972 contributor to VBG who was not a Kodak employee. Contributions appear to have been made through a payroll deduction plan. After inquiry by the GAO, Kodak said that there was no connection between the company and the fund, but to avoid any misinterpretation, the payroll deduction plan was terminated. The $45,200 expended by the fund went to the following candidates:

Nixon	$30,000
Sen. Baker (R-Tenn)	10,000
Sen. Thurmond (R-SC)	1,000
Sen. McClellan (D-Ark)	500
Rep. Quillen (R-Tenn)	3,000
Rep. Kuykendall (R-Tenn)	500
Rep. Broyhill (R-Va)	200

IRRC reports discussed stockholder resolutions involving three companies whose officials had pleaded guilty to the corporation's making an illegal contribution to the Nixon campaign in 1972—Northrop, Gulf Oil, and Goodyear Tire & Rubber. The Northrop resolution, proposed by shareholder John M. McCrea, asked that the company's "political nonpartisanship" be affirmed to the stockholders through several measures, including full disclosure of the operations of the "Northrop Good Citizenship Committee," and the avoidance of corporate political endorsements. The Gulf resolution, proposed by William Katzenstein, Jr., requested the corporation to adopt a policy of discharging employees who make illegal contributions; a second Gulf resolution, proposed by the Project on Corporate Responsibility, would prohibit all corporate political contributions.

The Goodyear case, involving three proposed resolutions by Earl Raps, called on the corporation to take corrective and disciplinary actions regarding illegal contributions of corporate funds to political campaigns. The three resolutions asked that: (1) Goodyear employees or directors who authorized the illegal contribution to the Nixon campaign in 1972 be disciplined through forfeiture of future salary increases until the amounts forfeited equal the total

---

[h]The corporation is also cited in Senate Select Committee, *Final Report,* p. 553.

illegal contribution (a sum totalling $40,000); (2) employees or directors who authorize further violations of election laws shall be dismissed; and (3) an annual listing of contributions made by the corporation in the preceding year be provided shareholders.

Resolutions affirming the political nonpartisanship of three of the nation's largest banks were also discussed by IRRC. The banks were Chase Manhattan, Manufacturers Hanover, and First National City, all of New York City; the resolutions, by one shareholder, were identical in asking the following practices be "avoided": handing out to employees contribution cards for a single political party; requesting an employee to send in a contribution, with no payee designated, for forwarding to a party or committee; and distributing contribution cards in a manner likely to favor one party. The management of all three banks opposed the resolution on grounds they did not engage in such practices. Corporate managements normally oppose such stockholder resolutions, and normally the stockholder resolutions are soundly defeated, as were these.

Stockholder resolutions in early 1975 concerning corporations and their role in the political process took on "new or modified approaches in their efforts to influence corporations' behavior,"[i] according to IRRC. Primarily the resolutions were designed either to "affirm the political nonpartisanship of the corporations and direct that certain practices be avoided, or . . . require disclosure of political contributions the corporations have made." Resolutions were submitted to 27 corporations, and modified or rewritten resolutions from 1974 were submitted to Standard Oil Co. of California, Phillips Petroleum Co., and Marathon Oil Co.; one 1974 resolution to Northrop Corp. was rescheduled after Northrop's annual meeting was postponed when two top officers pleaded guilty to using corporate funds for illegal political contributions.

Suit Against Bethlehem Steel Ads

The U.S. Court of Appeals in Philadelphia upheld in April 1974 the suit against the Bethlehem Steel Corporation (and its Board of Directors, chaired by Stewart S. Cort) by a stockholder—Philadelphia attorney, Richard A. Ash—who contended that the corporation illegally spent $500,000 in political ads to help the Republican Party in the 1972 campaign.[52] The suit had earlier been dismissed in U.S. District Court in Philadelphia in October 1972.

The District Court had dismissed the case chiefly on grounds that the material in question was nonpartisan since it did not specify a candidate or

---

[i]"Corporations and the Political Process," *Analysis No. 1*, March 4, 1975 (Washington, D.C.: Investor Responsibility Research Center, Inc., 1975). This report provides background information on federal campaign finance laws, state campaign finance laws, corporate practices, and the role of corporate money in electoral campaigns.

candidates by name, and that the expenditures had thus not violated Section 610 of the FECA of 1971. The Court of Appeals, however, held there was ". . . no evidence Congress thought the American public so unperceptive that it would recognize a statement as supporting or attacking a particular candidate only by use of his name. . . ." Such a requirement, the opinion continued, would "eviscerate" Section 610.

In June 1975 the U.S. Supreme Court overturned the appeals court ruling. In a unanimous decision, the high court said that stockholder complaints such as Ash's must henceforth be taken to the Federal Election Commission, not the federal courts. The 1974 Amendments to the FECA, the court noted, provided this as one of the roles of the commission; moreover, nothing in the Federal Corrupt Practices Act, then in effect, permitted private individuals to invoke enforcement of Section 610.

Justice William J. Brennan, Jr., who wrote the opinion said that the criminal laws against illegal corporate contributions were not meant primarily to benefit investors but rather are concerned with the "potential corrupting influence" of corporations.

The Court also said that since corporations are the "creatures of state law," state courts should handle relations between stockholders and corporations.[53]

Incorporating Political Committees

One lesson Democrats learned from the 1968 presidential contests was that top campaign officials sometimes need financial protection from creditors demanding payment of campaign bills. In 1968 the presidential bids of Senators Eugene McCarthy and Robert Kennedy ended deep in debt, and both campaign organizations proved unable to pay up. To collect, some creditors brought suit against ranking campaign officials, putting these individuals in financial jeopardy.

To avoid this in 1972, the campaign organization of Senator Hubert Humphrey sought to acquire the status of a nonprofit corporation. This offered the advantage of permitting the organization to write into its incorporation papers a provision limiting the personal financial liability of campaign officials for debts incurred by the organization.

However, incorporation presented a legal risk, since federal law prohibits corporations from making political contributions or expenditures for any federal office. A campaign organization collects and expends money for campaign purposes. Recognizing this problem, the Humphrey camp asked the Justice Department for an opinion on whether incorporation would make its campaign expenditures illegal. Attorneys for Humphrey argued that campaign associations fall outside the intent of the law, which is really aimed at direct economic intervention by corporate business and labor in politics. When the Justice Department agreed that the law would not apply to campaign associations, the

Humphrey organization went ahead and incorporated.[54] The organizations supporting several other presidential contenders, including George McGovern, took the same step.

Of course, the FECA requirements on extension of credit to political candidates by regulated industries, leading to regulations of the Civil Aeronautics Board, the Federal Communications Commission, and the Interstate Commerce Commission, reduced substantially potential liability of political committee officials by reducing the opportunities for incurring large debts in regulated industries.

Dairy Contributions

A classic illustration of how money may talk when special interests deal with the government was provided by the dairy industry in the first Nixon administration. The story embraced the so-called "milk deal"—the sudden increase in the government subsidy of milk prices in seemingly apparent response to campaign contributions and congressional pressure. It included a criminal antitrust investigation of one dairy co-op allegedly thwarted by an Attorney General who was also the President's de facto campaign manager, and supposed efforts by the co-op to buy its way out of a civil antitrust suit. None of these charges were proved, however.

The deep involvement of dairymen in politics flows from their great stake in federal policy, with an almost direct connection between government decisions and the prices of dairy products. The dairy lobby in 1972 essentially consisted of the three largest milk co-ops in the country: Associated Milk Producers, Inc. (AMPI) with 40,000 members and headquarters in San Antonio, Texas; Mid-America Dairymen, Inc. (Mid-Am), of Springfield, Missouri, with about 20,000 members; and Dairymen, Inc. (DI), of Louisville, Kentucky, with about 10,000 members.

Together, the three co-ops came in the late 1960s to constitute the richest new source of political money in years. Each set up a political arm or "trust," said to rely for political funds on voluntary contributions from farmers:[j] The contributors to SPACE, for example, were dairy producers, milk haulers, and employees of Dairymen, Inc. Dairy producers contributed by authorizing deduction of stipulated amounts from the proceeds of the sale of milk marketed for them by the cooperative. Milk haulers contributed by authorizing a deduction from their hauling check, and employees of DI

---

[j]AMPI formed TAPE in February 1969 (replaced by CTAPE after April 7, 1972); DI established SPACE in March 1969, organized in virtually the same way as TAPE; and with advice and encouragement from AMPI and DI, Mid-Am formed ADEPT in the middle of 1970.

contributed through a payroll deduction. Under the governing trust agreement, contributions were limited to a maximum of $8 per month, or $96 per year from each donor. This maximum insured the anonymity of the donors, since under federal law (both FCPA and FECA) only those who gave larger donations in a year had to be identified.

In 1972 alone AMPI reported political spending of nearly $1 million, with about $900,000 cash on hand at year's end. The only other special interest organization to spend more was the AFL-CIO's COPE. In combination, the three giant co-ops are known to have given more than $1.8 million to presidential and congressional candidates for the 1972 campaigns.

The dairy scandal of 1972 appeared to have antecedents in the 1968 campaign. The dairy lobby had access, through such long-time allies as Hubert Humphrey, to policy-making officials in the Kennedy and Johnson administrations. When some of these officials left office, they went promptly onto the milk lobby's payroll as executives, lawyers, and lobbyists (for example, former Johnson administration officials Jake Jacobsen, James R. Jones, and George Mehren were among others hired by AMPI). Before LBJ announced his decision not to seek reelection in 1968, AMPI (which was MPI at that time) paid $90,711 for the printing (and approximately $14,000 additional publication expenses) of an illustrated book containing the text of 23 messages by Johnson to Congress, entitled *No Retreat from Tomorrow*. MPI concealed the printing expenditure under fictitious bookkeeping entries, and deducted it as a necessary business expense for public relations. Furthermore, the co-op's checks apparently ended up in 1968 DNC coffers as reimbursements, since the committee had already paid the printer. The IRS rejected the deduction, but a resulting Justice Department investigation of AMPI's (and MPI's) 1968 political spending was strangely moved into the department's inactive files, and not rediscovered until 1974, after the statute of limitations had expired. In response to an independent audit by a Little Rock, Arkansas law firm, requested by AMPI head, George Mehren,[k] IRS—whose books on AMPI had remained closed since 1968—undertook a new audit. However, all the co-op's illegal expenditures since 1968 had gone undiscovered until 1973.

During the Senate Watergate Committee's investigation of the dairy lobby's influence on price decisions, a 1972 memo from Representative James R. Jones,

---

[k]See "Report of Wright, Lindsey & Jennings to Board of Directors of Associated Milk Producers, Inc., March 13, 1974." The 157-page report, made public on March 14, 1974, was commissioned by AMPI's board of directors in August 1973, shortly after the corporation came under investigation by a Little Rock, Arkansas Federal Grand Jury for 1968 contributions, and by the Watergate special prosecution force and Senate committee for 1968-72 contributions. The document and an accompanying audit report by Haskins & Sells (for the period September 1, 1967-June 30, 1973) were submitted to the U.S. District Court in Kansas City, Missouri, where the Justice Department was conducting its antitrust suit against AMPI, and to the other investigative forces.

D-Oklahoma, to Mehren surfaced. It alleged that two AMPI officials (David Parr and Harold Nelson) had offered him a retainer in late 1968, during the time they were pressing then lame-duck President Johnson to raise milk prices for the following year. Jones, then a White House aide, had refused the job but accepted a renewed offer a month later at the end of Johnson's term, becoming a lawyer for AMPI. The memo, which Jones later repudiated, claimed credit for prompting LBJ's approval of a milk price support and was written to protest an AMPI move to stop his annual retainer. In repudiating his memo, Jones said the milk price decision had been taken at the end of 1968 by Agriculture Secretary Orville Freeman with no known influence exerted by LBJ. Although Agriculture Department documents support this, the memo adds support to the basic picture of close ties between the dairy lobby and White House officials. AMPI also paid dozens of phony bonuses to employees that wound up as $1,000 contributions totalling over $54,000 to Johnson's President's Club. After Johnson dropped out of the race, AMPI reportedly gave some $80,000 in bonuses and advances to employees and outside agents and told them to donate the money to political campaigns, chiefly Hubert Humphrey's. Later, two AMPI officials were convicted of passing $22,000 in corporate funds to Humphrey's 1968 presidential campaign.

After supporting Humphrey with over $150,000 in 1968, AMPI faced a problem in January 1969 with Nixon now in power. Leaders of the dairy industry felt it was imperative to win friends in the Nixon administration, and in August 1969 gave a secret $100,000 contribution in $100 bills, to Herbert W. Kalmbach, Nixon's personal attorney and chief fund raiser. The illegal gift came from the co-op's treasury and presumably also violated the $5,000 limit on campaign contributions. AMPI concealed the donation on its books through an elaborate laundering scheme involving exaggerated payments to its lawyers and public relations men. Kalmbach added the $100,000 to a $1.7 million surplus left over from the 1968 Nixon campaign that later financed undercover White House political activities, such as payments to Tony Ulasewicz and to the 1970 gubernatorial campaign of Albert Brewer against George Wallace in Alabama. In addition to seeking access to the White House, AMPI sought three objectives: (1) 90 percent price supports; (2) a presidential address at their Kansas City gathering; and (3) public identification with the President.[1]

Efforts to influence the administration continued because of the dairymen's reported disappointment with the results of the $100,000 contribution. Sometime before September 9, 1970 the three co-ops offered $2 million to Nixon's reelection effort, through White House staff member Charles Colson, who was dealing with special interest groups. Also in 1970 AMPI contributed

[1]These are noted in Herbert Kalmbach's logs on August 2, 1969—the day he received the $100,000—and on earlier dates.

approximately $135,000 to Republican candidates through the special fund handled by Jack Gleason and Herbert Kalmbach.[55]

The $2 million offer was referred to in a letter from AMPI attorney Patrick J. Hillings to the President in December 1970. Hillings complained of the President's failure to cut off imports of four dairy products. Two weeks later Nixon slashed import quotas on two of the products and reduced them on two others. The White House maintained Nixon never saw Hillings' letter but acknowledged the President had learned of the $2 million promise six months earlier. It also pointed out that the President's quotas were less favorable to the dairy industry than the drastic quotas recommended by the Tariff Commission.

The "Milk Deal"

The central event in the dairy scandal was the alleged "milk deal" of March 1971. The President played a leading role in this affair. The question was whether Nixon had raised milk price supports in return for campaign contributions. The alleged milk deal was investigated by the Senate Watergate Committee, and during the House Judiciary Committee's impeachment inquiry, for the issue seemed to be one of bribery.

The affair began with the level of milk price supports. On March 12, 1971 Secretary of Agriculture Clifford Hardin announced that there was insufficient reason to raise the subsidy.[m] Within two weeks, however, the dairy industry had persuaded the administration to recant. On March 23, before any hearings on bills introduced to raise the support level, the President reversed the secretary's decision and took steps to raise the support level. Then on March 25 Hardin, claiming that an increase in dairy farmers' costs had been detected, announced in a press release that the price support level would be raised after all, from $4.66 to $4.93 per hundred pounds—approximately 85.1 percent of parity. (In March 1970 price support levels had been raised from $4.28 to $4.66, or 85 percent of parity—the largest increase ever at the beginning of a marketing year.) The reversal meant a windfall variously estimated at from $300 to $700 million for dairy farmers in the new year. The bill was paid by consumers in higher milk prices and by taxpayers in greater subsidies to dairy farmers.

After Hardin's original declaration, the dairymen mounted a lobbying campaign on all fronts. Pressure was brought on the administration through Congress. Legislation was quickly introduced to raise the support price to 90 percent of parity—$4.93 or higher; 30 bills were filed in the House sponsored or supported by 29 senators and 88 representatives, including some of the most powerful members. The White House "White Paper," released January 8, 1974,

---

[m]The Commodity Credit Corporation (CCC) Board of the Department of Agriculture had unanimously favored the $4.66 level, after careful consideration of the situation, on March 3, 1971.

claimed 125 representatives sponsored legislation, but the Watergate Committee report found only 88, and fewer than 29 senators. Of these sponsors, 13 senators and 50 representatives had reportedly received $187,000 in campaign funds from dairy groups in the previous three years. The bill introduced by Senator Gaylord Nelson, D-Wisconsin, reportedly was written by dairy lobbyists.

Other means of persuasion were also employed. Most of the bills' sponsors were Democrats; most Republican allies of the dairymen privately urged the administration to raise price supports on its own. Letters from dairy farmers flooded Congress and the White House. The dairymen also hired a former Assistant Secretary of Agriculture in the Johnson administration and later an AMPI consultant, Dr. George Mehren, to lobby at his old department. Mehren took over as AMPI general manager in January 1972.

The dairymen also found a friend in Treasury Secretary John Connally. Two AMPI officials testified that Connally met with co-op representatives in mid-March and told them that new money would have to come if they wanted price supports boosted. Connally also is reported to have told the dairymen to go ahead with their new contributions because the rise was assured.[56] Connally later denied making either statement. He acknowledged urging Nixon to boost price supports but said he knew nothing of the dairy contributions at the time.

The culmination of the lobbying campaign was an audience at the White House on March 23. Sixteen dairy executives made their case at a one-hour meeting with the President. AMPI had given $10,000 to the Nixon campaign the previous day. Subsequent facts, including release of the March 23 White House tapes, show Connally received a phone call from Nixon minutes before the meeting with the dairymen, during which he urged the President to endorse an increase to 85 percent of parity. The actual meeting was uneventful; although parity was discussed, the President made no commitment to the dairymen. He expressed gratitude for the agricultural community's political support, and promised to try to attend their next annual meeting. Whereas a March 22 memorandum to the President from John Whitaker (John Ehrlichman's former assistant for agriculture) reminded Nixon of the dairy lobby's strength and their decision to spend political money heavily, Nixon made no reference to the $2 million (or any financial) pledge during the March 23 meeting.

Later that day the President held a follow-up meeting with Connally, Hardin, and other administration officials. Connally again urged Nixon to support higher parity, warning that Congress would legislate higher price supports unless he did it first. Nixon agreed to meet the dairymen's requests if they promised not to seek more price raises, at least until 1973. The President decided to raise price supports that afternoon but did not make his decision public.

Still later on March 23 the White House passed word to the dairy officials that it expected a reaffirmation of their $2 million campaign commitment in light of the forthcoming hike in price supports. In testimony before the House

Judiciary Committee, Kalmbach said that the dairymen were required to reaffirm their pledge before Nixon would announce the increase in milk price supports. (This testimony suggested to the committee that whether or not the contributions actually influenced the price support decision, Nixon's acceptance constituted bribery. However, the President refused to produce materials subpoenaed by the committee relating to conversations he had with various aides during the dairy negotiations, so a case for bribery could not be established.) The dairymen tried to raise a quick $300,000 contribution at a predawn meeting on March 24, but could only raise $25,000. That night they renewed their $2 million pledge and contributed the $25,000. The next day the price support boost was announced.

The co-ops contributed another $45,000 two weeks later and another $247,500 by the end of 1971. A memo from Gordon Strachan to Haldeman on September 11, 1971, noted that $232,500 had been contributed to date by the dairymen: TAPE gave $187,500 to 75 committees; ADEPT gave $15,000 to six committees; and SPACE gave $30,000 to 12 committees. Additionally, on September 2 AMPI had responded to an earlier request by Colson for a $5,000 contribution and gave that amount to People United for Good Government. The money was later used to reimburse a loan made to Colson that funded the "Plumbers" break-in of the offices of Dr. Fielding—Daniel Ellsberg's psychiatrist.[n] Their generosity continued in 1972, including $45,000 given in the last ten days of the campaign, a donation the dairymen avoided reporting before the election by exploiting a loophole in the law.

Most, but not all, of the money came from the three biggest co-ops. In 1972 the Lehigh Valley Cooperative Farmers, a Northeastern farm group, secretly gave $50,000 in $100 bills toward Nixon's reelection. The Lehigh group subsequently admitted the money was an illegal corporate contribution and was fined $5,000; its president at the time received a suspended fine of $1,000. Altogether, dairy co-ops contributed a total of $682,500 to Nixon's 1972 reelection.

The dairymen's initial donations to the Nixon cause were given to established Republican committees. But publicity arising from the money's suspected tie to the price support turnabout made the co-ops adopt more devious ways. Nearly all the rest of their donations in 1971 were given in $2,500 amounts to 93 dummy committees set up in Washington, D.C. These paper organizations served to evade the FCPA regulations limiting the yearly amount of political contributions to $5,000, and also the tax laws requiring gift tax on contributions in excess of $3,000 to one political committee. The names of the dummy organizations had been supplied to the dairymen by the late Murray Chotiner,

---

[n]*Hearings Before the Committee on the Judiciary*, House of Representatives, pp. 43-51. The $232,500 was also listed separately by the FCRP (on a list of pre-April 7 contributions sent to Rose Mary Woods) under the heading "house account."

an attorney and close political adviser of the President, and Chotiner's law partner, Washington, D.C. AMPI attorney, Marion Harrison. Dairy contributions reportedly were also channelled through the two men into the campaign.

Democrats made remarkably little of the suspected "milk deal." Many had also accepted campaign money from the dairymen and had supported legislation to raise milk price supports.

But not everyone was silent. Ralph Nader and three consumer groups sued the government to force a roll-back of the price support hike. They charged that the increase was authorized in response to campaign contributions and congressional pressure instigated by the dairy co-ops. During the protracted lawsuit, the White House tried to withhold key documents and tape recordings, citing executive privilege. However, in the end much material was surrendered and the lawsuit revealed a good deal about the dairy lobby's activities. Further light was shed by a study[57] of AMPI's political dealings commissioned in 1973 by its new board of directors—faced with increased investigation by congressional committees and the Justice Department, supposedly to discredit their predecessors and steal the thunder of AMPI's critics. The report showed a history of secret, illegal contributions to both parties—predominantly to Democrats from dairy states—concealed generally under fictitious bookkeeping entries or phony bonuses to employees who would then contribute the money to favored candidates.

The milk price decision was investigated by the Senate Watergate Committee, the Special Prosecutor's Office, and the House Judiciary Committee. The controversy finally forced the White House to issue a "White Paper" in 1974 defending the decision. While conceding that the President had been reminded of the dairymen's $2 million pledge before the March 23 meeting, the White House denied that the campaign pledge or donations had influenced the decision. It attributed the policy reversal to the need to increase milk production, the normal pursuit of farmers' votes, and the need to prevent the Democratic-controlled Congress from legislating even higher price supports. It claimed that a presidential veto of such legislation could have been overridden and, moreover, would have alienated the farm vote and perhaps proven disastrous in some Midwestern states. Nixon referred to congressional pressure as "a gun to our heads," in a November 17, 1973 press conference before the Associated Press Managing Editors.

Yet, AMPI's general manager later testified that while the dairymen had substantial congressional support it was not enough to override a veto. For that matter, Nixon's raising of the subsidy was no less expensive than most of the plans under consideration in Congress. With this heavy congressional pressure on the President, it could have been politically damaging either to let the Democrats in Congress take credit for the increase or to veto such legislation.

The "White Paper" also raised two other issues. First, it inadvertently suggested that political factors had been involved in spite of a declaration of

Secretary Hardin in 1972 that he had ordered the price increase strictly on economic grounds. Second, it contradicted an earlier declaration by Nixon that before the 1972 election he refused to listen to any information about contributions.

The Antitrust Case

The dairymen's $2 million pledge presumably was known to John Mitchell, who was active in the Nixon campaign while still Attorney General. Late in 1971, after considerable delay, Mitchell overruled repeated recommendations of his antitrust division for criminal prosecution of AMPI for monopolistic practices. Instead, Mitchell cited "the difficulties of obtaining a (criminal) conviction" and opted for a civil antitrust suit, a milder action. The civil suit was filed on February 1, 1972.

There is evidence the antitrust investigation worried the White House. Presidential assistant Colson wrote White House Chief of Staff Haldeman on September 24, 1971, warning of "very serious adverse consequences" if the Justice Department "goes too far."[58] Kalmbach later testified he assumed Colson meant the dairymen might halt their donations. The antitrust case was put on the agenda to be discussed at a "political matters" meeting between Mitchell and Haldeman. All this raised the question of whether Mitchell vetoed a criminal prosecution for legal reasons or to protect people who had promised money for Nixon's reelection.

Even though the administration was suing AMPI, a few days after the suit was filed, Kalmbach asked AMPI's new general manager George Mehren for another donation. While its sister co-ops continued to give, AMPI contributions unaccountably ceased the previous September at $202,000. Mehren said later the suit looked like extortion to him and he refused Kalmbach. Subsequently, Mehren testified that after his insistence that future AMPI donations be made public to avoid accusations of a payoff, Kalmbach withdrew his request without explanation. Mehren also testified AMPI decided to make no further presidential campaign contributions lest it seem to be trying to influence settlement of the suit.

But later AMPI was accused of taking the initiative to buy its way out of prosecution. Former AMPI lobbyist Bob A. Lilly said Mehren offered $150,000 in 1972 to the Nixon campaign to sidetrack the investigation. According to Lilly, Mehren wanted to make it clear to the administration that AMPI was not "welching" on their commitment (presumably, the $2 million) and sought assurances in return that the Justice Department would "slow down the antitrust action" and then "reduce it to just a wrist slap."[59]

In testimony Lilly indicated AMPI's $150,000 was to be part of a combined $300,000 payment from the three giant co-ops. The other two co-ops had a stake in AMPI's suit as they were party to some of the marketing arrangements the government was protesting. Another former AMPI official, Dwight Morris, testified he had been told by AMPI's president that Kalmbach had agreed to take the $300,000 but had backed out when the I.T.T. affair—another antitrust controversy—broke into the headlines.

These charges were supported when investigators found $150,000, consisting of 30 checks for $5,000 each, signed by Mehren and then voided, that could have been intended as AMPI's payment. The payee lines had been left blank, presumably so the names of dummy committees could be inserted later. The checks were signed April 4-5, 1972. Lilly said they were due for delivery on April 6— the last day before the new campaign law took effect ending the use of conduit committees to avoid disclosure.

AMPI may have made yet a second attempt to buy its way out of the suit. During late October and early November 1972, CTAPE made a $352,500 contribution to two Republican congressional campaign committees. Of that, $221,000 was transferred to Republican National Committee (RNC) committees, which then forwarded $200,000 to the FCRP. Supposedly, the $200,000 was intended for congressional candidates and transferred to the Nixon campaign simply as repayment of an advance to the congressional campaign committees. But two former AMPI officials testified the money was intended for Nixon's reelection from the start. In fact, Mehren told Watergate Committee investigators that faced with White House pressure for continued presidential contributions, and fearing his refusal would jeopardize the co-op, he had sought advice from his former employer, LBJ. During an October 21, 1972 meeting at his ranch, the former President not only advised Mehren to meet any prior commitment his predecessor may have made on AMPI's behalf, but also suggested the trust should balance its total contributions for the year to both parties, noting that contributions to congressional committees could be beneficial to presidential campaigns without linking the dairy trust to presidential support. Johnson also was said to have referred to a dairy pledge of $250,000 to his previous campaign, which had not been delivered. However, an agreement to pay Johnson $94,000 a year to lease a twin-engine, 13-passenger plane for AMPI's use (the LBJ ranch was 50 air miles from AMPI headquarters) had been implemented by Mehren's predecessor, Harold Nelson, just days before his ouster. AMPI's 51-member board had disapproved the lease arrangement, but the minutes had been falsified to reflect approval. LBJ apparently told Mehren that he welcomed the arrangement as a supplement to his retirement income.

An additional $95,000 was contributed to the Nixon campaign by DI and Mid-Am: in August 1972 leaders of the two co-ops met with Connally and made a $50,000 commitment to Democrats for Nixon; and just before the election, the two co-ops gave $45,000 to the FCRP. These contributions, plus the disputed $200,000 AMPI donation, brought the three major associations' known spending on the Nixon campaign to $632,500.

Table 12-2 lists the contributions by the major dairy trusts relating to the 1972 election.

Democratic Presidential Candidates

While the co-ops were dealing on a large scale with the Nixon administration,

Table 12-2
Legal and Illegal Contributions by Major Dairy Trusts Related to the 1972 Election

Nixon	$ 682,500[a]
Democratic presidential candidates:	
Wilbur Mills	185,600
Hubert Humphrey	17,225[b]
Fred Harris	10,000
Henry Jackson	4,500
Edmund Muskie	2,750
George Wallace	2,000
Vance Hartke	1,850
Valentine, Sherman & Associates (VSA) services to Humphrey and other Democratic candidates and officials (paid by AMPI)	137,000[c]
Democratic congressional and senatorial campaign committees	109,500
Republican congressional and senatorial campaign committees	152,500[d]
Total	$1,305,425

Source: Senate Select Committee on Presidential Campaign Activities, *Final Report*, No. 93-981, 93rd Cong., 2nd sess. (Washington, D.C.: U.S. Government Printing Office, June 1974), pp. 579 ff.

Note: The additional sum of $8,893, not included, was spent on political activity by three other dairy committees ($6,784 of it dispensed to various candidates) representing Dairylea Co-op, Inc. of New York, the Land O'Lakes Dairy, and the National Milk Producers Federation.

[a]Although both the "White Paper" and an affadavit of Alexander Keema verifying contributions by three major dairy trusts during 1971 and 1972 to 1972 presidential candidates show that Nixon received $427,000 from TAPE/CTAPE, ADEPT, and SPACE, the above figure consists of the following:

$100,000[c] — Secret 1969 AMPI contribution to Kalmbach
237,500 — AMPI and the three dairy trusts, 1971 gifts to presidential committees
95,000 — FCRP and Democrats for Nixon, 1972 (from ADEPT and SPACE)
200,000 — Additional CTAPE fund, October 1972
50,000[c] — Secret LeHigh Valley Cooperative Farmers contribution to Nixon, 1972
It is possible (looking at the Watergate Committee's attempt to trace the dairy contributions) that $95,000 given to nonpresidential Republican committees in 1971 went to Nixon's campaign, which would make total dairy support of the president in excess of $777,000.

[b]Includes $12,500 from TAPE/CTAPE; $3,500 from SPACE; and $1,225 from ADEPT.

[c]Illegal contributions.

[d]CTAPE gave $352,500 to two Congressional committees; $221,000 was transferred to RNC, which then transferred $200,000 to FCRP (included in Nixon total above).

they did not neglect the Democrats. Officially, they gave a total of $93,925 to Democratic presidential contenders; the Senate Watergate Report indicates $109,500 to Democratic congressional and senatorial campaign committees; $137,000 in computer services by Valentine, Sherman and Associates; and more to Humphrey and Mills.

The dairymen's strongest support of a 1972 Democratic candidate was to Representative Wilbur Mills; they constituted the chief financial backers now on the public record of Mills' presidential campaign, contributing $55,600. In addition, Mills received a $6,000 donation from an individual dairy farmer. Mills was one of the dairymen's chief allies in Congress and wielded immense power as chairman of the House Ways and Means Committee. He also received $75,000 from corporate assets of AMPI, $15,000 from corporate assets of Mid-Am, and $40,000 in donations from AMPI members, employees, and officers given to Mills' campaign before April 7, 1972, when the new disclosure law took effect. Most of Mills' campaigning was done before April 7.

According to Bob Lilly, AMPI general counsel Dave Parr wanted to raise $2 million in cash to help elect Mills president.[60] Parr apparently believed in the fall of 1971 that Mills could become President. At least five AMPI employees were detailed to Mills' presidential drive and corporate funds were said to have been used for Mills' campaign expenses. AMPI was also reported to have helped finance the Arkansas Voter Registration Association, said to have been organized by Mills and an accountant. Mills said he was unaware of any corporate donations to his campaign.

George Mehren said he stopped illegal corporate contributions immediately when he took over as AMPI general manager in 1972. Mehren said he also squelched two other proposals by Parr to raise money for Mills: (1) a payroll checkoff of co-op employees, and (2) $100 donations from employees disguised as expense account items. Both schemes would have violated the ban on corporate campaign contributions. Mehren said he vetoed them even though Parr reminded him that "we owed [Mills] a good deal."

Senator Hubert Humphrey, who seems to have supported legislation favorable to the dairy industry consistently since 1949, received more than $40,000 in contributions from the dairy cooperatives in 1971 and 1972. The Senate Watergate Committee concluded that dairy trusts gave Humphrey $5,125 in 1971, and $12,100 in 1972, with $12,500 of the total given by TAPE and CTAPE. The Humphrey campaign also received $25,000 in corporate contributions from AMPI in the form of payment of bills to Valentine, Sherman and Associates.

On August 1, 1974 Associated Milk Producers, Inc. pleaded guilty to one count of conspiracy and five counts charging illegal campaign contributions in 1968, 1970, and 1972, and was fined the maximum of $35,000. The action in Judge George L. Hart, Jr.'s court had centered on political contributions of

$280,900 in cash, disguised on AMPI books as legal fees and other expenses, and unspecified amounts in services by co-op salaried employees who worked in various political campaigns. The criminal information had dealt with the $100,000 that went to Kalmbach in 1969, and with $100,500 that went to the 1968, 1970, and 1972 Humphrey campaigns. Other amounts included $50,000 in 1972 that benefitted various Democratic party candidates for federal elective office in Iowa; $8,400 for the 1970 reelection campaign of Senator Edmund Muskie of Maine; $7,000 for the 1972 campaign of Senator James Abourezk of South Dakota; $5,000 for the 1972 presidential campaign of Representative Wilbur Mills of Arkansas; and $10,000 contributed to the 1970 campaign of former Republican Representative Page Belcher of Oklahoma.

The Justice Department's antitrust suit was settled August 14, 1974, with AMPI promising not to use coercion against nonmembers. Coercion of independent milk producers was one of the major means the co-op had used to gain control of big milk markets. It also agreed: to give members at least one opportunity each year to leave the organization; to refrain from selling cheap milk in some areas to punish nonmembers by driving down their prices; to file reports with the Justice Department each year for the next ten years, and to allow government enforcers to inspect its records on request; and not to buy from any milk hauler who is the sole means of getting a nonmember's milk to market. The Justice Department noted that it had won all the points in the consent decree that it had felt it might win by taking the case to trial. One of the toughest provisions won would sharply reduce the co-op's economic power by prohibiting its purchasing any milk plant for ten years without advance approval of the Justice Department.

The 1974 congressional elections saw the milk lobbies pump thousands of dollars into congressmen's campaigns. But some of the contributions were returned because of the bad publicity, and observers predicted that in the future, more discretion would be used by the dairymen. AMPI's political arm, CTAPE, had $1,654,895 cash on hand as of August 15. To that point, CTAPE had contributed $388,292 or $1,711 per day, with the bulk of the contributions expected in the few weeks before the elections.

The political arms of the two other largest dairy cooperatives, SPACE and ADEPT, had $2,340,775 cash on hand as of mid-August 1974. Since election day, 1972, the three committees had contributed at least $100 to each of 82 sitting United States senators and representatives, for a total of $213,000. The total included $50,000 to five Democrats on the House Agriculture Dairy Subcommittee, $15,970 to three of the remaining 15 Democrats on the full committee, and $5,750 to two of the 16 Republicans.

In the Senate, four Democrats on the Agriculture subcommittee together got $36,850 while one of the four Republicans received $15,600. From November 7, 1972 to May 31, 1974 the dairymen contributed $102,450 in gifts of at least $500 each to members of the congressional subcommittees immediately concerned with dairy prices and marketing, plus $21,720 to other members of the full Agriculture committees.

With this strategy, the dairymen planned to concentrate on new legislation, and to combat dairy imports in the wake of a hostile year for the dairy industry. Dairymen contended the U.S. Tariff Commission improperly failed to impose countervailing duties on dairy imports. They thus sued the commission, and stated that if the suit failed, they would push for new legislation.[61]

A GAO audit report on Dairymen, Inc.'s political committee, SPACE, was released on November 8, 1974.[62] The committee reported $130,108 cash on hand; $693,193 receipts, and $493,965 expenditures during the period from April 7, 1972 to May 31, 1974. The audit disclosed at least 112 "illegal corporate contributions"—authorized deductions from DI payments to incorporated dairy producers and haulers—to SPACE during the period covered, totalling $25,265; this was based on 25 percent of contributors GAO surveyed (75 percent did not respond). GAO referred the matter to the Attorney General even though SPACE returned the funds to the 112 corporations.

Connally's Role

John Connally, who had resigned as Secretary of the Treasury on June 12, 1972, was involved with the dairy interests; he was indicted on July 29, 1974, charged with taking money to help the dairy lobby and giving false testimony to a Grand Jury, but was later acquitted.

In pretrial hearings Connally testified he refused an offer of $10,000 in May 1971 from AMPI lobbyist Jake Jacobsen to aid candidates of his choosing. Jacobsen confirmed the story, but later, on February 21, 1974, was indicted for perjury; the charge was dismissed on May 3, and on July 29 Jacobsen was indicted for making an illegal payment to a public official. Subsequently, Jacobsen testified against Connally, in exchange for leniency, saying Connally had accepted the $10,000 as a payoff both for his support of the milk price hike and his help in the settlement of the antitrust suit. Jacobsen said that after charges of a "milk deal" were raised in the press, Connally had returned the $10,000 to Jacobsen and they agreed on the cover story that Connally had refused the money.

Other evidence seemed to implicate Connally in the alleged antitrust payoff. According to Bob Lilly, AMPI's decision to give another $150,000 to the Nixon campaign was made after a meeting with Connally. George Mehren testified that the meeting concerned the antitrust suit and campaign funding.

The indictment against Connally alleged that he received two $5,000 payments in exchange for recommending to Nixon that the milk price supports level be raised; that three meetings and two telephone calls transpired between Jacobsen and Connally; that Connally agreed to have $10,000 in cash ready to give to Jacobsen so he could make it available for inspection if called upon; and that Connally made false testimony before a Grand Jury on April 11, 1973.

Harold S. Nelson, AMPI's former general manager, pleaded guilty on August 1, 1974 to conspiring to pay off Connally for his help in securing the 1971 increase in milk price supports, and for making illegal corporate contributions of $330,000 over the past six years. Nelson previously testified there was no limit on the amount of money dairy co-ops were prepared to give Nixon. Of their original $2 million commitment to the 1972 election, AMPI paid $492,500. Nelson blamed White House ineptness in establishing dummy committees for smaller contributions to evade detection of the contribution's source. When Mehren took over as general manager of AMPI in January 1972, Nelson, Parr, Lilly, and AMPI comptroller and TAPE trustee Robert O. Isham were replaced. It was the influence of these men, according to an AMPI counsel, that was responsible for the illegal contributions, and now that influence was gone from the organization.

Jacobsen pleaded guilty on August 7, to one count of offering a gratuity ($10,000) to a public official (Connally). In plea bargaining Jacobsen agreed to retract earlier testimony that Connally twice rejected offers of milk money, in exchange for the prosecution dropping all seven charges involving his misapplication of $125,000 of savings and loan funds. Connally pleaded innocent on August 9, 1974 to his indictment. On November 23 Chief Judge George L. Hart, Jr. of U.S. District Court denied motions for dismissal of four of the five counts against Connally.

In April 1975 Connally went on trial in Washington, D.C. before Judge Hart, charged with having accepted $10,000 in payoffs for backing the 1971 milk support price increase. During the three-week trial, the government—in a case brought by the Special Prosecutor's Office—sought to prove that Connally had taken the sum from AMPI, passed on to him by his long-time friend Jake Jacobsen. The defense contended that only circumstantial evidence linked Connally to the payoff. The jury found Connally innocent of the charges.

The government's case hung largely on the testimony of Jacobsen, the only witness to accuse Connally of taking the AMPI bribe money. In his testimony Jacobsen, who had agreed to testify against the former Texas governor in his August 1974 plea bargaining, claimed Connally, a millionaire, asked him for money shortly after the milk price support increase in the spring of 1971. Jacobsen said he had gotten $10,000 from AMPI for that purpose in April 1971 and had turned the money in two installments of $5,000 each: on May 14, 1971, after Connally helped win the price support hike and on September 24, 1971, after Connally asked John Mitchell to help settle the antitrust suit. Both payments had been made in Connally's Treasury office, Jacobsen alleged.

The Texas attorney testified that when a Federal Grand Jury and the Senate Watergate Committee learned of the gift, he and Connally had agreed to say that the money never left Jacobsen's safe-deposit box in an Austin, Texas bank. Connally gave him $10,000, Jacobsen said, in a cigar box on October 29, 1973; he later worried that the bills might not be old enough to have been in circulation in 1971 and gave Jacobsen a fresh batch of money, according to Jacobsen's testimony.

Both men had testified to the Grand Jury and the Senate Watergate Committee that Jacobsen had offered the money to Connally to pass on to political candidates as he saw fit. Connally denied throughout, however, that he had ever accepted the money.

Connally's defense attorney, Edward Bennett Williams, introduced evidence from Jacobsen's 1972 bankruptcy statement. It showed that in the summer of 1971, when Connally had insisted that he had rejected the $10,000 offer from AMPI, Jacobsen had paid off $10,000 on indebtedness at an Austin bank. In late 1971, when AMPI gave Jacobsen a third $5,000 to pass on to Connally, the bankruptcy statement showed that Jacobsen had paid $5,000 on an indebtedness to a bank in Fredericksburg, Texas.[63]

Following Connally's acquittal, the Special Prosecutor's Office moved to have two perjury counts and one conspiracy count still pending against Connally dismissed. Jacobsen faced a maximum penalty of two years in prison and a $10,000 fine on the charge of offering a gratuity to a public official.

Labor in Politics

For organized labor, 1972 opened with Alexander E. Barkan, director of the AFL-CIO's Committee on Political Education (COPE), declaring that the union's goal in the election was the defeat of Richard Nixon, long one of labor's targets.[64] By mid-summer, at the Democratic Convention, Barkan and George Meany were among the leaders of the ABM (Anybody But McGovern) fight and McGovern ran against Nixon in the fall as the first Democratic presidential nominee in 20 years without official endorsement from the higher echelons of union labor. There was nonetheless substantial backing for McGovern from segments of labor that refused to go along with the Meany-Barkan position.

Money from COPE was available, however, in those congressional and senatorial races, mostly Democratic, which had been designated as important to labor's cause. Three important Senate seats—those of Republicans Margaret Chase Smith of Maine, J. Caleb Boggs of Delaware, and Jack Miller of Iowa—fell to Democratic opponents receiving heavy labor backing, and Senator Claiborne Pell, a Democrat of Rhode Island, probably was reelected because of union money and manpower.

Labor's coolness toward McGovern stemmed from a variety of factors. His voting record on certain labor issues was criticized; Barkan in particular was bitter about an incident in 1966 when McGovern appeared to have promised a key vote on cloture, and then reversed himself.[65] McGovern's defense and foreign policy views were disturbing to other labor leaders, such as Frank Fitzsimmons, whose International Brotherhood of Teamsters, not affiliated with AFL-CIO, endorsed Nixon. The McGovern-Fraser Commission on the reform of delegate selection to the Democratic National Convention irked certain labor leaders. The changes brought about by the commission appeared to reduce labor's role in the party generally and at the convention. Actually, delegate surveys indicate that there were more union officials represented at the Miami Beach convention than had been at Chicago four years earlier when Hubert Humphrey, a labor favorite, was nominated—five percent of the delegates in 1972 to four percent in 1968. Probably more important was the fact that the selection process was made more competitive and this required labor to work hard for delegate strength.

Beyond all this were intangible antagonisms. Meany and many other old-guard labor leaders regarded McGovern as the candidate of permissive and intellectual elements in the Democratic party; the frictions were cultural and generational. At about the time Barkan was announcing early in 1972 that Nixon was labor's target, he was also saying that "we aren't going to let those Harvard-Berkeley Camelots take over our party."[66]

At that point in 1972 McGovern had the support of five percent of Democratic voters, and appeared far from securing the nomination. During the prenomination period, some labor money went to several Democratic presidential candidates—particularly Senator Humphrey. (See Table 12-3.) Before union leaders realized it, the South Dakota Senator had the nomination within grasp, and it was too late for them to concentrate stronger backing behind one man; the result was the ABM effort at Miami.

As Appendix W indicates, in the prenomination period, the candidate receiving the most support from the political action committees of labor was their long-time favorite, Hubert Humphrey; he was given much more money than his nearest rival, Edmund Muskie. One of Muskie's largest supporters—$5,236 reported—was the American Federation of State, County and Municipal

Table 12-3
Labor Support of Democratic Candidates, 1972 Prenomination Period

Hubert Humphrey	$156,952
Edmund Muskie	30,231
Vance Hartke	19,875
Wilbur Mills	4,000

Sources: Based on data combined and adjusted from: Senate Select Committee on Presidential Campaign Activities, *Final Report*, pp. 530-33; and *Alphabetical Listing of 1972 Presidential Campaign Receipts*, vols. I and II, Office of Federal Elections, General Accounting Office (Washington, D.C.: U.S. Government Printing Office, November 1973).

Employees through its political action committee, Public Employees Organized
to Promote Legislative Equality (PEOPLE), and affiliates. The fastest-growing
union in the AFL-CIO, with over 700,000 public workers on its rolls, this union
broke with the Meany position after the convention and supported McGovern,
giving $18,056. Other labor money in the presidential primaries went to Vance
Hartke and Wilbur Mills. Hartke, who chairs the Senate Subcommittee on Surface Transportation, was supported mainly by three transportation unions. The
Mills labor money came entirely from the Seafarers who later endorsed Nixon
and contributed a controversial $100,000 to him just before the election. Henry
Jackson is strangely missing labor support in 1972, in view of the fact that he
later became a labor favorite.

At the convention George Meany and Alexander Barkan were reported as
instrumental in distributing an unsigned pamphlet entitled "Why Labor Can't
Support George McGovern." The pamphlet achieved a measure of notoriety
when a dummy group, termed Labor for America Committee, was formed with
money from the Finance Committee to Re-Elect the President for the sole purpose of a mailing of the pamphlet by the Nixon campaign. The FCRP invested
at least $4,400 in the mailing.[o]

Following the convention the AFL-CIO's executive council, by vote of
27 to 3, adopted a neutral posture in the presidential race, the first time it had
taken a stance other than support of the Democratic nominee since the AFL-
CIO was formed in 1955. The neutral posture left member unions free to
endorse either presidential candidate on their own, if they chose. But AFL-
CIO state and local councils were bound constitutionally to abide by the national organization's policy, according to Meany.

With that the labor movement proceeded to fragment. Three of the four
largest unions in the AFL-CIO (the Steelworkers, Electrical Workers, and Car-
penters) remained neutral. Nine of the 17 building trade unions were among
those that endorsed Nixon, along with the Teamsters. The other giant in the
labor movement, the United Auto Workers, like the Teamsters, does not belong
to the AFL-CIO; the UAW endorsed McGovern and helped establish a National
Labor Committee to Elect McGovern-Shriver as an alternative to the AFL-CIO's
COPE.

By the time the campaign ended, 32 of the 116 unions in AFL-CIO joined
this committee. The 32 pledged to McGovern included many of the federation's
larger unions and 14 of the 33 unions with presidents on the executive council;
union sources said the council's declaration amounted more to a vote of confidence in Meany than a vote against McGovern.

Some AFL-CIO state and local chapters also went their own way. At least

---

[o]The committee's address was a post office box rented by Mrs. Myles Ambrose, wife
of the former commissioner of customs, according to Senate Select Committee *Final
Report*, p. 157.

ten of the state central groups defied Meany and endorsed McGovern. Furthermore, some ignored Meany's demands that they recant. The fact that some
defied Meany reportedly led to retaliation by some of the unions belonging to
the state groups. Construction unions, many of which backed Nixon, were
accused of cutting off funds to the state offices defying Meany. Meany denied
the charge that he had instigated withdrawal of the funds to quell the rebellion.

In all, organized labor gave at least $878,828 to McGovern's pre- and post-
nomination campaigns, and about $164,750 to Nixon's. The McGovern total,
surprisingly, is nearly twice as much as Humphrey received in 1968 when he
had labor, including COPE, solidly behind him. Indeed, the amounts were
extraordinary when considered against Humphrey's $540,900 in 1968[P] — a
year that saw a continuation of the trend throughout the 1960s for growing
expenditures by labor committees.

In addition to the known contributions, labor union political action committees made loans to the McGovern campaign, as follows:

Committee for Good Government (UAW)	$ 50,000
United Automobile Workers VCAP	150,000
Communication Workers of America	100,000
International Association of Machinists & Aerospace Workers—Machinists Non-Partisan Political League	100,000
Retail Clerks International Association—Active Ballot Club	75,000
Miscellaneous	7,878
Total	$482,878

Some of these loans were repaid and some were converted into contributions.
For example, $60,000 of the $200,000 UAW loans were repaid. Adding the
remaining $140,000 ($90,000—VCAP and $50,000—C.G.G.) to the direct con-
tributions of $171,000, the aggregate total outlay would be $311,000 for
UAW assistance to the McGovern campaign.

Nixon's largest single labor support came from the Seafarers Union whose
president, Paul Hall, had been indicted in 1970 for violation of the then existing election finance law. The case was dismissed in May 1972 by the U.S.
District Court sitting in Brooklyn for failure on the part of the Justice Department to prosecute the case. Justice then decided not to appeal the dismissal.

On October 31, 1972 the Seafarers Political Action Donation Committee
(SPAD) applied for a loan of $100,000 to the Chemical Bank of New York.
The loan was approved on the next day by the vice-president in charge of
"political loans," Frank Fredericksen, and a check was made payable to the

---

[P]Of that amount, $167,531 was given before Humphrey's nomination, whereas most
of McGovern's labor money in 1972 was after his nomination.

FCRP. The check was then delivered to Herbert Brand, president of the Transportation Institute of Washington and a member of the Maritime Committee to
Re-elect the President, who turned it over to the FCRP on the day before the
election.

Fredericksen later said he approved the loan without checking with any
higher officers of the bank—including Chairman of the Executive Committee
of Chemical Bank Harold Helm, also a co-chairman of the FCRP—because it
had appeared legal to him. Furthermore, Fredericksen said that he was unfamil-
iar with the ban (in Section 610) on union money raised through "commercial
transaction." Section 610 also required that unions raise political contributions
only through the voluntary acts of the members. The FCRP did not list the
Seafarers' gift until their year-end statement, although the law required a special
report within 48 hours of any contribution of $5,000 or more received in the
last 12 days before an election.[67]

Another Nixon supporter was the Teamsters union, although the exact
amount of its contribution remains in dispute. Former Teamsters President
James R. Hoffa, who was paroled from Lewisburg Prison by Nixon in December
1971, alleged that the union donated $600,000 to $700,000 to the former
President's reelection campaign. This was denied by the current Teamsters
President Frank E. Fitzsimmons, who claimed that the contributions by his union
totalled only $18,000 to Nixon, as reported to the GAO by the Teamsters; with
affiliates, the Teamsters gifts total $19,550 on the record.

Fitzsimmons was one of only two top union officials who contributed $500
or more personally to a presidential candidate, a survey by the Watergate investigators revealing he gave Nixon $4,000. A Teamsters colleague, Salvatore
Provenzano, gave Nixon $2,000. The Senate Committee solicited the views of
the top officials of 70 unions—those with memberships of at least 50,000—in
seeking to measure the personal financial involvement of labor leaders in the
1972 election. All of the officials contacted, nearly 200 individuals, responded
to the questionnaires.

In 1972 disbursements by a number of the major committees were off
sharply. An exception to this was the UAW committees that backed McGovern
handsomely. By contrast, the Seafarers who backed Nixon spent considerably
less than they had in politics in 1968. COPE was the largest spender among the
labor committees in 1972, reporting expenditures of $1.4 million. Table 12-4
lists the gross disbursements of major labor committees from 1960 to 1972.

Labor's political spending in 1972, as disclosed under federal laws, totalled
$8.5 million in adjusted gross expenditures, $2.3 million in direct costs for
salaries and fixed expenses, and $6.2 million transferred mainly to federal
candidates and their campaign committees. The 1972 campaigns were no exception to the rule that labor spends little on presidential campaigns ($1.2

Table 12-4

Gross Disbursements of Major Labor National-Level Committees, 1960-72

	1972[a]	1968	1964	1960
AFL–CIO COPE	$1,397,338	$1,207,000	$989,000	$794,000
UAW–V–CAP	891,333	309,000	269,000	61,000
ILGWU	603,230	1,077,000	426,000	316,000
Steelworkers	401,207	240,000	251,000	239,000
Machinists	198,945	572,000	260,000	193,000
Seafarers	388,599	947,000	121,000	
Railway clerks	268,491	128,000		
United transportation	261,564			
Communications	129,365	195,000	123,000	82,000
Retail clerks	239,449	164,000	81,000	

[a]Source: *Annual Statistical Report of Contributions and Expenditures Made During the 1972 Election Campaigns for the U.S. House of Representatives* and *Annual Statistical Report of Receipts and Expenditures Made in Connection with Elections for the U.S. Senate in 1972.* For other years and for AFL–CIO COPE in 1972, source is the Citizens' Research Foundation.

million) compared with its disbursements at the congressional and local levels.[q] In fact, campaign spending by unions on national elections, including congressional races, tends to be greatly overrated. Union political auxiliaries collect an average of five or six cents per union member at the national level. Thus, the collective contribution of a 100,000 member union to a candidate can be surpassed by a $10,000 gift from a single wealthy individual.

But while the cash labor puts into politics is relatively little—the unions' disbursements on the two presidential candidates in 1972 represent only a

[q]Labor committee reports under the FECA indicate less than $500,000 went to state and local candidates. The amounts given to senatorial and congressional candidates in in dispute because certain primary figures are lacking. Common Cause has calculated about $3.6 million given to such candidates in what it calls the general election period. But the methodology is faulty because only funding of candidates who were running in the general election was summarized, and the general election period was not defined. See Campaign Finance Monitoring Project, *1972 Federal Campaign Finances: Interest Groups and Political Parties*, vol. II (Labor), (Washington, D.C.: Common Cause, 1974), p. x. The Citizens' Research Foundation has calculated $120,000 given in the January–February 1972 period. See Herbert E. Alexander and Caroline D. Jones, eds., *CRF Listing of: Contributions of National-Level Political Committees to Incumbents and Candidates for Public Offices, 1971 and January–February, 1972* (Princeton, N.J.: The Citizens' Research Foundation, 1972), p. 26. Figures between March 1 and the remainder of the prenomination period are unclear.

fraction of the totals spent on the general election—it would be difficult to
exaggerate the political value of labor's enormous manpower pool, particularly
for voter registration and get-out-the-vote activities on election day. The AFL-
CIO Industrial Union Department and affiliates may put as much as $4 to $5
million into citizenship activities, including registration drives. Although these
are considered nonpartisan, they are conducted among union members and their
families in areas where Democratic registration is high; because of their nonpartisan character union dues money can be used. McGovern lost this kind of
assistance, though he benefitted indirectly from such activities on behalf of
other supported Democrats. But no doubt McGovern was hurt by lost money
as well as lost manpower by the defection of COPE. Union aid may also include detailing union officials full time to help staff a candidate's campaign
organization. What it means when labor puts its machinery into high gear for a
candidate was rather vividly demonstrated in 1968. Humphrey was trailing
far behind Nixon in the early fall polls; once labor swung into action behind
the Democratic nominee, he began to move up against his rival on the November election day.

Meany's liaison with a Republican President did not last. Within a year
of Nixon's reelection, he grew disenchanted with the President and was openly
attacking him for Watergate, his economic policies and his policy of detente.
Finally Meany broke with Nixon altogether, declaring that he had dishonored
his office through Watergate and other scandals, and the AFL-CIO launched
a massive campaign for Nixon's impeachment.

Meany's strategy for control of a Democratic Congress worked. In spite of
the Nixon landslide, the Democrats actually gained two seats in the Senate and
lost only 12 in the House. As noted, the three Republican senators who were
unseated lost to COPE-supported Democrats; in the House, all five Republicans
who lost were challenged by liberal Democrats backed by the AFL-CIO's
political arm.

Labor failed, however, to defeat the two long-time Senate foes against whom
it mounted its heaviest assaults: Senator John McClellan of Arkansas, against
whom labor contributed some $72,806 to his primay opponent, David Pryor;
and Robert P. Griffin of Michigan, against whom labor spent $104,589 in the
campaign of his opponent, Frank J. Kelley (the highest union outlay to any
congressional candidate). McClellan's investigations of labor union corruption
and mismanagement in the 1950s, coupled with his conservative voting record,
brought enmity in labor circles. Griffin was never forgiven by labor for his
sponsorship of the 1959 Labor-Management Reporting and Disclosure Act,
commonly known as the Landrum-Griffin Act.[r]

---

[r]For a hostile view of labor's political activity, see Douglas Caddy, *The Hundred Million Dollar Payoff* (New Rochelle: Arlington House Publishers, 1974).

Labor Money

To channel direct financial assistance to federal candidates, the unions organize auxiliaries, usually managed by officials of the parent union and financed by voluntary contributions from union members. However, the amounts of money raised are relatively small: at the national level, an average of five to six cents per union member is collected. It takes many gifts to aggregate the big sums sometimes contributed to candidates. A single large contributor may give as much to one candidate—say $1,000 or $5,000—as a single international union representing the contributions of thousands of individuals. In fact, the actual money labor puts into politics tends to be overrated; probably more important is the manpower provided by unions, particularly for registration and election-day activities. The labor movement generally grasped early the need for strenuous precinct work, with all the drudgery of registration and vote drives, and at times has carried on the work in uncongenial atmospheres, such as in the South.

Election Reform

Organized labor has traditionally not been counted in the vanguard of the campaign finance reform movement. Union leaders liked the hazy distinction between the "hard" and "soft" money they could contribute to candidates, that is, the voluntary contributions from their membership that could go directly to a campaign versus the money in their political education funds, created from union dues, that in areas such as get-out-the-vote drives and registration efforts could indirectly play a large role in helping a candidate. But after the evidence produced in the Watergate investigations of how massively business had injected funds into the Nixon reelection effort, major spokesmen for union labor became convinced that labor could never outspend business, and they joined the coalition for reform. Both the AFL-CIO and the UAW called for public financing of federal campaigns.

The Auto Workers' Leonard Woodcock told the Senate Subcommittee on Privileges and Elections in September 1973 that, in his view, the only way to insure "the immunity of our political system from the twin diseases of corruption and malfeasance . . . [was] to opt for direct public financing of federal elections."[68]

Andrew J. Biemiller, AFL-CIO legislative director, spoke of the challenge labor felt from business when he told the same committee that

. . . we have never liked making political contributions. It is an activity that has been forced upon us. If we did not contribute to friendly

candidates, we would risk the election of anti-labor candidates and the
enactment of laws contrary to the interests of working people.

... [What] we are saying to this committee is: "Stop us and
every other campaign contributor. The risks are too great for us to
unilaterally stop making campaign contributions as long as the other
side continues." We want the Congress to put the AFL-CIO out of the
business of making campaign contributions.[69]

Most of the members of Congress that labor has supported with political
money voted for election reform. Thomas E. Harris, who was associate general
counsel of the AFL-CIO, was one of the U.S. Senate appointees to the Federal
Election Commission.

Contribution to a Union

While looking into union activity, the Watergate investigators found one instance where the flow of money was the reverse of the usual pattern—from the
McGovern campaign to a union. The case was that of El Pueblo con McGovern,
a campaign committee composed of union leaders and supporters; the entire
amount of money the committee raised—$75,200—was contributed to it by
various McGovern campaign committees, including the McGovern Central Control fund, which gave the committee $42,500.

El Pueblo con McGovern spent about half of the total given it—$36,593—
in reimbursing the United Farm Workers, AFL-CIO, or its satellite groups
(the Caesar Chavez workers' organization centralized in California) for office
rental, supplies, buses, and personal services. In August 1973 the McGovern
Central Control Fund gave to the Farm Workers Political Education Fund a
remaining cash balance, $4,134 as "a gift," from termination of the El Pueblo
con McGovern.

GAO Audits

A provision of the Federal Election Campaign Act of 1971 directs the
General Accounting Office to make audits and field investigations with respect
to reports and statements filed under the Act. These audits in the 1972 election
helped shed new and more direct light on union practices that had gone on for
some years in apparent violation of the law.

Unions are prohibited from making contributions to federal candidates
from funds derived from members' dues. They may use such funds, however,
for purposes of political education—communications with members and their

families, nonpartisan registration drives and get-out-the-vote campaigns. Contributions to federal candidates must come from voluntary contributions by the members, and be kept in a separate bank account from the education funds. GAO audits, however, disclosed instances of the commingling of these funds and other apparent violations.

An audit of the report of the North America Committee on Political Education (AMCOPE) of the Amalgamated Meat Cutters and Butcher Workmen, located in Chicago, showed that AMCOPE had transferred $500 from its education account to the Utah Labor Committee for McGovern-Shriver. Additionally AMCOPE deposited in its voluntary account $1,000 of union dues received from a local union. AMCOPE also made contributions from its education funds in two states, Indiana and Texas, where union gifts to state candidates are prohibited.

An audit of the Akron, Ohio political education committee of the United Rubber, Cork, Linoleum and Plastic Workers of America disclosed that both voluntary and educational funds were commingled in the same bank account. However, the audit revealed that the committee did have administrative procedures and controls to separately account for the two funds. After this was brought to the committee's attention by the General Accounting Office, it agreed to establish a separate bank account for its voluntary political funds.

Both of these audits were referred to the Attorney General, although not as "apparent violations" of the law because the supervisory officers did not have responsibilities for Title II of FECA, and the transmittal merely revealed what the audits showed.

National Right to Work Committee

A persistent critic of union spending has been the National Right to Work Committee (NRWC), a Washington-based organization which describes itself as "A Coalition of Employees and Employers." While the House of Representatives was considering various alternatives in election finance laws in the winter of 1973, Reed Larson, the executive vice-president of NRWC, wrote to Congressman John H. Dent, the chairman of the House Subcommittee on Elections, a letter outlining his committee's position. The committee held that all of the various proposals had a common shortcoming, failing "to deal adequately with the most serious of all election campaign abuses, namely, the use of compulsory union dues for partisan political purposes." The National Right to Work Committee wanted an amendment to Section 610, which would, in effect, ban the use of union dues for the establishment of any sort of political education committee. The amendment would also have outlawed use of funds obtained coercively by corporations from their stockholders for political purposes.[70]

Suit Against Political Use of Union Dues

A group of California union members brought a class-action suit in December 1971 in an attempt to deny a tax exemption to any labor union that used compulsory union dues for political purposes—claiming they were being denied their constitutional rights when such money was used to support political candidates and philosophies with which they may not agree. The suit was filed in the U.S. District Court, District of Columbia.[71]

The suit, supported by the Legal Defense Fund of the National Right to Work Committee, was brought on behalf of 22 members of the International Association of Machinists and of the United Automobile Workers employed at McDonnell-Douglas and North American Rockwell plants in California. Judge Charles R. Richey dismissed the workers' complaint, basing his decision on a Supreme Court ruling in 1961,[72] which noted a reluctance "to impose such an injunctive remedy" on political activities by unions. Such an injunction, the Supreme Court had held, would itself "work a restraint on the expression of political ideas which might be offensive to the First Amendment." Both the Supreme Court and Judge Richey noted that other avenues were open for the individual union members to seek remedies when they felt their money was being used to support candidates or parties whom they opposed.

Judge Harold Leventhal of the U.S. Circuit Court of Appeals, writing for a unanimous Court, upheld the District Court ruling.[73] He noted that the union members were entitled to legal protection in dissenting from paying dues they believed would be used for political purposes that they opposed. But he recalled Judge Richey's opinion that the Supreme Court cases, which had established workers' rights to such protection, also spelled out carefully the remedies to which they were entitled, and the broad stroke of denying tax exemption to the union was clearly not one of them.

Judge Leventhal pointed out they could stop the expenditures for political causes of the portion of their dues ascribable to political actitivies. Or a dissenting employee could obtain a refund for such portion. The remedies, he wrote, "were limited to restitution and to injunction directed against specific union activities."

The tax exemption granted labor unions on dues receipts was not based on support of "each aspect of their activities, but rather on the concept that what was involved was essentially a pooling of the individual resources of the members, as contrasted with the entrepreneurial profit of corporations." Unions have enjoyed this tax exemption since 1909, the court noted.

In 1969 and 1971 there were moves in Congress to terminate the union exemption, on grounds that dues were being used for political activities. Congress rejected the moves on both occasions. "What was involved," concluded Judge Leventhal, "was the determination by Congress to keep the tax exemption of dues and contributions in a neutral stance, rather than to embroil the

tax laws and the agencies administering them into involvement with and surveillance of the political activities of the unions."

Pipe Fitters Ruling

The Pipefitters Local Union No. 562 of St. Louis, Missouri was indicted
along with three of its officers in 1968 for conspiracy to violate 18 U.S.C.,
Section 610, which prohibits a labor organization from making a contribution
or an expenditure in connection with a federal election. The charge was that
from 1949 through 1962 the union maintained a political fund to which union
members were required to contribute; the fund was subsequently chartered as
a separate "voluntary" organization, but union officials maintained control
and there were no significant changes in the style of collections.

After the Court of Appeals for the Eastern District of Missouri rejected the
union's challenge, and held that the fund was merely a subterfuge, the case
then came before the U.S. Supreme Court in June 1972. The Court upheld
the union's case, asking that the indictments be dismissed.

In the opinion written by Justice William Brennan, the Court noted that
the FECA of 1971, which had gone into effect while the arguments to the
Supreme Court were being made, had added a paragraph to Section 610 that
expressly authorized unions to establish, administer, and solicit contributions
for political funds. In effect, said Justice Brennan, the law as newly written
repealed the provisions under which the indictment had originally been
brought.[74]

13

The Impact of Watergate: Part II

Corporate Prosecutions

In the fall of 1973 the Office of the Special Prosecutor filed suit in U.S. District Court in the District of Columbia against American Airlines, Inc., Goodyear Tire and Rubber Company, and Minnesota Mining & Manufacturing Co., alleging violations of federal laws in making illegal contributions of corporate funds to Nixon and other presidential candidates in the 1972 campaign. Over the next two years, 21 companies pleaded guilty to this charge (in several cases the prosecution was not by the Special Prosecutor); the companies and, in most instances, their chief officers were fined in varying amounts. Appendix X lists the corporate contribution cases and their disposition.

In total, these firms were charged with contributing close to $960,000 illegally. The bulk of it, almost $850,000, had gone to the Nixon campaign.[a] In addition, Hubert Humphrey's 1972 presidential bid received over $50,000 illegally from the dairy trusts; Wilbur Mills' campaign received $20,000; Henry Jackson's $11,000; Edmund Muskie's $1,000; and George McGovern's an undetermined amount of the $16,040 that the Greyhound Corporation admitted went to both Nixon and McGovern. Some $6,000 in illegal corporate gifts were made to several congressional campaigns by a number of companies. All of this was revealed in the investigation into illegal corporate giving conducted by the Office of the Special Prosecutor.[b]

As the cases developed, a deliberate pattern of devious activity by the

---

[a]The Greyhound Corporation said a total of $16,040 had been given illegally to the campaign committees of both Nixon and McGovern, but there was no way to reconstruct each gift. The $850,000 Nixon figure does not include whatever his "share" of the Greyhound money may have been.

[b]On May 25, 1974, the first anniversary of the Watergate Special Prosecution Force, the Special Prosecutor's Office issued simultaneously an annual report of activities ("Watergate Special Prosecution Force Report") and a status report ("Watergate Special Prosecution Force Status Report"—expanding and updating through May 20, 1974 earlier reports). Of special interest in the annual report is the description of investigations by the Campaign Contributions Task Force (ten attorneys and six support staff) into campaign fund raising for the 1972 election and subsequent administration decisions. In addition to prosecutions arising out of criminal charges filed against corporations and individuals (see Appendix X), the task force "has recorded the first instances of successful prosecution of two longstanding criminal statutes: Chapter 18, section 600 (Promise of Government Appointment for Political Contribution) and Chapter 18, section 611 (Contribution by Government Contractors)."

corporations designed to mask the sources of contributions became apparent, in many instances involving a "laundering" of funds through foreign sources.

American Airlines made an illegal $55,000 contribution to the Nixon campaign for which it was fined $5,000; unlike most of the other guilty corporations no officer was fined since American had been the first to volunteer details of its illegal activity to the Office of the Special Prosecutor. (American's chief executive officer George A. Spater had also made a legal contribution of $20,000 to the Nixon campaign.) The corporate money had come from a $100,000 check drawn originally on American's account at the Chemical Bank in New York.[c] From there it went to the Swiss account of a Lebanese agent, Andre Tabourian, and was charged on American's books as a "special commission" to Tabourian in connection with "used aircraft sale to Middle East Airlines." It then returned to the United States and into an account maintained at Chase National Bank in New York. Tabourian then came to New York, withdrew the money in cash, and gave it to an American Airlines official who put it in an office safe. Later George Spater had $55,000 of it, in $100 bills, put in an unmarked envelope and delivered to the Finance Committee to Re-Elect the President (FCRP).

The American Airlines contribution was made in response to a Kalmbach request for $100,000—the sum usually named—at a time when the company had several matters pending before various agencies of the federal government, including a proposed merger between American and Western Airlines. Kalmbach was at that time the counsel to United Airlines, a principal competitor, and the personal attorney for President Nixon. Spater later testified before the Senate Watergate Committee that he found himself in the position of being worried on the one hand about giving the money illegally to his competitor's counsel and, on the other, not giving it to the reelection effort of the President when the decision on the proposed merger was at stake.[1]

Both federal and state laws were violated by Minnesota Mining & Manufacturing Co. (3M) in the 1972 campaign, and evidence was also brought to light of an illegal secret fund through which the company had made political contributions totalling $635,000, one fifth of that to Nixon, over a period of a decade. In the 1972 campaign two Democratic contenders, Hubert Humphrey and Wilbur Mills, also received $1,000 each in illegal 3M funds.

The company was initially fined $3,000 and the chairman of the board, Harry Heltzer, $500, (in October 1973) on federal charges of having contributed $36,000 to the Nixon campaign and the $2,000 to the two Democrats, all in 1972. The 3M contribution came from a secret cash fund kept in the safe of Irwin Hansen, vice-president of finance, that had been first create n 1963 at the request of Burt S. Cross, then 3M's president.

---

[c]Chemical Bank also figured in the matter of a questionably legal $100,000 loan it made to the Seafarers' Union just before the November election by which the Seafarers then made a $100,000 donation to the Nixon campaign. The chairman of Chemical's Executive Committee, Harold H. Helm, was also co-chairman of FCRP.

The fuller account of the uses to which this fund was put emerged in January 1975, when 3M pleaded guilty to five counts of illegal contributions in violation of Minnesota law, and the list of contributions was made public. The company was fined $5,000, Hansen $3,000. Nixon had received a total of $136,400 from the company fund, starting with $75,200 in his 1968 campaign. This was followed by a $5,000 gift in 1970, $20,000 in 1971, and $36,200 in 1972 (under Minnesota law, only the last contribution constituted grounds for prosecution; violations occurring before January 22, 1972, could not be charged). Other politicians who received 3M funds, the state investigation found, included Senators Humphrey and Walter Mondale, D-Minnesota; Senator Lowell Weicker, R-Connecticut, of Watergate Committee prominence; and former Congressman Clark MacGregor, R-Minnesota, who succeeded John Mitchell as chairman of the Committee to Re-Elect the President (CRP) in the summer of 1972. More than 390 contributions were made from the fund between 1963 and 1972.

The charges were brought by the Minnesota Attorney General after acquiring the case in October 1974 from the Ramsay County (Minneapolis-St. Paul) attorney's office. Attorney William Randall surrendered the case in the face of conflict of interest charges—Randall acknowledging that he was a substantial 3M stockholder. When the files of the 3M offices were subsequently searched, Randall was one of the many politicians listed who had benefited from the secret fund, having received $1,000 in his 1966 reelection campaign for the county post.[2]

The scene moved again into federal court where a grand jury sitting in St. Paul indicted 3M and two of its board members on criminal income tax charges involving the fund. It was the first indictment of its kind resulting from the Watergate investigations into illegal corporate contributions. Such tax violations are felonies carrying jail terms of up to five years for conspiracy and up to three years for filing a false tax return.[3] Cross and Hansen, the indicted board members, subsequently pleaded innocent of the charges and were released on $1,000 personal recognizance bail.[4]

The money for the secret fund was raised initially by overstating prepaid insurance, later by paying a Swiss attorney who submitted false billings for his services. Company officials said that $136,000 remaining in the fund was returned to the company when the first charges arose; and the FCRP returned $30,000 of the 1972 Nixon contribution (the other $6,000 had been for six $1,000 tickets to a "Salute the President" dinner). A stockholder's suit brought against 3M resulted in Heltzer paying the company $70,000, as did Cross, while Hansen paid $34,000. William L. McKnight, chairman of the company from 1949 to 1966, paid $300,000, and Wilbur M. Bennett, director of civic affairs, paid 3M $1,000.[5] In all, the evidence brought to light by 3M's illegal gifts to the 1972 presidential campaign—amounting to $38,000—cost former and present company executives and board members at least $489,000, exclusive of legal fees and any fines that may ultimately be imposed out of the federal income tax indictments pending at this writing.

The $40,000 contribution to Nixon from Goodyear Tire and Rubber Co.
came from funds in an account maintained for years in a Swiss bank for rebates
received from foreign manufacturers buying Goodyear supplies. Goodyear was
fined $5,000; Russell DeYoung, who also had made a personal contribution to
the Nixon campaign of $5,000, was fined $1,000.[6]

Braniff Airways made a bogus payment to an agent in Panama in order to
arrange its $40,000 illegal contribution to the Nixon campaign. The gift was
made possible without reporting for tax purposes, according to a company
attorney, through the "peculiarities of airlines accounting." Braniff was fined
$5,000, its board chairman Harding L. Lawrence $1,000; he reimbursed Braniff
for the $5,000 fine, while other officers paid the company $3,218.85 for lost
interest, and $19,181.09 for legal fees incurred. Both Lawrence and C. Edward
Acker, the Braniff president, had also each made legal personal gifts to the Nixon
campaign. It was after these gifts, Lawrence told Watergate investigators, that
Maurice Stans told him he felt Braniff executives could do more because the
company was doing better than the rest of the industry, and CRP's chief fund
raiser suggested a donation in the neighborhood of $100,000 would be more
appropriate.[7] Stans denied having said this, or even having made the Braniff
solicitation.

The Gulf Oil contributions, totalling $125,000 ($100,000 to Nixon,
$15,000 to Wilbur Mills, $10,000 to Henry Jackson) were arranged through
a Gulf subsidiary in the Bahamas, and charged to the firm's "miscellaneous
expense account." Gulf was fined $5,000 and Claude C. Wild, Jr., a former vice-
president who had handled the transaction, was fined $1,000. At the Watergate
hearings, Wild testified that he had originally arranged for $50,000 to be given
to the Nixon campaign; he then produced another $50,000 after being told that
$100,000 was being suggested as the level the large American corporations
should arrange to provide.[8] Wild subsequently resigned from Gulf.

The circumstances of the transfer of Gulf money to the Mills campaign
were related by the man who acted as the middleman, Carl Arnold, a Washington
lobbyist for the gas and oil interests. A friend of Mills, Arnold was in the process
of raising money for the Arkansas congressman's presidential bid when he
approached Claude Wild at Gulf. Wild subsequently delivered the $15,000 in
cash in a sealed envelope to Arnold, a former official of the American Petroleum
Institute. Arnold said he never openned the envelope, but simply called the
Mills campaign committee and asked that someone come around to pick it up.
Arnold said he never asked about the source of the funds, nor, he said, did Mills.
When the Special Prosecutor's Office later brought charges against Gulf, Mills
ordered that the $15,000 be returned.[d]

Arnold also figured in the distribution of part of the illegal corporate gifts

---

[d]Richard M. Cohen, " 'Johnny Appleseed' of Campaign Funds," *Washington Post*, January 6, 1975. (For a list of returned corporate contributions, see Appendix X and Table 13-1.)

made by Ashland Oil; a total of $270,000 in contributions was made from 1970 to 1972. Ashland made a $100,000 illegal gift to the Nixon campaign, which Ashland arranged through an oil drilling subsidiary in Gabon on the west coast of Africa, entered on the corporate books as a "capital expense," and paid through the company's bank account in Geneva. Orin E. Atkins, chairman of Ashland's board, testified that it had not excited anyone's curiosity when an Ashland official walked into a Swiss bank and asked for $100,000 in cash. He said that an Ashland vice-president took the funds to Washington and personally delivered the cash to Maurice Stans, who dumped it in his desk drawer. Atkins said the funds from the Gabon subsidiary were used because this company had some undeveloped land that probably would never be written off for tax purposes, and thus would never come under the scrutiny of the Internal Revenue Service. He added that Ashland had been more concerned about violating the tax laws than those governing political contributions.[9] For the Nixon contribution, the company was fined $5,000, Atkins $1,000, and he reimbursed Ashland $7,175 in legal costs and $7,179 in lost interest; the $100,000 contribution was returned by FCRP in July 1973.[e]

Ashland later admitted to another $170,000 in illegal gifts to politicians of both major parties from 1970 to 1972, for which Chief Judge George L. Hart, Jr., U.S. District Court, District of Columbia fined the company the maximum of $25,000.[10] Lobbyist Arnold figured in the distribution of this cash, $50,000 of which went to Democratic National Committee Chairman Robert Strauss between 1970 and 1972 while he was serving as party treasurer; $6,864.65 to Hubert Humphrey; $2,500 to the 1972 reelection campaign of Senator John G. Tower, R-Texas; and $10,000 to former Republican Governor of Kentucky, Louis B. Nunn, in his unsuccessful 1972 senatorial bid. Both Strauss and Humphrey told Watergate investigators that they thought this had come from individual donors, as did campaign aides of both Tower and Nunn;[11] the FCRP thought the same.

In February 1975 the Special Prosecutor's Office subpoenaed the finance reports of the Democratic Party for 1970 and 1971, covering the period when Strauss accepted the Ashland gift. Strauss later created a special DNC panel to consider whether the party should refund the contribution. Still unresolved as of this writing is whether Strauss was liable for not properly reporting the gift; the statute of limitations was shortened from five to three years in the 1974 Amendments, and applied to that section of the law, so Strauss could no longer be charged.

When two of the federal regulatory agencies—the Securities and Exchange Commission and the Civil Aeronautics Board—began to look into the matter of illegal corporate contributions in late 1974, further disclosure, not limited to the 1972 elections, ensued. An SEC suit, for example, helped bring to light the full

---

[e]For a list of returned corporate contributions, see Appendix X and Table 13-1.

extent of 3M's illegal corporate contributions over a ten-year period. Another SEC suit similarly led the Phillips Petroleum Company to admit that the scope of its illegal political activities went well beyond the financial involvement in the 1972 campaign to which it had already admitted illegal contributions.

Phillips and its chairman of the board, W.W. Keeler, had pleaded guilty in December 1973 to making an illegal contribution of $100,000 to the Nixon Campaign; the company was fined $5,000, Keller, $1,000, and the FCRP refunded the contribution. In an SEC suit that followed more than a year later, it was disclosed that Phillips had an additional cash fund generated through foreign transactions and kept secretly at the corporate offices in Oklahoma, which over a ten-year period had made contributions totalling some $585,000 (not including the $100,000 to FCRP) to various political activities.[12]

The Carnation Company and its chairman of the board, H. Everett Olson, pleaded guilty on December 19, 1973 to using corporate funds for $7,900 in contributions to the Nixon campaign, and $1,000 to the 1972 Senate-House majority (Republican) dinner; $2,900 was given in response to a fund-raising letter from the FCRP, and $5,000 was solicited by a Los Angeles civic leader who requested Olson to purchase tickets at $1,000 each to a Nixon fund-raising dinner in southern California. Both Nixon contributions were made in the form of personal checks by Carnation executives, who were reimbursed in cash by the company's senior vice-president. The cash was obtained by charging a $7,900 "travel expense" on the books to a transportation expense account. The company, which had voluntarily admitted the gifts but had not disclosed them publicly, was fined $5,000; Olson was fined $1,000.[13]

Diamond International Corporation gave $5,000 to a Nixon campaign committee in 1972, and $1,000 to the Muskie campaign in December 1971. On March 7, 1974 the corporation and its vice-president of public affairs, Ray Dubrowin, were fined $5,000 and $1,000 respectively. Dubrowin had arranged the Nixon donation by drawing two checks from the corporate account, dated February 23, 1972 and March 27, 1972, and made payable to the First National City Bank of New York, which then issued two $2,500 treasurer's checks to the Effective Government Committee of the FCRP. The Muskie contribution, also converted to a cashier's check, was solicited by Maine's Democratic Governor Kenneth M. Curtis, in a fund-raising letter inviting attendance at a $1,000-a-ticket reception honoring Senator and Mrs. Muskie. Dubrowin told Watergate investigators that a major consideration in making the Muskie contribution was the corporation's business dealings with the state of Maine.[14]

The Northrop Corporation, the aerospace firm that did $370 million of Defense Department business in fiscal 1973, made illegal contributions totalling $175,000 to the Nixon campaign. Of that sum, $100,000 was given before the April 7 deadline, half on April 5, 1972. The remainder was part of the money Herbert Kalmbach raised in the summer of 1972 at White House request as payments to the original Watergate defendants. When he testified at the Watergate coverup trial in November 1974 Kalmbach told of approaching Northrop President Thomas V. Jones, an old friend, and requesting an additional $50,000; after he got the envelope with the cash, he discovered that it contained $75,000. Jones "laughed off" the discrepancy, and told him to keep the money since he had pledged much more to the Nixon campaign. Kalmbach broke down in tears on the stand as he related this account of how he felt he had used a friendship to get money for illegal purposes.[15] Jones and the corporation were subsequently fined $5,000 each, the first contributors to be charged under Section 611 of federal law prohibiting contributions by corporations doing business with the government. Northrop Vice-President James Allen was fined $1,000.

In an affadavit filed in connection with a shareholder's suit, it was later disclosed that Northrop had maintained a secret political fund of up to $1.1 million over a period of 13 years. The money was laundered through a Paris-based consultant, William A. Savy, in the guise of payments for legitimate consulting work. Savy kept only $130,000 of the total transmitted to him over the 13-year period, the remainder, known as the "Savy fund," went to various political campaigns in California and nationally from 1961-73.

The tentative settlement of the suit, announced in November 1974, called for Jones to relinquish the presidency of Northrop within 18 months, but stay on as chairman and chief executive officer. The settlement also called for selection of four new independent, outside directors, to be approved by Federal District Judge Warren J. Ferguson. In the future, the terms specify, at least 60 percent of Northrop's board will be outside directors, meaning individuals without significant financial interest in the company. The terms also provide for revision of the executive committee so that five of its six members will be outsiders. Additionally, the precedent-setting settlement states that the company will carry out a blanket prohibition against use of any Northrop funds and facilities on behalf of candidates, parties, or office holders at the federal, state, or local level for at least two years; this policy can be changed only with shareholder approval.

At the time the tentative settlement was announced, Jones had repaid $122,000 to the company, and the terms required that he pay another $50,000. Vice-President Allen was directed to repay $10,000.[16]

Still another in the long series of judgments against Northrop came in March 1975, when Pentagon auditors discovered that the 1972 illegal gift had been charged to overhead on United States Air Force contracts. Northrop was ordered to refund the money.

The Lehigh Valley Cooperative Farmers, Inc. made a secret $50,000 cash contribution to the Nixon campaign from its corporate funds in April 1972. The donation, covered up by co-op officials and not reported by the FCRP until over a year later, was made in exchange for an appearance by Agriculture Secretary Earl Butz at the cooperative's annual dinner. The co-op represented nearly 1,000 Pennsylvania, New Jersey, and Maryland dairymen in 1972. Arrangements for

Butz's appearance were made by Francis X. Carroll, the co-op's former Washington lobbyist. After an invitation for an appearance by Vice-President Agnew was turned down, a number of surrogates were approached, and the CRP was reportedly offered from $35,000 to $75,000. All but Butz refused.

Carroll delivered $25,000 in cash to CRP messengers in Washington on April 20, where he then met Butz at the airport and accompanied him to Allentown, Pennsylvania for the dinner. The second $25,000 was paid in early May at CRP headquarters. The $50,000 cash went into a secret fund later used to pay the original Watergate defendants. Carroll had received and cashed corporate checks, made payable to him and charged to expense accounts in company records. The first $25,000 was approved by then President and General Manager Richard L. Allison; authorization from the co-op board was never sought or obtained for the second payment, although Allison approved both. The second $25,000 was treated as a loan to Carroll, but he did not sign a note for it until June 1973, and apparently never repaid the amount. Allison and Carroll both left the co-op, and on May 6, 1974 Lehigh Valley pleaded guilty to charges of making an illegal campaign contribution and was fined $5,000. Allison received a $1,000 suspended fine on May 17, and Carroll was given a suspended sentence on May 28 for aiding and abetting an illegal campaign contribution.[17]

National By-Products, Inc., an Iowa-based firm that distributes animal fats, proteins, and hides, was charged by the Special Prosecutor's Office with making a $3,000 illegal corporate contribution to the FCRP. The case was brought in the U.S. District Court, Southern District of Iowa. On June 24, 1974 the corporation pleaded guilty to the charge and was fined $1,000.

Two leaders of a dairy farmers cooperative went to jail for their role in the illegal campaign contributions of the Associated Milk Producers, Inc. (AMPI)—an organization that ended up playing the role of both special interest and corporate offender in the 1972 campaign. The corporation was fined $35,000 on August 1, 1974 for making illegal campaign contributions of $100,000 to Nixon, $50,000 to Senator Hubert Humphrey, and $5,000 to Representative Wilbur Mills.[f] Harold S. Nelson and David L. Parr became the first individuals in the string of corporate prosecution cases to be given jail sentences. The two men pleaded guilty—Parr on July 23, 1974, and Nelson on July 31; on November 1 Judge George L. Hart, Jr. gave each man a three-year sentence and a $10,000 fine, then suspended all but four months of the sentence. Judge Hart told the men he was not attempting to reform or punish; his aim rather was to deter similar actions by others.

Norman Sherman, a former press secretary to Humber Humphrey during his vice-presidency, pleaded guilty on August 12, 1974 to his role in aiding illegal corporate political donations by AMPI. He was fined $500.

Sherman was a partner in a Minnesota-based firm, Valentine, Sherman &

---

[f]For a discussion of the dairy funds, see pp. 486-500.

Associates, which specialized in computerized political services—providing, for example, combined lists of voter registrations and telephone numbers, a valuable tool in an election campaign. Founded in 1969 by Sherman and Jack Valentine (also fined $500), VSA first worked in Humphrey's 1970 senatorial campaign, and was also employed in his 1972 presidential bid. Some $25,000 of the services provided Humphrey by the firm, it was charged, came from illegal corporate funds of AMPI.

Sherman's story is revealing. He said that his firm approached AMPI with a view to producing lists for the dairy cooperative, which might be used for a variety of purposes, political and otherwise; AMPI officials later said that their interest was "purely political." Sherman claimed moreover that he thought the approach was perfectly legal, that he was not asking for an illegal political contribution, but simply seeking another customer to share the very expensive costs of the computerized data VSA provided. Another error he conceded was in not paying as much attention as the firm should have to the "Incorporated" in AMPI, although he knew full well that corporations were barred by law from contributions.[18]

When the first payment from AMPI arrived, however, it was in the form of a corporate check. At first Sherman and Valentine hesitated to cash it, fearing it might be illegal—but then did so because they were badly in need of the money, and their attorney had told them it was legal (the attorney, they discovered later, had also been retained by the milk producers).

Over two years later—during which AMPI's role in promoting a rise in milk price supports with a large Nixon donation had surfaced—Sherman and Valentine were summoned before a grand jury, and subsequently pleaded guilty in U.S. District Court in St. Paul.

In passing sentence, the judge said he felt there had been mitigating factors, and it appeared to him that Sherman and Valentine had not intended to violate the law. He noted particularly that their former attorney had assured them they were acting legally in cashing the check, but then quoted from a letter from the Special Prosecutor's Office, "one might well wonder whether the defendants received the benefit of objective and disinterested advice."[19]

Sherman has subsequently speculated that the fact of his association with former Vice-President Humphrey might have "inevitably attracted and, in the Watergate climate, possibly even required" the attention his case got.

"I became, I think, the most readily available token Democrat needed to offset the otherwise totally Republican line-up. Valentine, like a Siamese twin, necessarily became a target by association."

Like many others in 1972, Sherman got caught up in a system, was victimized by it, and now feels he paid the price for behaving according to habit and tradition, not taking the law very seriously, not expecting the law to be enforced, taking ethical short-cuts, and giving too little thought to consequences.

The largest fines for contributions to the 1972 campaigns were assessed in the case against American Ship Building Company and its chairman George M. Steinbrenner, III, who was also the principal owner of the New York Yankees. This was regarded by the Special Prosecutor's Office as the strongest of the campaign contribution cases under investigation. Archibald Cox had originally invited companies that were guilty of illegal contributions to step forward voluntarily with information about their contributions. The volunteers, it was announced, would be charged only with misdemeanors; others that were found to have violated the law would be charged with felonies. In most cases the companies had come forward voluntarily.

Steinbrenner, however, was indicted in April 1974 on 14 felony counts. He at first vowed to fight the charges, but later relented; all but two were dismissed when he agreed to enter a guilty plea. Steinbrenner pleaded guilty to a conspiracy, and to the charge of devising a "false and misleading explanation" of $25,000 given to the Nixon campaign, and of trying to "influence and intimidate employees of his company." Steinbrenner admitted that he had arranged contributions totalling $32,200 to Nixon's campaign. Also cited were contributions totalling $29,000 to two Democratic congressional campaign dinners, a $1,000 gift to the campaign of Senator Vance Hartke, D-Indiana, and $5,650 to the 1974 campaign of Senator Daniel K. Inouye, D-Hawaii (which was returned). On August 23, 1974 Steinbrenner was fined $15,000, while American Ship Building was assessed $20,000 for two violations of the Federal Election Campaign Act. Steinbrenner also was suspended for two years from any association with the New York Yankees by the baseball commissioner.

The illegal schemes devised by Steinbrenner involved giving fictitious bonuses to "loyal" employees, along with lists of various committees to which they should make donations; it was agreed that the political contributions would be for less than the bonuses in order to cover taxes paid by the recipient. The committees, with such names as "Loyal Americans for Government," the "Stable Society Council," and "Dedicated Americans for Effective Government," were all associated with the Committee to Re-Elect the President. Steinbrenner's corporate lawyer, Thomas H. Melcher, Jr., also pleaded guilty to a misdemeanor in aiding and abetting Steinbrenner in the complex bonus system scheme. A Securities and Exchange Commission investigation estimated that Steinbrenner between the years 1970-73 had made total illegal contributions in excess of $120,000.

In addition to the illegal sums for which Steinbrenner was found guilty, he had also given $75,000 from his personal funds, a legal contribution, to the Nixon campaign.[20]

House Majority Leader Thomas P. ("Tip") O'Neill shed further light on the manner in which Steinbrenner was approached for a contribution to the Nixon campaign:[21] An active Democratic fund raiser during the 1968 campaign, Steinbrenner was told by Herbert Kalmbach that he ought to "get with the right people" in the 1972 campaign. Since 1968 Steinbrenner's firm had been investigated by the IRS and the Justice Department; in 1972 he reluctantly became a Democrat for Nixon and initiated the contributions for which he was convicted. When O'Neill approached Steinbrenner for a McGovern contribution, Steinbrenner begged off, saying "they are holding the lumber over my head." Upon hearing the story, O'Neill became convinced that Steinbrenner had experienced a "plain, old-fashioned god-damned shakedown," and he began thinking that Nixon would actually be impeached. O'Neill later became a moving force in the congressional proceedings, which culminated in the vote to impeach.

A Columbia, South Carolina architectural firm, LBC & W, and its president, William Lyles, Sr., received fines in September 1974 totalling $7,000 for illegal contributions of $10,000 to the Nixon campaign. The Special Prosecutor's Office also found a system of fictitious bonuses used in this case, with the money going eventually into a contributions fund.

The Greyhound Corporation was similarly found guilty of reimbursing officers of the corporation for their contributions to presidential candidates. Senior officials of the bus company were encouraged to contribute personal funds to the presidential candidate of their choice, and then awarded a supplemental bonus twice the amount of the contribution of each executive who gave, again to cover taxes. The Greyhound payments totalled $16,040 to various committees organized on behalf of both Nixon and McGovern. Greyhound was considered in the volunteer category and on October 8, 1974 was fined $5,000 on a misdemeanor, a judgment questioned by some in view of the fact that the company had been told by the FBI that it was under investigation before it went to the Special Prosecutor.

In one instance, an illegal corporate contribution in one state was used to help finance the Nixon reelection campaign in a neighboring state. Time Oil Company of Seattle, Washington, a small firm engaged in distribution and sales to cut-rate gasoline stations, pleaded guilty on October 23 to making illegal campaign contributions to both Nixon and Senator Henry Jackson, that state's senior senator.[22] Time Oil President Raymond Abendroth also entered a guilty plea to two counts charging illegal contributions of $6,600 to the Nixon campaign, $1,000 to Jackson's. U.S. District Court Judge George L. Hart, Jr., fined the company $5,000 and Abendroth $2,000.

Eight months later it developed that the Nixon money had gone into Oregon, when former Congressmen Wendell Wyatt of that state pleaded guilty to not reporting expenditures from a $5,000 cash fund he had controlled while heading the Nixon reelection effort in Oregon. The fund, he later testified, had been established with monies from Time Oil's illegal contribution.[23]

In December the former president and founder of HMS Electric Corp., Charles N. Huseman, was found guilty of an illegal $5,000 contribution to the Nixon campaign and was fined $1,000. The electrical contracting company, based in Washington, D.C., has since been purchased by another firm and its name changed.[24]

A Baltimore construction firm, Ratrie, Robbins & Schweitzer, Inc., and its two top executives, Harry Ratrie, president, and Augustus Robbins, III, executive vice-president, pleaded guilty in January 1975 to making an illegal $5,000 corporate contribution to the FCRP. The firm also had been under investigation in connection with the kickback scandals that led to Vice-President Agnew's resignation; a company lawyer said that federal prosecutors in Baltimore had given the company a "clean bill of health."

United States District Judge Hart fined the corporation $2,500, half the maximum penalty for this violation, and imposed no fine on either Ratrie or Robbins. They were placed on probation for one month after their lawyers told Judge Hart that the men had consulted with their company's accountant, who told them the contribution was legal.[25]

The First National Bank of Albuquerque, New Mexico, pleaded guilty in March 1975 to having made illegal campaign contributions in 1972, and was fined $15,000 for gifts totalling $8,000. The case was unusual in that the fine was greater than the amount of the illegal contributions; it was prosecuted by the Justice Department rather than the Office of the Special Prosecutor. The bank had made one gift of $1,000 to a "Victory '72 Dinner" for Nixon and Agnew, while the remainder of the contributions went to various state Senate and House candidates in New Mexico.

Also charged by the Attorney General, the Singer Company of Maryland pleaded guilty in June 1975 to having made an illegal contribution of $10,000 to the FCRP in 1972, and was fined $2,500 on the misdemeanor charge.[26] In the course of the hearing before U.S. District Judge R. Dorsey Watkins, the federal prosecutors dropped felony charges against Singer that sought to implicate the company in a criminal fraud conspiracy involving J. Walter Jones, an Annapolis banker alleged to have been Vice-President Spiro Agnew's "bag man."

Three days after the sentencing, however, a Singer executive was indicted on conspiring with Jones to make the illegal contribution. Martin Leader, finance manager of Singer's Simulated Products Division, was named in the three-count indictment. A month later the indictment was dropped when Leader pleaded guilty to a misdemeanor charge in the illegal contribution.[27]

Singer faced a maximum fine of $5,000 for its guilty plea. Judge Watkins levied the $2,500 after agreeing with the arguments of Singer attorneys that the company's action was less serious than the crimes committed by other corporations charged by the Special Prosecutor's Office, since the contribution did not involve the top management of the company or a corporate slush fund.

Jones, who had been the chief Nixon–Agnew fund raiser in the state of Maryland in 1972 had refused to cooperate with the U.S. Attorney's Office in its investigations leading to Agnew's resignation from the vice-presidency in 1973. In June 1975 Jones was scheduled to face trial on charges of conspiring with Leader to make the illegal 1972 contribution from Singer.

The picture of corporate contributions that unfolded during 1973, 1974, and 1975 suggested that some corporations maintained secret funds for political uses on a scale unlike anything imagined previously. During the last year of the Johnson administration and the first of the Nixon administration—1968 and 1969—there was a series of federal prosecutions of corporate political practices. In all, the Justice Department obtained 15 indictments and 14 convictions of businesses, many of them in southern California, for deducting, as legitimate business expenses, payments that were in effect political contributions; these cases had been uncovered by the Internal Revenue Service and referred to the Justice Department. Another series of indictments against a group of banks was brought in 1971, and still another against a number of Arkansas electric companies in the summer of 1973 charging violation of the federal election laws. But in none of these was there anything like the roster of American big business, representing many sectors of the economy, that was involved in the contributions to the Nixon campaign.

Many of the officials convicted of involvement in this effort said that they had contributed corporate funds illegally because the solicitations had come from high officials such as Stans and Kalmbach, whom they saw as close to the President. Their concern, they claimed, was not in obtaining favors, but over governmental discrimination against them if they did not meet the implied quota for contributions. American Airlines' George Spater told the Watergate committee:

> I believe that the present system places unfair pressures both on candidates and on corporate executives . . . most contributions from the business community are not volunteered to see a competitive advantage, but are made in response to pressure for fear of the competitive disadvantage that might result if they are not made. The process degrades both the donor and the donee. . . . It is particularly dangerous when the pressure is implicit in the position of the individual making the solicitation.[28]

Spater said he was motivated by "fear of the unknown," likening his state of mind to "those medieval maps that show the known world and then around it, Terra Incognita, with fierce animals." Gulf's Claude Wild said he decided to arrange the contribution so his company "would not be on a blacklist or at the bottom of the totem pole" and so that somebody in Washington would answer his telephone calls.[29]

Some of those involved said that fund raising for the Nixon reelection effort differed from other such campaigns because of the enormous amounts of money suggested and the fact that cash was unquestioningly accepted. Some contributions in cash were so large that it must have appeared obvious, except to the most insensitive person, that they might have come from corporate funds rather than individuals.

In the words of the Senate Watergate Committee, "there is evidence that a number of them [the solicitors] either were indifferent to the source of the money or, at the very least, made no effort whatsoever to see to it that the source of the funds was private rather than corporate. . . . [T]here is no evidence that any fund raiser who was involved in these contributions sought or obtained assurances that the contribution was legal at the time it was made."[30] Later, when such contributions were exposed, the FCRP sought and received affadavits from the companies stating that FCRP had had no knowledge that the money was corporate and therefore illegal. Moreover, the corporate money was returned.

A published example of corporate resistance to solicitation came in a report that American Motors Corporation officials said they flatly refused, when asked for $100,000 and then a week later for $50,000.[31] Other executives of companies, among them, Union Oil Company and the Allied Chemical Corporation, were also reported to have turned down appeals to raise large amounts from employees.[32]

The New York Times undertook a telephone survey of the heads of scores of major corporations and found that most of the prime defense contractors had been solicited by Nixon fund raisers to produce money. Numerous executimes of companies refused flatly, some gave only from their private funds, and some gave only after April 7 and on the record. Apparently, the customary amount suggested as a target for the largest companies was $100,000, but the requests were scaled down for smaller ones. Some Democrats were approached, mistakenly or not, and some gave directly or later to Democrats for Nixon. A distinct pattern of high pressure was discerned by some.[33]

Certainly Watergate and its aftermath trail of businessmen confessing to illegal contributions damaged the business community. But, ironically, the image of the greedy businessman as the corrupter, seeking favors from the politician, has been changed in some minds. If extortion is involved, the businessman becomes the victim, not the perpetrator.

The consequences of these businessmen's actions have since become apparent in other ways. Eight of the top executives involved in disclosure of illegal corporation spending in 1972 have left their companies. In some instances they headed the companies. Four have left corporate posts: Russell Young, chairman of Goodyear Tire and Rubber Company; Claude C. Wild, Jr., a vice-president of the Gulf Oil Corporation; William Keeler, chairman of Phillips Petroleum; and John H. Melcher, Jr., executive vice-president of American Ship Building Company, the last on an extended leave of absence. Some of the companies denied any connection between the departures and the campaign-fund scandals; some of the men involved were near retirement age. The other four who left were on the boards of the corporations they served as outside directors.

George Spater, the former chairman of American Airlines who was not fined personally (he was the first executive to volunteer and accept the offer by Prosecutor Cox), went to live abroad. He was reportedly residing in Britain in the home occupied by novelist Virginia Woolf when she was working on the papers of her husband, Leonard.[34]

In view of the number of corporations convicted, one wonders whether there were more in 1972 that were not caught. For the most part, those who chose to volunteer the information at the invitation of Archibald Cox were found guilty. Inescapably, this leaves the suggestion that some did not step forward and some were never unearthed.[g]

In January 1975 a bill to amend sections 610 and 611 was introduced by Congressman George E. Danielson, D-California (of the House Judiciary Committee) that would significantly increase the penalties for illegal corporate contributions. The proposed amendment would provide that every corporation, labor organization, or government contractor making an unlawful campaign contribution be fined in an amount equal to the illegal contribution, in addition to any other fines or penalties. As Danielson pointed out, most of the corporations prosecuted for their illegal campaign contributions of 1972 got back the full amount of the contribution, and at most were fined the maximum $5,000 permitted by law for each count.[35]

Throughout, the FCRP maintained that it never solicited corporate contributions as such, only asking corporate executives to take responsibility to raise money from among other executives for the campaign. Target amounts were suggested, it was admitted, but no quotas were imposed. Targetting, however, suggests quotas that if unmet suggest problems for those not complying. The FCRP consistently held that no government contracts were awarded on the basis of contributions made, and that no harm came to corporations refusing to arrange for collections; some pointedly refused to consider giving. However, any amount was accepted in any form, cash or otherwise. In some cases corporations laundered the money but the FCRP itself had no laundry, did not encourage corporations to launder the money, and claims it had no knowledge if or when it occurred. Some corporations readily falsified information in lists of contributors supplied to fund raisers. When it was found that corporate money was involved, it was returned immediately. Subsequent disclosures showed that some corporations had maintained "slush funds" for years, and gave to Democrats as well as Republicans. The Ashland Oil Comapny gift to the Democratic National Committee (DNC) illustrates that both parties were caught up in the system, and unbelievably failed to question the true sources of so much cash.

The Nixon solicitations in 1972 were marked by excesses—excessive seeking of money, excessive requests for larger sums than were offered or were necessary for a healthy campaign. Because the campaign represented an incumbent

---

[g]For an extended discussion of the law, see William French Smith, *Corporate Political Contributions: The Law and the Practice* (Washington, D.C.: National Association of Manufacturers, May 1973).

administration, requests for funds were taken seriously, and were perceived by
some to border on extortion. Of course, extortion implies preying on innocent
or naive men, and the corporate executives were neither. Forms of solicitation
need not be criminal to be questionable. Because some corporations had maintained "slush funds" and had experience with and available means of laundering
money, one can readily assume that some company officials were eager to contribute, even by means they knew to be illegal, but in 1972 objected to the target amounts they considered excessive. Some corporate officials came forth
voluntarily and willingly when Special Prosecutor Cox invited confession, and
sought to put an end to the kind of corporate practice. Therefore, assuming no
intent to extort, a lesson for fund raisers representing incumbents is the need to
exercise moderation in approaching potential donors, whether or not direct
benefits in terms of policies, contracts, jobs, or favors can be perceived by the
donor, the recipient, or the public. Moderation was not the style in some fund
raising for the Nixon campaign, and a pattern of perceived pressure was reported
by so many corporate executives—of Chrysler, Ford, American Motors, Union
Oil, Allied Chemicals, Iowa Beef Processors, Gulf and Western, and others—that
they all could not have misjudged the zeal of some fund raisers caught up in an
effort to exceed all previous money drives, in an atmosphere that seemed to
exploit incumbency, with its implied (and inferred) power.

From the stories of the political slush funds maintained by some of America's largest corporations—touched off by the operations and criminal investigations started in mid-1973 by the Special Prosecutor's Office—a widening circle
of investigations began, which, by mid-1975, were being conducted by four
government agencies and one Senate subcommittee. The focus shifted from the
relatively limited area of illegal contributions to politicians in this country, to the
issue of multimillion-dollar efforts practiced by corporations seeking to obtain
contracts or influence abroad. In perspective, $100,000 to a presidential cam-
paign is not much compared with millions of dollars given in Italy, Korea, and
other countries.

The Securities and Exchange Commission, seeking to determine whether
corporate money had been spent abroad and not reported to stockholders,
auditors, or the government, found that Northrop had spent some $30 million
in payment to about 425 foreign agents. SEC action also brought to light a
$10 million secret slush fund maintained by Gulf Oil Corporation, which earlier
had pleaded guilty to $125,000 in illegal 1972 gifts. The commission charged
that $5.4 million in cash had gone into political campaigns between 1960 and
1974 from this fund, which was maintained through Gulf's Bahamas subsidiary.[36]
The SEC also found that Gulf Oil Corporation had made illegal gifts of $4 million
to South Korea's governing Democratic Republican party, with $3 million paid
before the 1971 election in which President Park Chung Hee's party was kept in
power by a thin majority.

In addition to the SEC investigations, the Civil Aeronautics Board, the

Internal Revenue Service, the Pentagon, and the Senate Foreign Relations Subcommittee on Multinational Corporations undertook investigations relative to their particular areas of interest. The CAB's concern was with possible violation of their strict accounting rules by airlines such as Braniff or American in the establishment of their secret funds. The CAB investigations were triggered by the suicide of the board's enforcement chief, William Gingery, on the eve of a Senate inquiry in February 1975. Gingery apparently believed he had failed in his duty to uncover illegal airline expenditures, and further suspected that large payments were being made for illicit purposes abroad.[37] He left behind a note accusing the agency of blocking a probe into illegal political contributions. The acting CAB chairman, Richard J. O'Melia, denied he had ordered investigations closed, and in turn charged his predecessor, Robert D. Timm, with having done so. Timm denied the charges. The investigations that then ensued revealed that American Airlines had an illegal fund of $275,000, which it had been spending since 1964 on scores of federal and state candidates. It was also learned that Braniff had a fund, totalling perhaps as much as $927,000, which it had used for similar purposes. The Braniff activities were technically the more serious of the two—involving the issuing, according to the CAB, of "at least 3,626 unreported flight tickets," from the sale of which the secret political fund was built up.[38] When the report of the Senate inquiry became known several months later, it charged that the CAB had prematurely ended an investigation into possible illegal campaign contributions by 34 airlines.[39]

The IRS wanted to know if some of the funds spent by American corporations abroad were illegally claimed as business expenses. The Pentagon sought accountings for its award of government contracts; many of the stories of bribery and corruption that emerged centered on arms sales. The Senate investigative effort, chaired by Senator Frank Church, D-Idaho, focused on the political impact of American business spending abroad; Gulf's chairman, Bob R. Dorsey, conceded to the Senate group that the corporation's $3 million spent on the 1971 Korean election might well have made the difference in keeping Park in power.[40]

The spate of new disclosures brought demands for some form of regulation of the multinational corporations. Some argued for new legislation that would require these corporations to disclose any payments they make to agents or politicians as well as to disclose any subsidiaries they set up overseas, while others suggested the establishment of an international code of conduct. The latter approach, apparently favored by the State Department, is being discussed at the United Nations and at the Organization for Economic Cooperation and Development.[41] A former assistant Secretary of the Treasury (now director of the Center for the Study of American Business at Washington University, St. Louis), Murray Weidenbaum, suggested diminishing the immense power government agencies exercise over business in the rewarding or withholding of contracts, subsidies, product approval, and the like.[42] Still another suggestion, by the president and chief executive officer of the Bendix Corporation, W. Michael Blumenthal, was that business itself establish a professional organization—similar to the American Medical Association, the bar associations, or the American Institute of Architects—which would devise and sustain standards of business ethics.[43]

Contributions Returned

As disclosures emerged during 1972 and 1973, the Finance Committee to Re-Elect the President returned the money that had been contributed to it improperly both by corporations and by individuals. Most of this money—totalling some $1,615,000—had been available to the Nixon campaign since before April 7, 1972; some, however, such as that of C.V. Whitney, was returned in 1971. The sum of $465,000 was returned to corporations that had made illegal contributions to the campaign, as shown in Table 13-1.

The FCRP also returned more than $1 million to seven individuals. Robert H. Allen of Texas was refunded the $100,000 in laundered money he had provided. Robert L. Vesco was refunded $250,000, including the $200,000 in cash

Table 13-1
Contributions Returned by Finance Committee to Re-Elect the President, 1971-73

Corporation or Individual	Amount of Contribution	Date Returned
American Airlines	$ 55,000	7/11/73
Ashland Oil, Inc.	100,000	7/17/73
Braniff Airways, Inc.	40,000	
Goodyear Tire & Rubber	40,000	8/10/73
Gulf Oil	100,000	7/26/73
Minnesota Mining & Mfg.	30,000	9/11/73
Phillips Petroleum Co.	100,000	8/17/73
Total Corporate Repayments	$ 465,000	
Robert H. Allen	$100,000	1/24/73
Walter T. Duncan	305,000	5/73
Ernesto Lagdameo	30,000	7/72
C. Arnholt Smith	200,000	3/28/72
Eric Ho Tung	15,000	9/7/72
Robert L. Vesco	250,000	1/31/73
Cornelius Vanderbilt Whitney	250,000	12/2/71
Total Individual Repayments	$1,150,000[a]	

[a]Does not include $100,000 returned to Howard Hughes by Rebozo.

he had donated while he was under investigation by the Securities and Exchange Commission.

C. Arnholt Smith, long-time friend and financial backer of Nixon (his support helped Nixon launch his first congressional bid in 1946), was refunded $200,000 in March 1972, shortly after he contributed it. His gigantic California business empire, including the U.S. National Bank of San Diego, was under investigation by the SEC, the Justice Department, and the Civil Aeronautics Board. Smith was subsequently indicted on five counts of unlawful corporate political contributions to Nixon's 1972 campaign and the 1970 campaign of Senator George Murphy, R-California. Already facing a federal court trial on a 25-count indictment for fraud, Smith pleaded not guilty to the charges of illegal campaign contributions on January 20, 1975. In March 1975 Smith was found guilty on two of the five counts, both charging that he had funneled corporate money to the 1970 Murphy campaign, by having associates in his business make the contributions and then later reimbursing them from company funds. The counts involving the 1972 Nixon contributions were dismissed after the jury told the judge that it could not agree.[44]

Walter T. Duncan, the Texas land speculator who also had "given" $300,000 to the Humphrey campaign, was refunded the $305,000 he had contributed to the Nixon campaign.

The FCRP also returned a $30,000 contribution from the former Philippine ambassador to the United States, Ernesto Lagdameo, and his associates. Maurice Stans told Watergate investigators the CRP decided not to accept the Lagdameo gift because of doubts about the legality of a foreign contribution; the sum was refunded out of pre-April 7 cash held by campaign aide Frederick C. LaRue.[45]

Cornelius Vanderbilt Whitney was given back the $250,000 he had contributed to Nixon in 1971. The money was refunded for fear its exposure in confirmation hearings might be linked to a reported promise made by John Mitchell, then Attorney General, that Whitney's name would be submitted for consideration for an ambassadorship to Spain. Whitney never got the appointment, apparently in part because of his advanced age.[46] He told investigators that the money was refunded because he did not want it to adversely affect the appointment.[47] Whitney did contribute $50,000 to Nixon in 1972, when he was no longer under consideration for the diplomatic post.

Also returned because of doubts over the legality of acceptance was $15,000 from Eric Ho Tung, born in Hong Kong. A November 1973 audit of the FCRP showed his $15,000 contribution returned shortly after its receipt because he was a foreign national.

Another contribution to Nixon, which was returned—not included in this compilation—was that of billionaire Howard R. Hughes. The $100,000 cash, held in a special secret fund for three years by Charles G. (Bebe) Rebozo, was returned in the spring of 1973 when it became the object of an IRS investigation.

In addition, the FCRP claims that more than $2.5 million in contributions offered were rejected, including $1 million from Italian financier Michele Sindona. All such rejections were based on instances in which either proposed conditions (such as nondisclosure) were attached to the potential gift, or the individual was considered by FCRP officials to have a questionable reputation or occupy a position, which might lead to pressure or suggested improprieties after a gift was made.

Democratic Contributions Returned

A few contributions were returned by Democratic presidential candidates of 1972, chiefly those who ascertained they had received an illegal corporate gift. But the usual response by candidates and their staffs was that they were never aware of the true source of the contributions, that they had appealed to corporate officials for personal contributions, knowing that corporate funds could not be given.

When the Special Prosecutor's Office brought charges against Gulf Oil Corporation, Congressman Wilbur Mills returned (from his personal account) the $15,000 he had received from that company. Senator Henry Jackson returned the $10,000 he had gotten from Gulf; he also returned $4,000 to a Los Angeles businessman, Leo Harvey. Harvey had given the Jackson campaign $10,000— $3,000 in his own name, $3,000 in his wife's name, $3,000 in his secretary's name, and $1,000 in his bookkeeper's name. The matter was referred by the GAO to the Justice Department, but no prosecution occurred.

The McGovern campaign returned $14,000 to Dominick Etcheverry of New York—a retired school teacher, administrator for the NCEC. Etcheverry had contributed $20,000 to the campaign on the condition that they meet and discuss McGovern's stand on issues, but the meeting never occurred, so Etcheverry stopped payment on the check. The McGovern campaign returned $14,000, which had already been drawn on the check.

Stans and the FCRP[h]

Maurice H. Stans was Secretary of Commerce when he resigned in February 1972 to become chairman of the Finance Committee to Re-Elect the President. Prior to this time the finance effort of the Nixon campaign had been conducted by a number of earlier committees under the direction of Hugh Sloan, Jr. and Lee Nunn, presumably without any direct participation by Stans.

---

[h]This section is based upon a number of interviews with the author on December 19, 1972; February 8, 1973; August 29, 1973; July 3, 1975; and July 11, 1975.

Stans acknowledges that when he became finance chairman he recognized the opportunity afforded by the law to raise a substantial amount of money before April 7, 1972. He believed that many contributors would want to take advantage of the option to keep their contributions confidential by giving before April 7, 1972. Stans organized accordingly, and by directing solicitations in the intervening period to major potential sources, the FCRP succeeded in raising $20 million before April 7. This was one third of the total raised for the entire campaign, and it gave the FCRP a substantial amount of the "early money" that presidential campaigns in other years had difficulty in raising.

Prior to joining the FCRP, Stans arranged with the campaign management for a separation of functions to prevent overlapping between the campaign organization (CRP) and the FCRP; representatives of the CRP and the FCRP would work together only on the budget committee. Under this plan, neither Stans nor the members of the FCRP would have any part in campaign strategy or tactics; and the CRP would have no responsibility for the solicitation or handling of money. The CRP would make commitments for the costs of running the campaign and would call upon the FCRP to pay all approved bills and to provide any funds requested. The FCRP would raise the money and meet the requirements of the CRP in any form they were presented. This helps to explain why Stans and the Finance Committee claim no knowledge of the activities, proper or improper, of the CRP, since they had agreed not to question the actions of the campaign management.

As of April 7 the previous structure involving hundreds of committees was terminated, and there were set up instead approximately 60 committees, one to perform the actual fund raising and disbursing in each state, plus five national committees dedicated to financing specific campaign functions such as radio, television, and other media. It was then arranged with each of the state committees to send to Washington all contributions in excess of $100 (excepting those placed in the states to enable contributors to avoid gift taxes), so they could be recorded, deposited, acknowledged, and reported through a centrally controlled computer system. Contributions of $100 or less were retained locally, and any additional campaign costs for each state were covered by monthly lump sum payments from Washington to the state affiliates, geared to the cash flow requirements of a campaign budget for each state approved by the national CRP. It was an efficient operation designed to comply with the new law, and it worked well except for the out-of-routine transactions that occurred.

As Watergate and its related disclosures unfolded in 1972 and 1973, Stans and the FCRP became the target of many accusations and insinuations of wrongdoing, ranging from the charge that he was the mastermind of the Watergate burglary to the accusation that he and the FCRP had been guilty of illegal fund-raising practices. This was a natural consequence of the climate of suspicion created by Watergate. Stans denies any complicity in the Watergate break-in or cover-up, or in such highly publicized matters as the dairy industry or I.T.T. contributions, and subsequent events have not established any links. He was charged, along with John Mitchell, with criminal conspiracy in connection with cash contributions by Robert Vesco, but was acquitted on all counts after a 70-day trial in New York early in 1974.

In January 1973 the FCRP was charged with eight misdemeanor offenses and was fined $8,000 for failure to report certain pre-April 7 payments to Gordon Liddy and Herbert Porter. The complaint, rising out of GAO investigations, named Hugh Sloan, Jr., the FCRP treasurer, as the person responsible for the failure to report, but did not charge him.[i] The FCRP pleaded nolo contendere and paid the fine.

Following this, Stans and the FCRP were accused in public hearings and in the press of a wide range of other illegal activities. It was asserted that the FCRP had an overseas "laundry" to which it sent illegal contributions and brought them back into the United States under fictitious names. It was accused of using coercion and even extortion in the raising of contributions, by taking advantage of persons known to be in trouble with the government; inversely, it was accused of making deals with such companies and individuals to relieve them of their problems in return for contributions. It was accused of the sale of ambassadorships and other government positions. It was accused of making corporate solicitations. It was accused of having received many large contributions that it failed to report; and it was charged with a wide range of other infractions of the law.

The Senate Watergate Committee and the Office of the Special Prosecutor investigated these charges and few indictments were made. Of course, some violations may have been found but reduced in plea bargaining. Whereas the FCRP had no laundry with which to disguise the source of funds,[j] a number of contributors "laundered" contributions on their own before delivering them, without any known participation in that process by the FCRP. The FCRP claims it had no list of companies in trouble with the government, practiced no coercion

---

[i]Sloan later noted that his being named in the charge was evidently agreed to by the CRP and the Justice Department without his knowledge. He learned of it only after the plea had been entered, and would have contested the action as an inaccurate assessment of responsibility had he been aware of the situation at the time.

[j]One other use of the term "laundering" surfaced in connection with a deposition given by Henry M. Buchanan, an accountant who worked with the FCRP (he is a brother of Patrick J. Buchanan, one of President Nixon's speech writers), and released on June 27, 1973. The deposition was given in connection with the Common Cause suit seeking disclosure of sources of pre-April 7 contributions. H.M. Buchanan described an outside bank account opened in 1971 at the direction of Hugh Sloan. According to Buchanan, funds were deposited, and in five instances checks were drawn and cashed, at the direction of Jeb Magruder, to pay secretly a salary supplement to an unidentified CRP employee who felt he was not earning as much as he deserved. This use of the term "laundering," however, differs from the described corporate laundering of funds through foreign banks to convert intended contributions into cash in order to disguise the time source of funds.

or extortion of contributors and offered no deals to contributors to help them with government problems. Ironically, the major published instances in which the words "coercion" or "extortion" were used were those of executives of corporations that had made illegal contributions, that had laundered their contributions in other countries, and that it was learned later had a history of making illegal contributions and had made substantially similar contributions to the 1968 Nixon campaign. Under these circumstances, insinuations of extortion in 1972 were hard to evaluate. Stans and the FCRP claim not to have offered or sold ambassadorships or government positions and apparently were careful to avoid circumstances in which such transactions might be inferred. Stans admits recording every expression of interest in a government policy or job by any prospective contributor and reporting that interest to the White House after the election, whether or not the individual made a contribution.

One transaction in 1970 by Herbert Kalmbach, apparently with the approval of the White House, did involve the sale of an ambassadorship, and Kalmbach pleaded guilty to the charge; but this occurred about a year before the FCRP was formed. Stans claims that neither he nor anyone authorized by the FCRP solicited illegal contributions from corporations; the FCRP did develop a group solicitation plan—described elsewhere—whereby officers and employees of corporations and organizations could be solicited by an officer of the corporation; while these may have been set up on a partisan or bipartisan basis, there is no proven record of anyone connected with the FCRP suggesting that company funds be given. Subsequent disclosures showed that about 20 corporations did make illegal contributions, either by using corporate funds or by reimbursing employees for contributions made by them. The FCRP returned a total of $465,000 to seven corporations when it was learned that the contributions were illegal.

In the course of postelection developments, Stans was also accused of having raised money during the time that he was Secretary of Commerce, particularly in 1970, but no evidence of such actions on his part was forthcoming. In one instance Herbert Kalmbach testified in open court that Stans had participated in soliciting a contribution in 1971, but the contributor and the intermediary in that instance both provided affidavits later stating that Stans did not so participate and was not aware of the contribution.

Allegations were also made that Stans asked contributors to give in the form of cash. The prosecutors in the Vesco case (the Mitchell-Stans trial in New York) sought to establish that practice by questioning contributors across the country, but all of them apparently stated that Stans had indicated the contribution could be made in any form that the contributor chose.

To meet the contention that the FCRP was hungry for money, Stans claims that more than $4 million in contributions was either returned or rejected. This included the return of illegal corporate contributions and of contributions from individuals whose integrity was in question, and the refusal to accept contributions from persons attaching conditions to them.

In March 1975 Stans did plead guilty to five misdemeanor infractions of the election laws in Federal Court in Washington and in May was fined a total of $5,000 for them (he later asked the CLT for reimbursement for the fine). The court found that these were nonwillful violations of the laws, involving two counts of unknowingly receiving illegal corporate funds and three counts of late reporting.

One of the illegal contributions was for $40,000, which Stans received from an official of Goodyear Tire and Rubber Co., and the other was for $30,000 from Minnesota Mining and Manufacturing Co., both given in March 1972. Stans states that both companies later supplied him with the names of individual employees allegedly contributing the funds, but eventually admitted that the lists were false and that the funds were corporate funds. The two companies also acknowledged a long-standing practice of making illegal contributions to others as well.

Goodyear and 3M pleaded guilty to making illegal contributions and both companies and certain of their officers were fined. Officers of the companies acknowledged before the Senate Watergate Committee that they had given corporate funds illegally—they thought safely since it was before the April 7 disclosure date—and then had drawn up false lists of contributors. When the true sources of the funds were made known to Stans, the FCRP immediately returned each of the contributions.

The three remaining misdemeanors were for failure to report on three transactions which Stans claimed he understood were not of a type to require reporting. These consisted of: $30,000 offered to Stans in June 1972 by Ernesto Lagdameo, former ambassador from the Philippines; a transfer of $81,000 in the summer of 1972 by Stans and Hugh Sloan, Jr. to Frederick LaRue for LaRue to hold; and contributions totalling $39,000, given on November 3, 1972 and January 17, 1973 by the former Governor of Montana, Tim Babcock.

Some of the money in these three transactions became involved in the Watergate cover-up; in fairness, no evidence establishes that Stans had knowledge of it. The $30,000 Lagdameo money was part of $75,100 that Stans transferred to Herbert Kalmbach a few weeks after the Watergate break-in, at a time when Kalmbach was gathering up money to pay the burglars and their counsel; Kalmbach testified that he concealed this purpose from Stans, saying only that he needed money for an important White House project, which he would not disclose and concerning which Stans would have to trust him. Some of the $81,000, which Stans and Sloan gave to LaRue to hold, was paid by LaRue to Kalmbach without the knowledge of Stans or Sloan, and apparently used by Kalmbach for payments to the burglars. Of the money from Babcock, $14,000 went directly from Stans to LaRue and may have been similarly used by LaRue after he took over Kalmbach's role of financing the cover-up.

Stans was the third former member of Nixon's cabinet, after Mitchell and

Kleindienst, to be found guilty following the 1972 campaign. Stans explained his guilty plea at the time as follows:

> I pleaded guilty today in Federal Court to five misdemeanors under the election financing laws in 1972. In each of these transactions I made a good faith judgment at the time that the Finance Committee was complying with the law, but it now turns out that was not the case. I have done this after long deliberation and full advice of counsel, for these reasons:
>
> (1) This disposition, I believe establishes once and for all that I had no guilty involvement in the Watergate burglary, the Watergate coverup, the Segretti sabotage, the ITT case, the White House plumbers affair, or the 1971 dairy industry dealings. At no time have the Special Prosecutor or the Justice Department alleged that I played any guilty part in those matters, and this action puts that conclusion on the record. This is important, in view of the many baseless public charges against me in recent years.
>
> (2) The plea relates to three instances in which campaign receipts or disbursements were not reported on time and two instances in which I nonwillfully and unknowingly took in illegal contributions, out of the hundreds of thousands of contributions and expenditures in the 1972 campaign. During the campaign I took every possible step to adhere to the law and instructed the Finance Committee's entire organization to do so, too. The violations now disclosed were not willful, and at the time they occurred were not believed to be violations. . . .[48]

Stans claims he was inadvertently caught in minor charges of a nature that had not previously been prosecuted in the history of the Corrupt Practices Act, and that the court found were not willful. In his testimony before the Senate Watergate Committee in June 1973, he contended that he was innocent of any wrongdoing, with the possible exception of minor technicalities. At the conclusion of his testimony he asked the committee in its report to "give me back my good name." While that seemed unlikely at the time to the members of the committee, and the Senate *Report* did not make a judgment because he was then under investigation, the extensive investigations of Stans and the FCRP by the Senate Committee and the Special Prosecutor seem to have established that their methods of operation, apart from their known infractions, were acceptable.

Stans was, without dispute, the most successful political fund raiser in American history, Mark Hanna and Matthew McCloskey notwithstanding. Considering his roles in 1968 pre- and postnomination for Nixon, when at least $35 million was raised centrally, and in 1972, when more than $60 million more was raised, the record is clear. This leaves the question of judgment in raising so much money if it was not needed. Nixon fund raisers claim they could have raised $100 million in anti-McGovern money, if they had wanted to. One fund raiser suggested that Stans could have raised another $10 million readily had he not been distracted by the Common Cause suit. By agreement, and because money was so easy to raise for an incumbent President, funds were turned over by the finance managers to the political operatives at their request, without questioning the reasons for which it was needed or the purposes for which it would be spent. The matters of why so much cash was accepted, apparently with no questions asked, and once raised, why the cash was not better controlled on all levels of distribution, remain. More than $4 million came in cash, some from individual contributors of good reputation. It is notable that so many fund raisers were so insensitive as not to ask the source of so much cash, especially when it was presented by corporate officers; and that cash was turned over to members of the CRP and White House inner circle merely for the asking, with no questions raised. It was not illegal to give or accept or pay out cash, and the practice of using cash was an important legacy of the traditional way of doing business in politics; no other campaign in history is known to have used it so lavishly, however. The 1974 Amendments prohibit cash contributions in excess of $100.

In addition to Stans, the major fund raisers were Herbert Kalmbach and Lee Nunn. Nunn was responsible for at least three solicitations that later became controversial: those of Cornelius Vanderbilt Whitney, Gulf Oil, and some of the dairy money.

The name of Hugh W. Sloan, Jr. surfaced often in the Watergate developments and hearings. Sloan worked at the Republican National Finance Committee (RNFC) prior to Nixon's nomination in 1968, in the joint RNFC-presidential campaign finance activities. He was hired for the White House staff on January 20, 1969, as staff assistant to the President. In March 1971 Sloan left the White House to work on the reelection effort. He became chairman of the finance arm of the reelection organization on October 1, 1971. In February 1972, when Maurice Stans took over as chairman, Sloan became treasurer of the FCRP, a position he held until he resigned on July 14, 1972.

Sloan told Common Cause attorneys (in sealed testimony made public May 4, 1973) that the CRP had solicited "somewhere between $1 and $2 million" in secret cash contributions between 1971 and early 1972, and that the daily records and working papers were subsequently destroyed,[49] although summary reports covering the transactions were available. On June 6, 1973 he gave the Senate Watergate Committee a detailed accounting of nearly $1.8 million in cash disbursements made by the finance committee during the spring of 1972, but said he did not know at the time what the funds were being used for, and had been told not to concern himself with the matter. Sloan also described the "nightmare" of handling millions of dollars ($5-$6 million received in two days prior to the April 7 disclosure date), and said he had chosen to resign from the FCRP rather than perjure himself or take the Fifth Amendment during testimony in the Watergate trial about his disbursement of funds to

Gordon Liddy. Following his resignation from the FCRP, and after his legal
position relating to pending civil suits was clear, he was employed by that committee intermittently as a consultant. By then the election was won and Sloan
assisted Stans in the winding down and settlement of finances and also with
some of the legal questions raised.

The Vesco Case

One of the most controversial contributions to the Nixon campaign was for
$250,000 all but $50,000 in cash, from New Jersey financier Robert Vesco.
Vesco, along with former Attorney General and Nixon campaign manager John
Mitchell, and former Secretary of Commerce and head of the FCRP Maurice
Stans, was indicted by a federal grand jury in New York City in May of 1973.
Vesco fled to Costa Rica before the indictment, and has thwarted all efforts to
extradite him. He had been charged in a civil action by the Securities and Exchange Commission in November 1972, with looting $224 million from foreign
mutual funds he controlled.

Mitchell and Stans were indicted on 15 counts[k] for criminal conspiracy,
obstruction of justice, and perjury in their testimony to the grand jury in connection with Vesco's $200,000 cash contribution. These were the first indict-
ments of former cabinet officers since the Teapot Dome scandal during the
Harding administration; it was the first time former cabinet officers had stood
trial together in United States history. Also indicted was Harry L. Sears—Vesco
attorney, former New Jersey State Senate Republican majority leader, Nixon
New Jersey campaign manager, and associate of former New Jersey Governor
Cahill. Also a casualty of the Vesco affair was SEC chairman G. Bradford Cook,
who resigned after controversy developed over the revelation that he had participated in expunging certain references to the Vesco contribution from the
SEC civil charges against Vesco.

Vesco's problems with the SEC became widely known when a federal judge
in New Jersey dismissed his suit in May 1971, to block the SEC probe into financial manipulation within the Vesco-controlled International Controls Corporation (ICC) in Fairfield, New Jersey, and Investors Overseas Services, Ltd. (IOS)
in Geneva, Switzerland. A few months later Vesco was released on bail in
Geneva from a complaint alleging improper business conduct in that country.
It was revealed later that Sears, an ICC director, had succeeded in arranging for
then Attorney General Mitchell to phone the American embassy in Berne to
express interest in Vesco's release. Shortly after the November election, the
SEC filed suit charging that Vesco and others had misappropriated IOS money,

---

[k]One conspiracy count and two obstruction of justice counts jointly against the two
men, plus six perjury counts against each.

and asking the court to place IOS and ICC in receivership for protection of investors.[1]

In the early stages of the SEC investigation, FCRP Vice-Chairman Daniel Hofgren routinely approached a Vesco business associate for a contribution. Hofgren denied knowing about the SEC investigation. About this same time Sears asked Mitchell on behalf of Vesco to arrange an appointment with SEC Chairman William J. Casey. Sears also visited Stans and discussed a Vesco contribution, but no meeting with Casey was forthcoming.

Vesco decided that he wanted to give $500,000 but Sears dissuaded him from giving so much because, as he said, "(it) would have been open to an unfavorable interpretation," in light of the SEC probe.[50] Sears testified that he met with Stans on April 3 "to finalize the arrangements" for the contribution, which was to be given to Stans in New York on April 6, the day before the new campaign act went into effect. Sears further testified that at some point another Vesco associate asked Edward Nixon to call CRP to confirm that the contribution was wanted in currency and he understood second-hand that Nixon had done so.

When Stans failed to make his expected April 6 trip to New York, Sears and ICC president Laurence B. Richardson, Jr., flew to Washington on April 10 in an ICC plane with a briefcase containing $200,000 in cash, which they delivered to Stans. Less than two hours later Sears met with Mitchell to inquire again about the SEC appointment, and on May 11 Sears met with Casey and Cook to discuss the case. It was agreed at the meeting that Cook, who was then SEC counsel, would personally look into the Vesco situation.

On January 31, 1973 the $200,000 unreported cash contribution and the $50,000 reported contribution were returned to Vesco by FCRP with a letter suggesting that the refund was "[in] your best interest, as well as ours," and explaining, "[it] has come to our attention that you ... are under investigation by the SEC." De Van Shumway, spokesman for FCRP, said that the decision to refund the contribution was made shortly after the SEC civil suit was filed, but had no explanation for the delay until January 31 (five days after the *Washington Star-News* reporter James Polk broke the story about the contribution) to return the money. Stans said the delay was caused largely by the FCRP lawyers in deciding how the accompanying letter should be worded.

Stans asserted that even though the Vesco money had been received on April 10, it was not reported because he believed a contribution pledged prior to April 7 qualified under the law as a contribution constructively made before that date. This interpretation of the law, Stans asserted, was followed "on advice of counsel." The GAO did not agree, referred the case to the Attorney General for apparent violations of the law, and the FCRP later was fined the maximum of $1,000 on each of three counts.

---

[1]See Robert A. Hutchison, "The Looting of I.O.S.," *Fortune*, March, 1973, pp. 126-40, for an account of Vesco's rise and fall in international finance.

Mitchell-Stans Trial

The trial of Mitchell and Stans, before Federal Judge Lee P. Gagliardi in New York City, began on February 19, 1974. By then Vesco had become a fugitive in the Bahamas and Costa Rica with both nations refusing to extradite him. Sears, the Vesco attorney, was granted immunity, and testified at the Mitchell-Stans trial for both the defense and the prosecution. During 31 days of testimony, 59 witnesses were heard, including two former chairman of the SEC; both of the President's brothers, Edward and F. Donald Nixon; John W. Dean, III; and Rose Mary Woods, the President's long-time personal secretary.

Mitchell and Stans were acquitted of all criminal charges on April 28.[51] The government contended that Vesco had promised to contribute a large sum of money to the FCRP if Stans and Mitchell would exert their influence at the SEC, and that Stans wanted the contribution in cash in order to keep it secret. Edward C. Nixon, President Nixon's younger brother, testified that Stans had not asked for cash but said he would take the contribution in any form Vesco wanted to give it.

Sears testified that he had gone to Washington with ICC president Laurence Richardson on April 10, 1972—three days after the disclosure deadline—and delivered to Stans an attache case containing $200,000 in $100 and $50 bills. Two hours later, he said, he arranged with Mitchell a meeting with SEC chairman William Casey. Mitchell denied any recollection of that meeting; the defense further contended that if Mitchell had called Casey, he was merely doing what any congressman might do for a constituent, but not breaking the law.

The government then contended, primarily in testimony by John Dean, that Mitchell had on a number of occasions shortly before the November election talked about the SEC investigation, with a view to keeping new impending subpoenas quiet. In the testimony of G. Bradford Cook, former SEC counsel, the prosecution tried to show how Cook, who said that in talking with Stans about his desire to become the SEC head he had also discussed the Vesco case, sought to get an embarrassing paragraph in the SEC suit deleted from the record. The paragraph discussed the movement of $250,000 in cash transferred by Vesco from the Bahamas to his New York bank, and moved around by associates, ultimately to his New Jersey office where it was hidden in the base of a lamp. More importantly, the original paragraph, which stressed lack (and refusal at SEC hearings) of disclosure regarding disposition of the $250,000, was changed; in the SEC suit filed on November 27, 1972, it said merely that unaccounted for "sums of cash had been transferred between Vesco and other groups . . . ."[52]

The bulk of the Mitchell and Stans defense was the question of their credibility as against that of Sears, Cook, and Dean, a defense that was reportedly very persuasive to the jury. Stans told the jury that when he had testified before the grand jury earlier, the testimony that led to his perjury counts, the near-fatal illness of his wife had caused him to become hazy as to certain dates and events, and he had not been given time to refresh his recollection. One juror later commented: "I think Vesco was the real culprit of this whole thing."[53]

A matter with broader implications for the picture of 1972 campaign contributions emerged during the testimony of Rose Mary Woods. She was called to show that a list of contributors to the FCRP before the April 7 cutoff did not include Vesco's name and thus support the contention by the prosecution that Mitchell and Stans were attempting to hide his $200,000 contribution. On cross-examination, however, a second list of pre-April 7 contributors emerged, one that did include Vesco's name, circled and with a question mark. Miss Woods said the list was meant to be of persons who might receive White House dinner invitations at a later date.[54]

Following the acquittal of Mitchell and Stans, several attempts at extraditing Vesco from Costa Rica by United States authorities were made. The newly elected President of that country, however, subsequently charged the Nixon administration of being "less than sincere" in its efforts to return Vesco to the United States to stand trial.[55] In early 1975 Vesco remained in Costa Rica amid some internal criticism of his finding refuge there.

The Babcock Case

One case involved the former Governor of Montana, Tim M. Babcock. In December 1974 Babcock pleaded guilty to being the middleman for $54,000 in illegal campaign contributions from Armand Hammer, the president of Occidental Petroleum, a Los Angeles-based company that in 1974 signed a $20 billion trade contract with the Soviet Union. Babcock, who was at the time of the contributions a vice-president of an Occidental subsidiary, made the contributions in the names of four other Occidental officials, when in fact the money came from Hammer as part of a $100,000 contribution from the Occidental president to Nixon. Hammer had previously contributed $46,000 in cash the period before the April 7 disclosure went into effect.[56]

On January 31, 1975 Babcock was sentenced to serve four months in the federal prison at Lompock, California. In passing sentence U.S. District Court Chief Judge George L. Hart, Jr. told the former governor:

> When you broke the law, you knew you were breaking it, and thereafter you tried to cover it up [a reference to Babcock's having used the "cover" of the four other names], . . .
>
> Mr. Babcock, in your case you were not some untrained underling who had to dance to the tune of a boss. You were independently wealthy . . . . You could have told Hammer you had no intention of assisting him in breaking the law and [could] have been impervious to any penalty of any sort that meant anything.[57]

Investigators said the only apparent reason for the use of Babcock as a go-between was to preserve Hammer's anonymity.

Howard Hughes, Bebe Rebozo, and $100,000

One of Watergate's remaining mysteries is the matter of the $100,000 gift from millionaire recluse Howard Hughes to the Nixon campaign, which Charles G. (Bebe) Rebozo, Nixon's close friend, claims he kept intact, in $100 bills, before returning them to Hughes in 1973.

The mystery is replete with conflicting evidence as to when the $100,000 was delivered to Rebozo, where it was delivered, and for what purpose. It is not certain that all of it was meant for the 1972 campaign. Some of it may have been a "payment past due" from the 1968 campaign; by another account, part was meant for the 1970 congressional elections.

One of the story's deepest roots can be traced back to the 1956 election, when a principal in the 1972 effort used Hughes' money to bankroll an operation that the then vice-president could use in his fight against the "Dump Nixon" campaign.[m] Another element dates from the same year—a $205,000 loan from Hughes Tool Company to the president's brother, Donald, the purpose of which is not clear.

Apart from Nixon and Hughes, the story also involved other familiar figures, among them the President's personal secretary, Rose Mary Woods, and his personal lawyer, Herbert Kalmbach. It was the first time, as the Senate Watergate Committee developed the story,[n] that Nixon's long-time friend, Bebe Rebozo, figured in any significant way in the investigations. Others who played a key role in some accounts were:

> *Robert Maheu,* the general manager of Hughes' gambling and hotel interests at the time the gift was made, who, by the time the story broke, had been fired by Hughes and was suing him for libel

---

[m]In 1956 Harold Stassen organized what became known as the "Dump Nixon" movement, and had a poll conducted, which showed that certain other Republicans, notably Secretary of State Christian Herter, would add more strength to the ticket than Nixon would. Robert Maheu, testifying in 1974 in his suit against Hughes, told how, with Hughes money, he had infiltrated the Stassen camp, and learned of the survey. He recruited a group of ex-FBI agents (Maheu was a former agent) to conduct a "counter-poll." The results, radically different from the one conducted for Stassen by a professional survey organization, showed Nixon the strongest candidate. Maheu turned them over to the late Senator Styles Bridges of New Hampshire who released them. Maheu said this was the beginning of what he termed his "influence" within the Nixon organization. ("Maheu Says Unit Aided Nixon in '56," *The New York Times*, May 11, 1974.)

[n]When the Senate Watergate Committee went out of existence, its files on the Hughes-Rebozo matter were turned over to the Office of the Special Prosecutor. No action by that office had been taken at this writing.

Richard Danner, another Hughes aide and an official in the 1968 Nixon campaign; he had introduced Nixon to Rebozo early in Nixon's political career

Edward P. Morgan, a Hughes lawyer

Paul Laxalt, former Republican governor of Nevada

Robert H. Abplanalp, millionaire friend of Nixon and Rebozo

Robert Bennett, president of a Washington public relations firm; he was responsible for setting up the multiple dummy committees through which large dairy contributions were channelled to Nixon's reelection campaign;[58] and the firm managed Hughes' interests and a Hughes trust account in Washington, D.C.

Although denials by one party or another of motives, timing and location frequent the testimony obtained by Senate Watergate investigations at virtually every step of the way, the Senate staff constructed the following sequence of events.

In the summer of 1968 Nixon and Rebozo met with Danner and discussed a possible contribution from Hughes for that year's campaign. Danner subsequently took the matter up with Morgan who relayed it on to Maheu in Las Vegas, where Hughes was then living, secluded in a top floor penthouse of one of his hotels. Maheu said Hughes wanted to make a gift, provided that Nixon personally—but privately—acknowledged it. Morgan took this news back to Washington where he met in September 1968 with Rebozo and Danner to discuss the candidate's acknowledgment of the gift.

In testimony given in the Maheu civil suit against Hughes, Danner said that Rebozo at one point that fall virtually decided to drop the idea of the gift as he had been told that Nixon's brother Donald would be involved in delivery of the money, along with another Hughes aide, John Meier.[59] Danner said Rebozo told him he wanted nothing to do with these two men relating to political contributions.

Adding greatly to the confusion is the fact that the Hughes gift was made in two installments of $50,000 each (and some have theorized that there were more than two installments, and a total greater than $100,000).° The first attempt at making the initial $50,000 contribution came in December 1968, with Nixon

---

°It should be noted, at the risk of adding even more confusion, that Hughes made other contributions to Nixon that were reported, both in 1968 and 1972. In the former year he contributed a reported $50,000, while in 1972 his reported contributions amounted to $150,000. The $100,000 that lay in Rebozo's safety deposit box was never disclosed until 1973.

then President-elect. According to Danner, in early December Maheu and then
Governor Laxalt went to Palm Springs, California, where Nixon was staying at
the home of Walter Annenberg, with a view to giving the money directly to Nixon.
They were informed, however, that the President-elect's schedule would not permit such a meeting.

Two cash sums of $50,000 each apparently were put together by the Hughes
organization at this time.[P] Nadine Henry, Hughes' long-time personal secretary,
on instruction from Maheu, gathered together one sum of $50,000, while Maheu
also got $50,000 from the cage at the Sands casino in Las Vegas. And records
show that fifty consecutively numbered $100 bills deposited in the Las Vegas
bank used by the Hughes casinos during this same period were among those that
Rebozo had identified as being used in the first delivery.

In the Senate investigators' reconstruction, the first $50,000 did not actually
get to Rebozo until some nine months later, in mid-September 1969, in Key
Biscayne, Florida. Maheu authorized the payment in early September (what had
happened to the two earlier $50,000 sums is simply not clear), and Danner said
that was when he had made the first payment.

Rebozo, however, claimed that the initial payment was not made until July
1970, and was meant as a contribution for that year's congressional campaigns;
after consultation with Rebozo, Danner changed his story and said he agreed on
the latter date. A further discrepancy arose as to where the payment was made—
Rebozo said San Clemente definitely, Maheu said Key Biscayne definitely, while
Danner said that he had made one of two deliveries at San Clemente, and that
July 3, 1970 was the only time he was at the Western White House. (Danner
joined the Hughes organization on a full-time basis in January 1969, after his
role in the 1968 Nixon campaign.)

Still more conflicts are evident in the testimony as to when and where the
second payment of $50,000 was made.[q] Rebozo claimed both payments were
in 1970, while Danner and Maheu offered inconsistent accounts. The attempts
by Watergate investigators to pin down dates and places were unavailing; the
matter of when the money arrived had considerable relevance in seeking to
determine why it was given. If, for example, the first payment was in July 1970,
as Rebozo claimed, its legitimacy as a 1970 congressional campaign contribution
is far more believable. If made in the summer of 1969, however, it raises the
question of whether it was a final payment on a 1968 campaign pledge, again

---

[P]Hughes' gifts to Democratic contenders in 1968 were also reported. Maheu testified
that $25,000 was given to Lawrence O'Brien, shortly after Robert Kennedy's death, to ful-
fill a promise made before the assassination. He also said he had made a gift on Hughes'
behalf to Hubert Humphrey, a contribution Humphrey said he did not remember receiving.
(Wallace Turner, "Defamation Trial of *Maheu v. Hughes Corporation* Opens on Coast,"
The New York Times, February 27, 1974.)

[q]The total sum may have been $100,100 since the Watergate staff, when it photo-
copied the money, came up with 1,001 bills.

legitimate, or whether it might have been a payment for favors rendered in July 1969, when the purchase by Hughes of Air West was sanctioned by the federal government; five years later Hughes was indicted of stock manipulation in effecting this takeover, but the indictment was subsequently dismissed.

Another element as to possible motivation behind the second $50,000 surfaced in 1974 when it was revealed that Danner, the man who all agreed had delivered both payments—whenever or wherever—had visited then Attorney General John Mitchell in Washington in March 1970.[60] Danner asked Mitchell for help in a casino purchase Hughes wished to make of The Dunes, by seeking a reversal of a 1968 Justice Department ruling prohibiting Hughes from buying any more casinos (he then owned five). Over objections of his Justice Department aides, Mitchell told Danner he saw no problems, and to go ahead with the purchase. The Dunes purchase subsequently fell through, but Maheu later testified that he had authorized the second $50,000 only after Danner returned from the meeting with Mitchell.

Rebozo's story was that he had taken the two deliveries from Danner to be a contribution to the 1972 election campaign. He said he had put the two envelopes in a safe deposit box at his Key Biscayne bank, after having removed from the money paper bands that said "Las Vegas" on them. He testified that he had decided not to turn the money over to the 1972 campaign effort after the Hughes-Maheu split in December 1970, and that the bills remained intact in his safe deposit box until he returned them to Hughes in the summer of 1973, after learning that the IRS was looking into the matter of the contribution.

Rebozo's account was disputed, however, by Herbert Kalmbach, in March 1974 testimony before the Senate Watergate Committee. Kalmbach said that Rebozo had sought his advice, shortly after he learned of the IRS probe, because the money was not intact, and that part of it had been given or loaned to Rose Mary Woods and F. Donald Nixon. Both parties denied this, while Rebozo stuck to his story. According to Kalmbach, the President told Rebozo to talk with him about this money.

Both Nixon and Rebozo, seeking to reinforce their claim that the money had not been touched, said that an FBI agent had examined the bills before they were returned. But when the agent, Kenneth Whitaker, testified before the Senate Watergate committee he said he was unable to verify that it was the same money given by Danner three or four years earlier because the bills were not new, nor were the serial numbers consecutive.

About a week before Rebozo returned $100,000 to the Hughes organization, he met with Robert Abplanalp. Rebozo said it was just a luncheon meeting; the Senate investigators theorized, but never established, that he turned to Abplanalp for help in making up whatever money might have been used from the original $100,000.

The Hughes gift was clearly a matter of great concern to the White House. When it first became public, in August 1971, there was apparently consternation, and reportedly something akin to panic when, several months later, Hank Greenspun, editor of the *Las Vegas Sun*, asked whether the Hughes contribution had been used to help buy San Clemente. Kalmbach was dispatched to see what Greenspun might know, particularly of the Hughes relationship with Donald Nixon. He found out nothing, but the White House subsequently learned, reportedly first from Robert Bennett, that Greenspun could well have hard evidence in his possession—hand-written memos by Hughes to Maheu, which Maheu had taken with him when Hughes abruptly fired him in December 1970. Bennett was president of the Washington public relations firm that represented Hughes (and also, it was later revealed, served as a cover for the CIA).

Bennett also figured in another Hughes contribution to Nixon, reported at $100,000, in which signed blank checks were given to the CRP. Sally Harmony, who was G. Gordon Liddy's secretary, said that she had typed in the names of various fund-raising committees on the checks, but could not recall the total amount. Bennett was the Hughes agent who signed the checks; he said the amount had been fixed in advance at $50,000 and that the use of blank checks was strictly a clerical matter. Other sources, however, said the total amount of money involved was $100,000.[61]

In early 1972 both Jack Anderson and *The New York Times* said they had hard evidence of connections between Hughes and Rebozo.[62] The day after the *Times* report on February 3, Gordon Liddy presented a revised version of his campaign espionage scheme, this one at $500,000, to John Mitchell and others. Magruder, who was at the meeting, said later that Mitchell showed enthusiasm for using the project to break into Greenspun's office in Nevada, as well as Lawrence O'Brien's office in Washington. Liddy's proposal was subsequently further modified to the effected $250,000 Watergate burglary scheme.

The role of Bennett's firm was unclear, but Watergate Committee investigators placed it somewhere near the mystery of the Hughes-Rebozo fund; they felt the fund could be larger than $100,000, involving several deliveries of $50,000, all of it reportedly available as testified to by Maheu and others. More than two deliveries would help explain some of the discrepancies.

As for the motivations for the break-in, it has been noted that two phones were tapped—O'Brien's (unsuccessfully) and that of R. Spencer Oliver, Jr., chairman of the association of Democratic State Chairmen, who was not a staff member of the DNC, but merely had offices there for convenience. Robert Oliver, Spencer's father, was employed at Mullen and Company, Bennett's PR firm, as was E. Howard Hunt at the time of the break-in. When Bennett came to Washington to work for Mullen and Company, he brought with him the Hughes Tool Company as a client. And the man within the firm who specifically represented the Hughes interests was Oliver senior. Somewhere in this mix, investigators have postulated, may lie the ultimate reason for the Watergate break-in—perhaps a hunt for evidence relating to the Hughes $100,000, thought to be in the Democrat's possession, which the burglars were instructed to remove.

The waters got even murkier in July 1974, when a few days after the judge in the Maheu civil suit said he wanted Hughes' lawyers to produce more of the 500 hand-written memoes from Hughes to Maheu they claimed for their case, Hughes' headquarters in Los Angeles were broken into by a professional safe-cracking team, and two chests full of Hughes' personal papers were stolen. Within a few weeks, an extortion demand was made by a mysterious phone call, asking $1 million for return of the papers. The demand was rejected on grounds the papers would probably have been copied.

The real explosion from this burglary, however, did not occur until seven months later, in March 1975, when it was revealed, first by *The Los Angeles Times* and then in a detailed account by *The New York Times'* Seymour Hersh, that among the papers stolen were those outlining the multimillion dollar contract, by some estimates upwards of $300 million, between the Hughes organization and the CIA to build the Glomar Explorer, the ship that attempted to salvage a sunken Russian submarine from three miles deep in the Pacific. This set off a new round of speculation about the degree of involvement between Howard Hughes and the Nixon administration. Senator Frank Church of Idaho, who was chairing the Senate's investigations into the CIA, announced that his committee was preparing to look further into the matter of Hughes' campaign contribution.

Hughes had been in the business of secret campaign contributions since at least the 1940s. According to Noah Dietrich, the man who helped manage Hughes' financial affairs for over three decades, Hughes managed to funnel hundreds of thousands of dollars to politicians, in apparently legal fashion, with contributions from foreign subsidiaries.[63]

Additional Funds

Although he testified in the Common Cause suit against the FCRP that he had never been a fund raiser, Bebe Rebozo figured in a number of other contributions besides that of Howard Hughes to the 1972 campaign; the total, counting the Hughes money, would appear to be near the half-million dollar mark.[64]

Shortly after Nixon took office in 1969, he asked Rebozo to contact oil millionaire John Paul Getty for a major contribution. Rebozo subsequently arranged with Getty for Kalmbach to meet him and the CRP filings reflect a 1972 Getty contribution of $125,000. Rebozo also arranged an appointment for Kalmbach with former U.S. Ambassador to Ireland (1965-68) Raymond Guest, a contact that produced $200,000 for the FCRP.

On April 5, 1972 Rebozo opened an account with a $10,000 deposit of two checks from contributors at the Key Biscayne Bank & Trust Co.; the next day— one day before disclosure deadline—he had $10,000 from the account wired to the FCRP. The FCRP took over this account in its name and Rebozo subsequently deposited $29,740 in additional contributions which the FCRP then transferred to Washington.

At first Rebozo omitted any reference in his Senate testimony to a pre-April 7 gift of $50,000, which he received from A.D. and J.E. Davis, brothers who own the Winn-Dixie store chain; when asked about the Davis gift some months later, he acknowledged that he had received it in $100 bills on April 5. Fred LaRue picked up the Davis gift from Rebozo in October 1972, six months later, and said he was not told the source of the funds. LaRue sent part or all of this money to the Nunn campaign in Kentucky for a Senate seat.

Use of the Money

A number of allegations were raised by Senate Watergate investigators about the improper uses Rebozo might have made of campaign contributions he controlled—including payment for improvements and furnishings on Nixon's Key Biscayne home, and paying of expenses and gifts for Nixon. Herbert Kalmbach testified before the Watergate Committee that on April 30, 1973 Rebozo told him of spending part of the $100,000 Hughes contribution he was holding on F. Donald Nixon, Edward Nixon, Rose Mary Woods, and others. In their efforts to verify Kalmbach's testimony, the committee subpoenaed financial records from Rebozo and his Key Biscayne Bank & Trust Co.; Rebozo refused to provide all documents requested. The committee then subpoenaed third-party documents and records relating to services provided to the President or Rebozo during the period in question, and prepared a detailed analysis of the testimony and evidence gained during their limited but revealing survey. The following facts were produced:

1. Rebozo ordered and paid for expenses totaling over $50,000 for President Nixon during the periods following both the 1968 and 1972 Presidential elections.

2. These payments were made by Rebozo despite the fact that all other expenses of President Nixon were paid for by check issued against his bank accounts or by debit memos drawn against his bank accounts. Rebozo has the authority to draw against the President's account at the Key Biscayne Bank by issuing debit memos for cashiers' checks and bank transfers. Although he has regularly used this procedure, he did not do so for these transactions.

3. Substantial payments furnished by Rebozo on behalf of President Nixon were made in cash and, when Rebozo paid the same companies for work done for his own benefit, he paid by check.

4. Expenses paid for by Rebozo included $45,621.15 for

improvements and furnishings at the President's 500 and 516 Bay Lane properties in Key Biscayne, Fla. The records reflecting expenditures for these improvements were withheld from the firm of Coopers & Lybrand and do not appear in their August 1973 examination of the President's assets and liabilities, which covered the period from January 1, 1969, to May 31, 1973.

5. Currency totaling at least $23,500 was deposited by Rebozo in trust accounts not in his name to pay for the President's expenses, thus concealing the true source of these payments. All currency so deposited was in $100 bills.

6. In addition to Rebozo's role as the President's personal agent regarding the Key Biscayne property, President Nixon was aware of and concurred in at least some of these improvements to his properties.

7. Substantial funds used to pay for expenses and gifts of President Nixon were transmitted to trust accounts in the name of Rebozo's attorney, a process which concealed the source of the funds.

8. The sum of $4,562, which originated as campaign contributions, was passed by Mr. Rebozo through three bank accounts and a cashier's check, none in his name, to purchase jewelry given by the President as a [birthday] gift to his wife. [The money went toward a pair of diamond earrings bought for $5,000 from the New York jeweler, Harry Winston; Nixon apparently paid the balance himself.]

9. Throughout the period during which these expenditures were made on the President's behalf, Rebozo had access to substantial amounts of cash retained from campaign contributions received.

10. The Coopers & Lybrand examination of the President's assets and liabilities as of May 31, 1973, reflects no liabilities payable to Rebozo.

11. Rebozo did not file a U.S. gift tax return for calendar years 1969, 1970, 1971, or 1972 as [may have been] required by the Internal Revenue Code, section 6019(a).

12. The President reimbursed Rebozo in the amount of $13,642.52 for a portion of the cost of construction of a pool on the President's property. This reimbursement occurred after Rebozo returned funds to representatives of Hughes and despite the fact that Coopers & Lybrand report reflected no liability payable to Rebozo.

13. During November 1972, Rebozo expended at least $20,000 in currency on the President's behalf.

14. According to Rebozo's testimony and financial records, the only apparent sources available to Rebozo for a substantial portion of the $20,000 in currency used in November 1972 were campaign contributions.[r]

---

[r]Senate Select Committee, *Final Report*. pp. 1031-32; see pp. 1030-53 for discussion.

Special Interests

A number of instances relating to campaign contributions emerged in 1972 and afterwards where the questions raised were often a matter of ethics as well as of legality of the gifts, and where it was conjecture as to whether the subsequent treatment accorded the giver resulted from the contribution. This is a problem area troubling many observers of political finance. U.S. District Judge George L. Hart, Jr. noted, when he instructed the jury in the bribery case (not relating to the 1972 elections) against Senator Daniel B. Brewster, D-Maryland, in 1972, that it was "entirely proper and legal" for donors to make contributions only in the hope that the legislators receiving the gifts would continue to maintain general positions agreeable to the donor. The law seeks to draw a further distinction between "bribery"—where there is evidence that the recipient of the money actually was influenced or changed a view—and "illegal gratuity," a legal term describing a gift made "for or because of" an act, even if the recipient would have performed the act anyway in the normal course of his duties. Both are against the law, although there has not yet been a conclusive ruling on "illegal gratuity" in the matter of political contributions. This highlights the problem of drawing the line between those contributions, which are to be encouraged as a legitimate and desirable aspect of citizen participation in politics, and those that are, or verge on, bribery.[s]

Some cases of presumed special interest drew the attention of the Watergate investigators, others did not. Some questions, for example, involved foreign money given to the Committee to Re-Elect the President, an ironic twist in light of the fact that one early "cover story" for some of the Cuban-American members of the Watergate break-in team was that they were looking for evidence of money from Fidel Castro's government allegedly given to support the Democrats. The ensuing investigation brought to light sizable gifts to the Nixon campaign from representatives of Philippine interests; $30,000 of that money was given by Ernesto Lagdameo, former Philippines ambassador to the United States, and then a Philippines businessman, along with two of his associates, Jesus Cobarrus, Sr., and Eugenie Lopez, Jr., a nephew of the Philippines vice-president. The $30,000 was subsequently returned by the FCRP because of its doubts over the legality of accepting it.[65] Another contribution, this one $25,000, given pre-April 7, came from Ramon Nolan, a roving representative for Philippine sugar interests. The Philippines had the largest foreign share of the United States sugar market in 1972, a quota set in earlier years by the American government at twice the level allocated to any other nation.

---

[s]For discussion of this, see Lawrence Meyer, "The Fine Line Between Contributions and Bribes," *Washington Post*, March 17, 1973; and Brooks Jackson, "Bribery and Contributions," *The New Republic*, December 21, 1974. On the question of political temptation, Lincoln Steffens once observed that Adam blamed Eve who in turn blamed the Serpent, whereas the real fault, in Steffens' view, was and continued to be with the apple.

On November 1, 1972 the Comptroller General referred to the Justice Department the matter of "five $3,000 contributions on August 31, 1972, to the [FCRP] and its affiliated committees by Mr. Eric Ho Tung, whose residence was in Hong Kong."[66] The FCRP had already refunded the contribution to Mr. Ho Tung, who was not a United States citizen, on September 7, 1972, and reported the refund in its 15-day preelection report.

A number of Greeks were contributors to the Nixon campaign. When the White House was looking for cash in March 1973 to pay the Watergate defendants, the name of Thomas A. Pappas emerged. Pappas is a Greek-born industrialist from Boston, who holds dual citizenship in his native country and the United States, and who gave the FCRP $101,673, all but $1,000 of which was in pre-April 7 contributions; he also contributed $22,600 in-kind in 1973. Pappas was also an active fund raiser for Nixon who reportedly once approached Aristotle Onassis for a Nixon gift but was turned down on grounds that Onassis felt it improper "to interfere in American political affairs."[67] (Mrs. Jacqueline Kennedy Onassis made a $2,500 contribution to McGovern.) Pappas was a friend of the late Nikos J. Vardinoyiannis—a Greek shipowner who contributed $27,500 to the CRP, $12,500 of that after a Greek company he headed was chosen to supply fuel to the U.S. Sixth Fleet.[68]

On March 20, 1973 John Dean talked with John Ehrlichman about E. Howard Hunt's demand for $130,000, and Ehrlichman suggested he call Mitchell in New York. During the ensuing telephone conversation Dean asked Mitchell if he had talked to Pappas, and Mitchell said he had. Dean then asked (in a code adopted because Martha Mitchell had by then picked up another extension and was listening): "Is the Greek bearing gifts?" Dean reported that Mitchell responded, "I want to call you tomorrow on that."[t]

The following day, Nixon told Dean he knew where he could get a million in cash if need be, and a few minutes later, Dean mentioned that LaRue had talked to Pappas. The President said, "I know." The following exchange then took place:

Dean: And Pappas has agreed to come up with a sizeable amount,
           I gather, from, from—

Nixon: Yeah.

Dean: Mitchell.

Nixon: Yeah. Well, what do you need, then? You need, uh, you
           don't need a million right away, but you need a million. Is
           that right?[69]

---

[t]The March 20 phone call is related by Walter Pincus, *The New Republic*, August 3, 1974, p. 10.

Within a few minutes after Pappas' name had come up, according to White House records, Haldeman called Ehrlichman on a matter noted in his telephone memoranda as "re: Urik Oil Co." That company is associated with Pappas, who was then chairman of the Board of Pappas Esso Oil Refinery In Greece, and a member of the National Petroleum Council.

Pappas' $22,600 gifts-in-kind were the personal fund-raising expenses he listed in a report of his contributions to CRP on February 14, 1973. These included seven round-flight trips to Greece in 1972, costing $9,079, plus airline expenses for an October 1971 trip to meetings in Paris and Switzerland. Also listed were costs for air travel in the United States ($3,041), incurred at a Boston fund-raising dinner for Nixon ($5,517), and at the Miami Convention ($521).

Pappas grew close to Spiro Agnew after Nixon's choice of Agnew for vice-presidential candidate in 1968. At that time, there were unsubstantiated reports that Pappas raised, and himself provided, large sums of money for the 1968 campaign in appreciation of Agnew's nomination.

Another instance emerged of a $20,000 gift in cash, which originated as a loan from Greek shipping owner Angelos Maroulis to American tanker owner Leo Berger for transmittal as a contribution to the Nixon campaign. The transmittal agent was Helen Bentley, then head of the Federal Maritime Commission, which regulates rates and routes for United States shipping. A number of other instances saw foreign nationals "laundering" United States corporate money on its way illegally to the FCRP. Immediate denials were issued by the FCRP when these matters were made public, stating it had not known the money had been laundered, and had playe d no part in any laundry. As early as September 1972 FCRP spokesmen denied instances of foreign laundering of campaign funds, calling such charges as those found in the House Banking and Currency Committee reports[70] a dishonest and insulting attempt by Democrats to hurt the President's reelection efforts in the last days of the campaign.

There were allegations, although no proof, that money from the Swiss bank account of the Shah of Iran, perhaps running to $1 million or more, found its way to the Nixon campaign after being transferred to a bank in Mexico City.[u] Watergate investigators also probed extensively into reports that money from other Arab states went to the Nixon campaign; one trail, apparently without hard evidence, led them into the connections of the Saudi Arabian banker Adnan M. Khashoggi with C.G. (Bebe) Rebozo. This was spurred by the taped White House conversation in which Nixon talked about "two or three hundred thousand dollars" available for legal fees for H.R. Haldeman and John Erlichman. This sum was two to three times as large as the cash known to be in Rebozo's

---

[u]Columnist Jack Anderson made these allegations, which he said came from the report of a former Justice Department official to Watergate investigators. See Anderson, "Kissinger to Press Shah on Oil Costs," *Washington Post*, November 1, 1974. The story was later denied by CRP. But if such money had been given it could have gone to the Rebozo fund and not been passed to the CRP. The Office of Special Prosecutor probed these matters, with no findings at this writing.

safe deposit box at that time. Khashoggi had been an arms sales middle man helping United States corporations such as Northrop sell fighter planes in the Mideast.[71]

Michele Sindona, the multimillionaire Italian financier, confirmed in 1974 earlier reports that he had made an offer of a $1 million contribution to the Nixon reelection campaign.[72] After the 1972 election Sindona's name emerged in connection with the troubled affairs of the Franklin National Bank of New York, of which he was the largest shareholder. His 1972 offer was turned down by Stans, because Sindona did not want the proposed contribution made public, which would have violated the law then in effect.

Sindona told a reporter from the *Corriere Della Sera* of Milan that he had wanted to make the contribution because he wanted to meet Nixon, and believed that his reelection "might have helped us all." He acknowledged that he had requested his proposed contribution be kept secret, but said his gift was intended to show his fellow Italian businessmen that someone who had "Wall Street listening to him," rather than "the gangsters," was finally taking an interest in United States politics. The financier also discussed with *Corriere Della Sera* his purchase of the majority interest in the Societa Generale Immobiliare, previously owned by the Vatican, later resold. The multinational real estate company numbers among its holdings the Watergate complex.

Under federal law in 1972,[73] it was a felony to solicit, accept, or receive a political contribution from a foreign principal or an agent of a foreign principal. The law also prohibited an agent of a foreign principal from making a political contribution on behalf of his principal or in his capacity as agent of the principal. The legality of political contributions by foreign nationals hinged on the definition of the term "foreign principal." The Department of Justice held that the term "foreign principal" did not have the same meaning as "foreign national." Since the term "principal" connoted the existence of an agency relationship, it was the department's view that a foreign national was a foreign principal only if the principal had an agent within the United States. Therefore, it was not considered a violation of the statute to accept a direct political contribution from a foreign national who did not have an agent within the United States. The term "foreign principal" included governments of foreign countries, foreign political parties, persons outside the United States who were not United States citizens, and partnerships, associations, corporations, organizations or other combinations of persons organized under the laws of, or having their principal place of business in, a foreign country.

The thrust of the Foreign Agents Registration Act Amendments of 1966 was to require disclosure of the political activity of foreign agents within the United States. Congress did not consider the issue of direct political contributions by foreign nationals when it enacted that act or its 1966 amendments. None of the other major acts of Congress dealing with political campaigns and elections—the Corrupt Practices Act, the Hatch Act, or the Federal Election

Campaign Act of 1971—amended federal law to prohibit direct contributions by foreign nationals. This had the effect of permitting political contributions from individuals who neither resided in the United States nor had the right to vote in elections within the United States. Thus, political contributions were sometimes made to candidates of both parties by foreign nationals who were associated with or employed by firms doing business in the United States.

In additon, in 1972 hundreds of thousands of dollars, including illegal contributions from corporate funds, were laundered through foreign banks and foreign companies. These abuses illustrated that the statute which sanctioned direct contributions by foreign nationals undercut other elections laws such as the disclosure requirements and the prohibition on corporate contributions. Since foreign banks generally are not subject to United States law and enforcement processes, laundered funds are difficult to trace.[v]

The FECA Amendments of 1974 revised the law to apply directly to foreign nationals, who were defined as in the Foreign Agents Registration Act of 1938, or as any individual who is not a citizen of the United States and who is not lawfully admitted for permanent residence. The amendment is based on the notion that foreign nationals who cannot vote in American elections ought to be excluded from influencing elections by contributing money. Of course, this prohibition does not apply to Americans living abroad.

A number of other instances surfaced that involved alleged relationships between money contributed in 1971-72 and possible favored treatment. While none of these were proved, and some may be completely unfounded, they suggest the climate that led reformers and others to be suspicious about many large campaign gifts.

1. In a series of meetings of trucking executives around the country, held at a time when the industry was fighting a government proposal that would have caused more competition among various modes of freight transportation, more than $600,000 was raised in campaign contributions for Nixon's reelection effort.[w] One trucker, John Ruan of Des Moines, Iowa, who was secretary of the American Trucking Association, headed the industry fund drive. Ruan, president of Ruan Transport Co., himself gave $50,000 to the Nixon campaign. The executives of at least nine trucking firms met the drive goal of $25,000 per company. The money was the largest centrally organized single-industry collection apart

---

[v]For an extended discussion and recommendations, see Senate Select Committee, *Final Report,* pp. 573-75.

[w]James R. Polk, "$600,000 From Truckers Led Nixon's Industry Gifts," *Washington Star,* November 6, 1973. In 1974 a bill allowing heavier trucks on the interstate highway system passed Congress after a lobbying drive that included some last minute contributions before the election among some 117 members of the House. Earlier the House had rejected the weight increase but reversed itself and President Ford signed the legislation. ("Successful Truck-Bill Lobbying Included Campaign Fund Drive," *The New York Times,* January 7, 1975).

from the dairy industry gifts. The dairy groups totalled more over a several-year period if early "access" money is counted, but the truckers' funds were concentrated into several months before the November election. The truckers have long had an industry collection system and have participated handsomely in presidential campaigns since at least 1960.

2. A gift of $18,000 was made by the two top officials of Overseas National Airways, Inc., a jetliner charter company carrying both military and civilian groups, four months after the 1972 election, when CRP was reporting a $5 million surplus.[74]

3. A letter was written to then Attorney General John Mitchell from a major figure in the pharmaceutical industry, Elmer H. Bobst, honorable chairman and a director of Warner-Lambert, saying he had a close friend with a $100,000 gift if the Federal Trade Commission acted as the industry wished in a merger challenge. The FTC was at that time challenging a merger between Warner-Lambert and Parke, Davis.[X] This contribution was never made.

4. A $30,000 contribution was made to the Nixon campaign by Calvin Kovens, indicted and found guilty with James Hoffa of conspiracy and mail fraud; Kovens was paroled unexpectedly shortly after Charles Colson was asked to see what Nixon could do to help.[75]

5. The head of a black management consulting firm in Washington, Samuel E. Harris, said he learned that he needed to make a second $1,000 contribution to Nixon to get on the FCRP "white list" and be considered a "fully recognized contributor."[76] The FCRP claimed it had no "white list."

6. McDonald's Hamburgers, whose chairman, Ray A. Kroc, contributed $250,000 to the Nixon campaign, won a subsequent favorable ruling from the government. This permitted McDonald's to raise prices while price controls were in effect. There were mitigating circumstances in that the approval followed agreement to put on an extra slice of cheese, permitting treatment of the claim as a new product. McDonald's also benefitted after the election from Nixon administration efforts, which were successful, to establish a lower teen-age minimum wage,[77] but no relationships were established.

7. Senator Warren C. Magnuson, chairman of the Senate Commerce Committee, publicly charged that the Nixon administration had promised to postpone effective federal regulation on flammability of carpeting in order to get campaign contributions from carpet manufacturers. He alleged that Maurice Stans set up a secret White House meeting with industry and government representatives for the purpose. Stans and the other participants denied any favors had been sought or given, or that contributions had been solicited. Several carpet manufacturers were very large contributors to the Nixon campaign.[78]

Many such allegations and intimations were made during the election

---

[X]The case is mentioned in "Special Report: Nixon and Big Business," *FACT*, vol. III, no. 13 (June 23, 1972), 5.

campaign and its aftermath, but no connections between contributions from special interests and subsequent favorable government treatment were proved. None of the actors in these cases were officially charged with improper actions. Such allegations reflected an atmosphere of suspicion, triggered by day after day of new disclosures and exposures. The climate created pressures for new legislation by dramatizing the potential for abuses among large contributors, special interests, and campaign fund raisers.

The Grain Deal

Although it remains a controversial topic in terms of its impact on American consumers, and smacks of a classic attempt at gaining government influence through campaign contributions, the grain deal in the summer of 1972[y] and subsequent gifts by executives of the grain interests to the Nixon campaign apparently involved no favored treatment for the contributors. The company that probably gained the most from the sale of United States government-subsidized wheat to the Soviet Union was the Continental Grain Company, whose president Michel Fribourg gave $1,000 to the McGovern campaign in the spring of 1972. Four top officials of Cargill, Inc., who gave a total of $10,000 to the Nixon campaign on September 18, 1972, the day before a company vice-president testified before Congress, were from the one company that some sources report actually lost on the grain deal.[z] One Minneapolis grain executive who sold no wheat to the Russians was Dwayne Andreas; he gave a total of $144,137 to the Nixon campaign, $25,000 of which wound up as money used by the Watergate burglars.

The contributions by the Cargill executives came to light in October, when campaign reports were filed. The company's board chairman denied any impropriety, calling the timing of the donations sheer coincidence.

---

[y]Some 12 million tons of wheat and 7 million tons of other grains were sold by six grain export firms at a rate below the $60 per ton world price, for a total $1.4 billion. After the deal was announced and the magnitude of Russia's purchases realized, the domestic price of wheat spiralled to $180 per ton. See Joseph Albright, "Some Deal," *The New York Times Magazine,* November 25, 1973.

[z]Days earlier, according to GAO reports, an additional $2,000 was given to CRP (on September 10) and $2,000 more to a Nixon dinner committee (on September 18) by Cargill executives. The Cargill accountants reported that the company actually lost about $661,000 on the Soviet sale (Albright, "Some Deal.")

14 The Aftermath

Trial by the Polls

For many years observers perceived little about the relationships between public opinion polls and the success or failure of political fund-raising campaigns. Although the realization came earlier, 1972 illustrated in important respects just how well fund raising may succeed if the candidate is doing well in the polls (Nixon); how fund raising may lag if the candidate is not doing well in the polls (Lindsay); how fund raising wanes as public support—as reflected in the polls—wanes (Muskie); and how poorly fund raising fares when the candidate does poorly in a primary election (Humphrey). Of course, the candidate's recognition factor is important, although that can be improved if sufficient funds, time, and luck are available to improve the candidate's visibility in a positive way (McGovern).

Events in 1972 also brought out another phenomenon related to public opinion. Before the Watergate revelations, the public seemed prepared to be cynical about the political process—and how that process was financed. A 1972 survey showed that 46 percent of the American voters felt they could trust the government only "some of the time." More than half—59 percent—believed that the government was run on behalf of a "few big interests" instead of for all the people. And 38 percent agreed with the statement that "quite a few" of the people running the government were dishonest.[1]

These feelings were expressed at a time when the great majority of the American public was not seriously disturbed by the Watergate scandals. Pollster Louis Harris said, in an October 1972 survey, that voters rejected the idea that White House aides had ordered the Watergate bugging by a 50 to 25 percent margin. By an even greater margin—66 to 16 percent—voters rejected the idea that President Nixon was involved in the scandal.[2]

The Nixon campaign did not seem to suffer any substantial loss of votes as a result of the limited Watergate revelations made before November 1972. As late as April 1973 the Gallup Poll reported that 53 percent of the voters thought the Watergate bugging and cover-up were "just politics—the kind of thing both parties engage in."[3]

During the primary and general election periods, Senator George McGovern and his supporters tried to make an issue of the ways that the Committee to Re-Elect the President (CRP), as well as his Democratic primary opponents, were raising funds. But this seems not to have had much impact on the electorate. In October 1972 Louis Harris found that only 18 percent of the voters agreed with the Democrats' charge that "Republicans are hiding $10 million in campaign contributions, mostly from big business, given in return for favors from the Nixon Administration."

Fifty-seven percent of the respondents in the same poll called the controversy over campaign contributions "mostly politics." Harris probed further and found that 34 percent of the voters agreed that "these are the same kind of charges that come up in every election and it is just the usual mud-throwing that goes on."[4] This evidence showed voters were not then outraged at what some considered to be common unsavory practices.

The Watergate revelations of 1973 and early 1974 changed public reaction to the scandal itself and to the voters' perception of the campaign finance process. The erosion of confidence in President Nixon himself was one effect, as successive revelations and events made it appear that his top aides and perhaps even the President himself had been deeply involved in the Watergate cover-up. That erosion of confidence is obvious from Nixon's standing in the polls. Just after his second inauguration, in late January 1973, Nixon enjoyed approval of 68 percent of the American electorate, according to the Gallup Poll.[5] By July 1974 Nixon's approval rating in the Gallup Poll had plummeted to 23 percent.[6] But immediately after the election, few even of his most vociferous critics would have suggested that Nixon should be ousted from office. By the first days of 1974, however, Gallup indicated 46 percent of American voters believed the President should resign, and 37 percent believed he should be impeached.[7] By mid-July 1974, 73 percent of the American public thought Nixon had either planned the Watergate bugging, or knew about it and participated in the cover-up;[8] by mid-August 64 percent favored impeachment, 55 percent favored removal from office, and by a vote of 44 to 35 percent, the public preferred to have then Vice President Ford as chief executive for the remaining two years of Nixon's second term.[9] These findings indicate massive changes in public opinion, resulting from new revelations and daily headlines on Watergate topics.

But the Watergate revelations did more than erode confidence in Richard Nixon and his administration. They also substantially lowered public confidence in political institutions. In November 1973 the University of Michigan's Survey Research Center (SRC) asked a representative sample of voters some of the same questions it had asked in 1972, and found that 66 percent of the respondents said they could trust the government only "some of the time"—a 20 percent rise from the year before. Fully 72 percent of the 1973 respondents felt that government was run on behalf of a "few big interests"—a rise of 13 percent since 1972. And 53 percent of the respondents believed that "quite a few" of the people running the government were dishonest—a rise of 15 percent since 1972. These findings show a substantial change of opinion in just 12 months. More important, they show a deepening cynicism about political institutions and the people who run them.[a]

In a major survey of citizen confidence and concern regarding American government and institutions, conducted in late 1973 for a Senate subcommittee, Louis Harris found high levels of disaffection, cynicism, and disenchantment, with significant decreases of trust in the executive branch and in institutional leadership generally.[b] The public tended to be poorly informed, yet ready for straight talk given by strong leaders; the people sought greater accountability, less secrecy, more integrity, and increased candor. The respondents felt that lobbies are not representative, are selfish, have undue influence, and that too many public officials represent various special interests rather than the public interest. On the issue of political finance, the public felt that contributions should be fully disclosed, should not be in cash or under the table, that election law is a mockery, and that some public financing is desirable if adequate safeguards are provided.

The Watergate revelations also made a significant difference in how Americans regard campaign financing—and what they thought should be done about it. Many of the Watergate-related revelations involved illegal or at least unsavory campaign finance practices: the alleged seeking of influence by financier Robert Vesco; the large dairy contributions and the rise in milk prices; hundred dollar bills and huge sums of cash delivered to the CRP. These revelations increased public awareness of the need for honesty and probity in campaign financing and government—and heightened the intensity of public desire for reform. In the summer of 1973 the Harris organization found that 43 percent of the respondents to a survey listed "integrity in government" as one of the two or three biggest problems facing the country. (Only five percent had placed it in the same category in a similar survey conducted in May 1972.)[10]

---

[a]William Chapman, "66% Feel Distrust in Government," *Washington Post,* January 8, 1974. Watergate was also found to be having an impact on children. See F. Christopher Arterton, "The Impact of Watergate on Children's Attitudes toward Political Authority," *Political Science Quarterly*, vol. 89, no. 2 (June 1974), 269. Also see Patrick J. McGeever, "'Guilty, Yes; Impeachment, No': Some Empirical Findings," *Political Science Quarterly*, vol. 89, no. 2 (June 1974), 289; Gerald B. Finch, "Impeachment and the Dynamics on Public Opinion: A Comment on 'Guilty, Yes; Impeachment, No'," *Political Science Quarterly*, vol. 89, no. 2 (June 1974), 301.

[b]Senate Subcommittee on Intergovernmental Relations, "Confidence and Concern: Citizens View American Government," *Hearing* on *A Survey of Public Attitudes,* 93rd Cong., 1st sess., December 3, 1973 (Washington, D.C.: U.S. Government Printing Office, 1974). The Harris Survey updated an SRC series on trust in government reported in Arthur H. Miller, "Political Issues and Trust in Government: 1964-1970," *American Political Science Review (APSR)*, vol. LXVIII, no. 3 (September 1974), 951-72. See also Jack Citrin, "Comment: The Political Relevance of Trust in Government," *APSR*, vol. LXVIII, no. 3 (September 1974), 973-88; and Miller, "Rejoinder to 'Comment' by Jack Citrin: Political Discontent or Ritualism?", pp. 989-1001.

At the same time public support for reform of campaign financing was clearly increasing. Between June and September 1973–a period of many Watergate revelations–a Gallup Poll showed that the percentage of the public that supported a system of public financing of campaigns, with all contributions from private sources prohibited, rose from 58 percent of the electorate to 65 percent.[11] By August 1974, the poll showed, two Americans in three (67 percent) were in favor of government financing of campaigns for federal office; 24 percent opposed the proposed change, and nine percent were undecided.[12] Compare this response to a somewhat different question asked by SRC interviewers ten years earlier, in 1964, when there was far less consciousness of the problems of campaign financing: SRC reported then that only 11 percent of the electorate in that year favored the idea of the government helping to pay for political campaigns, while 71 percent were opposed.[13]

Gallup, Harris, and the other pollsters offered perhaps the best chronicle of the loss of public confidence in Richard Nixon and his administration. By mid-September 1973 Nixon suffered a six-point drop in his Gallup Poll rating, setting another low record of 32 percent support.[14] A Harris Poll of about the same time showed 51 percent in favor to 34 percent against Congress beginning impeachment proceedings[15] –a sharp change of opinion from one month earlier when the same question had elicited a 50 to 39 percent rating *against* beginning the proceedings.[16] This drop in public confidence reflected reaction to Nixon's withholding the White House tapes from the Senate Watergate Committee. By January 1974 Nixon's support had dwindled to 26 percent, close to the lowest of his term in office.[17]

The next month evinced a two-point rise after the State of the Union message, but that small vote of confidence was only recorded from fellow Republicans. Table 14-1 shows the high and low points for Nixon and the previous five Presidents.

Along with his own fortunes, Nixon seemed to be affecting the credibility of his party. By June 1974, in a poll measuring congressional strength, the Democrats had a commanding lead–57 percent over 30 percent for the Republicans.[18] Nixon's strong point, foreign policy, was reflected to some degree in

Table 14-1
High and Low Ratings for Nixon and the Previous Five Presidents

	High	*Low*
Nixon	68	24
Johnson	80	35
Kennedy	83	57
Eisenhower	79	49
Truman	87	23
Roosevelt	84	54

his June Middle-East tour, with 54 percent favoring his actions in foreign affairs, but only 18 percent agreeing with his domestic policy. Although his overall ratings remained about the same as in a previous survey, approval among college-educated respondents, who are generally more interested in foreign policy, rose eight percent, while it dropped among high school- or grade school-educated respondents.[19]

In July Gallup showed the lowest figure for Republican identification since the poll started to ask party affiliation questions in 1940. The percentage of Americans identifying themselves as Republicans had dropped to 23 percent, but the Democrats' 44 percent did not show a gain from two years earlier. The significant figure was the rise of voters who referred to themselves as independents—33 percent.[20]

The tape controversy was strongly in the public mind, with a July Harris Poll showing 69-22 percent in favor of Nixon's handing over the tapes. Harris showed a similar 69-29 percent unfavorable reading of how well people thought the President was doing his job.[21] The same period saw 55-29 percent registering confidence in Democrats over Republicans for Congress.[22] This effect on the 1974 elections was one of the main causes of Republican pressure for Nixon's resignation, which came a few days later on August 9, 1974.

Two days after Nixon's resignation, a Gallup Poll showed 79 percent of the respondents thought Nixon did the best thing by resigning, with 13 percent feeling he should have stayed in office. Fifty-five percent were against criminal prosecution of the former President.[23] Mid-August showed a rise in public confidence in the Congress—from 30-47 percent in April, to 48-35 percent. Much of this was attributed to the televised sessions of the House Judiciary Committee hearings, and the conduct of its members.[24] President Ford received a vote of confidence in a mid-August poll, 71 percent in favor of the manner in which he took the reins of government, only three percent against, and 26 percent undecided.[25] By this time 56 percent were in favor of Nixon being prosecuted, 37 against, and seven percent undecided. Of these respondents, Democrats registered 70-25 percent in favor of a trial, and Republicans were 33-59 in favor of prosecution.[26]

In early September Gallup reported that 58 percent of the respondents were in favor of Nixon being tried on criminal charges. Taken before Ford pardoned Nixon, the poll showed 36 percent thought he should not be tried, and six percent gave no opinion.[27] This same period showed the Democrats holding a wide lead in the coming congressional elections; 54 percent said they would prefer to see Democrats win, to 35 percent preferring Republicans. Another question showed that 39 percent thought Democrats could do a better job against inflation, to 18 percent for the Republicans.[28]

The traditional honeymoon soon seemed to be over for President Ford with a slight drop in approval of the way he was handling the presidency to 66 percent, from the 71 percent high after taking over from Nixon. After the Nixon pardon Gallup showed Ford's rating had plummeted to 50 percent by early October, with disapproval up to 28 percent from an earlier low of three percent. The 21 point decline in approval is the sharpest ever recorded for a President during his first two months in office. Most of the disapproval was registered among Democrats.[29]

Nixon Appointments

Although the practice of rewarding large contributors with federal jobs is not new, the matter took on particular interest following the 1972 election. It became the focus of one set of investigations by Special Watergate Prosecutor Leon Jaworski. Herbert W. Kalmbach, the former President's personal lawyer, was sentenced to jail for having promised an ambassadorship in 1970 in return for a campaign contribution (a violation of federal statute) as well as for his role in raising a fund of $3.9 million from incumbent ambassadors, among others, for use in the 1970 congressional campaigns without creating a proper committee structure for the purpose.

In the months following his reelection, President Nixon sent to the Senate the names of 319 persons whose appointments to various high level federal positions were subsequently confirmed.[30] Appendix Y lists 52 of these appointees, or 17 percent, who were recorded as having made a large contribution to the Republicans; their gifts totalled $772,224. Of this, $703,654, or 91 percent, went to the Nixon campaign, and 36.7 percent of that came in during the pre-disclosure period. Several of these Nixon appointees also contributed to the Democrats, who received eight gifts totalling $5,973. Three Nixon appointees gave in excess of $50,000: Ruth Farkas gave $300,000 post-April 7 to Nixon; Kingdon Gould, Jr. gave $112,900, of which $100,900 went to Nixon; and John N. Irwin II gave $53,000, of which $50,000 went to Nixon. Of the total given by Nixon appointees to Republicans, $581,405 or 75 percent was given by ambassadorial appointees.

The percentage of presidential appointees making large contributions in 1972 is higher than that recorded in the three previous presidential elections studied by Citizens' Research Foundation (CRF), although caution must be applied in drawing conclusions because of the more comprehensive disclosure law. Following the 1960 election, with a change of party control of the White House, of 253 appointees requiring Senate confirmation, 35, or 14 percent, were large contributors giving in sums of $500 or more. Four years later with President Johnson, there were 187 appointees, and 24 large contributors, or 13 percent. In 1968, with another shift of party power, there were 345 appointees, 34 of whom, or ten percent, contributed, giving $325,975 to the Republicans, and $500 to the Democrats.

The 1972 appointees are only those appointed after the November election, and do not include a number of incumbent ambassadors, appointed during Nixon's first term in office, who made major contributions to his reelection campaign. Their gifts are analyzed elsewhere and are listed in Appendix R.[31]

Seven of the incumbent ambassadors did figure publicly, however, in the illegal fund-raising effort in the 1970 congressional campaigns to which Herbert Kalmbach pleaded guilty, as did two former White House political aides, Jack A. Gleason and Harry S. Dent. The operation involved a misnamed political committee called the Public Institute—also called "Operation Townhouse"—which had neither a chairman nor a treasurer, and which did not file disclosures, all violations of the federal statute then in effect, the Corrupt Practices Act; it funneled as much as $3.9 million to some 20 or more Republican candidates for the Senate, House, and governorships. Partial information about the operation had emerged in 1970 when several candidates who received the contributions listed them in federal or state campaign fund reports as coming "care of Jack A. Gleason"; some aspects of the story surfaced in the Watergate investigations.[32]

Gleason had handled the operation, which was set up in the basement of a Washington town house. Dent, a South Carolinian who was widely regarded as the principal operative of Nixon's "southern strategy," was an adviser on which races should be supported by the funds, along with two other White House aides, Charles W. Colson (later imprisoned for his role in the Daniel Ellsberg trial) and the late Murray Chotiner. Former White House Chief-of-Staff H.R. (Bob) Haldeman was in overall charge according to testimony given by both Gleason and Dent in their trial before U.S. District Judge George L. Hart, Jr. in Washington.

Kalmbach pleaded guilty to his role and on July 1, 1974 began a 6-to-18 month prison sentence; he was freed by order of U.S. District Court Judge John J. Sirica in January 1975. Dent, who resigned as counsel to the Republican National Committee a few days before his guilty plea (to one count of aiding and abetting a political committee that had no treasurer) in November 1974, was sentenced in December to one month on unsupervised probation by Judge Hart who called him an "innocent victim" in the fund-raising plan. In January 1975 Gleason was also sentenced to one month on unsupervised probation by Judge Hart, who noted that Gleason, not a lawyer, had been advised both by White House superiors and "a prestigious New York law firm" that his activities were legal.[33] Gleason had pleaded guilty in November to aiding and abetting the illegal fund-raising operation.

The seven envoys who gave generously in 1970 (and their 1970 contributions as revealed at least partially on available federal and state records) were: Walter Annenberg, Great Britain ($15,000), Kenneth Franzheim, II, New Zealand ($10,000), Shelby C. Davis, Switzerland ($5,000), John P. Humes, Austria ($10,500), John D.J. Moore, Ireland ($5,000), J. William Middendorf, II, the Netherlands ($4,500), and Kingdon Gould, Jr., Luxembourg ($5,000).

The Nixon ambassadorial appointment that generated by far the most controversy and had the most impact was that of Dr. Ruth Farkas as ambassador to

Luxembourg in 1973. Dr. Farkas, a sociologist and a director of Alexander's Department Store in New York, testified in her confirmation hearings before the Senate Foreign Relations Committee that over half of the $300,000 contribution that she and her husband had promised to the Nixon campaign was delayed until January 1973, by prearrangement, to await a more favorable market for stocks. The committee held up action until an audit confirmed that the $300,000 had been pledged before the election, and the full Senate subsequently confirmed her nomination without dissent. This was before the Watergate cover-up began to collapse.

Dr. Farkas testified before the Foreign Relations Committee on March 13, 1973, denying any connection between her contribution and her appointment, and stating that she made the gift because of her respect for Nixon's actions as President. In letters dated the next day submitted to the committee, Dr. Farkas and Rep. Louis C. Wyman, R-New Hampshire, detailed how Wyman, who had known her for several years, arranged a meeting for her in Washington with Maurice Stans. At that meeting, with Wyman present, Stans explained to Dr. Farkas how a contribution of $300,000, to be legal, must be split up into gifts to individual committees not exceeding $5,000 and he said he would provide her with a list of committees. Dr. Farkas and her husband subsequently wrote a total of 76 checks in amounts of $2,000, $3,000, $4,000 and $5,000 to some 31 different committees (chiefly state Finance Committees to Re-Elect the President). Dr. Farkas wrote 17 checks totalling $50,000 in October 1972; her husband wrote 28 in November 1972 totalling $97,000, and 31 in January 1973, totalling $153,000.[c]

When Herbert Kalmbach appeared under oath before the House Judiciary Committee's impeachment inquiry in July 1974, he told a different and expanded story. Kalmbach testified that White House aide Peter Flanigan had told him that he should contact Dr. Farkas regarding a campaign contribution in exchange for the ambassadorship to Costa Rica. The arrangements for that meeting were also made by Representative Wyman (the Kalmbach meeting was not mentioned in either of the letters from Wyman or Dr. Farkas). At the meeting Mrs. Farkas reportedly balked at the Costa Rica offer, saying, according to Kalmbach, that she was interested in Europe and "isn't $250,000 an awful lot of money for Costa Rica?"[34] (Dr. Farkas had actually been in line for that Central American embassy in 1969, but her name was suspended by the White House after it was disclosed that Alexander's Department Store was being investigated by the IRS in connection with an attempted tax write-off for a contribution in

[c]Letters and checks are reproduced in Senate Committee on Foreign Relations, *Hearing on the Nominations of William B. Macomber, Jr. to be Ambassador to Turkey; Marshall Green to be Ambassador to Australia; Dr. Ruth Lewis Farkas to be Ambassador to Luxembourg; V. John Krehbiel to be Ambassador to Finland; and Michael P. Balzano, Jr., to be Director of Action*, 93rd Cong., 1st sess., March 13, 1973 (Washington, D.C.: U.S. Government Printing Office, 1973), pp. 44-48, 75-76.

the 1965 New York City mayoralty race; Dr. Farkas was not personally involved in the matter, however.)

Kalmbach was jailed for fund-raising activities relating in part to "ambassadorial auction." He was indicted and then convicted after plea bargaining and pleading guilty to a misdemeanor in promising a European ambassadorship in 1970 in return for $100,000 in campaign contributions from J. Fife Symington, a Maryland Republican. A promise of a federal job in return for financial support is a violation of federal law. Kalmbach had become a major witness against Nixon officials and helped the Office of the Special Prosecutor and the Watergate Committee in their work. In pleading guilty, Kalmbach admitted helping the 1970 "Operation Townhouse" by raising money from traditional Nixon givers, including W. Clement Stone and the wealthy Nixon-appointed ambassadors.

Peter Flanigan was subsequently nominated as ambassador to Spain in 1974 by President Nixon, and the appointment was reaffirmed by President Ford. Flanigan's nomination drew strong opposition during confirmation hearings, and the nomination was not acted upon by the Senate after he acknowledged that he had singled out Mrs. Farkas as "a good prospect" for solicitation. Flanigan asked President Ford not to renew the nomination in the 94th Congress and Ford agreed. Congressman Wyman, who began as a heavy favorite to move up to the U.S. Senate seat vacated by Norris Cotton, was hurt after information about his role in the Farkas appointment came to light during his New Hampshire campaign. On Election Day, November 1974, he and Democrat John A. Durkin were in what proved to be a razor-slim contested election. Court suits and appeals to the U.S. Senate resulted in months of wrangling about who had won the election; the issue was resolved in August 1975 when the Senate declared the seat vacant and called for a new election. Press reports of Ambassador Farkas' testimony before the Watergate grand jury in the spring of 1975 indicated that she had recanted her sworn statement to the Senate Foreign Relations Committee about her contribution having nothing to do with the ambassadorship. She allegedly told the grand jury that she now believed the contribution was expected because of her appointment. In the new account, Mrs. Farkas reportedly claimed that Wyman had "tricked" and "seduced" her and her husband into the agreement, a charge that Wyman promptly denied, saying there never had been "explicit" promise of the post. The Special Prosecutor's Office continued to look into the allegations as part of its ongoing investigation of Watergate-related matters.[35]

Mrs. Farkas' predecessor as the ambassador to Luxembourg was Kingdon Gould, Jr., who served in that post throughout much of Nixon's first term. Gould, co-owner of a large parking lot chain in the Washington, D.C. area, gave $100,900 to the former President's reelection campaign in 1972, and was subsequently named United States ambassador to the Netherlands. In his confirmation hearings, Gould testified that his 1972 gift had been $51,000, neglecting to add that another contribution of $50,000 had been made in his wife's name,

Mary T. Gould. The full size of the contribution came out only after his nomination to The Hague had been confirmed by the Senate unanimously.

Two contributors seeking appointments as ambassadors, which they never received, were described in executive session of the Senate Watergate Committee by public relations executive Robert Gray, a Nixon fund raiser. John Safer, a well-known sculptor, Washington, D.C.-area real estate developer, and 1968 fund raiser for Eugene McCarthy, gave $250,000 (pre-April 7) to the Finance Committee to Re-Elect the President (FCRP). Gray, who had solicited the contribution, testified Safer wanted to be considered for an ambassadorship, and was given "a set speech [used] when making solicitations in this context," that there would be no appointment for his contribution, although his interest in one would be conveyed to the proper persons.[36] Safer's interests, both in making the contribution and in government service, were communicated to Maurice Stans and to Herbert Kalmbach, who reiterated that his interest would be forwarded to the proper persons but there could be no guarantee he would be given a post. In another instance, Gray's public relations firm, Hill & Knowlton, was retained by an Iowa businessman, Roy Carver, board chairman of Bandag, Inc. Carver sought to gain "greater visibility on the Washington scene" and was "anxious to be considered as an ambassador."[37] To achieve "consideration" Carver would call Gray periodically to find out what was the largest contribution to Nixon and who had given it, apparently so that he could give the highest amount and thus achieve recognition. Carver finally gave approximately $257,000 worth of Bandag, Inc. stock to the FCRP on November 2, 1972. In return he was given several State Department and White House interviews, but no appointment.[38]

Still another case of an ambassadorship sought and failed, that of Cornelius Vanderbilt Whitney, which occurred in 1971, is reported elsewhere.[39]

The process of "ambassadorial auction"[d]—which went to new extremes in the Nixon administration—has spurred several, as yet unsuccessful, efforts to control such a practice. In the wake of the Farkas appointment, both the Senate and the House considered possible restrictions. A proposal by the House Foreign Affairs Committee would require nominees to ambassadorial or ministerial posts to report to Congress all political campaign contributions for four years before their names were submitted to the Senate for confirmation. The Senate Foreign Relations Committee prepared draft rules on ambassadorial nominations: one rule would call for the committee to oppose confirmation of nominations where prima facie qualifications were large contributions; a second

---

[d]For a discussion of the process of "ambassadorial auction," see Charles W. Yost, "Ambassadorships for the Highest Bidders," *Washington Post,* November 29, 1972. Also see Gordon Strachan's memo to H.R. Haldeman, containing reference to "commitments" to large contributors seeking ambassadorships, in "Political Matters Memoranda, December 16, 1971," House Committee on the Judiciary, *Statement of Information: Appendix IV,* 93rd Cong., 2d sess. (Washington, D.C.: U.S. Government Printing Office, May-June, 1974), pp. 69-70.

would limit the number of noncareer ambassadors to 15 percent of the total number, or about half the present ratio. The rules were not put into effect by the Senate committee after objections to such restrictions were made by the Department of State and some senators, and major contributors continued to be named to ambassadorial posts after routine, almost perfunctory, screening by the Senate Foreign Relations Committee. In April 1974, during the confirmation hearings of industrialist Leonard K. Firestone as ambassador to Belgium his gift of $110,000 to the 1972 Nixon reelection campaign was praised by Senator John Sparkman, D-Alabama, as a "show of public spirit." Sparkman was acting chairman of the committee in the absence of J.W. Fulbright, D-Arkansas, who was then occupied with what proved to be a losing primary campaign. Fulbright had been one of the most influential critics of the ambassadorial "sales." The nomination of Firestone, a director of Firestone Tire and Rubber Co., was reported out of committee shortly thereafter. He was confirmed the next day by a voice vote in the Senate.

Later, however, the Congress enacted a requirement that reports of political contributions, made by nominees for ambassadorial or ministerial posts (and by their immediate families), which were filed with the Senate Committee on Foreign Relations and with the Speaker of the House at the time of their nomination, also be published in the *Congressional Record*.[e]

One nonambassadorial appointment of interest was that of William Simon, first as Under Secretary of the Treasury, then additionally as administrator of the Federal Energy Office during the energy shortfall in the Winter of 1974, then finally as Secretary of the Treasury. Simon contributed $15,000 to the Nixon reelection campaign in the pre-April 7 period. At the time of the contribution he was a general partner of Salomon Brothers, a major New York investment banking firm; he and 16 other partners of the firm contributed at the same time a total of $100,000. Simon's $15,000 gift was the largest of the 17 that made up the $100,000 total.

Maurice Stans claims that from the time he became finance chairman in February 1972, no commitments of any kind were made to contributors in the way of appointments to ambassadorships or any other government positions. Individuals who made direct offers of contributions in return for appointments, of which there were five or fix, were rebuffed, and their contributions were rejected. Persons who expressed an interest in a government appointment were told that their names would be submitted to the White House at the close of the campaign

---

[e]See, for example, "Statement of Political Contribution of Certain Nominees," *Congressional Record*, December 19, 1974, pp. S22360-61, authorized by "State Department/ USIA Authorization Act, Fiscal Year 1975," Public Law 93-475, sec. 4, approved October 26, 1974. PL 93-475, sec. 4, amends section 6 of the Department of State Appropriations Authorization Act of 1973. The reporting period to be covered is defined as "beginning on the first day of the fourth calendar year preceding the calendar year of his nomination and ending on the date of his nomination."

as candidates for such positions, regardless of whether or not they made any contribution. At the close of the campaign Stans did submit to the White House a list of 63 such persons, of whom one third were noncontributors or nominal contributors.

Stans also states that at the time he agreed to become finance chairman he insisted on a policy of dealing with the matter of appointments for contributors and received guidelines from H.R. Haldeman to the effect that (1) no commitments of any kind could be made by anyone connected with the Finance Committee, (2) the White House was interested in any recommendations that the FCRP might make or any expression of interest on the part of contributors, (3) any such candidates would be subject to full review by the White House, the State Department, and the FBI as to their credentials and qualifications, and (4) appointments could be made only in the event of vacancies and then only by determination of the President. Stans insists that throughout the campaign he adhered to these principles, and he knows of no instance in conflict with them.

Transition Costs

In the aftermath of the public and congressional outcry over the Nixon pardon, President Ford's request for some $850,000 in government funds for the former President's transition to private life met immediate opposition, and was soon slashed sharply.

Under the Former Presidents' Act, Nixon was entitled to a government pension for life of not less than $60,000 a year and annual office and staff maintenance expenses of not less than $96,000.

The Ford request for funds under both the Former Presidents' and Transition Acts, was to cover the transition expenses through the fiscal year ending June 30, 1975. But a Senate subcommittee on appropriations, chaired by Senator Joseph M. Montoya, D-New Mexico, made it immediately clear that the amount was far too great. The proposed sum included $450,000 in the transition budget ($171,000 as pension), and $400,000 in staff salaries and other allowances. The total request of $850,000 for an 11-month period compared with $542,000 actually spent by former President Lyndon Johnson during his first 18 months out of office. It was disclosed at the Senate hearings that the federal government had already been paying salaries amounting to almost $450,000 a year for 22 employees, including Nixon's personal valet and maid.[40]

The subcommittee voted unanimously to slash the request. By the time the bill was signed by President Ford in December, the amount that Congress approved was down to $200,000 for the 1975 fiscal year—$55,000 in pension for the last six months of fiscal 1975. One of the major items cut from the bill by a House subcommittee was a request for funds to build or buy a vault in California to store the White House tapes and other documents from the Nixon administration, material that was in litigation.

The chairman of the House panel, Tom Steed, D-Oklahoma, said that the subcommittee "couldn't see recommending $110,000 for a vault and $50,000 a year for guards to preserve papers and tapes there was no assurance we'd ever get the public benefit of."[41]

A few months later, in early 1975, trustees of the foundation charged with building the Richard M. Nixon presidential library decided to abandon the project, reportedly with Nixon's consent.[42]

Watergate-related Litigation

Within days of the June 17, 1972 incident at the Watergate, the first of a series of legal suits based on the break-in and wiretapping, and later on evidence that ensuing investigations produced, was filed. On June 20 the Democratic National Committee brought a $1 million civil suit against the CRP. Subsequent suits filed by leading Democrats, including both Lawrence F. O'Brien and Robert S. Strauss (successive national chairmen), by the Democratic State Chairmen's Association, and by Spencer Oliver, the State Chairmen's Association official whose phone was tapped, brought the amount being asked of the Republicans by the Democrats to more than $6 million.

After first fighting the suits and filing countersuits, the Republicans later made offers to settle the suits (in amounts that ranged from $500,000 up to $1.25 million) as evidence mounted and the possibility of losing arose. The first offers were either rejected by the Democrats outright or delayed because of wrangling within the party over what settlement should be made with the Republicans. In January 1974, for example, a dispute arose between Oliver and Strauss. Strauss was willing to settle for the Democratic National Committee (DNC) at $775,000. Oliver, however, stated that he wished his suit, for $5 million in damages, to be considered and settled separately. In June 1974 Representative Shirley Chisholm, D-New York, also balked at the settlement proposed by refusing to sign a waiver that would bar future lawsuits against Republicans who had engaged in dirty tricks in the 1972 campaign. A tentative settlement proposed in February had requested all the Democratic presidential and vice-presidential contenders to sign such a waiver. Herself a 1972 presidential contender, Chisholm said she was considering a libel suit against Donald H. Segretti, who was then serving a prison term for his campaign role.

The Republicans filed countersuits; a notable one was the $5 million countersuit for libel filed by Maurice Stans against O'Brien. Some six suits were filed by both sides, with alleged damages totalling more than $13 million.

The CRP also sued John W. Dean, III in August 1974. The trustees of the 1972 Campaign Liquidation Trust filed suit in Montgomery County Court, Maryland, to recover $15,200 that they claimed had been turned over to him by the FCRP. Dean had testified before the Senate Watergate Committee that former White House Assistant Gordon Strachan had given him the money, which—

except for $4,820 he had borrowed for his wedding and honeymoon—had remained in his office safe.

Concurrently, other suits related to the Watergate affair were being filed. In July 1973 a class action lawsuit seeking $1 million in punitive damages from CRP and its finance committee was filed in U.S. District Court in Cleveland, Ohio. The action was brought by Barbara Smialek, a radio talk show hostess ("Penny Bailey") who had contributed to the Nixon campaign, charging that the CRP had misappropriated funds to pay for illicit activities. Disenchanted Republicans in Missouri similarly filed; in both Ohio and Missouri recovery was denied in final actions. Still another similar suit was filed in Houston, Texas in September 1974 by John J. and Rose V. Moran who had contributed $101,508 to Nixon. They asked $3.6 million in damages, claiming that the CRP had used donations for illegitimate purposes; that case is still pending.

Two hours after President Nixon resigned his office on August 9, a Philadelphia man, Kent Saldan, filed a $25 million damage suit in federal court seeking to overturn results of the 1972 presidential election on grounds of "fraud and corruption." Also named were the CRP and its finance committee. Saldan is chairman of the American Constitutional Rights Committee, a group organized earlier in the year to "pursue the Watergate matter" and seek Nixon's resignation. The Saldan suit claimed any damages awarded would be "divided equally among all voters who file for it within one year after the judgment."

These suits were evidence that some contributors to the Nixon campaign were disturbed by some of the uses to which their money had been put: first, to incur costs for illegal activities such as the DNC break-in; second, to pay "hush money" and lawyer's fees out of the CRP surplus; and third, to settle with the Democrats, causing the money to assist the opposition party. The Republican National Committee (RNC) received many such complaints when seeking contributions in 1973 and 1974.

Shortly after the election the RNC was offered the CRP surplus, hoping to use it to fund a new political committee for the purpose of recruiting good candidates for future Republican campaigns for the Congress and at the state level. Before plans were implemented, it became apparent that the CRP surplus would be dissipated on legal fees and Watergate-related costs. The RNC soon realized that if it accepted CRP surplus funds, it would be drawn into the DNC and other suits. Accordingly, in late February 1974 the FCRP was succeeded by the 1972 Campaign Liquidation Trust (CLT), with the transfer of $3.6 million, intended to cover legal fees and other expenses of the major lawsuits pending. Three trustees were appointed to administer the trust: Maurice Stans, Charles E. Potter—former Republican senator from Michigan—and Guilford Dudley, Jr.— a Nashville, Tennessee insurance executive and large contributor. When the Liquidation Trust considered whether to pay the legal fees of Stans and John N. Mitchell in their defense in the Vesco case, Stans refrained from participating in the matter; a decision was made to pay their legal costs. Stans resigned and was replaced as a trustee by Paul Barrick, former FCRP treasurer, in August 1974. The trust paid fees and expenses only after audits by an accounting firm confirmed the amounts due.

On August 9, 1974 the DNC and the CRP reached an agreement in court to settle their Watergate lawsuits. The CRP, represented by the CLT, was to pay $775,000 to the Democratic Party, its former National Chairman O'Brien, and the Association of State Chairmen, which it did. O'Brien agreed to turn his share ($400,000) over to the Democratic Party, although he withheld it pending settlement of his legal fees. The DNC agreed that it would not file any future Watergate-related suits, and the Republicans agreed to drop all libel countersuits. The Oliver lawsuit was still pending.

Other legal actions ensued. In one, a citizen's criminal complaint was filed against former President Nixon in September 1974 by five members of a Hawaii-based political movement calling itself The New American Revolution. It sought to allege as crimes the three counts brought by the House Judiciary Committee in its impeachment hearings.

James McCord, one of the five Watergate burglars, filed a $10 million damage suit at the U.S. District Court for the District of Columbia in December 1974 against his original attorneys, accusing them of "legal malpractice" in the handling of his defense. Among his attorneys was F. Lee Bailey. McCord charged his lawyers with conflicts of interest and with negligence for asking him to remain quiet and accept clemency offers. This civil suit was rejected by the Court.

The American Bar Association, confronted with the type of atmosphere McCord's suit reflected, and troubled with criticism over enormous legal fees, attempted in the fall of 1974 to take a look at the legal profession's "image" in the eyes of the United States public.[43] The results tended to bear out the fears. A large majority of those questioned in a survey by National Opinion Research Center—some 62 percent—said that they thought most lawyers charged more for their services than they were worth, and a narrower majority felt that all legal fees were unfair. Attorneys came in for criticism for taking too much time to get things done, and a big majority—76 percent—felt that many matters currently handled by lawyers could be done just as well and less expensively by accountants, bank officers, and insurance agents.

Legal Fees

As a result of Watergate and the protracted litigation stemming from it, a new category of campaign expenditure was added to the 1972 account books—legal fees. What the final total will be when the last settlement is in on the last suit is uncertain, and an exact figure may never be known because of the confidentiality of lawyer-client relations regarding some fees, and because there was some volunteered service. But a final estimate of more than $3 million in paid legal fees from campaign funds does not seem unreasonable.

The FCRP, which raised more than $60 million for the Nixon reelection campaign, and had some $4.5 million left over after the election, spent much of the surplus on legal fees and related expenses. Early in 1973, after the investigations and litigation began to proliferate, the Budget Committee of the Nixon campaign adopted a formal policy with respect to legal fees incurred by employees of CRP and FCRP in explaining or defending their actions in 1972. Under this policy, reimbursement would be made for legal expenses incurred in connection with all such matters for which there were not criminal charges, thus covering legal costs related to civil suits or to appearances before various investigating bodies. If formal criminal charges were pending, the individual's expenses would be reimbursed only if he were later adjudged innocent or if the offences did not involve felonies. This general policy was approved by the FCRP counsel as being consistent with normal corporate practice. In mid-1975 the FCRP's successor organization, the 1972 Campaign Liquidation Trust, had paid or knew that it owed more than $2 million in legal fees. It had also paid $775,000 to the Democratic National Committee in settlement of the civil suit brought by the DNC after the break-in. Pending was the amount that might be won or settled in the accompanying civil suit by R. Spencer Oliver, the former executive director of the Association of State Democratic Chairmen whose phone had been tapped by the Watergate burglars.

The trustees of the CLT decided in August 1974, with minor modifications, to carry on the policy to provide financial aid for legal fees limited, however, to innocent actions of those persons who had, in fact, been employed by the CRP or the FCRP. This raised questions about whether to pay fees for Kenneth Parkinson, since he was outside counsel, and insured that the attorneys' fees for H.R. Haldeman and John Ehrlichman would not be paid by the trust. At the time of their sentencing, Haldeman and Ehrlichman were reportedly attempting to raise $400,000 and $300,000, respectively, to cover their legal expenses, including those for anticipated civil suits and appeals.[44]

Because of the reporting requirements of the FECA, there is much more detail about legal spending in the aftermath of Watergate than would otherwise have been the case. Quarterly reports to the GAO show more than 30 legal firms retained in all. The Washington law firm of Wilkinson, Cragun & Barker, for example—which handled most of the legal work for Maurice Stans as well as for the FCRP—had billings that ran more than $500,000 by early 1975. Mitchell's legal fees in the Vesco trial totalled $471,390; should his Watergate cover-up trial and ensuing appeal action proceed at a similar rate, he could be faced at the end with a $1 million legal bill, of which he could be reimbursed for less than half unless he wins his appeal in the Watergate cover-up case. Stans' bill from the Vesco case was $380,793, and he had additional legal fees in the Washington court action involving his pleading guilty to five misdemeanors involving both campaign receipts and expenditures.

In addition to the legal expenses in such matters, the CLT also had to defend a number of other litigations arising out of Watergate. For example, the Associated Milk Producers, Inc. brought suit for return of their $100,000 illegal contribution. The matter of returning contributions raised potentially enormous problems, since a suit settled in favor of a contributor claimant might be used as precedent for literally thousands of other such requests. The FCRP defended and won several class action suits to force the return of contributions in whole or in part.

Costly legal fees were not limited to the Republicans. The Democrats also ran up large bills in connection with the civil suits they brought against the CRP following the break-in at the DNC. Initially, they set out to borrow money to help pay legal fees when the civil suits were first brought. Some $75,000 was raised for this purpose, and subsequently returned to the contributors from the $775,000 settlement they reached. In addition, they had a $65,000 attorney's bill, pending as of March 1975. Moreover, a staff lawyer had cost them $30,000, while the miscellanea of legal services—reports, legal secretaries, transcripts, and the like—cost at least $25,000 more. This totalled nearly $200,000, not counting Lawrence O'Brien's legal fees in this suit, which amounted to between $75,000 and $80,000. He considered withholding the legal fees from his part of the settlement, and he did withhold his whole $400,000 portion from the $775,000 settlement pending an IRS ruling on whether it constituted income. The State Chairmen's Association also had legal fees, as did R. Spencer Oliver. The association got $105,000 as part of the $775,000 settlement, while Oliver's, as noted, is pending at this writing. Democratic officials pointed out that their civil suit was not brought out of a desire to make money—much of their settlement could end up going for legal fees and costs—but rather as a way of getting out the facts about Watergate,[45] which they expected would pay political dividends.

The trail of Watergate-associated legal fees stretches almost interminably, it seems, if one counts the area of illegal corporate contributions in which a number of the executives fined had to pay back the legal fees to their company. For example, the chairman of Ashland Oil reimbursed his firm for $7,175, and officers of Braniff Airways paid their company $19,181 for legal costs growing out of illegal corporate gifts. From such figures, a sense of the legal fees involved in the other cases of illegal corporate gifts can be gained; these, of course, are not political expenditures or reported as such.

President Nixon's legal expenses were extensive. While still in office—the GAO reported in May 1974—the federal government paid $382,474 in fees, salaries, and expenses for the team of White House lawyers who defended him up to that point. The figure went higher, with lawyers J. Fred Buzhardt and James D. St. Clair remaining on the payroll for a short time after Nixon's resignation. Rabbi Korff, whose group took over the job of raising funds for Nixon's legal fees when he left office, reported in March 1975 that Nixon's lawyers had run up $345,155 in bills since he resigned, primarily for his effort to keep control of his presidential tapes and papers.[46] Korff said that the total bill, barring unforeseen new legal action, might go as high as $400,000. Combining the GAO figure, the Korff estimate, and the further sums paid Buzhardt, St. Clair, and others during the summer of the Judiciary Committee hearings, a final total in excess of $1 million in Nixon's legal fees, public and private, seems not unlikely.

In further assessing legal costs of the 1972 election and its aftermath one should note the added expenses to taxpayers—although not political money— of the special staff of the Senate Watergate Committee, which at its peak numbered 90 persons; of the staff of the Office of the Special Prosecutor; and of the added staff of the House Judiciary Committee. The Judiciary Committee spent, by one estimate, $1,172,124; the Ervin Committee, reportedly $1.5 million;[47] and by mid-1975, the Special Prosecutor's office, $5.5 million.

The taxpayers seem clearly to have borne the greatest burden what with the various special government responses as well as the veritable army of attorneys and their staffs involved in the White House defense. In the GAO's May 1974 report on amounts spent on legal actions, $130,000 in costs were noted as billed to eight other federal agencies: Justice, Defense, HUD, Labor, HEW, Transportation, Agriculture and the FCC.[48] These amounts seem minimal, particularly insofar as the Department of Justice is concerned.

Impeachment Groups: Pro and Con

As the possibility of the impeachment of President Nixon gained credence with the swearing in of Gerald Ford as Vice-President in the fall of 1973, a number of "powerful and established organizations"[49] were at work supporting the impeachment effort. Primarily through direct mail efforts and newspaper ads, they attempted to persuade and inform the public about the impeachment process, or to urge congressmen to endorse impeachment. These groups, the AFL-CIO, the American Civil Liberties Union (ACLU), the National Emergency Civil Liberties Committee, the Americans for Democratic Action (ADA), Ralph Nader's "Public Citizen," and the National Committee for an Effective Congress were joined by newly established groups such as the National Committee on the Presidency, which was determined to secure the approximately 60 additional congressional votes needed to attain House majority approval on the impeachment vote, and the National Campaign to Impeach Nixon, which was described as "the left wing of impeachment politics."[50]

On October 14, 1973 the 245,000 member ACLU, whose board of directors had called for Nixon's impeachment on September 30, took a full-page ad in *The New York Times* detailing "why (impeachment) is necessary" and "how it can be done." Response was immediate and favorable, 751 respondents volunteering their services in the cause and 410 persons contributing more than

$10,000 in less than a week.[51] By May 1974 the newspaper advertising campaign had brought in about $150,000, of which $40,000 was spent on additional advertising.[52]

One of the major forces in the impeachment drive was the AFL-CIO, and Nixon loyalists suggested that union campaign contributions had made members of the House Judiciary Committee, which was studying grounds for impeachment, beholden to this lobby. Labor had contributed $189,000 to Democrats on the committee during the 1972 campaigns, compared with $2,100 to committee Republicans. Committee Chairman Peter Rodino, for example, had received about one-quarter of his 1972 campaign fund ($113,169) from labor, and was in fact the largest single House recipient of labor money, $28,923.

Labor had come a long way in less than a year since the 1972 election when AFL-CIO president George Meany got the powerful organization to go neutral rather than support McGovern. On October 24, the day after Nixon announced he would turn his tapes over to Judge Sirica, Meany made a public statement: ". . . Nothing that happened yesterday changes our opinion that the President has so destroyed the people's confidence in government that he should resign or be impeached."[53] Two days earlier at the AFL-CIO convention a unanimous vote for impeachment had been adopted. The federation also published in early November a 19-point "bill of particulars" against Nixon and mailed five million copies to union members nationwide.

Other pro-impeachment voices spoke from the conservative side. One such group was Conservatives for the Removal of the President (styling itself CREEP 2). It was headed by Howard Phillips, who had earlier been appointed by Nixon to head the Office of Economic Opportunity, but had subsequently resigned.

Common Cause maintained a neutral stance on impeachment but called for open proceedings in the House Judiciary Committee and provided the committee with pertinent legal memoranda and procedural information.

Committee for Fairness to the Presidency

In the summer of 1973, as the Senate Watergate Committee continued to hear ever more damaging testimony about President Nixon's role, Rabbi Baruch Korff of Massachusetts, who claimed to have tried without success to have letters protesting criticism of the President published in *The New York Times,* decided to raise funds to help back up his views. With some of his own money, plus funds borrowed and solicited from friends, he bought a $5,700 ad in the *Times* entitled "An Appeal for Fairness." In less than a month, Korff said, he had received $84,000 in cash and pledges from 10,000 individual contributors. With this he launched the National Citizens' Committee for Fairness to the Presidency. Over the next six months the committee claimed it raised about $400,000 from 160,000 people, which bought newspaper ads and other publicity denouncing the "liberal" press and Nixon's "enemies" in the Congress.[54] By the spring of 1974 the committee listed 217 affiliate groups and more than 350,000 contributors.[55]

Another prominent pro-Nixon organization, called Americans for the Presidency, was established by Donald M. Kendall, a personal friend of the President, and chairman of PepsiCo Inc., who had put together and managed a CRP effort in 1972 to organize the support of American business. The organization placed ads in 117 newspapers, listing nationally known sponsors including the Rev. Norman Vincent Peale, Mrs. Mamie Eisenhower, Bob Hope, and Teamsters Union President Frank E. Fitzsimmons. In May 1974 the group reported that it had collected $25,000 used for the ads and operating expenses.[56]

Following Nixon's resignation, the Korff group turned its efforts toward helping the former chief executive with his legal and medical bills, which shortly mounted to about $500,000, according to Korff.[57] For this purpose Korff organized the President Nixon Justice Fund. By October 1974 the legal fund—to which Nixon's lawyer directed submitted bills—was nearly $100,000 in debt. At that point it owed $77,773 to the firm of Herbert J. Miller, Nixon's lawyer, plus a $31,000 loan to another Korff-organized defense committee for the former President. Korff said the bills to the Miller firm plus $30,000 previously paid them, were for fees in the suits involving the challenged agreement on Nixon's White House tapes and papers plus a number of subpoenas served on Nixon.[58] In the following month the organization, which had changed its formal name to the President Nixon Justice Fund, was able to pay another $30,000 toward the legal fees.[59]

In addition to the two committees, Korff organized a third, the United States Citizens' Committee (USCC), which, he claimed in November 1974, had a paid membership of about 3,000. Dues varied from $500 for charter membership to $10 for annual student membership. The USCC published a monthly newsletter, commenting on Nixon's legal and medical plight, and frequently criticizing the news media.[60]

In February 1975 former press secretary Ronald L. Ziegler said that Nixon still had legal fees of $225,000 facing him and that some $100,000 had been collected by that time for legal defense funds. Ziegler said, ". . . [Nixon was on a] very tight budget. If he had to turn only to his own resources to pay for current and anticipated legal costs, he would be in a very serious financial position."[61]

The Agnew Resignation

Although untainted by Watergate, Vice President Spiro Agnew was forced to leave office by a scandal of his own making. While the Agnew case was dramatic, in that it reached to the highest levels of the federal government, it had all the dimensions of classic political corruption, illustrating anew the dangers of hidden money. It was ironic that Agnew, the administration's self-appointed champion of morality and a politician admired for his candor, stood accused of tax evasion and related white-collar crimes.[62]

What began as a routine investigation of corruption in Baltimore County in 1972, where a Democrat, N. Dale Anderson, had succeeded Agnew as County Executive, led ultimately to the Vice President's doorstep. About the same time that Agnew's Maryland campaign finance reports were subpoenaed, on August 10, 1973 the Salute to Ted Agnew Night Committee (which had supported President Nixon and other federal candidates in 1972) was indicted, on August 14, for violating the Maryland Fair Election Practices law. This case was discovered to fit a larger pattern of contributions to Agnew from persons already under investigation for alleged kickbacks and bribes, and led to the Grand Jury investigation of Agnew for alleged bribery, extortion, and tax fraud. Agnew's resignation from office was one of the conditions of a plea bargaining agreement under which he would plead no contest to the single count of tax evasion while the federal government would publish a 40-page account of how he had extorted bribes for ten years, 1962-72, during which he served as Baltimore County Executive, Governor of Maryland, and Vice President. According to witnesses, Agnew had used political office to hand out county and state contracts in exchange for personal payoffs from seven engineering firms and one financial institution, pocketing well over $100,000.[f] In 1967 alone he failed to pay taxes on money from such kickbacks that amounted to $29,500.

As the account was put together by the United States attorney in Maryland, George Beall, one of whose witnesses was a prominent political fund raiser, I.H. Hammerman, II, Agnew followed what had allegedly been customary with Maryland governors and taken advantage of the state law that left the awarding of engineering contracts to the discretion of the governor and state roads commissioner, rather than providing for competitive public bidding. The man who had been Agnew's public works staff man in Baltimore County, Jerome B. Wolff, went to Annapolis with Governor Agnew as state roads commissioner and became Vice President Agnew's science adviser. Agnew, Wolff, and Hammerman worked out a plan whereby any kickback money went 50 percent to the Governor, with the remainder split evenly between the other two men. The kickbacks followed Agnew to the vice-presidency. According to the government account, Agnew argued that the demands of his vice-presidential office would increase his personal expenses—although his salary was $62,500 annually plus

---

[f]On October 2, 1973 Maryland's Governor Mandel named an 11-member task force to study the awarding of state contracts without competitive bidding. Under the chairmanship of Professor Abel Wolman of Johns Hopkins, the results were published on December 15, 1973 in "Report of the State of Maryland Task Force on Non-Competitive Contracts."

$10,000 for expenses—while noting that he would do what he could for contractors with respect to federal work.

The evidence of Agnew's implication in the scandal, gathered in Maryland, was brought to the attention of Attorney General Elliot Richardson in July of 1973. Richardson, concerned over the mounting evidence at the Ervin Committee hearings that could conceivably lead to the impeachment of the President, felt this made it imperative that Agnew—who stood to be convicted as a felon—resign the vice-presidency.

When he was first confronted with the evidence by Richardson, Agnew denied the allegations, and he continued to plead his innocence through August and September. He was put under increasing pressure from the White House and the Justice Department to resign. He himself maintained his innocence to the end, but finally, facing a possible prison term, he accepted the plea bargaining conditions that would leave him technically free to proclaim he had done nothing wrong; he pleaded "no contest" which is the legal equivalent of a guilty plea without the admission.[g]

A week after his resignation and admission of income tax evasion, Agnew addressed the nation on television, on October 15, 1973, asserting his innocence, claiming he "made the plea because it was the only way to quickly resolve the situation." In discussing his own case, he blamed the system of political financing for catching people up, expressing the hope that as an aftermath to recent events a new system for financing campaigns would be established. He spoke in favor of public funding for every candidate and urged state and local governments to amend their laws to prevent abuses and corruption.

Agnew left office with sizable debts on a home he had heavily mortgaged, owing back taxes and heavy legal fees. In December 1974 he was disbarred—a further blow to his fortunes. Among the fund-raising efforts to help the former Vice President in his financial difficulties was one launched by Frank Sinatra, a close friend of Agnew, who reportedly wrote and called a number of his friends, asking them to contribute up to $3,000 each to help defray legal expenses.[63]

In January 1974 the GAO disclosed that a total of $89,222 had been spent on Secret Service protection for Agnew after he had left office, a move for which President Nixon had no legal authority.[64]

In September 1974 Agnew became involved with land developer and political speculator Walter Dilbeck of Evansville, Indiana, and an Arab investment group from Kuwait. Agnew acted as developer's agent for Dilbeck at a $100,000-a-year-plus-expenses salary. The plans for the large-scale development

---

[g]For two investigative works on Agnew written by Washington reporters—the first inspired during the last days of Agnew's 1970 campaign to drive "radical liberals" out of Congress, the second inspired by his resignation—see Joseph Albright, *What Makes Spiro Run* (New York: Dodd, Mead & Company, 1972), and Richard M. Cohen and Jules Witcover (of the *Washington Post*), *A Heartbeat Away* (New York: The Viking Press, 1974).

project, assessed as high as $8.25 million, fell through, as did Agnew's relationship with Dilbeck after Agnew reportedly was paid most of his salary.[65]

Watergate

The Ellsberg Break-in

One of the more sensational disclosures from the Watergate maze was that there was a link between that break-in and one at the office of the psychiatrist of Dr. Daniel Ellsberg, who was being tried, along with Anthony Russo, for releasing to the press the top secret "Pentagon Papers" on the history of the American role in Southeast Asia. During their trial it was revealed that members of the same team caught burglarizing Watergate had also, some nine months earlier in September 1971, broken into the office of Dr. Lewis J. Fielding, Ellsberg's psychiatrist.

The "Pentagon Papers" began appearing in the press in June 1971, leading to a sharply increased concern in the White House over "national security" leaks. Within a week after *The New York Times* published the first story of a three-part series on June 13, 1971 (the *Washington Post* and other papers then followed suit), Nixon authorized the formation of the unit known as the Plumbers, operating out of the White House basement. The team, created ostensibly to "stop security leaks and investigate other sensitive security matters,"[66] was supervised by John Ehrlichman, with help from Charles Colson, headed by Egil Krogh (later convicted and sentenced), and employed G. Gordon Liddy and E. Howard Hunt.

Seeking to gain material to discredit Ellsberg, a team, outfitted with CIA equipment at White House request, and led by Liddy and Hunt, burglarized Dr. Fielding's office in Los Angeles; the CIA had prepared an earlier, inadequate psychiatric profile of Ellsberg. The results both of the burglary and the final profile were unrewarding from the White House point of view.

The financing of the Fielding burglary, as determined by Watergate Special Prosecutor Archibald Cox, was convoluted. Colson arranged a $5,000 no-questions-asked loan from Washington public relations executive Joseph Baroody, who had been a Nixon campaign fund raiser and organizer. Colson repaid the loan with funds from the Associated Milk Producers, Inc., delivered at his request to a dummy committee headed by Washington attorney George Webster.[h] The dairy money was converted to cash, given to a messenger Colson sent, and paid to Baroody September 21, 1971—less than a month after he was asked for the loan.

---

[h]A number of Washington, D.C. paper committees were set up by Colson to receive secret campaign donations, including part of the dairy lobby's contributions made allegedly in return for the administration's increase in milk price supports.

The Ellsberg-Russo trial had been under way for about five months when, on May 2, 1973, Judge W. Matthew Byrne, Jr. asked for a dismissal and mistrial motion, making it clear he was penalizing the government for its prosecution of the case. On April 27 he had disclosed publicly for the first time the fact of the Liddy-Hunt involvement in the Ellsberg case. Only two days before that Nixon had permitted the Justice Department to tell Judge Byrne of this involvement. He had previously ordered Assistant Attorney General Henry Petersen to "stay out of" that possible link to Watergate on national security terms. With Petersen's threat to resign, however, Nixon relented. When asking dismissal, Judge Byrne further revealed that on two occasions in early April he had met in San Clemente with Ehrlichman, and once with Nixon. Ehrlichman had asked Byrne if he would like to be considered for directorship of the FBI once the Ellsberg case was settled. Although Byrne was interested, another qualified nominee was accepted for the position before he could be considered.

The Tapes Suits

When President Ford announced his pardon of former President Nixon in early September 1974, one aspect of the matter provoked particularly widespread criticism—the agreement that Nixon would be the one to determine which, if any, of the famous White House tapes could be released from his custody. News of the agreement touched off a flurry of legal activities and congressional action.

The Special Prosecutor's Office, which had not been consulted in advance on the agreement, immediately began negotiations with the White House where the tapes (and cartons of other documents involved in the agreement) were still being stored. The White House itself backed off; Justice Department lawyers announced that the agreement was not "self-executing," meaning that as long as the Ford Administration did not move to begin turning over the tapes to Nixon, the agreement had no force. Senators Sam Ervin of North Carolina and Gaylord Nelson of Wisconsin introduced a bill that passed overwhelmingly, in effect nullifying the agreement. In October Judge Charles R. Richey of Federal District Court, District of Columbia, issued a restraining order on the agreement.[67]

Nixon meanwhile had also filed suit seeking enforcement of the agreement. Two groups of writers, historians, political scientists, and filmmakers filed suits asking that the agreement be declared illegal. And convicted Watergate burglar James McCord also sued to rule the pact illegal on grounds that he needed access to certain of the tapes in connection with a civil suit he had filed on another aspect of the Watergate case.[68]

The Watergate cover-up trial of Mitchell, Haldeman, Ehrlichman, Mardian, and Parkinson was concurrently underway, and Judge John J. Sirica ruled that certain of the tapes requested by the prosecution might be introduced in evidence. They proved devastating to the defense case, particularly to Haldeman's case. They also showed clear evidence of alterations in and deletions from the edited transcripts released by the White House in April 1973—the transcripts that, in Nixon's words, purported to show "everything that is relevant" and "tell it all"; passages excluded would have been highly damaging to Nixon's defense against impeachment.[69]

It was in the new tapes also that there surfaced evidence that Charles G. (Bebe) Rebozo may have controlled a sum of money two or three times as large as the $100,000 from Howard Hughes that Watergate investigators then knew about; the tapes revealed Nixon offered Haldeman and Ehrlichman money from a special fund—seemingly set up to provide favors to long-time Nixon campaign contributors—to recoup their legal fees in April 1973 (they declined his offer).[70]

In December 1974 the House passed unanimously the bill requiring the federal government to take possession of Nixon's papers and tapes; it was then signed by President Ford.[71] Also in December U.S. District Court Judge Gerhard Gesell ruled that there could be public broadcast of the tapes played during the cover-up trial. Gesell said in his ruling that he saw no legal barrier to making the tapes public. Nixon's attorneys subsequently appealed the ruling on grounds that this could intrude on presidential privilege, invade the former President's privacy, and could be embarrassing to those on tapes "in candid conversations never intended to be publicly aired."[72] The three television networks, the public broadcasting system, and a recording firm had been told by Gesell that they must come up with a plan "which does not permit over-commercialization of the evidence." The initial plan submitted by these groups, however, was rejected by Gesell; it did not, in his view, protect against commercialization or undignified use of the material. He then turned the matter over to Judge Sirica, where it may be raised again—Gesell had taken the case because Sirica was too occupied with the cover-up trial at the time the tapes question was first raised.[73]

Nixon's attorneys also continued to press the larger matter of the former President's ownership of the tapes and other documents, in spite of the congressional action. When Judge Charles Richey ruled in U.S. District Court, District of Columbia, that the materials belonged to the government and not to Nixon, the attorneys sought an appeal route that they hoped would take the issue as directly as possible to the Supreme Court.[74]

The Cover-Up Trial

The Watergate cover-up trial began on October 1, 1974. It ended exactly three months later on New Year's Day, 1975, when—for many millions of Americans—the news that Nixon's top aides had been found guilty came as an interruption in the Rose Bowl game. John Mitchell, H.R. Haldeman, John

Ehrlichman, and Robert Mardian were found guilty on all counts after the jury had deliberated for 15 hours over a period of three days. A fifth defendant, Kenneth W. Parkinson, counsel to the CRP after the Watergate break-in, was acquitted. The jury findings came, fittingly, on the day that one of the most sweeping campaign reform laws in United States political history took effect.

For each of the five, the government sought to prove the following:

John Mitchell.   That he had approved the campaign espionage plan which led to the Watergate break-in and afterwards helped in the cover-up by suggesting evidence be destroyed and approving payment of hush money.

H.R. Haldeman.   That he sought to get CIA leaders to put pressure on the FBI to limit the investigation of the burglary, and that he, too, approved payments, from his secret $350,000 fund in cash.

John Ehrlichman.   That he helped Haldeman in the CIA matter, ordered destruction of evidence, and tried to get the CIA to pay money to the burglars.

Robert Mardian.   That he had been in meetings in which hush money, destroying evidence, and false cover stories had been discussed and plotted.

Kenneth Parkinson.   That he had participated in the cover story and had relayed demands for money.

The defendants denied all charges, testifying on their own behalf. Their attorneys hammered at the credibility of the government witnesses, and in fact, most of the major prosecution witnesses—Jeb Magruder, Frederick LaRue, E. Howard Hunt, and John Dean—conceded on the stand that they had, at one time or another, lied to investigators about their role in the affair — above all, Dean, who tied each of the defendants to the conspiracy, and whose credibility was most severely challenged by defense attorneys.

Against this, however, were the White House tapes that the public first heard about in the summer of 1973 at the Senate Watergate hearings, and that Judge John Sirica permitted the prosecution to play to the jurors over strong defense objection. On the tapes, played on earphones to judge, jury, defendants, lawyers, and spectators at the trial, Haldeman and Nixon were heard discussing the use of the CIA to thwart the FBI and discussing hush money. Ehrlichman was heard, with Haldeman and Nixon, trying to put together the cover-up "scenario." Mitchell played a less prominent role on the tapes, but the others talked about him and his knowledge in advance of the espionage plan.

Nixon, ill with phlebitis in California, was unable to appear at the trial, although his testimony was sought by both Haldeman and Ehrlichman. Their defense lawyers, in final arguments, sought to depict the former President as the "maestro" who orchestrated the Watergate cover-up. Mitchell's lawyer said that the former Attorney General and director of CRP had only done what he did because he was loyal to Mr. Nixon and trusted him completely.

The jury's verdict was apparently a popular one with most Americans—70 percent questioned in a Gallup Poll after the guilty verdict was in on four out of five men said they agreed with the finding. The public was almost evenly divided (43 percent for, 44 percent against) on granting them pardons, in light of the one granted Nixon by Ford. Americans also were divided on whether the men should be jailed or fined—34 percent for jail, 30 percent for fines, 15 percent for both jail and fines.[75]

The possible penalties the defendants could have received ranged from five years in jail for Mardian to 25 years for Mitchell and Haldeman. All four men announced that they planned to appeal, a process expected to go on two to three years and conceivably to reach the Supreme Court.

The question remained as to whether Special Prosecutor Henry S. Ruth, Jr., who succeeded Leon Jaworski, should prepare a final report detailing all his office knew about the Nixon role. Both Ruth and Jaworski, in testimony before a subcommittee of the House Judiciary Committee in January 1975, said they doubted the constitutionality of any legislation that would authorize the Special Prosecutor's Office to issue any such report. They said that although there was further "incremental" evidence against Nixon, they did not have substantial evidence that had not already been made public. Ruth said the unpublished evidence, however, involved many other persons whose rights would be invaded, and he was certain the constitutionality of a law requiring a final comprehensive report would be challenged in court.[76]

LaRue Sentenced to Prison

Frederick C. LaRue was sentenced in March 1975 to six months in prison (reduced by the court from an original sentence of from one to three years) for his role in the cover-up. LaRue was an aide to CRP Director John Mitchell, and in that capacity was responsible for funneling thousands of dollars in $100 bills to the Watergate burglars. Under a special arrangement with the prosecutors, LaRue pleaded guilty to a single count of a conspiracy to obstruct justice. He was the first participant to plead guilty in the cover-up—in an indictment handed down only ten days after the break-in at the DNC—and the last of eight men convicted in the case to be sentenced. He entered prison on April 1, 1975.

Strachan Case

The case against Gordon Strachan ended in March 1975, when the Special

Prosecutor's Office asked that all criminal charges against him be dropped. A former White House aide (deputy to H.R. Haldeman), Strachan achieved perhaps his greatest notice in the summer of 1973 when, in his Senate Watergate testimony, he advised young people to "stay away" from the federal service. Originally he had been named in the conspiracy indictment against the top White House aides, including Haldeman, Ehrlichman, and Mitchell. Strachan had been accused of obstruction of justice, conspiracy to obstruct justice, and lying to the Watergate grand jury about a $350,000 cash fund used in the payoff of the original Watergate defendants. His case was separated from the others, after he contended successfully that evidence against him would be tainted because he had cooperated with the Prosecutor's Office on the promise of limited immunity.

Freeing of Dean, Magruder, Kalmbach, and Colson

With the verdict in on the Watergate cover-up trial, but before passing any sentence on the four men found guilty—Mitchell, Haldeman, Ehrlichman, and Mardian—Judge John Sirica freed three men whose testimony had helped convict them—John Dean, Jeb Stuart Magruder, and Herbert Kalmbach. Sirica gave no explanation for his action. Dean had served four months of a one- to four-year sentence. Kalmbach had completed the minimum of his six- to 18-month sentence. Magruder had served seven months of a ten-month to four-year term. A good portion of their time while in custody was spent in prosecutors' and lawyers' offices and at trials.

Although Judge Sirica gave no reason for the move, he was known to favor setting examples for convicted men who have cooperated in helping the courts establish the full truth of circumstances surrounding their crimes, a cooperation that the Special Prosecutor's Office had received from the three newly freed men.[77] Perhaps their release was meant to be a signal to one or more of the four defendants to come forward and tell all before sentencing. None did. Three weeks later Judge Gerhard A. Gesell freed Charles W. Colson from prison after he had served seven months of a one- to three-year term. The judge cited "serious family difficulties which have greatly aggravated the severity of the sentence imposed."[78]

Lecture Tour Controversy

Several of the men who had figured prominently in the Watergate matter undertook profitable lecture tours after Nixon had resigned from office—and the matter of fees, particularly those of Ron Ziegler and John Dean, stirred up considerable controversy.

Ronald L. Ziegler, former Nixon press secretary and one of the few men in the upper echelons of the White House who was never charged with a crime, was invited to speak at Boston University, but the invitation was rescinded, partially because of student and faculty resentment of the $2,500 fee Ziegler was to receive. Boston University President John R. Silber later reissued the invitation, but offered Ziegler the school's maximum speaker's fee of $1,000 plus expenses. Ziegler declined to accept, and the speech was cancelled. He did speak, however, at Michigan State University over the protest of the student government, which originally was to pay half of the $2,500 fee negotiated by Ziegler's agent. When the students withdrew their support, the school's administration said they would pay the full fee asked.[79]

John Dean began a lecture tour within a few weeks after he was freed from jail in January 1975 that was calculated to net him $100,000. For his first appearance at the University of Virginia he was paid $4,000, and tickets to the speech were $1.50 and $2.50. The campus newspaper protested the speech as did a small group of students, chiefly on the grounds that the fee was too high. Dean went on to speak at Georgetown University in the face of a protest petition signed by more than 1,000 faculty and students, which said that in paying Dean $3,000 "we feel that we are tacitly encouraging the practice of rewarding serious and sensational crime."[80]

In addition to his lecture earnings, Dean received a $300,000 advance for his book about Watergate, while his wife, Maureen, received a $150,000 advance for a book on her life and courtship with the White House counsel.

Senate Watergate Committee Recommendations

In its final report the Senate Watergate Committee made a series of recommendations bearing on presidential practices and campaign finance, as an outgrowth of its investigations.[81] The amendments to the Federal Election Campaign Act, which took effect January 1, 1975,[82] incorporated eight of the committee's 11 recommendations on campaign financing in one form or another —some as recommended, others with changes. These dealt mainly with limitations on cash contributions, limits on campaign contributions, the establishment of a Federal Election Commission, and a flat ban on solicitation or acceptance of foreign gifts. The committee recommended, for example, that individual contributions be limited to $3,000, and group contributions to $6,000; as finally enacted, the comparable limitations were $1,000 and $5,000. Many of the provisions were a foregone conclusion, at least so far as the committee was concerned, because the Senate had already passed a campaign finance measure by the time of the committee report.

The committee, however, also recommended that public funds not be used to finance presidential campaigns: five of the seven members of the committee preferred a tax alternative, whereby a 100 percent tax credit up to $25 on a single return ($50 on a joint return) would be given to political contributors. This plan would have avoided the arbitrary allocations of a subsidy, permitting instead citizen determination of where the money would go in accordance with patterns of individual contributions given to candidates and committees of the donor's choice.

At the close of the 93rd Congress, Senator Ervin introduced a bill proposing a series of reforms designed to prevent further abuses of executive power, which reflected the recommendations published throughout the Watergate Committee *Report*. The wide-ranging reform effort was reintroduced by Senator Abraham Ribicoff, D-Connecticut, in the Watergate Reorganization and Reform Act of 1975 when Congress reconvened in January 1975.[i] With the exception of those specific campaign reform provisions enacted in the FECA Amendments, the bill addressed itself to the recommendations of the Watergate Committee. The bill's co-sponsors included three of the five remaining "Watergate Senators" (Ervin and Gurney had not sought reelection)— Inouye of Hawaii, Montoya of New Mexico, and Weicker of Connecticut. Missing as sponsors were Senators Baker of Tennessee and Talmadge of Georgia.

In the area of political finance, the bill proposed that the maximum for tax credit on political contributions be increased to $25 per individual ($50 on a joint return), and abolished tax deductions for such contributions with a view to encouraging small contributions. The bill would make it illegal for any government official who must be confirmed by the Senate or is on the White House payroll to solicit or receive campaign gifts while in office and for one year after leaving office. Whereas the committee had recommended that violations of major FECA provisions, such as participating in illegal corporate or union contributions, be upgraded to a felony, both the FECA Amendments and the proposed reorganization bill would increase the fine for illegal campaign contributions by corporations and labor unions.

The Watergate reorganization proposal extended beyond political finance in proposing the establishment of a permanent office of Public Attorney independent of the executive and judicial branches of government; a Congressional Legal Service under the direction of a Congressional Legal Counsel to guard against executive usurpation of legislative functions and protect congressional interests in court; extended coverage of the Hatch Act—the law that limits participation in political campaigns by federal employees—to the Justice Department, including the Attorney General; and new standards regarding congressional investigations and hearings.

---

[i]S. 495: "A bill to establish certain federal agencies, effect certain reorganizations of the federal government, and to implement certain reforms in the operation of the federal government recommended by the Senate Select Committee on Presidential Campaign Activities, and for other purposes." Referred to the Committee on Government Operations. See *Congressional Record*, January 30, 1975, S1211-17.

Other proposals in the bill focused on matters that were clearly related to some of the financial excesses that came to be put under the Watergate umbrella. The bill would require annual disclosure by the President and Vice President of income, taxes, business transactions, debts, and expenditures on their behalf. It would expand coverage of that section of the law that makes it illegal to award federal grants and loans to try to influence an election. It would sharply limit access by White House officials to Internal Revenue records.

Further, the proposed act would create several new criminal provisions, such as a prohibition against the use of campaign funds to finance any violations of the federal election laws. Another proposal, designed to protect persons dependent on federal funds from overzealous campaign solicitations, would prohibit solicitation of, or political contributions by, any person receiving a federal grant, loan, or subsidy from Congress in excess of $5,000 (during that calendar year).

Watergate and the Media

One of the major participants in the Watergate drama was the United States media. The investigative reporting of the *Washington Post's* Carl Bernstein and Bob Woodward turned up key evidence early in the case that linked the Watergate burglars to CRP and the White House, and helped win the *Post* the Pulitzer Prize.[83] The televised hearings of the Ervin Committee, and later the Rodino Committee, undoubtedly played a large role in the shaping of public attitudes to a point where a President had the lowest poll ratings for that office in a quarter century. That same President often used television himself. Nixon, the chief executive who probably had the fewest press conferences for his time in office of any President since the practice was inaugurated, also called on the TV networks more frequently than any President to give him free time for speeches to the American people. In the Watergate affair he took to television to explain the resignations of Haldeman and Ehrlichman, to defend and explain away in a series of white papers his deepening involvement, and, at the end, to announce that he was resigning. Thanks to television, the resignation speech was seen by more people than any other event in American history— with the exception of man's landing on the moon: Some 100 million citizens watched the speech in the United States, it has been variously estimated, while 125 million Americans watched the moon landing in July 1969.[84]

For its role in Watergate the press was both castigated and praised. As might be expected, the nature of comments about the press role was often best understood by their source. Nixon's own antipress feelings have been amply documented; his animus went well back into his early years in politics. Bernstein and Woodward, in *All the President's Men*, vividly report how Nixon was furious about news leaks on Watergate early in 1973, urging his aides to try to stop them.[85] But among those who blamed the United States press for its effort to "get Nixon" were such strange bedfellows as Robert Welch of the John Birch Society and Leonid M. Zamyatin, director general of Tass, the Soviet press agency, both of whom attacked a press conspiracy.[86]

Criticism of the press came too from within its own ranks. Finlay Lewis, a Washington correspondent from the *Minneapolis Tribune*, writing in the special issue of the *Columbia Journalism Review* (*CJR*) devoted to "Watergate and the Press," argued that the press, for all its good work in helping uncover Watergate, had also its share of errors, one of which, by CBS, led to a libel suit against the network.[87] In the same issue, Ben Bagdikian, the *Review's* national correspondent, discussed the need for newspapers to provide analysis and interpretation as a supplement to live TV coverage of something like the Watergate hearings.[88] Several months earlier *New York Times* columnist James Reston had raised the issue of the need for "all the analysis we can get of Presidential power and television power. . ."; CBS had just announced it would replace its "instant analysis" with a policy of "delayed reaction."[89] Jules Witcover of the *Washington Post*, also in *CJR*, wrote of some of the ways the White House press corps might have performed better in their coverage.[90]

In the early stages of Watergate, while the *Washington Post* was featuring its coverage in front-page stories, many other newspapers buried the stories on inside pages, and came around to great urgency only when the news value of the exposures made prominent coverage inescapable. According to a survey by Bagdikian, in the last half of 1972 "no more than 14 reporters of the 2,200 assigned to Washington" began investigating Watergate and reporting on it.[91]

However, probably no previous domestic story ever commanded so much continuing attention and the efforts of so many investigative reporters. Much of the reporting covered the financing of the Nixon reelection campaign, and one reporter, James R. Polk of the *Washington Star-News*, won a Pulitzer Prize for his national news reporting. Polk's winning entry included ten stories on political finance, and won mention particularly for disclosures he made of the secret Vesco donation to the Nixon campaign, and exclusive reports on the handling of secret funds by Herbert W. Kalmbach, Nixon's former personal attorney.

In the course of the Democrats' civil suit against the CRP, and the ensuing countersuit, attorneys from the reelection committee attempted, unsuccessfully, to force newsmen and their publications to provide notes and records, and to give depositions.

The CRP attorney, Kenneth Wells Parkinson, issued subpoenas to reporters and executives of the *Washington Post*, the *Washington Star-News*, *The New York Times* and *Time* magazine. Lawyers for the newsmen argued before D.C. District Court Judge Charles Richey that the constitutional rights of the reporters and publications would be violated if they were forced to turn over investigative materials. *The New York Times* publisher, Arthur Ochs Sulzberger, who was not subpoenaed, interposed himself between the court and his reporters, arguing that files and notes developed by the *Times* reporters were not their property, but that of the Times corporation, and thus the reporters could not present them.

The newmen's briefs were answered in court by CRP litigators with charges, for example, that the *Post* brief was "in poor taste" and "outrageous." The CRP further argued: "Reduced to bare essentials the pleas of these [newsmen] is a unified demand of the Fourth Estate for exemption from the duty to appear and give testimony in virtually all civil litigation."[92]

Nevertheless, Judge Richey ruled in favor of the newsmen, stating in part:

> This court cannot blind itself to the possible chilling effect the enforce-
> ment of these subpoenas would have on the flow of information to the
> press and, thus, to the public. This court stands convinced that if it
> allows the discouragement of investigative reporting into the highest
> levels of government, that no amount of legal theorizing could allay
> the public's suspicions engendered by its actions and by the matters
> alleged in this lawsuit. . . .[93]

The press provides a crucial link in the flow of information to the public in the matter of the campaign disclosure laws enacted at the federal level and in so many states as a response to Watergate. As Timothy Harper noted in *The Quill*: ". . . for all practical purposes, disclosure is meaningless unless the press does its part. Every candidate can follow a disclosure law to the letter, but the public will never know where the money came from or where it went unless newsmen relay the information."[94] Unless the press makes a point of who gave what to whom—as was done so well in the Watergate affair—the public will not gain full benefit from the disclosures now required at the federal and state levels.

FECA Amendments of 1974

On May 16, 1973 President Nixon sent a special message to Congress proposing the creation of a nonpartisan commission to study campaign reform. The move came during a time of maximum pressure from Watergate and related scandals; the public hearings of the Senate Watergate Committee were to begin the next day. Nixon was by no means out in front in his calls for reform. A week earlier, on May 8, a House Republican leader, John B. Anderson of Illinois, had introduced a bill (H.R. 7612) that he co-sponsored with Democrat Morris Udall of Arizona calling for an independent Federal Election Commission.

In spite of these events, it was one month short of two years before a new election law became fully operational, with President Ford's April 14, 1975 swearing-in of the six members of the Federal Election Commission established by the 1974 Amendments to the Federal Election Campaign Act. Along with the creation of the commission, the other major "firsts" in the bill were the establishment of overall limitations on how much could be spent in political campaigning, and the extension of public funding to campaigns for presidential nomination and for the workings of the national conventions.

In the period leading up to the 1974 enactment, pressures for change were many. Startling patterns of campaign finance were disclosed under the FECA requirements. The Watergate, Agnew, and related scandals exposed practically every election corrupt practice. The media covered closely the development of election legislation, and generally editorialized in favor of reform, including favorable support of the concept of public funding. Common Cause continued its role, lobbying and monitoring congressional political fund reports. In mid-1973 a new group, the Center for Public Financing of Elections, was established as an independent, single-purpose lobby group and focal point for pressure. Interestingly, some large political contributors were among its supporters. A coalition of 30 such groups, ranging from environmentalists to labor unions, and including the National Committee for an Effective Congress, the League of Women Voters, and the National Women's Political Caucus, held periodic meetings to plot strategy.

Although the Anderson-Udall impetus came in the House, the actual passage of legislation in 1973 came only in the Senate. On July 30, by an overwhelming 82-8 margin, the Senate adopted a reform bill designed to improve the FECA of 1971.[j]

The bill (S.372) was sponsored by Senator John Pastore, D-Rhode Island. Hearings were first held on expenditure limitations (by the Commerce Committee) and then on disclosure and other portions (by the Rules and Administration committees). The Rules Committee's version of the bill was then strengthened considerably during debate on the Senate floor. The pattern with most campaign finance legislation in the Senate in the past decade has been that weaker bills are reported out and then strengthened on the floor. In the course of debate, the Senate defeated, 53-38, an amendment by Senators Edward Kennedy and Hugh Scott to extend public financing beyond the provisions in the Revenue Act of 1971.

In the fall the scene shifted to the House, where the greater frequency with which its members must face reelection had traditionally made it a more conservative body on questions of campaign reform. There the Pastore bill faced Representative Wayne Hays of Ohio, chairman of the Committee on House

---

[j]S.372, 93rd Cong., 1st sess., 1973 (the "Federal Election Campaign Act Amendments of 1973") contained provisions that would strictly control campaign spending and contributions, strengthen disclosure requirements, and establish an independent bipartisan monitoring and enforcement agency. The bill did not provide for public campaign financing.

Administration, cautious in the matter of reform, and opposed to public financing of elections. The bill was referred to his committee's Subcommittee on Elections where hearings were held on it and the Anderson-Udall bill in October and November. Although neither bill concerned public funding, considerable time was devoted to discussion of that issue. When the first session of the 93rd Congress adjourned, Hays pledged that he would have a bill reported out early in 1974.

Meanwhile, in November the Senate was considering H.R. 11104—a House bill to temporarily increase the public debt ceiling. Under a unanimous-consent agreement between the leadership of the two parties, six hours of debate on amendments dealing with public funding of campaigns were permitted—the primary target was a proposal offered by Senator Kennedy, which called for public funding of both presidential primary and general elections as well as Senate and House general elections only. On November 27, passage (57-34) of an amended version of Kennedy's proposal sent the debt ceiling bill back to the House, where the Rules Committee filed a resolution disagreeing with the Senate amendments. The House adopted this resolution, 347-54, on November 29 and Senate Finance Committee Chairman Russell Long, D-Louisiana, promptly moved that the Senate request a conference with the House. Senator James Allen, D-Alabama, a vehement opponent of public finance, led a parliamentary attack by filibustering. In early December two attempts at cloture having failed, the effort to enact public financing was dropped for that session.[k]

Nixon again urged that Congress set up a commission to study campaign reform proposals in his November 17 press conference in Orlando, Florida with the Associated Press Managing Editors. But the Democratic-controlled Congress did not want to accede to another study group; it wanted to pass a law to amend the 1971 Act.

Campaign reform was a major item on the agenda as the second session of the 93rd Congress got underway, although just when a House version might get out of the House Administration Committee was an open question. As the year opened, the Subcommittee on Elections was still going through the markup process. In his State of the Union message, in which he declared "one year of Watergate is enough," Nixon took note of the congressional delay on reform and announced that he would submit an administration proposal on campaign reform.

The White House proposals came on March 8, 1974, in a televised address to the nation, and they pleased very few congressional leaders, including those of Nixon's own party. Anderson in the House, and Senate Minority Leader

---

[k]See U.S., *Congressional Record*, 93rd Cong., 1st sess., vol. 119 (November 30) S21495-21505, S21575-21578; (December 1) S21631-21634; (December 2) S21638-21647; (December 3) S21707-21726—for the extended Senate debate.

Hugh Scott—the principal co-sponsors of bipartisan reform bills then under consideration—indicated at a White House briefing that they disagreed fundamentally with the Nixon plan. It was viewed by many as combining "safe" reforms everyone wanted with others that were unpassable. As for public finance, Nixon called it "taxation without representation."[95]

Congressman Hays kept pushing back the date of his promised bill, in spite of pressure to act more quickly from Common Cause and other reformers. His committee did not begin markup sessions until March 26. On April 11, 1974, after 13 days of debate, the Senate passed by a 53-32 vote a campaign reform bill (S.3044), combining provisions of S.372 with a call for public funding of presidential and congressional primary and general election campaigns. It survived one last filibuster attempt by Senator Allen to kill it, with a rare vote of cloture on April 9. The Senate bill provided that candidates for the House, Senate, and the presidency would be limited to federal funds to pay for their general election campaign costs, and would have to rely on a mixture of small private contributions and matching federal grants for primary contests.

In what many saw as deference to Allen before the cloture vote, the Senate adopted his amendment reducing the amount a candidate could spend—to eight cents per voter in primaries, 12 cents per voter in general elections. Some supporters of public financing warned that this was an impractically low figure. Applied to the eligible voter population in 1972, for example, it would have meant that Nixon and McGovern would have been limited to about $14 million each, very low amounts considering what they actually spent.

Another amendment adopted was one offered by Senator James Buckley, C-New York, requiring an immediate certification by the Federal Court of Appeals of any court test of the constitutionality of the bill's provisions, an opportunity of which he and other opponents availed themselves when the final version of the campaign reform bill became law.[1]

On July 30, 1974 the House version of a campaign reform bill (H.R. 16090) —which Hays had pledged would be out early in the session—was reported to the floor. It was approved, 355-48, on August 8, a few hours before Nixon announced his resignation. The House version differed sharply from the Senate bill by being much more limited in scope; but although it called for public funding for presidential—not congressional—elections, it added public financing of presidential nominating conventions.

Another delay was created by Hays when he balked over naming the House

---

[1]Buckley was joined in his court challenge on January 2, 1975 by former Senator Eugene McCarthy, Representative William Steiger, millionaire political activist Stewart R. Mott, the Committee for a Constitutional Presidency, the Conservative Party of New York, the New York Civil Liberties Union, the American Conservative Union, and *Human Events*. Suit was filed in the District of Columbia, U.S. District Court. See U.S., *Congressional Record*, 94th Cong., 1st sess., vol. 121 (January 16) H 173-178, for a reprint of the pleadings.

members of the conference committee because of dissatisfaction with certain of the proposed Senate members, particularly those like Pastore, Long, and Kennedy who had been in the forefront of the campaign reform legislation.

The conferees finally began meeting in September, but the impasse between House and Senate members on the public finance issue was not settled until early October. As finally passed by the committee, the bill included only presidential elections in the public funding. The reform bill was passed, 60-16, by the Senate, and 365-24 by the House; it was signed by President Ford on October 15, 1974, to take effect January 1, 1975. A long-time opponent of public funding, the President expressed doubts about some sections of the law, but said "the times demand this legislation."[96] The law is outlined in Appendix C.

When the law took effect January 1, 1975, it did so with the Federal Election Commission, the enforcement device of the new legislation, not yet fully named. Only two of the six members on the commission had then been named, and one of those was to be withdrawn and replaced by another. In the absence of the commission, the Clerk of the House and the Secretary of the Senate continued to carry out their roles in administering the FECA of 1971. By then, a number of 1976 presidential candidates had announced and were going about the matter of raising money geared to the new law.

The law specified that four members of the commission would be nominated by Congress, two by the President. The original nominee of Senate Majority Leader Mike Mansfield was Joseph F. Meglen of Billings, Montana—Mansfield's treasurer in his two previous Senate campaigns. When objections were raised to Meglen's qualifications for the $38,000-a-year post, and he rethought the obligation to move to Washington for what was essentially a full-time job, he had his name withdrawn. The Senate then nominated Thomas E. Harris of Arkansas, former associate general counsel of AFL-CIO. Senate Minority Leader Scott named Joan D. Aikens of Swarthmore, Pennsylvania, the head of the Pennsylvania Council of Republican Women. The two nominees from the House were both former Congressmen—Robert O. Tiernan of Rhode Island named by Democratic Majority Leader Thomas P. (Tip) O'Neill, and Vernon Thomson of Wisconsin, nominated by Republican leader John J. Rhodes. Ford's two nominees were also former Representatives: Thomas B. Curtis, Republican of Missouri; and Neil O. Staebler, Democrat of Michigan. The members of the commission were finally sworn in by the President on April 14, 1975, and Curtis was elected chairman of the group, with Staebler named vice-chairman.[m]

Apart from provisions of the 1974 Amendments under attack in the courts, two negative features of the law require mention because they apply to matters

---

[m]A discussion of the history and impact of the 1974 Amendments can be found at David Adamany and George Agree, "Election Campaign Financing: The 1974 Reforms," *Political Science Quarterly*, vol. 90, no. 2 (Summer 1975), 201-20.

extensively described in this book. One is the shortened statute of limitations, reduced from five to three years, thus limiting adjudication of some investigations such as that of Robert Strauss for his handling of the Ashland Oil contributions between 1970-72, when he was treasurer of the DNC.

The other is the provision relieving the supervisory officers under the 1971 law of responsibility to compile political fund data for 1973 and 1974, and failing to mandate the Federal Election Commission to make such compilations in the future. While the FEC has authority to undertake such compilations, and in its early dicussions seems committed to do so, the 1973 and 1974 data will remain untabulated by official government publications, thus making more difficult trend analyses of political money at the federal level.

Common Cause Audit and Role

In the spring of 1974 Common Cause became the subject of an inquiry as to whether it had violated the 1971 election law by failing to register as a political committee. The audit was requested by Representative Wayne L. Hays, chairman of the House Administration Committee, and two senior Republican members of the committee, Representatives Samuel L. Devine and William L. Dickinson. Devine had, in effect, challenged Common Cause two years earlier when he sought to exempt corporations and unions from a ban on gifts by government contractors, at a time when that specific section of the law was the basis for a Common Cause court suit. As to Chairman Hays, he and John Gardner, the chairman of Common Cause, had been sparring with increasing bitterness after April 1972, when Gardner named Hays as one of the candidates who had not filed reports on time in violation of the new election law. Hays had countered during an appearance by Gardner before his committee in June 1972, and the exchange there was harsh, with the congressman making accusations of "bold, bareface lies," and using similar language.[97]

The skirmishing continued in spring 1973, Gardner accusing Hays of deliberately stalling on action for an election reform bill, Hays retorting that he would not be rushed into pushing "bad legislation" just because Common Cause wanted it. In March 1974, on the day of a major Democratic fund-raising dinner in Washington, Common Cause took a full-page ad in the *Washington Post* headlined, "There's Another Political Scandal in Town, But This One Belongs to The Democrats." It sharply attacked Hays, scoring his "shabby manuevering" in delaying the pending election reform bill.[98] In May, Hays, Devine, and Dickinson asked the GAO to investigate Common Cause, saying it was "actively involved in almost all aspects of politics and it is hard to imagine that some of their efforts don't inure to the benefit of some Federal candidates."[n]

---

[n]Portion of a letter to GAO excerpted in "Common Cause Candidate Aid to Be Checked," *RCC Newsletter*, June 24, 1974, p. 6. This article in the newsletter of the

Common Cause President Jack T. Conway, in a letter made available to the press, wrote to the Office of Federal Elections at GAO that the organization would be "happy to cooperate" with the investigation. The letter said that the charges were "totally unfounded" and that the allegations by the three congressmen "constitute an attempt to divert public attention from their own failures as key Members of the House Administration Committee to provide much needed campaign finance reforms."[99]

The Office of Federal Elections (OFE) investigated Common Cause activities in some detail. It closely reviewed Common Cause financial records, its newspaper ads for the period under investigation (April 7, 1972-June 30, 1974), its program of publishing candidates' views on issues, and its campaign monitoring project, which analyzed candidates' political fund reports, to determine whether the group had endorsed or opposed candidates. In a report issued in October 1974, the OFE concluded:

In our opinion, Common Cause neither accepted contributions nor made expenditures for the purpose of influencing the nomination or election of candidates. Although Common Cause's activities . . . may have had some effect upon elections, we believe that the purpose of the expenditures for newspaper advertisements, publicizing candidates' views, and publicizing information on campaign financing reports was to promote the views of Common Cause on issues of importance to its membership. In no case did we find that Common Cause supported or opposed the nomination or election of any candidate.[100]

On this basis, the Office of Federal Elections held that Common Cause was not a "political committee" under the federal election law and thus not subject to its requirements. The OFE found that during the 27-month period of its review, Common Cause had receipts and expenditures of $11,874,176 and $11,513,701, respectively.

When the FECA Amendments went into effect on January 1, 1975, the law contained a section that raised an important question. Section 308 states that "Any person . . . who expends any funds or commits any act directed to the public for the purpose of influencing the outcome of an election . . . shall file reports with the [Federal Election] Commission." This provision could be interpreted as a warning to some nonpartisan groups, such as Common Cause, that had never been considered seriously to be political committees, to refrain from any activities that might somehow influence elections. No doubt, some politicians unhappy with public disclosure and hostile to Common Cause would have liked to force such organizations to disclose their finances on the same basis as political committees. In any case, the provision was enacted,

---

Republican congressional campaign urged readers to send to either Devine or Dickinson any information they might have about Common Cause influencing an election.

and on January 9, 1975 Common Cause voluntarily filed the Registration Form
and Statement of Organization designed for political committees. In doing so,
Common Cause crossed out the words "political committee" on the title page
of the form, stated the form was filed under Section 308 of the FECA Amendments, and wrote in several places: "Common Cause is a non-profit, non-partisan
organization and does not support or oppose candidates for any elective office."

The key words in the statute are "for the purpose of." Any organization
accused of not filing could defend itself by claiming that its activities were not
"for the purpose of" influencing an election, even though some incidental influence might result as the unintended byproduct of its activity. Nevertheless, the
Common Cause filing is expected to bring consequences for other such groups
exempt, so far, from filing.

Within months of registering, Common Cause was accused by Hays on
April 8, 1975 of failing to file its March 10 disclosure.[101] Hays berated the organization for violating the law after itself criticizing various candidates and
political committees for their lack of compliance. Hays said on the floor of the
House he hoped Common Cause would now have a better appreciation of what
it takes to comply with the complex federal law Common Cause had so much to
do with enacting. Common Cause missed the March 10, 1975 filing because
the 1974 Amendments changed that periodic reporting date to April 10, when
the organization did actually file. However, when the establishment of the
Federal Election Commission was delayed by the slowness of the appointing and
confirming process, the Secretary of the Senate, the Clerk of the House, and the
Comptroller General on December 31, 1974 announced that during the interim
period until they transferred responsibilities to the commission, the 1971 law
would remain in full force and effect, and candidates and treasurers would continue to file as previously. Common Cause answered by denying any violation
of the law, stating Hays was incorrect since Common Cause registered under the
new law, which set the April 10 filing date, and it would have been inappropriate to file on March 10 because Common Cause was not registered under the
old law.[102] Hays then charged Common Cause with "stonewalling," noting that
both the Clerk of the House and the Secretary of the Senate notified the organization it should have filed on March 10.[103]

The Financial Future

Watergate and ensuing revelations of the misuse of political funds were a
spur to the FECA Amendments. Abundant signs emerged in the 1974 congressional elections that many large contributors had been made exceedingly gun-shy
by the Watergate atmosphere. Republican fund raisers, in particular, found
money hard to raise.[104] The combination of disclosures, exposures, indictments,
convictions, and new laws slowed the free flow of money.

A number of candidates found it politically popular to impose a voluntary limit on the amount they would accept from an individual contributor. Former Attorney General Ramsey Clark, seeking a senatorial nomination in New York in 1974, adopted a limit of $100, as did others.[o] Some candidates imposed voluntary limits either of $1,000, the individual contribution limit adopted in the 1974 Amendments, or of $3,000, the limit appearing in Senate bills in 1974. The new law would seem to spell an end to the very large contributor, barring successful constitutional challenge of the limitations.

In an unusual communality of interest, conservative Senator James Buckley of New York and former Senator and antiwar leader Eugene McCarthy were among those who brought suit questioning the law's constitutionality. The constitutional implications of the regulation of political finance took on new perspectives, following major analytical works[105] on the subject and acquired new dimensions, as the Buckley-McCarthy suit at the federal level fell in the same period that numerous suits were being brought and decided on the state level. Some decisions in state courts found provisions of some laws unconstitutional under state constitutions.[p] The judicial phase of regulation is certain to refine—perhaps modify—the thrust of recent change.

Reform is not neutral, but works to change institutions and processes, sometimes in unforseen ways. The reform of our election laws—regulating elections that in turn help determine who will be elected to write other laws—has become a priority issue since the revelations about 1972 campaign abuses. Election laws are used as instruments to achieve certain political goals. Laws that regulate relationships between candidates and political parties, and between citizens and politicians, and that affect the relative power of interest groups (including parties), are bound to influence the entire political process and change the ways in which citizens, candidates, parties, and other groups participate in elections. The changes of the past several years are certain to have direct consequences for the two-party system, and to bring structural modifications in the institutions that participate in electoral activity.

The 1974 federal law seems likely to have the unforeseen effect of spotlighting and increasing the impact of the political action committees of special interest groups. Simple arithmetic explains why this is so. The individual contributor may now give no more than $2,000 to any individual candidate ($1,000 maximum each in the primary and general election). But a political action committee—which aggregates many smaller contributions—may give a total of

[o]Senator Charles Mathias, R-Maryland, who also adopted a $100 limit, actually returned a total of over $14,000 to contributors who had inadvertently made a contribution over $100; see Karlyn Barker, "Mathias Gifts Returned to Contributors," *Washington Post*, September 23, 1974.

[p]For example, *Deras* v. *Myers*, the Supreme Court of the State of Oregon, 404-407, May 14, 1975; *Bare* v. *Gorton*, 84 Washington 2nd 380 (1974).

$10,000 to a candidate ($5,000 in a primary, $5,000 in the general election).
This figure was set as a ceiling because it was acceptable to Alexander Barkan,
national director of the AFL-CIO's COPE, labor's major political action committee.[106] Scores of political action committees are allied under the aegis of
labor, dairy, construction, trucking, and other interests—each local or affiliate
permitted to donate up to the $5,000-$10,000 level to a federal candidate as
long as the committee has been registered for six months or more, receives
contributions from more than 50 persons, and makes contributions to five or
more federal candidates. The special interest committees were very active in
the 1974 campaigns even before the new limitations took effect. Because of
the decrease in large individual contributions brought on by the prevailing
atmosphere and by the limitations some candidates voluntarily imposed, the
proportion of total receipts received by congressional candidates from special
interest money appeared to be larger than ever before.

The rush to fill the vacuum created by the limitations on individual contributors had been building momentum before Watergate. In 1964 giving by
special interest groups amounted to $5.7 million; it went to $6.8 million in
1966; $11.4 million in 1968; $11.4 million in 1970; $12.4 million in 1972; and
in 1974 reached $16.8 million.

The redistribution of sources of campaign finance was by no means the
only reaction to Watergate that surfaced in the 1974 election, and more continue to show up. Although the final report of the Senate Watergate committee
emphasized that "it had received no evidence suggesting any complicity in
wrongdoing on the part of the Republican National Committee. . .",[107] voters
did appear to blame the Republican Party as much as they did Nixon. Analyses
showed a wide shift away from the Republicans in November voting, a switch
marked in every region, ethnic group, and economic classification; but it was a
shift that observers termed negative—against the Republicans, not so much for
the Democrats.[108] This was reinforced by a Gallup Poll in the spring of 1975,
which showed that while the proportion of respondents identifying themselves
as Democrats had gone from 43 to 46 percent since the summer of 1972, the
Republican percentages had fallen from 28 to 22 percent—the lowest point
since such surveys were begun in 1935.[109]

Both the Democratic and the Republican leaderships became embroiled
in debate over their respective parties' proper direction—first the Democrats
as they surveyed the wreckage of the McGovern campaign, then the Republicans
as they confronted the havoc wrought by Watergate.

Less than a week after the McGovern defeat, moderate and "old line"
Democrats began to mobilize to wrest control of the party. Author Ben Watten-
berg, a Jackson supporter, announced the creation of the Coalition for a Democratic Majority (CDM), with ten organizing members and 71 sponsors. The
new organization included many supporters of Senators Muskie, Humphrey, and
Jackson, representing more traditional Democratic views than those of the

McGovern supporters. The coalition ran newspaper ads in December 1972 headed "Come Home, Democrats." The full page ads, which cost about $14,000, beckoned traditional Democrats to return to the party, and charged that the "New Politics" had failed.[q] Top union officials were among the ad sponsors, and COPE funds helped pay for the ads. The CDM was successful in December 1972, in its goal of ousting Jean Westwood from the leadership of the DNC and installing Robert Strauss as chairman.

The McGovern wing of the party formed its vehicle, starting in January 1973, when the Democratic Planning Group (DPG), a Washington-based effort that termed itself "A communication/information center for progressive Democrats," was established. The DPG was sponsored by, among others, Stewart Mott— McGovern's largest contributor in 1972, and a critic of Strauss. Throughout 1973-75 the newsletter published by the DPG criticized Strauss on various issues— party reforms, what it termed his "deal" with John Mitchell over settlement of the Democratic civil suit, delegate selection proposals, the charter commission, and the arrangements for the miniconvention. In spite of intraparty feuding, the Democrats still have been able to raise money through annual spring dinners, and the telethons have been relatively successful.

The Republican leadership debates came after the 1974 congressional campaigns, when the GOP suffered large losses in Congress and in the states. Debate was between those urging the party to open its ranks and to appeal to various political persuasions (a view championed by President Ford) and those who argued that defining and adhering to one political philosophy was the chief hope of Republican salvation. The chief spokesman for this view was former California Governor and conservative champion Ronald Reagan.

An institution born out of the Watergate scandals was the Office of the Special Prosecutor and there was debate over whether it ought to become a permanent institution, available, for example, to carry out the criminal enforcement responsibilities of the Justice Department under the new campaign finance laws.[110] The men who had held that office, in particular Archibald Cox and Leon Jaworski, emerged from relative obscurity to become instant folk heroes, able to have impact on public opinion even after they left office. Jaworski's remarks after stepping down from the post were given treatment usually accorded senior statesmen.

In a series of speeches and news conferences in February 1975, Jaworski said he thought that Nixon's holding on to the Watergate tapes had proved his undoing, that "what hurt Nixon the most was when people found out he had hid the truth."[111] The former Special Prosecutor urged Nixon to do some "soul searching," to make a statement giving American people the truth about Watergate.[112] Jaworski praised the American people for their role in demanding

---

[q]See, for example, *The New York Times*, December 7, 1972, p. 14.

action in the Watergate scandal, saying that if they had not, it could have grown into outrages as great as those in Nazi Germany.[113]

On April 6, 1975 the statute of limitations ran out on further prosecution of certain 1972 violations; an amendment to the 1974 Act shortened the period of vulnerability from five to three years.[114]

Most of what happened in Watergate's aftermath seemed to indicate that many of the fixed patterns to which American politics had grown accustomed were in a state of flux, and many were likely dead forever. Old institutions were questioned, and new ones, such as the Special Prosecutor's Office, were examined for their possible future usefulness. Ways of collecting and spending campaign money seemed immutably altered, and limited government funding a certainty at the federal level. The Federal Election Commission was launched to preside over new laws and new practices. In the course of issuing its regulations and advisory opinions, the commission will help define permissable practices, and thus will set the course of future political activity. The extent to which the commission is flexible or restrictive will set the legitimate bounds of the expansiveness or narrowness of future politics. Regulations can be stifling if a legalistic approach is taken, or they can be permissive without being lax, if a broader approach is adopted. The broader approach must encompass an understanding of the voluntary and participative aspects of American electoral politics. Excessive regulation will only confirm to those who already believe—erroneously— that money in politics is necessarily dirty and every use of it has to be regulated and monitored. The goal should be to encourage citizen participation, including financial participation, in every way compatible with fairness and equity. It is very easy to turn people off from financial participation in politics, whether as donors or as solicitors or as treasurers of political committees.

It is ironic that the attempted cover-up produced more information about who gave what and who spent what—and why—than for any election in American history. Political observers and political scientists will be studying the records left by Watergate and the 1972 election for years to come. Out of this new openness, backed by the obvious needs for renewed trust in government and increased levels of confidence in the electoral process, it may be possible to do much about correcting imperfections in the system. If could be Watergate's lasting and positive legacy.

Appendix A: Federal Election Campaign Act of 1971

The Federal Election Campaign Act of 1971:[1]

1. Limits the amounts candidates for federal offices can spend on radio, television, cable television, newspapers, magazines, billboards, and automated telephone systems in any primary, runoff, special, or general election to ten cents times the voting-age population of the geographical unit covered by the election, or $50,000, whichever is greater.

2. Provides that no candidate can spend more than 60 percent of his media expenditure limit on broadcast advertising.

3. Provides that the broadcast media cannot charge candidates more than the lowest unit rate charged any other advertiser for the same class and amount of time or space for a period extending 45 days preceding a primary election or 60 days preceding a general or special election. At other times, rates cannot exceed the charges made for comparable use for other purposes. Rates for newspapers or magazine advertising cannot exceed the charges made for comparable use for other purposes.

4. Includes an escalator provision to reflect increases in the federal government's price index. (By the time of enactment the limit was officially calculated at 10.43 cents per voting-age population.)

5. Defines "election" to mean any general, special, primary, or runoff election, nominating convention or caucus, delegate selection primary, presidential preference primary, or constitutional convention.

6. Broadens the definition of "contribution" and "expenditure."

7. Places a ceiling on contributions by any candidate or his immediate family to his own campaign of $50,000 for President or Vice President, $35,000 for senator, and $25,000 for representative, delegate, or resident commissioner.

8. Stipulates that the appropriate federal supervisory officer to oversee election campaign practices, reporting, and disclosure is the Clerk of the House for House candidates, the Secretary of the Senate for Senate candidates, and the Comptroller General for presidential candidates and miscellaneous other committees.

9. Requires all political committees that anticipate receipts in excess of $1,000 during the calendar year to register with the appropriate federal supervisory officer, and to include such information as the names of all principal

603

officers, the scope of the committee, the names of all candidates the committee supports.

10. Requires candidates and their committees for the Senate and House to file duplicate copies of reports with the Secretary of State, or a comparable office, in each state for local inspection.

11. Requires each political committee and candidate to report total cash on hand and total receipts by category. Contributions and loans in amounts of $100 or more must be itemized, giving the full name, mailing address, and occupation and principal place of business of the contributor, along with the date and amount of the contribution. Each transfer of funds from any committee must also be itemized, as much all receipts from dinner and such events in amounts of $100 or more from any one source.

12. Requires each political committee and candidate to report total expenditures, as well as to itemize the full name, mailing address, and occupation and principal place of business of each payee, plus date, amount, and purpose of each expenditure in excess of $100; to itemize the same for each expenditure for personal services, salaries, and reimbursed expenses in excess of $100.

13. Requires each political committee and candidate to report the amount and nature of debts and obligations on a continuing basis until extinguished.

14. Requires the supervisory officers to prepare an annual report for each committee registered with the supervisory officers and furnish such reports to the Public Printer for sale to the public.

15. Requires candidates and committees to file reports of contributions and expenditures on the 10th day of March, June, and September every year, on the 15th and 5th days preceding the date on which an election is held and on the 31st day of January. Any contribution of $5,000 or more is to be reported within 48 hours if received after the last preelection report.

16. Requires a full and complete financial statement of the costs of holding a presidential nominating convention within 60 days after the end of the convention.

17. Prohibits any contribution to a candidate or committee by one person in the name of another person.

18. Defines explicitly the role that unions and corporations can take in political campaigns, get-out-the-vote drives, and voter registration activities.

19. Authorizes the office of the Comptroller General to serve as a national clearinghouse for information on the administration of election practices.

20. Requires the Civil Aeronautics Board, the Federal Communications Commission, and the Interstate Commerce Commission to promulgate regulations with respect to the extension of credit without collateral by any person, business, or industry regulated by the federal government to any person on behalf of any candidate for federal office.

21. Prohibits funds appropriated for the Office of Economic Opportunity from being used for any political activity.

Appendix B: Revenue Act of 1971

The Revenue Act of 1971[1] provides tax incentives:

1. That political contributors, if they choose, can claim a tax credit against federal income tax for 50 percent of their contributions, up to a maximum of $12.50 on a single return and $25.00 on a joint return (the 1974 Amendments to the FECA increased these amounts to $25.00 and $50.00 respectively).

2. Alternatively, the taxpayer can claim a deduction for the full amount of contributions up to a maximum of $50.00 on a single return and $100.00 on a joint return (the 1974 Amendments increased these amounts to $100.00 and $200.00 respectively).

3. Eligible as contributions are gifts to candidates for election to any federal, state, or local elective office in any primary, general, or special election, and gifts to any committee, association, or organization operated exclusively for the purpose of influencing or attempting to influence the election of such candidates, for use to further such candidacy.

The act also provides a tax checkoff:

1. That every individual whose tax liability for any taxable year is $1.00 or more can designate on his federal income tax form that $1.00 of his tax money be paid to the Presidential Election Campaign Fund.

2. Married individuals filing joint returns can designate $2.00 of their tax money.

It provides for funding in the presidential general election campaign:

1. Major candidates, defined as those nominated by political parties whose presidential candidate received 25 percent or more of the popular vote in the preceding presidential general election, are entitled to receive from the fund 15 cents for each person over age 18; given the latest population data, that would have provided $20.4 million to a major party candidate in 1972 (the 1974 Amendments revised the amount to the same amount as the limitation, $20 million).

2. Minor candidates, defined as those nominated by a party receiving 5 percent or more but less than 25 percent of the total votes in the preceding or current presidential election, are entitled to receive the same proportion of this $20.4 million as their vote was of the average major party vote (the 1974 Amendments revised the minor party proportion to the major party amount). A minor party candidate qualifying for the first time would have to campaign on

loans or contributions, would be reimbursed after the election, and would be free to use the money to repay loans or to return contributions to donors.

3. Candidates accepting checkoff funds would be limited to that amount and could not raise or spend additional funds.

4. Candidates not accepting checkoff funds can raise or spend money with the same limitation, plus a 20 percent overage for fund-raising costs.

5. Total payments from the fund to a party, however, cannot exceed the amounts actually incurred in running the campaign, and various reports and audits are required.

6. The Comptroller General of the United States was delegated the responsibility of determining the amounts spent or incurred by each party (the 1974 Amendments relegated this responsibility to the Federal Election Commission).

7. The Comptroller General would be assisted in these functions by an advisory board consisting of two members representing each major party and three public members agreed upon by the other members.

8. If the amounts in the fund were insufficient to make the payments to which the political parties were entitled with respect to a presidential campaign, payments would be allocated to the party accounts in the ratio of the balances in their accounts.

9. Surpluses remaining in the fund after a campaign would be returned to the Treasury after all parties had been paid the amounts to which they were entitled.

Note: The FECA Amendments of 1974 made provision for government funding of presidential prenomination campaigns, and for national nominating conventions; see Appendix C.

Appendix C: Federal Election Campaign Act Amendments of 1974

The Federal Election Campaign Act Amendments of 1974[1] established the following contribution limits:

1. $1,000 per individual for each primary, runoff, and general election, and an aggregate contribution of $25,000 to all federal candidates annually.

2. $5,000 per organization, political committee, and national and state party organizations for each election, but no aggregate limit on the amount organizations could contribute in a campaign nor on the amount organizations could contribute to party organizations supporting federal candidates.

3. $50,000 for President, $35,000 for Senate, and $25,000 for House races for candidates and their immediate families.

4. $1,000 for independent expenditures on behalf of a candidate.

5. Barred cash contributions of over $100 and foreign contributions.

The Amendments established the following spending limits:

1. Presidential prenomination—$10 million total per candidate for all primaries. In a state presidential primary, limited a candidate to spending no more than twice what a Senate candidate in that state would be allowed to spend (see below).

2. Presidential general election—$20 million per candidate. (Amount tied into the Cost of Living Index and will rise accordingly.)

3. Presidential nominating conventions—$2 million each major political party, lesser amounts for minor parties.

4. Senate primaries—$100,000 or eight cents per eligible voter, whichever was greater.

5. Senate general elections—$150,000 or 12 cents per eligible voter, whichever was greater.

6. House primaries—$70,000.

7. House general elections—$70,000.

8. National party spending—$10,000 per candidate in House general elections; $20,000 or two cents per eligible voter, whichever was greater, for each candidate in Senate general elections; and two cents per voter (approximately $2.9 million) in presidential general elections. The expenditure would be above the candidate's individual spending limit.

9. Applied Senate spending limits to House candidates who represented a whole state.

10. Repealed the media spending limitations in the Federal Election Campaign Act of 1971 (PL 92-225).

The Amendments made the following exemptions from the above spending limits:

1. Expenditures of up to $500 for food and beverages, invitations, unreimbursed travel expenses by volunteers, and spending on "slate cards" and sample ballots.

2. Fund-raising costs of up to 20 percent of the candidate spending limit. Thus, the spending limit for House candidates would be effectively raised from $70,000 to $84,000 and for candidates in presidential primaries from $10 million to $12 million.

They made the following provisions for public financing:

1. Presidential general elections—voluntary public financing. Major party candidates (those receiving 25 percent or more of votes) would automatically qualify for full funding before the campaign, based on votes the party received four years before. Minor party and independent candidates (those receiving 5 percent or more of votes) would be eligible to receive a proportion of full funding based on past or current votes received (amount tied into the Cost of Living Index and will rise accordingly); but would not be eligible until after the election if qualifying occurs in current election year. If a candidate opted for full public funding no private contributions would be permitted.

2. Presidential nominating conventions—optional public funding. Major parties would automatically qualify. Minor parties would be eligible for lesser amounts based on their proportion of votes received in a past or current election.

3. Presidential primaries—matching public funds of up to $5 million per candidate after meeting fund-raising requirement of $100,000 raised in amounts of at least $5,000 in each of 20 states or more. Only first $250 of individual private contributions would be matched. The candidates of any one party together could receive no more than 45 percent of total amount available in federal money. No single candidate could receive more than 25 percent of the total available. Only private gifts raised after January 1, 1975 would qualify for matching for the 1976 election. No federal payments would be made before January 1976.

4. All federal money for public funding of campaigns would come from the Presidential Election Campaign Fund. Money received from the federal income tax dollar checkoff would be automatically appropriated to the fund.

The Amendments made the following stipulations for disclosure and reporting dates:

1. Required each candidate to establish one central campaign committee through which all contributions and expenditures on behalf of a candidate must be reported. Required designation of specific bank depositories of campaign funds.

2. Required full reports of contributions and expenditures to be filed with the Federal Election Commission ten days before and 30 days after every election, and within ten days of the close of each quarter unless the committee

received or expended less than $1,000 in that quarter. A year-end report was due in nonelection years.

3. Required that contributions of $1,000 or more received within the last 15 days before election be reported to the commission within 48 hours.

4. Prohibited contributions in the name of another.

5. Treated loans as contributions. Required a co-signer or guarantor for each $1,000 of outstanding obligation.

6. Required any organization that spent any money or committed any act for the purpose of influencing any election (such as the publication of voting records) to file reports as a political committee. (This would require reporting by such lobby organizations as Common Cause, Environmental Action, Americans for Constitutional Action, and Americans for Democratic Action.)

7. Required every person who spent or contributed over $100 other than to or through a candidate or political committee to report.

8. Permitted government contractors, unions, and corporations to maintain separate, segregated political funds. (Formerly all contributions by government contractors were prohibited.)

They made the following provisions for enforcement:

1. Created a six-member, full-time bipartisan Federal Election Commission to be responsible for administering election laws and for the public financing program, with two ex officio members (the Secretary of the Senate and the Clerk of the House of Representatives).

2. Provided that the President, Speaker of the House and President ProTem of the Senate would appoint to the commission two members, each of different parties, all subject to confirmation by Congress. Commission members could not be officials or employees of any branch of government at the time of appointment.

3. Made the Secretary of the Senate and Clerk of the House ex officio, nonvoting members of the commission; provided that their offices would serve as custodian of reports for candidates for House and Senate.

4. Provided that commissioners would serve six-year, staggered terms, and established a rotating one-year chairmanship.

5. Provided that the commission would: receive campaign reports; make rules and regulations (subject to review by Congress within 30 days); maintain a cumulative index of reports filed and not filed; make special and regular reports to Congress and the President; and serve as an election information clearinghouse.

6. Gave the commission power to render advisory opinions; conduct audits and investigations; subpoena witnesses and information; and go to court to seek civil injunctions.

7. Provided that criminal cases would be referred by the commission to the Justice Department for prosecution.

They established the following penalties:

1. Increased existing fines to a maximum of $50,000.

2. Provided that a candidate for federal office who failed to file reports could be prohibited from running again for the term of that office plus one year.

3. Set January 1, 1975 as the effective date of the act (except for immediate preemption of state laws).

4. Provided that no elected or appointed official or employee of the federal government would be permitted to accept more than $1,000 as an honorarium for a speech or article, or $15,000 in aggregate per year.

5. Removed Hatch Act restrictions on voluntary activities by state and local employees in federal campaigns, if not otherwise prohibited by state law.

6. Prohibited solicitation of funds by franked mail.

7. Preempted state election laws for federal candidates.

8. Permitted use of excess campaign funds to defray expenses of holding federal office or for other lawful purposes.

Appendix D: The GAO Report

Under provisions of the Federal Election Campaign Act (FECA) of 1971, the Comptroller General, the Secretary of the Senate, and the Clerk of the House were each required to prepare an annual report of the receipts and expenditures of all candidates and committees reporting to them. Many special interest, party, and multicandidate committees reported to all three supervisory officers, hence are included in each of the reports. As to discrete data, the House and the Senate were each dealing with individual candidates largely independent of one another and operating largely within traditional norms. Their data lent itself more readily to computerization. On the other hand, the General Accounting Office (GAO), dealing with the presidential candidates, found itself confronted with hundreds of interlocking committees; for example, there were 716 registered McGovern committees—with extensive movement of funds back and forth amongst many of them. Some presidential committees, however, operated within highly individualized frameworks, with unsophisticated reporting techniques developed by amateurs. For these and other reasons, serious problems inhere in the GAO data, hence the totals compiled by GAO cannot be accepted as definitive.

The GAO divided the reporting committees into three categories: those organized on behalf of a specific presidential candidate; those organized by or affiliated with a political party; and those not affiliated with either a candidate or a party, such as business and labor political committees. The party and nonparty committees were required to file with GAO if any of their receipts or expenditures were related to any presidential (or vice-presidential) campaign, but the GAO properly did not include the total expenditures of these party and nonparty committees in its compilation of spending by each presidential candidate, for two reasons: (1) Except for the major party national committees and their satellites, only a fraction of their activity was attributable to any presidential campaign; and (2) the report forms made it difficult to separate out the amounts attributable to, say, a presidential candidate spent by a state party committee.

Of course, the GAO totals could not include receipts and expenditures prior to April 7, 1972. For all but five of the 18 Democratic candidates and for two of the three Republican candidates, the political and financial high points of their campaigns occurred before that date. For example, Muskie spent about $7 million but the GAO report lists him for only a little more than $1 million. In addition to this inescapable problem resulting from the effective date of the law—which also affected the compilations of the Clerk of the House and the Secretary of the Senate—several candidates tried to avoid the provisions of the FECA by raising money or prepaying some campaign costs prior to April 7; this technique was used by Nixon and Jackson, among others. The investigations of the Watergate Committee, the Office of the Special Prosecutor, and various court actions uncovered some of this pre-April 7 income and expenditures, which Citizens' Research Foundation (CRF) has merged with the data reported to GAO. Unless one is fully alert to the necessary adjustments, the GAO totals can be misleading.

While the effective date problem was a once-only situation, the problem of differences in reporting was a continuing one. The GAO's report of total receipts and expenditures for each candidate was compiled by adding the income and outgo as reported by each committee, aggregating the year's reports to arrive at a yearly total. The various committees, however, were including very different data in their reported line item totals; even the bottom line figures could not be accepted at face value, for entries were sometimes on the wrong line or column totals were left blank. In its introductory statement, GAO properly warned the data were mainly unaudited and reported as submitted by political committees.

The GAO attempted to exclude reported transfers among committees, since transfers should be treated as income by the committees first receiving the money and as expenditures by the committees finally spending the money. Enormous transferring of funds occurred amongst the McGovern committees, especially in the general election period; many items were not identified as "transfers" on the summary pages, and hence were not correctly listed by GAO: CRF identified $802,000 of such transfers listed as loans, and another $439,000 as "other receipts." The only way to overcome this problem was to examine carefully all the supporting schedules to determine how each committee interpreted the summary sheet line items and then adjust those line items as necessary to insure conformity among all the reports. Given the mass of data, the GAO did not undertake an analysis of such magnitude, but mainly totalled whatever was reported.

Other distortions occurred because of the method of reporting loans and loan repayments. When a loan was received, it was included in the total reported receipts and the use of that money for campaign expenses was included in the total reported expenditures. If the campaign later received contributions used to pay back the loan, those contributions were also included in the total reported receipts, and the loan repayment was then included in the total reported expenditures. Since the GAO did not uniformly adjust raw figures, the income and expenditures from properly reported and subsequently repaid loans were sometimes double counted. To illustrate the magnitude of the problem: the major McGovern committees showed loans of $9.6 million but repayments of $5.2 million.

Another but smaller problem of upward distortion occurred with gifts of stock. One practice was for contributors to donate the current value of a stock but request payment back of its original cost to the contributor. When this was done, the total value of the stock was listed as a contribution; then, when the stock was sold and the contributor reimbursed for the original cost of the stock to him, that reimbursement was listed as an expenditure. The inescapable result was that both receipts and expenditures were overstated by the difference between the original cost and the later sale price of stock contributed in this way. This distortion occurred in other 1972 campaigns, but was a significant item in the McGovern campaign, wherein Stewart R. Mott's gifts were made in this manner, totalling $750,000 as listed contributions but netting $400,000 after McGovern committees returned the "basis" or cost. While the common disclosure forms designed by all three supervisory officers were inadequate for reporting loan and gift of stock information, the problem at GAO was magnified because of the large amounts of money involved.

The GAO listed $5,774,000 in the category of "other receipts." A few contributors were (incorrectly) reported in this section; there were occasional entries of interest on Treasury notes and bank deposits that represented bona fide income; but most of this category had to be "adjusted," that is, subtracted out. Refunded expenditures, which bulked large, did not represent incremental income.

Another distortion affected only two of the presidential candidates; this occurred because the reporting forms did not provide any easy way to distinguish spending (or receipts) directed toward winning nomination from spending (or receipts) directed toward winning the general election. The GAO staff picked the date of each party's convention as the dividing line: all receipts and expenditures prior to that date were presumed to be for "influencing the nomination" and those after that date for "influencing the election." This seemingly logical division is not realistic, however, because bills are often paid weeks or months after the expenses are incurred. Furthermore, the summer lull after the presidential primaries and the national conventions is a time to get caught up with prenomination bills and to plan ahead (more than actually spend) for the general election campaign. The GAO's date decision affected only the two winning candidates, McGovern and Nixon, and because of the lack of necessity for separating Nixon's prenomination from his general election finances, only the McGovern totals were irreparably distorted. The Nixon data, however, more graphically demonstrate the fallacy of using an arbitrary date. For example, GAO reports a Republican total of $13.5 million as "expenditures influencing nomination," a designation that distorts Nixon's post-April 7-pre-convention period.

CRF's analysis of McGovern's primary and general election spending was done on a committee-by-committee basis. Thus, the expenditures of "Delegates for McGovern" and 200+ other such committees, organized in support of the

nomination and terminating before the general election campaign got underway, were treated in their entirety as prenomination spending. Since most
committees were clearly distinguishable in their orientation (through an
analysis of their spending, the dates when obligations were incurred, termination dates, etc.) this approach posed few problems. Only in the specific
instances where a prenomination committee continued on through the
general election was a cutoff date used; July 31 was found to be realistic.

All of these elements—plus time to review work products carefully—combined to produce CRF totals for McGovern that are quite different from
those of GAO. Without adjustment for understated transfers, loan repayments,
gifts of stock and refunded expenditures, analysis of a primary-general election
cutoff date, and with frequent keypunch errors, the GAO's McGovern expenditures contrast notably with CRF's calculations. (See Table D-1.)

Table D-1
GAO vs. CRF Reports of McGovern Expenditures

	Post-April 7 Prenomination Spending	*General Election Spending*
GAO	$6.8 million	$38.2 million
CRF	9.3 million	29.8 million

The GAO report of total receipts and expenditures obviously does not
include debts, since debts are not money received or expended. However, in
calculating the total cost of a campaign, the campaign's debts must be added to
its expenditures. Because few businesses would give candidates more than
limited credit (after the experience of 1968) debts were not a major factor in
1972—but they did affect some totals. Humphrey, for example, owed more
than $100,000 to creditors at the end of 1973 (in addition to his campaign's
large outstanding loans). Debts owed to lenders (i.e., outstanding loans),
and debts owed to businesses (i.e., unpaid bills), are totally different in their
effect on expenditures and costs. Loans received and used are already included
in income and expenditure figures, and adjustments have to be made only if
and when the loans are repaid; debts owed to creditors have not been included
in the income and expenditure data and have to be added to the latter for a
true cost figure.

Computerization of Political Finance Data:
Theory Versus Fact

Confronted with almost 100,000 pages of candidate and committee reports, the GAO turned to an outside agency under contract to prepare, edit, and computerize the data for its annual report. In-house computer specialists were also used to supervise and monitor the work, but oversight was inadequate. The Clerk and the Secretary produced their reports entirely in-house, with demonstrably better results, although the Clerk found it necessary to issue a sizable revision of the committee totals.

In theory, the GAO's massive, two-volume printout would provide a definitive body of data on which reporters, political scientists, and historians could draw. In fact, every seasoned reporter and experienced researcher who has dealt with political finance reports knows they must be approached with extreme wariness, because there is little uniformity in reporting procedures used by various candidates and committees. In spite of lengthy manuals of instruction to committee treasurers, in spite of desk checks and opportunities to amend erroneous reports some monumental reporting errors were allowed to stand. CRF did not assess the totals of any category, as reported on the summary page, without carefully examining the individual items and supporting schedules. While the GAO staff sometimes pursued the smallest details—following up with a committee that reported a $38 deficit to find out how the debt would be handled—some glaring discrepancies went unchallenged: One Sanford committee, for example, reported a $1,145.97 balance at the end of one reporting period; the next report showed $51,892.97 on hand at the beginning of the period; yet, the report showing the additional amount of $50,747.00 was accepted without question until a field audit took place. Auditors sometimes reviewed each report by itself, picking up internal inconsistencies and mathematical errors, but not examining one committee's reports for sequential consistency, nor the reports of various committees of one candidate to match up, for example, the reported transfers in and transfers out between them. Most auditors had an understanding of the complexities of the data, but they were not continually involved in the computer project. This meant that some reports were turned over to keypunchers without proper input from auditors. The results were distorted accordingly.

The AFL-CIO is listed in the GAO printout as having receipts in excess of $11 million, direct expenditures of more than $9 million, and less than $50,000 transferred out to candidates and committees. Actually, COPE reported receipts and expenditures of about $1.4 million. Further, by studying the body of the reports as against the summary sheets, one can determine that transfers out to candidates and committees were in excess of $1 million. Even these figures require refining, however. Although COPE lists all receipts as "individual contributions—unitemized," other affiliates of COPE reported transferring to COPE more than $500,000; hence, COPE's "adjusted receipts" were slightly more than $500,000—a significant proportion of which came from certificates of deposit, representing a carry-over of funds from previous years.

A better understanding is gained from Table D-2.

Table D-2

A Comparison of Financial Data Reports: GAO, COPE, and CRF

	Receipts		Expenditures		
	All Receipts Except Transfers	Transfers	Direct Expenditures	Transfers	Gross Expenditures
GAO printout	$11,310,662	$ 0	$9,221,952	$ 45,000	$9,266,952
As reported by COPE	1,252,519	0	1,352,338	45,000	1,397,338[c]
As interpreted by CRF	674,622[a]	577,897[b]	187,183	1,210,155	1,397,338[c]

[a]Includes $152,074 in matured certificates of deposit purchased in 1971, hence reflected in 1971 receipts.

[b]As reported by other labor committees, e.g., $136,170 from ILGWU, $101,733 from AFT, $137,550 from RCPL, and so on.

[c]As amended in 1973; year-end report originally showed $1,270,075 and was so reported by House and Senate printouts.

The most cursory examination would have indicated something amiss in the GAO's summation of the COPE data:

Cash on hand, 4/7/72 (as reported by COPE)	$ 21,682
Receipts (GAO's figure)	11,310,662
	$11,332,344
Expenditures (GAO's figure)	$ 9,221,952
Cash on hand, 12/31/72 (as reported by COPE)	$ 4,125

It is possible to account for the discrepancies set forth above of COPE receipts and expenditures. Most important, the keypunchers aggregated the "calendar year to date" items, unmindful of the obvious arithmetic progression of figures that COPE erroneously reported. Second, COPE failed to identify the "transfers-in," as required by law. Third, COPE reported as "transfers-out" only those funds given to the COPE Education Fund (a nonreporting group and not a political committee at all, by legal definition). And finally, COPE actually transferred-out to reporting congressional and senatorial candidates and committees almost $1 million, but reported this on the summary sheets as "other expenditures." An additional $220,000 was transferred-out to national and state labor committees, again recorded as "other expenditures."

A few other random examples of the unreliability of the published data demonstrate that, although the COPE summation is the most garing example, it is by no means an isolated case: Republican National Committee receipts—$6.5 million in the GAO printout compared with a reported $4.8 million (a margin of error of over 30 percent); the Republican National Finance Committee expenditures—$5.5 million as against a reported $4.2 million (again, a 30 percent margin of error). Hubert Humphrey's direct expenditures were inflated by over 50 percent. The committees supporting Terry Sanford originally submitted garbled reports that defied computer and expert alike, but the printout again erred by at least 30 percent.

In these instances it was possible to identify the manifest errors because of prior knowledge of the data involved; again and again, aggregates were added to aggregates, producing a pyramided, meaningless total.

The GAO made no claim that the data represented a sophisticated analysis; indeed, the preface of the publication in question contains the disclaimer that "the data . . . should be utilized as a guide and summary and, where necessary, verified from the source of the reports."[1] Dealing with a huge mass of data, some errors were inevitable. Clearly identifiable errors are relatively harmless, even amusing. There are instances where the printout lists as contributions the zip code numbers of McGovern contributors; they were credited with high five-figure donations instead of the modest amounts actually given. Officials at the AFL-CIO, however, were not amused by the mishandling of their data. Given the magnitude of known errors, the entire publication becomes suspect; yet, it stands as an historic document and an example of the kinds of data, more carefully presented, necessary for historic studies.

To its great credit, the GAO published in October 1972 a preelection compilation of contributors of $25 or more—the first time a federal agency had issued such an election report. This was prepared carefully, directly from edited reports. It was a fine example of innovation—publishing data voluntarily, not required by statute, but within the spirit of the law.

Many of the problems faced by the GAO were inevitable. The annual report was a "first-time" project, prepared under a complex new law. The disclosure forms and some policies were agreed upon jointly by the three supervisory officers, so GAO did have full independence to chart its own course. But the focus on the presidential elections put the GAO in the spotlight; Watergate and partisan charges and countercharges about filings and audits demanded much time. The GAO policy was not to change arbitrarily the reported data, but to get political committees to adjust, correct, and amend their own reports to the GAO's satisfaction; this policy was designed both to educate those filing reports and to achieve full compliance with the law. It took time and experience to improve the process. More effective desk checks of reports when filed, and better sanctions to motivate campaigners to make the necessary changes on the reports in timely fashion, would have minimized many of the problems.

Appendix E: Summary of GAO Audits in Compliance with the FECA, June 5, 1972-December 16, 1974

Table E-1

A Summary of GAO Audits in Compliance with the FECA, June 5, 1972–
December 16, 1974

Committees[a]	No Violations (Simple Audit)	Technical Violations	Referrals to the Justice Department[b]
Party			
Democratic	13	40	12
Republican	16	65	13
Communist		1	2
American		1	
Other		2	2
Presidential			
(Democratic)			
McGovern	2	36	42
Humphrey		2	4
Muskie	1	16	2
Wallace			1
Chisholm			2
Sanford		1	1
Mills		1	
Yorty		1	
Jackson		3	
(Republican)			
Nixon	1	45	8
Ashbrook		1	1
(American)			
Schmitz		1	
Vice-Presidential			
(Democratic)			
Arnold	3	1	
Eagleton		1	
Gravel		1	
Peabody		1	
Shriver		1	
(Republican)			
Agnew	1		2
Labor	5	15	8
Business/Professional	3	19	4
Newspapers[c]			2
Individuals			3
Miscellaneous	4	5	2
Total Committees			
420	49	260	111

[a]Each committee is counted only once although in some cases, such as the McGovern for President–D.C. Committee and the Finance Committee to Re-Elect the President, several audits were made. In both of these cases, the committees are counted under the Referrals to Justice Department category, although some reports found only technical violations. The GAO reports often covered more than one committee. This table counts committees audited, not numbers of reports.

Table E-1 (Cont.)

[b]Several referrals to the IRS or to state attorneys general are not listed here; however, in most of these cases, a committee would be referred to the United States Attorney General simultaneously.

[c]*The New York Times* was investigated twice for failing to obtain the proper certification for an advertisement: once for the Haiphong Mining ad, and once for an ad placed by the National Committee for Impeachment. Also, in six of its reports on various committees, the GAO cited 12 newspapers for failing to obtain proper certification.

Appendix F: Remarks by Democratic National Chairman Lawrence F. O'Brien on Signing of Voluntary Primary Spending Limitations by Democratic Presidential Contenders

DEMOCRATIC NATIONAL COMMITTEE

Lawrence F. O'Br.en, *Chairman*

FOR RELEASE: 2 P.M.
THURSDAY, DECEMBER 2, 1971

OFFICE of COMMUNICATIONS   John G. Stewart, *Director*
DNC-71-103ph E. Mohbat, *Press Secretary*

REMARKS BY DEMOCRATIC NATIONAL CHAIRMAN LAWRENCE F. O'BRIEN
ON SIGNING OF VOLUNTARY PRIMARY SPENDING
LIMITATIONS BY DEMOCRATIC PRESIDENTIAL CONTENDERS

We are here today to conclude an important agreement among announced and potential candidates for the Democratic presidential nomination.

This voluntary agreement places strict and verifiable limits on the amount of money Democratic contenders will spend on television, radio, newspapers, and billboards in the upcoming presidential primaries. These limits will hold expenditures considerably below the levels reached in the Democratic and Republican primaries of 1968.

Several months ago, Senator Humphrey, Senator Jackson, Senator McGovern and Senator Muskie agreed in principle to a voluntary spending limitation of five cents per registered voter per state. We have now reached agreement on the operational details. All other potential Democratic contenders, as they are identified, will be asked to subscribe to these terms. I am most hopeful -- indeed, confident -- of their unanimous acceptance of these spending groundrules.

You have material setting forth the specifics of the agreement that will be signed today. Let me, however, emphasize several points:

First, this voluntary agreement is unique to American presidential politics. Nothing like it has ever been attempted before, much less brought into being. It has been made possible by a common belief among Democrats that sanity must be restored to the expenditures of money in the quest for high public office. Campaign spending in 1968 -- both in the primaries and general election -- was an outrage. The American people know it was an outrage. And the Democratic Party has decided to do something about it.

Second, this agreement is an integral part of the more comprehensive reform effort that the Democratic Party has spearheaded for the 1972 presidential campaign. We have totally reformed the party's delegate-selection process and the national convention. Democrats -- especially Senator Mike Mansfield -- led the way in winning the vote for 18-year-olds by congressional action. We have now passed for a second time campaign spending limitations covering all federal elections. The National Voter Registration Act is currently on the Senate calendar. The dollar check-off provision for public financing of presidential campaigns is awaiting final action by the two Houses.

2600 Virginia Avenue, N.W., Washington, D.C. 20037   (202) 333-8750 • night: 333-0161

-2-

If these reforms are viewed collectively, they represent the most far-reaching and fundamental reshaping of American politics since the first decade of the 20th Century.

Third, the agreement to be signed today, and the other reforms I have described, arise from a growing conviction among Americans that the old ways of conducting our political affairs are no longer acceptable. The time has arrived for an end to the era of back-room deals and of campaigns financed by massive contributions from vested interests. . .at least so far as the Democratic Party is concerned.

We invite President Nixon and the Republican Party to join us, even though, at the moment, there is scant evidence of the GOP's support for this effort to redeem the basic premise of American democracy -- that government by equally representative of and responsive to all the people, not just to those favored by wealth and influence.

Finally, I wish to acknowledge the unwavering support of Speaker Carl Albert and Majority Leader Mansfield in reaching agreement on the document we sign today, as well as their splendid leadership in guiding through the 92nd Congress the reform legislation that I trust will soon be on President Nixon's desk. Without their wisdom and determination at many points in the legislative process, these historic proposals would have perished somewhere along the way.

To the Democrats who will sign the primary spending limitation agreement, I express my deepest gratitude for your willingness to submerge personal ambitions and self-serving considerations in the greater cause of restoring common sense and decency to American presidential politics. Yours is an example that our Republican friends will be hard pressed to match.

This is truly a day when one is proud to be a Democrat.

#   #   #

TEXT OF AGREEMENT

December 2, 1971
Washington, D. C.

We the undersigned agree to this voluntary method of limiting expenditures for television, radio, newspaper advertisements and billboards in the 1972 Democratic presidential primaries, and join in setting forth the following specifics of the understanding:

1. Expenditure limits in 1972 for buying time on radio and TV in states with presidential primary elections will be not more than 5¢ per registered voter in each state as of January 1, 1972. Direct expenditures by the candidates and indirect expenditures by committees or individuals on behalf of their candidacy or pledged delegates are included.

2. The individual state limitations will not be transferable among the states, except there will be a contingency pool up to one-third of which may be applied to increase the expenditure in any single state. Allocations to the contingency pool will be made by reducing each state's allowable expenditure by five per cent. In specific areas where there is a media market overlap, expenditures will be allocated on the basis of the primary election dates. For example, if a candidate elects to enter both the New Hampshire (March 7th) and Massachusetts (April 25th) primaries, he is limited to the New Hampshire allocation plus no more than one-third of the contingency poll prior to March 7th -- the date of the New Hampshire primary.

3. This agreement will be self-policing. The reporting requirements under FCC regulations provide adequate public records by which the good faith compliance can be monitored. Additionally, the candidates urge individual radio and television stations prior to election day to make available a public statement of the actual purchase of broadcast time by each candidate or on behalf of each candidate.

4. The participants to this agreement further agree to a voluntary method of limiting the campaign expenditures for newspaper advertising and billboards in the 1972 Democratic presidential state primaries.

-2-

Expenditure for these forms of advertising shall be limited to not more than 5¢ per registered voter in each state as of January 1, 1972. Direct expenditures by the candidates and indirect expenditures by committees or individuals on behalf of their candidacy or pledged delegates will be included within this limitation.

The individual state limitations will not be transferable among states. Expenditures shall be counted in the state of publication and principle distribution or display.

5. The Democratic National Committee will circulate this agreement, and a list of those candidates who enter into this agreement, to the news print media and the radio and television stations in all presidential primary states.

Table F-1
Primary States

	Date	5¢ Per Registered Voter (Minus 5%)
East		
New Hampshire	3/7	$ 18,000
Rhode Island	4/11	22,000
Pennsylvania	4/25	257,000
Massachusetts	4/25	124,000
D.C.	5/2	12,000
Maryland	5/16	76,000
New Jersey	6/6	151,000
New York	6/20	353,000
South		
Florida	3/14	133,000
North Carolina	5/2	92,000
Alabama	5/2	75,000
Tennessee	5/4	81,000
Arkansas	6/27	39,000
Midwest		
Illinois	3/24	254,000
Wisconsin	4/4	117,000
Ohio	5/2	185,000
Indiana	5/2	114,000
Nebraska	5/9	33,000
West Virginia	5/9	45,000
South Dakota	6/6	17,000
West		
Oregon	5/23	46,000
California	6/6	413,000
New Mexico	6/6	20,000
5% contingency pool		$ 142,000
(Not more than 33 1/3%)		(47,333)
Total media spending limit (All primaries plus contingency pool)		$2,819,000

Appendix G: Results of the Muskie Direct Mail Efforts

MUSKIE FOR PRESIDENT   **1972**
(202) USA —   **1972**   or write
       1972   K Street NW, Washington, D.C. 20006

March 31, 1972

SUBJECT: Results of Direct Mail Efforts

TO: Bernhard/Mitchell/Brink/Kline

MAIL LIST	DATE MAILED	COST	QUANTITY MAILED	NO. OF RESPONSES	AMOUNT RECEIVED	PROFIT
A	5/14/71	20,990	171,545	2,212	42,296	21,306
B	7/15	3,769	39,000	718	15,518	11,749
C	8/26	3,667	48,644	1,264	16,124	12,457
D	10/18	2,613	19,988	88	1,341	(1,272)
E	12/5	9,396	79,732	1,626	41,444	32,048
F	12/27 1/5/72	58,678	460,652	4,670	111,603	52,925
TOTAL		99,113	819,561	10,556	228,326	129,213
OTHER						
TV Announcement 1/4/72				2,080	23,008	

Appendix H: Political Contributions of Stewart R. Mott in 1972

Table H-1
Political Contributions of Stewart R. Mott in 1972

Presidential

Shirley Chisholm	$ 2,100
John Lindsay	6,000
Eugene McCarthy	5,000
Paul McCloskey	6,000
George McGovern	400,000
Anti-Edmund Muskie, negative research and advertisements	39,000

$458,100

Senatorial

James Abourezk, SD	$ 1,000
Edward Brooke, MA	200
Lee Metcalf, MT	200
Walter Mondale, MN	200
Claiborne Pell, RI	500
Floyd Haskell, CO	500

$ 2,600

Congressional

Herman Badillo, NY	$ 1,100
James Burch, VA	1,000
Phillip Burton, CA	100
John Conyers, MI	100
Ronald Dellums, CA	100
Charles Diggs, MI	100
John Dow, NY	100
Don Edwards, CA	100
Walter Fauntroy, delegate, D.C.	100
William Green, PA	500
Kenneth Heckler, WV	500
Robert Kastenmeier, WI	100
John Kerry, MA	1,000
Edward Koch, NY	400
Howard Lee, NC	1,000
Allard Lowenstein, NY	1,000
Paul McCloskey, CA	1,000
P.J. Mitchell, MD	500
Alberta Murphy, AL	500
Richard Ottinger, NY	100
David Pryor, AR	2,500
Charles Rangel, NY	200
Ogden Reid, NY	100
Henry Reuss, WI	100
Donald Reigle, Jr., MI	100
Frank Smith, MS	500
Gerry Studds, MA	1,000
Yancy White, TX	500

Table H-1 (Cont.)

Congressional (Cont.)

Charles Wilson, TX	$	500
Senate and House candidates (unspecified)—amounts given directly, plus expenses		5,000
Senate and House candidates (unspecified)—amounts given through National Committee for an Effective Congress		13,992
		$ 33,892

Miscellaneous

Albert Blumenthal, NY	$	500
Tony Olivieri, NY		500
Cissy Farenthold (gov), TX		1,000
Dan Walker (gov), IL		1,000
Center for Political Reform		66,000
Democratic Planning Group		6,000
October 9 mini-campaign—Vietnam		80,000
Opposition to DNC telethon		6,000
People Politics (fund-raising cost)		22,000
Vote for Peace (TV program)		75,000
		$258,000

Administrative expenses

Presidential campaigns	$	40,000
Party reform and delegate selection		10,000
Miscellaneous issues (including some not specified above)		20,000
		$ 70,000
Grand total		$822,592

Investment-loss deductions (not included in hard money total)

The Informed Delegate (newsletter)	$	17,000
New Democrat Magazine		5,200
The Reliable Source (publication)		3,000
Total		$ 25,200

Appendix I: Lists of CRP-paid Expenses Termed "White House Support"

Table I-1
Lists of CRP-paid Expenses Termed "White House Support"

Consolidated Schedules, May 31, 1973

	Cumulative	Current
White House Support		
Advanceman costs	$ 663,199.71	$ 119.17
Advertising	4,605.84	
Art	1,695.76	
Audio	71,166.32	
Banner and signs	12,327.75	
Consultants	74,196.07	
Data processing	18,918.57	
Film and film production	54,949.55	
Flowers	990.47	
Gifts	338,151.30	1,600.00
Hotel	228,370.23	1,392.82
Lighting costs	44,926.74	
Mailing lists	4,393.95	
Mailing services	27,099.92	
Microfilm costs	277.79	
Miscellaneous	48,637.85	
Miscellaneous office expense	23,184.41	
Office supplies	10,145.58	
Photos	52,399.21	
Postage and delivery	71,754.83	
Prepaid expenses	4,000.00	
Printing costs	168,617.63	
Publications—news services	169,930.54	
Receptions	148,951.61	966.86
Reimb. White House staff costs	39,951.16	
Survey and polls	352,929.26	
Tapes and taping	7,702.06	
Telephone	49,603.45	
Telegraph	17,420.99	
Television	137.00	
Transportation—air	545,514.29	38,697.50-
Transportation—other	28,391.81	1,156.70-
Schedule total	$3,284,541.65	$33,461.95-

Committees—Presidential and First Family Travel, Department 70 Schedules, May 31, 1973

	Cumulative	Current
White House Support		
Advanceman Costs	$ 514,008.80	$ 119.17
Advertising	884.80	
Art	1,471.26	
Audio	45,677.14	
Banner and signs	6,083.02	

Table I-1 (Cont.)

	Cumulative	Current
Consultants	$ 31,423.83	
Film and film production	2,678.32	
Flowers	892.50	
Gifts	304,725.29	
Hotel	83,923.02	
Lighting costs	28,648.94	
Miscellaneous	32,946.28	
Office expense	953.28	
Office supplies	4,578.87	
Photos	18,800.44	
Postage and delivery	24,050.00	
Printing costs	25,622.73	
Publications–news services	34.00	
Receptions	45,233.00	349.32
Reimb. White House staff costs	19,779.01	
Tapes and taping	5,968.50	
Telephone	1,892.88	
Telegraph	238.86	
Transportation–air	208,671.77	
Transportation–other	9,848.03	
Schedule total	$1,419,034.57	$ 468.49

Committees–White House Staff Expenses, Department 71 Schedules, May 31, 1973

	Cumulative	Current
White House Support		
Advanceman costs	$ 58,820.41	
Advertising	119.00	
Consultants	10,279.10	
Film and film production	2,521.69	
Flowers	76.67	
Gifts	3,996.45	
Hotel	13,721.75	$ 788.16
Miscellaneous	112.40	
Office supplies	682.50	
Photos	111.09	
Postage and delivery	10,109.17	
Printing costs	23,296.94	
Publications–news services	1,431.25	
Receptions	11,193.99	
Reimb. White House staff costs	4,705.90	
Tapes and taping	740.00	
Telephone	4,780.91	
Television	209.00	
Transportation–air	36,090.98	
Transportation–other	2,292.31	
Schedule total	$ 185,291.51	$ 788.16

Table I-1 (Cont.)

Committees—Public Relations Operations, Department 72 Schedules, May 31, 1973

	Cumulative	*Current*
White House Support		
Advanceman costs	$ 3,119.83	
Advertising	917.00	
Audio	2,823.81	
Banner and signs	575.00	
Consultants	16,999.06	
Data processing	18,918.57	
Film and film production	46,613.94	
Gifts	10,045.30	
Hotel	4,443.29	
Mailing lists	4,393.95	
Mailing services	27,099.92	
Microfilm costs	167.79	
Miscellaneous	591.67	
Miscellaneous office expense	10,299.20	
Photos	26,912.03	
Postage and delivery	36,486.21	
Prepaid expenses	4,000.00	
Printing costs	111,576.46	
Publications—news services	167,765.89	
Receptions	5,883.54	
Reimb. White House staff costs	6,378.70	
Survey and polls	109,040.19	
Telephone	50.81	
Telegraph	11,134.59	
Transportation—air	7,669.05	
Transportation—other	30.00	
Schedule total	$ 633,935.80	

Committees—The Vice-President, Department 73 Schedules, May 31, 1973

	Cumulative	*Current*
White House Support		
Advanceman costs	$ 87,250.67	
Advertising	2,685.04	
Art	224.50	
Audio	22,665.37	
Banner and signs	5,669.73	
Consultants	15,494.08	
Film and film production	3,135.60	
Flowers	21.30	
Gifts	19,384.26	$ 1,600.00
Hotel	126,282.17	604.66
Lighting costs	16,277.80	
Microfilm costs	110.00	

Table I-1 (Cont.)

	Cumulative	Current
Miscellaneous	$ 14,987.50	
Miscellaneous office expense	11,931.93	
Office supplies	4,884.21	
Photos	6,575.65	
Postage and delivery	1,109.45	
Printing costs	8,121.50	
Publications—news services	699.40	
Receptions	86,641.08	$ 617.54
Reimb. White House staff costs	9,087.55	
Survey and polls	243,889.07	
Tapes and taping	993.56	
Telephone	42,878.85	
Telegraph	6,047.54	
Television	72.00–	
Transportation—air	293,082.49	38,679.50–
Transportation—other	16,221.47	1,156.70
Schedule total	$1,046,279.77	$34,718.60–

Appendix J: Total Contributions and Loans of W. Clement and Jessie V. Stone, 1968-72

Table J-1
Total Contributions and Loans of W. Clement and Jessie V. Stone, 1968–72

1968 Contributions

Republican	$2,852,699	($2,813,699 to Nixon)
Democratic	— —	
Miscellaneous	1,000	

1969 Contributions

Republican	$ 18,616
Democratic	— —
Miscellaneous	— —

1970 Contributions

Republican	$ 234,592
Democratic	— —
Conservative	15,000
Miscellaneous	— —

1972 Contributions

Republican	$2,133,254.40	($2,051,643.45 to Nixon)
Democratic	8,411.54	
Miscellaneous	— —	

Total 1968–72 Contributions

Republican	$5,239,161.40	($4,865,342.45 to Nixon)
Democratic	8,411.54	
Conservative	15,000.00	
Miscellaneous	1,000.00	
	$5,263,572.94	

1970 Loans

Republican	$522,000
Conservative	300,000

Total 1968–72 Loans

Republican	$522,000
Democratic	— —
Conservative	300,000
Miscellaneous	1,000
	$823,000

Table J-1 (Cont.)

N.Y. Post 7/13/73

Total contributions 1968-72		$5,680,503.45		
Total loans 1968-72		1,234,203.70		

1968

Presidential:

R	Nixon	$2,813,699	*Washington Post, 7/15/73, Mintz.*	$2,813,699

Congressional:

R	Kaplinski H-8-Ill	1,000	
R	RCB Club	1,000	
	Legislative offices (unspecified)	4,000	6,000

Party Committees:

R	RNAC	5,000	
R	RNC	3,000	8,000

Other Committees:

R	Ogilvie-Gov-Ill	25,000	
M	UN-Rep-AM	1,000	(not included in total)	25,000

$2,852,699

1969

Congressional:

R	RCB Club	3,000	3,000

Party Committees:

R	RNC	3,616	3,616

Other Committees:

R	Holton-Gov-Va	12,000	*Washington Post, 7/15/73, Mintz.*	12,000

$ 18,616

(cont.)

Table J-1 (Cont.)

1970

Congressional:

		Amount	Notes
R	Beall S-Md	$ 5,000	
R	Brock S-Tn	15,000	
C	Buckley S-NY	15,000	Also lent $300,000 to Buckley, which was repaid. Stone later said he had not lent $300,000 but had guaranteed bank loans up to $100,000. *Washington Post* 7/15/73, *Washington Post* 7/26/73.
R	Bush S-Tx	10,000	
R	Carter S-NM	20,000	
R	Cramer S-Fla	10,000	Stone later said the amount was $2,500. *Washington Post* 7/26/73.
R	Danforth S-Mo	2,500	
R	Garland S-Va	500	*Washington Post* 7/15/73
R	Smith S-Ill	17,500	Also lent $500,000 to Smith, $200,000 was repaid. *Washington Post* 7/15/73.
R	Taft S-Ohio	7,500	
R	Weicker S-Conn	10,000	
R	Wold S-Wy	10,000	
R	Anderson H-16-Ill	100	*Washington Post* 7/15/73.
R	Farber H-19-NY	500	
R	Parker H-7-Md	1,000	
R	Phillips H-6-Mass	2,500	
R	Powell H-24-Ohio	1,000	
R	Schlafly H-22-Ill	33,492	*Washington Post* 7/15/73
R	Uccello H-1-Conn	2,500	
R	Wilkinson H-4-Okla	45,000	Also lent $22,000 to Wilkinson. Stone later said the loan was $10,000 and it was fully repaid. *Washington Post* 7/15/73, *Washington Post* 7/26/73.
R	RCB Club	3,000	(Additional congressional money may have been given through Jack A. Gleason's Operation Townhouse. "About half of the money for the townhouse operation came in campaign donations written directly to the Senate races by such givers as Henry Ford II, insurance

$　212,092

Table J-1 (Cont.)

1970

executive W. Clement Stone, and ambassador to England Walter H. Annenberg. The other $1.5 million came from Kalmbach's cashier's checks." *Washington Star* 7/11/73, James R. Polk.

Party Committees:

R	Rep-St-C-Mass	$ 2,500

Not included are contributions/loans to the Illinois Republican State Central Committee. "In Illinois, he said, he has made loans to the Republican state central committee of $1.2 million and has given it or loaned it another 'quarter of a million dollars.' The unpaid loan balance is $709,000, he said." *Washington Post,* 7/14/73, Mintz.

Other Committees:

R	Meskill-Gov-Md	10,000
R	Reagan-Gov-Calif.	25,000
		35,000
		$ 249,592 (Contributions)
		822,000 (Loans)

"Specifically, Stone said he contributed $810,659 to a long list of candidates in 1970, and another $1,234, 203.70 in loans." *N.Y. Post* 7/13/73.

$ 2,500

1972

Presidential:

R	Nixon pre 4-7	$2,000,000
R	Nixon	51,643.45
		$2,051,643.45

Congressional:

R	Boggs S-Del	3,000
R	Chafee S-RI	500
R	Domenici S-NM	500
R	Griffin S-Mi	5,200
R	Hirsch S-SD	500
R	McClure S-Ida	500
R	Percy S-Ill	2,500
R	Tower S-Tx	2,500
D	Randolph S-W.Va.	8,411.54

(cont.)

Table J-1. (Cont.)

1972					
R	Callahan H-2-Calif.	$ 250			
R	Crane H-12-Ill	100			
R	Fetridge H-9-Ill	250			
R	Hoellen H-11-Ill	1,000			
R	Steelman H-5-Tx	500			
R	Young H-10-Ill	10,400			
R	Rep-Cand-Conf	2,500	$ 38,611.54		*Washington Post* 7/18/73.
Party Committees:					
R	Rep-Campn-C	3,000			
R	Rep-Assoc-C	9,000			
R	RNC	3,000			
R	RNFC	3,000			
R	URF of Ill	6,000			
R	Rep-Vctry- C	3,000			
R	Nat'l-Rep-Heritage-Centr-C	2,910.95			
R	Rep-Conv-Gala	5,000			
R	RNFOC	500			
R	RNFAC	2,500	37,910.95		
Other Committees:					
R	McLaughty-Gov-Vt	1,000			*Washington Post* 7/18/73, Mintz.
R	Ogilvie-Gov-Ill	1,000			*Washington Post* 7/18/73, Mintz.
R	Carey-SA-Ill	11,500	13,500.00		*Washington Post* 7/18/73, Mintz.
			$2,141,665.94		

Appendix K: Samples of Loan Agreements, Loan Conversions, and Loan Repayments Used in the McGovern Campaign in 1972

I

McGovern '72 Shriver

1910 K Street, N.W., Washington, D.C., 20006 · (202) 333-4900

October 17, 1972

Mr.

Dear

November 7 is rapidly approaching. The remaining days represent
in a very real sense the most critical period of our entire campaign
effort. Every political barometer now indicates that Senator McGovern
is indeed recording significant gains in popular support. Overflowing
crowds greet the Senator at every step. Literally hundreds of thousands
of letters have poured into our headquarters here in Washington. The
polls, at times our nemesis, are all reporting a very favorable trend.
Indicative of this movement, the results of interviews conducted by
Cambridge Survey Research on October 12 and 13 show that Senator McGovern
has cut a 27 point deficit in Michigan to 8, a 33 point deficit in
Ohio to 13, a 20 point deficit in New York to 10, and a 12 point deficit
in California to 1.

As you know, not since the election of 1932 have the American
people had such a clearcut choice in selecting their next President.
You who have been so helpful to this campaign are aware of the many
differences that exist between George McGovern and Richard Nixon not
only on the major issues confronting this country, but in morality,
integrity, and honesty as well. Unfortunately, however, many Americans
do not really know Senator McGovern and what he stands for. Lack of
exposure is the major barrier that stands between George McGovern and
the Presidency. To counteract this disadvantage, we must utilize all
of the media and particularly television, in a mass communications
effort during the next few weeks.

Over 30 million Americans watched George McGovern speak on the
Vietnam war one week ago; over 30 million people saw and heard the
real George McGovern, not an image defaced by his opponents. We must
continue to provide the electorate with as much opportunity as possible
to meet the real George McGovern for only then can they make a credible
decision when they enter the voting booths on November 7.

Serving only to intensify the frustration of those of us who know
and believe in the real George McGovern is a knowledge of the actions
and attitudes of the present administration. Never in American history

-2

has there been leadership so beholden to special interests, so guided by
political expediency, nor so oblivious to the common good. With utter
contempt for the laws of our society, Nixon and his Committee to Re-elect
the President have been caught employing what the New York Times, in its
editorial of October 12, termed "police state tactics."

Those of us intimately involved in the campaign who reside in the
nation's capital and are considered by many to be more politically sophisticated
than the average American have been shocked, day after day, as investigative
reporters release further details of espionage and of sabotage of the whole
political process. We are enclosing for your information a copy of the letter
we have sent to the Attorney General of the United States which is self-
explanatory.

There is no question that your generosity has played a vital role in
allowing the candidacy of the Senator to come as far as it has. Your loan,
when added to the seventy others solicited under the one-to-four repayment
plan program, totalling $3,700,000, provided the initial money to fund the
presidential campaign, its voter registration efforts, and its direct mail
in the early difficult weeks after the Convention. My associates on the
National Finance Committee take pride in the fact that in an unprecedented
manner, we have met these loan obligations to date.

However, as we enter the final three weeks of the campaign the necessity
of setting aside in escrow one out of every four contribution dollars to meet
loan repayments in accordance with the terms of our agreement will force us
to cut back on our budget for TV, radio, and newspaper advertising. In order
to give our candidate the maximum communications exposure possible in these
final weeks, Miles Rubin, Morris Dees, and I have agreed to convert 50% of
our one-to-four loans ($360,000 face value) to contributions. We feel that
we must impose on your generosity once again and ask you to do the same.
You may be interested in knowing that Miles, Morris and I will have each
contributed (exclusive of our substantial loans) well in excess of $100,000
each to the McGovern campaign in addition to the full-time efforts of Miles
and Morris for the past half year and myself for a year and a half.

To facilitate the conversion process, you will find enclosed a "forgiveness"
form, and a stamped return envelope. It is suggested that you distribute
the resulting contribution among the committees listed (see enclosed) with a
maximum of $3000 being assigned to any one committee. We would appreciate
your immediate attention and your early response to enable us to plan TV for
next week.

Sincerely,

Henry L. Kimelman
National Finance Chairman

P.S. We have already had indications from six other lenders that they
      are going along with our recommendation.

enclosure

II

October 27, 1972

McGovern for President Committee, Inc.
1910 K Street, N.W.
Washington, D. C. 20006

Gentlemen:

The undersigned refers to the sum of $_____ owed to him by
you as of this date and hereby informs you that he has this day
assigned $_____ of said amount receivable to the independent
McGovern Campaign Committees set forth on Schedule A attached, as
contributions in the indicated amounts.

This letter shall serve as an assignment and transfer, without
guarantee or recourse, of the indicated amounts to the indicated
committees.

Very truly yours,

III

Number_____

District of Columbia
Washington, D.C.

AGREEMENT FOR LOAN REPAYMENT

The McGovern for President Committee, a non-profit corporation,
organized under the laws of the District of Columbia, (herein called the
"Committee"), agrees to repay without interest the loan to the Committee
from _____ (herein called the "Lender") in
the amount of _____ or in such lesser amount as this agreement provides on the following basis: The Committee will pay pro-rata
to the above Lender and all other lenders holding similar obligations,
which the Committee covenants and agrees will not exceed $4,500,000 prin-
cipal amount (herein called "Borrowed Funds"), a sum equal to twenty-five
percent (25%) of all cash "contributions" as defined in Section 301 of
the Federal Election Campaign Act of 1971 received by the Committee, less
the Borrowed Funds. The obligation to repay portions of this loan is
conditioned upon the receipt of cash contributions, less Borrowed Funds
sufficient to meet the disbursement schedule set forth below.

It is understood that there will be established a trust account
with the National Savings & Trust Company of Washington, D.C., into
which, commencing on August 1, 1972, there shall be paid on a current
basis all funds properly allocable but limited to the repayment of this
and similar Borrowed Funds which funds shall be fully disbursed on
December 31, 1972. Pro-rata settlement to the Lender and other lenders
of similar Borrowed Funds will be made from the trust account every two
weeks beginning August 28, 1972, with the final payment being made
December 31, 1972, the date all obligations under this agreement termi-
nates. The records of this account shall be subject to inspection by
the Lender at any time

Date:_____   McGOVERN FOR PRESIDENT COMMITTEE
                                     A Non-Profit Corporation

                                     By_____
                                        Henry L. Kimelman
                                        Chairman of the Board

Appendix L: Summary of Guggenheim Productions, Inc. Expenses for the McGovern General Election Broadcast Campaign, 1972

Production Descriptions		Cost Program	Cost Dubs
Spots			
Original package, TV spots		$ 85,000	$205,745
Fund-raising spots & tags		24,574	inc. above
Original package, radio spots		30,000	5,608
Package of "negative" TV & radio spots		25,000	46,890
5-minute "Eleanor McGovern" spot		13,500	2,232
"Sen. Kennedy" spots		3,500	12,712.50
"Sen. Humphrey" spots		3,500	inc. above
Total spots		$185,074	$273,187.50
Programs			
Biography	Broadcast Oct. 1	$ 21,000	$ 14,731
Vietnam speech	Broadcast Oct. 10	19,379	6,886
"California" confrontation program	Broadcast Oct. 15	12,500	1,400
Economics speech	Broadcast Oct. 20	24,305	1,400
Corruption speech	Broadcast Oct. 25	18,247.50	6,290
"People" film (A Candidate's Journal)	Broadcast Oct. 31	100,000	8,276.75
Second Vietnam program	Broadcast Nov. 3	14,159.60	
Splicing together program for – – –	Nov. 5	27,141.40	
Cancelled program, plus editing biography for – – –	Nov. 6	12,177.69	
Transferring film to tape		5,200	
New confrontation program	Never Broadcast	766.05	
Nixon-McGovern debate	Never Broadcast	37,240	
Total programs		$292,116.24	$ 38,923.75
Other			
Screening for Sen. McGovern in Los Angeles		$ 977.50	
Telethon expenses		880	$ 875
Dubs for Ark., So. Cal., Paris still unpaid			562
Total		$479,047.74	$313,548.25

Total postconvention expenses incurred	$792,595.99
Preconvention expenses paid by McGovern for President, Inc.	42,327.00
Grand total	$834,922.99[a]

Payments reported on part 9 of Sept. 10, 15-day, and 5-day reports	$735,432.00
Payments reported on part 9 of this report	110,000.00
Total payments to Guggenheim Productions, Inc.	845,432.00
Grand total of expenses incurred	- 834,922.99
Amount owed to committee by Guggenheim Productions, Inc. (Part II)	$ 10,509.01

[a]Does not include advertising commissions.

Appendix M: Examples of McGovern
General Election Broadcast Purchases, 1972

Table M-1
McGovern General Election Broadcast Purchases, 1972: Example I

| Television | Network Buy | Week of October 17-23 (Week 6) | |
		Net Time	Edit Charges
CBS:			
10/17	5 min.	$ 8,889	$ 2,235
10/18	60 sec.	42,500	250
10/19	5 min.	11,296	2,235
10/20	60 sec.	32,300	250
10/22	5 min.	13,200	2,235
10/23	5 min.	13,926	2,235
10/23	5 min.	12,754	2,235
10/18	5 min.	5,202	470
10/19	5 min.	5,250	470
10/22	60 sec.	7,905	125
		$153,222	$12,740
		$165,962	
NBC:			
10/22	60 sec.	$ 28,050	$ 297.50
10/17	5 min.	13,600	148.75
10/23	60 sec.	22,950	297.50
		$ 64,600	$ 743.75
		$ 65,343.75	
ABC:			
10/17	5 min.	$ 5,553.05	$ 5,826.50
10/19	60 sec.	30,600.00	300.00
10/22	5 min.	5,553.05	212.50
10/20	1/2 hr.	34,510.00	1,275.00
		$ 76,216.10	$ 7,614.00
		$83,830.10	
Network Gross Time plus editing charges:		$367,026.75	
3% Commission:		$ 11,010.80	

Table M-2

McGovern General Election Broadcast Purchases, 1972: Example II

Summary of Network Television Buy

Week 6: October 17-23

Net time	$294,038.10	Gross time	$345,927.17
Editing fees	21,097.75	Editing fees	21,097.75
Net plus editing	315,135.85	Gross inc. edit	$367,024.92
3% commission	11,010.75		
Expense incurred	$326,146.60		

Week 7: October 24-30

Net time	$356,247.00	Gross time	$419,114.11
Editing fees	21,643.00	Editing fees	21,643.00
Net plus edit	377,890.00	Gross inc. edit	$440,757.11
3% commission	113,222.71		
Expense incurred	$391,112.71		

Summary of Network Radio Buy

Week 6: October 17-23

Net time	$ 26,385.44	Gross time	$ 31,041.69
Production fees	382.50	Production fees	382.50
Net plus prod.	26,767.94	Gross inc. prod.	$ 31,424.19
3% commission	942.73		
Expense incurred	$ 27,710.67		

Week 7: October 24-30

Net time	$ 49,344.59	Gross time	$ 58,052.46
Production fees	425.00	Production fees	425.00
Net plus prod.	49,769.59	Gross inc. prod.	$ 58,477.46
3% commission	1,754.32		
Expense incurred	$ 51,523.91		

Appendix N: Examples of Candidate Authorizations and Certifications for Media Expenditures within the Limits

I

mcgovern · shriver '72

1910 k street, n.w. · washington, d.c. 20006 · (202) 333-4900

TO WHOM IT MAY CONCERN:

I am a candidate of the Democratic party for the office of the President of the United States.

As required by P.L. 92-225, Reg. 11.1, Sec. 4.12c, I hereby authorize--without any restrictions or limitations---the following person to make certifications on my behalf in compliance with Reg. 11.1, Sec. 4.12a:

        Mr. Thomas Collins
        Rapp, Collins, Stone & Adler, Inc.
        475 Park Avenue South
        New York, New York   10016

August 15, 1972   Senator George McGovern

As permitted by rulings from the General Accounting Office (Reference 8330-E; C5-1659 of June 8, 1972) and Federal Communications Commission (Reference 8330-E; C5-1444 of June 13, 1972); I, Thomas Collins, authorize the use of a facsimile of my signature on certifications under Section 104(b) and (c) of the Federal Election Campaign Act of 1971. In making this authorization, I understand that I am personally responsible for each certification in the same manner as if I had affixed my signature by hand and accordingly have satisfied myself that the proper control procedures exist for the use of the facsimile.

                         Thomas Collins

II

THE WHITE HOUSE

WASHINGTON

July 20, 1972

MEMORANDUM FOR: C. LANGHORNE WASHBURN
                    FINANCE COMMITTEE TO
                    RE-ELECT THE PRESIDENT

Sections 104(b) and (c) of the Federal Election Campaign
Act of 1971 require that a candidate for the office of
President, or a person specifically authorized in writing
by such candidate, certify to any person making a charge
for use of any newspaper, magazine, outdoor advertising
facility or broadcasting station on behalf of his candidacy
that payment of such charge will not violate the expenditure
limitations imposed by Title I of the Act.

In accordance with this requirement and the regulations
and guidelines found in 11 CFR 4.12(c) and the answer to
Question 1, Part VII of the March 16, 1972 Federal
Communications Commission Public Notice entitled "Use
of Broadcast and Cablecast Facilities: Candidates for
Public Office", I hereby authorize you to make such certifications on my behalf for my campaign for nomination and
election to the office of President. In that these regulations
and guidelines also require a statement of any restrictions
or limitations on your authority to act in this regard, by
this memorandum I notify you that none are imposed.

As permitted by rulings from the General Accounting Office
(Reference 8330-E; C5-1659 of June 8, 1972) and Federal
Communications Commission (Reference 8330-E; C5-1444 of
June 13, 1972); I, C. Langhorne Washburn, authorize the use
of a facsimile of my signature on certifications under Section
104(b) and (c) of the Federal Election Campaign Act of 1971.
In making this authorization, I understand that I am personally
responsible for each certification in the same manner as if I
had affixed my signature by hand and accordingly have satisfied
myself that the proper control procedures exist for the use of
the facsimile.

                                    C. Langhorne Washburn

III

SAMPLE CERTIFICATION

I_____ certify that the payment of the charge in

the amount of $_____ by __ (name and address of media firm)_____

for the use of advertising space on behalf of the candidacy of (name &

political affiliation of candidate) in the (primary, run-off, or general

election) for (title of office, including Congressional District if

appropriate) in the state of _____ will not violate

the candidate's expenditure limitation under paragraph (1) (2) or (3)

of Section 104 (a) of the Federal Election Campaign Act of 1971, Public

Law 92-225. The advertising referred to in this certification is

(description of advertising)_____

and is for display or publication on (date of publication) in (name &

address of newspaper). The line rate for this advertising is $_____.

Date signed

_____

Signature of candidate (or a person.
authorized in writing by the candidate
to so certify).

Appendix O: Sample Letter Addressed to Hugh Sloan, Jr. Authorizing Contributions in Stock to CRP

Mr. Hugh Sloan, Jr.
c/o The Committee for the Re-election
  of the President
1701 Pennsylvania Avenue, N.W.
Washington, D.C. 20006

Dear Mr. Sloan:

  I hand you herewith the following securities:

Certificate Number	Number of Shares	Issuer

  I am delivering this stock to you as my agent to effect transfer thereof as herein set forth. You are authorized and directed to divide this stock into certificates with values of not to exceed $3,000 each, on the date of transfer, and to cause one of the certificates, as my agent for such purpose, to be transferred to each of the following named separate entities:

  It is my intent by these instructions to make a separate and individual contribution of not to exceed $3,000 to each of the hereinabove specifically named entities.

  Please confirm this arrangement by signing a copy of this letter.

      Sincerely,

      _____

_____

Better Society Committee
Stable Society Council
Improved Society Support Group
Dedicated Americans for Effective Government
Loyal Americans for Government Reform
Active Volunteers for Improved Government
Dedicated Friends of a Better America
Supporters of Good Government
United Friends of a Balanced Society
Dedicated Volunteers for Reform in Society

Stable Society Committee
Improved Society Council
Reform in Society Support Group
Dedicated Americans for a Better America
Supporters of a Balanced Society
Active Volunteers for Effective Government
Dedicated Friends of Government Reform
United Friends of Good Government
Loyal Americans for Reform in Society
Dedicated Volunteers for Effective Government

Improved Society Committee
Dedicated Americans for Improved Government
Active Volunteers for Government Reform
United Friends of Government Reform
Dedicated Friends of a Balanced Society
Loyal Americans for Effective Government
Better America Support Group
Reform in Society Council
Supporters of a Better Society
Dedicated Volunteers for Government Reform

Appendix P: Memo from Henry L. Kimelman Explaining Contributions of Appreciated Property

McGOVERN FOR PRESIDENT 410 FIRST STREET SE WASHINGTON, DC 20003

To: Members, Finance Committee   1 November 1971

From: National Finance Chairman

Subject: Contributions of Appreciated Property

The attached letter from Attorney Stanley S. Weithorn sets out the way in which individuals can contribute appreciated property to the McGOVERN campaign without incurring any income tax liability whatsoever. We believe it is self-explanatory.

For example, if you or any other potential contributors, own securities which cost $5,000 and have a fair market value of $10,000.00 at the time of the gift to one of the McGOVERN Committees, the Committee will purchase it from you for $5,000.00 and sell it immediately for $10,000.00 effecting a net benefit to the campaign of $5,000.00. You as the donor realize the cost return of your $5,000.00 investment and the campaign benefits from your $5,000.00 contribution. You personally will save anywhere from approximately 30% to 70% (short term or long term) of the tax liability which would ordinarily be levied on this gain.

The above has been confirmed to me personally by Stewart Mott, of New York, who was rendered the same opinion by his counsel, Mudge, Guthrie, etc. (the old Nixon law firm) and by Myer Feldman of Ginsberg, Feldman and Bress, a leading and prestigious law firm in Washington, D.C.

Henry L. Kimelman
National Finance Chairman

661

FRANCIS B. UPHAM, JR.(1894-1962)
IRWIN F. DEUTSCH
JOEL M. HANDEL
HERBERT S. MEEKER
RAYMOND RUBIN
ROBERT STURZ
PIERRE A.TONACHEL
STANLEY S. WEITHORN
—
EDWARD P. BANK
JOEL K. BOHMART
LAWRENCE LEVY
ROBERT G. PIERCE

UPHAM, MEEKER & WEITHORN
ATTORNEYS
CHRYSLER BUILDING, NEW YORK, N. Y. 10017

TELEPHONE: (212) OX 7-6640
CABLE ADDRESS: UPFRANK
TELEX: 125404

October 28, 1971

Mr. Henry Kimmelman
McGovern for President
410 First Street, S.E.
Washington, D.C. 20003

Dear Mr. Kimmelman:

This letter is intended as a written confirmation of the legal opinion that I had given orally to Abner Levine at an earlier date.

The question at issue relates to the Federal income tax consequences to the donor of a gift of appreciated property to a political organization, under a "bargain sale" arrangement. Specifically, I have focused on a factual situation whereunder appreciated property is sold to a political organization for an amount equal to the tax basis of the donor.

Under such circumstances, it is clear that the sale price realized may be offset completely by the tax basis of the property (without proration of that basis), so that no gain is realized by the donor in connection with the sale portion of the transaction.*

This rule was most clearly annunciated in the case of Elizabeth H. Potter, 38 T.C. 951 (1962). The Internal Revenue Service subsequently acquiesced in the result of the Potter case.

---

* With respect to the gift portion of the transaction, the donor will, of course, be subject to gift tax, to the extent not offset by the annual exclusion and the lifetime exemption.

Because the use of the bargain sale technique in the charitable area was considered, by the Treasury Department, to constitute an abuse, Congress, in The Tax Reform Act of 1969, altered the prior rule so as to provide that, in the event of a bargain sale of appreciated property made to a charitable organization by any person, the tax basis of the transferror is prorated between the "sale" portion and the "gift" portion of the property's value. Consequently, gain is now realized by the transferror in connection with the "sale" portion of the transaction, in accordance with Internal Revenue Code Section 1011(b).

In the course of its deliberation on this question, the Senate Finance Committee issued S. Rep. No. 91-552, 91st Cong., 1st Sess., 80 (1969), which provides, in part, as follows:

"If property is sold to a charity at a price below its fair market value - a so-called bargain sale - the proceeds of the sale are considered to be a return of the cost and are not required to be allocated between the cost basis of the 'sale' part of the transaction and the 'gift' part of the transaction."

Thus, the rule of prior law has been recognized by the judiciary (in the Potter case), by the executive (through the Internal Revenue Service's acquiescence in the Potter case) and by the legislature (through its issuance of the above quoted Senate Finance Committee report). That becomes particularly important in light of the fact that the 1969 statutory change relates solely and exclusively to bargain sales made to charitable organizations. Specifically, I.R.C. §1011(b) provides:

"(b) Bargain Sale to a Charitable Organization. - If a deduction is allowable under section 170 (relating to charitable contributions) by reason of a sale, then the adjusted basis for determining the gain from

Mr. Henry Kimmelman   -3-   October 28, 1971·

        such sale shall be that portion of the adjusted basis
    which bears to the fair market value of the property."

        It is therefore quite clear that a bargain sale
    of appreciated property made to <u>other</u> <u>than</u> a charitable or-
    ganization (such as a political organization) is <u>not</u> sub-
    ject to the rule of proration but, instead, continues to
    be subject to the rule of prior law, as described above.

        If you have any further questions with respect
    to this matter, please do not hesitate to communicate with
    me.

                            Sincerely,

    SSW/jd
    cc: Mr. Abner Levine

Appendix Q: Split Contributions to Candidates for the Same Office and/or Political Committees at the Same Level by Individuals Who Gave $10,000 or More in 1972

This appendix lists those 116 split contributions to candidates for the same office and/or political committees at the same level by individuals who gave $10,000 or more in 1972. These included presidential splits: splits in which contributions were given to the individual candidate committees of Nixon, Muskie, Humphrey, Jackson, McGovern, Mills, Yorty, Lindsay, Wallace, Sanford, Hartke, Bayh, McCloskey, Chisholm, McCarthy; National Party Committee splits: splits given to opposing national party committees; congressional splits: splits in which contributions were given to specific congressional candidates on the same level; state splits: splits in which contributions were given to specific state candidates or committees on the same level.

Table Q-1
Split Contributions to Candidates for the Same Office and/or Political Committees at the Same Level by Individuals Who Gave $10,000 or More in 1972

	Presidential		Splits
	Nixon and Democratic Candidates		
Nixon $465,145.98	Muskie $144,422		19
Nixon $270,576.08	Humphrey $202,460		14
Nixon $1,067,811.36	Jackson $301,387.92		19
Nixon $79,645.56	McGovern $74,146.74		7
Nixon $146,878.46	Mills $10,000		4
Nixon $29,000	Yorty $2,500		2
Nixon $100,000	Lindsay $10,000		1
Nixon $17,000	Wallace $7,500		1
Nixon $14,150	Sanford $3,000 (loan)		1

Table Q-1 (Cont.)

	Presidential		Splits
	Nixon and Democratic Candidates		
Nixon $565,232.22	Humphrey $353,450	Jackson $138,000	6
Nixon $28,500	Muskie $15,500	McGovern $80,150	4
Nixon $54,019	Muskie $5,500	Hartke $750	2
Nixon $5,000	McGovern $18,850	Humphrey $2,400	1
Nixon $22,000	Humphrey $17,500	Muskie $500	1
Nixon $8,500	Humphrey $11,000	Mills $1,000	1
Nixon $47,167.80	Humphrey $2,500	Bayh $50,000	1
Nixon $15,000	Mills $1,000	Wallace $5,000	1
Nixon $115,097.60	Mills $51,000	Jackson $10,000	1
Nixon $6,000	Mills $500	Muskie $250	1

Table Q-1 (Cont.)

Presidential

Nixon and Democratic Candidates

						Splits
Nixon $90,300	McGovern $16,500	Humphrey $26,600	Jackson $2,000			1
Nixon $10,000	Jackson $1,000	Lindsay $1,000	Mills $6,000			1
Nixon $38,000	Humphrey $50,000	Muskie $10,000	Bayh $500			1
Nixon $10,000	Jackson $10,000	Humphrey $3,000	McGovern $2,100	Muskie $5,000	Hartke $250	1

McCloskey and Democratic Candidates

				Splits
McCloskey $159,681.00	McGovern $324,375.05			14
McCloskey $11,500	Lindsay $344,167			2
McCloskey $5,300	McGovern $66,875.37	McCarthy $8,600		2
McCloskey $9,825	McGovern $319,365	Chisholm $10,000		1
McCloskey $27,100	McGovern $317,252.76	Muskie $8,000		3

Table Q-1 (Cont.)

Presidential					Splits
McCloskey and Democratic Candidates					
McCloskey $6,000	McGovern $407,747.50	McCarthy $5,000	Lindsay $6,000	Chisholm $2,100	1
Nixon, McCloskey, and Democrats					
Nixon $3,000	McCloskey $4,000	McGovern $2,000	Lindsay $1,000		1
Congressional					Splits
Committees					
NRSC $3,000	DSCC $1,000				1
NCRDC $5,000	RCB Club $2,000				1
Senate Candidates					
Texas	D-Sanders $12,685.01	R-Tower $9,883.75			4
Louisiana	D-Ellender $61,000	I-McKeithen $11,000			2

Table Q-1 (Cont.)

Congressional

	Senate Candidates		Splits
Georgia	D-Nunn $2,142.01	R-Thompson $2,030.97	1
Virginia	D-Spong $1,500	R-Scott $3,000	1
Rhode Island	D-Pell $3,000	R-Chafee $3,000	1

House Candidates

H-4-Ariz	D-Brown $500	R-Conlan $500	1
H-3-La	D-Bauer $500	R-Treen $500	1
H-24-NY	D-Reid $1,250	R-Vergari (& Peyser 23) $1,000	1
H-17-Cal	D-Stewart $1,000	R-McCloskey $3,000	1

State

Texas-Governor	D-Smith $4,000	R-Grover $31,000	1

Table Q-1 (Cont.)

	Congressional			Splits
	State			
California Committees	D-Brisco $1,000	R-Fay $1,000	R-Grover $18,000	1
	Rep-St-Centr-C-Cal $1,000	Dem-St-Centr-C-Cal $3,250		1
State Senate	D-Alquist $1,000	R-Nejedly $1,000		1

Appendix R: Contributions of Officials of 13 Selected Groups, 1972

There are cases throughout the 13 groups in which individuals serve in more than one capacity in the organization. For example, an officer may also be a director or a trustee. In these cases, the official number of officers, directors, trustees, etc. is given, but the individual's contribution is counted only in the first category in which he appears.

Some individuals are officials of more than one of the 13 groups. In these cases, the contributions are included in each individual group; however, the final total eliminates all contribution duplications.

Table R-1
Contributions of Officials of 13 Selected Groups, 1972

Group or Association	Total Members	Contributing Members	Contributions				Additional Factors
			Republican	Democratic	Miscellaneous	Total	
American Bar Assn.							
Officers	1	--	$ --	$ --	$ --	$ --	--
House of Delegates	305	42	28,450	33,473.95	--	61,923,95	2 Splits
Officers & Delegates	7	--	--	--	--	--	--
American Medical Assn.							
Officers	6	1	200	--	--	200	--
Trustees	11	--	--	--	--		--
Officers & Trustees	1	--	--	--	--		--
American Petroleum Inst.							
Officers	5	--	--	--	1,415	--	22 Splits / 1 R&M
Directors	182	94	816,043	107,107			1 Split
Officers & Directors	8	4	2,600	1,000	515	928,680	
			818,643	108,107	1,930		
American Iron & Steel Institute							
Officers	12	--	--	--	--	--	--
Directors	44	17	24,450	2,860	500		1 Split / 1 R&M
Officers & Directors	2	2	2,500	--	--	30,310	--
			26,950				
Association of American RR							
Officers	15	--	--	--	--	--	--
Directors	20	9	12,650	--	2,875	15,525	--
Officers & Directors	1	--	--	--	--	--	--

Table R-1 (Cont.)

Group or Association	Total Members	Contributing Members	Contributions Republican	Democratic	Miscellaneous	Total	Additional Factors
Business Council							
Officers	1	—	$ —	$ —	$ —	$ —	—
Executive Committee	112	88	980,709	154,955	9,742		3,000 D Loan 19 Splits 5 R&M
Officers & Executive Committee	5	5	33,414	—	2,000	1,180,820	1 R&M
			1,014,123				
Chiefs of Foreign Missions & Special Missions							
Career Officers	80	3	1,400	—	—		
Noncareer Officers	36	20	1,104,764	10,500	—	1,116,664	2 Splits
			1,106,164				
Manufacturing Chemists Assn.							
Officers	6	1	1,000	216	—		
Directors	31	9	13,250	150	—		1 Split
Officers & Directors	2	2	2,700	—	—		
			16,950	366		17,316	
National Assn. of Electric Cos.							
Officers	4	—	—	—	—	—	
Directors	31	10	6,900	1,000	—	7,900	
Officers & Directors	2	—	—	—	—	—	
National Assn. of Manufacturers							
Officers	—	—	—	—	—	—	
Directors	128	56	232,860.37	14,414	6,925		4 Splits 2 R&M
Officers & Directors	44	23	73,467	500	1,600		1 Split 2 R&M
			306,327.37	14,914	8,525	329,766.37	

(cont.)

Table R-1 (Cont.)

Group or Association	Total Members	Contributing Members	Contributions				Additional Factors
			Republican	Democratic	Miscellaneous	Total	
National Association of Real Estate Bds.							
Officers	--	--	$ --	$ --	$ --	$ --	1 Split
Directors	206	22	27,101	2,175	5,802		1 R&M
Officers & Directors	6	2	500	6,000	--	41,578	--
			27,601	8,175			
National Coal Assn.							
Officers	--	--	--	--	--	--	--
Directors	38	10	14,300	--	--		10,000 R Loan
Officers & Directors	4	1	4,000	--	--	18,300	--
			18,300				
U.S. Chamber of Commerce							
Officers	16	7	7,250	2,600	--		2 Splits
Directors	50	23	47,526.32	5,000	1,432		4 Splits
Officers & Directors	--	--	--	7,600	--		
			54,776.32			63,808.32	
Totals	1,406	435	$3,323,583.69	$339,950.95	$32,206	$3,695,740.64	58 Splits 11 R&M R–$10,000 Loan D–$ 3,000 Loan

Appendix S: American Centimillionaires, 1972

In 1968 *Fortune* published a list of 66 centimillionaires, each with wealth of at least $150,000,000 (see Arthur M. Louis, America's Centimillionaires, *Fortune,* May 1968, pp. 152-57, 192-96.) In 1972, 63 of them were still living. Of the 63, 51 persons, or 81 percent, made political contributions in 1972. This appendix lists those 51 individuals and their contributions of $100 or more.

Table S-1
American Centimillionaires, 1972

No. of Contributors: 51

Contributions:

Republican	$5,550,896.19	
Democratic	496,521.54	
Miscellaneous	23,600	
Total	$6,071,017.73	

No.	Name	Party	Amount
1.	Getty, J. Paul Los Angeles, Calif.	Rep.	$ 128,000
2.	Hughes, Howard R. Houston, Tex.	Rep. Dem.	150,000[a] 3,000
3.	Ludwig, Daniel K. N.Y., N.Y.	Dem.	2,500
4.	Mellon, Paul Washington, D.C.	Rep.	62,500
5.	Hunt, Nelson Bunker Dallas, Tex.	Rep. Dem.	16,500 5,000
6.	McKnight, William L. St. Paul, Minn.	Rep.	500
7.	Mott, Charles Stewart Flint, Mich.	Rep.	8,500
8.	Smith, R.E. (Bob) Houston, Tex.	Rep.	3,000
9.	Allen, Charles, Jr. N.Y., N.Y.	Rep.	22,000
10.	Dorrance, John T., Jr. Camden, N.J.	Rep.	39,600
11.	Englehard, Mrs. Charles W., Jr.[b] Far Hills, N.J.	Rep. Dem.	3,000 19,200
12.	Hess, Leon N.Y., N.Y.	Rep. Dem.	252,500 228,500
13.	Hewlett, William R. Palo Alto, Calif.	Rep.	26,500
14.	Packard, David Los Altos, Calif.	Rep. Dem.	91,000 1,000
15.	Houghton, Amory, Sr. Corning, N.Y.	Rep.	12,000

Table S-1 (Cont.)

16.	Lilly, Eli Indianapolis, Ind:	Rep.	$ 7,500
17.	Mars, Forest E. The Plains, Va.	Rep.	15,500
18.	Mauze, Abby Rockefeller (Mrs. Jean) N.Y., N.Y.	Rep.	52,000
19.	Rockefeller, David N.Y., N.Y.	Rep. Dem. Misc.	74,000 500 500
20.	Rockefeller, John D., III N.Y., N.Y.	Rep. Dem.	64,500 3,000
21.	Rockefeller, Laurence S. N.Y., N.Y.	Rep. Misc.	77,500 2,200
22.	Rockefeller, Nelson A. N.Y., N.Y.	Rep.	82,500
23.	Rockefeller, Winthrop Little Rock, Ark.	Rep.	115,700
24.	May, Cordelia Scaife Pittsburg, Pa.	Rep. Misc.	107,500 2,000
25.	Scaife, Richard Mellon Pittsburg, Pa.	Rep.	1,068,000
26.	Wallace, DeWitt Pleasantville, N.Y.	Rep. Misc.	140,600 7,900
27.	Payson, Joan Whitney (Mrs. Charles) N.Y., N.Y.	Rep.	149,000
28.	Whitney, John Hay N.Y., N.Y.	Rep. Misc.	59,750 1,000
29.	Abercrombie, James S. Houston, Tex.	Dem.	1,000
30.	Benton, William N.Y., N.Y.	Dem.	32,250
31.	Blaustein, Jacob Baltimore, Md.	Dem.	1,000
32.	Daly, Edward J. Oakland, Calif.	Rep. Dem. Misc.	90,800 51,300 1,000

(cont.)

Table S-1 (Cont.)

33.	Dillon, Clarence Douglas N.Y., N.Y.	Rep. Dem.	$ 62,000 5,500
34.	Duke, Doris N.Y., N.Y.	Rep. Dem. Misc.	5,000 3,000 1,000
35.	Copeland, Lammot DuPont Wilmington, Del.	Rep.	29,500
36.	DuPont, Henry B. Greenville, Del.	Rep.	2,000
37.	Ford, Benson Dearborn, Mich.	Rep. Dem.	28,250 560
38.	Ford, Josephine (Mrs. Walter Buhl, II) Grosse Pointe, Mich.	Rep.	4,300
39.	Ford, William C. Dearborn, Mich.	Rep. Dem.	2,000 30,000
40.	Frick, Helen Clay Pittsburg, Pa.	Rep.	79,000
41.	Grant, William T. N.Y., N.Y.	Rep.	1,750
42.	Hope, Bob Hollywood, Calif.	Rep.	60,000
43.	Houghton, Arthur A., Jr. N.Y., N.Y.	Rep. Dem.	6,000 50,000
44.	Johnson, J. Seward New Brunswick, N.J.	Rep. Dem. Misc.	42,000 18,550 6,000
45.	Kiewit, Peter Omaha, Neb.	Rep.	100,912
46.	McDonnell, James S., Jr. St. Louis, Mo.	Rep.	37,529.79
47.	Norris, Dellora F. Angell (Mrs. Lester J.) St. Charles, Ill.	Rep.	10,950
48.	Robins, El Claiborne Richmond, Va.	Rep. Dem. Misc.	18,000 2,750 2,000
49.	Stone, W. Clement Chicago, Ill.	Rep. Dem.	2,133,254.40 8,411.54

Table S-1 (Cont.)

50.	Sulzberger, Iphigene (Mrs. Arthur Hays) N.Y., N.Y.	Dem.	$	24,500
51.	Taper, S. Mark Beverly Hills, Calif.	Rep. Dem.		8,000 5,000

[a]Not included is $100,000 in cash that was held for three years by Bebe Rebozo and then returned to Hughes.

[b]Contributions are from Mrs. Charles W. Englehard, Jr. Mr. Englehard is deceased.

Appendix T: New Rich of the Seventies

In 1973 *Fortune* published a list of 39 individuals who had amassed the bulk of their fortunes in the five years since the 1968 list of the 66 centimillionaires discussed in Appendix S. (See Arthur M. Louis, "The New Rich of the Seventies," *Fortune*, September 1973, pp. 170-75, 230, 232, 236, 238, 242.) Excluded are individuals who became wealthy entirely through inheritance. The cutoff point for the 1973 list is $50 million. Of the 39, 28 persons, or 72 percent, made political contributions in 1972. This appendix lists those 28 individuals and their contributions of $100 or more.

Table T-1
New Rich of the Seventies

No. of Contributors: 28

Contributions:

Republican	$1,118,754.47	
Democratic	321,865.28	
Miscellaneous	4,000.00	
Total	$1,444,619.75	

1.	Stern, Leonard N. N.Y., N.Y.	Rep.	$ 1,000
2.	Carver, Roy J. Muscatine, Ia.	Rep.	300,971.31
3.	Davis, Leonard N.Y., N.Y.	Rep. Dem.	4,500 232,500
4.	Petrie, Melton J. Secaucus, N.J.	Rep. Dem.	26,500 2,500
5.	Cohen, Arthur G.[a] N.Y., N.Y.	Rep. Dem.	40,500 61,500
6.	Eckerd, Jack M. Clearwater, Fla.	Rep.	4,500
7.	Goodwin, Leo, Jr. Ft. Lauderdale, Fla.	Rep.	2,000
8.	McNeil, Henry S. New Brunswick, N.J.	Rep. Misc.	112,000 1,500
9.	Roush, Galen James Akron, Oh.	Rep.	13,000
10.	Carlson, Curtis L. Minneapolis, Minn.	Rep. Dem.	3,265.75 1,000
11.	DeMoss, Arthur S. Valley Forge, Pa.	Rep.	5,500
12.	Hanson, John K. Forest City, Ia.	Rep.	1,000
13.	Manoogian, Alex Taylor, Mich.	Rep.	43,866.50
14.	Frey, Edward J. Grand Rapids Mich.	Rep.	108,000
15.	Riebel, Richard E. Grand Rapids, Mich.	Rep.	400

Table T-1 (Cont.)

16.	Grainger, William W. Chicago, Ill.	Rep.	$ 25,000
17.	Krieble, Robert H. Newington, Conn.	Rep.	1,200
18.	Lane, William N. Lake Forest, Ill.	Rep.	1,000
19.	Levy, Lester A. Dallas, Tex.	Dem.	2,000
20.	Long, Joseph M. Walnut Creek, Calif.	Rep. Misc.	10,000 2,500
21.	Mitchell, George P. Houston, Tex.	Rep. Dem.	5,750 2,000
22.	Terra, Daniel J. Kenilworth, Ill.	Rep.	273,500
23.	Walton, Sam M. Bentonville, Ark.	Rep. Dem.	1,000 250
24.	Blake, S. Prestley Somers, Mass.	Rep.	500
25.	Broad, Eli Los Angeles, Calif.	Rep. Dem.	24,300.91 15,580.28
26.	Fingerhut, Manny Minneapolis, Minn.	Dem.	2,535
27.	Meyerhoff, Harvey M. Baltimore, Md.	Rep.	3,500
28.	Rossi, Anthony T. Bradenton, Fla.	Rep. Dem.	106,000 2,000

[a]Made a $100,000 combined contribution with his father-in-law, Charles C. Bassine, to Bayh. For purposes of this analysis, we have attributed $50,000 to Cohen.

Appendix U: Data Preparation for Chapter 11

The raw data used in Chapter 11 came from a computer tape supplied by the General Accounting Office (GAO). This tape was a copy of one used by the GAO to print out the listing contained in their *Alphabetical Listing of 1972 Presidential Campaign Receipts*, published in 1973 pursuant to the Federal Election Campaign Act of 1971.[1] The information contained on the tape corresponded exactly to the information printed in the readily available GAO document.

The data consisted of 72,439 records, each representing a single contribution, loan, or transfer made to a political committee registered with the GAO. Each of these contributions, loans, or transfers was in amounts in excess of $100. Each was made between April 7, 1972 and December 31, 1972. Each complete record contained 12 pieces of information divided into 12 fields as follows:

1. The last name of the contributor
2. The first name of the contributor
3. The middle name or initial of the contributor
4. A title of the contributor: Mr., Mrs., Ms., Hon., etc.
5. A city or town from which the contribution was made
6. A two-letter abbreviation of the state from which the contribution was made, based on the Post Office-authorized two-letter state abbreviation
7. A zip code for the address
8. The amount of the contribution
9. The classification of the contribution: direct contribution, indirect contribution, or contribution-in-kind, and loan
10. An abbreviated name of the recipient committee
11. The recipient committee's official code number
12. The date of the contribution

All these records had been sorted alphabetically by the GAO on the sequential basis of the content of (1) the first field, (2) the second field, and (3) the third field. This sequence was important because occasionally a first name (normally in the second field) would be erroneously typed in the first field and would thereby affect the alphabetizing process.

Although the GAO performed a monumental task in compiling this data, the final product was far from perfect and needed editing and recoding before it could be used. For example, the listing contained a number of records that were unreadable entries, the alphabetizing in many cases had been defective, there were gaps—notably in state identification codes—where sufficient information existed to recover the missing data, and, most of all, the listing contained a large number of contributions that were either transfer payments or contributions by nonindividuals. Furthermore, since each contribution was listed separately, it was impossible on the basis of the raw data to machine-aggregate the contributions of a single individual so that conclusions could be reached about *contributors*, as well as about individual *contributions*. This problem was especially important since a significant number of donors made multiple contributions and most of the very large contributors to a single candidate divided their contributions among many different committees to avoid paying a gift tax. Finally, since the listing of contributions specified only the recipient *committee*, it was extremely difficult to machine-aggregate the contributions by *candidate* or *category of recipient*.

It was necessary, therefore, to edit the original data by performing three basic operations: (1) cleaning; (2) attaching a code that would indicate that certain sets of contributions were made by the same individual; and (3) attaching a code that would indicate that certain sets of contributions were made to the same *candidate* or *category of recipient* (e.g., a national committee, a state party, a nonparty fund, etc.).

I.   Data cleaning

   A.   Removals
      The original GAO list of 72,439 records contained approximately 3,500 records that were not contributions of individuals. These records included the following:

      1.   Contributions by commercial firms (most often advertisements in convention program books)
      2.   Contributions by partnerships
      3.   Contributions by political action committees or good government funds
      4.   Contributions by corporate or labor union political committees
      5.   Committee transfer payments
      6.   Bookkeeping entries appearing as contributions

   These were all removed from the listing so that the edited tape contained only records of contributions by individuals.

   A small number of repaid loans, designated in the original listing with a (-) sign, were also removed.

Finally, in a number of entries, the entire record contained undecipher-able data. When no relevant information could be salvaged, these records were also removed from the listing.

The resultant list contained 68,658 records, for a net loss of 3,781 records.

B.   Information recovery, corrections, and relocations
    1.   Revising state names
        The original GAO listing contained several hundred records in which the state field was blank, but which also contained sufficient informa-tion elsewhere in the record to indicate what the state should have been. This information included: other contributions clearly made by the same person, zip codes, and city names that permitted identi-fication of the respective state. Using such information, several hundred state codes were recovered. Extreme care was taken, how-ever, not to fill in state names when there was a reasonable chance that the record could belong to more than one state: (Columbus, Georgia vs. Columbus, Ohio; Jackson, Michigan vs. Jackson, Missis-sippi). The rule followed was: if the name in the city field corre-sponded to that of a major American city, then it was presumed that the contribution was from that city and the appropriate state was entered. If the name was that of a middle size city, or smaller, then one additional piece of information was required to assign a state code—such as identical names of contributors on two contributions from the same city. State codes were not assigned on the basis of a recipient committee's location if that was the sole criterion available for judgment, although that information was used as a piece of sup-porting evidence when other factors corresponded.

    2.   Erroneous state codes
        The GAO's two-letter state code supposedly corresponded to the Post Office-authorized two-letter state abbreviation code. However, there were (1) numerous records that contained erroneous abbre-viations ("CN" instead of "CT" for Connecticut, for example), (2) dual abbreviations "NE" and "NB" for Nebraska, and, most impor-tant, (3) misapplied abbreviations: "MI" being used inconsistently for Michigan (the correct state), Mississippi, and Missouri, "AK" being used inconsistently for Alaska (the correct state) and Arkansas, and so forth. A special study was made of all state designations of this variety: MI, AK, MA, and NE to verify the accuracy of the designation when possible.

Finally, all foreign-origin contributions were supposed to be recorded as "ZZ". However, many GB's (for Great Britain), FR's (for France), etc., appeared in the listing. These were converted to ZZ.

The same standards were applied here for corrections, as above for recovery of information. The original state code, even though in error, provided some additional information as to the true identity of the record.

3. Faulty alphabetizing
    The way in which the data was originally compiled and the nature of the alphabetizing program interacted in many instances to create erroneous alphabetizing. An extensive examination of the data was conducted to correct for the following problems that led to erroneous listings:

    a) First name in last name field
        For example: "Bernard P. Hogan" was listed under "Bernard," not "Hogan." In any circumstances when there was reasonable ambivalence regarding which was the first or last name, the record was left unrelocated.
    b) Information in addition to the last name appearing in the last name field
        For example: parts of the first name, the designation "Esq.", etc., occasionally appeared tagged on to the last name. Since the machine considered such information in the original alphabetizing process, records of the same person might be located elsewhere in the alphabetical listing.
    c) A split record
        Occasionally the computer split the record in such a way that the first letters in the field were not the first letters of the last name. For example one record alphabetized among the "A's" appeared as: ABETH BOUKAS CONSTANTINE AND ELIZ. Clearly this should have read: BOUKAS CONSTAN—TINE AND ELIZABETH.
    d) Variant treatment of split or apostrophied last names
        Since the alphabetizing program used by the GAO treated blanks in the same field as distinguishing bits of information, a split name (VanPelt, e.g.,) might be alphabetized in two different places, depending whether it had been split or run together: VAN PELT or VANPELT. With apostrophied names, a third characteristic was introduced, so that O DONNEL, O'DONNEL, and ODONNEL would all be

located in different places in the listing even though these three different designations might refer to the same person.

Records in categories a, b, and c above were relocated as follows:

a) When the same person appeared elsewhere on the list, the record containing one variant of the spelling was relocated next to the other variant of the spelling.

b) When the same person did not appear elsewhere on the list, the record was relocated in approximate alphabetical order. (Technical considerations occasionally precluded an exact alphabetic relocation).

Records in category "d)" above were relocated only when the same person appeared elsewhere on the list, as in "a)" immediately above.

In summary, records were relocated so that contributions made by the same person were physically next to each other in the edited tape.

II. Sequencing and aggregating (motting) contributions from the same contributor

A sequence number, running from 00001 to 68658 was attached to each physical record in the edited file and a second code number was attached to enable the computer to identify when two or more contributions were made by the same person. When this was the case, an identical code number was attached to the respective records. Each record on the edited tape, then, included: (1) an absolute sequence number, and (2) a special code number identical to the code number on the previous record when both records denoted contributions made by the same person. The attachment of this special code number (to enable the computer to aggregate contributions by the same contributor) we called "motting" in honor of Stewart R. Mott, who made a large number of multiple contributions. Motting did not involve changing any existing data, merely attaching the special code number.

A. Who were motted?

All persons clearly identifiable as being the same person were motted. This did not include "Jr.," "III," etc. Such records were motted within themselves (when there were more than one Jr., for example)

but were not motted with plain listings. "Sr's." were motted with
plain listings; "Jr's." were not motted with "II's."

Whenever there was solid evidence that two people were married, they
were motted if and only if (1) they made a joint contribution (Mr. &
Mrs. John Smith, John & Mary Smith, e.g.) or (2) the wife made a
contribution in her full married name, Mrs. John Smith. In these cases
all contributions made by each person were then motted, even though
some contributions made by one or both did not fit the above criteria—
as long as there was at least one joint contribution or one contribution
made by the wife in her full married name. Hence, the following would
all be aggregated together:

Smith	John	Mr.
Smith	John	Mr.
Smith	John	Mr. & Mrs.
Smith	Mary	Mrs.
Smith	Mary	Mrs.

The following would also be aggregated:

Smith	John and Mary	
Smith	John	Mr.
Smith	Mary	Ms.

Whenever contributions did not fulfill the above requirements, the contributions were not motted, even though there was strong evidence that
the two were married. Hence, the following would be motted into two
sets of two, possibly separated by a number of names, not one set of
four:

Smith	John	Mr.
Smith	John	Mr.
Smith	Mary	Mrs.
Smith	Mary	Mrs.

B. Other criteria for motting
There were five important pieces of information that provided evidence
about the identity of the contributor: name, city, state, zip code, and
the recipient of the contribution. The last of these was the least reliable
since contributors made contributions to more than one candidate and
to more than one committee.

Whenever the names, city, state, and zip code were identical, the records were motted. They were also motted when the cities and zip codes were different if the names were identical and the indicated locations were near—and in the same state. (This may have resulted in a few mottings of different people, but we reasoned that frequency of the same person stating a home and office address on different contributions was sufficiently high to warrant this rule.)

When the names were only partially the same, either from spelling variations, the use of initials, etc., the records were motted when there was substantial evidence to warrant it. In this case such evidence would include identical city, state, and perhaps zip code. If some of these were lacking, a rule of reasonableness was used that might include further evidence such as type of contribution and recipient committee. As the evidence from the name declined, more was required from the other pieces of evidence to institute the motting. Over all, the rule was, when in doubt, don't mott.

We estimate that an extremely small number of records were motted that should not have been and that a somewhat larger number were not motted that should have been. The impact of this circumstance on the overall results is probably very slim because the total population is so large that it would take an enormous number of errors to affect the totals. Very few large individual contributions were listed: when one person gave a lot of money, it was invariably broken up into many small contributions; it is unlikely that a large percentage of contributions by one contributor would be missed.

Whenever the text and the tables refer to "aggregated" contributions, they refer to contributions "motted" in this fashion.

III. Aggregating the recipient committees

To be able to say that a certain amount of money was given to "McGovern" or "Nixon," etc., it was necessary to combine the enormous number of recipient committees in some meaningful way. To enable the computer to do this easily, the edited tape was given a committee code that was the same for various types of committees. The committees were aggregated under the following categories:

A. Candidate committees
Committees were aggregated by candidates in two categories for each candidate:

1. Committees where the candidate's name or some other clear, un-
    ambiguous title ("Re-Elect the President," e.g.) left no doubt about
    the fact that that committee was specifically for a given presidential
    candidate. The candidate data presented in Chapter 11 and the con-
    clusions drawn are based exclusively on this category of committee.
2. Committees where this clear indication was lacking, but where the
    GAO had designated that committee as "belonging" to a candidate
    —largely according to where the funds had been transferred. This
    latter category of committee was often a local or county committee
    which presumably had sent a majority of its money to a given can-
    didate. These committees were omitted from the calculations in
    Chapter 11.

B. Party national committees were given separate categories and combined
    with their respective convention fund-raising committees.
C. State and Local committees were aggregated by party designation, if not
    obviously belonging to a candidate.
D. A number of joint committees (Nunn and Nixon. . . , for example) were
    given separate categories.
E. Nonparty committees were combined into one category.

These were the principal aggregations of the data.

IV. Significance of the data

Although the data used are "complete" in one sense of the word, several
points should be made about their use and their overall significance.

This study is limited exclusively to individual contributors who made a direct
contribution of more than $100 to a presidential committee after April 7,
1972 and before January 1, 1973. Organizational transfers and other non-
individual contributions were excluded. The analysis was limited to committees that raised money purely for presidential candidates[a] and to the respective national committees. Whenever the same person made more than one
contribution, all of his or her contributions were treated as if one contribution had been made—as long as these contributions were all made to the
same candidate and came from the same state. (The one exception to this
procedure came in the treatment of time flows.) The overall results must be

---

[a]Since much Nixon money in Kentucky was raised through committees listed jointly
with other candidates, and since such committees were not included in our analysis, there is
a bias introduced against Kentucky in our Nixon data.

placed in the context of three significant factors that introduce a degree of bias into the findings.

A. The April 7 cutoff point at the beginning of the listing introduces a number of obvious biases and potential biases: (a) Many large contributions were made before this date, as reported elsewhere in this book. Since more were made to Nixon than to McGovern, a bias is introduced to the candidate totals. (b) Since the contributions before April 7 were, on the average, larger than those made after April 7, the overall dollar breakdowns in size of contributions to Nixon is biased in favor of the smaller contribution. (c) Since the large contributions made after April 7 were, in their geographical breakdown, much less evenly distributed than the other contributions, those made before probably also followed this erratic pattern. If so, the April 7 cutoff point introduces a geographic bias to the overall result. (d) Since the April 7 date occurred in the middle of the primary season, some presidential hopefuls were reporting data from only the end of their campaigns. In many cases these contributions probably did not reflect the overall finance picture. A bias is also introduced with respect to some states whose primaries occurred early, and where a large amount of money had been raised for in-state primary efforts. Major primaries occurring before April 7 were New Hampshire, Florida, Illinois, and Wisconsin.

B. Since the reporting procedures of some McGovern committees were consistently less precise that the reporting procedures of Nixon, marginally more data is missing on McGovern's contributions than on Nixon's. This is especially true of missing dates, but is also true of missing states. Thus, a very small Nixon bias is present when grand totals are compared that rely on state or date information. Since the average size of the nondated and nonstated contribution is significantly smaller than the size of the data-complete contribution, the effect on grand totals is miniscule, but a slight bias is introduced when comparing McGovern's smaller contributions with Nixon's.

C. The $100 cutoff point probably also introduced a significant bias since it was so easy to circumvent by making two smaller contributions to two different committees. There is some statistical evidence—based on distribution patterns—to support the contention that this practice was more widespread with Nixon than with McGovern. If this is an accurate conclusion, a significant bias is introduced when comparing the Nixon totals of small contributions to the McGovern totals. As with all other biases noted above, care is taken when conclusions are drawn to discount or incorporate the bias in weighing significance.

Appendix V: Business and Professional Committee Contributions to 1972 Presidential Candidates

This appendix divides business and professional committees into categories by type of association. First are political action committees of corporations. Second are political action commmittees of financial institutions, that is, banks, savings and loan associations, insurance companies. Third are professional and trade groups' political action committees. Fourth are political action committees of health associations. And fifth are miscellaneous committees. A breakdown of contributions from each committee to the 1972 presidential candidates is given in tables V-1 through V-5.

Table V-1
Business Groups' Political Action Committees' Contributions to Presidential Candidates, 1972

Corporation	McGovern	Humphrey	Hartke	Nixon	Schmitz
Black & Veatch (Good Govt. Fund)	$	$	$	$ 1,000	$
Cerro Corp. (Cerro Leadership Employees Civic Fund)				19,000	
Consolidated Natural Gas Co. (Consolidated Voluntary Non-Partisan Pol. Fund)				500	
Consolidated Natural Gas Service, Inc. (Consolidated Pol. Action Comm.)				1,000	
Eastman Chemical Co. (Volunteers for Better Govt.)				27,000	
Fluor Corp. (Fluor Employees Pol. Fund)				4,000	
General Dynamics Corp. (Effective Citizenship Program)	720.49				
General Electric Co. (Non-Partisan Pol. Comm.)	750			4,000	
General Telephone Co. of Cal. (Good Govt. Club)				5,000	
Gould, Inc. (Better Govt. Assoc.)		1,000		20,000	
Hawaii Telephone Co. (Hawaiian Telephone Employees Good Govt. Club)				2,500	
Hughes Aircraft Co. (Hughes Active Citizenship Fund)	3,807.61	1,015		23,876.65	343
Kerr-McGee Corp. (Kerr-McGee Employees Non-Partisan Pol. Comm.)				10,153.75	
Land O'Lakes Creameries, Inc. (Midwest Pol. Act. Cooperative Trust)		200			
Lockheed Aircraft Corp. (Lockheed Employees Good Citizenship Program)	8,000			50,000	
LTV Aerospace Corp. (Active Citizenship Campaign Fund)				3,108.91	

Table V-1 (Cont.)

Corporation	McGovern	Humphrey	Hartke	Nixon	Schmitz
Medusa Corp. (Medusa Employees Good Govt. Comm.)	$	$	$	$ 160	$
Meredith Corp. (Employees Fund for Better Govt.)				2,000	
Minnesota, Mining & Manufacturing Co. (Voluntary Pol. Contribution Plan)				1,250	
Northrop Corp. (Northrop Good Citizenship Comm.)	1,000				
Olin Corp. (Olin Executives Voluntary Non-Partisan Pol. Fund)				4,180	
Pacific Lighting Service Corp. (Pacific Lighting Pol. Assist. Comm.)				3,840	
Rex Chainbelt, Inc. (Employees Voluntary Political Contribution Plan Comm.)				10,000	
Santa Fe Railway Co. (Civic Trust 80)				3,781.02	
Sherwin Williams Co. (Comm. for Good Govt.)			1,000	6,000 cash[a]	
Standard Oil (Good Govt. Prog.) Okla., Tex., Ind.				125	
Texas Eastern Trans. Corp. (Employees of)				635	
Texas Instruments Co. (Constructive Citizenship Program) Tex., Mass.				30,000 cash[a]	
TRW, Inc. (TRW Good Govt. Fund)		5,000		21,025	
Union Oil Co. (Political Awareness Fund)				15,500	
Union Pacific Railroad (Fund for Effective Govt.)			250	7,860	
White, Weld & Co. (White, Weld Non-Partisan Pol. Comm.)				8,000	
Youngstown Sheet & Tube Co.				195	
Totals	$14,278.10	$7,215	$1,250	$285,690.33	$343

[a]Amounts from Committee to Re-Elect the President filing, September 28, 1973, under court stipulation in a Common Cause suit.

Table V-2
Financial Institutions' Political Action Committees' Contributions to Presidential Candidates, 1972

Association	McGovern	Humphrey	Jackson	Mills	Nixon
Associated Credit Bureau, Inc. (Consumer Reporting & Collection Executives PAC)	$	$	$	$	$ 5,000
Chemical Bank, N.Y. (Fund for Good Govt.)	409				6,822.12
Citizens Savings & Loan Assoc. (Citizens Savings PAC)					275
First Boston Corp. (First Boston Good Govt. Fund)					2,500
First National City Bank (Citicorp Employees Voluntary Political Fund)					20,000
Independent Insurance Agents (Amer. Insurance Men's PAC)					400 (Agnew)
Johnson Corp. Employees Federal Credit Union					275
Long Island Trust Co. (Litco Good Govt. Fund)					2,625
Lumbermen's Mutual Casualty Co. (Kemper Campaign Fund)					12,500
Merrill, Lynch, Pierce, Fenner & Smith (Effective Govt. Assoc.)		500	1,000		15,500
National Assoc. of Life Underwriters (Life Underwriters PAC)				2,000	200
Savings & Loan League (Savings Assoc. PAC)					500
Smith, Barney & Co. (SB Better Govt. Comm.)				2,000	20,000
Trust Co. of Georgia (Good Govt. Group)					2,000
Union Bank, Cal. (Good Govt. Assoc.)					2,200
Wells Fargo Bank (Good Govt. Comm.)	2,347.50				101
West Virginia Bankers Assoc.				1,000	
Totals	$2,756.50	$500	$1,000	$5,000	$90,898.12

Table V-3
Professional and Trade Groups' Political Action Committees' Contributions to Presidential Candidates, 1972

Association	McGovern	Mills	Nixon	Hartke
American Assoc. of Woolen Importers, Inc.	$	$200	$	
American Waterways Operators, Inc. (Barge & Towing Industry Comm. for Pol. Action)			1,000	
Fire Chiefs Assoc. of Mass.			250	
National Education Assoc. (NEA Employees for McGovern, Falls Church, Va.)	250			
National Telephone Co-op Assoc. (Telephone Education Comm. Organization)	200			
National Tool, Die & Precision Machine Assoc. (Tool, Die & Precision Machine Industry PAC)			3,000	
Natural Gas Retailers (Gas Employees PAC)		400		
Totals	$450	$600	$4,250	

Table V-4
Health Associations' Political Action Committees' Contributions to Presidential Candidates, 1972

Association	Mills	Nixon	Hartke
American Medical Assoc. (AMPAC, National)	$	$ 6,000	$
American Medical Assoc. (California Medical PAC)		17,000	
American Medical Assoc. (Florida Medical PAC)	1,500		
American Medical Assoc. (Professional Comm. for Good Govt., California)		200	
American Podiatry Assoc. (Podiatry PAC)			250
American Society of Internal Medicine	1,000		
Totals	$2,500	$23,200	$250

Table V-5
Miscellaneous Business-Professional Contributions to Presidential Candidates, 1972

McGovern:	$ 3,712.45
Hartke:	1,000.00
Nixon:	18,155.30

Appendix W: Labor Union Political Action Committee Contributions to Presidential Candidates, 1972

Table W-1
Labor Union Political Action Committee Contributions to Presidential Candidates, 1972

Union	McGovern	Humphrey	Muskie	Hartke	Mills	Nixon-Agnew
AFL–CIO COPE	$	$ 500	$	$ 4,000	$	$
Amalgamated Clothing Workers	50,746	1,000		250		
Amalgamated Laundry Workers	700					
Amalgamated Meatcutters & Butcher Workmen	56,400	600		250		
Amalgamated Transit Union	200					
American Federation of Musicians		2,000				
American Federation of State, County & Municipal Employees	18,056	600	5,236	250		
American Federation of Teachers	30,536	100				
American Postal Workers Union				125		3,500
Brotherhood of Locomotive Engineers		377				
Brotherhood of Railway, Airline & Steamship Clerks, Freight Handlers, Express & Station Employees	5,000	2,500		10,000		10,000
COPE-California		39,500				
COPE-Indiana		200				
COPE-Oregon				500		200
Communications Workers of America	123,369	8,200				
Distributive Workers of America	8,147	135				
Graphic Arts International Union	16,090					
International Association of Machinists & Aerospace Workers - Machinists Non-Partisan Political League	113,000	375				
International Brotherhood of Electrical Workers	11,122	110				

Table W-1 (Cont.)

Union	McGovern	Humphrey	Muskie	Hartke	Mills	Nixon-Agnew
International Brotherhood of Painters & Allied Trades		1,000				19,550
International Brotherhood of Teamsters - DRIVE						
International Chemical Workers Union	1,350					
International Ladies Garment Workers Union	66,792	4,500				
International Molders & Allied Workers Union	2,500					
International Union of Automobile Aerospace & Agricultural Implement Workers of America (UAW-Comm. Good Govt. & UAW-V-CAP)	171,176		24,995			
International Union of Electrical Radio & Machine Workers	3,493			250		
International Union of Rubber, Cork, Linoleum & Plastic Workers	16,442	8,140				
Laborers' International Union of North America						25,000
Marine Cooks & Stewards Defense Fund		2,000				
Marine Engineers Beneficial Association-MEBA Political Action Fund		2,000				1,500
National Union of Hospital & Health Care Employees	35,218					
Oil, Chemical & Atomic Workers International Union	32,975	2,225				
Operating Engineers						2,000
Retail Clerks International Association-Active Ballot Club	74,802	11,926				
Retail, Wholesale & Department Store Union	1,500	10,000				
Seafarers International Union of North America				1,000	4,000	100,000
Service Employees International		1,000				
Textile Workers Union of America	1,250			250		

(cont.)

Table W-1 (Cont.)

Union	McGovern	Humphrey	Muskie	Hartke	Mills	Nixon-Agnew
Transport Workers of America-Transport Workers Union Political Contributions Comm.	15,575	1,000				
United Brotherhood of Carpenters & Joiners of America	3,500	500				
United Furniture Workers of America	2,900					
United Glass & Ceramic Workers of America		365				
United Paperworkers International Union						3,000
United Steelworkers of America	520	41,699				
United Transportation Union-Transportation Political Education League		14,400		3,000		
Miscellaneous Unions	15,319					
Totals	$878,828	$156,952	$30,231	$19,875	$4,000	$164,750

Note: Combines data from survey reported in Senate Select Committee on Presidential Campaign Activities, *Final Report*, No. 93-981, 93rd Cong., 2d sess., June 1974 (Washington, D.C.: U.S. Government Printing Office, 1974), pp. 530-33; and from FECA filings recorded in *Alphabetical Listing of 1972 Presidential Campaign Receipts*, vols. I & II, Office of Federal Elections, General Accounting Office (Washington, D.C.: U.S. Government Printing Office, November 1973).

Appendix X: Illegal Corporate Contributions in the 1972 Presidential Campaigns

Table X-1
Illegal Corporate Contributions in the 1972 Presidential Campaigns

Corporation	Campaign	Amount of Contribution	Plea (Date)	Court Action
American Airlines	Nixon	$55,000 (refunded by FCRP)	Guilty (10/17/73)	$5,000 fine
American Ship Building Co. George M. Steinbrenner, III, Chrm. Bd. John H. Melcher, Jr., Exec. Vice Pres., Counsel	Nixon	$25,000	Guilty (8/23/74) Guilty (8/23/74) Guilty (4/11/74)	$20,000 fine $15,000 fine $2,500 fine
Ashland Petroleum Gabon, Inc. Orin E. Atkins, Chrm. Bd., Ashland Oil, Inc.	Nixon	$100,000 (refunded by FCRP)	Guilty (11/13/73) No contest (11/13/73)	$5,000 fine $1,000 fine
Associated Milk Producers, Inc. (AMPI) Harold S. Nelson, Gen. Mgr. David E. Parr, Spec. Counsel	Nixon Mills Humphrey	$100,000 5,000 50,000	Guilty (8/1/74) Guilty (7/31/74) Guilty (7/23/74)	$35,000 fine 3 yr. sentences, suspended-4 mo., $10,000 fines
Braniff Airways Harding L. Lawrence, Chrm. Bd.	Nixon	$40,000 (refunded by FCRP)	Guilty (11/12/73) Guilty (11/12/73)	$5,000 fine $1,000 fine
Carnation Company H. Everett Olson, Chrm. Bd.	Nixon	$7,900	Guilty (12/19/73) Guilty (12/19/73)	$5,000 fine $1,000 fine
Diamond International Corp. Ray Dubrowin, Vice-Pres.	Nixon Muskie	$5,000 1,000	Guilty (3/7/74) Guilty (3/7/74)	$5,000 fine $1,000 fine
Greyhound Corporation	Nixon McGovern	total $16,040 to both candidates' committees	Guilty (10/8/74)	$5,000 fine
Goodyear Tire & Rubber Co. Russell DeYoung, Chrm. Bd.	Nixon	$40,000 (refunded by FCRP)	Guilty (10/17/73) Guilty (10/17/73)	$5,000 fine $1,000 fine

Table X-1 (Cont.)

Corporation	Campaign	Amount of Contribution	Plea (Date)	Court Action
Gulf Oil Corporation	Nixon Mills Jackson	$100,000 (refunded by FCRP) 15,000 (refunded) 10,000 (refunded)	Guilty (11/13/73)	$5,000 fine
Claude C. Wild, Jr., Vice-Pres.			Guilty (11/13/73)	$1,000 fine
HMS Electric Corp. Charles N. Huseman, President	Nixon	$5,000	Guilty (12/3/74)	$1,000 fine
LBC & W, Inc. architect. firm William Lyles, Sr., Pres. & Chrm. Bd.	Nixon	$10,000	Guilty (9/17/74) Guilty (9/17/74)	$5,000 fine $2,000 fine
Lehigh Valley Cooperative Farmers Richard L. Allison, Pres.	Nixon	$50,000	Guilty (5/6/74) Guilty (5/17/74)	$5,000 fine $1,000 suspended fine
Francis X. Carroll, Lobbyist			Guilty (5/28/74)	$1,000 suspended fine
Minnesota Mining & Mfg. Co. (3M)	Nixon Humphrey Mills	$30,000 (refunded by FCRP) 1,000 1,000	Guilty (10/17/73)	$3,000 fine
Harry Heltzer, Chrm. Bd.			Guilty (10/17/73)	$500 fine
National By-Products, Inc.	Nixon	$3,000	Guilty (6/24/74)	$1,000 fine
Northrop Corporation Thomas V. Jones, Chrm. Bd. James Allen, Vice-Pres.	Nixon	$150,000	Guilty (5/1/74) Guilty (5/1/74) Guilty (5/1/74)	$5,000 fine $5,000 fine $1,000 fine
Phillips Petroleum Co. William W. Keeler, Chrm. Bd.	Nixon	$100,000 (refunded by FCRP)	Guilty (12/4/73) Guilty (12/4/73)	$5,000 fine $1,000 fine
Ratrie, Robbins & Schweitzer, Inc. Harrie Ratrie, President Augustus Robbins, III, Exec. V.P.	Nixon	$5,000	Guilty (1/28/75) Guilty (1/28/75) Guilty (1/28/75)	$5,000 fine $1,000 fine $2,500 fine

(cont.)

Table X-1 (Cont.)

Corporation	Campaign	Amount of Contribution	Plea (Date)	Court Action
Singer Company[a] Raymond A. Long Martin A. Leader	Nixon	$10,000	Guilty (6/11/75)	$2,500 fine
Time Oil Co. (Seattle)	Nixon Jackson	$6,600 1,000	Guilty (10/23/74) Guilty (10/23/74)	$5,000 fine $2,000 fine
Raymond Abendroth, President				
Valentine, Sherman, & Associates	Humphrey	$25,000 worth of computer services, paid by AMPI		
Norman Sherman (former press sec'y to Humphrey)			Guilty (8/12/74)	$500 fine
John Valentine			Guilty (8/12/74)	$500 fine

Total contributions	$958,540	
Nixon	842,500	(excluding Greyhound amount)
Others	109,000	(excluding Greyhound amount)
Returned by FCRP	465,000	

[a]Prosecuted by the Attorney General.

Appendix Y: Contributions Among
Selected Nixon Appointees, 1972-73

Table Y-1 names those 58 individuals who contributed $100 or more in 1972 and who were appointed to offices in the Nixon administration in 1972-73. Contributions by husbands or wives are included under the appointees' names. It is not suggested that a contribution was a reason for any appointment.

In all, a total of 319 appointees were analyzed for contributions. The names were taken from lists of appointments published by the *Congressional Quarterly Almanac*, 1972, pp. 96-100, and the *Congressional Quarterly Almanac*, 1973, pp. 990-96. In the analysis, only noncareer ambassadors were analyzed for contributions. For a specific breakdown of these totals, see the section on Chiefs of Foreign Missions and Special Missions (Noncareer), Appendix R.

Table Y-1

Contributions Among Selected Nixon Appointees, 1972-73

Name	Appointment	Contribution
Alexander, Donald C. Cincinnati, Ohio	Commissioner, Internal Revenue Service	$ 400 Rep.
Anders, William A. Washington, D.C.	Member, Atomic Energy Commission	800 Rep.
Barrett, A.C. Biloxi, Mississippi	Member, Federal Maritime Commission	500 Dem.
Bowers, Jack L. San Diego, California	Assistant Secretary, Navy Department	750 Rep.
Brewer, W. Donald Denver, Colorado	Member, Interstate Commerce Commission	1,000 Rep.
Brinegar, Claude S. Rolling Hills, California	Secretary, Transportation Department	485 Dem. 700 Misc.
Callaway, Howard H. Pine Mountain, Georgia	Secretary, Army Department	5,500 Rep.
Casey, William J. Washington, D.C.	Member, Securities and Exchange Commission	500 Rep.
Clements, William P., Jr. Dallas, Texas	Deputy Secretary, Defense Department	22,341 Rep. 500 Dem. 25,000L Rep.
Cohen, Edwin S. Washington, D.C.	Under Secretary, Treasury Department	500 Dem.
Cook, G. Bradford Chicago, Illinois	Chairman, Securities and Exchange Commission	12,000 Rep.
Crawford, Harold R. · Washington, D.C.	Assistant Secretary, Department of Housing and Urban Development	300 Rep.
Conner, William C. Fort Worth, Texas	Judge, U.S. District Court	29,999 Rep. 2,500 Dem.
Crowe, Phillip K. Oslo, Norway	Ambassador to Norway	1,000 Rep.
Delury, Bernard E. Floral Park, New York	Assistant Secretary, Labor Department	900 Rep.
Dent, Frederick B. Washington, D.C.	Secretary, Commerce Department	10,500 Rep.
Dobbin, Tilton H. Owings Mills, Maryland	Assistant Secretary, Commerce Department	3,500 Rep.

Table Y-1 (Cont.)

Name	Appointment	Contribution
Donaldson, William H. New York, New York	Under Secretary, State Department	$ 10,000 Rep.
Farkas, Ruth Lewis New York, New York	Ambassador to Luxembourg	300,000 Rep.
Farland, Joseph S. Washington, D.C.	Ambassador to Iran	25,000 Rep.
Fogel, Herbert A. Philadephia, Pennsylvania	Judge, U.S. District Court	150 Rep.
Ford, Gerald R. Grand Rapids, Michigan	Vice-President of the United States	128 Rep.
Frizzell, Dale Kent Topeka, Kansas	Assistant U.S. Attorney General	569 Rep.
Gallegos, Bert A. Falls Church, Virginia	Assistant Director and General Counsel, Office of Employment Opportunities, Executive Office	120 Rep.
Gould, Kingdon, Jr. Laurel, Maryland	Ambassador to the Netherlands	112,900 Rep.
Guin, J. Foy, Jr. Russellville, Alabama	Judge, U.S. District Court	1,000 Rep.
Harvey, Matthew J. Tyler, Texas	Assistant Administrator, Agency for International Development	1,000 Dem.
Hull, Hadlai A. Washington, D.C.	Assistant Secretary, Army Department	20,027 Rep.
Ingersoll, Robert S. Winnetka, Illinois	Ambassador to Japan	3,000 Rep.
Irwin, John N., II Washington, D.C.	Ambassador to France	53,000 Rep.
Keating, Kenneth B. New York, New York	Ambassador to Israel	4,500 Rep.
Krehbiel, V. John Pasadena, California	Ambassador to Finland	29,500 Rep.
Lubar, Sheldon B. Milwaukee, Wisconsin	Assistant Secretary, Department of Housing and Urban Development	9,360 Rep.
Lynn, James T. Cleveland, Ohio	Secretary, Department of Housing and Urban Development	1,000 Rep.

(cont.)

Table Y-1 (Cont.)

Name	Appointment	Contribution
Macomber, William B., Jr. Washington, D.C.	Ambassador to Turkey	$ 500 Rep.
Marsh, John O., Jr. Washington, D.C.	Assistant Secretary, Defense Department	500 Rep.
Marshall, Anthony D. New York, New York	Ambassador to Trinidad & Tobago; Ambassador to Kenya	48,505 Rep.
Mendolia, Arthur I. Greenville, Delaware	Assistant Secretary, Defense Department	1,000 Rep.
Moore, George M. Silvers Springs, Maryland	Member, Tariff Commission	200 Rep.
Nangle, John F. Brentwood, Missouri	Judge, U.S. District Court	750 Rep.
Neumann, Robert G. Washington, D.C.	Ambassador to Morocco	500 Rep.
Parker, Daniel S. Janesville, Wisconsin	Administrator, Agency for International Development	15,875 Rep.
Peterson, Peter G. Washington, D.C.	Secretary, Commerce Department	2,000 Rep.
Richardson, Elliot Washington, D.C.	Secretary, Department of Health, Education & Welfare	2,100 Rep.
Rush, Kenneth Walla Walla, Washington	Deputy Secretary, Defense Department	2,500 Rep.
Sampson, Arthur F. Camp Hill, Pennsylvania	Administrator, General Services Administration	250 Rep.
Simon, William E. Summit, New Jersey	Deputy Secretary, Treasury Department	17,500 Rep.
Sommer, A.A., Jr. Cleveland, Ohio	Member, Securities and Exchange Commission	200 Dem.
Stowe, David H. Bethesda, Maryland	Member, National Mediation Board	288 Dem.
Tauro, Joseph L. Marblehead, Massachusetts	Judge, U.S. District Court	1,000 Rep.
Thompson, Mayo J. Houston, Texas	Member, Federal Trade Commission	2,000 Rep.

Table Y-1 (Cont.)

Name	Appointment	Contribution
Tiemann, Norbert Lincoln, Nebraska	Administrator, Federal Highway Administration	$ 200 Rep.
Train, Russell E. Washington, D.C.	Administrator, Environmental Protection Agency	8,500 Rep.
Volpe, John A. Wakefield, Massachusetts	Ambassador to Italy	3,000 Rep.
Walker, Charles E. Pittsburgh, Pennsylvania	Deputy Secretary, Treasury Department	150 Rep.
Warner, John H. Washington, D.C.	Secretary, Navy Department	5,000 Rep.
Whittaker, John C. Winston, North Carolina	Under Secretary, Interior Department	150 Rep.
Wiley, Richard E. Arlington, Virginia	Member, Federal Communications Commission	300 Rep.

Contributions:

Subtotals	Republican	$772,224
	Democratic	5,973
	Miscellaneous	700
Total		$778,897

Loans:

Total	Republican	$ 25,000

Notes

Chapter 1
Introduction

1. Herbert E. Alexander, *Money In Politics* (Washington, D.C.: Public Affairs Press, 1972), pp. 99-100.
2. "Campaign Fund Tax Check-off Gains in Users," *Congressional Quarterly,* vol. XXXII, no. 27 (July 6, 1974), 1742-44.

Chapter 2
The Impact of the New Federal Election Laws: Part I

1. See *A Study of Election Difficulties in Representative American Jurisdictions: Final Report* (Washington, D.C.: U.S. General Accounting Office, January 1973); *A Study of State and Local Voter Registration Systems: Final Report* (Washington, D.C.: U.S. General Accounting Office, August 1974); *Election Administration Bulletin* (Washington, D.C.: U.S. General Accounting Office, May 1974); *Federal-State Election Law Survey: An Analysis of State Legislation, Federal Legislation and Judicial Decisions* (Washington, D.C.: U.S. General Accounting Office, July 1973); *Survey of Election Boards Data Base* (Washington, D.C.: U.S. General Accounting Office, May 1974); *Survey of Election Boards: Final Report* (Washington, D.C.: U.S. General Accounting Office, May 1974); *Survey of Election Boards: Summary of Written Comments* (Washington, D.C.: U.S. General Accounting Office, July 1974); *Describe, Analyze, and Compare the Currently Available Methods of Vote Counting Equipment and to Make Appropriate Recommendation: Final Report,* Prepared for: U.S. General Accounting Office, Office of Federal Elections, Clearinghouse on Election Administration (Vienna, Virginia: Analytic Systems, Incorporated, October 1974); *Experimental Voting System Supplement,* Prepared for: U.S. General Accounting Office, Office of Federal Elections (Vienna, Virginia: Analytic Systems, Incorporated, December 1974); *Election Laws Examination With Respect to Voting Equipment,* Prepared for: U.S. General Accounting Office, Office of Federal Elections (Vienna, Virginia: Analytic Systems, Incorporated, January 1975); Roy G. Saltman, *Effective Use of Computing Technology in Vote Tallying,* Prepared for: Clearinghouse on Election Administration, Office of Federal

Elections, General Accounting Office (Washington, D.C.: Information Technology Division, Institute for Computer Sciences and Technology, National Bureau of Standards, March 1975).

2. *Washington Post*, May 2, 1972 at A4, col. 1 (cited in Jeffrey M. Berry and Jerry Goldman, "Congress and Public Policy: A Study of the Federal Election Campaign Act of 1971," *Harvard Journal on Legislation*, vol. 10, no. 2 (February 1973), p. 361.

3. Campaign Expenditures Committee, House Report No. 93-286, 93rd Cong., 1st sess. (Washington, D.C.: U.S. Government Printing Office, June 1973), pp. 22-25.

4. *A.C.L.U.* v. *Jennings*, 366 F. Supp. 1041 (D.D.C., 1973).

5. *United States* v. *National Committee for Impeachment*, 469 F. 2d 1135 (2d Cir., 1972).

6. Nicholas M. Horrock, "F.B.I. Harrassed A Leftist Party," *The New York Times*, March 10, 1975.

7. See Brooks Jackson, "Senate Unit Passed Funds to Democrats," *Washington Post*, September 8, 1974; and "Democrats Linked to Secret Funds," *The New York Times*, September 8, 1974. See also Senate Select Committee on Presidential Campaign Activities, *Final Report*, No. 93-981, 93rd Cong., 2d sess. (Washington, D.C.: U.S. Government Printing Office, June 1974), p. 743.

8. Interview with Philip S. Hughes, director of OFE, June 22, 1973.

9. See Martin Tolchin, "Inquiry Clearing Rep. Chisholm of Election Campaign Charges," *The New York Times*, April 24, 1974; see also Shirley Chisholm, *The Good Fight* (New York: Harper & Row, Publishers, 1973), pp. 159-60.

10. See "Hansen Campaign Violations," *Congressional Quarterly*, February 22, 1975, p. 366.

11. "Rep. Hansen Gets 60-Day Sentence," *The New York Times*, April 19, 1975; J.Y. Smith, "Hansen Is Ordered to Prison," *Washington Post*, April 19, 1975.

12. "Judge Saves Hansen From Jail; Terms Representative 'Stupid'," *The New York Times*, April 26, 1975.

13. See Herbert E. Alexander, "Campaign Finance Reform: What Is Happening—Particularly in the Individual States?", *Vital Issues*, vol. XXIV, no. 1 (September 1974); American Law Division of the Congressional Research Service Library of Congress, "Analysis of Federal and State Campaign Finance Law," Prepared for the Office of Federal Elections of the General Accounting Office, October 1974; Citizens' Research Foundation, "State Statutes Regulating Political Finance," August 1974.

14. Arthur Andersen & Co., *Financial Management System for Political Campaigns*, New York, August 1, 1972.

15. *Federal Elections Campaign Media Manual* (Washington, D.C.: Campaign Media Consultants, Inc., 1972).

Chapter 3
The Impact of Watergate: Part I

1. Eugenio Martinez, "Mission Impossible: The Watergate Bunglers," *Harper's Magazine,* October 1974, pp. 50-56.

2. Senate Select Committee on Presidential Campaign Activities, *Final Report,* No. 93-981, 93rd Cong., 2d sess. (Washington, D.C.: U.S. Government Printing Office, June 1974), p. 31.

3. Carl Bernstein and Bob Woodward, *All the President's Men* (New York: Simon & Schuster, 1974), p. 48. See also Report of the Office of Federal Elections to the Comptroller General of the United States, *Audit of the Finance Committee to Re-Elect the President,* August 26, 1972.

4. James McCord Testimony before Senate Select Committee, May 18, 1973, *Hearings* Before the Select Committee on Presidential Campaign Activities of the United States Senate, 93rd Cong., 1st sess., book I (Washington, D.C.: U.S. Government Printing Office, 1973), p. 196.

5. Senate Select Committee, *Final Report,* pp. 52 ff.

6. GAO Press Release, April 27, 1973.

7. "Meeting: The President, Haldeman and Ehrlichman, EOB Office," *The White House Transcripts,* A New York Times Book, with an introduction by R.W. Apple, Jr. (New York: Bantam Books, Inc., 1974), appendix 14, p. 331.

8. James R. Polk, "Arab Money in U.S. Politics Probed," *Washington Star,* December 19, 1974.

9. Jack Anderson, "Shah Link to Nixon Campaign Hinted," *Washington Post,* June 10, 1974.

10. Anthony Ripley, "Ex-Aide Says Haldeman Controlled 3d Cash Fund," *The New York Times,* April 27, 1974.

11. Senate Select Committee, *Final Report,* p. 108. See also Alexander M. Bickel, "Watergate and the Legal Order," *Commentary,* January 1974, pp. 19-25.

12. William Chapman, "Alabama Probing 1970 Use of Funds Against Wallace," *Washington Post,* August 1, 1973; William Claiborne, "Wallace Primary Foe's Aides Admit Getting GOP Funds," *Washington Post,* October 8, 1973.

13. John Hanrahan, "Wallace Men Say GOP Tried to Block Drive," *Washington Post,* March 9, 1973.

14. Senate Select Committee, *Final Report,* pp. 164-66.

15. Norman Kempster and Martha Angle, "Infiltrator Won Democrats' Confidence," *Washington Star-News,* October 10, 1973.

16. Senate Select Committee, *Final Report,* p. 189.

17. Ibid., p. 197.

18. Ibid., pp. 190-92.

19. Ibid., pp. 192-96; see also Lawrence Meyer, "GOP's Campaign Spy Worked Three Camps," *Washington Post,* October 11, 1973.

20. Ibid., p. 198.
21. Bill Kovach, "Chotiner Agrees He Paid Newsmen," *The New York Times,* August 29, 1973; Jules Witcover, "McGovern's Mata Hari: Suspected Once, Ignored Often," *Washington Post,* August 21, 1973; Senate Select Committee, *Final Report,* pp. 199-200.
22. Senate Select Committee, *Final Report,* p. 152; see also Barry Sussman, *The Great Cover-up: Nixon and the Scandal of Watergate* (New York: The New American Library, 1974), pp. 201-2.
23. Senate Select Committee, *Final Report,* pp. 200-201.
24. Ibid., pp. 202-3.
25. Ibid., pp. 203-5.
26. Ibid., pp. 109 and 210.
27. Bob Woodward and Carl Bernstein, "Stans Scathes Report," *Washington Post,* September 14, 1972.
28. Marjorie Boyd, "The Watergate Story: Why Congress Didn't Investigate Until After the Election," *The Washington Monthly,* April 1973, pp. 37-45.
29. Senate Select Committee, *Final Report,* p. 73.
30. Ibid.
31. See Sussman, *The Great Cover-Up,* p. 263.
32. House Committee on the Judiciary, *Report,* No. 93-1305 ("Impeachment of Richard M. Nixon President of the United States"), 93rd Cong., 2d sess., August 20, 1974 (Washington, D.C.: U.S. Government Printing Office, 1974).
33. *Common Cause, et al.,* v. *Finance Committee to Re-Elect the President, et al.,* Civ. Act. 1780-72 (D.D.C., June 28, 1974).
34. *Nader* v. *Saxbe,* 497 F.2d 676 (D.C. Cir. 1974).
35. Ibid.

Chapter 4
Spending in the 1972 Elections

1. See "Printouts," footnote h, Chapter 2, this book.
2. Herbert E. Alexander and Caroline D. Jones, eds., *Political Contributors of $500 or More in 1971 and January-February, 1972,* (Princeton, N.J.: Citizens' Research Foundation, 1972); *Political Contributors of $500 or More Voluntarily Disclosed by 1972 Presidential Candidates,* (Princeton, N.J.: Citizens' Research Foundation, 1972).

Chapter 5
The Prenomination Campaigns

1. From lists compiled from SANE, Campaign '70, the Cambodia T.V. broadcast, and McGovern's own lists of over 150,000 names.

2. See Jonathan Cottin, "Report/McGovern swept convention states on work of silent majorities." *National Journal,* vol. 4, no. 27 (July 1, 1972).

3. Kevin P. Phillips, "Muskie's Cinema Angels," *Washington Post,* November 20, 1970.

4. *Federal Election Campaign Act of 1973,* appendix A, *Hearings* before the Subcommittee on Commerce, U.S. Senate, 93rd Cong., 1st sess. (1973), table 11. Hereafter referred to as FCC, *Survey 1972.*

5. Ben A. Franklin, "Record Spending Indicated in Primary Campaigns," *The New York Times,* March 22, 1972.

6. Ibid.

7. See R.W. Apple, Jr., "Humphrey Surge Perils Muskie's Wisconsin Drive," *The New York Times,* March 6, 1972.

8. See Robert Walters, "Muskie's 'Fat Cats' Have Fur Ruffled," *Washington Star,* April 26, 1971.

9. Theodore White, *Breach of Faith: The Fall of Richard Nixon* (New York: Atheneum/Reader's Digest Press, 1975), p. 278.

10. Senate Select Committee on Presidential Campaign Activities, *Final Report,* No. 93-981, 93rd Cong., 2d sess. (Washington, D.C.: U.S. Government Printing Office, June 1974), pp. 869-90.

11. "Humphrey Says Dairy Gifts Almost Made Him Retire," *The New York Times,* May 19, 1975.

12. "Memorandum Re Senator Humphrey's Expenditure of Personal Funds in Connection With His 1972 Campaign For the Democratic Presidential Nomination," Joe A. Walters and Frank J. Walz, counsel (Minneapolis, July 2, 1974). See also "Humphrey Responds to Watergate Draft Report Charges," Humphrey press release, June 27, 1974.

13. Report of the Office of Federal Elections to the Comptroller General of the U.S. on the Committee for the Nomination of Hubert H. Humphrey, Inc., October 12, 1973, p. 6.

14. FCC, *Survey 1972.*

15. See Herbert E. Alexander, *Financing the 1968 Election* (Lexington, Mass.: D.C. Heath and Company, 1971), pp. 173 ff.

16. Senate Select Committee, *Final Report,* p. 883.

17. Flora Rheta Schreiber and Stuart Long, "How It Was for Mr. Humphrey," *The New York Times,* October 13, 1974.

18. Nick Kotz, "A Political Switch-Hitter Strikes Out," *Washington Post*, May 31, 1973.
19. James Polk, "Nixon Campaign Refunds $305,000 to Donor," *Washington Star*, March 9, 1973.
20. Richard M. Cohen, "Agnew Ends Partnership With Dilbeck," *Washington Post*, February 8, 1975.
21. Lloyd Shearer, "Spiro Agnew—He's Becoming a Millionaire in Real Estate," *Parade*, January 19, 1975, pp. 4-5.
22. Shearer, "Spiro Agnew," p. 5.
23. Robert Walters, "Rewards of Running," *Washington Star*, March 11, 1973.
24. FCC, *Survey 1972*.
25. "A Jarring Message from George," *Time*, March 27, 1972, p. 25-26.
26. "Wallace's Well-Financed List-Building Efforts," *Congressional Quarterly*, September 4, 1974, p. 3.
27. "Washington Whispers," *U.S. News & World Report*, December 30, 1974, p. 3.
28. Quoted in "Jackson Again Declines to List His Contributors," *The New York Times*, March 22, 1972.
29. Quoted and reported in "The Arab Factor," *National Journal*, January 8, 1972, p. 68.
30. See Lewis Chester, Godfrey Hodgson, and Bruce Page, *An American Melodrama* (New York: The Viking Press, 1969), pp. 493-95.
31. See Thomas P. Ronan, "Lindsay Alliances All But Defunct," *The New York Times*, December 23, 1973.
32. Murray Schumach, "Mayor Bids Backers Adieu with Songs, Dances, Quips," *The New York Times*, December 16, 1973.
33. Senate Select Committee, *Final Report*, p. 905, fn. 8.
34. Ibid., p. 904.
35. Ibid., pp. 911-20 and 922-23.
36. Ibid., pp. 908-10.
37. Quoted in Robert Walters, "The Scandal of Wilbur D. Mills," *Washingtonian*, November, 1974, p. 95.
38. James R. Polk, "Truckers Gave in Cash to Mills 1972 Effort," *Washington Star*, July 22, 1974; "Cash Donations to Mills Revealed," *Washington Star*, August 1, 1974; "2 Perot Executives Gave Mills $100,000, Watergate Files Show," *The New York Times*, August 2, 1974.
39. Dr. Hunter S. Thompson, *Fear & Loathing On the Campaign Trail '72* (San Francisco: Straight Arrow Press, 1973), p. 208.
40. Shirley Chisholm, *The Good Fight* (New York: Harper & Row, Publishers, 1973), pp. 43-51.
41. Report of the Office of Federal Elections on the Shirley Chisholm for President Committee and Affiliated Organizations, November 7, 1974.

42. Dom Bonafede, "Political Report/CRP Continues Uncertain Existence as It Grapples with Watergate Controversy," *National Journal,* May 26, 1973, p. 764.

43. Ben Franklin, "Record Spending Indicated in Primary Campaigns," *The New York Times,* March 22, 1972.

44. "Report of the Office of Federal Elections to the Comptroller General of the United States on the Ashbrook for President Committee, Washington, D.C.," June 12, 1974.

45. See Lou Cannon, *The McCloskey Challenge* (New York: E.P. Dutton & Co., Inc., 1972).

46. *The Los Angeles Times,* January 30, 1972.

47. "McGovern Dominating Coast Media Coverage," *The New York Times,* June 6, 1972.

Chapter 6
Financing the Conventions

1. Herbert E. Alexander, *Financing the 1968 Election* (Lexington, Mass.: D.C. Heath and Company, 1971), p. 74.

2. *Hearings* Before the (Senate) Select Committee on Presidential Campaign Activities: Watergate and Related Activities, book 2 (Washington, D.C.; U.S. Government Printing Office, 1973), p. 790.

3. Commission on the Democratic Selection of Presidential Nominees, *The Democratic Choice,* 1968.

4. Commission on Party Structure and Delegate Selection, *Mandate for Reform: A Report of the Commission on Party Structure and Delegate Selection to the Democratic National Committee* (reprinted in *Congressional Record,* September 22, 1971, E 9841-55).

5. Ibid.

6. Americans for Democratic Action, *Let Us Continue . . .; A Report on the Democratic Party's Delegate Selection Guidelines,* (Washington, D.C.: 1973), p. 20.

7. "Additional Recommendations and Related Commentary" of the Rule 29 Committee, December 20, 1974, p. 1.

8. *Wigoda* v. *Cousins,* 302 N.E. 2d 614.

9. Federal Election Commission, AOR 1975-1 Convention Financing, June 24, 1975; *Federal Register,* July 15, 1975, p. 26660.

10. The figure on a check dated August 5, 1971, from "Sheraton Harbor Island Corporation" to the "San Diego Convention and Visitors' Bureau."

11. Alexander, *Financing the 1968 Election,* p. 158.

Chapter 7
The General Election Campaigns

1. Senate Select Committee on Presidential Campaign Activities, *Final Report,* No. 93-981, 93rd Cong., 2d sess. (Washington, D.C.: U.S. Government Printing Office, June 1974), p. 19.
2. Don M. Larrimore, "Nixon Campaign Tried to Enlist Retired Americans Now in Italy," *Washington Post,* October 26, 1972.
3. Report of staff of House Banking and Currency Committee, October 31, 1972; update of a September 12 confidential report, issued to members of the Committee by Chairman Wright Patman.
4. Jack Anderson, "White House Fund Exposed," *Philadelphia Bulletin,* November 14, 1974.
5. See James R. Polk, "Top 154 Givers Produced $21.3 Million," *Washington Star,* September 30, 1973.
6. Christopher Lydon, "Big Donor Wants Nixon Impeached," *The New York Times,* May 15, 1974.
7. Senate Select Committee, *Final Report,* p. 519.
8. Thomas E. Patterson and Robert D. McClure, *Political Advertising: Voter Reaction to Televised Political Commercials,* Study No. 23 (Princeton, N.J.: Citizens' Research Foundation, 1973), pp. 32ff.
9. Ibid., p. 35.
10. Republican National Finance Committee, 1972 Annual Report, p. 7.
11. Ibid., p. 3.
12. Ibid.
13. David K. Wilson, "The Chairman's Report," Annual Report of the Republican National Finance Committee, December 31, 1973.
14. Senate Select Committee, *Final Report,* p. xxxii.
15. "Why McGovern Is Changing His Campaign Strategy," *U.S. News & World Report,* September 18, 1972, p. 31.
16. "Democrat Check Fails to Clear in Mix-Up," *Washington Star,* September 14, 1972.
17. "Money Matters," *Together With McGovern & Shriver* (published by the McGovern Central Committee), October 1972.
18. Ben A. Franklin, "Some Wealthy Donors Deserting McGovern," *The New York Times,* August 9, 1972.
19. See Stephen D. Isaacs, *Jews and American Politics* (Garden City, N.Y.: Doubleday & Company, Inc., 1974), pp. 1-6.
20. Martin F. Nolan, "Kennedy scuttled plan to share funds raised." *Boston Globe,* October 12, 1972.
21. Clare Crawford, "Personal Appeal From Ted Kennedy," *Washington Star,* September 5, 1972.

22. Ben A. Franklin, "$2-Million Loans Made to McGovern," *The New York Times*, September 13, 1972.

23. George Gent, "Presidential Campaign Stirs the Arts Communities," *The New York Times*, September 26, 1972.

24. Ibid.

25. Douglas E. Kneeland, "McGovern Adopts Fund-Raising Role," *The New York Times*, September 7, 1972.

26. Arthur Greenspan, "The Money of Politics," *New York Post*, November 25, 1972.

27. Paul R. Wieck, "Abroad With McGovern," *The New Republic*, November 4, 1972, pp. 12-15.

28. Jack Anderson, "McGovern's Mail Volume Monitored," *Washington Post*, June 29, 1974.

29. Ben A. Franklin, "650,000 Donors Aided McGovern," *The New York Times*, November 26, 1972.

30. Senate Select Committee, *Final Report*, pp. 553-58.

31. Donald A. Petrie, letter of resignation as Treasurer of the Democratic National Committee, submitted to Chairman Jean Westwood, November 2, 1972.

32. Les Brown, "Democratic-Telethon Ban Is Defended," *The New York Times*, June 29, 1974.

33. Report of the Office of Federal Elections on The Democratic National Telethon Committees, November 1, 1974.

34. "Americans Abroad Also Waging Campaign," *The New York Times*, October 14, 1972.

35. "Second Report of the Office of Federal Elections to the Comptroller General of the United States Concerning the McGovern for President-D.C. Committee and Other Related Committees," October 31, 1972.

36. News release from GAO, June 27, 1973, containing copies of an exchange of correspondence between Hughes and Shumway.

37. *Congressional Quarterly*, October 28, 1972, p. 2792.

38. "Communist Party Agrees to Buy Two Spots on Radio for Gus Hall," *The New York Times*, October 16, 1972.

39. Martin Waldron, "Trotskyite Nominee Stumps in Texas," *The New York Times*, January 2, 1972.

40. Agis Salpukas, "Socialist Labor Party Plans Presidential Campaign," *The New York Times*, April 11, 1972.

Chapter 8
Specialized Expenditures

1. *Federal Election Campaign Act of 1973*, appendix A, *Hearings* before the

Subcommittee on Commerce, U.S. Senate, 93rd Cong., 1st sess. (1973), table 11. Hereafter referred to as FCC, *Survey 1972*.

2. "Broadcast Spending: Presidential, Senate Costs Drop," *Congressional Quarterly*, May 12, 1973, p. 1134.

3. See "Broadcast Spending," p. 1136, and FCC, *Survey 1972*, tables 3, 4, 5, & 6.

4. See "Broadcast Spending," p. 1135, and FCC, *Survey 1972*, table 11.

5. FCC, *Survey 1972*, table 11.

6. Ibid., table 14.

7. Ibid., table 11.

8. Ibid.

9. Ibid.

10. Ibid., table 14.

11. Ibid., table 11.

12. Ibid., table 14.

13. Ibid.

14. Ibid., table 11.

15. Ibid.

16. Ibid. table 18.

17. Ibid., table 14.

18. Ibid., table 11.

19. Ibid., table 14.

20. Ibid., table 11.

21. Ibid.

22. Ibid.

23. Ibid.

24. Ibid.

25. Ibid.

26. See "Political Commercials: On the Spot," *Newsweek*, October 2, 1972, pp. 20-21.

27. See Maurice Carroll, "TV Ads on Voting Studies in N.J.," *The New York Times*, January 28, 1973; see also Thomas E. Patterson and Robert D. McClure, *Political Advertising: Voter Reaction to Televised Political Commercials*, Study No. 23 (Princeton, New Jersey: Citizens' Research Foundation, 1973).

28. "Political Commercials: On the Spot."

29. "Politics vs. TV: A Quadrennial Test Quickens," *Broadcasting*, October 16, 1972, p. 17.

30. "McGovern Hitting Hard with TV in the Stretch," *Broadcasting*, October 30, 1972, p. 19.

31. "McGovern Aides Second-Guess his Air Campaign," *Broadcasting*, November 13, 1972, p. 13.

32. See "Political Advertising: Making It Look Like News," *Congressional*

Quarterly, November 4, 1972, p. 2900; see also Walter DeVries and
V. Lance Tarrance, *The Ticket-Splitter: A New Force in American Politics*
Grand Rapids, Michigan: William B. Eerdmans Publishing Company, 1972).

33. "The Making of Presidents Is Hard Work in Radio-TV," *Broadcasting,*
October 23, 1972, p. 18.
34. FCC, *Survey 1972,* table 22.
35. Ibid., table 23.
36. Ibid., table 24.
37. Ibid., table 23.
38. Ibid., table 24.
39. Ibid., table 22.
40. Ibid.
41. Ibid., table 23.
42. "Radio: A Political Story 'Give-Away'," by Bill Moroney, *Washington Post,* October 5, 1972.
43. "Politics vs. TV: A Quadrennial Test Quickens."
44. "The Making of Presidents is Hard Work in Radio-TV."
45. *Broadcasting,* November 13, 1972, p. 21.
46. See "Court Backs TV and Radio Refusal of Political Ads," *The New York Times,* May 30, 1973.
47. "Carl Albert Endorses TV Debate Between the President and McGovern," *Washington Post,* July 26, 1972.
48. "Democrats Press Nixon on Debates," *Washington Post,* October 19, 1972.
49. "McGovern Would Pay for Debates; Offer Rejected," *The New York Times,* October 19, 1972.
50. "HHH, GSM Take to the Tube," *Broadcasting,* June 5, 1973, p. 38.
51. "Yorty Wants In," *Broadcasting,* June 5, 1972, p. 38.
52. FCC, *Survey 1972,* table 1.
53. Ibid.
54. Ibid.
55. Ibid.
56. Ibid.
57. Ibid., table 2.
58. Ibid., table 17.
59. Ibid., table 14.
60. Federal Communications Commission, *Survey of Political Broadcasting:* Primary and General Election Campaigns of 1970 (Washington, D.C.: U.S. Government Printing Office, 1971) tables 18, 19, 26, and 27.
61. FCC, *Survey 1972,* table 13.
62. Ibid.
63. Ibid., tables 25 and 26.
64. Ibid.
65. Ibid., table 30.

66. Ibid., table 28.
67. Ibid., table 27.
68. Ibid., table 29.
69. Letter dated October 12, 1972, on file with the OFE at GAO.
70. Report to the Comptroller General by the Office of Federal Elections on the November Group and Guggenheim Productions, February 21, 1973.
71. Testimony of Phillip S. Hughes, director, Office of Federal Elections, before the Committee on Rules and Administration, June 7, 1973, pp. 2-3.
72. "BoA offers plan to disburse political advertising payments," *Editor & Publisher*, April 29, 1972, p. 14.
73. Congressional Quarterly, *Almanac 1973*, vol. XXIX (Washington, D.C.: Congressional Quarterly Inc., 1974), p. 723.
74. Ben A. Franklin, "Congressmen's Free Mail Under Increasing Attack," *The New York Times*, October 17, 1972.
75. Robert E. Taylor, "Judge's Ruling on Franking Stirs Furor in Congress," *Philadelphia Bulletin*, October 15, 1972.
76. Joseph P. Albright, "Money is Still the Flypaper of Political Campaigns," *The New York Times Magazine*, September 1, 1974, p. 36.
77. Herbert E. Alexander, *Financing the 1968 Election* (Lexington, Mass.: D.C. Heath and Company, 1971), pp. 113-16.

Chapter 9
The Impact of the New Federal Election Laws: Part II

1. David W. Adamany and George E. Agree, *Political Money: A Strategy for Campaign Financing in America* (Baltimore and London: The Johns Hopkins University Press, 1975), pp. 140-41.
2. Internal Revenue Service, *Statistics of Income—1972, Individual Income Tax Returns*, Doc. no. T22.35/2: In 2/972 (Washington, D.C.: U.S. Government Printing Office, 1974).
3. Democratic Study Group Staff Analysis, January 4, 1972.
4. Technical Information Release, Internal Revenue Service, Washington, D.C. June 21, 1972.
5. Roslyn A. Mazer, "Taxing Political Contributions: The IRS Balks at Reform," *Catholic University Law Review*, vol. 23, no. 2 (Winter 1973), p. 324; see also ibid., fn 13 [Lehrfeld, *The Gift Tax Implications of Political Contributions*, 54 A.B.A.J. 1032 (1968)].
6. Mazer, "Taxing Political Contributions," p. 327; see also ibid., fn 31 [Fernschreiber & Granwell, *Avoiding Gift Tax on Political Contribution: Obstacles and Opportunities*, 50 TAXES 671 (1972)].
7. Reported by Jack Anderson, "IRS Ruling May Hinder Campaign Donation Law," *Philadephia Bulletin*, August 13, 1972.

8. Jerry Landauer, "How Political Donors Avoid Gift, Gains Taxes by Contributing Stock," *Wall Street Journal*, September 27, 1972.

9. Herbert E. Alexander, *Financing the 1968 Election*, (Lexington, Mass.: D.C. Heath and Company, 1971), p. 170.

10. Winston Groom, "Court Tax Ruling Strikes at Big Political Gifts," *Washington Star*, June 8, 1974.

11. See *Edith R. Stern* v. *United States of America*, 304 F. Supp. 376ff. (E.D. La. 1969), and 436 F.2d 1327 (5th Cir. 1971).

12. Mazer, "Taxing Political Contributions," p. 331.

13. Letter from Henry L. Kimelman, national finance chairman, McGovern for President, to members, finance committee, November 1, 1971.

14. Susanna McBee, "IRS Acts to Tax Gains on Political Stock Gifts," *Washington Post*, August 2, 1973.

15. Mazer, "Taxing Political Contributions," p. 329; see also ibid., fn 41 [Boehm, *Political Expenditures*, 231, TAX MANAGEMENT A-41 (1970)].

16. Ibid. [Treas. Reg. § 1.501 (c) (4)-1 (a) (2) (ii) (1959)].

17. Paul Valentine, "Watergate Cash Taxable, Experts Say," *Washington Post*, July 19, 1973.

18. Mitchell Rogovin, "Revenuers vs. Republicans," *The New Republic*, July 7, 1973, pp. 16ff.

19. Rev. Rul. 74-21, December 20, 1974.

20. Rev. Rul. 74-22, December 20, 1974.

21. Rev. Rul. 74-23, December 20, 1974.

Chapter 10
Sources of Funds

1. See *CRF Listing of: Political Contributors of $500 or More Voluntarily Disclosed by 1972 Presidential Candidates* (Princeton, N.J.: Citizens' Research Foundation, 1972).

2. *CRF Listing of: Political Contributors and Lenders of $10,000 or More in 1972* (Princeton, N.J.: Citizens' Research Foundation, 1975).

3. "Blount Paid $325,000 on '72 Campaign Debt," *Washington Post*, January 29, 1975.

4. Alexander W. Keema, III, "Campaign Finance Reform: Limiting Campaign Contributions," *GAO Review*, Summer 1974, pp. 55-61.

5. Keema, "Campaign Finance Reform," p. 58.

6. Senate Select Committee on Presidential Campaign Activities, *Final Report*, No. 93-981, 93rd Cong., 2d sess. (Washington, D.C.: U.S. Government Printing Office, June 1974), p. 507.

7. Reported by UPI in *The Trentonian*, November 22, 1974.

8. See Ronald Sullivan, "Two G.O.P. Fund Raisers for Cahill Indicted on Charges of Bribery," *The New York Times*, April 20, 1973; see also Rose DeWolf, "Corruption Charges Threaten Cahill's Campaign," *Sunday Bulletin*, June 3, 1973.

9. "State's High Court Weighs Colsey Future as Lawyer," *The New York Times*, May 9, 1973.

10. Fred Ferretti, "Jersey G.O.P. Club Faces U.S. Audit," *The New York Times*, May 28, 1973.

Chapter 12
Business and Labor in Politics

1. News Release and text of remarks by Henry Ford, II, chairman of the board, Ford Motor Company, at the company's Community Service Awards program at Cobo Hall, Detroit, October 18, 1973.

2. Senate Subcommittee on Privileges and Elections, *Hearings on Public Financing of Federal Elections*, September 18, 19, 20, and 21, 1973 (Washington, D.C.: U.S. Government Printing Office, 1973), testimony of Charles F. Hood, pp. 362-66.

3. The Business Roundtable, "Statement on Federal Election Reform," May 20, 1974, p. 3.

4. "A Statement by the Board of Directors of the Public Affairs Council," Washington, D.C., (released) July 25, 1973.

5. Dom Bonafede, "Campaign '72 Report /GOP money men expect to raise $41 million for Nixon campaign," *National Journal*, vol. 4, no. 22 (May 27, 1972), 890.

6. Editorial entitled ". . . And to Sabotage the Campaign Spending Law," *Washington Post*, October 2, 1972; Editorial entitled "Raid on Election Reform," *The New York Times*, October 3, 1972.

7. "Political Fund Bill Is Killed in Senate," *Washington Post*, October 15, 1972; also *Common Cause Report From Washington*, vol. 3, no. 1 (November 1972), 7.

8. Public Affairs Council memorandum to PAC membership, October 4, 1974.

9. Memorandum by Joseph J. Fanelli, manager, Public Affairs Department, U.S. Chamber of Commerce, sent to Public Affairs executives, October 11, 1974.

10. Letter from Richard D. Godown of NAM to Henry Petersen, September 13, 1972 and Petersen reply, September 15, 1972.

11. Public Affairs Council memorandum, January 28, 1972.

12. U.S. Chamber of Commerce Newsletter, March 30, 1972.

13. Letter to then Rep. James Abourezk (D) of South Dakota, from Assistant Attorney General Hentry E. Petersen, Department of Justice, Washington, D.C., May 18, 1972.

14. Quoted in *Common Cause Report From Washington*, vol. 3, no. 1 (November 1972), 2, 4, 7.

15. Ibid., p. 4.

16. Weed-Scott Report, December 1972, p. 2.

17. Senate Select Committee on Presidential Campaign Activities, *Final Report*, No. 93-981, 93rd Cong., 2d sess. (Washington, D.C.: U.S. Government Printing Office, June 1974), p. 545.

18. Ibid.

19. Ibid., p. 548.

20. Ibid., p. 549

21. Ibid., fn. 9.

22. Ibid., p. 550.

23. Business and Industry Committee for the Re-election of the President, *City Chairman's Guide*, section I, introduction (letter from Donald M. Kendall).

24. Ibid., section XIV, "Sample Partisan Speech."

25. Senate Select Committee, *Final Report*, p. 362 (Dean testimony).

26. Confidential Memorandum to H.R. Haldeman from Fred Malek, December 23, 1971, entitled "Redirecting the White House to Support the President's Re-election," in committee files. Ibid., pp. 361 ff. Published in "Executive Session Hearings Before the [Senate] Select Committee on Presidential Campaign Activities," Washington, D.C., January 31, February 8, April 8, and May 28, 1974 (Washington, D.C.: U.S. Government Printing Office, 1974), pp. 8320-24.

27. Ibid.

28. Ibid.

29. Ibid.

30. Ibid.

31. Malek, Confidential Memorandum to H.R. Haldeman, March 17, 1972, entitled "Departmental Responsiveness," in committee files.

32. See Lawrence Meyer, "White House Campaign in '72 Under Legal Cloud," *Washington Post*, June 8, 1974.

33. Malek, Confidential/Eyes Only Memorandum for H.R. Haldeman, June 7, 1972, entitled "Responsiveness Program—Progress Report," in committee files.

34. See Bob Kuttner, "Safety Rules Delay Linked to Campaign," *Washington Post*, July 16, 1974.

35. See editorial, "How to Buy Votes," *Washington Post*, June 3, 1974.

36. Ibid.

37. Senate Select Committee, *Final Report*, pp. 419-23.

38. Ibid., pp. 526-43.

39. Ibid., p. 528; pp. 473-81

40. *Miller* v. *American Telephone and Telegraph Company*, 507 F. 2d 759 (C.A. 3, 11/4/74).

41. See "Dismissed Executive Seeking Order on Southwestern Bell Files," *The New York Times,* November 25, 1974; and "Suit Against Southwestern Bell Delayed for a Ruling," *The New York Times,* November 26, 1974.

42. Nicholas Horrock, "U.S. Investigating 2 A.T.&T. Concerns," *The New York Times,* February 9, 1975.

43. "Officials Linked to Bell Scandal," *The New York Times,* March 2, 1975.

44. "C&P Audit to Seek Political Violations," *Washington Post*, May 12, 1975.

45. Robert Lindsey, "A.T.&T.'s Earnings Down 10%; Political-Fund Inquiry Ordered," *The New York Times,* April 17, 1975.

46. House Judiciary Committee, Statement of Information: Appendix IV ("Political Matters Memoranda": August 13, 1971–September 18, 1972), May–June, 1974 (Washington, D.C.: U.S. Government Printing Office, 1974).

47. *The New York Times,* June 19, 1973.

48. *Center on Corporate Responsibility, Inc.* v. *George P. Schultz et al.,* Civ. A, No. 846-73, U.S. District Court, Washington, D.C., December 11, 1973. (As Amended December 12, 1973.)

49. See also Timothy S. Robinson, "Corporate Center Wins Court Round," *Washington Post,* December 12, 1973.

50. "Corporate Political Activity," Analysis No. 4A, Supplement No. 2, April 16, 1973.

51. Ben A. Franklin, "Inquiries Into Nixon's Re-Election Funds Turning Up a Pattern of High Pressure," *The New York Times,* July 15, 1973.

52. *Ash* v. *Cort,* 496 F.2d 416 (3rd Cir. 1974).

53. 495 F.2d 416, reversed (*Cort et al* v. *Ash.* Syllabus. No. 73-1908. Argued March 18, 1975. Decided June 17, 1975).

54. An exchange of letters by Richard Berryman on Humphrey's behalf, dated February 23, 1972, and Henry E. Petersen, Assistant Attorney General, Department of Justice, dated March 6, 1972.

55. See *Hearings Before the Committee on the Judiciary, House of Representatives,* book VI, part I: Political Contributions by Milk Producers Cooperatives: The 1971 Milk Price Support Decision (Washington, D.C.: U.S. Government Printing Office, 1974), pp. 8ff.

56. Senate Select Committee, *Final Report,* p. 639 (Lilly testimony); *Hearings Before the Committee on the Judiciary*, p. 401.

57. "Report of Wright, Lindsey & Jennings to Board of Directors of Associated Milk Producers, Inc., March 13, 1974.

58. Senate Select Committee, *Final Report,* p. 762 (Strachan Exhibit No. 7).

59. Ibid., p. 725.

60. Ibid., p. 922.

61. See Morton Mintz, "Dairymen Readying New Gifts," *Washington Post*, September 1, 1974.

62. Report of the Office of Federal Elections on The Trust for Special Political Agricultural Community Education, Louisville, Kentucky, November 8, 1974.

63. James M. Naughton, "Both Sides Tell Connally Jurors in Final Arguments That They Must Decide Whom to Believe," *The New York Times*, April 17, 1975.

64. Theordore H. White, *The Making of the President 1972* (New York: Atheneum Publishers, 1973), p. 229.

65. Ibid., pp. 212-13.

66. Ibid., p. 38.

67. Senate Select Committee, *Final Report*, pp. 512-13.

68. Senate Subcommittee on Privileges and Elections, *Hearings on Public Financing of Federal Elections*, September 18, 19, 20, and 21, 1973 (Washington, D.C.: U.S. Government Printing Office, 1973), p. 350.

69. Ibid., p. 346.

70. Letter from Reed Larson, executive vice-president, National Right to Work Committee to the Honorable John H. Dent, chairman, Subcommittee on Elections, Committee on House Administration, December 13, 1973 (11 pp.). See also Reed Larson, "Political Unions," *Washington Post* (Editorial), September 27, 1973.

71. "Suit Attacks Political Use of Compulsory Union Dues." *The New York Times*, December 15, 1971.

72. *Marker* v. *Connally*, U.S. District Court, D.C., Civil Action No. 2486-71.

73. *Marker* v. *Shultz*, U.S. Court of Appeals, D.C., No. 72-1499, August 8, 1973.

74. *Pipefitters* v. *United States*, (slip opinion), No. 70-74, U.S. Court of Appeals, 8th Circuit, June 22, 1972.

Chapter 13
The Impact of Watergate: Part II

1. Senate Select Committee on Presidential Campaign Activities, *Final Report*, No. 93-981, 93rd Cong., 2d sess. (Washington, D.C.: Government Printing Office, June 1974), pp. 447-51.

2. Bernie Shellum and Jack Coffman, "3M admits guilt in campaign gifts," *Minneapolis Tribune*, January 23, 1975. Also Senate Select Committee, *Final Report*, pp. 484-86.

3. Richard M. Cohen, "3M, 2 Executives Indicted in Gifts Fund of $634,000," *Washington Post*, January 24, 1975.

4. "Tax Counts Denied in 3M Case," *Washington Post*, February 4, 1975.

5. Anthony Ripley, "Minnesota Mining Had $334,000 Fund for Political Gifts," *The New York Times*, January 1, 1975.

6. Senate Select Committee, *Final Report,* pp. 465-68.

7. Ibid., pp. 462-63.

8. Ibid., pp. 467-70.

9. Senate Select Committee, *Final Report,* pp. 459-62.

10. Anthony Ripley, "$170,000 in Illegal Gifts Admitted by Ashland Oil," *The New York Times,* December 31, 1974.

11. Richard M. Cohen, " 'Johnny Appleseed' of Campaign Funds," *Washington Post,* January 6, 1975, and *The New York Times,* ibid.

12. Henry Weinstein, "Oil Concern Sued for Election Fraud," *The New York Times,* February 25, 1975.

13. Senate Select Committee, *Final Report,* p. 464.

14. Ibid., pp. 464-65; George Lardner, Jr., "Firm Guilty of Muskie, Nixon Gifts," *Washington Post,* March 8, 1974.

15. "Hush Money Role Related by Kalmbach," *Washington Post,* November 13, 1974.

16. "Settlement Data on Northrop Set," *The New York Times,* November 21, 1974; "Judge Takes Case of Suit on Northrop Under Advisement," *The New York Times,* November 24, 1974.

17. Senate Select Committee, *Final Report,* pp. 481-84.

18. Norman Sherman, "Sherman Recalls Year of Misery," *Minneapolis Tribune,* January 26, 1975.

19. Ibid.

20. Senate Select Committee, *Final Report,* pp. 451-59; William E. Farrell, "Steinbrenner Spared Jail, Fined for Campaign Gifts," *The New York Times,* August 31, 1974; "Hartke, Inouye Got Gifts," *Washington Post,* September 21, 1974.

21. Jimmy Breslin, *How the Good Guys Finally Won* (New York: Viking Press, Inc., 1975, pp. 15 ff.)

22. "Seattle Firm, Head Fined on '72 Gifts," *Washington Post,* October 24, 1974.

23. Timothy S. Robinson,"Ex-Rep. Wyatt Guilty in Funds Case," *Washington Post,* June 12, 1975.

24. "Electric Firm Figure Fined in Nixon Gift," *Washington Post,* December 4, 1974.

25. "Two Guilty on Gift to Nixon Campaign," *The New York Times,* January 29, 1975.

26. Fred Barbash, "Singer Pleads Guilty, Is Fined $2,500," *Washington Post,* June 12, 1975.

27. "Singer Official Guilty in Nixon Fund Case," *Washington Post,* July 11, 1975.

28. Senate Select Committee, *Final Report,* p. 451.

29. Ibid., p. 470.

30. Ibid., pp. 446-47.

31. Morton Mintz and Nick Katz, "Automen Rejected Nixon Fund Bid," *Washington Post,* November 17, 1972.

32. Michael C. Jensen, "The Corporate Political Squeeze," *The New York Times,* September 16, 1973.

33. Ben A. Franklin, "Inquiries Into Nixon's Re-election Funds Turning Up a Pattern of High Pressure," *The New York Times,* July 15, 1973.

34. Michael C. Jensen, "Election '74: Where Have All the Fat Cats Gone?", *The New York Times,* November 3, 1974.

35. *Congressional Record,* January 30, 1975, pp. H399-400.

36. Eileen Shanahan, "Gulf Oil Accused by S.E.C. of Hiding $10-Million Fund," *The New York Times,* March 12, 1975.

37. Leonard Curry, "The Multinational Corporation," *The Nation,* May 24, 1975, p. 619.

38. Robert Lindsey, "Two Airlines Face New C.A.B. Charges on Campaign Gifts," *The New York Times,* March 13, 1975.

39. David Burham, "Senate Study Says C.A.B. Broke Rules for Airlines," *The New York Times,* June 30, 1975.

40. Richard D. Lyons, "Gulf Oil Admits It Illegally Gave 5-Million Abroad," *The New York Times,* May 17, 1975.

41. Robert M. Smith, ". . . And Reform Is Not An Easy Task," *The New York Times,* June 15, 1975.

42. Murray L. Weidenbaum, "On Causes of Business Corruption," *The New York Times,* May 4, 1975.

43. W. Michael Blumenthal, "New Business Watchdog Needed," *The New York Times,* May 25, 1975.

44. Everett R. Holles, "Nixon Ally Found Guilty on Coast," *The New York Times,* March 21, 1975.

45. "Nixon Donation From Second Filipino Revealed," *Washington Star,* June 13, 1973.

46. Senate Select Committee, *Final Report,* pp. 504-5.

47. James R. Polk, "Probe of Diplomatic Rewards Focuses on 4," *Washington Star,* May 18, 1974.

48. Statement of Maurice Stans, March 12, 1975.

49. *Money & Politics,* ed. Lester A. Sobel (New York: Facts on File, Inc., 1974), p. 15.

50. Joseph F. Sullivan, "Sears Declares He Arranged Gift," *The New York Times,* March 1, 1973.

51. "Mitchell and Stans Are Acquitted on All Counts After 48-Day Trial," and "A Historic Trial: Few in Such High Posts Have Faced Such Serious Charges," *The New York Times,* April 29, 1974.

52. Martin Arnold, "Cook Says Chat With Stans Led to Shift in Vesco Suit," *The New York Times,* March 28, 1974.

53. Marcia Chambers, "Jurors Couldn't Believe Federal Witnesses," *The*

New York Times, April 29, 1974.

54. Martin Arnold, "Miss Woods Praises Mitchell and Stans," *The New York Times,* March 19, 1974.

55. John M. Crewdson, "Costa Rican Chief Questions U.S. Sincerity in Its Efforts to Extradite Vesco," *The New York Times,* October 8, 1974.

56. James R. Polk, "Ex-Governor Linked to Donation," *Washington Star,* September 5, 1974.

57. Timothy S. Robinson, "Babcock Sentenced in '72 Violation," *Washington Post,* February 1, 1975.

58. Senate Select Committee, *Final Report,* p. 641.

59. Ibid. pp. 936-37.

60. George Lardner, Jr., "Mitchell Tied to Hughes Bid," *Washington Post,* June 23, 1974.

61. "Blank Checks From Hughes to Nixon Fund Alleged," *The New York Times,* January 10, 1974; George Lardner, "Witness Filled in Highes Gift To Nixon," *Washington Post,* January 10, 1974.

62. See Jack Anderson, "Two Ghosts Haunt Nixon's Campaign," *Washington Post,* January 24, 1972; Wallace Turner, "Hundreds of Copies of Hughes Memos are Readily Available in Las Vegas," *The New York Times,* February 3, 1972.

63. Noah Dietrich and Bob Thomas, *Howard, The Amazing Mr. Hughes* (Greenwich, Conn.: Fawcett Publications, Inc., 1972), p. 243.

64. Senate Select Committee, *Final Report,* pp. 998-1001.

65. James R. Polk, "Philippine Cash Surfaces," "Sugar Envoy Mum on Donation," and "Nixon Donation From Second Filipino Revealed," *Washington Star,* June 11, 12, and 13, 1973.

66. Report of the Office of Federal Elections to the Comproller General of the United States on the Finance Committee to Re-Elect the President, November 1, 1972.

67. James R. Polk, "Tanker Owner Explains Bentley Cash for Nixon," *Washington Star,* September 6, 1974.

68. Rowland Evans and Robert Novak, "Greek Gifts for President," *Washington Post,* July 20, 1972; and Seth Kantor, "Jaworski Eyes Probing Foreign '72 Gifts," *Washington Post,* January 25, 1974.

69. House Committee on the Judiciary, *Report,* No. 93-1305 ("Impeachment of Richard M. Nixon, President of the United States"), 93rd Cong., 2d sess., August 20, 1974 (Washington, D.C.: U.S. Government Printing Office, 1974), p. 71.

70. See Patman Committee, pp. 63 ff.

71. Special Report—two articles by James R. Polk, "Prospecting for Arab's Wealth," and "Arab Money in U.S. Politics Probed," *Washington Star,* December 18 and 19, 1974.

72. "Sindona Said to Vow to Save Franklin," *The New York Times,* July 2, 1974.

73. 18 U.S.C. 613.
74. James R. Polk, "Post-Election Gift Solicited," *Washington Star,* July 29, 1973.
75. James R. Polk, "Mitchell Handled Cash From Miamian Paroled Early," *Washington Star,* June 15, 1974.
76. Richard M. Cohen, "Candidate's Accounts of Gift Differ," *Washington Post,* June 8, 1974.
77. Nick Kotz, "Politics Enters Teens' Pay Scale," *Washington Post,* October 6, 1972; and "McDonald's Price Increase Linked to Donation," *Washington Post,* November 3, 1972.
78. Morton Mintz and William Chapman, "Carpet Lobby Said to Pay GOP for Aid," *Washington Post,* October 7, 1972; Mintz, "Campaign Giver Denies Return Aid," *Washington Post,* July 21, 1973.

Chapter 14
The Aftermath

1. Conducted by the University of Michigan, Survey Research Center, November 1972.
2. "Majority Dismiss Watergate and G.O.P Fund Charges," *The Harris Survey,* October 19, 1972.
3. George Gallup, "The Gallup Poll: Nixon Popularity Down 14 Points from '73 High," *Washington Post,* April 23, 1973.
4. "Majority Dismiss Watergate and G.O.P. Fund Charges."
5. Gallup, "The Gallup Poll: Approval of Nixon Levels Off at 2%[sic]," *Washington Post,* January 6, 1974.
6. "Poll Finds G.O.P. at Lowest Point," *The New York Times,* July 18, 1974.
7. Gallup, "Gallup Finds Nation Evenly Divided on Nixon Resignation," *Washington Post,* January 21, 1974.
8. Gallup, "The Gallup Poll: Nixon Support Stayed Low," *Washington Post,* August 11, 1974.
9. Ibid.
10. Louis Harris, "The Harris Survey: Integrity Now the Watergate Issue," *Washington Post,* June 26, 1973.
11. Gallup, "The Gallup Poll: 67% Support U.S. Funding of Campaign," *Washington Post,* September 19, 1974.
12. Ibid.
13. University of Michigan, Survey Research Center, 1964.
14. Gallup, "The Gallup Poll: Nixon's Popularity Shows New Decline," *Washington Post,* September 23, 1973.
15. Harris, "The Harris Survey: Impeachment Gains Support on Tape Issue," *Washington Post,* October 4, 1973.

16. Ibid.

17. "Nixon at New Low in Poll; 26% Approve His Efforts," *The New York Times*, February 3, 1974.

18. Gallup, "The Gallup Poll: Elections Held Today Would Give Democrats A 'Veto-Proof' House," *Washington Post*, June 23, 1974.

19. Gallup, "The Gallup Poll: President Registers No Gains," *Washington Post*, July 5, 1974.

20. "Poll Finds G.O.P. at Lowest Point," *The New York Times*, July 18, 1974.

21. Harris, "The Harris Survey: 69% Backed Tape Turnover Ruling," *Washington Post*, July 29, 1974.

22. "Democrats Leading G.O.P. in Polls 55-29%," *The New York Times*, August 11, 1974.

23. "79% in Poll Back Resignation," *The New York Times*, August 11, 1974.

24. Gallup, "The Gallup Poll: Rating of Congress Rises Sharply," *Washington Post*, August 29, 1974.

25. "Support for Ford Declines Sharply," *The New York Times*, September 12, 1974.

26. "A Gallup Poll Finds 56% Want Nixon to Face Criminal Charges," *The New York Times*, September 2, 1974.

27. "The Gallup Poll: 58 Pct. Favored Trial of Ex-President," *Washington Post*, September 22, 1974.

28. "Democrats Holding Wide Lead in Campaign, Gallup Poll Finds," *The New York Times*, October 6, 1974.

29. Clifton Daniel, "Ford's Gallup Rating Off," *The New York Times*, October 13, 1974.

30. Listed by *Congressional Quarterly* in *1972 CQ Almanac*, pp. 96-100; and in *1973 CQ Almanac*, pp. 990-96.

31. At Chiefs of Foreign and Special Missions, see p. 675; see also pp. 386-87.

32. See "Nixon Aide Guilty on Political Fund," *The New York Times*, November 16, 1974; Lou Cannon, "Harry Dent Resigns Position As General Counsel of GOP," *Washington Post*, December 7, 1974; James R. Polk, "Dent Put on Probation," *Washington Star*, December 12, 1974.

33. "Ex-Aide to Nixon Put on Probation," *The New York Times*, January 18, 1975.

34. House Committee on the Judiciary, Impeachment Inquiry, *Testimony of Witnesses*, book III, 93rd Cong., 2d sess., July 12, 15, 16, 17, 1974 (Washington, D.C.: U.S. Government Printing Office, 1974), p. 650.

35. See Christopher Lydon, "Mrs. Farkas Said to Blame Wyman for Deal for Post," *The New York Times*, July 2, 1975; Lydon, "Wyman Disputes Charge of Envoy," *The New York Times*, July 3, 1975; Lawrence Meyer, "Prosecutor Probing $300,000 Donation," *Washington Post*, July 4, 1975.

36. Senate Select Committee on Presidential Campaign Activities, *Final Report*, No. 93-981, 93rd Cong., 2d sess. (Washington, D.C.: U.S. Government

Printing Office, June 1974), pp. 494-95. See also James R. Polk, "Donors Courted Envoy Posts?" *Washington Star*, June 28, 1974.

37. Senate Select Committee, *Final Report*, p. 495.

38. Ibid., p. 496.

39. See p. 531.

40. David E. Rosenbaum, "Hostility Voiced As Hearings Open," *The New York Times,* September 12, 1974; "The Imperious Ex-Presidency," *Parade/Philadelphia Bulletin,* October 27, 1974.

41. James M. Naughton, "House Panel Seeks to Cut Over Half of Nixon Funds," *The New York Times,* September 18, 1974.

42. "Trustees May End Nixon Library Plan," *The New York Times,* December 26, 1974.

43. See Barbara A. Curran and Francis O. Spalding, *The Legal Needs of the Public* (Preliminary Report of a National Survey by the Special Committee to Survey Legal Needs of the American Bar Association in Collaboration with the American Bar Foundation), (Chicago: The American Bar Foundation, 1974); see also Warren Weaver, Jr., "Lawyers Criticized in A.B.A.'s Survey," *The New York Times,* September 3, 1974.

44. Harry F. Rosenthal, "Watergate Brings Staggering Legal Fees," *Philadelphia Bulletin,* September 23, 1974.

45. Communication from Eric Jaffee, Treasurer, Democratic National Committee, March 24, 1975.

46. "Nixon's Legal Bills Put at $297,294.60," *Washington Post*, March 29, 1975.

47. David Rosenthal, "The Watergate Bill," *New York Post,* August 14, 1974.

48. Letter to Representative Edward R. Roybal from Elmer Staats, Comptroller General, May 13, 1974.

49. Charlotte Evans, "About That 'Impeachment Lobby'," *Washington Star,* February 4, 1974.

50. "Impeachment Lobby: Emphasis on Grass-Roots Pressure," *Congressional Quarterly,* May 25, 1974, pp. 1368-73.

51. Tom Wicker, "How to Impeach With Honor," *The New York Times,* October 31, 1973.

52. "Impeachment Lobby," p. 1372.

53. Reprinted in *COPE Memo,* October 24, 1973.

54. John Saar, "Rabbi Begins Drive: Be Fair to Nixon," *Washington Post,* August 23, 1973.

55. Dom Bonafede, "White House Report/Anti-impeachment Plans Focus on Law, Politics and Media," *National Journal Reports,* May 11, 1974, pp. 690-91.

56. Ibid., p. 691.

57. Richard Cohen, "Korff Fund Pays Nixon Fees," *Washington Post*, November 25, 1974.

58. "Korff Fund for Nixon Is in Debt," *Washington Post,* October 31, 1974.

59. Cohen, "Korff Fund Pays Nixon Fees."

60. Ibid.

61. "Politics Out For Nixon, Ziegler Says," *Washington Post,* February 14, 1975.

62. See *U.S.* v. *Spiro T. Agnew,* Crim. A. No. 73-0535, U.S. District Court, District of Maryland, October 10, 1973.

63. Steven V. Roberts, "Sinatra Reported Working Hard Among Friends to Raise Money to Aid Agnew," *The New York Times,* December 4, 1974.

64. Majorie Hunter, "G.A.O. Challenges Guard for Agnew," *The New York Times,* January 30, 1974.

65. "Agnew Denies That He Got Leniency," *The New York Times,* August 31, 1974; "Agnew Linked to Land Deal," *Washington Post,* September 1, 1974; Lloyd Shearer, "Spiro Agnew—He's Becoming A Millionaire in Real Estate," *Parade* in the *Philadelphia Bulletin,* January 19, 1975; Richard M. Cohen, "Agnew Ends Partnership With Dilbeck," *Washington Post,* February 8, 1975. See also Chapter 5, p. 161.

66. See President Nixon's May 22, 1973 address to the nation, reprinted in *Watergate: Chronology of a Crisis,* vol. I (Washington, D.C.: Congressional Quarterly, Inc., 1973), pp. 90 ff.

67. Anthony Ripley, "U.S. Judge Delays Accord on Nixon Tapes and Data," *The New York Times,* October 22, 1974.

68. Timothy S. Robinson, "Notables Sue for Access to Nixon Tapes," *Washington Post,* October 25, 1974.

69. James R. Polk, "Impeachment Article Supported," *Washington Star,* November 24, 1974.

70. George Lardner, Jr., "Nixon Offered Fund to Haldeman, Ehrlichman," *Washington Post,* December 5, 1974.

71. "Congress Passes Nixon Tapes Bill," *The New York Times,* December 10, 1974; "Ford Signs Bill on Nixon Papers," *The New York Times,* December 20, 1974.

72. Timothy S. Robinson, "Nixon Attorneys Fight Broadcasting of Tapes," *Washington Post,* December 20, 1974.

73. Harry F. Rosenthal, "Gesell Rejects Plans to Broadcast Tapes," *Washington Post,* January 9, 1975.

74. Timothy S. Robinson, "Stay Order Argued in Nixon Case," *Washington Post,* February 2, 1975.

75. The Gallup Poll, "U.S. Divided on Pardons In Cover-Up," *Washington Post,* February 2, 1975.

76. Lawrence Meyer, "Report on Nixon Opposed," *Washington Post,* January 31, 1975.

77. "For Three, Sufficient Punishment," *Time,* January 20, 1975, p. 30; "The Watergate Jailbreak," *Newsweek,* January 20, 1975, p. 18.

78. Timothy S. Robinson, "Judge Frees Colson After 7 Months," *Washington Post,* February 1, 1975.

79. David H. Kogut, "Ziegler Reinvited to Speak But Offer is Cut to $1,000," *Washington Post,* January 31, 1975.

80. Bart Barnes and Ronald Taylor, "Dean to Earn $100,000 on Lecture Tour," *Washington Post,* January 31, 1975; James T. Wooten, "Dean Speech Tour Opens in Virginia," *The New York Times,* February 3, 1975.

81. Senate Select Committee, *Final Report,* pp. 96-106, 211-13, 442-44, 563-77, 1071-74, 1084-86.

82. See Appendix C.

83. See *Year of Scandal: How the* Washington Post *Covered Watergate and the Agnew Crisis,* compiled and edited by Laura Longley Babb, Washington Post Writers Group (Washington, D.C.: The Washington Post Company, 1973), a documentation of the *Washington Post's* role in uncovering the Watergate scandal.

84. Les Brown, "Nixon Talk Fails to Set TV Record," *The New York Times,* August 10, 1974.

85. Carl Bernstein and Bob Woodward, *All the President's Men* (New York: Simon & Schuster, 1974), p. 269.

86. George Seldes, "The New Gadflys," *The New York Times,* September 18, 1974.

87. Finlay Lewis, "Some errors and puzzles in Watergate coverage," *Columbia Journalism Review,* vol. XII, no. 4 (November/December 1973), 26.

88. Ben Bagdikian, "Newspapers: Learning (too Slowly) to Adapt to TV," *Columbia Journalism Review,* vol. XII, no. 4 (Nov./Dec. 1973), 44.

89. James Reston, "Politics, Watergate and Television," *The New York Times,* June 13, 1973.

90. Jules Witcover, "How Well Does the White House Press Perform?", *Columbia Journalism Review,* vol. XII, no. 4 (Nov./Dec. 1973), 39.

91. Cited by David S. Broder, "The Press' Role: A Critical View," *Washington Post,* May 8, 1973, and George Seldes, "The One-Party Press," *The New York Times,* September 5, 1973; and originally printed out by Ben Bagdikian at an editors' convention in May 1973.

92. "Excerpts From Subpoena Ruling," *Washington Post,* March 22, 1973; see also "District Judge Quashes Watergate Subpoenas," *Congressional Record,* March 27, 1973, S5824.

93. Ibid.

94. Timothy Harper, "Disclosures on the Campaign Trail," The *QUILL,* March 1974, p. 24. From The *QUILL,* published by the Society of Professional Journalists, Sigma Delta Chi.

95. Christopher Lydon, "President Urges Campaign Reform With Gift Limits," *The New York Times,* March 9, 1974; David S. Broder, "Dodging vote reform," *Chicago Sun-Times,* March 13, 1974.

96. John Herbers, "Bill to Reform Campaign Funds Signed by Ford Despite Doubts," *The New York Times,* October 16, 1974.

97. Natalie Davis Spingarn, "Can a Nonpartisan Lobby Find a Role in Politics?", *Washington Post,* November 19, 1972.

98. Advertisement, *Washington Post,* March 21, 1974.

99. Letter from Conway to L. Fred Thompson, director, OFE, dated May 14, 1974.

100. "Report of the Office of Federal Elections on Common Cause, Washington, D.C.," October 23, 1974.

101. *Congressional Record,* April 8, 1975, p. H2520.

102. Ibid., April 14, 1975, p. H2733.

103. Ibid., April 16, 1975, p. H2812.

104. See Joseph P. Albright, "The Price of Purity," *The New York Times Magazine,* September 1, 1974, p. 12. Also David E. Rosenbaum, "Big 1972 G.O.P. Contributors Giving Less, While Wealthy Democrats Donate More," *The New York Times,* November 4, 1974.

105. Albert J. Rosenthal, *Federal Regulation of Campaign Finance: Some Constitutional Questions,* Milton Katz, ed., (Princeton: Citizens' Research Foundation, 1972); Howard R. Penniman and Ralph K. Winter, Jr., *Campaign Finances: Two Views of the Political and Constitutional Implications* (Washington, D.C.: American Interprise Institute for Public Policy Research, 1971); Winter, *Watergate and the Law: Political Campaigns and Presidential Power* (Washington, D.C.: AEI, 1974).

106. Albright, "The Price of Purity," p. 37.

107. Senate Select Committee, *Final Report,* p. xxxii (introduction).

108. David E. Rosenbaum, "Wide Voter Shift From G.O.P. Shown," *The New York Times,* November 7, 1974.

109. George Gallup, "GOP Affiliation Sliding and Prospect Not Bright," *Trenton Times Advertiser,* April 13, 1975.

110. Lloyd N. Cutler, "Yes," and Ronald Goldfarb, "No": "A Permanent 'Special Prosecutor'," *Washington Post,* December 2, 1974.

111. "Jaworski Says Keeping Tapes Proved to Be Undoing of Nixon," *The New York Times,* February 18, 1975.

112. Lesley Oelsner, "Jaworski Urges Nixon To Speak Up," *The New York Times,* February 23, 1975.

113. "Jaworski Praises Americans' Action In Watergate Case," *The New York Times,* February 28, 1975.

114. "Limitation Statute Ends on Nixon Drive Donors," *The New York Times,* April 8, 1975.

Appendix A
Federal Election Campaign Act of 1971

1. P.L. 92-225

Appendix B
Revenue Act of 1971

1.   P.L. 92-178

Appendix C
Federal Election Campaign Act Amendments of 1974

1.   P.L. 93-443

Appendix D
The GAO Report

1.   *Alphabetical Listing of 1972 Presidential Campaign Receipts,* vol. I, Office
     of Federal Elections, General Accounting Office (Washington, D.C.: U.S.
     Government Printing Office, November 1973), p. 2.

Appendix U
Data Preparation for Chapter 11

1.   *Alphabetical Listing of 1972 Presidential Campaign Receipts,* vols. I and II,
     Office of Federal Elections, General Accounting Office (Washington, D.C.:
     U.S. Government Printing Office, November 1973).

Index

Index

About the Author

Herbert E. Alexander is the Director of the Citizens' Research Foundation in Princeton, N.J., a position he has held since 1958. He received the B.S. from the University of North Carolina, the M.A. from the University of Connecticut, and the Ph.D. in political science from Yale University in 1958. He taught in the Department of Politics at Princeton University, 1956-58, and was a Visiting Lecturer at Princeton University, 1965-66, and a Visiting Lecturer at the University of Pennsylvania, 1967-68. During 1961-62 he was Executive Director of the President's Commission on Campaign Costs and from 1962-64 he was a Consultant to the President of the United States. Dr. Alexander was also a Consultant to the Comptroller General of the United States and to the Office of Federal Elections at the General Accounting Office during 1972-73. In 1973 Dr. Alexander undertook consultancies with the New Jersey Election Law Enforcement Commission and with the U.S. Senate Select Committee on Presidential Campaign Activities, and in 1974 with the New York State Board of Elections and the Illinois Board of Elections.

Dr. Alexander has written extensively on matters relating to money in politics. He is the author of *Financing the 1960 Election* (1962), *Financing the 1964 Election* (1966), *Financing the 1968 Election* (1971), *Money in Politics* (1972), "The Switch in Campaign Giving" (with Harold B. Myers), *Fortune*, November 1965, and "A Financial Landslide for the G.O.P." (with Harold B. Myers), *Fortune*, March 1970. He has written several articles for books, among them: "Financing the Parties and Campaigns," in *The National Election of 1964*, ed. Milton C. Cummings (Washington: Brookings Institution, 1966); "The Problem of Money: Financing the 1960 Election," in *Party Politics and National Elections*, ed. Demetrios Caraley (Boston: Little, Brown, 1966); "Financing Presidential Campaigns," in *History of American Presidential Campaigns, Vol. IV*, ed. Arthur M. Schlesinger Jr. (New York: McGraw-Hill, 1971). Dr. Alexander has also edited and contributed to *Studies in Money in Politics, Vol. I* (1965), *Vol. II* (1970) and *Vol. III* (1974), published by the Citizens' Research Foundation.